FROM THE CAST-IRON SHORE

P9-COO-810

My official college portrait. By Everett Kinstler, 1995.

FROM

the

CAST-IRON

SHORE

In Lifelong Pursuit of Liberal Learning

FRANCIS OAKLEY

University of Notre Dame Press
Notre Dame, Indiana

University of Notre Dame Press
Notre Dame, Indiana 46556
undpress.nd.edu

Copyright © 2019 by the University of Notre Dame

All Rights Reserved

Published in the United States of America

Library of Congress Cataloging-in-Publication Data

Names: Oakley, Francis, author.
Title: From the cast-iron shore : in lifelong pursuit of liberal learning /
Francis Oakley.
Description: Notre Dame : University of Notre Dame Press, [2018] |
Includes bibliographical references and index. |
Identifiers: LCCN 2018043818 (print) | LCCN 2018050212 (ebook) |
ISBN 9780268104030 (pdf) | ISBN 9780268104047 (epub) |
ISBN 9780268104016 (hardback : alk. paper) | ISBN 0268104018
(hardback : alk. paper) | ISBN 9780268104023 (pbk. : alk. paper) |
ISBN 0268104026 (pbk. : alk. paper)
Subjects: LCSH: Oakley, Francis. | College teachers—United States—
Biography. | College presidents—United States—Biography. |
Williams College—History.
Classification: LCC LA2317.O26 (ebook) | LCC LA2317.O26 A3 2018 (print) |
DDC 378.0092 [B] —dc23
LC record available at https://lccn.loc.gov/2018043818

∞ *This paper meets the requirements of ANSI/NISO Z39.48-1992*
(Permanence of Paper).

To my wife,
children,
and grandchildren

CONTENTS

PART III

Williamstown

PRELUDE

Somewhere or other as I recall—I don't seem to be able to find it in his autobiography—Edward Gibbon, describing his feelings when he had completed the sixth and final volume of his great *The History of the Decline and Fall of the Roman Empire*, wrote: "I walked under the lindens with lassitude and elation." Having recently, at the age of 83, turned into Yale University Press the manuscript of the third and final volume of an attempt to reshape the way in which we have characteristically understood the unfolding of Western political thought from late antiquity to the mid-seventeenth century, I thought I could lay claim to having acquired some dim sense at least of what he was feeling. But lindens are few and far between in the northern Berkshires and elation I was keeping on a nervously short leash until I had heard what the more astringent of the scholarly reviewers might have to say about my earnest efforts. As for lassitude, it proved to be very short-lived. Even while I was going through the dreary business of assembling a bibliography and checking up on the accuracy of my footnotes, memories of my childhood came pounding imperatively on the portal of consciousness and demanding some sort of expression. Without having planned to do so, then, I ended up backing into the writing of a species of memoir.

Although I have enjoyed writing it, it would be disingenuous for me, as it was, in fact, for Gibbon, to claim that "my own amusement . . . [was] my motive." I have to acknowledge, rather, that I don't fully comprehend the nature of the urgencies that produced the effort involved. It was not simply, I think, the nostalgia of old age peering back affectionately at the sometimes strange doings of one's younger self and at the concatenation of developments and events that shaped one's earlier years. Instead, I think, it was something more anxious than that, a compelling urge to detect some sort of pattern in the complex and intricate doings that filled long years characterized above all by their persistent busy-ness, to discern, if you wish, some coherent shape and direction in the gradual unfolding of a life. We all, I suspect, are moved to engage in such an effort. We tell stories of our past and in so doing edge unwittingly towards the shaping of some sort of narrative of the trajectory of our living overall. But comparatively few of us are moved to commit that narrative to writing and to risk sharing it with others. If I do that, it is probably because I love to write and have characteristically done most of my thinking with pen in hand and a readership in mind. If I have certainly thought in order to write, I suspect that I have also written in order to think. At the same time, conscious as I am of the degree to which, in our day, the promiscuous composition of memoirs has become something of a tired cliché, it was not without some foot-dragging that I allowed myself to be drawn into writing one of my own. I did my best, in effect, to resist the urgencies of the personal past. But in vain. What follows, then, is the fruit of my shamefaced capitulation. The unaccustomed freedom from the tyranny of the footnote has been one of the unexpected joys attendant upon this sort of writing. But recognizing that the reader might conceivably be interested in going to the source of words quoted in the text, I have appended at the end of the book a listing of such sources, each cued to the particular page on which it is invoked.

PART I

Liverpool

CHAPTER ONE

The Secure Realm of BEFORE

"Oh God, oh Jesus, oh Sacred Heart. Boy, there's two gentlemen to see you." These are the words that the Brendan Behan of *Borstal Boy* had his landlady screech up the stairs when the hard men of Special Branch showed up on the doorstep of his North Liverpool lodgings to take him into custody. In so doing, they moved quickly enough to preempt his frantic attempt to rid himself of a suitcase crammed with gelignite, detonators, and other incriminating paraphernalia associated with the Irish Republican Army's 1939 bombing campaign in England. This launched him, at the age of sixteen, on the trail that was to lead him to time in Walton Jail, arraignment in court, trial, sentencing to several years in Borstal (juvenile reform school), eventual expulsion from England, and the launching of a successful literary career. That 1939 campaign is forgotten today almost as totally as is the subsequent IRA campaign of raids in the 1950s on British military installations in England and Northern Ireland with the object (sometimes embarrassingly successful) of seizing arms and ammunition for use in future assaults on the hated imperial establishment. And yet, as I now realize, it was a remarkably extensive campaign, generating apprehension and alarm in a whole series of English cities from London to Manchester, Birmingham, Liverpool, and Coventry, and inevitably stirring up, so far as English attitudes towards the Irish were concerned, a renewed wave of anger, fear, and loathing.

Tear gas bombs precipitated panic in cinemas; in London, railway and Tube stations were damaged by explosions; in Manchester and Liverpool, power lines, bridges, jails, and other public buildings were targeted. Among the worst incidents were a bombing in Coventry that went awry, injuring some sixty bystanders and killing another five, and a massive explosion in Liverpool that totally destroyed the Central Post Office on Mount Pleasant.

In 1939, at the time the sixteen-year-old Behan was apprehended, we were living across town in the South Liverpool suburbs and the post office incident is firmly embedded among my early memories. It is so less, I think, because of the event itself, however dramatic it must have been, than because of the *sotto voce* anxiety my parents unwittingly conveyed to their offspring, worried as they were about the degree to which such unhappy goings-on could stir up rancid anti-Irish sentiment once more. And their anxiety, as I was later to discover at elementary school, was wholly warranted. For we were an Irish family, perhaps the more self-consciously so because we bore an English surname. My siblings and I had been fated to grow up in England rather than Ireland simply because my father, at a time of high unemployment in both Britain and the Irish Free State, had been fortunate enough to have been offered the job of assistant foreman in the packing and shipping department of a bobbin and shuttle factory that served the needs of the Lancashire and Indian cotton mills. He knew a lot about timber and was a known quantity because his father's sawmill had earlier shipped timber to that factory. It was situated in Garston, at the most southerly end of the complex of docks stretching along the tidal waters of the Mersey estuary navigable by ocean-going vessels. To that factory he rode his bike six days a week, and they were long days beginning at 6:30 in the morning. But he had a family of six to support and counted himself lucky to have the job at all. Of his four children, one girl and three boys—Molly, Vincent, Noel and I—I was the youngest. And while I had been born in Allerton, a place that was later to emerge as Beatles or, at least, Lennon-McCartney territory, my parents had subsequently moved into another council (that is, municipally-funded rental) house in the neighboring borough of Garston. It was a somewhat more gritty area than Allerton and, in the infinitely subtle social gradations embedded in the working and lower-middle class pecking order of the day, the address was (socially-speaking) a less desirable one. In effect, it suffered from what my urban sociologist daughter now tells me is known in her business as "territorial stigma." But the house was slightly bigger than the Allerton one and it had the further advantage of being within reasonable walking distance of our Catholic parish church and its affiliated elementary school on which our lives were very much centered, and it was also closer to my father's place of work. Moreover, territorial stigma notwithstanding, on clear days the front garden afforded to us coastal flatlanders a faraway and beckoning glimpse of the mountainous ramparts of the Clwydian Range in Flintshire, rising up beyond the River Dee in North Wales, with the summit of Moel Famau looming, remotely mysterious, in the center.

"Immigrant," I suspect, was a term that my mother and father would have found offensive had it been applied to them. Until overtaken by the years of war they still thought of themselves, I sense, as "just being here for a while" and as destined, sooner or later, to "go home." Certainly, we children were all taught, if pressed on the matter, to describe ourselves as "Irish and proud of it," and that identity we took very much for granted. But what exactly it meant was far from being clear. We were called upon in effect, and however unwittingly, to navigate the muddied cultural waters and complex cross-currents of the Irish diaspora in England, and our task was made the more challenging by the fact that our father and mother were themselves very different kinds of Irish people. My father, Joseph Vincent Oakley, was a small-town product. He came from Athlone in County Westmeath, which was by virtue of its strategic location on the River Shannon a military garrison town, constituting the halfway crossing point for the principal road and railway connections linking Dublin in the east to Galway in the west. He had Protestant relatives somewhere in the neighborhood of Cork, and his family, though hardly of the "ascendancy class," was certainly of Anglo-Irish stock. His branch of the family had, it seems, "gone native" in the early 1800s by embracing Catholicism, the precipitating factor being the remarriage of a widowed ancestor, William Oakley by name, to a Catholic woman. While the family produced some schoolteachers over the course of the nineteenth century, their normal engagement appears to have been in some type of small business. My paternal grandfather followed along in that track, operating a small sawmill that cut, processed, and shipped out timber harvested largely on the Clanricarde estates that reached down to the Shannon from the west. And my father, one of the older sons in a family of twelve, worked in that enterprise (for little more, it seems, than pocket money) into his twenties, when the firm itself went bankrupt. Having learned to drive, and not lacking entrepreneurial instincts of his own, he embarked then upon the operation of a livery service in the Irish midlands, combining that enterprise, for they were clearly a very musical family, with what was advertised as "the Oakley String Band," which provided incidental music for silent films and played for dances throughout the same region—Athlone and Roscommon, Tullamore and Mullingar. The "band" was, in fact, no more than a trio composed of himself on the cello, his younger brother Paddy on the violin, and his sister Florrie on the piano. And his last job in Ireland, which came to an end with the establishment of the Irish Free State in 1922 and the departure from Athlone in February of that year of the long-standing British garrison, was as a civilian employee of the British Army working, I believe, for the quartermaster's office in charge of stores. And it was in Athlone, I think, that he met my mother, a junior civil servant whose assignment at that time was that of secretary to the British Army officer commanding the Athlone garrison.

While my father was of ultimately Anglo-Irish stock and did not speak a word of Irish, he had many of the characteristics, nonetheless, that foreigners attribute (somewhat indiscriminately) to the Irish. That is to say, he spoke with a rich brogue, sang melodiously with a fine, well-schooled bass voice (that none of his sons, alas, inherited), had a lively sense of humor, was open and gregarious by nature (he could have been a Kerryman), was a good actor and a skilled raconteur, and was possessed of a great store of well-embroidered stories which we, as children, loved to hear him tell—especially those stemming from the Irish Troubles of 1919–21. One of those stories I particularly remember, though I would hesitate to vouch for its *total* veracity. In his livery service capacity, my father, having dropped off a customer in Mullingar and while driving back to Athlone, found himself, having rounded a bend in the road, suddenly stopped by armed men at what appeared to be the site of a recent Sinn Féin Volunteers ambush of a Black and Tan (British paramilitary auxiliary police) vehicle. His flustered explanations of who he was and what he was doing on the scene were met with great skepticism. Though not a very political person, he was of moderately nationalist sympathies, strong enough certainly, as a younger man, to have joined the Irish Volunteers, then under the leadership of Sir John Redmond. The Volunteers were one of those poorly-armed paramilitary groupings that sprouted up in Ireland, north and south, in the context of bitter disagreement about the implementation of the Home Rule Act of 1914. But he had dropped out of the Volunteers later in the year when the group had split, the majority concurring with Redmond's view that they should put aside purely Irish considerations and (perhaps) join the British Army to share in the fight against the German menace, the minority moving off in a more radically nationalist direction, coming to be known first as the "Sinn Féin Volunteers" and, eventually, as the "Irish Republican Army" (IRA). Whether or not any of that personal history came out on this unfortunate occasion I don't know. But, for one reason or another, he was treated as a suspicious person and forced to drive at gunpoint back to Athlone so that his claimed identity could be verified. The person who was finally able to vouch successfully for him and to get him off what threatened to be a singularly unpleasant hook (the Black and Tans had the reputation of being exceedingly brutal interrogators) was none other than his parish priest, and I have always found it odd that Black and Tan types were willing to take an Irish priest's testimony at face value. But then, as Messrs. Daedalus and Casey reveal in the course of the dinner party row that Joyce describes in *A Portrait of the Artist as a Young Man*, the Irish clerical establishment had long been ambivalent about Irish nationalist aspirations and had been directly at odds with the Fenians, the Irish Republican Brotherhood, and other groups of revolutionary disposition. So perhaps the willingness of Black and Tans to accept the word of a priest should not be the occasion of too much surprise.

If my father's Irishness was one thing, my mother's was quite another. She came from Connaught and was brought up on a tiny farm in County Galway in a village called Ballycasey, itself no more than a clutch of thatched cottages strung along a *boreen*, or little dirt road, many of them destined to be destroyed during the Troubles of 1919–21 in a British Army reprisal for the nearby ambush of a military convoy by a group of Sinn Féin Volunteers or the IRA. The nearest small town to Ballycasey is Headford, originally a Viking settlement, situated on the eastern shore of Lough Corrib, right across from Connemara. She was unquestionably, then, what the Behan of *Borstal Boy* (an irrepressibly cocky Dubliner) referred to condescendingly as "bog Irish." She was possessed of a wealth of peasant sayings that my brother Noel and I later wished we had somehow recorded. One, however, has adhered to the walls of my mind and may be adduced as an illustration. Singularly unimpressed by people who thought altogether too highly of themselves and whom she was prone to labeling as the "big I ams" of this world, she often commented witheringly, when such a person was drawn to her attention, that "Yes. He breaks eggs with a *big* stick."

In contrast to my father, she was a rather private person. While not exactly shy in the manner of some Connemara folk, she was certainly somewhat reserved in her social interactions. She spoke an Hiberno-English that was not heavily accented, though the syntax and rhythms of her speaking were clearly of alien provenance, and her vocabulary had a mildly macaronic quality. In her day at the turn of the century, her region was still, I believe, part of the *Gaeltacht*, or Irish-speaking part of the country. Certainly, she grew up as an Irish speaker. Later to be known as Julia Curran, her Irish name was Seabeán Ní Cureán, and she appears to have switched to English as her dominant language only after starting her schooling in the little, one-teacher elementary school she attended. There, English was the sole language of instruction; Irish was not taught. But the schoolmaster, concerned that his charges would never learn to read or write in the ancient native tongue they still spoke, held voluntary classes in the language after regular school hours, and I still have the Irish grammar book they used in those sessions.

Clearly a bright girl, whom I well know would have loved to have become a teacher herself, she had the gumption or whatever it took, having finished her formal schooling at the age of fourteen (and in this unlike her older sister Mary who married a neighboring farmer), to break free from Ballycasey and what she always referred to as "the country." At the age of fifteen she embarked on the great adventure of going to Dublin. There she enrolled in what was called a *Civil Service College* (I have her graduation certificate), which appears to have been a sort of Katie Gibbs secretarial school teaching typing, shorthand, the drafting of business letters and memoranda, the organization of an office, and the management of meetings, a set of skills which prepared her to undertake the type of vital responsibilities discharged today by those whom we call administrative assistants. She must have done quite well at all of this because she did indeed go on to become a junior civil servant working, if at some remove, under the British War Office. She was stationed in Dublin during the Easter Rising of 1916 when martial law was imposed on the city, and I have the curfew pass issued to her at that troubled time so that she could make her way, if summoned during the proscribed hours, back to the office in Dublin Castle where she worked. All of this, ironically, at a time when her father and brother were Sinn Féin sympathizers and her future brother-in-law—my Uncle Tommy Devaney—was active enough in the IRA to be picked up by British soldiers and, in the course of interrogation, beaten so savagely that he was granted a small pension later on after the Irish Free State had been established. At some point, I don't know exactly when, she was transferred to Athlone, where she stayed until the departure of the British military garrison in February 1922. At that time, she declined an opportunity to remain in the British civil service, which would have involved a posting to Belfast in the six counties of the North. Instead, having married my father, she left Ireland and moved with him to Liverpool when he took up his new job there. Having as a teenager in the immediate postwar years spent summers helping with the haymaking and harvest in the area between Tuam and Lough Corrib in County Galway, where my uncle and aunt (her older sister) farmed a smallholding, and having visited my grandfather in the village where my mother grew up, I have a poignant sense of the cultural distance she had to traverse to become the person I knew as the beloved mother of my childhood. And an acute sense, accordingly, of the determination, force of character, and independence of spirit that impelled her onward through the trajectory of her life.

Living in England, we were separated by both distance and war from grandparents, uncles, aunts, and cousins, and I had the opportunity to meet, and then but fleetingly, only one of my four grandparents and less than half of my uncles, aunts, and first cousins. Being part of two successive generations of emigration, and with remarkably few photographs or mementos linking me to a longer past, I have sometimes felt as if I were the product of a species of spontaneous generation. Perhaps because of this separation, my immediate family was a pretty close-knit one. But a minimum of fuss was made over birthdays (I cannot remember any of us having a birthday party), and we were not overly demonstrative in our expressions of mutual affection. Familial interchange, certainly, was not punctuated with all the "love yous" that American TV dramas would seem to suggest are the common currency of affective exchange between parents and children today. But if we didn't necessarily dispose of the language to describe the feeling, we children had never a moment's doubt that we were cherished, and we relaxed into the comfort of that knowledge like puppies nestling into the softness of a welcoming pillow. Most of all me, I somewhat guiltily suspect. For as the "baby" of the family I was almost certainly fussed over more than the others, and my siblings, sometimes to their irritation, were expected to put themselves out in order to keep a watchful eye on me. "What's the little one-een up to?," I can hear my mother calling out to my brother, using what I think of as a typically Irish double diminutive. For we were, indeed, an Irish family. That being so, for my expatriate parents the pull of "home" was strong. I am dubious about the authenticity of some of my earliest "memories" which may well be retroactive constructions based on overheard family talk or the perusal of family snapshots. But one of the earliest memories I know to be authentic concerns Ireland. It dates to the summer of 1936 when I was four years old. That summer, for the first time since I had been born, my parents, having scraped and saved, were able to bring all six of us to Dublin, where we stayed with my father's sister Florrie (of Oakley String Band fame) and her husband Dick. While I was very excited at the prospect of this trip, my memories of the whole grand adventure, which involved sailing overnight to Dublin (today an eight-hour trip but in the old ships significantly longer), are quite fragmentary in nature. The things that have stayed in my mind are the experience of standing impatiently after dark in a long queue at the Pier Head in Liverpool waiting to board the packet steamer; trying to sleep on a ship's bunk with my father in a crowded cabin with the lights on; playing in the back garden of my uncle and aunt's house in Drumcondra (north Dublin), a small semidetached house not unlike our own in Liverpool, but one that they owned; and so on. I was fascinated by the fact that my uncle, who had very bushy eyebrows, had the habit of twisting the right one while holding forth or telling us stories. He and Florrie, who had no children of their own, made a gratifyingly big fuss over us and I was somehow further impressed by the fact that they were both chain-smokers. I have a penumbral recollection of walking along O'Connell Street near Nelson's

Pillar, then an iconic part of the Dublin cityscape but destined in 1966 to be blown up (allegedly) by a group of ex-IRA men celebrating, it seems, the anniversary of the 1916 Easter Rising. That recollection, however, may well be one retrojected from one of my later visits to Dublin after the war. During one such visit I had the pleasure of playing violin duets with my Uncle Paddy (also of Oakley String Band fame), who had gone on to make a successful career in music and to play in the first violin section of the Radio Éireann Symphony Orchestra. Though they, too, lived in Drumcondra not far from Florrie, I have no recollection of having met him and Aunt Fanny or their children Eileen and Moira during our 1936 visit to Dublin. Nor, oddly, do I carry in my mind any pictures of our return trip home even though it took place in the daytime and it must have been very exciting for a young boy able to observe all the fascinating nautical to-ings and fro-ings as the ship slipped its hawsers, maneuvered out of Dublin harbor, and finally made its way into the Mersey estuary which, in those days, was almost always busy with merchant ships sporting the exotic flags of a host of far-off foreign realms.

Among the other memories I carry with me from those childhood years in the late 1930s, a few stand out as exemplary. The first two evoke across the gulf of time a powerful sense of loss. One day at school, Mr. Quinlan, father of a little friend who had missed the last two days of school because of sickness, knocked on the door of our classroom, entered, and spoke in low tones to our teacher. She, in turn, called me up to the front of the class and Mr. Quinlan took me out into the hallway. There he told me, with gentle sadness, that little Bernard had just died of diphtheria—still in those days an ever-present scourge. Beyond an evanescent sense of numbness, I don't remember how I dealt with that frightening news. I was told that I didn't need to worry about Bernard. He was now safe in the loving arms of his father in heaven and was looking down, with interest and affection, on the doings of his old friends here below. That must have brought with it some sense of reassurance because I can recall no protracted process of grieving. The other loss was less traumatic. Because our respective ages more or less matched, my brothers and I were all good friends with the neighboring McKernan children. The youngest McKernan child, another Francis, was a close chum of mine and had sat next to me when we were both in what was referred to as "the Babies' Class"—that is, kindergarten. The parents had earlier emigrated from Garston to the United States, but, after the premature death of her husband, their mother had brought the children back to England. Now, with the prospect of war in Europe becoming daily more threatening, she decided that they would do well to return to America. At a rather formal going-away party marked by the exchange between us of appropriate gifts, we all bade our opposite numbers farewell. With the exception of Eddie, the oldest of them and Vincent's opposite number, the ensuing separation proved to be permanent. In Eddie's case, the fortunes of war brought him back to Liverpool in transit to the south coast early in 1944 as the build-up to D-Day quickened, and one evening he arrived unexpectedly for supper at our house. He was a private—First Class—in a US Army infantry unit belonging to the Yankee Division (one of my prized possessions became the shoulder flash bearing that division's insignia which he gave me on that occasion). He looked well fed and handsome in a nicely fitted uniform made of the sort of fine material that only officers in the British Army could expect to lay claim to. One can only speculate rather gloomily about how miserable, in those pinched and hungry times, we must all have looked to him. Conscious, no doubt, of the stringency with which food was then rationed, he had brought with him from the relative cornucopia of an American force's PX a parcel of goods—from chocolate and cigarettes (Camel) to Spam and salami. We had already made the acquaintance of Spam; we were accustomed to frying it like bacon and thought it was the food of the gods. Salami, however, was an unknown quantity. In my mother's rather limited cooking repertoire, frying was the default mode. So the following week, having sliced the salami and deciding that it might well be raw, she fried it. Before her startled eyes it dissolved into a pool of grease leaving only a spider's web of meaty fiber to be eaten and leaving us all totally mystified about how Americans prepared and ate this strange stuff.

My other exemplary memories from the late prewar era are more positive in nature. One is that of the thrilling sense of a new world opening up before me when I began going with my brothers and sister to our local suburban public library and was able to take out books myself. While we had all grown up, somewhat mysteriously, as early and voracious readers, we really did not have all that much to read at home. No more, in fact, than a couple of dozen books, the best of them being a splendidly illustrated compilation of classic stories entitled, quite appropriately, *The Golden Wonder Book*. Illustrated with handsome line drawings, it was replete with tales of "old, unhappy, far-off things, and battles long ago." Of those, the one that I think touched me most as a child was the old Irish legend of the children of Lir, turned into swans by their wicked stepmother, with the little ones seeking shelter from the cold winds and fierce waves under the protective wings of their older sister Finnuala. A good half of those books, however, were part of a dreary self-help series that my poor father had been able to acquire by accumulating coupons from a weekly magazine to which he subscribed. The magazine was entitled *John Bull* (improbable reading for an Irishman) and the books thus acquired were the sort that breezily promise that if you can only lay your hands on a hammer and nails, a few stout planks, some canvas, and a bit of rope, and then faithfully follow the instructions given, then you, too, can build yourself a yacht and embark upon the wine-dark sea, sailing for Byzantium.

All of this we took, of course, with a large pinch of salt. We needed more convincing reading fodder than that and we found it in our suburban library, situated no more than a mile from where we lived and within easy walking or, later, biking distance. It speedily became our spiritual home. Located in a handsome stone building erected courtesy of the philanthropy of Andrew Carnegie (or of the foundation he had been far-sighted enough to establish), it was possessed of a nice reading room with a long wooden table, green-shaded table lamps, and wooden chairs distinguished by their truly Division I level of creakability. The creaking was enough, in fact, when the chairs were filled with a bunch of squirming boys, to drive even the most placid of librarians to the very brink of nervous collapse. As I now realize, the library quickly and permanently imprinted on my impressionable mind an indelible sense of what a *real* library should look and feel like. It was possessed of a good collection of children's literature, as well as fiction and poetry in general, and, as I discovered as a teenager struggling to master the piano, of a creditably challenging collection of Elizabethan and Jacobean keyboard music. For me, as for my sister and brothers, it was nothing less than an imaginative lifeline. Or, to shift the image, it opened up for us an enticing portal for travel into Keats's "realms of gold" wherein "many goodly states and kingdoms" we could see. It was nothing less, in fact, than our own

Charm'd magic casements, opening on the foam
Of perilous seas, in faery lands forlorn.

And, later on, it was to provide a route of escape from the lonely, pinched, grim, grimy, and, until the Luftwaffe was contained, dangerous realities of life in wartime Britain.

The second of these exemplary memories is somewhat different in nature. Crisp, clearly delineated, and gently illumined by the glow of a pale English sun sinking towards the west at the end of an improbably perfect summer's day, it stands out beckoningly in my mind because of its freshness and specificity. I have always adored summer picnics, whether at Glyndebourne before the opera, or at Marlborough, Vermont, in the days when Casals was still playing at the festival there, or at Tanglewood in the southern Berkshires, summer home to the Boston Symphony Orchestra, or, for that matter, at the Saratoga track in New York state before post time during the racing season, for horses have loomed large in our lives. And I trace that attachment back to the happiness I felt as a child when my mother excitingly punctuated the normal routines of family life by treating us to picnics. Sometimes she included on those occasions our playmates Ken and Gordon Anderson, who lived next door to us in the other half of our semidetached house. She did so, I think, because she felt sorry for them. Their father, a Scots veteran of the Great War and a tram conductor by trade, was also an abusive drunk whose violent behavior towards his poor wife and children seemed to be steadily escalating. It did so to such a degree, in fact, that on more than one occasion, when Anderson had put his wife and children out in the cold, my father had to intervene, pounding on the door and threatening to call the police unless he let them back in and refrained from hitting them. Later on, as I grew older and began to dwell on such things, any restiveness I might have begun to feel about the comparatively strict ground rules that governed our living at home tended to be tempered by the alarm and gloom I had come to feel about the misery and chaos prevailing in the Anderson household.

Ken and Gordon were not with us, however, on the specific, almost iconic, occasion I remember so clearly and which dates, I think, to the summer of 1937 when I was not quite six years old. Present on that occasion were just the members of the family—my sister, Molly, the eldest, my brothers Vincent and Noel, and myself—with my father cycling up from work to join us at the end of his day. The southern end of Liverpool is plentifully supplied with open public park space, with Springwood, Calderstones Park, and Clarke Gardens being quite close to where we lived. My parents' favorite spot was the last—a former estate, still not heavily frequented, that had been donated to the city council in the 1920s. It surrounded Allerton Hall, a handsome Palladian-style mansion built in the 1730s of fine dressed sandstone, and was situated about three-quarters of a mile up the road to Woolton on which we lived. It was, in fact, not far from Menlove Avenue, at the other end of which the ur-Beatle, John Lennon, was later to grow up. At that time, in the depths of the Great Depression and before the onset of the War, the mansion itself stood empty, derelict, and subject to vandalism. The fearsome carving of a ferocious lion's head above its main entrance (reproduced in black polished metal on its door knocker) gave it a forbidding aspect and we children, at least, were tempted to assume that it had to be haunted. So we tended to give it a wide berth. But the surrounding grounds were inviting rather than forbidding and provided the perfect site for a late-afternoon picnic.

We trooped up there one late-summer afternoon carrying two large baskets. One was filled with ceramic cups, saucers, and plates, as well as a teapot filled with tea and wrapped in a towel to keep it hot, for we didn't possess anything as fancy as a Thermos flask. The other contained utensils, a tablecloth, a sweet sandwich cake, and a lot of cucumber and salmon sandwiches—tinned salmon, of course, for it was not until much later in life that I encountered the real thing. For all I knew at that time, salmon might well be something one caught in cans. We were more or less ready to eat, with the tablecloth spread out on the grass in the shade of a large tree and cups, saucers, and plates set out neatly on it, when my father finally arrived to join us. The weather was wonderfully clear, if in a muted English sort of way with none of the harshly direct sunlight one encounters in southern Europe or across the Atlantic, and the afternoon sun glimmered gently through the leaves and branches of our protective tree. My mother was wearing a straw hat and a navy blue dress with white polka dots. I thought, admiringly, that she looked very pretty. And indeed she did. She cannot have been more than thirty-nine or forty at that time and had not yet become the rather stern, strict, anxious, and anxiously controlling person that the wartime years were to make of her. For it was in those later years that she took to fretting about the possible long-term and deleterious effects on our health that might stem from the inadequacies of our wartime diet, about the damage that upheavals and interruptions in our schooling might be doing to our life prospects, and, above all, about the well-being and safety of her oldest son, Vincent, then serving in the British Army. And, in this last matter, not altogether without cause. As a recruit in the Seaforth Highlanders, stationed in winter at Fort George on the bleak North Sea coast of Invernesshire (the eastern terminus of the old Highland Line), and in the days before penicillin was available to effect its miracles, he very nearly died of an acute dose of double pneumonia. We had, of course, no telephone and learned of his plight only when a police constable arrived at our house to share the dire news, impart some instructions to my parents, and give them train tickets so that they could make the long trip up to Scotland (very slow and difficult in wartime) in order to say goodbye to him. When they arrived, they found that he was indeed at death's door and had been given the last sacraments by the Catholic chaplain. But somehow or other he succeeded in beating the odds and recovering, spending what sounded like several enjoyable weeks as a pampered convalescent soldier at a stately Scottish home where he had the pleasure of playing violin duets with the daughter of the family. Though he was downgraded medically after his recovery, and transferred from the infantry to the Royal Army Ordnance Corps, that did not prevent him from being shipped off to the Middle Eastern theatre of operations where he was to remain until after the war. There he saw out the last months of his service living under canvas at Tel El Kebir in the Suez Canal Zone not far from Ismailia. He was at best never more than an intermittent letter writer. Even if he had been, the vagaries of military postal operations might still have ensured the debilitating pattern of long, anxious, and tension-wracked weeks with no word of him alternating with periodic deluges of accumulated correspondence. My mother found that pattern very difficult to cope with, and, as the weeks of silence wore on, the atmosphere at home would become increasingly tense and funereal. So much so that I swore to myself that if I was ever living away from home in the future, I would be sure to write on a weekly basis even if I had little or no news to convey. And that promise I strove mightily to keep over the thirty years between my departure for college in 1950 and my mother's death in 1981.

On the occasion of the picnic in question, however, all of that lay in the future. On that day, after we had enjoyed our tea, Vincent's role was a more benign one—that of busying himself with the organization of a little cricket game. Later on, we played hide-and-seek in the darkness of the woods that occupied about a third of the estate. Those woods amounted, I suppose, to little more than an enlarged copse of tall, mature trees. But to me at the time, they conveyed, if not a sense of "something far more deeply interfused," at least a powerful feeling of mystery. Years later when, while reading *The Lord of the Rings* to my own children at bedtime, I first encountered Tolkien's Ents—those mysterious ancient creatures, fundamentally treelike but still ambulant and possessed of language—what came immediately to mind were the tall trees of the mysterious Clarke Gardens woods, and that despite the fact that the New England county in which we were living at the time was itself eighty percent forested.

At the time we went on that iconic picnic it was still less than twenty years since the Great War had stumbled to its exhausted conclusion. It had left its dreadful mark upon many of the families we knew, and to English people at large its searing memory was still altogether too fresh to ignore. There was a small, well-kept cenotaph close to where we lived and on Armistice Day each year, even while World War II was at its peak, a well-attended memorial service was held there and wreaths were laid. The British Legion was still a very active organization and the participants in the service included not only detachments of soldiers and the Home Guard but also a quite large contingent of veterans, around fifty in number, all wearing their medals, still marching impressively well, and responding smartly to drill commands. The Great War had been so appalling a catastrophe that people in the late 1930s found it exceedingly difficult to come to terms with the dawning realization that something similar might well be about to happen again. And yet, as the decade wore on, the shadows were palpably lengthening for the all-too-brief interlude of peace that had begun in 1918. If Chamberlain's post-Munich proclamation of "peace in our time" had understandably been greeted with great relief, it was relief fated to be tugged at by a quickening undertow of doubt as the government's preparations for the eventuality of renewed war became increasingly apparent.

In Merseyside the looming spectre of war was brought home dramatically by a tragic incident in the middle of 1939. By that time, the Cammell Laird shipyards in Birkenhead "across the water" (i.e., across the Mersey estuary from Liverpool) were humming with renewed naval ship-building activity, and in June one of the vessels built there, the submarine HMS *Thetis*, sailed out into Liverpool Bay for its final diving trials. On that occasion it carried with it, along with its normal complement of about sixty hands, a goodly number of additional mechanics, shipwrights, technical observers, and other naval personnel. Diving about forty miles offshore, it was sent irretrievably to the bottom by some freakish combination of technological malfunction and human error, with an eventual loss of some ninety souls. Only four men were able to make it back to the surface by means of the Davis escape apparatus before that, too, malfunctioned and jammed. The vessel, by then a ghastly tomb, was eventually raised, refitted, and recommissioned as the HMS *Thunderbolt*. Under that name it was to see war service in the Atlantic and Mediterranean before being sent to the bottom again—this time in 1943 off Sicily and by Italian depth charges, with the loss of all hands.

The gloom generated by the desperate fate of the *Thetis* on its maiden voyage seems to have hung like a pall over Merseyside. It had certainly registered sharply on my mind. On a late summer seaside holiday that same year at Hoylake on the Cheshire coast, I found myself, my mind still filled with *Thetis*-related submarine lore, imagining that the long, low prominence of Hilbre Island, just off the coast, was in fact an enemy submarine, with the structure that stuck up in the middle of it being the conning tower from which we were being observed through binoculars by officers of the *Kriegsmarine*. And for adults, certainly, the contemporaneous quickening in the pace of preparation for a war that was becoming increasingly likely can have done little to dispel the gloom. Herr Hitler's name loomed large in overheard adult conversations; so, too, did worried talk about the Danzig Corridor, though the significance of that was not altogether clear to me.

For a curious young boy, however, mercifully unburdened by memories of the First War, much of this was intriguing rather than alarming.

So it was with great interest that I took note of the issuing of gas masks, the erection of simple warning devices which would, by changing color, signal the presence of droplets of mustard gas in the air, the arrival of a clever little stirrup pump to be deployed as a first line of defense against fire, and the affiliated issuing of long-handled rakes and shovels to be used for transferring burning incendiary bombs into buckets or piles of sand. Smallish objects, about a foot long, those bomblets were composed, apart from their aluminium tails, of highly volatile combustible materials and we had it drilled into us that they might explode if we were foolish enough to try to dowse them with water. As a measure to be limited strictly to the oncoming time of national emergency, we had also been issued with identity cards. I myself was inordinately proud of the fact that I was now NHWB 344-3, a designation which, along with my later army number, I still remember after more than seventy years, though I would be hard pressed, without checking it, to get my Social Security number right.

All of this, along with practice donning a gas mask and wearing it for fifteen minutes or so, I seem to have taken effortlessly in stride and certainly without any remembered degree of apprehension. Similarly the air raid practices at school. A cellar had been reinforced to serve as a shelter and there we would sit for a while, having all been taught (boys as well as girls) to knit in order to keep us busy. All my knitting (usually of large dusters to present to my mother) was in "plain"—in, over, through, off—as I recall. I never advanced far enough in my knitting career to master "purl." So much for the school air-raid shelter. But I must confess to having been really excited when the components of our own Anderson Air Raid Shelter finally arrived, along with illustrated instructions for its installation. Although I had diligently perused the latter and mastered their drift, it was still a startling sight, returning home after playing with a friend, to find that my father, helped by Vincent, had stripped the turf from a large, oblong-shaped area in our back garden ("backyard" in American parlance), stacking the sods neatly to one side, and that they were now engaged in digging down to a depth of almost three feet, piling the soil on the other side of the hole. The cast-iron frame, into which the back, front, and side pieces of the shelter would slot, was then installed at the bottom of the hole, and the arching side pieces, composed of stout, thick-ply, zinc-coated corrugated iron were put in place and bolted firmly together at the top where they joined. The front and back sections were then seated in the frame, and the whole thing was covered with a couple of feet of soil and sods. To that, in our case, were added a couple of handfuls of iris bulbs (which we had in abundance) that, blossoming the next spring, transformed the whole protective mound into a riot of purple flowers.

While these Anderson shelters could afford no protection against the misfortune of a direct hit or very near miss by a high-explosive bomb, they could certainly protect against blast, falling masonry, incendiary bombs, and the lethal rain of shrapnel from the exploding antiaircraft shells which blanketed both the city center and the ring of suburbs surrounding it. Unexploded antiaircraft shells sometimes made it to the ground—one such blew in the outer wall of the sacristy in our local parish church. Short of that, the shrapnel itself could be exceedingly dangerous. At the height of the blitz in Liverpool, one of our neighbors, a Mr. Rimmer who was serving as an air raid warden, though wearing his regulation tin hat (steel helmet) was destined to be killed outright by a large piece of shrapnel when he made the mistake of emerging from the communal shelter he was supervising in order to get in a quick smoke.

Rather grim preoccupations for a little boy, I suppose, but, at the time, before the war had actually started, preparations for war came through rather as intriguing than as in any way menacing. I divide my young life into two parts, the realms of BEFORE and AFTER. All such bellicose preparations belonged to the secure world of BEFORE, when my family was still intact and we were all together, when I was beginning my schooling in a relatively benign setting, and when, to the kindly eye of memory and the bleak realities of the Merseyside climate notwithstanding (winter fogs, high winds, rain squalls blowing in from the sea, and so on), the sun seems always to have been shining, as it did on the day of the picnic I remember so well. Late in the summers of 1938 and 1939 my parents rented a house in Hoylake for a fortnight's holiday. I have very happy memories of those weeks at the seaside. Playing in the sea was fun, even if the water tended to be cold and the jellyfish overabundant. So, too, was building elaborate sand castles on the beach and struggling desperately to defend them against the hostile incursions of the rising tide. Hoylake has a nice, long, well-kept promenade which stretches for about two miles from West Kirby eastward to Meols, punctuated at one spot by the Cheshire Coast Guard lifeboat station. Well off-shore one could see steady streams of oceangoing vessels making their way to or from the Liverpool docks. And on stormy days when the tide was in, the sea was rough, and beach time was precluded, we would all walk along the promenade dodging the waves that broke gratifyingly over the seawall and swept impressively across the pavement. On some evenings we would go down to the slipway at Meols where the small fishing fleet would come in with its catch. We would buy flatfish (sole or plaice) straight from the boats, and, after my mother had sautéed them (though the word itself was not part of her vocabulary), we would eat them with great gusto and within an hour or so of their being caught. Hilbre Island may still have loomed mysteriously offshore, but it was only on occasional moments in the charmed world of BEFORE that my imagination would project onto it the threatening profile of a lurking enemy presence.

CHAPTER TWO

The Shadowed World of AFTER

As an historian by calling, and one compelled by his interests to pursue topics across the traditional borderline between the medieval and the modern, I have always been skeptical about attempts to delineate too sharply the division between one historical epoch and another. The traditional periodization of European history into ancient, medieval, and modern (a Renaissance humanist invention) I have come to think of as a sort of creaking and groaning late-Ptolemaic system which calls for an increasingly baroque array of epicycles if it is to continue to function at all and to account at all plausibly for the complex phenomena involved. And yet, in my own life, and ironically so, I date the line dividing what I think of as the worlds of BEFORE and AFTER with startling precision. It coincides, in effect, with Hitler's invasion of Poland on September 1, 1939. With that moment, our holiday had to be cut short and we had to return home immediately that very day. The city's plans for the evacuation of over 100,000 children (an astonishing number) were to go into effect at once. My brother Noel's Jesuit grammar school—St. Francis Xavier's College—relocated in Flintshire, North Wales, and Molly's convent grammar school, run by the sisters of La Sagesse (an émigré French religious order) moved to less bleak surroundings in South Wales. As my oldest brother, Vincent, believed he had a vocation to the priesthood and was already committed to leaving for the archdiocesan seminary in Upholland (rural Lancashire), our family was suddenly truncated. Because of our youth, evacuation was deemed to be out of the question for children at the parish elementary school which I attended and, in view of the likelihood of air raids, the school was simply closed. So, within a couple of days, we went from being a household of six, bustling with the activity of four children, to a small family of three with a single seven-year-old child who had no school to fill in the long days and who was destined, it seems, to spend all too many lonely hours mooching around the house in the pallid grip of boredom.

For my mother and father all this was hard enough. They missed their children and worried about them. For the children, it varied. Vincent appeared to be basically happy at the seminary, where he seemed to spend a lot of time playing football (soccer) and, when the winter came on, learning to ice skate—an unusual avocation in the England of the day. All went well with Molly, too. She was older, after all, and was billeted with a very nice and welcoming family which had a daughter her own age, and she was to remain in touch with them long after she came home. Noel's experience, however, was altogether different. He was placed with an impoverished family which had taken in a young evacuee (and a papist at that!) because they actually needed the miserable six shilling weekly remuneration they were paid for so doing, and they were a good deal less than welcoming to a lonely eleven-year-old boy who had suddenly been uprooted from home and who couldn't even participate in familial conversation because it was conducted largely in Welsh. Even by wartime standards, moreover, they fed him poorly. Though in his letters home the poor kid tried to keep a stiff upper lip and to put a reassuring gloss on the situation in which he found himself, it gradually became clear to my parents that he was utterly miserable and struggling even to keep his head above water. Having visited him to assess the situation—and, in so doing, discovering that, skinny though he had already been, he was now actually losing weight—and having talked things over with the headmaster of the school, they eventually decided in the winter of 1939–40 to bring him home, the threat of air raids notwithstanding. Other parents had already done likewise. And, as the trickle of returnees grew to a steady stream, the school responded by instituting a schedule of classes in Liverpool, which continued to increase in scope until the whole school returned to its original site on Salisbury Street, close to the city center. It did so, ironically, just in time for the onset of the blitz.

For me, the sudden departure of my siblings, and especially my big brother Noel whom I dearly loved, ushered in some months of deep loneliness and much boredom, all of it exacerbated by the fact that I was deprived also of the easy, daily camaraderie of school life. Sporadic small classes were organized for us in people's homes, with teachers going from house to house to run them. But these lessons didn't amount to much—not enough, certainly, to meet the educational aspirations my parents had for their children and which distinguished them from most of their neighbors and friends. In the long row of council houses front-ing onto Woolton Road in the midst of which we lived, there were prob-ably a couple of dozen children. All but a handful of them finished their schooling at the age of fourteen, the small remainder going no further than sixteen. All, that is, except us. For us, my parents mysteriously had greater expectations and we were made to feel that we were destined for different and less predictable futures. Sometimes we chafed against that feeling for, during the school year at least, we were not as free as the neighboring children to while away the hours in play. Homework was taken with the utmost seriousness; so, too, was practice on the piano or violin, for money was somehow found to pay for our private lessons. My mother, then, was very worried about the possibility of a protracted gap in my schooling, fearing that it would leave me poorly placed to perform successfully in the competitive examinations for the Junior City Scholar-ship. Only with the help of one of these scholarships could I hope to go on to an academic high school and have at least a chance of getting into university. Otherwise my schooling would end at the age of fourteen. It was only the winning of such scholarships that had enabled Molly and Noel to move on to academically-oriented grammar schools. These schools, known as "direct grant" schools because they were in receipt of some government funding and were subject to government inspection, were nevertheless in essence private schools that charged tuition fees substantial enough to put them beyond my parents' means. If my own formal schooling was not to come to an abrupt halt, I had to be prepared well enough to compete successfully for one of those prized scholar-ships. In the context of my mother's great concern about the sudden closure of my school in 1939, I can recall her suddenly dissolving into tears when discussing the matter with a teacher after one of the periodic classes held at our house. So she threw herself into the breach and picked up the pedagogic slack. Lack of prolonged formal education notwithstanding, she proved herself to be an effective teacher, supportive but demanding. Indeed, I found the arithmetic book she favored (dating back to her own school days in Ballycasey) rather more difficult than the textbook we had used at school. Patient in explanation, she carefully led me through it, corrected my sums and the writing exercises she had set me to write, and from time to time suggested that I should write a story rather than an essay. One Sunday I did precisely that when she and my father were out and was enormously gratified when, upon her return, she was clearly impressed by what I had written.

The story in question was a simple one about a short ride on an aeroplane (something, of course, that I had never experienced) from the takeoff to the thrilling ascent up through the clouds, the joy of floating high above the ground, and the controlled descent again to landing. In it, describing our emergence from the clouds and our excited observation of the intricate and quintessentially English patchwork of fields interspersed with woods far down below, I had ventured to deploy, much to my mother's astonishment (or maybe apprehension), the word "panorama." Where I had picked it up, I don't know. But the whole story, I am sure, owed much to my delighted reading of the "Biggles" books by a certain Captain W. E. Johns. Intended originally, I gather, for adolescents, under wartime conditions these books had proved increasingly popular with younger boys, and I had been enthralled by the daring exploits of their hero, "Biggles," the nickname of James Bigglesworth. His early career as a young officer flying Sopwith Camels for the Royal Flying Corps during World War I drew him into perilously enthralling dogfights with his German counterparts in the air over the tragic network of trenches that defined the Western Front. Red Baron territory! The fictional Biggles was to enjoy a remarkably long career, living on, eternally young, to fly Spitfires and Hurricanes in World War II. But *my* Biggles was the heroic ace of the Great War, and I was later charmed to discover that he was also the hero of the little Parsee boy from Mumbai in Rohinton Mistry's novel, *Family Matters*. "Chocks off," Jehangir would proclaim, finding a new way to feed his beloved but bedridden grandfather. "Just a little left, Grandpa. Let's do an aeroplane." "First of all, Biggles is climbing into the plane," he said, dipping the spoon into the mush. The engine was revving, the chocks were off, and they were ready for takeoff. "The spoon taxied several times around the bowl and was airborne. After a straight ascent it began to swoop and swerve, banking sharply and looping the loop." Then, with a "Prepare for landing, Grandpa," it swooped down safely into the old man's mouth. Mission accomplished! But I should not have been surprised that the fictional Biggles of my Anglo-Irish youth had lived on to thrive in Mumbai. After all, he was the son of an administrator in the Indian civil service, had been born and brought up in India, loved the country, had many Indian friends, and even spoke fluent Hindi!

While I was pursuing my home schooling, the remainder of 1939 and the early months of 1940 proved to be a quiet time, punctuated only by the descent upon western Europe of a cruelly severe winter, bringing to us the type of heavy snowfall that one takes for granted in New England but that was excitingly unusual in our part of the British Isles. That period was punctuated also by the outbreak of war between the Soviet Union and Finland, which, having acquired our first wireless set (cause for great celebration), we were able to follow via the BBC, enthralled by the stiff resistance "the gallant Finns" were putting up against the monstrous regiment of Russian might. For me personally, at least until my parents finally bit the bullet and brought Noel home, loneliness and boredom loomed large and I sought to amuse myself with various distractions, most of them in some way war related. My favorite jigsaw puzzle was composed from RAF aerial photography of Hamburg (which we viewed as our sister city), and, having become familiar with the silhouettes of our own Spitfires and Hurricanes, I set out to memorize those of the leading German aircraft—Messerschmidts, Junkers, and Heinkels. I also drew a lot of ships, planes, and fighting men. Oddly enough, many of those soldiers wore uniforms and carried weapons dating back to the Boer War, details which had caught my attention in a wonderful series of bound illustrated magazines dating back to that era. These I had encountered and pored over in the welcoming home of my Uncle Peter and Aunts Rosie and Lily (Elmsly), whose dog I used to walk and play with. They were not blood relatives but the aging, unmarried children of a British Army captain whom my parents had befriended in Athlone. For Aunt Rosie, the kindly elder sister who ran the household, the imposition of a blackout to make things difficult for the Luftwaffe brought back fond memories of her childhood when her father had been stationed in British India up near the Khyber Pass. There, it turns out, they had had to maintain a comparable blackout regimen because the Pathans were prone to taking long-distance potshots at whatever glimmers of light they could detect in the military cantonments.

On the international scene, these rather quiet months were the period of the "Phony War," when the earlier fears of the horrors of gas warfare had begun to recede and the prospect of Guernica-like bombing attacks had begun to seem less likely. During this period, people became less religious about carrying their gas masks with them wherever they went, and we were regularly regaled with accounts of the utter impregnability and wonderful amenities of the Maginot Line, accompanied by reassuring pictures of French *poilus* sunning themselves beside their well-appointed bunkers. And we all sang, of course, that we were going "to hang out our washing on the Siegfried Line." Food rationing, it is true, was beginning to bite deep, scrap iron was at a premium and handsome wrought iron gates and railings were being carted off to be melted down, and the shortage of petrol drove private vehicles off the road, though some, with the help of cumbersome, coal gas–filled bags on the roof, put in a lugubrious appearance. As the spring of 1940 wore on, there was a sense of time almost standing still, and with Noel's return home, a matter of great joy for me, we began to detect glimmers, at least, of a return to something approximating quasi-normalcy.

But not for long. With the German invasion of Norway and Denmark in April 1940, and the British seizure of Narvik in response, the clouds of war began to thicken. And with the unprecedented catastrophes of May and June, unanticipated by Germans and Allies alike, the harsh realities of war were finally brought home to us in England. With the capitulation of Denmark, Belgium, the Netherlands, and France, and finally, after courageous and tenacious resistance, that of Norway too, Great Britain in June 1940—licking its own wounds after Dunkirk and in military disarray—had to face the grim prospect of standing alone against the assembled Axis powers, for Italy had now entered the war as a German ally. Before the nine o'clock news on Sunday evening, the BBC had adopted the practice of playing the national anthems of the fallen Allies. As the list grew depressingly long, it was reduced to playing only the opening bars of each anthem, with the "Marseillaise" being, in my youthful and doubtless bellicose estimate, unquestionably the best and most stirring. I memorized, accordingly, its thrilling words and began to imagine myself to be an honorary "enfant de la patrie." Unwilling to accede to Hitler's oblique overtones of peace (though there were clearly some English people of prominence who would have welcomed such a move), the country braced itself in the summer of 1940 for the impending Nazi invasion that was to continue to seem possible long after Hitler (as we now know) had abandoned the idea as unfeasible and had begun to turn his attention to the East. How seriously that threat of invasion was being taken was everywhere evident in England during the grim latter half of 1940 and the early months of 1941. And as a curious boy, I must now somewhat shamefacedly confess, I was excited and enthralled by the defensive steps being taken.

Some of those steps, like the evacuation of people from coastal areas, were limited to those southeastern regions that were most likely to be the initial targets for invasion and where it was anticipated the most decisive defensive battles would be fought. But others, so far as I know, were taken nationwide. Certainly they were prominent enough in the Merseyside area: the removal from the roads of all signposts carrying place-names, and also the removal of identifying names from railway stations; the erection across open flatland of seemingly endless rows of "dragon's teeth" anti-tank traps; the closing off of beaches with tangles of barbed wire, and the seeding (real or implied) of those beaches with life-threatening land mines; the guarding at night of important nodal points where roads converged and the blockading of those nodes with barbed wire and concrete blocks intended to force the traffic to slow down and wind its way at a snail's pace through the maze; the building of concrete pillboxes to cover the approaches to such spots; and the recruitment and deployment of Local Defense Volunteers armed with a bizarre variety of weaponry (privately-owned shotguns were not uncommon). At first distinguished only by an LDV armband worn over civilian clothing, the volunteers mutated quite rapidly into a uniformed and disciplined Home Guard, equipped (courtesy of Lend-Lease) with long, World War I–vintage American Springfield rifles, readily distinguishable from the Lee-Enfield 303s with which the regular army was then equipped. Indeed, the army continued to be equipped with Lee-Enfield 303s during my own army days in the 1950s until the Belgian-made NATO FN FAL rifle became standard issue.

All the preparatory steps in question were brought home clearly to us as our house was situated close to one such nodal point, where the Woolton Road narrowed from being a dual carriageway down to a single road before passing by Allerton Railway Station and under a bridge carrying the main London, Midland and Scottish (LMS) Railway lines to points east and south. The underpass was blockaded with concrete obstacles and barbed wire and guarded at nighttime, and the approaches to it on the Garston side were dominated by a newly constructed concrete pillbox situated in a field on the other side of the road, right opposite our house. Similarly, the Long Lane Recreational Ground around the corner, equipped with tennis courts and a bowling green but consisting largely in flat, open, and regularly mowed grassland available to the public for scratch cricket and football games, was now crisscrossed by deeply ploughed furrows, and the open space between the furrows was seeded with poles at least twelve feet high. This, it seems, was now standard practice with such large, flat open spaces, and it was intended to interdict their use as landing places for enemy planes or troop-carrying gliders.

To the period when such steps were being taken belongs the only time I have ever heard in Britain shots fired in anger. One night we were awakened by the sound of shouts from the sentries posted at the underpass by the station. There then ensued the sound of a car (or lorry) engine revving in high gear as the vehicle suddenly took off at speed. That in turn was followed by frantic shouts of "Halt!" and then by two or three shots. The flow of information at that time being very tightly controlled, no public mention was subsequently made of the incident, and we were left in the speculative dark about what, precisely, had happened.

For me and for my friends, all of these exciting goings-on were of compelling interest. Despite their ominous implications, and in this like the Blitz which was soon to follow, they were part of the exhilarating liberation from the ordinary that the early years of the war brought with them. We became habituated to seeing in the streets airmen from the various fallen nations who were being trained at a nearby RAF base to fly Spitfires. Most of them wore the standard RAF uniform with a shoulder flash indicating their nation of origin—Poland, Norway, the

Netherlands, Czechoslovakia. But, doubtless at General de Gaulle's insistence, the Free French stood out by virtue of wearing their own distinctive uniforms. All of this was very interesting. So, too, were the recently constructed pillboxes. And as they were not usually manned by day, it was in them that we gallantly fought our own imagined rearguard actions against overwhelming numbers of German invaders—otherwise known as "the Hun." Similarly enthralling were the military maneuvers in which fascinating pieces of equipment like Bren Gun carriers and the occasional tank were deployed. And only a little less so were the civil defense logistical exercises, in one of which I was lucky enough to become a participant. The objective of that particular exercise, or so in retrospect I assume, was to test the adequacy of the hospital and ambulance services under conditions involving fairly massive civilian casualties. Along with some of my comrades, I spent a happy day being shunted to and fro in ambulances and being fed tea and sweet biscuits by kindly nurses. To each of us was attached a large label detailing the nature of our injuries, thus signaling to which first aid post or hospital we should be taken. My injuries, described in technical terms I didn't understand, were clearly very severe because I ended up, having been shuttled to and fro between two hospitals, having my original label replaced by one that simply said "DEAD." My next trip, then, was across town to the city's morgue from which, after the requisite tea and biscuits and even a piece of milk chocolate, I was driven home. All in all, for a young, inquisitive boy, it was a most satisfactory and enjoyable day.

After Hitler turned his attention eastward and launched his ill-fated invasion of the Soviet Union in June 1941, the threat of an invasion of Britain receded and the frantic defensive scramble of the waning months of 1940 began to fade from popular memory. The barricades defending the approaches to nodal communication points were eventually dismantled (they hindered ordinary traffic as well as the movement of troops and military paraphernalia), though thousands of pillboxes were left in place, some of them (like the one on the edge of Clarke Gardens dominating Springwood Avenue) surviving down to the present. During the peak of the invasion threat, there must doubtless have been people of defeatist sentiment among the populace at large. Certainly, there was enough interest in Hitler's views to keep our local public library's copy of *Mein Kampf* tied up with a succession of borrowers, and the German propaganda broadcasts by one or another of the actors known as the figure Lord Haw Haw were widely listened to—though partly, I think, because they were quite amusing. And I can well remember the skepticism with which our own government's claims for the successes of the RAF in the Battle of Britain were often met with up north. In our own area this last was not altogether surprising given the fact that in daytime we never once saw RAF planes rising to attack even solitary German intruders. All of that said, however, the determination to resist and the will to fight off any German invasion was, at the time, quite palpable. In the summer of 1940 an astonishing 1.5 million men volunteered for duty in the Home Guard. In post-war years they were to be affectionately parodied as "Dad's Army," but they included in their ranks a significant number of battle-tested Great War veterans and would, I believe, have mounted a determined, if not necessarily effective, resistance had the expected invasion actually occurred. A government poster designed for use in the event of such an invasion but never disseminated said, simply, "Keep Calm and Carry On." I think that is precisely what the British public under such perilous conditions would have done. Certainly, with some inevitable exceptions, that is by and large how the public seems to have reacted when the Luftwaffe's campaign of bombing London and other major urban centers got underway late in the summer of 1940. To the degree to which that campaign was intended to destroy the morale of ordinary people, it clearly failed.

CHAPTER THREE

Trajectories of Fear

The basic historical record of the Liverpool Blitz is clear enough, though little attention was paid to it until several decades after the war. Liverpool—or, more accurately, Merseyside—was, after London, the most heavily bombed urban area in the United Kingdom. And not surprisingly so. The Commander-in-Chief of Western Approaches Command had his headquarters there in an extensive underground bunker complex from which was directed the Battle of the Atlantic, the longest continuous military campaign in World War II and one that reached its peak of frenzy from mid-1940 to the end of 1943. The Port of Liverpool was the home port and terminal point of an endless succession of trans-Atlantic convoys that alone kept Britain functioning during the darkest days of the war. And its Gladstone Dock complex afforded safe anchorage to the naval force of multinational composition that escorted so many of those convoys. During those years, the Mersey estuary was frequently crowded with merchant ships riding at anchor while they waited their turn to get into dock to unload their precious cargoes, protected in the meanwhile by a veritable canopy of barrage balloons intended to deter attack by dive-bombers or low-flying aircraft. An extraordinary sight and vivid testimony to the fact that Merseyside's eleven miles of docks and wharves were then handling over ninety percent of all war-related supplies entering Britain from abroad.

France capitulated to the German invaders in June 1940. In July, the Battle of Britain began. At the end of August, the Luftwaffe turned its attention from RAF airfields to London itself in the fruitless hope of destroying British morale and inducing the nation to respond positively to Hitler's peace feelers. Around the same time it became Liverpool's turn. The first substantial raid took place on the night of August 28 and, though varying in size and intensity, air raids, over three hundred in all, were destined to continue for almost a year and a half. The last truly damaging incursion occurred late in January 1942 when Hitler's military preoccupations had long since begun to shift eastward. Ironically enough, one of the houses destroyed in that last heavy raid was the one on Upper Stanhope Street where Hitler's half-brother Alois had lived before the First World War and where Hitler's nephew, William Patrick Hitler, had been born.

During those grim—though for a boy, I should confess, oddly energizing—eighteen months, the civilian casualty rate in Merseyside was very high; it involved approximately four thousand fatalities with many thousands more injured. The intensity of the raids fluctuated, peaking just before the Christmas of 1940 when, as we now know, the Luftwaffe threw into action some three hundred aircraft, and peaking again in May 1941. At the beginning of that latter month, and over the course of a horrible seven successive nights, the city and its environs were pounded by swarms of enemy aircraft peaking at almost seven hundred. While my memories of the whole eighteen months are uneven in nature, that awful May week (later to be memorialized in Nicholas Monsarrat's novel, *The Cruel Sea*) is unforgettable. The water mains had been destroyed, so the great fires raging at the city center burned on, day and night, illuminating what was for us in the southern suburbs the northwest quadrant of the sky and serving as an inextinguishable beacon for returning waves of German attackers. The Anglican cathedral was hit, an historic parish church, the municipal museum, and the Custom House utterly destroyed, several big stores were gutted by fire, the whole city center was torn apart, thousands of housing units were destroyed, and the damage done to the vital docking and harbor facilities was so extensive that it was not deemed prudent at the time to report on it fully. In the Huskisson Dock a munitions ship caught fire and finally blew up with such an appalling roar that we, three miles and more away, knew that something unusually terrible had happened. Across town in the Breck Road area where our Uncle Frank lived (again, no blood relative but an old musician friend of my father's from Athlone days who now played French horn with the Liverpool Philharmonic Orchestra), an ammunition train becalmed in a railway siding was set on fire by incendiary bombs. Wagon after wagon exploded, and the waves of blast from each successive explosion shattered the windows and progressively reduced to rubble the brick dwellings clustered in a neighboring housing estate. During that week my father, who had on rotation supervisory responsibilities over the fire watchers at his workplace, did not reappear for the better part of a day and a night, and he got home then only because the whole factory had to be evacuated when it was discovered that a high explosive bomb, which had failed to detonate, had burrowed down in the ground below his department and was lying there with its lethal fuse still intact.

Those air raids of May 1941 stand out in my memory because they were so ferocious. The norm, insofar as there was a norm, for enemy incursions varied in intensity, fell into a somewhat more predictable quasi-routine. Sometimes we would detect the throbbing drone of approaching enemy aircraft even before we heard the banshee wailing of the warning siren. At the time, rightly or wrongly, we were all convinced that we could distinguish between the steadier drone of RAF planes and the fluctuating sound of Luftwaffe engines (a mesmerizing "Where are you, where are you, where are you" sound, as the novelist Graham Greene, then fire watching in London, was later to describe it). So far as sound in general went, the unseductive music of the night, when an air raid reached its moment of peak intensity the racket was simply enormous—a continuous and cacophonous crepitation of exploding antiaircraft ordnance, punctuated by the eerie scream or whistle of high explosive bombs as they pursued their fearful trajectories down to earth, followed by a louder and deeper crump as they exploded, if not on some intended target, then often with devastating effect at random points of misfortune. More than once, crowded communal air-raid shelters in Liverpool were hit, with devastating casualties ensuing. Nor were the suburban residential areas immune to meaningless destruction by seemingly random sticks of bombs. As for the visual effects, we would sometimes turn off the lights, go into the bay-windowed front room (a parlor, though we didn't use that term), draw back the blackout curtains and peer out into the night sky. The sight was a mesmerizing one. The whole arc of the sky took on the appearance of a darkened lunar landscape, pitted, pocked, and cratered by the constant succession of exploding antiaircraft shells and lanced by moving fingers of light as searchlights, trying to pinpoint enemy aircraft, probed relentlessly into the nooks and crannies of the night. Once we saw an unfortunate German plane caught at the intersection of two such searchlight beams (being "coned" is, I believe, the term of art that fliers used for that surely terrifying experience). What the pilot did in this particular case was to crawl down one of the two beams like a silver moth seeking to reach (or to shoot out?) the source of light before somehow wriggling out of his moment of unwelcome prominence and reentering the redemptive embrace of darkness. After becoming habituated to such sights, the return of firework displays in the postwar years came inevitably as something of an anticlimax.

While those eighteen months were punctuated, on the one hand, by some moments of great drama, on the other they gradually fell into a predictable routine. The ululating wail of the siren sounding the warning that enemy aircraft were approaching, the throbbing sound of aircraft engines, and the steady note of the eventual "All Clear" became so familiar as to merge with the predictable routines of daily life and the fitful dreams of night. Like everyone else, we went about our business, got on with things, and more or less did what we were told to do in order to improve our chances for survival. We equipped our windows with blackout curtains and crisscrossed the panes of glass with adhesive tape in order to reduce the danger posed by flying shards of glass if the windows were blown in by the blast from a bomb. In addition, my father constructed reasonably stout shutters for the kitchen and the living room. The latter had a fireplace in which we burned coal and coke to heat both the room and the boiler that was the sole source of whatever hot water we had. It was the only heated room in the house. During the nights when it did not seem safe to go to bed, we more or less lived in those two rooms, especially after we had abandoned the practice of spending several miserable nighttime hours in the spider-infested dankness of our Anderson air-raid shelter. Observation of bomb damage to houses in our immediate vicinity had conveyed the lesson that when semidetached houses were badly damaged by blast, the thicker central dividing wall, buttressed by its chimney, tended to remain standing. So we fell into the practice of pushing a sturdy dining room table up against the central wall and close to the chimney and putting a pile of cushions and pillows under it so we could try to catch some sleep in warm surroundings and under whatever protection it offered. Wisely or unwisely, we ended up using that as our shelter. There we would lie, depending upon the intensity of the attack, dozing, talking, cowering, and, from time to time, reciting together a family rosary.

High explosive bombs seemed to us to follow a slanting trajectory. Only in the last few seconds would it become clear whether the bomb in question was going to hit us, was falling short, or was destined to pass overhead and hit the ground beyond—as did the nearest miss to our house, landing some four hundred yards away in a field and making an impressive crater but dissipating in the softness of the ground much of its dangerous blast effect. Incendiary bombs or bomblets, on the other hand, clustered in a container that spewed them out at some distance above the ground, were broadcast much more widely and indiscriminately. My brother tells me that one such, landing outside in the road on which our house stood, ignited its tar surface so that for a few moments, until it was extinguished with sandbags, it looked as if the Woolton Road itself could become a ribbon of fire. The local fire watchers who dealt with it wore their regulation steel helmets. But our drunken neighbor, feeling no doubt that he ought to do his bit, put in an impressive appearance wearing for protection one of his prized World War I souvenirs, an old-fashioned German *Pickelhaube*, or helmet crested with a formidable spike. Of that incident, however, I have no recollection. Despite the reported excitement of the moment, I appear to have slept soundly right through it. Some of the heavy bombs that we were accustomed to calling "screaming bombs" made a particularly unnerving sound as they descended, and that made our rough and ready assessment of their trajectories an even more fearful business. At such moments we instinctively held our breaths and our prayers would momentarily falter. But while the immediate reaction was one, of course, of breath-catching fear, we lived fervently in an enchanted Catholic sacramental universe, fraught with the outward signs of inward grace, and we still felt to the very depths of our being that no matter what happened we would endure together, if perhaps in a better place. We were instinctively attuned, it seems, to Julian of Norwich's late-medieval mystic sense that in the end "all shall be well, and all shall be well, and all manner of things shall be well." Ours was a kindly God and, as the Psalmist assured us, we his children could shelter under the shadow of his almighty wings. In the words of Psalm 90 (91), sung every day in the lovely service of Compline as darkness falls across the Christian monastic world, we were adjured to fear neither "the arrow that flyeth by day" nor "the terror that stalketh by night." God would cover us with his pinions and under his wings could we find our refuge:

> Scapulis suis obumbrabit tibi:
> et sub pennis ejus sperabis.
>   Scuto circumdabit te veritas ejus:
> Non timebis a timore nocturno,
>   A sagitta volante in die,
> a negotio perambulante in tenebris;
>   ab incursu, et daemonio meridiano.

At some level, in the embrace of such deep-rooted beliefs, one finds one's way almost instinctively to a certain calm and tranquility of spirit, something akin, perhaps, to Stoicism but without the latter's persistently pessimistic undertow. That spirit certainly carried on into the daylight hours after nights when our sleep had been interrupted by air raid warnings, the sound of bombers overhead, and the persistent racket of antiaircraft fire. In the mornings, moved by a spirit cognate to that of the young boy in John Boorman's splendid 1987 film *Hope and Glory*, we boys would sally forth to pick out the interesting pieces from the litter of shrapnel blanketing paths and roadways. For we all had shrapnel collections, I'm not quite sure why, and we conducted a lively trade of swapping pieces with the object of maximizing the quality and interest of our own particular collection and in an attempt, especially, to add what we all agreed was the *pièce de résistance*—namely, the aluminum tail of an incendiary bomb, for those tails tended to survive the combustion of the body of the bomb.

In order to round out the picture of what we experienced and felt during those far-off months of turmoil, several moments deserve mention. Surprisingly enough, they all stem from the daylight hours. First, the sudden appearance one evening while I was playing outside after tea, and almost simultaneously with the wail of the air raid warning and the opening up of firing by a nearby antiaircraft battery, of a solitary, low-flying German plane (I didn't recognize its make but I assumed it was a reconnaissance plane). It was following the line of the river, perhaps photographing harbor installations, and was flying so low, pursued by laggard bursts of antiaircraft fire, that one could see not only the silhouette of the pilot's head within the cockpit canopy but also the crosses on the side of the fuselage and even the swastika on the tail. It was an arresting sight to see a combatant going about his assigned task with such *sangfroid* and exhibiting so condescending a degree of indifference to the hapless enemies trying to encompass his destruction.

The second moment was very different in nature. I had gone off one afternoon to play with a friend, Bernard Smythe, a very independent-minded boy who was something of an explorer and intrepid wanderer by temperament and about whose possibly bad influence on me, or so I sensed, my parents were not altogether happy. That afternoon we had made our way for about two miles to what was known locally as the "Cast Iron Shore" (one of the local names that made their way into the Beatles' songs later on). It is a part of the South Liverpool shoreline stretching from Dingle to Garston Docks where, in the eighteenth century, the hulks of ships had apparently been beached to be broken up for metal scrap—hence the name. One stretch of it is occupied by Cressington Park, an area filled with large Victorian and Edwardian era houses. Many of these houses are subdivided into several flats today, but originally they were large stand-alone residences for well-to-do people, clustered in what was originally a gated community equipped with its own railway station and its own promenaded (though hardly salubrious) beach area. Our chosen destination was not Cressington Park, but instead the area of shoreline stretching beyond it on the Dingle side. There, a seawall had been built along the river, enclosing reclaimed land that was slowly being leveled with rubble and fill and was eventually to be transformed into municipal parkland. At the time it was still in very rough shape—a desolate, deserted, uneven landscape that was interesting to explore. That was precisely what we were doing when, in midafternoon, the air raid warning sounded. We heard no German planes and the antiaircraft batteries in the immediate vicinity did not open up. Looking down the river, however, past Dingle and close to the dock installations at the city center, we could see the tiny dot of an airplane being pursued, ineffectually as usual, by bursting antiaircraft shells. It was, I suppose, another reconnaissance plane, and after about three-quarters of an hour it disappeared, the shooting stopped, and the All Clear sounded. Where we were playing, there was absolutely no place to shelter, but the action was far enough away from us that we had never been in danger. Because of that, presumably, it never occurred to us that our parents had no way of knowing we were safe and that we had better make our way home straightaway in order to reassure them. So we played on and on. Even when it would have been time on a normal day to get home for tea, Bernard wanted to continue our explorations and I was foolish enough to go along with him. In the event, it was well after teatime when I finally got home and my heart sank when I saw that my father was already back from work. Upon my arrival, all hell broke loose. I was not in the habit of returning home late, certainly never as late as I was that day. Unable to pinpoint the precise focus of the air raid or which antiaircraft batteries had opened fire (a highly pertinent point of information because, as they well knew, falling shrapnel could be lethal), my parents had begun, with the worrying passage of time, to imagine the worst—the knock on the door, the grim-faced policeman bearing terrible news, the loss of their youngest through the sort of meaningless and accidental misfortune of war that the events of the past year had made so familiar.

And then I finally showed up, to be met with a highly combustible mixture of anger and relief. As I tried to bluster my way out of the singularly unpleasant corner into which I had painted myself, I must have slipped into cheekiness towards my mother, for my father, by disposition a gentle man, exploded into terrifying rage and slapped me hard with his open hand on one of my cheeks, sending me staggering. It was the only time, I think, that he ever hit me. I responded with a mixture of angry bluster and tearful bravado, hurling myself at him with clenched fists in a futile attempt to punch away at him. But I was only nine and he a six-footer. Sensing, I think, that I was momentarily consumed by an unhappy mixture of guilty petulance and angry humiliation, he simply held me firmly until I quieted down. The momentary *Sturm und Drang* dissipated as quickly as it had begun, and my mother gave me some special treat with my tea by way of signaling that what was past was, indeed, past. For both my parents relief was the dominant emotion and, recognizing that fact, I was determined never again to be guilty of anything so stupidly inconsiderate.

While the third moment worthy of memorialization was different yet again, it also attests, I am afraid, to the limits of such noble determination. It concerns a land mine. Land mines were a particularly fearsome and powerful type of high explosive ordnance deployed by the Luftwaffe and familiar to us because more than one had been dropped in our vicinity. They were adapted from the type of mine used at sea, and, given their large size, were each dropped with an individual parachute. The one in question had hit the ground about three-quarters of a mile away from our house but very close to where our friends the Elmslys lived. Fortunately, it had failed to explode on impact. Pending its defusion by a bomb disposal squad (a long, drawn-out affair because they were very hard pressed), a large section of housing in South Garston was cordoned off and the residents were evacuated, among them, of course, the Elmslys. They moved in with us and stayed two nights until the land mine had been neutralized and removed. It made for a big crowd in our small house and we had to sleep all over the place. But I remember it as a jolly time, an exciting break with the dullness of routine.

By the time all of this happened, my school, not that far from the area evacuated, was open once more and back in business. The next day, then, on our way home from school, a friend and I stopped to take a look at the proscribed and cordoned-off area in the hope of catching a glimpse of the dreaded land mine itself. There were two policemen and a knot of bored onlookers by the cordoned-off principal road (Duncombe Road) running through this particular residential area. But the entrances to the side streets, though roped off, were unguarded. So we slipped unnoticed under the rope and started making our way by a circuitous route down towards the spot where, we had been told, the land mine had hit the ground. As we plunged furtively into the heart of the area, the total absence of human beings, and even of dogs and cats, as well as the deepening and unaccustomed silence began to play tricks on our imaginations and to jangle our nerves. We were tempted, accordingly, to withdraw but, boyish curiosity warring with reluctant timidity, we somehow persisted in our quest. Later on in high school, when I first read the opening sections of Wordsworth's "Prelude," I was struck by an unexpected sense of familiarity. For there, of course, the poet relates the story of a boyhood escapade of his that unpredictably went awry. Like the young Wordsworth's purloining of a boat in order to row out into the magical darkness of a silent, moonlit lake, ours, too, was "an act of stealth and troubled pleasure." And, like Wordsworth's illicit adventure, ours also ended disconcertingly. Rounding the corner of a side street, we came suddenly within close view of the object of our quest. There it was, protruding unmistakably from the soft ground of the front garden of a house (on Whitehedge Road, I think); its parachute had snagged on a chimney pot and was spread out across the roof, flapping and rippling in the periodic gusts of wind. And the land mine itself, looking for all the world like the end of a huge, black cigar, was halfway embedded, and incongruously so, amid the carefully tended flower beds of a typically English front garden. It lay at an angle, inclining slightly towards the nearby wall of the house, in a position that oddly combined a measure of unwelcome intimacy with the projection of bone-chilling menace. It was the latter that caught our bemused and guilty attention and shook us to the core. The young Wordsworth had been driven into flight back to the shore by the gradual emergence before his startled eyes of a mountainous "grim shape" towering between him and the stars and seeming to pursue him,

> . . . a huge shape, black and huge [which],
> As if with voluntary power instinct
> Upreared its head.

It was the potential voluntary power of our own black and huge prominence, far bigger and more monstrous than we had imagined, that got to us. It was unnecessary to do any more than exchange terrified glances before turning on our heels and running headlong for safety down one of the side streets (Stormont Road?), half expecting to be hurled forward by a surge of blast from the malign device whose explosion our illicit presence might somehow have triggered. That didn't happen, of course, but we still didn't slow down. Ducking swiftly under the cordon and dashing by a startled passerby, we ran for a couple of hundred yards until we were well in the middle of the Long Lane recreation ground. Then, gathering our wits together, we made our way home, more or less in silence, across the park.

I cannot claim, with the young Wordsworth, that

> . . . for many days, my brain
> Worked with a dim and undetermined sense
> Of unknown modes of being.

Nothing so high minded as that. But the "certain darkness" he refers to did, I suppose, hang over my thoughts. We were an oddly chastened duo and, through a combination of fear of retribution and consideration for parental worries about the safety of their children under dangerous wartime conditions, we refrained, in accordance with a more or less tacit compact, from sharing with our respective parents the story of that particularly stupid escapade.

CHAPTER FOUR

Ad majorem dei gloriam

Although during these difficult years the exigencies of war intruded upon almost every aspect of our lives, much of what we did during the Blitz and the pinched, dreary years thereafter had in itself nothing at all to do with enemy hostilities or the epic global struggle of the Allies to turn the tide of battle in their favor. It was, in fact, my schooling that occupied most of my attention during those years, with my latter time at our parish elementary school unfolding against the backdrop of the devastating losses of merchant shipping and personnel in the Atlantic convoys of 1941 and 1942 (which meant for people in a port city like Liverpool the loss of many a relative, neighbor, or friend) and the backdrop of the seesaw campaigns in the deserts of North Africa which rendered familiar names like Tripoli, Benghazi, and Tobruk that were destined to return once more, seventy years later, to the front pages of our newspapers. They unfolded also against the successive catastrophes in Eastern Europe and the Far East—the stunning German advance to the very gates of Leningrad and Moscow, the attack on Pearl Harbor and subsequent loss of the Philippines and much of South-East Asia to Japanese occupation, as well as (and at the forefront of British minds) the sinking of the battleships HMS *Prince of Wales* and HMS *Repulse* and the appalling rout of Commonwealth forces in Malaya and Singapore. I followed all of these happenings on wireless news, in the local newspapers, and via the Pathé newsreels shown before films (my father loved the movies and often took us with him to our local cinema on Saturday evenings). And the more immediate presence of war was brought home on a daily basis by the passage along the Woolton Road of trucks filled with troops and of more sluggish convoys carrying the fuselages of fighter planes to the Rootes aircraft factory in nearby Speke, where they would be fitted with their engines. We were particularly taken, as time went on, with the appearance of twin fuselaged Lockheed Lightnings, as well as by the passage of trucks bearing Italian prisoners of war to the farms outside the city limits. Apparently relieved to be out of the fray, they usually made their way singing and didn't fail to whistle at any English girls they passed. The latter were prone to waving back excitedly, though not as excitedly as when trucks carrying American soldiers began to put in an appearance. This last understandably gave rise to ill feelings among their poorly paid and less well-attired British counterparts. I can recall that one truck carrying some of the latter had chalked on its side the sourly resentful message: "Don't wave girls, we're only British!"

But all of these goings-on notwithstanding, my own attention had to be focused, above all, on what was going on at school. Sometime in the 1942–43 school year I took the examination for a Junior City Scholarship and, in view of my mother's earlier worries, we were all mightily relieved when I was awarded one. In the autumn of 1943, then, I moved to my new school, St. Francis Xavier's College (SFX), a Jesuit school that, in the nomenclature of the day, was a direct-grant grammar school. I began my studies there not long after the great Soviet victory at Stalingrad and the turning of the tide in the Battle of the Atlantic, and just before the Eighth Army's decisive defeat of the German-Italian forces at El Alamein in North Africa. My grammar school years, (1943–50), were to straddle the period dominated by the ultimately successful Allied effort to crush the Axis powers and the unutterably dreary postwar years that were marked, in Britain at least, by national economic privation, continuing shortages of practically everything, the painfully slow restoration of public services (like street lighting), and the equally sluggish reconstruction of the basic infrastructure destroyed or run down during the years of war.

My early years at elementary school had provided good conditions for learning. The teachers were kindly and attentive, the setting and atmosphere relatively benign—though marred somewhat in my case by the amount of anti-Irish feeling that was prevalent among the boys and that led to my involvement in an unfortunate series of fights or scuffles. Liverpool, like Boston, numbers among its population a comparatively large proportion of people who are ultimately of Irish descent—most coming from families whose arrival dates back to the great migration that occurred in the 1850s in the context of the potato famine and during the decade or two immediately following. In contrast with the Boston Irish, however, who continue proudly to think of themselves as somehow Irish, by the time of the Second World War their Liverpool equivalents had long since ceased to think of themselves as anything other than English. It was a great irony, then, that so many of the boys who jeered at me, sneering that the Irish were dirty people who lived with their pigs, or were Nazi sympathizers guilty of refueling the very German submarines that were torpedoing Allied shipping, and so on, bore, unlike me, unambiguously Irish surnames like Murphy, Kelly, O'Flaherty, O'Brien, O'Donnell, and O'Connell. Whatever the case, it wasn't much fun. But the miseries involved were no more than intermittent, and they were dwarfed by the startling change of atmosphere that later occurred when my school, attached to the parish of St. Francis of Assisi, had to take in the boys and girls from the school attached to Holy Trinity parish, which could cater to their needs only into their eighth year. These were the children whom we came to dread and to whom we referred as the kids from "under the bridge"—the local equivalent of the American term "across the tracks." The bridge in question carried the railway line that ran parallel to the Garston dockside area and the children in question came from the old, grim, and slummy row housing crammed in between the railway and the river. They were a rough and tough lot, often ill-fed, ill-clad, and dirty (upon their arrival, head lice became a problem for all of us), as well as ill-behaved, adept at cruel bullying, and, as I would now in retrospect judge, frequently immature for their age. Though there were some striking exceptions, learning tended to bulk large neither in their own priorities nor in those of their parents, and our classes, two of them side by side in one open classroom, with a third separated from the other two by nothing more substantial than a flimsy glass partition, swiftly took on some of the characteristics associated with the word "bedlam." The male teachers at the school had been called up for military service, and they had been replaced by women who had left the teaching profession after getting married, sometimes long years earlier. Some of these women found it difficult or even impossible to cope with the obstreperous behavior of the new arrivals. The noise level, accordingly, could sometimes reach appalling dimensions, and I can remember wishing longingly for the headmaster, the only man still on the staff, to show up with his cane, punish the promoters of chaos, and restore order, if only for a while. He himself was an excellent teacher when he had the chance to take over a class (he was kind enough to give me some tutoring in arithmetic after school hours), but it was his unforgiving wartime fate to have to spend much of his time making punitive rounds from class to class simply in order to keep the lid on.

My departure for SFX, where Noel was still at school, was thus something of a welcome relief. The Junior City Scholarship not only took care of school fees but also included an allowance to help with the purchase of the requisite (maroon) school blazer, cap, and tie, and defrayed the costs involved in travelling to and from school via public transport—tramcar and, later, bus. The school had been founded not long after the Jesuits established themselves in a parish at Liverpool in the wake of Catholic Emancipation (1829) and the abrogation of the centuries-old Penal Laws that had burdened Catholics and excluded them from public life. It was situated close to the city center in what had been a prosperous mercantile district in the nineteenth century, but which, by 1943, had degenerated into a half-bombed-out slum. While the school building itself had incurred only minor damage during the Blitz, Salisbury Street, on which it stood, had taken a bit of a beating with the surviving houses sticking up unevenly like rotting teeth embedded in a singularly unattractive, rubble-strewn gum.

Upon that school we descended six days a week (half days on Wednesdays and Saturdays), boys from all over Merseyside and contiguous parts of the county of Lancashire. Some of those from the county bore surnames like Blundell and Scarisbrick that had a long and proud association with the stubborn regional tradition of Catholic recusancy, or refusal to conform to the Reformation religious settlement. We came by tramcar, train, bike, and bus, and, identified unmistakably by our school uniforms, had frequently to run something of a gauntlet between the tram or bus stop and the school gate, pursued by jeers of "college puddin'" from the local toughs. The trip from where we lived in Garston took about an hour and involved changing trams at the transfer point known as "Penny Lane"—like "Strawberry Fields" and the "Cast-Iron Shore," a local name later to be destined for immortality by virtue of its association with a Beatles song. And I have vivid memories from the years that ensued of desperately trying to memorize geometry theorems or Latin conjugations and declensions while seated, school-bound and petrified, at the back of a freezing and swaying tram. The school building on which we converged, a three-story piece of Victoriana now renovated and part of the Liverpool Hope University campus, was then a rather grim, gloomy, and grimy place, threadbare after years of economic depression and war, with large but dirty windows and a toilet and washroom facility which, while less appallingly noisome than the one at my equally old and run-down elementary school, had long since seen all its putative soap dispensers smashed and was almost permanently bereft of even the merest trickle of hot water.

It was not, physically-speaking, a particularly prepossessing or inviting facility. But some very good things took place, nonetheless, within its grimy walls. That they did so reflects, I believe, the quality and dedication of its teachers, the heart-of-the-matter intensity of its academic focus, and the unquestionable Jesuit commitment to the importance and nobility of the intellectual quest. There were only two Catholic grammar schools in Liverpool and, given that fact, the boys brought together at SFX were drawn from a broad array of social backgrounds, ranging from the marginally impoverished to the solid and comfortable middle class. Some came, accordingly, from families with little interest in the impracticalities of the type of academic education being offered, and it would have been all too easy for the school to "sell" its program, the demands being made, and the heavy burden of homework imposed, on the grounds that those things would enable the graduates to get "good jobs." But I cannot remember ever having heard anything to that effect. The emphasis, instead, seemed to be on the intellectual quest, not so much as an end in itself but as part of the ongoing effort of faith seeking understanding and as something directed to "the greater glory of God" (*Ad majorem dei gloriam*, or AMDG, the Jesuit motto). And in recognition of that fact, we were taught to inscribe "AMDG" at the top of all our essays and themes, with "LDS" (*Laus deo semper*, or "Glory be to God forever") inscribed at the end as a sort of spiritual QED.

In the Lower School (forms 1 to 5), boys were prepared for what was then called the School Certificate, which was awarded after an external public examination administered by a consortium of universities. The boys were unashamedly "streamed" by tested ability level into four separate classes to which were attached the totally transparent labels of A, B, C, and D. Some of the earlier cultural amenities (e.g., a school chorus and orchestra—how I would have loved to play in one!) had gone their way during the upheavals and stringencies of the war years. What remained was a rather stripped-down curriculum, its central focus being a narrowish group of strictly academic subjects in which the boys would have to present themselves for external examination: Latin, French, English, history, mathematics, and general science, with the addition at the age of thirteen of either chemistry and physics or Greek. This was a rather stark choice to have to make at that age. Mathematics was my best subject and I had enjoyed the general science taught in the first two forms, so I chose (unlike my brother Noel) to forego Greek and take chemistry and physics. The first of those sciences was taught very well, the second, alas, abysmally. I came to regret that choice later on when, having decided that I needed at least a smattering of Greek, I committed myself as a Williams faculty member to taking our introductory course in the subject. It met at 8:00 a.m. five days a week and was largely populated by young women students of daunting diligence and formidable competence. It was taught very skillfully and moved along rapidly. Remembering the glacial grind of the Latin classes of my high school days, I came away impressed with the speed at which language instruction can progress with bright, committed college students.

In addition to the core group of subjects at SFX, we were also taught religion, geography, and art, but as subsidiary subjects not examined for the School Certificate. The teaching of religion, oddly enough, did not bulk at all large. It was indifferently done and I can remember little or nothing about the form it took apart from the reading one year of Luke-Acts and the memorization of the Westminster Catechism—the English Catholic equivalent of the American Baltimore Catechism. Geography and art, on the other hand, I very much liked; both were well taught, the former in very traditional but interesting fashion with much drawing and memorization of maps, the latter in very creative and imaginative fashion. We painted, learned perspective drawing, and were let loose on elementary architectural design and the design of posters, furniture, decorative motifs for wallpaper, and so on. Perhaps inspired by Gustav Klimt and the Viennese Secessionists at the turn of the century, our teacher abhorred the distinction between arts and crafts and had us spend a lot of time drawing or designing knives, forks, spoons, cups, teapots, and saucers. He himself was very much "form follows function" in his aesthetic sensibilities and, under his influence, we were led to despise the over-elaborate Victorian furnishings with which we were surrounded and the gloomy, Gothic-revival buildings that seemed in Liverpool depressingly omnipresent. "Slaughterhouse Gothic!," we uppish boys would sniff dismissively, and it was to be some years before I could overcome such early prejudices and concede the sheer beauty of a truly great neo-Gothic building like the National Cathedral in Washington, DC, or, for that matter, of the Anglican cathedral in Liverpool, built out of the local sandstone, designed by Sir Giles Gilbert Scott, and situated on a commanding site overlooking the Mersey.

By my time, though the earlier school orchestra and chorus had both fallen by the wayside, we were still taught the traditional English and Scottish songs in periodic singing classes and, until my voice broke, I also contributed an undistinguished contralto to a small church choir that led the hymn singing at the end-of-the-week Benedictine service the whole school attended in the handsome SFX parish church. On those occasions, looking down from the choir loft while the reverend the headmaster delivered pedantic sermons on recondite topics like the Immaculate Conception, I can remember observing the occasional boy pursuing an alternative vision of immortality by surreptitiously carving his initials into the back of the pew in front of him. This was an offense, if one were caught, that carried the penalty of immediate expulsion. But as the condition of the pews itself testified, it was a traditional schoolboy practice that went back into the mid-nineteenth century. And there still runs through my mind the exultant sound of five hundred boys, fired up by the prospect of the impending deliverance from school at the end of the week, belting out to the melody of Ralph Vaughan Williams's splendid hymn "For All the Saints" the Latin words of a Marian hymn pleading (appropriately enough) for release of suffering souls from purgatory:

Languentibus in Purgatorio
Qui purgantur, adore nimio;
Subveniat tua compassio,
O Maria! O Maria!

For our physical, as opposed to spiritual, well-being we were exposed
to regular, well-planned, and quite rigorous sessions of physical education (gym), learning among other things how to do balance walking on
the Swedish beam and how to climb fifteen-foot ropes—both skills that
were to prove valuable later on when I became a soldier. But there was
no instruction in swimming (swimming pools were closed for much of
the war) and no coaching in the two sports in which the school competed: football (soccer) and cricket. Those who did well enough in those
sports to make it onto the school teams tended to have learned the appropriate skills from their fathers. As my Irish father had played neither
of those English sports and could give no such help, or perhaps because
I possessed no natural aptitude for them, I got nowhere with either of
those sports. So far as cricket went, that was a source of some sorrow for
I adored the game, serving in the sixth form as scorer for our first eleven
and following closely the performance of the leading professional teams.
My father and mother were also nonswimmers and, having had no formal instruction in that either, I never became more than an indifferent
swimmer, capable of little more than passing the not-very-stringent test
required at officer cadet school—that of swimming, fully clothed, one
length of an Olympic-sized pool.

While most of our teachers were Jesuits, either priests or younger
"scholastics" still making their way through the lengthy period of training and discernment before being ordained and, after that, admitted to
final vows, a few were laymen. Nearly all of the latter were Great War
veterans afflicted with various disabilities: one had been gassed and was
overtaken periodically by horrible bouts of racking coughing; one had
lost a leg, was equipped with a very creaky artificial limb, and, with a certain inevitability, was known among the boys accordingly as "Peg-leg";
another had lost the better part of a hand and we fixated, with morbid
curiosity, on the rigid, artificial fingers that made that hand at least partly
usable. Most, if not all, I realize at least in retrospect, were capable teachers and decent human beings, devoid, it seems, of any English snobbery

and comfortable and sympathetic in their dealings with the boys. But upper-level Latin and mathematics, while taught very well by Jesuit and laymen alike, tended to be taught by fear. And thereby hangs a tale.

While at SFX no corporal punishment was inflicted in class, no dramatic outbursts of pedagogical ire followed by punitive retribution, appropriate behavior on the part of the boys, a calm atmosphere conducive to learning, and the conscientious completion of one's work both in the classroom and at home was ensured by a baroque and, in the Jesuit fashion, highly rationalized, system of discipline that my own children refuse to believe could have existed, even sixty years ago. But it did, and its nature deserves a mention.

That system worked as follows. If a boy had not done his homework assignment properly or was guilty of misconduct, the teacher would characteristically tell the miscreant to see him after class. The boy would then be presented with what we called a "white bill," a small piece of paper signed by the teacher, with AMDG at the top and LDS at the bottom, indicating the boy's name, the nature of his misdemeanor, and the number of ferula strokes it warranted by way of penalty—"six ferulae," for example, or "twice-nine." The ferula was a small, bat-shaped implement made, we thought, of whalebone covered with rubber, though, in *A Portrait of the Artist as a Young Man*, Joyce portrays the boys at Clongowes Wood College, also a Jesuit school and one that a Dublin cousin of mine was later to attend, as believing it to be made of "whalebone and leather with lead inside." At the next break, the miscreant was required to take the bill to the prefect of discipline for registration, at which point he had the right to protest the punishment as unwarranted or unjust. This last was little more than a formality and, if the protest was viewed as frivolous, could lead to an increase in the severity of the punishment. The one time I myself tried on such an occasion to plead my innocence, the prefect of discipline, a splenetic Scotsman, coldly informed me that he usually found the masters to be right. I got the message and did not press my pathetic point. That formality completed, we had to take the bill at a set time to an office where one of the young scholastics would have the job of delivering the punishment itself, entering that fact into the record and returning the white bill to the teacher who had written it. The punishment was always delivered on the hands and could be severe enough to raise blood blisters. But, this being a boy's school and the maintenance of a stiff upper lip being essential, the main challenge was that of avoiding any whimpering, sign of tears, or loss of face. The reward was the extension of comradely respect and the strengthening of the species of tribal solidarity that, religion to the contrary, formed the bedrock of our communal ethic. The whole atmosphere was one very much informed by a sense of "us against them," and in such an atmosphere whining was almost as unacceptable as snitching. I was an interested student who wanted to learn and I don't believe I was, in general, a badly behaved boy. But during my four years in the Lower School (such punishments more or less ceased once one was in the sixth form), I received a total of around eighty-nine strokes (we all tried to keep tabs on our total), almost entirely for the petty misconduct of talking out of turn in class. None of this did I mention to my parents, knowing that, if I did so, they would simply reproach me for having misbehaved.

To that whole bizarre system, however, cruel though I suppose it was, a comic footnote attached. This being a traditional Catholic school of the pre–Vatican II era, there almost inevitably had to be some sort of indulgence option attached. And, indeed, there was. This took the form of the "red bill" subsystem. Red bills were quite handsome documents, formally printed in Latin on red paper, with AMDG at the top and LDS at the bottom, and they were awarded to students who had done well in the regular end-of-term examinations. All the teacher involved had to do was to fill in the number of ferula strokes to be remitted and to sign the bill. Not all teachers would accept such red bills when they were proffered by boys seeking remittance of punishment, but most would. Some of the more softhearted, in fact, would accept a red bill even if it had not been awarded to the boy presenting it but to a friend. Boys being ingenious gamers of almost any system, that inevitably opened up the way to a rather lively black market on which these instruments of indulgence were bought and sold for cash. I don't believe I ever sold such a bill, but for years I kept one folded up in my wallet as a souvenir and I much regret losing that bill along with the wallet itself. Had I still possessed it when my own children were themselves growing up and at high school, they might not have greeted my moving description of the disciplinary system at SFX with such knowing looks of total disbelief.

While most of us were proud to be at SFX, which enjoyed an enviable reputation among Liverpool grammar schools both as an academic powerhouse and for the prowess of its football team, I can't say that during our years in the Lower School we actually *liked* the place. The atmosphere was a bit too pressured for that and the shadow cast by the ever-present threat of punishment was such that the dark loom of Monday could cast a bit of a premonitory pall even over whatever time off we had at weekends. But life outside school, with all of its sustaining distractions, still went on. The established church notwithstanding, England, compared with the United States, is a markedly secular country. And that was so even when I was a child. But, against the odds, I had grown up in what amounted to a Catholic subculture. What I was the beneficiary of at home as a child, then, was what I once heard the distinguished sociologist of religion, Bob Wuthnow, refer to as a "heavy duty religious upbringing." Regular confession on Saturdays was followed by mass on Sunday mornings, the last of which was a *missa cantata* (full-scale sung High Mass). The parish choir was a good, well-directed one in which my father anchored the bass section, and I was accustomed from early childhood to hearing well-sung Gregorian chant and Palestrina motets. Sunday afternoon might bring with it a benediction service, while the evening certainly brought with it a choral service, sung in English and akin to the Anglican Evensong. And in Lent we made the Stations of the Cross. Both Lent and Advent were taken seriously as penitential seasons preparatory to the celebratory joys of Easter and Christmas. In our lives, the liturgical calendar was mapped onto and in many ways dominated the secular one. On Good Fridays, as the church bell tolled solemnly at 3:00 p.m., it was as if space and time had been transcended, and in our imaginations Christ died once more on the cross.

This being so, it is not surprising that, while still at elementary school, I had busied myself not only as a member of a Boy Scout troop in the Woolton area, but also as an altar boy at our parish church. In the latter capacity, when it was my turn, I had to make my way in the early morning darkness, and not infrequently in fog, on foot or (later) by bike to our parish church in order to serve at the first mass of the day. The church was a neo-Gothic structure in the thirteenth-century English style with partly stained glass pencil windows. It was not easy to black out, but the regulations were met by reducing light in the nave to a minimal glimmer cast downwards from carefully dimmed lamps and by illuminating the altar with little more than candlelight. Somewhat later on, when we were required at school to memorize large chunks of Milton's minor poems, I was to resonate nostalgically with his reference to

> . . . storied windows richly dight,
> Casting a dim religious light.

I thought I knew exactly what he had in mind. If I associated any darkness with religion, it was a benign and physical one, evocative of the beauty of holiness. As an altar boy I served also as acolyte at many a Requiem Mass and subsequent service of interment. Some of the beautiful words used in the latter ritual continue still to ring through my mind and retain their power to move, among them the antiphon said (or sung) just prior to burial:

> In paradisum deducant te Angeli:
> in tuo adventu suscipiant te Martyres,
> et perducant te in civitatem sanctam Jerusalem.
> Chorus Angelorum te suscipiat,
> et cum Lazaro quondam paupere
> aeternam habeas requiem.
>
> ———
>
> May the Angels lead thee into Paradise:
> may the Martyrs receive thee at thy coming,
> and lead thee into the holy city of Jerusalem.
> May the chorus of Angels receive thee,
> and mayest thou have eternal rest with
> Lazarus who once was poor.

Sad enough it may be, but for us altar boys the duty of serving on such occasions was not a cause for gloom. After all, it got us out of school for a while and brought with it the unaccustomed pleasure of a car ride, even if it was only to the Allerton cemetery and back.

Given the miserable surfacing of recent years, and not only in the United States, of appalling evidence of priestly pedophilia, perhaps I should report that, altar boy though I was, I myself encountered at the time nothing to suggest that anything of the sort was happening. In retrospect, moreover, and rightly or wrongly, it seems utterly foreign to what I sensed in the character of our priests and in their relationships with the laity in those far-off wartime years. Figures of authority those priests may well have been, and hemmed in also by a suffocating degree of adulation that could border almost on priest worship. But my own memory of the clergy in that small, largely working-class parish is that of two devoted, hard-working, and compassionate men who were good and attentive pastors to the flock they made a point of knowing so well.

In those same years I had also become a member of a Boy Scout Troop headquartered in Woolton, where we met above a fine but empty set of stables constructed out of the local sandstone and attached to a mansion left derelict during the Great Depression. While I was not passionately devoted to Scouting, I did enjoy many of the activities and, in pursuit of coveted badges, did my best to learn such skills as building and starting an outside fire with a minimum of equipment, cooking the basics over it with a minimum of utensils, and so on. I also enjoyed the Baden-Powellesque "wide games" that we played in the scrubby woods and deteriorating meadows of the surrounding estate. Not surprisingly, given their provenance, these games had a military feel to them, bearing a close resemblance in organization and objective to the maneuvers in which I was later to participate as a soldier during my infantry training days. The high point of our scouting year was a two-week camp under canvas up in rural Lancashire. The tents were cumbersome and of old-fashioned design, we slept rolled uncomfortably in blankets on the ground, the food was pretty awful even by wartime standards and, because of an ill-chosen location, we were dogged by an oversupply of aggressively stinging bumble bees. Not for us, in those days, the well-designed backpacks and tents or the comfortable sleeping bags and niftily miniaturized, propane-fueled, collapsible stoves that I associate with camping out later on along the Appalachian Trail in western Massachusetts, or when taking my children one by one for overnight togetherness campouts up on Stone Hill here in Williamstown. But, for a city-raised child, the experience was still a good and positive one. After two weeks of reasonably convivial discomfort, I was ready to return to what I now recognized as the real comforts of home. And perhaps that was an intended part of the whole exercise.

At about the same time as I had become a Boy Scout, and in this following in the footsteps of my brother Vincent, I had also taken up the violin, starting lessons with an elderly Dutchman, Kwast by name, who had played for years with the Hallé Orchestra in Manchester. I took to the instrument very well, passing with distinction several of the examinations set by the Associated Boards of the Royal College and Royal Academy of Music for which Mr. Kwast insisted on entering me and developing over time a powerful vibrato that sat well with my rather Romantic musical tastes. Blissfully unaware, however—or perhaps uninterested in—the academic demands and burden of homework with which we had to cope at school, and thinking perhaps that, like my Uncle Paddy, I might want to go the professional route into music, Kwast began to entertain ambitions for me. As a result, he began to insist on an amount of practice time that proved to be incompatible with the equally increasing amount of homework being required by SFX. As a result, then, with a mixture of relief and regret, I discontinued violin lessons at the age of sixteen. A year later I switched to piano lessons, and those I enjoyed much more. I found the piano more fun to play by myself, and those lessons left me, if only for a while, capable of turning in a reasonable rendition of Chopin's easier preludes. At the same time, I continued to play the violin. My sister Molly was an accomplished pianist and a capable accompanist, and we would both perform, along with my father who sang, at musical evenings that my parents put on for friends and neighbors. After my brother Vincent was finally demobilized from the army and living once more at home, we would also perform *en famille* pieces that Uncle Frank had arranged for our somewhat awkward combination of cello, piano, and two violins. I very much enjoyed those occasions and it didn't really hit me at the time that they were far from being the norm among my friends and acquaintances.

Several other things enriched my life during those years when I was in the Lower School at SFX. For one of my birthdays, my parents presented me with what was for those days a rather sporty Raleigh bicycle equipped with three speeds and dropped handlebars. With that, the world began to open up for me. Either with friends or with my brother Noel, I began to get out of the Merseyside urban agglomeration and to explore southern Lancashire and Cheshire. As it was the nearest stretch of real woodland and the largest in Cheshire, we liked particularly to ride our bikes to Delamere Forest, which is situated in the middle of the Wirral. This last is the peninsula of land framed by the Irish Sea and the twin estuaries of the River Mersey and the River Dee, an area referred to in the great fourteenth-century romance *Sir Gawain and the Green Knight* as "the wild land of Wirral" where "there lived but few that were loved by either God or man" but to which Sir Gawain was led nonetheless to explore in the course of his lonely quest for the Green Knight and the Green Chapel. Sir Gawain's quest, of course, had brought him up from the south and through North Wales. We came from the opposite direction. Near the city center, the Mersey narrows somewhat, but it is still almost a mile across to Birkenhead and the Wirral and we had either to make use of the sturdy, radar-equipped ferry boats that crisscrossed the river even in the worst of weather and the thickest of fogs, and which lent a glimmer of romance to a grimy port city, or to get there by riding through the Mersey Tunnel. For in those days cyclists were still (perhaps unwisely) permitted to use the Tunnel, and one would make one's perilous way, squeezed frighteningly close to the tunnel wall as huge lorries roared by, separated from one's right elbow by little more than eighteen inches.

Around the same time as I acquired my bike and newfound mobility, some friends and I took up tennis. I quickly became so attached to the game that, during the summer vacation, I used to play it for long stretches of time, as often as five days a week, sometimes with a girl to whom I was much attracted but in whose presence I was normally awkwardly shy. I suppose that lessons in the game were available at tennis clubs, but such amenities were beyond our reach and, in any case, it didn't seem to occur to us that lessons might be helpful. All our playing was done on inexpensive public courts, usually the grass courts at nearby Otterspool. We simply picked up the game, making up in gusto what we lacked in skill. Not the best way to learn because we also picked up some terrible habits. With time, I somehow acquired a pretty accurate fast serve and came to rely on it altogether too much in the effort to win games. I could not sustain a decently protracted rally and my choppy returns were all too often dependent on luck and an abundance of energy. Only years later, when I was almost fifty and had decided finally to take a few lessons, did I discover that I needed to do two simple things if I hoped to rally successfully: first, get my racket much further back in anticipation of a return; second, keep my eye on the ball. All those years, it turned out, I had instead been watching my opponent! And something similar had probably been true in my cricket playing too.

Oddly enough, while we didn't associate lessons or coaching with the ability to play sports well, we took it for granted that we would need them if we were to learn ballroom dancing. And that, by the time we were fourteen or fifteen, we were all determined to do. Being at an all-boys school, it loomed large in our pubescent longings as just about the only way to get to even remotely close quarters with girls. And that was surely a consummation devoutly to be wished. My mother and father were both good dancers and encouraged us to take lessons. When I did so, I discovered that I was not as clumsy as I had suspected and I readily mastered the waltz, foxtrot, and quickstep, as well as the samba and a somewhat shaky and evanescent ability at least to fake it with the rhumba and tango. As I did not stick with lessons long enough, that was about as far as I got and I altogether missed out on jitterbug. Like my future wife, who was a lovely and elegant dancer both in the ballroom and on ice skates, I came very much to enjoy dancing and it was to play a happy role in our social lives for decades.

One final thing worthy of note from those Lower School years was the return to Liverpool and arrival at SFX of the brothers O'Keeffe— Bernard, the elder, and Laurence, the younger, the latter known to his close friends as "Lol." In the early months of the war, before the torpedo-ing in the North Atlantic of the liner *City of Benares*, which went down taking to the bottom seventy-seven of the ninety evacuees it was taking to Canada and putting an end to that form of evacuation, the O'Keeffe brothers along with their sister Kathleen had been among the thousands of English children evacuated for safety to Canada. With their return, they brought with them a whiff of the exotic, intimations of more spacious realms that lay beyond the cruel sea, and a touch of worldliness lacking in the rest of us whose lives, after all, had revolved within the comparatively confined orbit of a provincial port city. I can well remember the newly arrived Lol, striding to and fro at lunch break across the school playground in full peripatetic mode, holding forth on Canada and his experiences in the New World, and trailed by a gaggle of fascinated boys hanging onto his every word. The brothers were alike, I think, only in their raw brightness and the multiplicity of their talents. Bernard, a fairly slim and neatly handsome fellow, was somewhat dreamy in demeanor and by temperament coolly reserved. Although I was to spend much time in the always-welcoming O'Keeffe household, I never came to feel that I really knew him. He was very talented musically, and was a fine pianist whom we all assumed (incorrectly, it turned out) was destined for some sort of a career in professional music. Lol, on the other hand, rumpled, untidy, and stockier in build, was very gregarious by nature, flatteringly interested in practically everyone he encountered, warmhearted by instinct and deeply loyal in his friendships. He was a gifted student of literature and a good pianist. After Oxford, he sailed through the challenging examinations required for direct entry into the administrative (senior) level of the civil service (in our day, a prestigious choice of career) and ended up in the Foreign Office. Over the years, in the interstices of his diplomatic activities, he somehow found the time to write and publish two novels and a monograph devoted to the role played by the domestic politics of ethnicity in the diplomatic relations among nations. In his later years, he served as British ambassador to Senegal and affiliated nations, as participant in one of the Vienna rounds concerning arms reduction, as British ambassador to Czechoslovakia (during the Velvet Revolution), and as director general of British Information Services (BIS) in New York City. This last appointment he adored, both because of the degree of independence that was attached to it and because of its natural fit with his gregarious temperament and the social skills that he and his (French) wife Suzanne possessed in such superabundance. During that period we more than once did house swaps with the O'Keeffe's, who were ensconced, courtesy of the British taxpayer, in a capacious apartment in Sutton Place on the fashionable upper East Side of Manhattan and were engaged in a constant round of entertaining. When Peter Jay (son-in-law of the then prime minister, James Callaghan, and not himself a career diplomat) became British ambassador to Washington, a controversial appointment, tensions rapidly developed between the two men, with Jay trying to cut by half the size of the BIS staff in New York and to bring the whole operation under a greater measure of ambassadorial control than heretofore. In response, and with, perhaps, unwise vigor, Lol struggled to defend the integrity and independence of his own piece of diplomatic turf. When Jay decided to make an official, if largely ceremonial, visit to New York, it was a potentially fraught occasion and the O'Keeffes scrambled to marshal their influential friends in the media to grace with their presence the truly splendid party they gave to honor and welcome the ambassador and his wife.

Claire-Ann and I were invited as houseguests for that occasion and had a wonderful time talking with the Jays, who were in reasonably gracious social mode, as well as with such luminaries of TV and print journalism as Walter Cronkite, Tom Brokaw, Midge Decter, and, I believe, her husband Norman Podhoretz, neoconservative editor-in-chief of the journal *Commentary*. The party showed every sign of having been a great success, ending, as it wound down and people departed, with the British ambassador to the United Nations, by that time very well lubricated, accompanying himself on the piano while he sang a somewhat lugubrious series of Welsh hymns. That notwithstanding, Jay was to persist in his attempt to cut British Information Services in New York down to size and his efforts seem in the end to have succeeded. Certainly, Lol's term as director general was cut short and, with the publication of an article about the contretemps in the pages of the *Economist*, the whole affair spilled out, unfortunately, into the open. The Tories, accordingly, seizing upon the matter as an opportunity to embarrass the Callaghan government, raised questions about it in the House of Commons and went on, even, to introduce a motion deploring "The removal from office of the director of BIS in New York by the prime minister's son-in-law because he [O'Keeffe] refuses to convert his daily digest of the British press to a pro-government propaganda medium." Lol may well have received his fifteen minutes of fame out of all of this, but, while it does not seem to have shadowed his subsequent career, it was the sort of publicity that no career diplomat would ever want to get.

He and I had become good chums shortly after he arrived at SFX and our friendship deepened during our time together in the sixth form and at Oxford. It matured, indeed, into one of those wonderful, lifelong friendships capable of surviving unscathed the separation of continents and the hostility of time. Although we were able to get together only infrequently, whether in England or the United States, and while those moments were more than once separated by the lapse of a good few years, our friendship was of the sort that made it easy to pick up the thread of conversation where we had left off, years earlier. On one two-day-long visit, when Lol was in New York on business and came to stay with me at Princeton (where I was spending a year's leave at the Institute for Advanced Study and commuting home on weekends), I can recall our talking animatedly and nonstop for the better part of twelve hours, the effort advanced, admittedly, by the consumption of an inordinate amount of Scotch. He was a very well-informed fellow with a broad and catholic array of interests, though in conversation, especially if a third party were present, he could become quite didactic, with his didacticism verging sometimes on the pompous. That could be an irritant for those whose liking for him was well under control. But it was the occasion, rather, of affectionate amusement for those of us who were genuinely fond of him. In him, any such pomposity had about it an endearingly Toad-of-Toad-Hall quality, lovable rather than deplorable, the more so in that it reflected none of the underlying narcissism with which A. A. Milne endowed his fictional Mr. Toad so superabundantly. Lol's didacticism, moreover, tended to be essentially object oriented, usually surfacing when he was holding forth enthusiastically, sharing in somewhat proprietary fashion his characteristically extensive knowledge of some historical site—Salisbury Cathedral, perhaps, to which he was deeply attached, or Stonehenge, which was very close to the cottage in Wiltshire that he and Suzanne had acquired. On one occasion, indeed, when we were walking around Stonehenge, he held forth so authoritatively and at such unconscionable length that we came eventually to be trailed by a growing body of enthralled onlookers who clearly assumed that he had to be some sort of official guide.

In the England of our school days, probably no more than 3 percent of the eighteen to nineteen-year-old cohort nationally went on to university. That group stemmed from the minority that, having taken the School Certificate, stayed on into the sixth form to prepare for the Higher School Certificate which was the *sine qua non* for university entrance. At SFX, the great majority of the boys left at the age of sixteen, having taken the School Certificate, with only a small cohort soldiering on to specialize for two sixth-form years in the classics, in mathematics and the natural sciences, or in history and literature. Lol and I belonged to the group of illuminati who pursued the last option. In comparison with our age group in French lycées or German Gymnasia, ours was a highly concentrated and specialized course of study—simply French and French literature, English literature, and history. Its downside was its obvious narrowness, its upside that it permitted the universities to start in the freshman year at a more advanced and specialized level. Its unscripted upside, too, was that it left room for the assembly at regular intervals of the entire sixth form, called together to participate in parliamentary-type debates on the great issues of the day. The pertinent motions, often political in nature, were picked by the headmaster himself, who also presided over these (sometimes tumultuous) affairs in the role of Speaker. He was clearly a Tory in his sympathies and that stimulated the more hardy among the boys (nearly all of them Socialist in disposition) to take advantage of the conventions of debate in order to rattle his ideological chain. I much enjoyed these occasions, developing a taste for the cut and thrust of debate and enough confidence to get to my feet, make my case, and stand my ground.

The further upside of the rather narrow course of studies we were pursuing was that it left us, as individuals, with a lot of free time which, if not wasted, could be put to good, general educational use. I don't think that any of us did waste that precious time, and, though it was a period of great tension at home, so far as school was concerned, I have very happy memories of my sixth-form years and of the wonderful intellectual horizons that were opening up before us. At home, the tensions were in some measure predictable, precipitated by the presence of too many large people crammed cheek by jowl in a pretty small space and all coming and going on different schedules. At the time, it was the expected cultural norm, at least for people of our class, for grown-up children working in the area to live at home and contribute their share to the family's expenses. And even if that had not been the case, the postwar housing shortage would probably have mandated that sort of living arrangement.

With the war years behind us, Vincent demobilized from the army and Noel from the Royal Air Force, our entire family of six was now living at home. That in itself was cause enough for moments of tension and ill temper, the more so because my mother's anxious need to control everything seemed, with the passage of time, to be growing. Exacerbating the general malaise, however, was the fact that Vincent, after getting back from the Middle East and enjoying his demobilization leave, simply didn't seem to know what to do with himself. He had taken his Higher School Certificate examinations at the seminary, had done quite well, and could have chosen to go on to university on the British equivalent of the GI Bill. But he was somehow not interested in doing that. In fact, he didn't seem to be interested in doing anything, betraying instead a worrying degree of passivity. It was as if, after almost a decade of sequential subjection to either priestly or military authority, he still needed to be told what to do. This caused my parents considerable distress. As the weeks lengthened into months with no sign of movement and no decisions arrived at, the tensions at home mounted accordingly. They eased somewhat when my father finally bit the bullet and found Vincent a job working for him. But by then, having, from the uneasy sidelines, watched the whole drama unfold, I had arrived at some conclusions. While I was not, I believe, an inconsiderate or particularly selfish boy and felt, indeed, somewhat guilty about entertaining such thoughts, it had become clear to me that my own desire for greater independence would mean that I would need to leave home once my schooling was over. Whether or not it was because of this onset of domestic turmoil, I found myself subject in those late-adolescent years to evanescent, if sometimes weeklong, bouts of depression (Churchill's "black dog"). These frightened me a bit, but I learned to cope with them by attempting doggedly to pursue whatever task was at hand, and by the time I left for college in 1950 they seemed to have stopped recurring. In subsequent years, I have been as little prone to depression as I have been to the species of dreary boredom that had overtaken me for a while in 1939–40 when I had suddenly to cope with the loneliness of being the only child left at home.

In the meantime, during those late-adolescent years, I was content to withdraw into my studies and into the world of music and imagination. All of us sixth-formers seemed to be reading voraciously and eclectically at large, and everyone, however untutored, seemed to be trying his hand at writing poetry. One of us was an opera buff, another, a Trollope fanatic, and I myself, thinking that it would be a wonderful thing to be a writer, took out a subscription to the *Times Literary Supplement* in an earnest if somewhat uncomprehending attempt to keep abreast of what was going on in the London literary world. P. G. Wodehouse's books were very much in vogue, and we all, it seems, were working our way through Jane Austen, reading, I suppose, not critically (her works were not required by the official English syllabus), but rather for interest and for fun, the way, I assume, they were written to be read. Our history teacher, who had an extensive personal library, took a genial interest in our reading habits, would suggest books for us to look at, and would lend them to us. Thus, most of us came to work our way through the "Catholic" authors—G. K. Chesterton, Evelyn Waugh, Graham Greene, and, by adoption, C. S. Lewis—and made a bit of a dent, too, on François Mauriac's *oeuvre*, though I must confess to having found his novels a bit depressing. I had become very interested in poetry and worked my way from *Palgrave's Golden Treasury of the Best Songs and Lyrical Poems in the English Language*, via the new Penguin series entitled *The Centuries' Poetry* that was edited by Denys Kilham Roberts and produced in cheap, wartime-standard paperbacks (the first books I ever purchased), and on into the collected works of such poets as Gerard Manley Hopkins, T. S. Eliot, and William Butler Yeats, the last of which I read again and again, memorizing the poems I most liked.

All of this extracurricular reading raised for us topics that we would earnestly discuss over coffee (not usually consumed in our sort of households, but, to us, a more "intellectual" drink than tea) in one of the Kardomah Cafés then springing up, or in the café of the Walker Art Gallery whose galleries we patrolled in the combined hope of meeting girls and acquainting ourselves with the visual arts. And that encouraged us, in turn, to imagine ourselves as budding intellectuals—French-style intellectuals, of course, for we were all snobbish Francophiles. France and not dreary old England, or so we thought, was the land where *real* intellectual life flourished. We dreamt, accordingly, of sitting, sipping strong, black coffee at the *Café Les Deux Magots* in Paris, puffing away at Gauloises, dressed (of course) in regulation black, and thinking cutting-edge existentialist thoughts, as dark as they were deep.

Not all our extracurricular activities, of course, were quite so high-minded. With few exceptions, we all went out dancing on most Saturday nights, the high point of our somewhat constricted social lives. And, during the unsupervised times at school allegedly devoted to "spiritual reading," an ongoing game of Pontoon went on, boys placing small bets in the hope of winning enough to finance a weekend date. Spending much time (as we had to do for our weekly essays) at the Picton Reference Library, the city's principal library collection situated in the city center, we also took the opportunity to "hang out" in town (though that accurately descriptive expression had yet to be coined). One of our favorite diversions was to go down to a "Scouse" equivalent of Hyde Park Corner which had sprung up on one of the cleared, but not yet rebuilt, bombed-out sites of which, at the time, there were still quite a few in the city. The fluctuating group of determined speakers who peopled that site ranged from obsessive millenarians prophesying the doom to come, to aggressive vegetarians excoriating the crimes of the carnivore, to representatives of the Conservative and Labour Parties jousting over the political issues of the day. But the ones I best remember were the representatives of the Communist Party, at that time quite strongly embedded in the ranks of some of the Liverpool labor unions, who heaped impartially a generous measure of vituperative scorn on Tories and Labour Party loyalists alike. Their staunch opponents, the earnest members of the Catholic Evidence Guild, who offered a sort of stripped-down version of Apologetics 101—nothing other, in fact, than a bit of boiled-over and boiled-down Bellarmine—also spoke there, as did those unfortunate young American Mormon missionaries who had had the bad luck of being assigned to duty in Liverpool, and who surely had to view their lot as nothing less than two years at hard labor. In that context they stood out not simply because they were Americans but also because they were young, good-looking, clean-cut, neatly dressed, healthy, and obviously well fed. And week after week, with whatever patience and good humor they could muster, they fought a losing battle against a wholly predictable barrage of ribald questions and interruptions focused almost exclusively on the joys and sorrows of polygamy.

Meanwhile, back in school, there were subjects to be mastered and examinations to be prepared for. And we took that challenge seriously. French literature was competently taught, if not inspiringly so. So, too, French language, so far as grammar and syntax were concerned. But it was taught very much as a dead, literary language like Latin, and our only real exercise in speaking it took place at the evening gatherings organized by the *Foyer français* in town. There we tried to put it to good use while (rather shyly) chatting up the girls who were our sixth-form equivalents at grammar schools like Bellerieve—a convent school that flourished the motto *Suaviter in modo, fortiter in re*, in which we sex-starved boys (inevitably) detected wholly improbable sexual overtones. English literature and history, on the other hand, were taught, not simply competently, but extremely well. The standard textbooks approved by the city's education authority were more or less ignored as being too thin. Instead, we were taught in more or less tutorial fashion with weekly essays (carefully graded) which called for a lot of independent reading and "research" in the Picton Reference Library. The same was true in history, where we were prepared in continental history for the medieval option and in English history for the Tudor-Stuart option. In both, we were privileged to have as our teacher W. F. F. Grace (nicknamed "Putty" Grace among the boys). He was a layman, a rather pious lifelong bachelor, almost certainly gay, an old boy of the school who, after military service in the Great War, had gone on to complete a PhD in nineteenth-century European diplomatic history at Cambridge under the supervision of Herbert Butterfield. When visiting his old school after obtaining his PhD, he had been asked, because of a sudden staff departure, to help out for a term. A quarter of a century later, he was still "helping out" in superb fashion and, having switched interests, had come to focus on the medieval period. I am not sure what the secret of his unquestionable pedagogic success was. He would simply come into class, sit on a desk, and start talking in an informal but altogether captivating manner. Beyond stipulating a topic for a weekly essay, he was not particularly directive in his advice about what we should read on the given topic. Again, as with our studies in English, we were thrown back on our own devices and imaginative resources and became acquainted, accordingly, with the study practices and library skills needed for independent work. But of Putty Grace I should properly acknowledge that, by an alchemy one can only admire without being able to emulate, he aroused in me, as in many other SFX sixth-formers, an abiding love for things historical in general and a consuming interest in the Middle Ages in particular. That love of the historical and fascination with its intriguing complexity may also have been stimulated, or so I am now inclined to think, by the fact that I had complexly intertwined in my mind, each competing for supremacy and each exerting its own emotional tug, three implicit master narratives of British history. One was Irish in provenance, the second of English Catholic inspiration, and the third, English and patriotic (jingoistic?) in feel, was the one embedded in our prescribed textbooks. The first, picked up at home, tilted in a "perfidious Albion" direction and resonated to the plaintive theme of centuries of English colonial oppression of Ireland. Its modern heroes, though they had ended up at odds, were Éamon de Valera and Michael Collins, "the big fellow." Its villains, unquestionably, were David Lloyd George and Winston Churchill, who, it was argued,

had threatened and cajoled the members of the Irish nationalist delegation to Westminster and tricked them into abandoning their hope for a
republican united Ireland and into settling instead for an unheroic Free
State in the twenty-six counties alone. That view of things was very much
at odds with the British history we learned at school, mostly because the
latter was really *English* history, with the Irish, Scots, and Welsh simply
being trundled on the stage every two centuries or so to be defeated. Also
at odds with the standard account conveyed by the prescribed textbooks,
which tended to glorify Queen Elizabeth and her vindication of Protestant England in the face of the alien and Catholic Spanish threat, was the
Chestertonian nostalgia inculcated at school for the old faith as it had
prevailed in England prior to the stripping of the altars. Similarly, the
glorification of the Elizabethan Catholic martyrs, especially Jesuits like
Edmund Campion, who had risked and lost their lives in the attempt
to keep the old faith alive among the Catholic recusants who had stubbornly refused, in the teeth of government oppression, to align themselves with the Elizabethan religious settlement. Though, significantly
enough, I don't remember having heard anything at all about those
Catholic laity and secular clergy who prided themselves on being loyal
Englishmen and proved willing to take the 1606 Oath of Allegiance and
to put up with the Elizabethan settlement in return for a restricted measure of toleration. Given the uneasy presence in the mind of views so
mutually antagonistic, it was hard for me, or indeed for any of us, to be
"God for Harry, England, and St. George" types. But if such views were
in tension one with another, I am inclined now to think that the tension
involved was a creative one that helped nourish in us a helpful measure
of skepticism and an incipient degree of comfort with interpretative
complexity. Certainly, by our sixth-form years, we had become sensitized
to the competing religious biases embedded in the historical writings of
such as Cardinal Gasquet, G. G. Coulton, and Hilaire Belloc.

At the end of two years, we all took the examinations for the Higher
School Certificate, and while we all secured entry to one or another of the
"redbrick" universities or Senior City Scholarships that ensured admission and financial support at Liverpool University, not all of us took up
those options. The school selected five of us to stay on for a third year in
order to compete for the Open Scholarships offered by the Oxbridge
colleges, and our long-suffering and uncomprehending parents were

somehow cajoled into permitting us to do so. These scholarships, funded by the college involved, were often quite ancient and, accordingly, did not carry with them much in the way of financial support. What they did carry with them, however, was a great deal of prestige both for the recipient and for the school from which he or she hailed, and in any case a state scholarship would make up on a family means-tested basis the size of the financial aid award needed. I have often wondered what would have happened had my parents insisted that I stay at home, take up the Senior City Scholarship, and continue my studies at Liverpool University. It was, after all, a first-rate place with an excellent history department numbering in the ranks of its faculty at that time two outstanding professorial appointees in medieval history, Geoffrey Barraclough and Hans Liebeschütz. As a student keen to focus on medieval history, I would certainly have been in very good hands. But the image of Oxford loomed large in the intellectual atmosphere of our school. In the absence of any Catholic university in Britain, the English Province of the Jesuits had long since established in Campion Hall its own constituent college at Oxford, and most of our Jesuit teachers were Oxford products and Oxford boosters. Even apart from that, we boys were all, it seems, in the grip of some sort of metropolitan mania. We were prone to thinking that everything worthwhile that happened in Britain took place in the environs of London or, at least, south of the grim Northern and Midlands industrial belt that constituted in our minds a sort of cultural and intellectual equivalent of the Mason-Dixon Line. There in the beguiling southland, Rupert Brooke's beloved England, lay the truly cultivated part of the country, so different from the roughness of our northern clime, a land of which we had little or no direct experience. Instead, it was one mediated to us largely by literature, news reports, and film. It was the land, or so we imagined, where everyone spoke with the authoritative, plate-glass, "Received Pronunciation" which the BBC had succeeded in establishing as socially *de rigueur*. This was the era, after all, in which the BBC's experiment in using Wilfred Pickles, a Yorkshireman with a mildly regional accent, as a news announcer had been met with irritated protests, some of them, I suspect, from people who spoke very much the same way as he did. Somehow, it seems, the news could not be taken seriously if announced in northern-accented English. Moved, then, by the unattractive stirrings of adolescent snobbishness and class-based insecurity, we were becoming awkwardly conscious, in those unutterably dreary postwar years, of what we interpreted as the stultifying provincialism of our lives in Liverpool.

There is a wonderful moment in Alan Bennett's play *The History Boys* when one of the boys, Posner, gripped, the author suggests, by "a premature disillusion," is moved in a confessional moment to confide in his teacher that

> I'm a Jew.
> I'm small.
> I'm homosexual.
> And I live in Sheffield.
> I'm fucked!

Had that play been written when we were still in school, whatever we might have made of the other things with which Posner felt himself burdened, I am confident that we would have resonated sympathetically with his dismay at growing up amid the northerly industrial grimness of Sheffield. After all, we ourselves were growing up in grimy old Liverpool, beginning to chafe against the cultural bit we felt it imposed on us, anxious to get away from the restrictions of home life, ready to spread our wings in glorious independence, and eager to find ourselves in the more exotic university world we had read about in novels like Waugh's *Brideshead Revisited*. Even when we finally got there, our preset image of the enchantment of Oxford life was so powerful as to trump the somewhat pinched and threadbare realities of conditions there in those immediate postwar years. It is true that no exotic figure like Sebastian Flyte thrust his elegant head through the open window of my room in order, impeccable manners notwithstanding, to vomit diffidently onto the floor. But, then, the rooms I occupied during the two years I lived in college were both on the first rather than the ground floor. And, though it may be a poor substitute, it is the case that my old school friend, Tony Galea, who was reading classics at Christ's College, Cambridge, contrived, having consumed too much cheap South African sherry at a party I threw to celebrate a visit of his to Oxford, to vomit *out of* my window onto the path leading down to Christchurch Meadows that runs between Corpus and Merton.

Our third year in the sixth form turned out to be even better than the other two. Lol O'Keeffe and I were the beneficiaries of a wonderful English tutorial given by a young Jesuit recently graduated from Oxford and on loan to SFX from Stonyhurst College, the order's premier public school in Britain. In that tutorial, tackling groups of Shakespeare's plays among other things in our weekly essays, we managed to work our way through most of the Shakespearian corpus—with the exception, I think, of *Timon of Athens*, *Titus Andronicus*, and *Pericles, Prince of Tyre*. In history, we soldiered on with the inimitable Putty Grace, burrowing further into the more recent scholarship and doing our best to absorb the unfamiliar perspective that informs Francis Dvornik's *Making of Central and Eastern Europe* and the new theoretical subtleties embedded in Walter Ullmann's *Medieval Papalism*. We also tackled parts, at least, of Augustin Fliche's monumental *La Réforme Grégorienne* and even struggled a bit with the canonistic technicalities of Barraclough's *Papal Provisions*.

Heady stuff for schoolboys it may well have been, but it all clearly added a measure of depth to what we wrote when we competed for our Oxford Open Scholarships. Lol and I, having entered for Open Scholarships in Modern Subjects, he at University College, I at Corpus Christi, did the written examinations at school and then went up to Oxford during the Easter vacation of 1950 for the vivas, or subsequent oral examinations, at our first-choice colleges. By early morning the next day, Lol had heard that he was in at University College but Corpus had not yet posted its results. So I spent the morning at Oriel College writing the first examination for an Open Scholarship in history. When I emerged at lunchtime, Lol was waiting for me with the glad tidings that the announcement of my election as a Scholar at Corpus had been posted at the porter's lodge there. So I withdrew from the competition for a scholarship at Oriel. Having somehow laid our hands on a couple of bikes, we then spent the afternoon riding all over Oxford in a mood of barely controlled exploratory euphoria.

The next day we embarked on a triumphal train ride back to Liverpool where we found that the other three who had been entered for Open

Scholarships had also been successful: Tony Murray, in mathematics, also at Corpus Christi College, Oxford, and Eric Bushell and Tony Galea, both in classics, at Peterhouse and Christ's College, Cambridge, respectively. We were neither the first nor the last at SFX to succeed in that competitive quest, but I think ours was, for a pretty small school, something of a banner year. The previous year, Chris McDonnell, who had started out like me at St. Francis of Assisi elementary school in Garston, had been elected to an Open Scholarship in history at Corpus, while John Sullivan had been elected to an Open Scholarship in classics at St. John's College, Cambridge. Viewed in retrospect, this success rate strikes me as extraordinary. There was nothing obvious in our social or educational backgrounds to suggest the likelihood of such an outcome. What we were attending, after all, was a small, provincial day school. McDonnell's and Sullivan's fathers were both dockers (i.e., stevedores) on the Liverpool docks, Bushell's and Galea's were elementary school teachers, Tony Murray's was a clerk in a local government office, Lol O'Keeffe's a constable in the Liverpool police force, and mine a foreman in a factory. Smart, I suppose, we undoubtedly were, at least in the sense that we were skilled examinees, for we had had to prove ourselves capable of scaling a rather steep and strictly meritocratic ladder. But things could easily have turned out otherwise, as they did for so many of our contemporaries. It is poignant to think about it now, but we would have got nowhere without the generosity, sacrifice, sympathy, and loving (if somewhat uncomprehending) support of our parents, or without the quality, thoughtfulness, interest, and dedication of our teachers. I would dearly like to think that we didn't let any of them down or squander the opportunities so generously bestowed upon us. Tony Galea, alas, died tragically in an autobahn accident while serving with the British Army of the Rhine, but given his ability, temperament, and drive, I find it hard to believe that, had he lived, he would not have made something significant of himself. Chris McDonnell, who took a First in history, and Lol O'Keeffe both went on to years of distinguished service in the senior ranks of the civil service (the War Office and Foreign Office respectively), in our day a much-admired calling. Eric Bushell went on to become a business executive. Tony Murray, John Sullivan, and I became academics—Tony became the principal of a teacher's training college and John Sullivan (who took a Starred Double First in classics at Cambridge) became a don of great distinction, first at Cambridge and then at Lincoln College, Oxford, before being lured away to a series of prestigious professorial appointments in the United States. As for what happened to me, we'll get to that later.

With our university future decided and no more examinations to be faced, the remainder of our third year in the sixth form was a relaxed and enjoyable one. As SFX did not itself offer instruction in German, though it viewed it as the language of scholarship, Lol and I were dispatched to a local technical college to make a start on getting some sort of a grip on that language. And a young Jesuit was assigned the task of mounting a mini course in philosophy for all of us. It took the form of a sort of assault course in various logical and epistemological conundrums. The purpose, I suspect, was to armor us against the wiles of the logical positivists and the lucidly persuasive arguments of A. J. Ayer's *Language, Truth and Logic*, which, at that time, had acquired among undergraduates the status almost of biblical revelation. It was all very stimulating and very much to my intellectual taste. But if there is any truth to the derisive description of philosophy as "the trade of professors and the sport of impertinent boys," I should ruefully confess that in that half term we never really got beyond the impertinent boys stage.

L.D.S.

PART II

Lissananny, Oxford, Toronto, Cambridge (MA),
Preston, Aldershot, Catterick, Gloucester, New Haven

CHAPTER FIVE

Poblacht na hÉireann

While the Fine Gael Party had traditionally leaned in a pro-Commonwealth direction, it was, ironically enough, a coalition government led by John A. Costello of Fine Gael that finally, in 1949, severed all remaining constitutional ties with the British Crown and declared the erstwhile Free State to be, in fact and not only in aspiration, the Republic of Ireland (An Poblacht na hÉireann). But after sixteen years of firm Fianna Fail Party rule under the leadership of Éamon de Valera, the Ireland that emerged from the years of hardship during the World War II Emergency remained very much de Valera's island. It was a country committed, after its years of wartime neutrality, to standing apart from international alliances and to an inward-looking striving for economic self-sufficiency. The acreage under tillage had more than doubled, farmers were required to grow a certain amount of wheat, and government subsidies supported the growing of the sugar beet needed to maintain an adequate supply of sugar. Insular in more than an economic or geographic sense, it was a country withdrawn into itself, hemmed in, culturally speaking, by the imposition of a fairly draconian system of book censorship and by its adhesion to a highly clericalist and traditionalist version of Catholic belief conducive to shaping a docile laity somewhat cowed in demeanor and an arrogant hierarchy that felt free to intrude itself into the political arena sometimes in a clumsily heavy-handed fashion. This it did, classically, in 1951 when, asserting bizarrely that the proposed scheme would "constitute a ready-made instrument for future totalitarian aggression," it came out in harsh opposition to the efforts of Dr. Noel Browne, minister of health, to reduce the high infant mortality rate in Ireland by introducing the Mother and Child Scheme—maternity care and health education for mothers as well as health care for children up to the age of sixteen. This was the Ireland with which I was to become quite closely acquainted during the years from 1946 to 1951. But its drawbacks and idiosyncrasies notwithstanding, it was a wonderfully welcoming country with which experience no less than heritage encouraged me to identify, and where I came to feel very much at home.

With the war finally over and travel restrictions more or less gone, it had once again become possible for us to get back to Ireland. In the summer of 1946, then, I accompanied my parents on a trip that took us first to Dublin, where we again spent time with my father's sister Florrie and his younger brother Paddy, then on to Athlone to visit with his older brother Tommy and his family. Not being accustomed to the mores of a small town (Athlone's population was no more than twenty thousand), I was astonished when old friends and acquaintances of his, who hadn't seen him for years, stopped my father in the street to greet him warmly by name. After Athlone, we headed west into Connaught to stay with my mother's older sister Mary, my Uncle Tommy Devaney, and their family of six. They worked a small farm in the tiny village of Lissananny, County Galway, situated about eight miles northwest of Tuam and close to the border with County Mayo. In that it took us from metropolitan Dublin via small-town Athlone to the rural fastnesses lying just to the east of Lough Corrib, the trip was an interesting one. At Athenry we switched from the Galway train to one going north to the ancient cathedral town of Tuam, there to be met by my Uncle Tommy and taken to Lissananny in a jaunting car—a traditional type of horse-drawn trap in which one sat sideways. Given the long lapse of years since my mother had seen her sister, our visit was clearly viewed by all as an important occasion worthy of ceremony. Both Tommy and his horse were well groomed and cleaned up, and Tommy was wearing his Sunday suit. When we arrived at his house, his father, still functioning in retirement as the patriarch of the family and shaved and suited up for the occasion, had been seated outside the gate in the wall surrounding the house and was helped to his feet to deliver in Irish on behalf of the family the traditional, formal words of welcome: *Céad mile fáilte*—"A hundred thousand welcomes." Thus began what was for me the first of several visits, for I returned by myself in subsequent summers, arriving in time to help with the haymaking and staying through the harvest. During that first visit we were driven over to Ballycasey where, for the first time, I met my grandfather, then in his early eighties. Still farming, he came through as a tough old fellow, with a full head of roughly cropped white hair and a twinkle in his eye. He no longer lived in the old thatched cottage where my mother had grown up, but had at some time been well enough off to build for his wife a largish, two-story house possessed of a parlor as well as the usual large kitchen-cum-living room. Unfortunately, my grandmother had died before it was completed and, at that point, all work on the house seems to have stopped. He had not bothered even to paint the window frames, which, when we visited, were beginning to crack and split, and he was using the parlor to store the dirty, oily wool from the previous year's sheep shearing. Canny, it seems, about wool prices, he was holding onto it in the hope of getting a better price the following season. He and my mother's younger brother Pawdy (short for Pádraig/Patrick) had fallen into the habit of camping out in what was basically an unfinished and deteriorating structure, more or less living in the kitchen on a residual diet of potatoes, bread, bacon, tea, and whisky. When she saw the conditions under which her father and brother were living, my mother was terribly upset and spent the next several days cleaning and scrubbing up the place in a futile attempt to make it more livable. Most of the young women had left Ballycasey for what they hoped would be a more promising city life, if not in Ireland then abroad, so Pawdy, like so many rural Irishmen, had never married. But I remember him as a warm, happy, and amusing fellow. When I was helping him move the sheep one evening, he began spontaneously to tell me a story about mysterious, supernatural happenings not in the next village, but in the one beyond that. Having assumed that I was being made privy to a piece of authentic Irish folklore, I was startled as the story unfolded to recognize that it was clearly based, beneath all his embellishments, on one of the Grimm's fairy stories which he must have encountered at school.

It was not with Ballycasey, however, but with Lissananny that I was destined over the next several years to become quite intimately acquainted. "Lis" (*lios*) in Irish means either "ring fort" or "fairy mound." While no remnants of fortifications were evident, there was, in one of my uncle's fields, a symmetrically circular, clearly man-made mound, about eight feet in diameter and three feet in depth with a flat stone positioned right at its center. As a young man, when working as a laborer on the roads, Uncle Tommy had been involved in an archaeological discovery somewhere in Galway, with the site yielding some very handsome Celtic brooches, and he had proudly shown me a copy of a scholarly article which described the site and the find and listed his name among those of the participants in the dig. But when I suggested that this particular mound on his own land warranted archaeological investigation, he would have none of it. Instead, he related to me a story of all the bad things that had happened in a neighboring village when someone was disrespectful (foolish?) enough to interfere with a similarly mysterious remnant from the ancient past.

Lissananny itself was strung along a twisting *boreen* and was not graced by a church, school, or shop. It was, in fact, little more than a collection of about twenty houses, many of them of the old, thatched cottage variety, small, picturesque, thick-walled, and cramped. The rest were rather ugly "modern" houses, some of them two storied and, in outside appearance, not unlike English council houses with slate roofs and walled gardens in which vegetables were cultivated for domestic consumption. The Devaney's, though one storied, was such a house, the original thatched cottage having been turned into a barn that housed the two cows on which they depended for their milk and butter. Unfortunately, like the other new houses, it was built of concrete with no damp course in the walls and, with the exception of the kitchen, had a slightly dank feel to it. I know that my clothes always felt a bit damp when I put them on in the morning. The kitchen was the large main room in which most of the living took place. It was warm and inviting enough, dominated as it was by the large, open fireplace in which a turf fire burned day and night and on which all the cooking was done. That room I associate especially with the figure of Grandfather Devaney, who would sit on a hard kitchen chair, lost in some sort of reverie, staring at the glowing turf fire and, with his stick, tapping rhythmically and incessantly the side of the hard sole of his right boot. He spoke little but would occasionally begin singing, to himself rather than anyone else, the words of one of the old, seemingly endless, narrative songs known as "Come all ye's." The house had a slate roof and was equipped with gutters and drainpipes which fed the abundant flow of rainwater into a cistern to supply water for use in washing and in the laundering of clothes. For just as there was no electricity (light was provided by oil lamps), so, too, was there no running water, no sewage system, no outhouse, even—this last providing something of a challenge for a city-raised boy unaccustomed to the practice of hopping over a loose stone wall in order to relieve oneself in an open field. Drinking water had to be brought in by bucket from a spring that bubbled up in a nearby field. Unfortunately, that spring was not fenced off from the rest of the field in which sheep were often left to graze. It is to drinking that water across the course of several summers that I am inclined to attribute my acquisition (presumably via fecal contamination) of the *h. pilori* bacterium which, while it would lie dormant for years, caused me periodic bouts of stomach pain until, in my late sixties, a test detected its presence and it was eliminated by a fortnight's course of heavy-duty antibacterial drugs.

If by modern city standards there was a lot that was lacking in the conditions of life prevailing at that time in places like Lissananny in the rural west of Ireland, there were also many things that attracted. Not least among them, to one who had grown up on bleak wartime rations in Britain, the freshness, quality, and quantity of the food available. The Devaneys kept hens, chickens, and milk cows, so fresh eggs, milk, and butter were in abundant supply, along with onions, carrots, cabbage, and first-rate potatoes grown in the vegetable garden adjoining the house. To my knowledge, the two milk cows were not tuberculin tested (a pertinent precaution given the salience of tuberculosis among the rural population), nor was the milk they produced pasteurized. But it tasted good, as did the pungent country butter my aunt made from it that went so well with the wonderful, coarse soda bread she baked in a flat Dutch oven suspended from the fireplace crane over the glowing turf fire. Although they raised a few bullocks and heifers and had a flock of about forty sheep (the former fattened for sale at market, the latter kept for the wool that was the main source of the family's cash income), they ate neither beef nor lamb. Even had they been able to afford to do so, that would have been an option precluded by the absence of electricity and, therefore, of refrigerated storage. But they also raised pigs, some for sale at market, and some to be slaughtered, cured, and eaten. So the staple meat, served with almost every dinner, was wonderfully tasty home-cured bacon, cooked and served in large thick slices. The only exception was the periodic Sunday meal when my aunt, having gone out into the farmyard, caught a hapless chicken, and wrung its neck, served that instead.

Fortified in this fashion, I came to enjoy the rhythms of country living and the regimen of agricultural work that went with it. I helped out with the rounding up and moving of the sheep and, in that wet climate, with the checking for and removal of the lethal maggots that could develop in their rear end from the eggs laid by the seemingly omnipresent large flies that we knew in England as "blue bottles." I was also called upon once to help load piglets onto the cart that was being taken to market. Given the amount of squealing and their frantic attempts to escape into the early morning darkness, it was hard not to suspect that they had somehow divined the dire fate that lurked in their future. But I didn't distinguish myself in my clumsy attempts to milk the cows or to help with the gathering and stacking of the turf needed to fuel the fire. While I was not altogether incompetent wielding the two-sided spade (a *sleán*) used to cut the sods of turf, my efforts to catch those rather sloppy sods when thrown to me by another cutter without splattering the messy stuff all over myself were clumsy enough to evoke a good deal of hilarity among my cousins. With the pitchfork and scythe, however, I did much better, wielding the former skillfully and even learning how to carry the latter while riding a bike—this last a maneuver not casually to be undertaken. And, tiring though it was, I came to enjoy the whole business of haymaking, from the cutting, turning, spreading, and gathering to the building of the conical haystacks that, from late summer onwards, were to be seen in all the farmyards in the region, some better (and even more aesthetically constructed) than others.

In the Lissananny of those faraway days, the sole source of traction, whether for ploughing, mowing, or haulage, was the horse. In the Devaney's case, this was a solitary mare. She was, as she had to be, a patient, hardworking beast who, as I found to my surprise when first handling the reins while she pulled the wagon, knew her own way home at the end of a long day and would firmly resist any attempt to steer her in any direction other than the one leading to the nice, dry barn where she clearly knew she could expect to get her well-deserved grain and hay. Given the frequency of rain in that part of the world, cutting and bringing in the hay during the fleeting intervals of sunny weather could involve very long days. After the hay was cut, we would fluff it up, rake it into long rows, turning it frequently, and then gather it up with pitchforks into large piles so that the wind could help dry it out. When it was ready, and we were given a day when the weather cooperated, everyone—men, women, and children—would turn out with pitchforks to load it onto the wagon to bring it back to the farmyard where the more experienced and skillful hands would have begun the task of building around poles the conical haystacks where the hay would keep dry for use in the winter months. One person would stand on top spreading the hay out into a neat circle around the pole and the rest of us had to be careful to turn over the pitchfork while hefting the hay up to him in order to avoid inadvertently stabbing his ankles. When the stack was over ten feet in height, it would gradually be shaped into a cone, thatched with straw to protect it from rain (I don't believe I ever saw a tarpaulin in Lissananny), and then stabilized against the wind and secured to the ground by "thumbropes," themselves made out of straw by twisting it around a stick. A half century later, and long after Irish agricultural practice had changed, I can recall seeing on TV, during reportage about the tragic warfare and massacres that accompanied the disintegration of Yugoslavia, shots of almost identical conical haystacks in the farmyards of the Bosnian countryside. It was as if time had stood still.

During those summers, I more than once biked over to Ballycasey with my cousins Pete and Paddy. I also accompanied my uncle Tommy on visits down to Tuam and Galway city, and we all went once en famille on what amounted to a pilgrimage to the Marian shrine of Knock in southeastern County Mayo. But most of the time, apart from the three-mile trips to the larger village of Kilconly to attend Sunday Mass at the parish church, was spent in Lissananny itself or on the additional fields called Lissalean that my uncle owned outside the village. The latter were mainly hay meadows, though one piece was given over to grazing because, I think, he didn't want to do anything to disturb some graves there that dated back to the potato famine of 1845–52 or, as they called

it, "the Great Hunger"—*An Gorta Mór*—when people who had starved
to death had been hastily buried in unconsecrated ground and their last
resting places marked simply by jagged pieces of stone. After working
hours, social life in Lissananny was very simple. The nearest pub or
place of assembly being in Kilconly, people in Lissananny were thrown
back on their own devices even during the summer months. One rather
cranky old man did own a wireless, but he kept himself very much to
himself and didn't let anyone else listen to it. So the main diversion
available was the traditional one of stopping by each other's houses in
the evenings for tea and talk. The protocol for so doing was firmly established. One didn't have to be invited in order to visit and one didn't
have to knock on the door when one arrived. Instead, it was the customary practice simply to lift the latch, open the door and step inside, and
greet those already there in formulaic fashion with the words: "God bless
this house." One would then be welcomed in to sit around the turf fire,
given a cup of tea, and drawn into the flow of conversation which could
often be quite lively and amusing. Words loomed large in Irish life and
talk dominated. But if one played any sort of readily available musical
instrument, one would also be called upon to perform. Once it became
known that I could play the violin, a fiddle was found for me and I had
to play. To my surprise, the villagers proved to be less interested in hearing traditional Irish songs and dances, quite a few of which I knew, than
being updated with renditions of the most recent pop songs, which, fortunately, I was usually able to knock off by ear. Subsequent and more recent visits to Ireland suggest to me that the reverse would be true today.
None of this, I suppose, seems very exciting, but there really was something quite enchanting about whiling away the evening hours in this
way, especially when it involved sitting around an aromatic turf fire in
the thick-walled, low-ceilinged, hobbit-like snugness of one of the old
thatched cottages. People were invariably (and incuriously) welcoming,
even to a "Yank" (all offshore returnees and visitors were referred to as
"Yanks" even if they didn't hail from America). And I was quickly made
to feel part of a pattern of village living which belongs now, I assume, to
a past that is forever gone.

My last visit to Lissananny was a brief one in the summer of 1951,
and it was little more than a coda to a long summer of hard and poorly
remunerated labor in County Offaly, in the southeastern midlands of Ire-

land. Late in the previous summer, just before I went up as a freshman to Oxford, my brother Noel and I, looking for a change of scene as well as a way to make a bit of extra money, had spent a fortnight at an agricultural camp in the Thames valley, not far from Staines. As had been the case in Ireland, the amount of English land given over to tillage for agricultural produce had been much expanded during the years of war and it had yet to contract again to prewar dimensions. As a result, the country had come to be dotted with agricultural "camps" intended to attract young people who could provide the supply of needed cheap seasonal labor which, under the conditions of low unemployment then prevailing, was hard to come by. Ours was such a camp. We were housed, barracks-style but reasonably comfortably, in large Nissen huts that had been erected when the camp was a wartime army establishment. We ate in a common canteen (the food wasn't all that bad) and spent our days either "budding" large fields of chrysanthemums or picking potatoes. The work was monotonous but not backbreaking or tiring enough to preclude us from going pub-crawling in the evenings in the lively drinking-spots strung along the banks of the Thames or, on weekends, going dancing in Staines. The atmosphere was, in fact, a bit holiday-like and during those two weeks we had a great deal of fun. Though no more than half of the campers were university students, the age of most of them coincided with the typical eighteen to twenty-two range for undergraduates. The group was made up of young women as well as men and, at the age of eighteen, it was my first "coeducational" experience since leaving elementary school. It was also broadly international in composition—mainly European, but the group also included one Indian student, a couple of Nigerians, and, five years after the end of World War II, at least one forlorn displaced person. He was an older, world-weary Rumanian fellow who probably viewed the rest of us as a bunch of immature idiots. I cannot recall all the names involved, but we speedily made some good, if fleeting, friendships with a lively French student from Brittany, Henri by name; a Dutch girl, Joep, and her Austrian boyfriend, Kurt, who had linked up in the course of an extended *Wanderjahr* that had taken them right across the continent; and, setting our hearts aflutter, some lovely Swedish girls, not Stockholm sophisticates but from a small town in one of the rural provinces. I loved the international complexion of the group and reveled in the lively and earnest conversations about differing national mores, politics, religion, and the "meaning of life" that sometimes went on well into the night as we sat around the dying embers of a large outdoor fire that was lit on several evenings of each week.

It was a wonderfully enjoyable, educational, and stimulating experience and, as one who as yet had been given no opportunity to visit the Continent, I was left with a strong appetite for involvement in things international. Perhaps because of that I perused, during my freshman year at college, the literature about summer jobs put out by the International Students Union and ended up signing on to work in Ireland during the summer months of 1951 for Bord na Móna (Peat Board), the semi-state company not long since established to promote, among other energy-related efforts, the mechanical harvesting of turf (peat) to fuel the generation of electricity in a series of power stations strategically located in the vicinity of some of Ireland's largest peat bogs. Despite the high rate of unemployment then prevailing in the Republic, Bord na Móna, headquartered in County Kildare, had experienced difficulty in recruiting enough labor to run its operations effectively, and the recruitment in 1951 of foreign student labor to work in the bogs during the long summer vacation was an attempted (if ill-conceived) response to that pressing need. But, so far as I was concerned, it didn't deliver anything remotely like the experience I had enjoyed so much during the summer preceding.

I was assigned to one of the Bord na Móna operations in the vast complex of peatland in the province of Leinster known as "the Bog of Allen," which stretches across parts of the counties of Laois, Offaly, Meath, Kildare, and Westmeath in the eastern midlands of the country. Our particular operation was situated within a few miles of Portarlington, a rather handsome, stone-built, former Huguenot settlement that lies right on the border between Offaly and Laois. As had been the case in our agricultural camp the previous year, we were housed on the grounds of what appeared to be an old army camp, but under conditions that were a good deal less satisfactory. There was the normal array of huts, but we were not housed in them. Rather, we were housed in a sort of tent village. The huts themselves were reserved for the cadre of regular employees who turned out to be Irish-speaking migrant laborers from the Aran Islands, a distant Irish version of the Turkish *Gastarbeiter* who were to make their appearance later on in Germany. Their goal was to

earn money that they could send back to their impoverished families on
the islands and, to that end, they would sometimes work in succession
and without any break two full, backbreaking shifts. They lived in a fair
degree of squalor (we had to share the toilet and shower facilities with
them) and, though we ate with them in the camp canteen, they kept
themselves very much to themselves, conversing exclusively in Irish.

Our group was totally male, no "coeducation" here, and turned out
to have only a small sprinkling of students from the Continent. The
only one of them I can remember at all well was a rather surly Belgian.
Instead, and oddly, it was almost exclusively English in composition,
though leavened by the presence of a rough, tough, and boisterous number of Catholic students from the northern six counties. They were all
from Queen's University Belfast and, Catholic loyalties notwithstanding,
lost no opportunity to convey that they didn't think much of the conditions of life prevailing in the Irish Republic. I myself shared a tent with
a couple of students from Manchester University, and it proved to be
a reasonably congenial arrangement. Indeed, the students as a whole
proved to be an interesting and decent lot and, while it would be stretching things a bit to describe our Bord na Móna experience as enjoyable,
we did manage to have some fun on our Saturday night excursions to
Portarlington. These necessitated a three-to-four-mile walk to and fro,
though on occasion we were able to hitch an illicit ride in empty wagons
on the mainline freight trains as they rumbled along to the railway siding in town. To do so, we would have to run hard and scramble on board
at a curve in the line where the trains always slowed down and, to avoid
being caught, jump off before the train finally came to a halt in Portarlington. I view this in retrospect as a rather foolhardy undertaking,
though at the time it smacked to us of high adventure, tempted, as we
were, to imagine ourselves as American hoboes riding the rails in an effort to escape the miseries of the Dust Bowl and Great Depression alike.

In my mind I retain a vivid picture of an incident that occurred on
one such Saturday night as we were making our way back to camp after
an evening's drinking, during which I had witnessed heavier and more
sodden drinking among the Aran islanders than I had ever seen before. On the way out of Portarlington, there is (or was) a humpbacked
bridge spanning a stream or canal. As we approached it, we saw the
extraordinary spectacle of one of the islanders laboriously peddling an

old-fashioned "sit-up-and-beg" bike right up to the crown of the hump and then, at that very moment, passing out. For a few seconds—it seemed an eternity—rider and bike stood upright, quite still, all lines of force, as it were, in momentary equilibrium, before the rider crashed sideways to the ground, his hands still gripping the handlebars. This was the cause of great merriment among his comrades who picked him up and, we had to assume, somehow got him back to camp. Had the next day not been a Sunday, I have no doubt that he would have been up on his feet for work at the crack of dawn.

On working days the routine followed a pattern of great regularity. The bog itself, the unforgiving site of our daylong labors, was a vast, flat, surprisingly parched, and desertlike wilderness. Having picked up at the cookhouse a packet of sandwiches (thick and dry), we lined up to be transported to the point of action in open wagons of the company's own narrow-gauge railway that crisscrossed the Bog of Allen. To this day, Bord na Móna claims to have the largest industrial railway network in Europe and to have in operation more mileage of track than Iarnród Éireann, the mainline Irish railway network. Nowadays the harvesting of the turf that is moved around on those narrow-gauge tracks appears to be mechanized from start to finish, producing "milled peat," which is scraped by machines from the surface of the bog. And Bord na Móna employs no more than a couple of thousand people nationwide. In our day, however, the whole process was much more labor-intensive. Big machines were used to cut down until they reached the layer of mud that lay beneath the seam of peat, a depth of about fifteen feet, thus creating huge and widening trenches. The sloppy peat thus cut would then be squeezed out like toothpaste to dry on the sections of bog not yet touched that lay adjacent to the rail tracks. The rest of the harvesting had to be done by hand and that is where we came in.

Our task was a twofold one. First, that of doing what used to be called "footing turf"—namely, breaking up the long rows and arranging the pieces into piles so that the wind blowing through them could further the drying process. Second, in sections where that process had been completed, throwing such piles onto a conveyor belt that kept moving remorselessly towards one while at the same time shifting the piles of turf sideways to a rail wagon for removal. While not complicated tasks, they both involved raw and unremittent manual labor, hard on the back and on the hands and nails. And, given the fact that we were paid by piece rates rather than by hours spent on the job, it was labor that was not particularly well remunerated. We were issued neither with protective gloves nor with water bottles. Under bog conditions, we could safely slake our thirst only at the price of stepping aside from the job at hand, thereby losing work time, and walking to the nearest barrel of chemically treated water, such barrels (not always kept filled) being placed at half-mile intervals along the track. Under such conditions, of all of us only the above-mentioned Belgian, who combined with his surliness marked Stakhanovite tendencies, succeeded in making a reasonable return for his efforts. But I needed whatever I could make and, in the end, did accumulate enough cash to see me through the rest of the long vacation without burdening my parents. I also made enough to pay my share of the cast's contribution towards making it possible to bring our Corpus production of T. S. Eliot's *Murder in the Cathedral* (during the Trinity term it had been a great success at Oxford) in September to the newly founded Edinburgh Festival as a fringe attraction.

   If the daily round of work for Bord na Móna was a bit grim and certainly monotonous, life back at camp was anything but that. Neither at our camp nor, it seems, at the others it set up, had the company planned at all well for the influx of invited foreign labor. By midsummer, angry letters of admonition and complaint about the deplorable conditions prevailing at some of the camps had begun to appear in the press. Our camp, which may not have been the worst, certainly left a great deal to be desired. Apart from the general squalor of the facilities, the food, even by the not very exacting English institutional standards of the day, was really pretty awful. More worryingly, there appeared to be something amiss with the camp's water supply. We had all begun to experience mild, dysentery-like symptoms which, with the passage of time, became cumulatively worse. Indeed, by the time I completed my tour of duty and departed, I was beginning to feel a bit weak and it took several days away from the camp before I began to feel normal again. Grounds, certainly, for concern, but it was not clear that there were any readily available avenues for complaint about it. The boys from Belfast certainly made their views known in rather threatening fashion, cornering the plant manager in the driveway to his house. But their efforts were without avail and resulted in no discernible change. Finally, for the matter was becoming a bit of a public embarrassment, Bord na Móna sent down a representative to speak to us and, one assumes, our discontented counterparts at other camps.

The man they sent was a small fellow, possessed of the diffident (if, it turned out, deceptive) demeanor of a subordinate office clerk. Dubliners, in those days at least, being frequently small of stature, he was what my mother would have called "a little maneen from Dublin." And he may well have been precisely that, though I assume he was out from the company's headquarters in neighboring Kildare. He was destined on this occasion to earn his keep the hard way. A meeting had been set up in the canteen after the evening meal. It was well attended and began promisingly enough with the concerns of the group being presented to him in reasonably civil fashion. When it became clear, however, that his *modus operandi* if it came to allegations of shortcomings on the company's part was to be consistently defensive and exculpatory, the atmosphere rapidly deteriorated. The boyos from Belfast had arrived in a characteristically boisterous mood, sitting together in a clutch with some, having dismembered a chair, wielding chair legs and projecting a stance of slightly comic belligerence. To express their disapproval of what the visitor had to say, they began to bang their chair legs rhythmically on the edge of the table at which they were sitting and the little maneen's voice was totally drowned out. Somehow or other, however, he succeeded in rescuing victory from the jaws of defeat. "I do hear," he said, raising his voice to make himself heard above the tumult, "I do hear that obscene and disgusting things have been scrawled on the lavatory walls." (At a place like that, of course, it would rather have been cause for comment had such things *not* been written.) "I am ashamed," he went on, more in sorrow it seemed than anger, addressing himself directly to the Belfast crowd and hitting his rhetorical stride, "I am ashamed that good Catholic boys like you would set so bad an example to these students from abroad. What sort of an impression of Ireland do you think you are giving to them?" And so on, and on, in a similar vein. By this point he had slipped into an affectingly homiletic mode, though perhaps not up to the standard of the Jesuit that James Joyce depicts delivering the hellfire sermon in *A Portrait of the Artist as a Young Man.* To the surprise of the rest of us, the chastening effect of his words on the Belfast rowdies was immediately evident. They quieted down and lapsed into a species of guilty sheepishness, while the little maneen wound up to his peroration and, mission handily accomplished, departed in scarcely concealed triumph.

In relation to our grounds for complaint, nothing at all appeared to be done (at least while I was still at the camp), not even about whatever it was that was wrong with the water system. When the summer began to draw to a close and it was time for me to leave, I did so with some relief. Stuffing my belongings into my army surplus rucksack (backpack), I set out to hitchhike across Offaly and Westmeath to Athlone in order to pick up the Galway train. I had no difficulty at all in getting the two successive lifts I needed to reach the Athlone railway station where, to my surprise (it was sheer serendipity), I spied my brother Noel standing on the platform outside his compartment and chatting up two dark-haired, gravely attractive Irish girls. They turned out to be students at University College Galway, and we had the pleasure of their company all the way to Athenry, where we had to bid them a reluctant farewell in order to catch another train heading north to Tuam.

When we got to Lissananny, my uncle and aunt seemed genuinely surprised, disturbed even, at what I had been doing for the rest of the summer. "Why," they exclaimed, "only criminals work for Bord na Móna!" And they were at pains to ensure that I ate heartily during my short stay with them. After a week, however, it was time for me to return home, though Noel, I believe, stayed a little longer. Although I had no premonition of it then, it was to be the last time that I was to see my uncle and aunt or Lissananny itself. While I was to do a great deal of travelling in the years immediately ensuing, it was more than thirty years before I saw Ireland again. By the time I did get back, in the autumn of 1984, it had ceased to be de Valera's self-sufficient island, enchanted and withdrawn. Instead, it was marked everywhere, and especially so in the West, by the rationalizing imprint reflective of membership in the European Union.

My reason in 1951 for leaving Lissananny so quickly and returning home was the need to pick up different clothes and head over to Manchester to the house of a friend from Corpus. There, those of us from the north who had been in the cast for the Oxford production of *Murder in the Cathedral* were to assemble in order to join the rest of the cast who, with a rented coach and a rented light board, had already set off from Oxford on the journey to Edinburgh. So, the full cast then assembled, we continued on north in high spirits, journeying via Carlisle and the stark high country just south of Hadrian's Wall and then through the Scottish Lowlands to reach our goal. Having added to my modest role in the chorus of the Men and Women of Canterbury an amended version of Eliot's Fourth Knight, it was my privilege across the two weeks following, and up and down Scotland, to deliver the first mortal blow to the hapless archbishop—in the Chapel of St. Salvator at the University of St. Andrews, during charity performances in the ruins of Arbroath Abbey and of the chapel at Holyrood Palace, and, most dramatically, in the east end of the nave of St. Giles Cathedral in Edinburgh. There we had capped the sobriety of the Calvinist communion table with the facsimile, at least, of a medieval high altar. To our surprise, this turned out to occasion in the correspondence columns of *The Scotsman* several expressions of outrage about the impropriety of permitting such an outward sign of creeping popery in the High Kirk. We should not have been surprised. We were staging our performance, after all, in the section of the cathedral where Jenny Geddes was famously reputed to have thrown her stool at the dean when he began in 1637 to read the collects from the newly-prescribed Book of Common Prayer—an unacceptable piece, it was thought, of Romanizing effrontery. And her historic act of defiance is memorialized on a wall plaque in the cathedral. But we needed that high altar. In our production it was to be the site of Becket's murder, effected in a highly stylized and carefully choreographed fashion. The members of the audience were seated in the eastern section of the nave and faced the altar. As their attention was fixed intently upon the other three knights who had burst in upon Becket, surrounding him menacingly with swords drawn, I in my capacity as the mysterious fourth knight suddenly stepped forth from the darkness behind the audience and out onto the center aisle. With dagger drawn, dressed throughout in black, I was equipped also with riding boots that rang out imperatively on the stones of the aisle as I made my way with quickening steps up to the altar, my movements orchestrated with the growling opening bars and my dagger's fatal thrust coinciding with the first, tympani-lashed, crescendo of Richard Strauss's *Thus Spoke Zarathustra!* The sword thrusts that followed were likewise orchestrated with the subsequent crescendos, and when the stricken archbishop finally sank to the floor all lights in the cathedral were sud-

denly cut and a spotlight situated across Parliament square simultaneously illuminated the great East window above the altar. It depicts the
ascension of Christ into heaven. If the putative theology implied by that
maneuver could well be questioned, its dramatic impact could not. For
me, certainly, it was a moment arresting enough to consign the residual
memories of my laboring work with Bord na Móna into "the dark backward and abysm of time."

CHAPTER SIX

Collegium Corporis Christi

Over the years, if not without a twinge of surprise, I have come to realize that I am a rather institutionally oriented sort of fellow. Institutions, after all, reflect the outpouring of human creativity and, unlike so many academics of recent generations, I have never been tempted to make important and honorable roles within an institution the object of some sort of "hermeneutic of suspicion." Instead, at least for me, they have tended to be an avenue for self-realization and fulfillment. Certainly, institutions of one sort or another have loomed large in my life. And among them, unquestionably, is Oxford. Not simply the beguiling Oxford of my formative undergraduate years in the early 1950s, but also the very different university community I have come to know quite well from the mid-1980s down to the present. In 1984, having just stepped down from almost eight years of service as dean of the faculty at Williams College in western Massachusetts, where I had been a member of the History Department since 1961, I was charged with the mission of establishing, organizing, shaping, and directing a residential junior year abroad program at Oxford for around two dozen Williams students. The program was to be run via a sort of loose collaboration with Exeter College, with which we had a long-standing collaborative arrangement at the postgraduate level, and our students accommodated at Ephraim Williams House. This was the name we gave (in honor of our founder) to a property which the college had just acquired on Banbury Road in north Oxford, midway between St. Hugh's and Summertown. It consisted of four large houses, the main one on Banbury Road itself, the other three on Lathbury Road and Moreton Street. Though originally totally separate residences, they had the advantage of being linked together in the back by a large garden area that formed a sort of interior quad. For some years they had together been the site of a residential language school teaching English largely to Italian high school students. But with the sale of the property to us, the language school was to vacate it no later than the end of the 1984 calendar year. As a piece of physical plant it was, we realized, in pretty run-down condition and would have to be thoroughly rehabilitated and refurbished. But as it was our hope to launch our own program there in the autumn of 1985, we were left with only eight months, not only to get the necessary work done on the physical plant, but also to shape the program, recruit a corps of instructors, gain access to the pertinent Oxford libraries, make arrangements for the social lives and medical care of our students, and so on. For the success of the rather frantic scramble to meet that deadline, great credit has to be given to two people. The first is Win Wassenar, an engineer by training, who was then director of the Williams Buildings and Grounds Department and who threw himself with great enthusiasm, energy, and skill into the tasks of picking and supervising the right architects and contractors and securing the necessary permissions from the Oxford municipal authorities. The second is Dan O'Connor, an old friend and colleague of mine, who was a member of the Williams Philosophy Department and who, when I was elected president of the college in March 1985 and had (somewhat reluctantly) to relinquish the prospect of spending the next two or three years back in Oxford, stepped down from his role as dean of the college (i.e., dean of students) and took my place as director of the Oxford program. The task he confronted was a difficult one, the more difficult in that he had to scramble as a total outsider to learn the arcane ropes at Oxford and to pick up from me the labor-intensive task of recruiting the first cadre of tutors in the broad array of subjects chosen by the first group of students selected for the program.

When, after the acquisition of the property, it had been decided to launch such a program, John Chandler, my predecessor as president, had appointed a faculty committee to frame a curriculum for it. That committee had been inclined to follow the pattern set by the only other formal study abroad program already at that time established at Oxford, that of Stanford University, which was operated in collaboration with Magdalen College. Like the other Stanford-operated study abroad programs around the world, the Stanford Oxford program functioned on the American two-semester calendar, thereby enabling students to sign up for just one semester. And its mode of instruction was the American seminar system. Our own program, however, was to be a yearlong affair and, once I was appointed as director, I succeeded in persuading the committee (and, subsequently, the faculty as a whole when the curriculum was brought up for a vote) that there was little point in sending our undergraduates to Oxford for a year unless we shaped the program in such a way that their experience would come as close as possible to that enjoyed by Oxford undergraduates themselves. So we adopted the Oxford three-term calendar and the Oxford tutorial mode of instruction. This placed a heavier burden on the director, who, instead of lining up a maximum of four instructors each semester to teach four seminars, would have to recruit a much larger and more varied group to staff a highly individualized set of tutorials. Thirty years of subsequent experience has shown, however, that the decision was a wise one. The more so in that it paved the way for the introduction, in 1988, into the Williams course of instruction on our home campus of the Oxbridge-style tutorials that have since become a signature feature of our course offerings.

During the winter months of 1984–85, having agreed to take on the assignment of director, I had made the first of several visits to Oxford to begin the task of organizing the program. At the time, I had been given the impression that the rector and fellows of Exeter, in return for the rather substantial fee that Williams had agreed to pay to the college, would play a central role in the business of providing or recruiting the necessary tutors. I was speedily disabused of any such assumption. The fellows themselves, when I visited each of them individually, seemed, with one exception, very much "out of the loop" about what we were proposing to do. They betrayed, certainly, no understanding of the fact that it was our intention to set up a high-quality, academically demanding program in which grades given for work done could in good conscience, and without fear of debasing the coinage, be included in the calculation of the student's cumulative grade point average. It was not our practice to do this with study abroad programs (which were usually focused on language acquisition) as we could not fully control the academic standards of those programs. In such cases, all we would give was nongraded credit towards the degree. When I discussed the matter with those Exeter fellows, it became clear that they viewed our proposed program, and not without suspicion, as some sort of pet project of the rector, for whom, it speedily became clear, their admiration was well under control. The exception among them was Paul Slack, an historian of seventeenth-century England of some distinction. He was at that time dean of the college, but was later drawn into the university's central administration and ended up as principal of Linacre College. He quickly grasped the value of what we were about, gave me good advice about how to find my way through the administrative maze that characterized Oxford as a federated, collegiate university, and proved over the years to be a good, helpful friend of our program. But even he felt constrained to make it clear that he himself could not get involved in the delicate business of recruiting tutors for us, either from the ranks of his colleagues at Exeter or from elsewhere in the university. As for the rector himself, Norman Crowther-Hunt, a peer of the realm who had served as minister of state in Harold Wilson's cabinet, he expressed surprise that we were taking on the burden of going the tutorial route. His own (quite condescending) vision of the instructional provision adequate for an American study abroad program at Oxford was that it needed to involve nothing more than the slapping together of a sort of circus of well-remunerated individual lecturers, people (he left us to conclude) like himself, charged with talking interestingly about their own favorite topics. That collection of lectures could then be billed as constituting a course. And it speedily became clear, as we discussed our putative project, that his own interest in the program hinged largely on the fact that it would provide an additional and, doubtless, much needed, source of revenue for Exeter. As an old American institution, we were clearly assumed to possess deep financial pockets and, in our innocence, to be willing to make ourselves available as some sort of providential cash cow for the native worthies. This was an attitude I was to encounter more than once at Oxford as I went about the business of setting up the program. I was led to conclude, accordingly, that if I wanted to avoid the risk of future directors being taken to the cleaners by some seemingly otherworldly donnish type, I would do well to refrain from appointing to the position any obvious Anglophile.

To forward the business of recruiting suitable tutors in the first few years, we looked beyond Exeter and secured, in return for an appropriate retainer, the services of a well-placed, knowledgeable, and well-connected don who could serve as a facilitator and an adviser to the director. Even with this element of local help, the task of recruiting tutors proved, for the first two or three years, to be something of a challenge, especially in such over-subscribed subjects as economics. With time, however, as the reputation of the program grew and the quality and seriousness of the Williams students became a known factor around the university, the pressure eased and we began to develop a solid cadre of tutors whose teaching had proved to be of high quality and to whom we could turn at need with a goodly measure of confidence.

Right at the start I had sensed the importance of establishing the academic reputation of our program within university circles at large and of making it clear that we could be relied upon to comport ourselves as good citizens within the Oxford community. With that goal in view, we set up a local advisory council composed of figures prominent on the Oxford academic scene. And, across time, we were fortunate enough to be able to appoint as council members not only Williams alumni like Keith Griffin, a prominent development economist who was at that time president of Magdalen, and Richard Repp, an Ottoman expert who was master of St. Cross College, but also the likes of Michael Brock, once my tutor at Corpus but now warden of Nuffield College, Sir Keith Thomas, a good friend and distinguished historian who was president of Corpus Christi College and president of the British Academy, and Sir Anthony Kenny, another president of the British Academy, who was also master of Balliol (and, later, warden of Rhodes House), and who had grown up (I discovered) within a mile of our old house in Liverpool and had been for a while at the Jesuit grammar school that I myself had attended. Under my chairmanship, the council met each year towards the end of Trinity term and its members gave us sage counsel and proved generously willing to be of help. With their aid and support, we were able to establish within university circles the reputation of the program as a serious, high-quality educational enterprise, and of Williams as a good, responsible citizen in relation both to the university community and to the city of Oxford itself. All of which, across time, served to distinguish us from the growing number of rather fly-by-night American study abroad operations which, cashing in on their geographic proximity to Oxford, were willing to advertise themselves in such a way as to suggest, quite improperly, that they were somehow connected with the university itself. As a result, though it understandably involved the payment of substantially increased fees, we were eventually able, when the university finally succeeded in rationalizing its own rather foggy rules governing the presence at Oxford of short-term foreign students, to have our Williams students formally classified as "visiting students" affiliated with Exeter College and accorded, therefore, all the privileges (including library access) enjoyed by normally matriculated Oxford undergraduates.

The sustained effort to get to that point and to secure the success of a program that was very close to my heart meant that I was usually in Oxford every academic year during my presidential years from 1985 to 1994, sometimes more than once. And after I stepped down from the presidency to return to teaching, I remained in close contact with the Oxford scene. In 1991, I had been elected an honorary fellow of my old college; in 1994, I spent the Michaelmas term at Oxford pursuing research in the Bodleian Library. During the 1999–2000 academic year I was there again, this time delivering the Berlin Lectures in my capacity as Sir Isaiah Berlin Visiting Professor in the History of Ideas. Those lectures were delivered in the Examination Schools on High Street and it was the first time I had set foot in that forbidding building since my viva there almost fifty years earlier. And, since then, I have returned to Oxford with some frequency, either to attend a Gaudy, a Founder's dinner, or some other event at Corpus, or on short research trips to use the Bodleian Library. So frequently, indeed, that I now have a favorite seat in the Upper Reading Room of the Old Bodleian. In the late 1960s or early 1970s when that building underwent extensive restoration, a frieze was uncovered that runs right around the room just below the ceiling. It depicts, in vividly colored fresco form, the portraits of scholarly illuminati from the distant past. When I first saw it, I discovered to my delight, and grouped closely together with one another, the portraits of several medieval intellectuals about whom, over the years, I have written quite extensively, among them Pierre d'Ailly (d. 1420); Jean Gerson (d. 1425), his pupil and successor as chancellor of the University of Paris; and Jan Hus

(d. 1415), the Czech national hero whom d'Ailly helped send to his death as a heretic. On my visits, then, it has become my habit to do my work seated at a nearby desk under what I have to hope is their approving gaze.

My more recent "take" on Oxford, then, is that either of a visiting scholar grateful for access to the incomparable humanistic resources that the Bodleian makes freely available or of an American academic administrator bemused by the complexity of the university's system of collegiate governance and, let it be confessed, mildly impatient with the somewhat foggy nature of its central administrative practices. And one of the things that this latter-day experience has brought home to me, by way of comparison, is the shabbiness and worn-out nature of the university and collegiate physical plant that was evident in the Oxford I first encountered when I came up as an eager freshman in October 1950. After the debilitating years of economic depression and war, deferred maintenance was then clearly the order of the day. The provision of fairly elaborate life-support systems in the form of the "scouts" or college servants who made our beds, cleaned our rooms, saw to our laundry, and waited on us at meals in Hall chimed oddly with the lack of up-to-date amenities in the college buildings themselves. Our rooms were not centrally heated; for warmth, we had to rely on small electric fires on which we also toasted the crumpets we ate with our tea. Nor was there any running water. For shaving and hand and face washing, we were dependent on a portable basin and the large jugs of hot water that our scouts brought to the rooms first thing in the morning. In the college's main buildings, if one wanted a shower or a bath, one had no option but to make one's way across a quadrangle or two to go to the pertinent facility. At Corpus, this was known as "the Plummer," a name immortalizing a distinguished Victorian fellow of the college who had made his scholarly reputation with fundamental contributions to our knowledge of Anglo-Saxon England and our understanding of the great *Historia ecclesiastica* written by the Venerable Bede. This last was the renowned Anglo-Saxon monk to whom those of us reading history and forced to master two books of his Latin text were apt to refer to derisively as "the *Venereal Bede.*" It was not uncommon, then, during the morning hours to see sleepy students clad in dressing gowns and bedroom slippers shuffling across the main quad towards the Plummer in pursuit of a morning bath. As food was still rationed in the impoverished England of the day, it was even more common to see a stream of students dashing into breakfast carrying in their hands a small dish with the week's miserable ration of butter and a small bowl with its equivalent in sugar.

Breakfast, as well as lunch and dinner, was eaten in the college's great Hall, seated on sturdy benches pulled up to the massive oaken tables that ran its length, one in the middle, the others up against the paneled walls on either side. At those side tables it was accepted practice, in order to get to the inner benches along the walls, simply to step up onto the table, picking one's way with great insouciance among the salt and pepper shakers, candles, cutlery, and tankards—all of the latter in those days were silver and some were of considerable antiquity. For the college was still using its silver on even the most ordinary occasions, and we drank our water at lunch or our beer at dinner from silver tankards, many battered from constant use but graced nobly with the college's crest. Some of them dated back even to the late seventeenth century. Amidst all of this, redolent of a storied past, and having had traditional table manners drilled into me at home, I was struck by the intemperate speed with which the public-school products among my fellow students put away their food. I was also taken by the fact that they often thought nothing of eating American-style with their fork in their right hand to facilitate, no doubt, the impressively sustained shoveling process.

In retrospect, the conditions under which we lived and the habits of life that went along with them strike me as a bit odd and I have to assume that our American and Commonwealth fellow students (all referred to as "colonials") found them to be precisely that. But the Americans, I suspect, coped with such things by deciding that they were appealingly quaint, perhaps even rather cute. I myself, of course, being habituated to the deprivations of wartime and the immediate postwar era, took such things for granted. And as I got to know some of my contemporaries and settled down into the unaccustomed rhythms of collegiate life, I found myself beginning to revel in the novelties of it all. I had arrived at Oxford with a set of glowing expectations (often literary in inspiration) that seem simply to have trumped in my mind the somewhat pinched and threadbare conditions of life then prevailing. I was entranced by the consciousness of being one of the privileged inheritors of an ancient institution with a noble history. I thrilled to the consciousness of being in direct academic descent from Chaucer's "clerk of Oxenford." And I was moved by the sheer beauty of my surroundings. That weighed more heavily than any inconveniences or discomforts. One of the books that we all, as sixth-formers, had read at school and that had helped mint the coinage of our intellectual conversational exchanges was Nikolaus Pevsner's *English Architecture*, and it had left us with a basic measure of stylistic literacy when it came to making sense of the precious architectural legacy with which England is so richly endowed. Certainly it helped us place and decode the marked variety of architectural styles on display at Oxford. My heart would lift as I rode my bike past All Souls and Queen's and into the beautiful curve of the High as it beckoned me towards Magdalen and the sheer perfection of its tower. I have often thought since that three or four years of visually attentive living in such a rich architectural setting is worth at least a handful of formal courses in art history.

Other things also conditioned my response to my new surroundings and served to tilt it in a positive and appreciative direction. Along with many of the other freshmen, I was assigned rooms in the old and quite roomy Corpus Annexe, which is situated diagonally across from the college itself, at the corner of Magpie Lane and Merton Street, overlooking the entrance to Christchurch Meadows, and in beguiling proximity to the tower of Merton Chapel with the sound of its bells marking the passage of the daylight hours. The corner suite on the first floor, which I shared with my SFX schoolmate Tony Murray who had come up to read mathematics, afforded a good view of all the intriguing comings and goings and to-ings and fro-ings in the street below. They were the rooms, it turns out, that had been occupied by Isaiah Berlin when he himself was a Corpus freshman some twenty years earlier, though I was to discover that fact only years later. With those accommodations, I was understandably well content. Why wouldn't I be? Apart from their strategic location, it was the first time in my life that I had a bedroom to myself; to have the further luxury of sharing a capacious study, equipped with a desk and bookcase for my sole use, served only to gild the lily. And, until I assimilated them insensibly into the rhythms of daily expectation, I was somehow moved by the liturgical tolling of the bells of Merton.

Coming, as I did, from a Jesuit grammar school where most of my teachers were Oxford products, the principal challenge I had expected to confront as a freshman was that posed by heightened expectations for academic performance. Such expectations existed, and they were real and exacting. But as I listened, somewhat anxiously, to the essays read aloud by my fellow history students (two of whom were old Wyckhamists and had, presumably, been superbly taught), I began to find, much to my relief, that I myself might actually enjoy some advantages of my own. I, too, it turned out, seemed to have been well and challengingly taught at school. Perhaps more important, that teaching had taken a more or less tutorial form in the sixth form. As a result, I had long since become habituated to the demands of independent work and to the salutary discipline imposed by the constant writing of analytical essays. When I embarked, then, on the task of reading for an Honours Degree in Modern History, I found the transition from schoolwork to the academic expectations characteristic of Oxford to be a smoother one than I had somewhat apprehensively anticipated.

In one area, that of lectures, I did flounder a bit, and as a result I gave up attending them for a couple of terms. The problem was in part one of my own making. I didn't quite realize that lectures were not simply a sort of spectator sport, and that in order to be effective the business of lecturing and attending lectures called for a reciprocal effort. That is, not simply effort on the part of the lecturer but also effort on the part of the student. An obvious point, I suppose, but as a freshman attending my first university lectures, I had been mesmerized by the sight of students who sat back in their seats, looking bored in a superior sort of way, and only occasionally leaning forward and picking up a pen to jot down a quick note. What, I wondered as I tried to figure out the nodal point of the lecture at hand that they seemed to have grasped so easily but which had utterly escaped me, was their secret? It finally dawned on me that there was, of course, no such secret, that those students were probably wasting their time, and that if one was to get anything worthwhile out of a lecture, however well or poorly delivered, one had to shoulder the responsibility of close and attentive listening and (preferably) full and detailed note-taking. It was to be some time, however, before I faced up to that fact. But when I did, I was certainly able to get a good deal out of lectures delivered by such as J. P. Plamenatz in political philosophy, who, it should be insisted, was much more sensitive to the historical context in which the great political philosophers had done their thinking than later critics of astringent Skinnerite persuasion would have us believe. I also benefited from what such luminaries on the history faculty as Richard Southern, Beryl Smalley, and Karl Leyser had to say, with Leyser, in particular, opening up a valuable window onto the world of German medieval scholarship that was closed to most of us by the inadequacy of our German or, indeed, by the lack of any knowledge of the language at all, for it was not widely taught in British schools. I also discovered that one could learn a great deal from some of those forbidding, highly specialized, and (apart from dons) poorly attended lectures in which scholars like Naomi Hurnard and Daniel Callus presented the unpublished results of their own current research.

Of course, there was another side to all of this, and it concerns the *nature* of Oxford lecturing. In his memoir, *Marginal Comment*, Sir Kenneth Dover, the eminent classicist who was for some years president of Corpus Christi College, discusses the formal efforts made at Oxford in the 1980s to improve the standard of lecturing there. My own memories from undergraduate days suggest that such efforts were long overdue. My sensibilities now sharpened by decades of academic experience at institutions in Canada and the United States, I would judge that the standard of lecturing at Oxford in the 1950s was really not very high. Henry Steele Commager of Columbia University, who was the Harmsworth Visiting Professor in American History in my second year, was unquestionably the best lecturer I encountered there. He was best both in the quality of what he had to say (about the lead-in to the Civil War) and in the way in which he said it. Given his long years of lecturing to students at a large American research university, his was an admirably skillful, well-organized, and finely tuned performance. In comparison, though doubtless there were some distinguished exceptions, the average Oxford lecture in my day, however learned and informative, tended to be flaccid in organization and ineffective in delivery. And neither characteristic was designed to encourage faithful attendance or attentive listening.

So far as my tutorials were concerned, and they were, of course, much closer to the heart of the learning process, I especially enjoyed Michael Brock's encouraging, energetic, and stimulating tutoring in my freshman year. Later on, indeed, I much regretted not having had him as a tutor for the field in modern English history where, never having done it at school, my basic knowledge was destined to remain uncomfortably thin. It is testimony to the kindly interest he took in students that Michael remained my point of contact with Corpus, taking an active interest in the progress of my career long after I had graduated. Among my other tutors, I particularly appreciated J. R. L. Highfield of Merton, to whom I was sent for tutoring in the late medieval and early modern stretch of English history, and C. H. Wilson (later to be principal and vice-chancellor of the University of Glasgow), who taught the political science field very much as political *philosophy*, via the seminar method, and in highly (if somewhat lazily) stimulating fashion. But it was Max Beloff who made the strongest impression on me. Although at that time he held the position of Reader in the Comparative Study of Institutions, he still did some undergraduate teaching and, having himself been a Corpus man, took on three of us who had chosen to do the special subject in slavery and secession. This focused quite tightly on the crucial period in American history that stretched from the 1840s to 1865, and it involved our first encounter with American historiography. Beloff himself had been born in England but his parents were Russian Jewish émigrés, and though he was a graduate of St. Paul's School in London and had read Modern History at Oxford, there was something decidedly un-English about the refreshing candor and bluntness of his response to our efforts, whether it was scathingly critical or gratifyingly laudatory. For he proved himself, in that term, to be capable of both. He tutored the two other students from Corpus together; I had him to myself. He had told us to write our first essays over the preceding vacation, and when I arrived, somewhat apprehensively, to read mine to him at our first tutorial, I encountered my two colleagues exiting, white faced, from theirs, having just been told in peremptory fashion that they were wasting his time and had better shape up. Not for him, it seemed, the passive voice, subjunctive mood, or conditional tense that I had been accustomed to hearing from tutors framing their comments. Instead he was all active, indicative, and imperative. That I was to find wonderfully invigorating and refreshingly different from what I had become (somewhat restively) accustomed to in the several tutorials on medieval topics that I had taken at Corpus with Trevor Aston. Aston, who was to succeed to the medieval position at Corpus previously held by the early medievalist J. M. Wallace-Hadrill, and was later to distinguish himself as the long-standing editor of *Past and Present*, which was for some years, so I would judge, the leading general historical journal in the Anglophone world. At the time, however, his position was that of a junior research fellow. In 1994, in the wake of the eye-catching remarks that Kenneth Dover made in his memoir about the tragic suicide that had put an end in 1984 to Aston's sadly troubled life, a few letters from former students appeared in the national press lauding his accomplishments as a tutor. That he may have developed over the years into a first-rate tutor I have no reason to doubt. But the Aston I encountered in the early 1950s, while clearly, in a disheveled sort of way, a very bright fellow, was also someone who had still to find his pedagogic feet. He was characteristically (and discouragingly) tepid in his commentary upon one's efforts and counterproductively parsimonious in his praise. At that time, I ended by judging his performance in a somewhat bleakly negative fashion. It was, I thought, disorganized, uninspired, and dispiriting, especially if one were to compare it with Roger Highfield's. And having been tutored on medieval history by both of them, so compare it I inevitably did.

While those of us at Corpus who were reading history grumbled *sotto voce* about such things, it would never have occurred to us to share such grumbles with our seniors. And the solicitation of student opinion about the effectiveness of the teaching the student was receiving was a novel departure that still lay far in the future. Immediately after Aston's election in 1952 as a full tutorial fellow at Corpus, one of the senior history dons there did say to me, "Aston is awfully good, isn't he?" To which my response (an embarrassed mumble) was taken, I assume, as confirmatory student approval of the appointment. Nor do I remember, apart from some restiveness about the political science requirement, much discussion about the nature of the curriculum which we were required to pursue and which, though it afforded a few options, was largely fixed. The comparative lack of choice, so alien to the American system of elective courses, we simply took for granted. I found our brief exposure to historical geography in the freshman year intriguing and, being of somewhat theoretical temperament, was stimulated by the need to come to terms with Adam Smith's *Wealth of Nations*, which was required as a set text. For similar reasons, because it really meant political *philosophy*, I was later very much taken with the required field in political science. It was structured around three formidable set texts that formed a sort of Procrustean bed on which the minds of students were to be stretched (or narrowed): Aristotle's *Politics* (in merciful translation), Hobbes's *Leviathan* (or, rather, a lengthy selection from that great work tendentious enough to come close to mandating a particular interpretation), and Rousseau's *Du contrat social* (in French). Imagining myself at that time to be a fellow of thwarted philosophical temperament for which the course of study mandated in history afforded no other outlet, I embraced the subject with alacrity. For me, indeed, it turned out to be something of a life changer, a moment of modest epiphany on the road to a personal intellectual Damascus. From my close encounter with those required texts I took away a great deal, especially from Rousseau. But I may have taken away even more from my anxious wrestling with Michael Oakeshott's lengthy introductory essay to the Blackwell's edition of *Leviathan*, which was the edition we had all been instructed to purchase.

If Oakeshott's essay is indeed a brilliant one, it was also one that I found great difficulty in understanding when I first encountered it as a nineteen-year-old. My first, somewhat breathless, take on it probably amounted in fact to little more than an instance of what Arthur O. Lovejoy once derided as "metaphysical pathos." That is, an instinctive, emotional response to "the loveliness of the incomprehensible," a response that, he wryly noted, has "stood many a philosopher in good stead with his public." "The reader doesn't know exactly what they [such philosophers] mean, but they have [for him] all the more on that account an air of sublimity, [and] an agreeable feeling of awe and exaltation comes over him as he contemplates thoughts of such immeasurable profundity." My explorations of the other philosophers I read around the same time were of much the same kind. Had there been in those days a combined philosophy-history curricular option, I would doubtless have pursued it. But no such option existed and my philosophical browsings, therefore, were strictly extracurricular. A fellow Corpus student who possessed distinctly High Church leanings had put me onto the Pusey House library, for which I acquired a reader's card, and I have happy memories of sitting there in what seemed to be an unheated reading room as darkness descended on early winter evenings, trying to make sense of the writings of existentialists like Gabriel Marcel or trying to penetrate the slightly incantatory opacity of Nikolai Berdyaev's prose. I did rather better, however, with my somewhat hostile reading of Ayer's *Language, Truth and Logic* (admirably lucid, I thought, but too clever by half), Jacques

Maritain's *A Preface to Metaphysics* (a book somewhat Bergsonian in feel), and Étienne Gilson's *Spirit of Medieval Philosophy* (his Gifford Lectures and surely the most compelling of his many contributions to our understanding of that subject). Around the same time I also read R. G. Collingwood's *Speculum Mentis*, which left me strongly drawn to the way he thought about the nature of historical understanding.

But if I was confident enough even in my freshman year, intellectually speaking, to reach out in this way beyond the sort of work required for the course of study in Modern History, and, indeed, cocky enough to entertain critical thoughts about my elders and betters, I was a good deal less sanguine, in the highly class-conscious Britain of the day, about my ability to navigate the unfamiliar social and cultural waters on which I had to embark once I got to Oxford. I was the less so since I had been permitted, because my father was nearing retirement, to defer my National Service until I finished university and had come up, accordingly, directly from school and at the age of eighteen. I did so only to find that most of my contemporaries at Corpus were older and more worldly-wise, sharing in common, as they did, the maturing experience of military life. I was, moreover, the son of immigrant parents who, bright though they undoubtedly were, had finished their own formal schooling at the tender age of fourteen. Unmistakably (and self-consciously) provincial as I was—in accent, dress, and (probably) demeanor—my own direct acquaintance with England and the modalities of English life was limited almost entirely to Merseyside and its immediate environs in Lancashire and Cheshire. Oddly enough, having spent much time there, from Dublin and its surrounding country in the east, via Westmeath in the center, to Galway and Mayo in the west, I was more broadly acquainted with Ireland, where I had come to feel very much at home, than I was with the length and breadth of England itself. Certainly the beautiful and quintessential England that lay to the south of the grim Northern and Midlands industrial belt was in many ways alien territory to me. Equally foreign were its characteristic mores and the reticent modes of social interchange prevalent there, saturated as they were with class feeling and the inclination to discriminate between "insiders" and "outsiders" to the detriment, of course, of the latter. That inclination seemed to come instinctively to those who had gone to public (i.e., private boarding) schools, perhaps especially (and somewhat anxiously) to those who had attended the less prestigious among those schools. So evident was all of this that I was sometimes tempted to think that English society had been modeled on the pyramidal, transtemporal hierarchy delineated in his *Celestial Hierarchy* by the anonymous fifth-century Syrian author whom we know as Pseudo-Dionysius the Areopagite. For it seemed, at times, to be a society in which the truly "inside" insiders presided at the apex of a hierarchy of descending exclusion, in which each rank of outsiders saw themselves as insiders in relation to the next and subordinate rank of outsiders. And so on, the whole system being fueled, it may be, as much by the reassurance of seeing others excluded as by the satisfaction of being included oneself.

In such a setting, clearly, I not only had much maturing to do but also a good deal to learn, culturally speaking, and to get used to. Had I gone to one of the larger and, perhaps, snootier colleges, where small, exclusive cliques based on social connections dating back to public school days were more prevalent, it might all have proved to be too much of a burden and I might have been tempted to withdraw almost entirely into things academic and intellectual, where I felt more secure, and to have become right at the start what in derogatory American parlance is called "a grind." But that, though I remained serious about my studies, I did not do. And happily so. At a residential university community like Oxford's, just as at residential liberal arts colleges in America, the rich cocurricular and extracurricular life of cultural and athletic activity, and the lively social interchange among students of different temperaments and different social, racial, regional, and national backgrounds that goes with it, forms an integral and powerfully educative part of undergraduate life. Not all the teaching and learning that goes on, after all, takes place in classroom, tutorial, laboratory, or lecture hall.

The Catholic Chaplaincy at Oxford was at that time a very active and lively operation. Through it I came to sing in a Gregorian chant choir directed by a learned Benedictine from St. Benet's Hall. Through it, too, I came to join a reel club and to love Scottish dancing and most other things Scottish. But it was college life itself that was mainly responsible for the broadening of my horizons. Though Corpus possessed a noble history as a center of classical learning, it was one of the smallest colleges at Oxford. Its very size worked to preclude the flourishing of exclusive cliques. The only one that was evident to me at the time was one formed by a group of ex–public school boys which orbited around a handsome and elegant fellow who (reputedly) had the background, connections, and financial wherewithal to do his National Service as a subaltern in the rarified ranks of the Brigade of Guards. That group seemed to inhabit its own exclusive world, and its members appeared to view the activities of the Corpus student body at large with a degree of detached disdain. But as a phenomenon, that group was also quite exceptional. Instead, the Corpus community I encountered as a somewhat shy and diffident eighteen-year old turned out to be an accessible and welcoming one. The great public schools were, of course, well represented among my contemporaries—notably Rugby, but also Winchester, Eton, Christ's Hospital, Charterhouse, Harrow, and others. So, too, however, were the first-rate grammar schools then to be found in almost every part of the country. There was an interesting group of Marshall and Rhodes Scholars from the United States, Canada, and Australia, a handful of students, black as well as white, from West Africa, Rhodesia, and South Africa, and a sprinkling of post-graduate students from the Continent. And an important factor, I think, given the college's particular history and tradition (which included in the eighteenth century a protracted phase of stubbornly Jacobite loyalties), was that it was also graced with a significant Scots presence, as invigorating as it was leavening.

I have no reason to believe that much (if any) social engineering had gone into the production of this mix, but it seemed nonetheless to work. It didn't prove hard to make new friends, and I already felt settled in and well on the way to becoming a loyal Corpus man by the end of my first term in 1950. At the end of that term, there was an informal concert in Hall at which dons and students alike contributed skits of one sort or another. One of my new friends, John Elton, a classicist who came from Winchester and with whom I had been playing violin duets, twinned up with me to do a spoof of an elaborately show-offy piece (much double-stopping!) written by an obscure central European composer who was distinguished for us largely by the fact that there were no vowels in his surname. When the affair was over, we were enormously gratified to be congratulated on our musical efforts by none other than Eduard Fraenkel, the Corpus Professor of Latin, sometime pupil of the great Wilamowitz himself, and one of that fine generation of distinguished German-Jewish émigré scholars who did so much to invigorate classical, medieval, and

Renaissance studies in the Anglophone world at large. This is clearly, I thought quietly to myself, the place for me.

I look back on my time at Corpus, on the range of activities I was drawn into, and on the good friends made there, with immense gratitude. I read papers to the Sundial Society (philosophical and literary) and the Pelican Society (historical—enterprisingly started by a fellow student, John Wilmer), serving for a year as president of the latter. I threw myself into rowing and performed (as a rather lightweight number four) in a pretty undistinguished but enjoyable second eight. I also took up cross-country, the start of a lifelong addiction to running that has left me finally with a cartilage-challenged right knee. But what stands out particularly is the recollection of the vitality at that time of the musical and theatrical life of the college, informal as well as formal. I have happy memories of playing Purcell late in the evening as part of an informal consort of recorders put together by another fellow Corpus man, Mark Sheldon, who was reading law, and of playing the Third Brandenburg Concerto as part of the violin section of a rather wheezy scratch orchestra, an experience oddly akin to that of rowing in a poorly balanced eight where stroke is not setting a good, crisp pace. A group of us were also taught to sing calypsos by Eldred Jones, a student from Sierra Leone who was to become a lifelong friend and whom I was to see again, over the years, in Oxford, London, New Haven, Toronto, and Williamstown. His academic expertise extended both to Shakespeare and to the newly burgeoning African literature of the day and, having become the founding and devoted long-term editor of the journal *African Literature Today*, he ended up as principal of Fourah Bay College in Freetown, his own alma mater and the oldest university college in West Africa. In 1985 he represented that college at my induction as president of Williams and gave a short but elegant speech, and on that occasion I had the enormous pleasure of bestowing upon him an honorary degree. On a more formal level, in my second year, I much enjoyed helping to provide, along with John Elton, Mark Sheldon, and others, the instrumental accompaniment for the Corpus Owlets' rather zany adaptation as a musical of Nicolas Udall's *Ralph Roister Doister* (often said to be the first comedy written in English). Its director was Alistair McIntosh, a fellow of multiple talents which extended from elegant print design to the orchestration of unusually effective choral speaking and the direction of plays in general.

At his prompting, another contemporary, a rather shy student who was reading law, composed for this mock-heroic effort a surprisingly lyrical and richly Romantic musical score that was great fun to play. Somewhere or other, I don't seem to be able to put my finger on the poem, Yeats writes of our movement along the arc of life from "the red flare" of youthful dreams into "the common light of common hours, until old age brings the red flare again." And there's something, I find, to that. But cutting occasionally through the jumble of my own aging dreams and rising proudly above their tumult, I still thrill to hear the wonderful descending violin obbligato written by that student for us to play in bold counterpoint to the rising cadences of Roister Doister's lugubrious and concluding lament.

At Corpus, we took advantage of the June weather to perform that play in the Fellows' Garden, which nestles snugly in the lea of a surviving stretch of the old city walls. And, because of Udall's connection with that school (he had been headmaster there until 1541 when he was convicted under the Buggery Act of 1533 of hanky-panky with his pupils), we were also invited to mount another performance, in the Fellows' Garden at Eton, from which one could catch a glimpse of the tower of Windsor Castle floating free, it seemed, on a thin layer of ground mist. It was all immense fun, and I similarly enjoyed playing, during that same Trinity term, in a small musical ensemble accompanying the songs in Alistair's OUDS (Oxford University Dramatic Society) production of *Twelfth Night*, which was played outside in the evening and as twilight descended. Only about ten years ago, while lunching with him in London, did I learn that the "Margaret Smith" whom he had cast (not without controversy, it seems) in the role of Viola was none other than the irrepressible Maggie Smith herself, who has since played so many splendidly achieved roles and served, after all, as the doyenne of *Downton Abbey*.

The theatrical event at the Corpus of my day that I am happiest to have been caught up in, however, was the one already mentioned that rounded out my freshman year. It was another of Alistair's efforts, his fine production of T. S. Eliot's *Murder in the Cathedral*, so successful at Oxford that he and those of us in the cast were inspired to take it up the following September to "the fringe" of the newly established Edinburgh Festival. Here the strength of the college's Scottish connections came powerfully into play. With their assistance, all sorts of obstacles were surmounted and practical problems resolved. Free accommodations were found for the men at Fettes College and for the women at another private school. And we were all made the grateful recipients of absolutely wonderful hospitality. Douglas Duncan, who brought to the role of Becket a finely modulated voice and superbly mature presence, happened to be the son of the current moderator of the Kirk Assembly through whose good offices the way was cleared for us to stage the first part of the play in the Senate House and the second in the High Kirk (St. Giles Cathedral) itself, with the cast solemnly processing at the intermission across Parliament Square to the cathedral and the audience dutifully following in its wake. Reviews in the *Scotsman* and other papers were quite laudatory, and the show was more or less sold out. Permission was similarly secured (I don't know quite how) to put on charity performances in the ruins of Arbroath Abbey and of the chapel at Holyrood Palace (a royal residence) before completing our tour with a week of performances in the Chapel of St. Salvator (John Knox's church) at the University of St. Andrews. Between the satisfaction of the performances themselves (very well received), the wonderful hospitality extended to us by the Scots, the fun of dancing eightsome reels on the deck of the ferry across the Firth of Forth, and late-night (post-show) partying on the chilly shore at St. Andrews, that fortnight on tour with the Corpus Owlets (the college's dramatic society) was truly memorable. So memorable, indeed, that there was not only a cast reunion, a seminar on Eliot and Becket at which I spoke, and a celebratory dinner at Corpus forty-five years later, but also, at the fiftieth anniversary, a revival at Oxford of the production itself, featuring many of the same, now aging, cast. But that latter effort I had alas to miss, having already committed to being in Scotland at that very time, delivering some lectures in Scottish history to a Williams alumni group touring the Highlands and Western Isles.

Oxford is a complex, federated university with the instructional task divided between a group of quasi-autonomous constituent colleges jealous of their privileges and the centrally controlled university departments supported in their work by the university's libraries, museums, and scientific laboratories. Under the Oxford system, the granting of degrees and the rigorous examinations that determined the class of degree to be awarded (at the undergraduate level there were four such classes of honours degrees as well as a sort of backup Pass option) lay in the hands of the university authority itself, with a rotating body of examiners, two grading each of the examinations written in each field. While it was the responsibility of the constituent colleges to teach the undergraduates and prepare them for the university examinations, one's performance in the essays written regularly for tutors, however good or bad, counted for nothing in the final determinations of whether or not one should be given a degree and, more to the point, the class of honours one should receive if one were being examined for an honours degree. Instead, everything depended on one's performance in almost a week of three-hour examinations, two per day on most days. Those examinations were taken in the June of one's final year and had come to be referred to as "Schools" because they were taken in the Examination Schools building on High Street. As our final year ground on, we came to view Schools with mounting apprehension as the very Trump of Doom. The whole system, it has to be confessed, was a highly stressful, rather brutal one, and, in each of my three years at Oxford, the weeks leading up to Schools were punctuated by a rash of desperate student suicides. After years, however, of observing and thinking about the standard American system, which involves a cumulative grade point average (GPA) reflecting the performance of a given student in every course taken from the first semester of freshman year onwards, I am less inclined than I once was to criticize the Oxford approach. For the GPA system unquestionably serves to discourage risk-taking in the choice of courses and to encourage a desiccating commitment to unremitting grind among academically ambitious undergraduates. And I have come, accordingly, to conclude that the Oxford system of our day, however miserable it may have been, did possess some correlative advantages. Certainly it suited the somewhat erratic trajectory of my own academic activities over the course of my three years of undergraduate work.

At Corpus, the term "collections" was used in two ways. First, to describe informal in-house examinations set by one's tutors to check on one's progress. These counted for nothing towards the degree. Second, to denote the annual occasions when we were called individually before the assembled dons, seated at the high table in Hall, with the senior tutor reading an assessment of one's performance to date and the president following up, as the case might be, with a few words of praise, encouragement, or admonition. Collections at the end of my second year took place in the immediate aftermath of the Corpus Owlets' triumphant production of *Ralph Roister Doister*. But after a few pleasant words of commendation for our efforts in that respect, the tone became more serious. I can't remember if it was the senior tutor or the president himself who delivered the central message on that particular occasion, but it proved to be at once both chastening and encouraging. I was told, with admirable (if kindly) bluntness, that they thought that I had a decent shot at getting First Class Honours in Schools and that they would encourage my aspirations to pursue an academic career. At the same time, however, they made it clear that if I were serious about such aspirations, I would need to trim my extracurricular sails at this juncture, withdraw from most (or all) of the activities that had so beguiled me, focus more intently on my studies, and maybe think about entering the competition for the Gibbs Prize Scholarship. I was also told, this time by way of encouragement, that I would not need to find a summer job that year, as the college could make some modest discretionary funds available to me so that I could stay up at Oxford over the long vacation and make a start on catching up on my academic work and filling in the gaps in my preparation for Schools.

That advice I took, as well as the generous offer of financial help, and I am eternally grateful to Corpus both for the forthrightness of the counsel given to me at a pivotal moment and for the support extended to make it possible for me to act on that counsel. It was for me the great turning point in the road that led me towards the academic calling that I have found so deeply fulfilling. And over the years, both as teacher and administrator, I have taken it as a model for how, in a humane and intimate collegiate setting, one should reach out to help shape the lives of the students entrusted to one's care.

The summer months that ensued, spent largely by myself in one or another of the Oxford libraries, marked for me the start of a very different Oxford experience. Those months gave me some inkling of what the scholarly life might really be like. They brought home to me the important lesson that if one were going to find satisfaction in the *vita contemplativa* of scholarship, one needed by temperament to be content with one's own company. Somewhat to my surprise, I found that I was, though I often felt lonely amid the bustling tourist life that engulfs Oxford in summertime—the more so in that I had had to move out of college. Oxford colleges in those days were unable to accommodate students for their full three years, and we were all required to move out of college and into digs around town for our final year. Those digs usually took the form of a bed and breakfast arrangement in one of the many houses around town owned and operated by former college servants. John Elton and I had lined up rooms in a house on the Abingdon Road about a mile from college and it was there that I spent those summer months. Until the Michaelmas term began, I was the only lodger there apart from a bank clerk in his forties who had grown up in one of the villages around Oxford and who struck me as a fellow living a constricted life of quiet desperation, one made bearable only by the weekends he spent careening up and down the country on an enormous Harley-Davidson motorcycle. Breakfast was included with the room, and I ate my other meals at pubs (*The Bear* on Bear Lane was my favorite), at various cheap cafés, or on Cornmarket Street at the British Council, which served lunch. Eldred Jones got married at the beginning of the summer and, with characteristic kindness, he and his wife Marjorie extended to me an open invitation to stop by at teatime at their flat on the Kingston Road in north Oxford. So I saw a lot of them that summer. Apart from the Joneses, there were no other Corpus students in residence during July and August, though there were a couple at University College whom I had got to know through my old school friend Lol O'Keeffe. One of them, whom I knew also through his girlfriend, Pat, who was reading history at St. Hugh's, was Vidia (V. S.) Naipaul, the Trinidadian who was destined in the course of time to win the Booker and Nobel Prizes in Literature. From time to time that summer, we would get together in a pub for an evening's drinking and I remember him from that time as a more charming and accessible fellow than he was later to become. In his cups he was prone to indulging extended, apocalyptic riffs about the decline and fall of Western civilization and to lament his (alleged) inability to write intelligently about literature. As he was reading for an honours degree in English, that presented something of a problem which he was trying to solve by electing as many of the purely philological options in the degree course as possible. After that summer, I believe I encountered him only twice. The first time, in the mid-1960s, was when he and Pat invited me along with the O'Keeffes for lunch at their South London flat. It was a lively and enjoyable occasion. Having begun to meet success with such books as *Miguel Street*, *The Mystic Masseur*, and *A House for Mr. Biswas*, Vidia was in high spirits, and so, too, was Pat, who had landed a job she very much liked teaching history at a nearby grammar school. And I was much impressed on that occasion by Vidia's focus on the writing task at hand, which was so intense that he had not in the previous six months ventured beyond the corner newsagent and tobacconist shop to which he could walk to pick up cigarettes and the paper. It was an altogether different story, however, when I encountered him, for the last time, towards the end of the 1970s at a dinner party the O'Keeffes gave (in his honor?) at the cottage they had acquired at Wiley in Wiltshire. On that occasion Vidia, who was by himself, came through as a more truculent and less user-friendly fellow, prone to bringing the party to a halt by dropping into the lively flow of talk such predictable conversation-stoppers as the question: "Why do all Americans lie?" By that time he was already beginning to distance himself from his old friends, and the O'Keeffes were later on to be very hurt when, though he, like them, was living in Wiltshire, he (or his new wife?) coldly refused all contact with them.

My laborious summer residence proved to be a success. I was able to do a good deal of catching up and to begin my final year with a pretty clear sense of the remaining challenges confronting me if I was to be adequately prepared for Schools. Before the Michaelmas term began, by way of decompression, I spent a wonderful week fell-walking in the Lake District with a Corpus classicist friend, Duncan Fishwick (later to become an expert on the Roman imperial cult), and some friends of his from the University of Manchester. We hiked over the mountains from valley to valley, staying at the youth hostels that were dotted conveniently around the region, and it was the beginning of my love affair with mountains. In subsequent years, some of my most enjoyable moments have involved hiking in mountainous terrain, whether in the Lakes again, or in the Pennines while I was stationed as a soldier in the North Riding of Yorkshire, or in the White Mountains of New Hampshire, or, eventually, in the Berkshire and Green Mountains and along the Taconic Range after we had settled down for good amid the ruggedly beautiful countryside of western Massachusetts.

That final year at Oxford was very different from the two preceding. Having withdrawn from the various beguiling activities that had made my first two years so stimulating and enjoyable, my final year was one filled with routine academic drudgery, enlivened by little except the award of the Christopher Bushell History Prize at Corpus and by election, on the larger university scene, to the Stubbs History Society. The selection process that led to that happy outcome (it was a bit of an honor) was characteristically occluded, but I expect that it was to Aston that I owed my election, for he had himself as an undergraduate been made a member of that august group. And it was in the context of its meetings that I first acquired the requisite academic ability to look intelligently engaged while listening somewhat restively to incomprehensibly specialized papers on such gripping topics as late medieval landholding patterns in the Welsh marches. But the year was not an easy one. I was a worried fellow and suffered a weeklong bout of insomnia during the Hilary term (a new and terrifying experience for me, and one that ended only after I had seen the doctor and been given a few sleeping pills). That encouraged me to seek solace, once more, up in the Lake District. So, with some Corpus friends, I spent an invigorating week there during the Easter vacation. It turned out to be still very wintry in the mountains, and, ill-equipped though we were for the snowy conditions still prevailing, we still managed to edge our perilous way up to the summit of Helvelyn via the slippery trail that rides along the spine of Striding Edge. Not the most sensible thing to do, I suppose, but it was an exhilarating experience.

After the rigors of the run-up to Schools, it was a great relief to get the actual examinations done and to sleep soundly on the nights between them. I emerged from the experience feeling that I had acquitted myself decently though with little sense of *how* decently, and I was content for a while to relax into the enjoyment of the post-Schools parties and the pleasure of leisurely afternoons spent punting on the Cherwell. But that did not last for long. The college had nominated me for a Goldsmiths' Company's Travelling Commonwealth Research Scholarship and I went up to London to interview for it—successfully, it turned out, to my great delight. The award was a fine one, bringing with it quite generous funding for two years of advanced study in any Commonwealth university. Having become very interested in medieval philosophy, my choice was to take up the scholarship at the Pontifical Institute of Mediaeval Studies in Toronto, a free-standing, papally accredited research institute founded about a quarter of a century earlier by Étienne Gilson of the Collège de France (at that time the leading scholar in the field), who continued still to serve as its director of studies. E. F. Jacob of All Souls, the late medieval scholar who was Chichele Professor of History, agreed to take me on as a DPhil candidate when I returned. We agreed that I should spend my time at Toronto learning Latin palaeography and getting a firm grip on the history of medieval philosophy. Then, having returned to Oxford, I would focus under his supervision on an appropriate dissertation topic. At the same time, Corpus made it clear that they would help me get started on that dissertation phase by appointing me to a Senior (i.e., postgraduate) Scholarship. My immediate future, at least, was thus provided for and that helped convince my parents to go along with my plans. In my mother's case that was not an altogether easy task, for she instinctively resonated to ancestral Irish memories suggesting that those who headed off to the New World were rarely seen or heard from again.

That she did so was not altogether surprising. Not long after she had moved with my father to England in the early 1920s, my father had somehow managed to find a job there for his youngest brother, Oliver. It was a simple laboring job and it had apparently not been to Ollie's taste, so they had all somehow managed to scrape together the cash needed to book him passage by sea to New York, where another elder brother, Jack, was pretty sure he could fix him up with something reasonable to do. After bidding him farewell at the Prince's Landing Stage in Liverpool, my parents anxiously awaited news of how things were turning out for him in America. They did hear something. It was a picture postcard (I would like to think it was a picture of the Statue of Liberty) bearing the simple message: "Have arrived, Love, Ollie." That was it—the last time they ever heard from him. Before I left for Canada, my father asked me, rather anxiously, to see if I could find him if I ever got to New York. When I did, I could find no trace of Ollie in the telephone directories for greater New York. In recent years, however, an English niece pursuing genealogical research via Ancestry.com discovered that Ollie had soldiered on, but he died in the 1960s in a Los Angeles veterans' hospital.

Two big issues remained. First, I needed to secure another two-year extension of my deferment from military service. That did not prove to be at all difficult. Second, I needed to find out whether or not I had qualified for the class of honours degree commensurate with the fine award I had been lucky enough to have had bestowed on me. For that I had to wait until July when two examiners were finished marking each of our examination papers (and had, presumably, tried to reconcile their grades where they diverged) and we were all summoned back to Oxford for our "vivas," or oral examinations. For those examinees whose written performance placed them unambiguously within a given class of honours (the vast majority, in fact), vivas were required but tended to involve little more than a five-minute formality. When I reported in the morning for mine, however, I was told to come back in the afternoon. That encouraged me to speculate nervously that I might be a credible candidate for a First, provided I didn't ruin everything by turning in a poor performance. In the event, when I showed up in the afternoon, attired in regulation sub fusc with white bow tie and Scholar's gown, I found myself confronting the full board of examiners, gowned and seated at a long table, while behind me several members of the public were sitting in as spectators to observe the proceedings. If it was a bit of a daunting experience for a twenty-one-year-old, it was also an invigorating one. One of the examiners had clearly been amused by a little dialogue I had written on one of my two general (i.e., European) history papers, involving two fictitious historians whom I had labeled "Barrachütz" and "Liebesclough" and designed to demonstrate the circular nature of one of the standard arguments usually advanced. "What," he said, "do you have against Barraclough?" To which I replied that I much admired Barraclough's work but thought he was simply wrong on the point in question. Another examiner seemed a bit suspicious about the long chronological gap dividing the questions I had chosen to answer on the late medieval and early modern paper in English history. "Mr. Oakley," he said, "are you allergic to the fifteenth century?" To which I truthfully replied that I wasn't (I was destined, after all, to become a late medieval specialist); I simply didn't like the particular questions asked about that period. And so it went on for a full fifty minutes or so. The questions I was asked were not all as edgy as the two opening ones, and I wasn't quizzed on all the papers. But while I left knowing that I hadn't messed things up, I also left without any clear sense of whether or not I had in any way forwarded my cause.

Events were to suggest that I had either forwarded my cause or, at least, not nudged the board's judgment in a negative direction. I did in fact get the First that I was convinced I needed if I were to embark on a successful academic career. But whether I was correct to be so convinced I am not at all sure. An Oxford First might, I suppose, have mattered had I chosen in the end to pursue a career in Britain. But I never got the sense in the American academic world that anyone paid much attention to it. My instructors at the Yale graduate school clearly preferred to make up their own minds about the quality of my intellectual efforts, and, when it came to the academic job market, what *they* had to say about my abilities seemed to be far more important than anything I might have achieved as a mere undergraduate. But I was quite ignorant about all of that at the time. The only thing I can say with any confidence about that First is that it encouraged me to appraise my academic efforts somewhat less negatively than had often been the case until that time. And, later on, I think it helped give me the confidence to take what I now view as creative intellectual risks in my scholarly writing.

With vivas out of the way, all that was left for me to do was to return home, get my things together for a prolonged stay abroad, and arrange for my sea passage to Canada. And that is what I did. Meanwhile, Eldred and Marjorie Jones were themselves sailing back to Sierra Leone on the MV *Aureol*, a ship of the Elder Dempster Line, and, as the port of departure was Liverpool, they stayed overnight with us before embarking. My parents had never met any black people before and were utterly (and predictably) charmed and captivated by them. It was a time of transitions and departures for all of us. In the month remaining, I took time out for yet another week of fell-walking and youth hostelling in the Lake District. This time I had as my trail companions Geoff Hulme, another Corpus friend, his (soon to be) fiancée Shirley, and her old school friend, Karolyn—this last a lovely girl whom I took to immediately and with whom I quickly hit it off. Like me, however, she was about to head off abroad for two years, in her case to a sort of finishing school in Lausanne where, along with perfecting her French, she was to pursue what sounded like a rather eclectic course of study that embraced not only subjects in arts and letters but also a training in standard secretarial skills. Bidding each other a reluctant farewell after a wonderfully enjoyable week, we promised to write, and we did indeed succeed in maintaining a protracted, if intermittent, correspondence over most of the following two years. I was to encounter her again after I had returned to England and was serving my time in the army. Geoff and Shirley had married during the winter of 1955–56 and I spent time with Karolyn on a few occasions when I stayed with them in London. By that time she was working for the BBC and she and I had fun exploring the amenities of London or, at least, those we could afford. But, sensing that she was beginning to get serious about me, I felt I had to share with her, somewhat awkwardly, the fact that I had by now acquired, however uncertain its prospects, a serious romantic attachment across the Atlantic. And with that, after some heart-wrenching moments, we were eventually to go our separate ways.

We were to encounter her again, at parties given by the Hulmes and other friends, while we were spending the 1969–70 academic year on leave in London. By that time she was married and the doting mother of two small children. Later on, the children grown, and having divorced and remarried, she moved with her new husband to France. And in the early 1990s, I was to see them both at the wedding of Geoff and Shirley's daughter—in Westminster Abbey, no less.

After our time in the Lake District, I returned home to pack and to spend a couple of weeks with my family before embarking from Liverpool in September for the ten-day transatlantic passage to Montreal. From that point, I was to go on to Toronto by train. Having grown up as a boy in a busy port city and being acquainted with quite a few people who had made their careers in the merchant marine, I was disposed to taking a rather romantic view of life at sea. Moreover, having sailed with some frequency to and fro to Ireland, whether from Holyhead in Anglesey to Dún Laoghaire or via the longer route from Liverpool to Dublin, I had come to enjoy the experience of being at sea and out of sight of land. So for me, that first protracted transatlantic transit smacked of high adventure. The ship I embarked on, the *Empress of Scotland*, was an old, stately, Canadian Pacific liner, originally of German registry but transferred into Allied hands, I believe, as part of the war reparations imposed on Germany at the end of the Great War. It had a fine, open promenade deck on which it was easy to get plenty of energetic exercise, and I much enjoyed the ritual, exercise concluded, of sitting on a deck chair, reading or (endlessly!) talking, wrapped warmly in blankets, and sipping the periodic cup of bouillon.

The departure from the Prince's Landing Stage at Liverpool and on out into the Irish Sea was familiar enough, but as we turned northward, passing the impressively green prominence of the Isle of Man, stopping briefly at Greenock to pick up by tender a few residual passengers, and then steering westward, first along the beckoningly green coast of Ulster and then out into the rougher open waters of the Atlantic itself, I thrilled to the novelty of the experience and celebrated the good fortune that had enabled me to embark on such an adventure. I speedily adjusted to the rolling and creaking of the ship as it encountered the long Atlantic swells, was relaxed at night into the deepest of sleeps, and managed to get in enough exercise during the day to do justice to three excellent meals, even in what used to be called steerage class. There were quite a few young people on board, some of them Canadians returning home after a period of study in Europe, and I was able to make several enjoyable (if evanescent) shipboard friendships. The days on board passed pleasantly enough; we were occupied by day with walking, talking, and playing deck tennis, and in the evenings with talking even more, eating, drinking, and dancing. The time spent in transit constituted a wonderfully relaxing interlude, easing the transition from the world I knew to the upcoming novelties and challenges of the unknown world that lay ahead. Those challenges, I am inclined to think, would have been far more daunting had it been customary in those days to cross the Atlantic, rapidly and peremptorily, by air.

But even leisurely sea passages must come to an end. After the excitement of spotting some large icebergs as we sailed south of Newfoundland, sober reality made its presence felt as we entered the Gulf of St. Lawrence and made our way past Prince Edward Island. Somewhere around that point, a Canadian immigration officer came on board with the first of the river pilots and settled down to go about his business. He did so in much more casual fashion than was to be called for later on after the restless movement (or attempted movement) from continent to continent of vast numbers of people became the order of the day. Though I explained to him that I was simply a travelling student who intended to spend no more than two years in Canada and then return home, he urged me to take "landed immigrant" status if for no other reason than it would enable me to travel to and fro to the United States without having to go through further formalities. His advice I accepted, so it was as an immigrant to Canada that I disembarked at Montreal, just as, four years later, it was as an immigrant to the United States that I disembarked on New York's west side from the old *Queen Elizabeth*, or, for that matter, just as it had been as immigrants, in fact if not in name, that my parents had disembarked at the Pier Head in Liverpool back in the early 1920s. Or just as, I suppose, centuries earlier, it had been as colonizing immigrants that my distant Oakley forebears had arrived as Protestant settlers in an overwhelmingly Catholic Ireland. Emigration, it seems, if not perhaps a dominant gene, had established itself as at least a recessive gene in the family's cultural DNA.

CHAPTER SEVEN

Oh, Canada!

When, in response to the ringing of the doorbell, Mr. McNamara (not his real name) opened the front door of his house on St. George's Street (north of Bloor in central Toronto), the man standing in the shadows on the wooden front porch, having simply said by way of introduction "You, McNamara?," clicked open a switchblade and walked him into the hall and then through an archway into the parlor. There, along with their mother, the two daughters of the house, dressed in bathrobes and their hair in curling pins, were sitting watching TV. The intruder, moving swiftly into the center of the room, grabbed the younger daughter by the curling pins, yanking her roughly to her feet and prodding her ample midriff with his knife, and turned to the rest of the family and uttered the inimitable words: "I'm not kiddin'." So far as I could later make out, that total of five words was all that was said until Mrs. McNamara, leaping to her feet, started berating the intruder, screeching at him *inter alia* that he really ought to be ashamed of himself. It's hard to know how the whole confrontation might have unfolded had not one of the other two students, who, like me, were renting rooms on an upper floor in the house, heard the doorbell ring and come down to see who was there. He was a rather gangly and clumsy Canadian eighteen-year-old who was busy failing his first year of medical studies and had, not uncharacteristically, been dozing on his bed. He came thundering down the stairs, tripped over his feet on the last section, and came tumbling down into the hallway. Unnerved by the commotion, the intruder had panicked and fled, jumping into a car and tearing away, while the clan McNamara poured out, yelling and screaming, onto the porch but failed, in the excitement of the moment, to catch the car's license number.

This was the version of events that I and the third lodger, a rather more diligent medical student from Trinidad, were able to reconstruct in the days that followed. Neither of us had been in at the time and a couple of Toronto policemen were wrapping up their investigation and delivering a stern warning to McNamara when we got back. He had emigrated from Ireland to Canada in the 1930s and it turned out that he had been selling Irish Sweepstakes tickets, a practice illegal in Ontario at that time. Word had apparently got out on the street that he had to have a ready stash of cash on hand in the house, one ripe for plucking without any likelihood of the police being summoned. Mrs. McNamara, however, unaware of her husband's illegal activity, had immediately called the police. The truth of the matter then tumbled out, leading to a noisy row between the couple and a prolonged period of tension in the family.

This aborted holdup was one of the more exciting events to punctuate the rather even tenor of the second academic year (1954–55) of my studies at Toronto. By the beginning of that year I had settled into research and, in largely uninterrupted fashion, was keeping my nose to the academic grindstone. Having moved out of the graduate residence on campus where I had spent my first year, I was now comfortably ensconced in the McNamara's house, a clean, well-kept, early twentieth-century structure with a wooden porch on the street side and a small garden (yard) in the back. My daily routine was quickly established and took on a certain almost liturgical regularity. Each day, by nine o'clock at the very latest, having with the other two lodgers been served a pretty good breakfast, I would be on my way to campus, walking south on St. George's Street, turning east on Bloor, and making my way past the array of small shops on one side and the university's football stadium and political economy building on the other until I got to the corner of Avenue Road. There I turned right, crossing the road and making my way past the Royal Ontario Museum and Victoria College, to arrive at the library of the Pontifical Institute of Mediaeval Studies, which fronts onto Queen's Park

Crescent East not too far north of the Ontario Legislative Building. The Pontifical Institute functions, along with the University of Toronto's nearby Centre for Medieval Studies, very much as the unofficial heart of medieval studies in North America. It was founded in 1929 by Étienne Gilson in collaboration with the Congregation of St. Basil, a Roman Catholic religious order. Originating in France, the latter had developed into an international order with a mission in secondary and tertiary education and with houses, schools, and colleges spread across Canada and parts of the United States. In the nineteenth century, it had founded St. Michael's College, originally a freestanding university but now (though still retaining its degree-granting authority in theology) one of the constituent colleges of the University of Toronto. The institute is situated at one end of the St. Michael's campus and, in my day, several Basilian fathers served on its faculty. It possesses a splendid reference and research library in matters medieval, and it was there that I was spending most of my days seated before a microfilm machine and painstakingly transcribing by hand, from microfilm of the four extant manuscripts, the text (and manuscript variants) of a hitherto unprinted but quite major reform tract written in 1403–4 by Pierre d'Ailly (1350–1420), a philosopher-theologian, sometime chancellor of the University of Paris, bishop, cardinal, and one of the leading ecclesiastics of his day. The work called for a good deal of patience. My initial task was the decoding of the heavily abbreviated late-Gothic cursive script in which the scribes had written. The manuscripts were fairly crabbed and occasionally messy (one looked on the microfilm as if some reader had spilled his soup on it). Moreover, given the fact that the meaning of the standard abbreviations sometimes fluctuated (depending on the region from which the particular scribe hailed), some of them were quite ambiguous. As none of the manuscripts was an autograph, I had to have recourse, accordingly, to the "genealogical" or "common faults" method, which relies on the presence of faults, omissions, differences in word order, and other textual variants in order to identify the relationships among the various manuscript renditions of the common text. That approach revealed that the manuscripts fell into two groups of two, neither possessing an obvious priority over the other, so I chose to base my critical text on the manuscript that needed least correction. In accordance with the normal requirements for a critical edition, I indicated in the footnotes all the variant readings present in the other manuscripts. The object in so doing was to liberate the reader from total dependence on the editor's judgment. With all variants available to him, he (the reader) could second-guess the editor's judgment and, in effect, construct a different preferred version of the text if he so wished.

When finished and printed in 1964 as a lengthy appendix to my first book (*The Political Thought of Pierre d'Ailly*), the Latin treatise in question ran to some hundred pages. It had taken me months to transcribe it properly and a few further months to run down and identify the provenance and accuracy of the myriad of unidentified or poorly identified references and loose quotations from other works embedded in the text. Dull old stuff, I suppose, not only to those who are not themselves medievalists, but also, I was to discover later, to some who are. Subsequent service on selection committees charged with the task of evaluating applications for research awards of one sort or another has brought home to me the disappointing lack of appreciation evinced even by scholars at large for basic palaeographical and editing work of the sort in which I was engaged in Toronto. I have found, indeed, that in comparison with other work it tends to be bracketed as a bit dreary, perhaps even unimaginative. It was not the sort of work I myself planned to pursue for the long haul; my own compelling interest lay, not in the establishing of texts, but in the interpretation of what they had to say. But it still struck me as being work of fundamental importance and as an appropriate point at which to launch my scholarly endeavors. I needed to be able to decode and read sources that had yet to make their way into print. I also needed to have printed texts of reliable accuracy at my disposal. Many printed medieval sources are still available only in early (late fifteenth-, sixteenth-, and seventeenth-century) versions marred by scribal misreadings and textual corruptions of one sort or another. One common fault, for example, is the inclusion as part of the text of marginal annotations that the manuscripts reveal to be the work of some later reader and not of the original author. Sometimes the printed text comes through as simply garbled on quite central points. Such was the case with the wording of a crucial section of the *Dialogus* of the great late-medieval philosopher-theologian William of Ockham, the only printed version of which dated to 1614 and which, as a young scholar, I was called upon to translate into English as part of an important anthology of political writings drawn from the medieval Muslim, Jewish, and Christian traditions. By leaning on the canonistic texts to which Ockham was referring in the corrupt section, I was able to propose a plausible emendation of the garbled printed text that had the virtue, at least, of rendering it intelligible. Intelligible it may have been, but it was not, as it turned out, accurate. Years later, a distinguished Ockham scholar was to solve the problem by exploring the manuscript tradition (involving no less than fifteen manuscripts), and that threw a redemptive light on the jumbled section of the 1614 printed version.

So I don't regret the long and often dreary hours I spent on my own editing project. Among other things, working on the project taught me to find my way around such fundamental and challenging sources as the Pseudo-Isidorean Decretals, the *Corpus Juris Civilis,* and the *Corpus Juris Canonici,* these last two being the great, standard collections of Roman and canon law. While teaching me, moreover, to be on my guard when making use of early-modern printed editions of medieval works, it also taught me the patience, discipline, and attention to detail that, in my anxiety to get to the heart of a given author's intent, I had previously probably lacked. None of this, of course, would have been possible without the invaluable, yearlong course in Latin palaeography that I had taken the previous year with Fr. Joseph Wey, at that time already laboring away at the formidable task of producing from multiple manuscripts the first critical edition of Ockham's *Quodlibetal Questions* that was destined to appear in print only a quarter of a century later. In that course, after confronting the mysteries of Roman cursive script (looking for all the world as if a chicken with inky feet had scuttled across the page) and the impenetrably patterned beauty of ninth-century Beneventan script (unpunctuated and continuous and reminiscent of certain types of Victorian wallpaper), the crabbed complexities of the late-medieval Gothic cursive with which I knew I would be dealing came almost as a relief. While the marvelously clear and often quite beautiful nature of the ninth-century Carolingian miniscule (the source of the lowercase letters in our modern print) stood out as nothing less than a major cultural achievement.

Palaeography was not my only academic preoccupation during that first year at the Pontifical Institute. Apart from the overall history of medieval philosophy, on which Étienne Gilson lectured with great energy and lucidity, I had the benefit of a few tutorials in Thomistic metaphysics that Fr. Gerald Phelan, a gifted teacher, was kind enough to give me, along with a wonderfully energetic seminar on Aquinas's ethics given by the German Dominican scholar I. Th. Eschmann, and a tightly-focused seminar offered by Fr. Armand Maurer on a section of Ockham's *Commentary on the Sentences of Peter Lombard* that related largely to epistemological issues. I also had to devote more time than I had expected to preparation for teaching the discussion sections of the basic course in Canadian government offered by the Department of Political Economy. Believing that I would do well to acquire some teaching experience while I was at Toronto, I had been brash enough to approach the chairman of that department (in which, after all, I was not enrolled) to see if there was any possibility of my doing some teaching in political philosophy, which I saw as one of my strengths. It turned out that political philosophy was taught at Toronto only as an upper-level course for majors, and it was small enough not to require discussion sections. But they were still looking rather frantically for someone to teach the sections attached to the large and basic Canadian government lecture course and, paying no attention, it seemed, to my ignorance of the subject, had offered me the job on the spot. Without quite realizing what a scramble it would involve or how much time it would take, I signed on. At the time I was only twenty-one and looked younger than my age. So I took the precaution, when teaching my first classes, of wearing a suit and tie to distinguish myself from the students. And even that did not prevent one rather cheeky young woman at my first class from asking me with ill-concealed incredulity if I was really "the professor."

Stressful though it could sometimes be, I think that taking on the task was, on balance, a valuable experience. It certainly brought home to me the educational challenges public (in Canada, "provincial") universities had to face when operating with nonselective systems of admission. The University of Toronto was a very large institution even then (it enrolls approximately eighty-three thousand students today). Introductory freshman courses of the sort that I was teaching in served the ancillary but sorely needed function of weeding out those students who could not cope with university-level academic demands. Among the students taking the Canadian government course, the range of ability and the quality of school preparation was enormous. In the discussion sections I taught, I had a number of truly gifted students. But the range of performance was depressingly wide and, during that year, I had to fail more students and give more "D" grades than in any subsequent time in my teaching career that spanned some forty-three years and four different institutions. Teaching the course also had the advantage of requiring me to read up on Canadian history more diligently and to acquaint myself at greater depth than might otherwise have been the case with Canadian politics and the characteristic pressure points in its constitutional structure. It was good to know that Canada is more of a confederation than a federation, with fewer powers in the hands of the central, federal government than is the case, for example, with the United States. It was also good to know how comparatively new it was as a nation-state; it was brought into existence by the British North America Act of 1867 and was less than a century old when I taught that course. And I was startled to learn in 1953 that it had reached its full territorial extent only four years earlier when (by a rather small margin) Newfoundland and Labrador had voted by referendum to become part of Canada. In some ways, indeed, the Canada I encountered still had a somewhat unfinished feel about it, though I did not share the bluntly negative appraisal handed down by an Australian friend who was working towards an MA in the University of Toronto's English Department. A sardonic fellow whom a couple of years at Cambridge and two further years teaching at one of the older English public schools had turned into something of a snob, he had come to dread returning to a homeland that he now viewed as irreparably provincial. So he had postponed his return home by going to Canada, only to react to it so negatively that he was now beginning to think that, by comparison, Australia looked quite good after all. He, I, and Robert Woof (an English friend and future Wordsworth scholar of note who, like me, was the recipient of a Goldsmiths' Company's Commonwealth Scholarship) had decided to spend the Christmas of 1954 at a (rather downscale) Ontario ski resort, only to be overtaken by an unexpected thaw and to find, equally to our dismay, that the nearest town was a dry town. As we lay on our bunks, then, listening to the unwelcome rain falling on the roof and sharing (in paper cups) a providential bottle of Scotch that our Australian friend had had the foresight to bring with him, he delivered himself of the condescending (if memorable) dictum: "Canada! What after all is it? No more than a railway in search of a nation!"

To me, happily, it was a good deal more than that. Toronto, though a less exciting and cosmopolitan city than it is now, and still somewhat monocultural (Scots Presbyterian) in feel, was, and is, an impressive, clean, and handsome city. In the early 1950s the massive inflow of immigrants that was eventually to transform it was only just getting underway. If suburban sprawl was already happening, I was not conscious of that fact, for my time was spent in the city's center. That was not as yet marked by the great clustering of high-rise buildings that dominate its skyline today. The core area around the Ontario legislature and the university had a spacious feel, fronting out onto the wide, ceremonial boulevard of University Avenue and onto Queen's Park Crescent, replete with plenty of trees and open green space. Bloor Street was already developing into a reasonably upscale shopping area and, along with Bay and Yonge Streets, it sported plenty of small places where one could eat quite well at reasonable prices. Nightlife, such as it was, was still rather cramped in style by the persistence on the books of a complex set of blue laws governing what alcoholic beverages one could drink, at what hours, and in what places. Sundays, as a result, had a heavy, subdued, and soberly nonconformist feel to them.

Although this was the occasion for a certain amount of derisive ribaldry among the American students at the university—"Toronto the Good!" they would sneer—it made little impact on me. I was too busy soaking up a new and appealingly vibrant cultural atmosphere, one comparatively unburdened by the sort of class consciousness that seemed still to weigh so heavily on English life, and one not marked by the social restraint and conversational obliquity so evident in parts, at least, of England. I may have been the first layman from abroad to go to study at the institute, and Fr. Reginald O'Donnell, a classicist who was the senior palaeographer there and the long-standing editor of its admired journal *Mediaeval Studies*, took me under his wing. Treating me as a colleague rather than a student and counseling me about what I needed to learn, he also introduced me to a broad array of faculty, not only at the institute itself but also at St. Michael's College. As the Basilians also had colleges in Rochester, New York, and Houston, Texas, the people I was meeting (along with a sprinkling of Europeans) were Americans as well as Canadians, and that was true also of the graduate students I got to know at the institute and in the University of Toronto at large. And I was delighted (relieved?) to find them refreshingly straightforward and encouragingly welcoming. Through the good offices of a Canadian friend at Corpus,

Gary Clarke, who turned out to be the scion of a prominent Toronto family, I also had the pleasure of meeting some people who did not move in university circles. Gary's family ran the highly respected publishing house of Clarke, Irwin & Company, and they were kind enough to fold me in with other, far more important, guests at sumptuous Sunday lunches at their home.

As I remember it, then, my adjustment to life in the New World proved, by and large, to be quick, easy, and basically trouble free. From time to time, when jarred by the inevitable instances of ugliness that go with city life, by the gaucheries sometimes evident in Canadian and American student behavior, or by the oblique flickers of anti-British resentment that one occasionally encountered (soon to be replaced, among Canadian academics at least, by a singularly unattractive form of knee-jerk anti-Americanism), I would feel twinges of homesickness, a wistful nostalgia for the comparative reticence of English discourse and for the beautiful variety of England's insular countryside to which I had become deeply attached. But I was young and, it seems, flexibly adaptable, and I quickly felt at least as much at home in Canada as I had in Ireland or as I was to feel, later on, in the United States. Further than that, and stodgy though Toronto could sometimes be, I was moved by the unaccustomed sense of possibility (partly illusory, it may be, but not altogether so) that seemed to dwell in the very air one breathed. I could not help being struck by the fact that Jane Timmins, one of the Canadian graduate students I had come to know, and one who, unlike the others, lived in a fine house in the fashionable Rosedale area north of Bloor, was one of the Timmins family which, only a few decades earlier and starting with nothing, had made a mining fortune in the northlands and after whom the small town of Timmins was named. Serving as best man at the wedding of Frank Howley, a recent English immigrant and older brother of Barbara, a graduate of Bellerive School in Liverpool who was one of our crowd at Oxford, I detected among the many English immigrants who were present on that occasion a similarly intoxicating sense of liberating possibility that they had found lacking in the Old Country (however attached to it they might be) and that had nudged them into making the wrenching but life-changing decision to leave family and homeland behind and to seek a new life across the Atlantic.

There was a parallel to all of this in the more cloistered world of higher education. One of the striking things evident there was the freedom students enjoyed of being able to delay for years the sort of choice about the specific specialty on which they proposed to concentrate that in England they would have been obliged to make at high school. At both the undergraduate and graduate levels, Canadian and American students enjoyed greater freedom to experiment and to change their minds about what truly interested them. Not for them, as with us, the Procrustean tracking into specialties in the high school years, with undergraduate work taking on, accordingly, some of the characteristics of the graduate course of study in North America. If that meant, of course, that it could both take them longer to come to terms with what exactly it was that they wanted to do and take them longer to attain a degree of mastery in the finally chosen specialty, no lasting penalty seemed in general to attach to that. In one or two fields, of course, and classics was one of them, there were some attendant drawbacks that should properly be weighed in the scales when judging the two systems. The mastery of the ancient languages made possible (or once made possible?) by the English public school practice of starting schoolboys on Greek and Latin in their tender years is simply not present among those who pick up the languages later and is (was?) sometimes the occasion for ill-placed condescension on the part of British classicists towards their American (or Commonwealth) colleagues. But here the observations made by Sir Kenneth Dover in his memoir while lauding the quality of the students he taught in a seminar at Stanford are apposite. Having noted that "it is . . . hard for any Classics department in an American university to find candidates in the home market who have what I would regard as a good knowledge of Latin or Greek," and having readily acknowledged that this "may shock people who went through a Classical education like mine," he also goes on to insist that this is but "one side of a coin whose other side shines brighter." "One consequence of the American approach [of postponed choice and late specialization]," he adds, "is that when they embark on graduate school [in Classics] they are capable of bad linguistic mistakes, their recall of vocabulary is weak and their ability to translate simple English into Greek or Latin poor by the standards of a British sixth form. But if they are highly intelligent, strongly motivated and passionately interested in the subject—and my Stanford students

possessed those virtues—their ignorance (sometimes mistaken for stupidity by thoughtless British critics) does not matter, because when they
are not sure of something, they look it up."

When I first read those words, I could not help thinking of John
Deck, a fellow student at the institute who, during a rather hardscrabble
undergraduate education, had acquired a decent knowledge of Latin and
Greek, and who was undoubtedly one of the most interesting friends I
made in Toronto. An American of German descent who hailed from a
gritty area in Buffalo, New York, he was an eccentric figure and a bundle
of contradictions. Possessed of a warm heart and a keen philosophic
mind, he also made much of his (alleged) ethnic and religious prejudices, speaking dismissively of "Polacks" and labeling contemptuously
as "neo-Catholicism" the mildly liberal "Commonweal Catholic" tendency evident at St. Michael's College. Whether he believed any of this,
I could never really tell. He liked to shock people and was possessed of
the sort of sly and sometimes cruel sense of humor that led him, for example, to attach (the not altogether undeserved) nickname of "Vapid" to
an eagerly obvious Canadian graduate student from one of the Maritime
provinces who in later life was destined to enter national politics and
even to serve a term as Canadian Secretary of State for External Affairs.
One of the eldest among six or seven siblings, John was already over
thirty when I met him, had developed a strong interest in the Neopla-
tonism of late antiquity, and was just about to begin work on a rather
challenging dissertation on Plotinus, later developed into a book entitled
Nature, Philosophy, and the One: A Study in the Philosophy of Plotinus
(1967). By any standards this was pretty refined and recondite stuff, and
when he described to me the trajectory of his own higher education to
date, I was astonished. Both as an undergraduate and then, again, as a
graduate student, he had needed to drop out for a year or so to make
some money working on the railroad. He had done it, first, to help finance his own studies and then, later, to help put a younger sister
through college. It was, to me, a bit of an eye-opener that the American
and Canadian approach to higher education was flexible enough to permit a student to do what he had done without imperiling his academic
future. In the Britain of those days, John would never, in all probability,
have graduated from university, let alone managed to complete a PhD,
embark upon an academic career, and succeed as a scholar pursuing a

very demanding academic specialty. That he was able to do so called, of course, for dogged determination and the passionate interest to which Dover alludes. But in the Britain in which I had grown up, interest and determination notwithstanding, the goal for which he had striven would almost certainly have eluded his grasp.

Such things made a deep impression on me. So, too, did the comparatively porous nature at the time of Canadian and American class distinctions. Such distinctions of course existed, and have perhaps become firmer over the course of the sixty years since the 1950s. But what in my English youth had seemed to be phenomena rooted in nature itself were now revealing themselves to me as no more than matters of shifting convention. Hallowed convention, it might be, but still no more than that. Naïve on such matters as I still doubtless was, this realization came to me as a bit of a revelation, perhaps even as something of a life changer. Having, over the course of two years, become accustomed to the variety and fluidity of Canadian and American life (which often brought back to mind the comfort and ease I had felt in Irish society), I was to find it difficult henceforth to take with total seriousness the traditional, class-conscious rigidities of English life. After I had returned from Canada in 1955 and was thrust into the highly traditional, old-fashioned, and sometimes stilted culture typical of officers' messes in the British Army, rather than becoming an unselfconsciously acculturated participant, I found myself slipping into the role of a somewhat detached (though not, I hope, too judgmental) observer. For me, what sociologists have described as the fundamentally dialectical nature of human society was hoving dimly into sight. The ultimately human-invented norms that had come to be externalized in society were beginning to lose for me their objectivized status and, with that, ceasing now to be effectively internalized in the consciousness.

Though such sociological notions were unknown to me at the time, such, so far as I can reconstruct them, were the *feelings* that overtook me during that first, important, and exceedingly stimulating year in Canada. In some ways it was a year of intellectual and emotional decompression after the highly pressured and demanding run-in to Schools and it was certainly a year filled with a multitude of new experiences. I had been in Toronto for no more than a couple of months when I met a beguiling American girl, Dana Breslin by name, though for some reason she preferred to go by the nickname of "Mike." I immediately fell for her. This proved not to be the best of ideas. She was a transfer student at St. Michael's College, a bit older than the usual undergraduate, and was beginning, I now realize, to set her mind on marrying and settling down. As a footloose twenty-one-year-old, I was neither a likely nor a convincing candidate for the pertinent role. But we did succeed in attaining to an affectionate friendship. She and her younger sister Cathy, at that time a freshman at St. Michael's and later to become a journalist and novelist, solicitous about the likelihood of my spending a lonely Christmas marooned in Toronto away from home, insisted with great kindness on my going home with them to the States for the holidays. Home for them was Pittsfield, the small town that functions as the county seat for Berkshire County in western Massachusetts, and Mike, owning a car, folded me into the carload of American students she was driving part of the way to their various destinations. The drive down was, for me, a very interesting experience, my first glimpse of southern Ontario, northern New York state and northwest New England. Having driven south on the Queen Elizabeth Way and crossed over into the United States, we headed east in what was rapidly becoming a winter wonderland, and on through what seemed to be the endless reaches of upper New York state. Like most Europeans, I had always, and almost instinctively, thought of New York in terms of the city itself and was fascinated to find out that it encompassed large and beautiful expanses of rolling agricultural land as well as the largest protected wilderness area in the East. At some point, I can't recall where, we crossed over into Vermont and began the descent on Old Route 7 into western Massachusetts. By the time we got there the snow was falling heavily and it was hard to see much of anything. When Route 7 merged with Route 2, at what I now realize was Field Park in Williamstown (the place that was destined, later on, to be my home for more than half a century), Mike pointed to the left and mentioned the presence there of an old and small liberal arts college called Williams. Somebody else in the car added, rather dismissively, that it was a "rich boys' college" and a bit of a "party school." While I now know that neither designation was altogether accurate even at that time, it remains the case that in a reputational survey published in the mid-1950s that ranked the better-known liberal arts colleges, Williams was not ranked among the top group, academically speaking, but slotted in well behind such celebrated women's colleges as Wellesley, Smith, and Mount Holyoke.

The Breslins had lost their mother a few years previously and their widower father, Dr. Breslin, a much beloved pediatrician in Pittsfield, could barely restrain his delight in having all three of his daughters at home—the youngest was finishing her high school years at a boarding school near Albany, New York. What ensued—at the first American home I had ever visited—was a wonderful, snow-clad, Hallmark card type of Christmas season, reminiscent of the sort of Dickensian white Christmas I had dreamt of as a child. The girls and I were invited to parties thrown by old friends of theirs; we also went tobogganing, I enjoyed my first (rather shaky) experience of ice skating, and Dr. Breslin and I played violin duets together—more fun to play, doubtless, than to listen to. After Christmas, Mike and I drove down to New York City, staying with Toronto friends in Bronxville but spending a good deal of time in the city itself. It was my introduction to the wonders of Grand Central Station, Rockefeller Center, St. Patrick's Cathedral, Central Park, and midtown Manhattan in general, still lavishly decorated for the holiday season, with Fifth Avenue packed with shoppers and tourists. In comparison, even at its best, Toronto seemed a quiet and sedate sort of place.

Among the many other friends I made that first year, two stand out. Both were members of the English faculty at St. Michael's College. And both stand out because of their expressed sympathy with the New Critical approach to literature. For, at that time, with the exception of Northrop Frye at Victoria College, the Toronto English faculty seemed in general to be wedded to something closer to a history of ideas approach to literary works. The first, and more junior of the two, was an American, Donald Theall by name, a Yale graduate who had been drawn to do his PhD work at Toronto by the presence of Marshall McLuhan on the faculty there. Marshall McLuhan was the second of the two friends I have in mind. Theall had imbibed his New Critical views in New Haven and McLuhan had done so in Cambridge, where he had been a student of I. A. Richards and F. R. Leavis. Both Theall and McLuhan were destined to move into more complex and ecumenical intellectual territory—Marshall to become something of a controversial public intellectual and Donald to chair the English Department at McGill University in the province of Québec and, later, to serve as president and vice chancellor of the newly founded Trent University in Ontario.

During my own Toronto years, the Thealls had two small children for whom, from time to time, I would babysit so that they could get a night out. Though I never babysat for the McLuhans (they had six children), Marshall used to invite a small group of us graduate students around to his house on Saturday evenings. Though the ostensible idea was to work our way together through part of Aquinas's *Summa theologiae*, those sessions tended to evolve rapidly into an occasion for listening to our host hold forth in return for drinking his beer. He was a very lively, imaginative presence, and it may serve to convey some general sense of the feel of our discussions if I report that when one, with a "No, but . . . ," indicated a measure of disagreement with one or another of his sweeping generalizations, Marshall's eyes would characteristically light up, and, with an animated "Yes, and . . . ," he would incorporate one's disagreement within an even larger and bolder synthesis.

While my own compelling interests lay elsewhere and were more traditionally historical in nature and certainly more sublunary than his, through those discussions and my reading of *Explorations*, a journal he ran in collaboration with Edmund Snow Carpenter (an anthropologist at the Royal Ontario Museum), I did get an invigorating sense of the lively intellectual currents coursing through Toronto that were eventually to give birth to what is sometimes called the "Toronto School of Communication Theory." Grounded ultimately in the pioneering work at Toronto of the classicist Eric Havelock and the economist Harold Innis, then developed by Carpenter, McLuhan, and (at some remove) Northrop Frye, the school has been described as forwarding "the theory of the primacy of communication in the structuring of human cultures and the structuring of the human mind." When I knew him, McLuhan had already published *The Mechanical Bride* (1951) but was only just beginning to hit his stride in the new field, and major contributions of his such as *Understanding Media* and *The Medium is the Massage* were not to appear before the 1960s. But the imagination, boldness, and intellectual vitality that were to fuel his subsequent rise to controversial prominence were already clearly on display.

In comparison with such heady soaring of the spirit, my own pressing intellectual concerns at that time were a good deal more earthbound. But they, too, were energized by the dawning realization that in coming to the Pontifical Institute I had entered into an intellectual and scholarly world different in kind from the one whose atmosphere I had breathed at Oxford. That was true in relation both to the philosophical and to the historical work being pursued there. So far as philosophy went, it was heavily Thomistic in intonation with the strain of Thomism dominant there being what is sometimes labeled as "existential," as opposed to the "transcendental Thomism" of such as Karl Rahner and Bernard Lonergan, or the "Wittgensteinian" or "analytical" Thomism later to be favored in England by philosophers like Anscombe, Geach, or Anthony Kenny. Wittgenstein, indeed, I cannot recall anyone at the institute even mentioning. If metaphysics was dead, nobody there seemed to have seen the obituary. It was a far cry from the analytical philosophical tradition so totally dominant at Oxford as to suggest that any other approach was démodé. Even the philosophic jokes were different. And if the differences in historical approach were not quite so dramatic, they were nonetheless real. In the University of Toronto History Department, Bertie Wilkinson and Michael Powicke were certainly pursuing the familiar approaches to medieval history to which I had been introduced as an undergraduate, but, given the sort of work I was to pursue at the institute in the history of philosophy and ecclesiology, I was to find myself inducted into the less insular world of international Catholic scholarship, German and Italian as well as French. It was all very stimulating and served as an instructive piece of consciousness raising about the degree to which particular institutional settings or cognitive communities as well as differing national traditions can, across time, shape, invigorate, or (less positively) insulate particular intellectual orientations, historiographic no less than philosophical.

The primary challenge confronting me as I deepened my familiarity with later medieval philosophy was, however, a somewhat more confined one. It was that of identifying a thesis topic substantial enough to meet the requirements for the Oxford DPhil. I was planning on doing and one that focused especially on the area of political thinking. I consulted, therefore, with Étienne Gilson, whose knowledge of the medieval intellectual scene was truly encyclopedic. He promptly suggested three possibilities, each of them involving the study of a particular thinker of importance whose works had not as yet been adequately explored and about whose thinking we really needed to know a great deal more. The first was Guido Vernani (d. ca. 1345), the acerbic critic who launched a frontal assault on Dante's *Monarchia* while referring to its author condescendingly and dismissively not by name but simply as *ille homo* ("that fellow") or *quidam* ("a certain person"). The second was Juan de Torquemada (1388–1468), the great papalist propagandist at the time of the Council of Basel (1431–49) whose *Summa de ecclesia* was to become a very influential high-papalist classic. The third was Pierre d'Ailly (1350–1420), not exactly a household name today but a nominalist philosopher of Ockhamist inspiration who, as a philosopher, was of much the same order of prominence in his day as Marin Mersenne or Bishop Berkeley were to be in the seventeenth century. My choice did not prove to be a difficult one. Vernani's work struck me as too slight to warrant full-scale thesis treatment. Torquemada, though essentially an ecclesiologist rather than a political thinker, looked a good deal more promising. But E. F. Jacob at Oxford, when I consulted him on the matter, indicated that he was sure (incorrectly, it turned out) that Torquemada was already being worked on "somewhere," as he put it, "in the Americas." Even had he not given me that cue, I was already beginning to think that d'Ailly would be a better choice. A prolific writer and expansive thinker whose writings (well over a hundred of them) ranged across philosophy, theology, ecclesiology, theopolitics, and even geography (Christopher Columbus turned out to have read and annotated several works of his in that last area), he represented an appropriately large topic and a bracing interpretative challenge. The more so in that, in the years of his maturity, having been chancellor of the University of Paris, he went on to become a bishop, cardinal, and one of the leading churchmen who, at the Council of Constance (1414–18), helped engineer the ending of the Great Schism of the West. One of his major writings, moreover, the *Tractatus de materia concilii generalis* (1403/4), which adumbrated the reforming role in the Church of regularly assembled general councils, had never been printed and was to afford me the opportunity the following year to put my palaeographic skills to use and to produce a critical edition. So I opted for d'Ailly and made plans to spend most of the summer of 1954 amid the incomparable holdings of the Widener and Houghton libraries

at Harvard, familiarizing myself with the philosophical, political, and ecclesiological contexts within which d'Ailly had done his thinking and embarking upon a preliminary canvas of his formidable body of writings.

But as the 1953–54 academic year drew to a close, I had another and
more exciting obligation to meet before settling down to that task. One
of the requirements of my Goldsmith's Travelling Research Scholarship,
and one provided for in the scholarship stipend, was that I should take
time out to familiarize myself by travel with the new continent in which
I was temporarily domiciled and with its peoples. With that on my mind,
I jumped at the opportunity when a Canadian graduate of St. Michael's,
now studying law at the university, asked if I would be at all interested
in partnering with him on an extended, exploratory trip out West. At
the time, it was not uncommon for West Coast purchasers of American
cars, who did not want to await delivery by rail from Detroit, to arrange
to have their new car driven out directly from the factory and delivered
to the car dealer through whom they had made the purchase. The plan,
as my friend envisaged it, was that we should try to get such a delivery
assignment, thus giving us a free trip to the West Coast, and then link
up with his sister and her friend who had both been working as nurses
in the desert resort town of Palm Springs and who were now ready to return home to Canada. Though they owned a car, they (and their parents)
were nervous about their undertaking the long, cross-continental drive
by themselves. Once we connected, the idea was to put in three weeks
of leisurely touring throughout the Western states before heading east
for home. Despite some predictable glitches, the plans eventually came
together, and in May (the Canadian academic year ends comparatively
early), we found ourselves leaving the General Motors factory in Detroit
and heading out to our destination in Los Angeles, driving nothing other
than an elegant white Cadillac, replete with the prominent fins that were
the distinguishing feature of that year's models. I have often wondered
since about the odd fact that the car's odometer was not connected, so
that, almost a week later, having put in long days of fast driving, and
having crossed the continent diagonally from Michigan in the northern
Midwest to Los Angeles in southern California, we delivered the vehicle
to the dealer with its odometer registering something less than a hundred miles. About that the dealer in question evinced neither curiosity
nor concern. All he wanted to do was to reassure himself, by means of a

minute inspection, that there were no signs of pebble scratches on the body of the car.

The federal legislation initiating the construction of the splendid interstate highway system of controlled access freeways that now exists, lay still at that time two years in the future. The roads, then, on which we drove across the country, and especially so in the West, were simply ordinary two-lane affairs, or two lanes with a third passing lane. As we drove on them across extended stretches of flat desert, or quasi-desert land, I was often struck by how comparatively deserted and extraordinarily straight they were. The Romans would have admired them. Leaving Detroit, we cut across Indiana to the town of Terre Haute and thence to St. Louis, where it was, I believe, that we picked up old, historic Route 66, which we were to follow most of the way to the West Coast. Terre Haute, an unexceptional sort of place, sticks in the mind because at the time it struck me (an essentially coastal sort of fellow apt to feel uneasy when definitively out of reach of large stretches of water) as somehow representing the dead heart of the vast continent we were traversing. And Route 66, as it threaded its diagonal way from Chicago, through Kansas, Missouri, and Illinois, and then pushing on through Oklahoma, New Mexico, and Arizona, all the way to Los Angeles, linking together rather than bypassing what seemed like an endless stream of small rural or quasi-rural communities, opened up for me a better window into the heartland of America than would travel today on the much superior, closed-access highways of the interstate system. Dubbed "The Mother Road" by the Steinbeck of *The Grapes of Wrath*, it had become either the *via dolorosa* or "the road to opportunity" for the countless Okies who, in the mid-1930s, had tried to escape along it from the terminal miseries of the Dust Bowl. Punctuated by a counterproductive oversupply of billboards and more than amply equipped with cheap motels and old, run-down campsites, it was to furnish me later on with the imaginative landscape across which I mentally traced the pubescent peregrinations of Nabokov's lovely Lolita and against which I set the tumescent tendernesses of his Humbert Humbert.

I much regret now that I didn't take more photographs along the way or at least keep some sort of a record or journal of our travels that summer. But I no more had the temperament at that time for journal or diary keeping than I do now, and I must rely on my somewhat jumbled memories to reconstruct the complex trajectory of our movements.

The girls had a much clearer idea of what they wanted to see than did we and, since the car was theirs, we sheepishly fell in with their plans. Summer temperatures at Palm Springs rise, I gather, into the unbearable zone and, in those days at least, the whole town more or less shut down for the summer months. When we left, it was the morning after many of the bars had put on drink-off sessions of what seemed like bacchanalian proportions. The first leg of our journey took us to the casinos, wall-to-wall slot machines, and high-kicking showgirls of Las Vegas, the Nevada resort town that was then considerably smaller than it is today but no less terminally tawdry. That behind us, we drove on to take in Lake Mead and the engineering marvels of the Hoover Dam in the northwest corner of Arizona, and, that under our belts, moved on to the stunning vistas afforded by the Grand Canyon. Following that, we spent a couple of enjoyable days with friends of the girls who owned a beautifully spacious modern house somewhere in the northern reaches of the state before threading our leisurely way up through the mountains of Colorado on the western side of the Continental Divide. Emerging eventually from the mountains, we settled into the long trip back to the coast again in order to spend some time exploring San Francisco, to the grace and beauty of which I was to become very attached during my repeated visits there later in life. But what, above all, I carry with me from that first visit has nothing to do with grace and beauty. It is, rather, the surreal and vivid memory of drinking some tropical-type cocktail graced with a miniature, collapsible parasol in a nightclub of heavily Hawaiian inspiration. There, the tables were grouped around what looked like a retired swimming pool, with the band playing on a raft moored in the middle. Intervals were signaled, as soon as the band's raft had been pulled to the side so that they could exit to the bar, by the onset of a fake thunderstorm accompanied by a tropical downpour happily confined to the pool itself. It was all as bizarre as it was memorable.

From San Francisco we made our way slowly up north, exploring the beauties of northern California and coming back to Route 101 where it becomes a scenic coastal road, often in full view of the Pacific, and continuing on into the state of Oregon. For some reason, rather than continuing north across Washington state and up to Seattle, we turned east at the Columbia River and the small town of Vancouver, and drove across Oregon into the mountainous country of Idaho. There, in response to his pressing invitation, we lingered for a very interesting overnight stay with the family of an American who was a student at the University of Toronto. His father was involved in the mining business and his home was in a secluded valley where some rare, exotic, and valuable metal (I can't remember which) was being extracted. It was the first functioning gated community I had ever encountered, a company town with a claustrophobic atmosphere and one that came close to being a heavily guarded compound. Driving on from there, we made one last extended stop so that we could take in the incomparable sights of Yellowstone National Park. After dutifully viewing the dramatic show put on by Old Faithful, we committed ourselves to the long grind of the eastward journey home. This was to take us across the seemingly empty Big Sky country of Montana, the austere beauty of which I loved, and thence, via the almost equally enormous reaches of South Dakota, into Minnesota, Wisconsin, Illinois, Michigan, and on, eventually, into Canada. Though for this stretch, increasingly anxious as I was to get back to Toronto, my memory of the precise route we took is really quite hazy.

Amid all the novelties of that long trip, all the unexpected revelations of the different ways in which people lived, as well as the new and often arresting sights seen, two very basic impressions had been forming in my mind. They seemed to crystallize during the latter part of our travels, and especially so during the long and monotonous transit across Montana and South Dakota. They amount, I fear, to little more than tired clichés, but they hit me then, understandably, with no little force. First, the sheer immensity of the United States, even if one brackets the South and Southeast, which fell outside the ambit of our travels. And, added to that, beneath the occluding carapace of commercially and media-reinforced uniformity, the marked variety of conditions under which people pursued their daily lives. To get a real sense of this, or so I concluded, one had to experience the country from the ground. Crisscrossing it by air from coast to coast, however frequently, simply doesn't do the job. Second, and complexly related to the first, the cultural rootage of the persistent strain of isolationism that across time rises and falls in American life but never really goes away.

Neither as a schoolboy nor as an undergraduate at Oxford had I been markedly political in my concerns. I could not help being conscious, of course, of the huge international upheavals spawned by the dawning of the Cold War era and by the inception of the endgame for the great European colonial empires: the Berlin blockade and airlift; the Korean War (when my brother Vincent was recalled for service but discharged again before being shipped out); the Mau Mau insurrection in Kenya which trailed on from 1952 to 1956, an exceedingly brutal struggle on both sides; as well as the bloody but ultimately successful British and Commonwealth Malayan counterinsurgency campaign that was mounted in 1948 in response to the revolt staged by the (largely Chinese ethnic) Malayan Communist Party. This last was a major campaign which ground on even after the ending of colonial rule and peaked around the mid-1950s when, especially under General Templer's successful leadership, the tide was turned. In the end it was to cost over 4,000 casualties among British and Malayan forces, around 1,800 of them fatalities. All of this I was aware of, but it was only after I had begun to live abroad that I began to focus more intently on such international upheavals, great and small, and upon the repercussions they generated in the sphere of domestic politics, whether in Britain, France, or the United States. In the last case, the fallout from the loss of China to Communist rule was still in 1954 generating intense partisan rancor and serving to encourage the depredations of the House Committee on Un-American Activities as well as Senator Joseph McCarthy's Senate Permanent Subcommittee on Investigations.

In the spring of 1954 I had begun to follow closely the climactic battle of Dien Bien Phu in Indochina. It had culminated on May 7 in General Giap's stunning and decisive defeat of the French and French Foreign Legion forces dug in unwisely on what turned out to be a killing field. I had admired President Eisenhower's wise refusal to commit American ground forces on the French side in what was essentially, after all, a failing campaign of imperialist reconquest. And, realizing that the French defeat was likely to have enduring repercussions that would be global rather than simply French in their impact, I had been intent on following the unfolding of the Geneva peace talks. But as we pushed eastward across Montana and South Dakota I could find out little or nothing about it from the regional newspapers we picked up or from the regional radio broadcasts we listened to. For that part of the country, the historic French defeat and the ongoing challenge of dealing with the Indochina situation might never have existed. In fact, Indochina itself might never have existed while even France did no more than hover un-certainly on the margins of consciousness. That this should be so was for me something of an eye-opener. And it certainly gave me some minimal comprehension of why isolationism, in the American heartland at least, might exert so ready an appeal.

Back in Canada, having parted from my travelling companions in Wel-land, Ontario, I spent a few days in Toronto getting my stuff together before departing for my summer's work in Cambridge, Massachusetts. After several intensely social weeks cooped up in a car with three other people, I was more than ready for a stretch of quiet time by myself, but I had promised to visit the home in New York state of an American graduate student I had come to know in Toronto and, as a result, I spent a couple of days at Canandaigua and was introduced to the beauty of the Finger Lakes region. I had also promised at least to stop by the Breslins' home in Pittsfield, where I promptly came down with some sort of infec-tion and ended up in bed with a fever—much, I could not help ruefully feeling, to the delight of the Breslin girls who threw themselves with great enthusiasm into the role of playing nurse. Being increasingly anx-ious to get started on my summer's work, I left for Cambridge rather earlier than Dr. Breslin wanted me to and while I still felt a bit drained and weak. Fortunately, I recovered quickly and settled down in a rather dingy rented room on Oxford Street, not that far from Harvard Yard, a room not altogether unlike the one on the Abingdon Road that I had inhabited as an undergraduate.

That done, I quickly settled into a rather productive routine. Each day I would make my way across to nearby Massachusetts Avenue where I would breakfast at a drugstore counter before making my way down to Harvard Yard and the Widener Library. A letter of introduction from Fr. O'Donnell of the Pontifical Institute cleared the way for the generous provision of both a reader's pass for the Harvard libraries and a carrel of my own in the Widener stacks. There I settled, and there I spent that entire summer, more or less, beginning with some contextual reading and with a canvass of the secondary literature on Pierre d'Ailly. The latter did not prove to be voluminous, the most important pieces of work being a couple of doctoral theses dating back to the closing decades of the nineteenth century. The first, by Paul Tschackert, was a solid German thesis that printed in its appendices some of d'Ailly's shorter tracts; the second, by Louis Salembier, was a Sorbonne thesis written in Latin. The interpretative perspective from which these two scholars had viewed d'Ailly's thinking was very outdated and often misleading, but they did provide a useful introduction to nearly the full range of his writings. Salembier, in particular, provided an extensive descriptive calendar of most of those writings, which proved to be invaluable as I set about the task of trying to skim through d'Ailly's entire *oeuvre* and, that done, embarking on the challenging task of reading, with due care and attention, those of his writings that seemed most pertinent to his political thinking.

I was a rather solitary figure most of the time, eating lunch and dinner by myself at one or another of the many inexpensive eating spots surrounding the Yard while I kept up with the news via the *Christian Science Monitor*, to which I had become attached. Cambridge at that time was enjoying a good phase; it was not the rather tacky and druggy place it was to become for a while in the late 1960s and early 1970s. It was crowded, lively, and cosmopolitan, and I was much stimulated by the vibrancy of its atmosphere. Having explored the campus and its environs, I discovered the Foreign Students Center, then located on Brattle Street, and fell into the habit of going there on the weekends in order to enjoy a bit of social life. It was an animated place, thronged with students from all over the world, and it organized, among other things, outings, picnics, parties, trips to the shore, and, on most Saturday evenings, informal dances. It also served, less attractively, as a bit of a magnet for a group of somewhat predatory long-in-the-tooth graduate students (or fringe hangers-on), one or two of whom had come to Harvard as older undergraduates on the GI Bill immediately after the Second World War, had stayed on to do graduate work, and were now stuck at the ABD ("all but dissertation") stage of their doctoral studies and seemed likely to remain permanently stuck at that stage. Living hand to mouth on a shifting array of part-time jobs, they seemed wholly trapped within the magnetic field of Cambridge student and quasi-student life, unable to break free of its spell. It was my first encounter with the "professional student" phenomenon evident, I suspect, on the fringes of most big research universities, and it wasn't reassuring.

But it was at that same Foreign Students Center that I met a nice, attractive, and rather genteel Lebanese graduate student who was doing a PhD in biochemistry at Boston University. Her name was Faiza Fawaz. We became good companions that summer—dancing, eating out together, or eating in her apartment meals that she herself cooked, and going to the theater and to the outdoor concerts of the Boston Pops Orchestra. Over the years, if intermittently, she would write to me (or, in later years, email me) to give me updates on her doings—her struggle with the rheumatoid arthritis that forced an interruption in her PhD studies; her marriage to a Danish chemist whom she met at the Yale Graduate School when she returned to the United States to complete her studies; their appointments at Brown University, he as the head of the Chemistry Department and she, having added to her PhD an MD, as clinical professor of medicine and chief of rheumatology at the Memorial Hospital of Rhode Island; their eventual retirement to the Mediterranean climate of Santa Barbara on the California coast; and, most recently, a deeply saddening goodbye message, alerting me to the fact that she was dying of pancreatic cancer.

My stay at Cambridge came to an abrupt end several days before I had planned to leave. I awoke one morning to the sound of torrential rain and of powerful winds buffeting the house. They presaged the arrival of Hurricane Carol which made its disastrous landfall in the greater Boston area, did a good deal of damage in Cambridge itself, and left us for two or three days without electricity. It was impossible to get any work done, so I packed up and left for Toronto just as soon as the Greyhound long-distance buses got going again. In my last couple of weeks, however, I had had the pleasure of meeting some of my distant cousins on the Curran (my mother's) side of the family. My sister Molly turned out to have been in correspondence with one of them and, when they heard I was in Cambridge for the summer, they made contact. So I had had a pleasant weekend visit to Cape Cod, where my distant cousin, Catherine (Curran) Dennis, lived with her husband Ralph. Ralph owned a car dealership and she taught English at a private school in the vicinity.

In 1958 when my wife and I were married in Connecticut, she, Ralph, and her brother Peter Curran and his wife (the latter lived in the greater New York area) were among the guests. And, over the years, Catherine, a rather refined person with intellectual and artistic interests, would drive up to Williamstown with a friend to visit the Sterling and Francine Clark Art Institute and stop by our place for lunch or tea.

While I was still at Cambridge, other distant cousins on the Curran side organized a get-together over dinner somewhere in South Boston. In the 1870s and 1880s, their forebears had immigrated to America from the Ballycasey area in County Galway and the recent generation, at least, seemed to have done quite well. One, I recall, was a doctor, and another a lawyer. The evening we spent together, a lively and enjoyable one, was marked, however, by two discordant moments, the second of which was quite revealing. The oldest person present, a rather grim-faced matriarchal figure, first brought the conversation to a temporary halt by looking at me rather bleakly and pronouncing that I didn't "seem very Irish." I wasn't sure what that was supposed to mean. None of them had ever been to Ireland or, indeed, to Britain. If they viewed the latter with a degree of ancestral suspicion, the former they saw entirely through the distorting and romanticizing lens of the Irish American experience. Distance in their case had certainly bred enchantment. The second discordant moment was rather different. It was occasioned by the current antics of Senator Joseph McCarthy, at that moment presiding in his capacity as Chairman of the Senate Permanent Subcommittee on Investigations, over the controversial Army-McCarthy hearings. The Currans of the diaspora were all clearly enthralled by the tangled soap opera that was playing out for weeks on national TV and was, in the end, to prove to be McCarthy's undoing. And they wanted to know what I thought about the whole affair. Unfortunately, I was foolish enough to oblige. Had I known then that a Gallup poll taken earlier in the 1950s had revealed that no less than 50 percent of Americans approved of the Senator's despicable tactics, I might have been more cautious or diplomatic. But, having peered from the Canadian side of the border at the bizarre goings-on over which McCarthy was presiding, and sharing the (somewhat condescending) Canadian perspective on that and related aspects of American political life, I had come to view with alarm and revulsion the career-destroying depredations involved. That view I was innocent enough to share with my Irish American cousins only to find, to my astonishment and dismay, that they all seemed to be staunch McCarthy admirers. It was only in the wake of the subsequent lively and reasonably good-natured dinner table discussion that it dawned on me that while McCarthy was no Bostonian, they still regarded him with quasi-tribal ethnic pride as "one of us." He was, after all, an Irish American of staunchly Catholic persuasion, and they seemed to take his deplorable antics as, above all, an admirable instance of "stiffing" or "putting it to" the WASPs. Years later, viewing Edward R. Murrow's "A Report on Senator Joseph McCarthy," my cousins' attitude came once more to mind. On that later occasion, I was struck by the fact that McCarthy's physical appearance, demeanor, and typical rhetorical moves were not unlike those characteristic of a certain rather boozy type of Irish American parish priest with whom they must have been comfortably familiar.

Having already discussed the scholarly endeavors that occupied me during my second year in Toronto, I need now, and by way of conclusion, refer to the most important thing that happened to me that year. It was the joy of meeting and getting to know my future wife. Going with some other graduate students to the St. Michael's College snack bar for coffee one afternoon, just before the start of the Christmas vacation, I saw a friend sitting with and chatting up two or three undergraduate women. We hastened to join him and, introductions having been made, lively conversation ensued. One of the undergraduates was a very attractive girl, blond-haired, blue-eyed, intellectually acute, and possessed of a smile so radiant that, for the sun, it had to be cause for envy. Claire-Ann Lamenzo by name, she turned out to be an American from Manchester, Connecticut, just outside the state capital at Hartford. Her Italian American father was an insurance executive in Hartford (working with, or under, none other than the poet Wallace Stevens) and her Yankee Irish mother owned and ran a nursery school. Claire-Ann was an English major and when, in conversation, it became clear that she was of New Critical interpretative sympathies (an approach I found puzzling because of its essentially ahistorical nature), I suddenly realized that she was the student whose praises my friend Don Theall had been singing. She had taken two courses with him and another (Tennyson) with Marshall McLuhan, for whose six children, I was later to learn, she had

been courageous enough to babysit, being herself the second of six. Attempts to organize the group as a whole to go on to dinner having proved
abortive, I was delighted to have her to myself, eating Wienerschnitzel
at a new Austrian-style restaurant on nearby Bay (or Yonge) Street. We
seemed instantly to have hit it off and went on to talk and talk, about
what I can't remember (there seemed no lack of topics), for three hours
and more before calling it a night. She was due to fly home first thing
the next day, and I promised myself to see more of her the following
semester.

"The best laid schemes o' Mice an' Men" do indeed, however, "gang
aft agley." She, it turned out, had an off-and-on relationship with a somewhat older fellow who was on the English faculty at a liberal arts college
in Hartford, and that relationship turned on again so sharply during the
course of that Christmas vacation that when she returned to Toronto in
the new year she was engaged to be married and, accordingly, off limits
to me. From time to time I would bump into her with groups of her
friends and we would chat a bit. But that was that. Fortunately, it wasn't
to be that for too long. After her fiancé visited her in Toronto and she, in
turn, returned home to visit with him in Hartford, they decided to break
off the engagement and I was free, accordingly, to get to know her better.
In the latter half of the spring semester I lost no time in doing precisely
that. With increasing frequency, we began to spend time together. We
explored Toronto, ate at small, inexpensive places around the city, and, as
the short Toronto spring made its presence felt, would go out to Toronto
Island, picking up sandwiches and making picnics on the shore of Lake
Ontario. And we talked. Oh, how we talked!—about the courses she was
taking, in art history as well as English, about the sort of historical work
I was intent on pursuing, about our families, about our childhood and
youth, about our hopes, fears, and aspirations, about practically everything under the sun. As we talked, and as time went on, it gradually became clear that we had been moving, without quite realizing it, from
lighthearted friendship or mere infatuation into something deeper, and
something that was beginning to lean yearningly towards the elusive
hope of permanence. Our companionship had an open and natural feel
to it. She was (to use or misuse later parlance) a firmly grounded, well-
centered sort of person with a calm intelligence that was less purely

academic than mine and with a strong, down-to-earth strain of common-sense on which, over the years, I have come to rely. As a younger girl, she had studied and performed ballet at the Wadsworth Atheneum in Hart-ford and she proved to be a lovely, graceful dancer. I was also entranced by her spontaneous *joie de vivre* (her performance of the Charleston was a thing to behold), and I began to think of her as my very own version of Chaucer's Blaunche, the Duchess, and mentally to apply to her the lovely lines of his that I had memorized romantically at school.

> I sawgh hyr daunce so comlily,
> Carole and synge so swetely;
> Laughe and playe so womanly,
> And loke so debonairly,
> So goodly speke and so frendly,
> That certes y trowe that evermor
> Nas seyn so blysful a tresor.

This was all, of course, quite wonderful. But across it fell the length-ening shadow of my imminent departure. I had already booked my pas-sage in early July for home and was trying to face up to the prospect of putting my academic work on hold for a couple of years while I dis-charged my obligation of military service in the British armed forces. Though I had received, earlier that year, the unsolicited offer of a faculty appointment at St. Francis Xavier University in Antigonish, Nova Scotia, and though, even without having completed the PhD, I could probably have found a position at some small Catholic college in the United States, the idea of staying in either country in order to avoid the obliga-tion of National Service in England simply did not arise. Although in the post-Vietnam era the thought that I would have been ashamed to do any-thing of the sort may well seem a bit quaint, that was, in fact, the case. And, Irish though they were, my parents would have shared the same feeling. My brothers Vincent and Noel, after all, had put in their time in the army and Royal Air Force, respectively, and in the end we were to-gether to have put in almost a decade of full-time military service and I don't know how many further years of service in the active reserve. I was, moreover, acutely conscious of the fact that I had received a first-rate education largely at the expense of the British taxpayer and, even apart from the legal requirement, I felt strongly that I, more than most, owed the country the duty of a period of service.

As we began, then, to brood about our uncertain future, we began to think accordingly—"plan" would be too strong a word—of Claire-Ann's going to England to do some postgraduate work after she finished up at Toronto in the spring of the following year. More proximately, we began to think of spending a farewell vacation together in Québec City, where I could board the ship sailing for home. And that we did, both of us lining up cheap accommodations at Laval University, she in a women's residence and I at a men's equivalent. So my time as a travelling student in Canada was to end early in July 1955 on a highly poignant note. The weather cooperating, we spent a wonderful week together, exploring Québec City and its environs, eating inexpensively at one or another of the many interesting little cafés there, reading and sunning ourselves on the Heights of Abraham overlooking the St. Lawrence River, the site of General Wolfe's great victory in 1758 during the Seven Years' War and now one of Canada's national urban parks. We even got dressed up one day to go for drinks and dancing (a "tea dance") at the stately old Château Frontenac Hotel. The week ended with my reluctant departure on the Canadian Pacific liner, the *Empress of France*, and that climactic moment, however miserable, was fraught with romance. The ship had sailed earlier in the day from Montreal, where almost its whole complement of passengers had boarded. It was simply to slow down in the river off Québec where the remaining passengers (I think there were only three of us) were to be taken out by tender to the ship. When we showed up at the quay, the sailor manning the tender permitted Claire-Ann to accompany me out to the ship. He did so, less, it turned out, from the goodness of his heart than because he wanted to try to put the make on her, which he lost no time in doing as soon as I was out of sight. Darkness was already falling as we left the quay and chugged out into midstream, there to hold until the *Empress of France*, painted creamy white all over except for a checkerboard pattern on her funnels, emerged from the gloaming, looming over us and steaming slowly alongside with a hatchway open just above sea level to receive us passengers. Frantic goodbyes hastily exchanged, I scrambled on board and struggled mightily to get up to the open boat deck in order to wave a last farewell. But I was too late. By the time I made it to the rail, the tender was already slipping away into the dusk and I was left with an overwhelming sense of loss.

It is a telling fact, my love of being at sea notwithstanding, that I can remember nothing at all about that long Atlantic voyage retracing in reverse the route from Liverpool along which I had sailed so excitedly two years earlier. Nothing at all, that is, except the turmoil of my inner feelings, for I was overcome by an enormous surge of doubt. What had I done? Why had I permitted old-fashioned notions of duty and honor to trump something that now seemed infinitely more important? Was I not, after all, being wholly unrealistic? What if, for perfectly practical reasons, Claire-Ann was unable to make her way to England? And, if she could do so, why should I take it for granted that I would not by then have been posted overseas to some currently uninviting location like Malaya or Cyprus? Why, moreover, should I believe that the inevitably fading memory of our time together would be enough to sustain her across a full year of separation? She was, after all, a very attractive girl; the one thing she would not lack on a university campus would be attentive male company. Would not the most likely endgame be the receipt, after a while, of a species of "Dear John" letter, fraught, no doubt, with nostalgic affection, but firm in its negativity about any possible future for the two of us? Such was the welter of thoughts and emotions that overcame me during that long and miserable Atlantic transit. Only when we sighted at last the emerald green coast of Ulster and began to slip down into the Irish Sea on the final leg for home did my unaccustomed gloom begin finally to lift. But until that moment I felt, in a way that I had never felt before and have never felt since, altogether alone and utterly bereft.

CHAPTER EIGHT

On Her Majesty's Service

On the Continent, the practice of compelling subjects and citizens to serve in the nation's armed forces had a long and often deeply resented history. In the United Kingdom, however, it came as something of a novelty when, in 1916 and amid the appalling carnage of the First World War, it was finally introduced. In 1939, as the shadow of the Nazi menace lengthened across Europe, it was reintroduced and, when the war was at its peak, it extended to all men (who were not in "reserved occupations" like mining or farming) from the ages of eighteen to fifty-one, as well as to single women from the ages of twenty to thirty. In the context of the Great War, conscription remained in effect for only three years and came to an end in 1919. After the Second World War, however, though the British Army was reduced in size to a force ranging between three hundred thousand and four hundred thousand, full-scale demobilization was simply not in the cards. The international turbulence occasioned by the dawn of the Cold War and the prevalence across the globe of grinding colonial conflicts of one sort or another precluded a return to a military establishment at the lower prewar levels. To maintain the armed forces at quasi-wartime levels, conscription proved necessary, and it was given a new legislative foundation in the National Service Act of 1948. It was to remain in force until 1960, with the last National Servicemen being demobilized as late as 1963. During that span of almost a quarter of a century, the length and terms of service fluctuated but, after the outbreak of the Korean War in 1950, the obligation came to be fixed at two years of full-time service plus three and a half years in the active reserve, this last involving annual two-week camps and periodic short training sessions during the course of each year, somewhat on the model of the peacetime National Guard in the United States. Such was the obligation that lay ahead of me in 1955 when I returned to Britain. I was to enter a rather bloated army, still equipped very much as it had been during World War II and, at a time when unemployment had dropped to a record low, having great difficulty in recruiting regular (professional) soldiers. As a result, it was reduced, in my judgment at least, to the over-rapid promotion of its noncommissioned officers (NCOs—corporals, sergeants, sergeant-majors). Certainly, the standard clichéd picture of the grizzled and experienced sergeant wisely guiding the inexperienced, wet-behind-the-ears second lieutenant, folkloric though it might be, was not readily evident in the army I got to know so well.

Mindful of the fact that I might conceivably want to return to America to complete my doctoral work, one of the first things I did after returning home in mid-July 1955 was to report in to the Ministry of Labour and National Service to request that my medical examination be scheduled as soon as possible. If I were to return to the United States and not miss the fall semester at graduate school, I needed to begin my military service no later than early September. In response to my request they were not, in fact, too quick off the mark and it was a full month before I was called in for the medical.

In the meantime, I enjoyed the warm welcome I received at home and was glad to see everyone again. Vincent, having married and secured a position with a small coastal shipping and shipbuilding firm in East Anglia, was now living on the Norfolk coast at Great Yarmouth. Molly and Noel, not yet married though heading into it (Noel with his Monica, Molly with her Sid), were still living at home and had begun their teaching careers which were to culminate for both of them in the headships of schools. Reunited with my family, I felt my spirits rising, the more so because a long, affectionate letter from Claire-Ann and, under separate cover, a copy of Dostoevsky's *The Brothers Karamazov*, which she loved and wanted me to read, were awaiting me when I arrived. Despite the geographical distance separating us, I felt very much in contact with her again and the gloom that had overtaken me during that long, miserable voyage receded still further into the past. And, across the course of the next year, the regular arrival of her eagerly awaited letters helped keep my spirits up during long and lonely months when we soldiers were not only segregated from female company but also altogether cut off, it sometimes seemed, from the normal world of civilized discourse. During the months of basic training our lives were to be constricted in many ways, but we were at least permitted to keep photographs of wives and sweethearts inside our lockers. And, like my comrades, that I did.

After two or three weeks at home, where I had the pleasure of lunching in town with John Elton, my old musical friend from Corpus who was now a classics master at a private school in Crosby (North Liverpool), I headed south to Oxford, where I updated E. F. Jacob on what I had achieved in Toronto and I touched base with Michael Brock, who was kind enough to take me to dine in the Senior Common Room. He also gave me a letter of introduction to the British Museum in London (my next stop as it still housed the British Library), where I got my first reader's card. There I settled in for more than a week's work trying to run down some of the vaguer and more stubborn references in d'Ailly's *Tractatus de materia* that had eluded me in Toronto. It was at that time that I first came to work in the Main Reading Room in the Great Rotunda, where Karl Marx had done so much of his writing, and in the North Library, where one had to sit if one were reading rare books. Over the years and in the course of several leaves and many a shorter research trip, I think I must have spent an accumulated total of more than two full years reading away happily in those hallowed precincts.

While in London, I had the good fortune of being able to stay with Lol and Suzanne O'Keeffe. They had married in Paris the previous year and now lived in a nice, roomy flat in Blackheath, South East London. Lol had now mutated into a senior civil servant assigned (somewhat to his displeasure) to Customs and Excise, though he was able, before long, to transfer to the Foreign Office, an assignment much better suited to his temperament and abilities. It was an enormous pleasure to spend time with these, my oldest friends. And Blackheath made so favorable an impression on me that Claire-Ann and I chose to live there during two successive leaves in the early 1960s and early 1970s when I was once more pursuing research in the British Museum.

Before leaving London to go on to Great Yarmouth to visit my brother Vincent and his wife Margaret (an Irish girl from County Mayo), I had lunch in Soho with a rather frail Faiza Fawaz, who had stopped over in London on her way back home to Beirut. She had had, alas, to discontinue graduate studies because of her illness. I didn't see her again for several years, and then I bumped into her in New Haven while I was teaching at Yale. She and her fiancé had just arrived there to finish up their PhD work. She seemed on that occasion more upbeat and much recovered, though she was to suffer from rheumatoid arthritis throughout her life.

Ideally, I would have liked to have done my service in the Royal Navy, but to do that one had to sign on for an extra year with no guarantee that one would be assigned to sea duty rather than becalmed in some dreary shore posting. So I settled for the army. Back in Liverpool, then, though after a rather nervous-making delay, I was finally called for my medical and pronounced fit for service. That done, I pressed my need for early call-up and the Ministry of Labour and National Service proved willing enough to oblige and issued the necessary orders. While I was told that I could eventually expect to be posted to the Royal Army Education Corps (a fairly nice, soft option that would bring with it a sergeant's stripes), I was being assigned first for twelve weeks of basic infantry training to the Loyal Regiment, North Lancashire, and was to report to the Regimental Depot in Preston on September 15. That I did, travelling up by bus and travelling very light, for my brothers' experience had alerted me to the fact that I would be required, as soon as I was outfitted with an army uniform, to parcel up my civilian clothes and mail them home. The Loyal Regiment, I discovered, was a fine old county regiment, festooned with battle honors and with a lineage extending back into the eighteenth century when, among other encounters, it had fought under General Wolfe in the Battle of Québec, scaling the Heights of Abraham and forcing the surrender of the city. In remembrance of that victory, the regiment celebrated Québec Day every September 13 and, in similar remembrance of Wolfe's death in that battle, all officers and noncommissioned officers wore a black shoulder lanyard. Indeed, although I was assigned to Ava platoon (that name memorializing a battle dating back to the First Anglo-Burmese War in the early nineteenth century), one of the platoons in the training company was named "Québec Platoon." As a result, less than two months after those idyllic afternoons spent with Claire-Ann, reading and sunning on the Heights of Abraham, Québec cast its alluring shadow once more across my life. And it was not to be the last time that I was to pick up distant reverberations of the Seven Years' War—or, as it tends to be called in these parts, the French and Indian War.

The Regimental Depot, situated at Fulwood Barracks in Preston and shared with the East Lancashire Regiment, was screened from the street by a high stone wall. It consisted of a big, square parade ground surrounded by solid granite buildings dating back to the early nineteenth century. They housed, along with our barrack rooms, a guard room, an infirmary and medical center, a quartermaster's store, officers' and sergeants' messes, classrooms, and the like. Centered on our side of the square was the flagpole from which, during the daylight hours, were flown the Union Jack and the regimental colors. There, in the dark of an early winter's morning, a bugler would march up, stand at attention, and sound "Reveille" to wake us all up. At the end of the day, at a similarly ceremonial moment, the bugler would take up his position in the same place and sound the "Last Post" (the British equivalent of the American "Taps"). At that moment, anyone walking around the precincts, civilians no less than military, was required to stand at attention facing the flags as they were lowered. These archaic rituals touched a romantic streak in my nature and helped make me feel more like a soldier. So, too, did the sacralized narrative of the regiment's history which it was each lieutenant's duty to instill in his platoon. Regular sessions were scheduled for such indoctrination. At them we learned of the history that lay behind the regiment's battle honors, with a special emphasis being placed in our case, for we were Ava Platoon, on the regiment's exploits in the First Anglo-Burmese War, a rather bloody affair that lasted from 1824 to 1826 and for which the Ava Battle Honor was awarded. It was while the lieutenant was talking about that victory in what had once been the Kingdom of Ava in Upper Burma that one of the recruits, a bluff Lancashire eighteen-year-old and a coal miner by civilian trade, put up his hand to ask a question. When called upon, he got to his feet and said that it didn't seem very honorable to him for British troops to be mowing down "naked savages." The lieutenant didn't brush him off. I sensed that he was pleased that a recruit possessed the fortitude to issue such a challenge. All he did was patiently explain that the Burmese were not exactly naked savages and, while their firepower was inferior to that possessed at that time by the British Army, they were in fact equipped with muskets and cannon. In any case, the narrative he was unfolding did not always involve the celebration of victories. It extended also to the dismal fate of the regiment's second battalion in World War II. Having fought in Malaya as a part of the rearguard attempting to slow down the Japanese descent upon Singapore, it shared the fate of the Singapore garrison and had to endure nearly four years of misery in Japanese prisoner of war camps. Only a minority, including the rather kindly and avuncular quartermaster sergeant at Fulwood Barracks, had survived. In this way we were inducted into a community saturated with a history it chose deliberately not to forget. For that history constituted the very core of its identity.

The buildings surrounding the barrack square at Fulwood were kept in very neat, tidy, and shipshape order. Behind them, however, symmetry gave way to a jumble of Nissen huts housing the cookhouse and eating area, the moderately revolting toilet and less than adequate shower facilities (the latter incapable, it seemed, of producing more than a trickle of water that was better than lukewarm), a football field, training areas, assault course, and NAAFI (Navy, Army and Air Force Institutes) canteen. The whole agglomeration, reasonably capacious, self-contained, and secluded, was for the next three months to constitute the totality of our little world. Our former and greater world, the one that stretched out beyond the barrack walls, was for us now, more or less, *terra incognita*. The only time the business of training took us back into the world, we passed through it as fleeting spectators, piled, during the latter part of our training, into open trucks and driven freezing down the length of the county to the huge firing range at Formby, situated on the Irish seacoast just north of Liverpool.

When I had first walked through the gateway into Fulwood Barracks and, later, over the course of the next two days while we were given another medical examination, issued with uniforms and various gear, and being otherwise processed, I had felt an elusive but nagging sense of familiarity and recognition. But it had taken me a while to pin it down. It was then that I realized that, after five years of enjoying the comparative freedom of university student life, my new circumstances and the conditions of living to which I was now having to adjust were bringing back, and quite forcefully so, more dismal memories of life at grammar school. I was beginning to recognize, in effect, that I had reentered the sort of world where one would be wise to keep one's head down and not draw unnecessary attention to oneself, a world in which one was likely to be found wrong or somehow wanting unless one was able to prove oneself to be in the right. And that recognition was to prove to be helpfully adaptive as we were chivvied impatiently through processing and repeatedly told that we were the most unpromising and unprepossessing shower of idiots that they (sergeants, corporals, and the like) had ever had the misfortune to see, let alone be called upon to try to turn into some poor facsimile of soldiers.

On our first day, having been medically examined, both of our arms were pumped full with a series of inoculations that left us feeling sore and brought on a quick but evanescent bout of feverishness during the night. I can still hear the intermittent groaning that broke the silence in our barrack room and punctuated what was a largely sleepless first night in the military. The next day, clearheaded again but feeling a bit weak and vaguely neurasthenic, we went through the rest of our processing, were outfitted with our uniforms, and had to parcel up our civilian clothes to be mailed home. While the general mood was one of bewildered (and, sometimes, dismayed) confusion, the whole ritual was punctuated by one redeeming moment of hilarity. It occurred while we were being issued our army paybooks and numbers (mine was 23179857), the basic identifying document that soldiers had to carry with them at all times. Into those paybooks a lance corporal was entering each recruit's personal details—home address, next of kin, religious affiliation, and so on. So far as the last was concerned, the range of choice was rather limited: "C of E" (Church of England), "NC" (Protestant Nonconformist—Baptist, Methodist, Presbyterian, Congregationalist, and the like), "RC" (Roman Catholic), and "J" (Jewish). While the vast majority of the recruits were eighteen-year-olds from Lancashire, there was a smallish group of us who, having gone to university, were a bit older and were drawn from a broader expanse of the country at large. As we shuffled through the line, one of that group, a rather innocent or innocently serious Jewish lad who was a graduate of the University of Leeds, caused a bit of a commotion. When asked to state his religious affiliation, he replied, truthfully enough (he was nonobservant) but perhaps a bit foolishly, "agnostic." With that, everything ground to a halt. The lance corporal simply didn't know what to do. To him everyone had to be C of E, NC, RC, or J. So he bellowed across the room: "Sarnt!" (That, not "Sarge," was the British Army abbreviation for sergeant.) "Sarnt!" he said, not without exasperation, "this fellow says he is a bloody agonistic [his pronunciation], what should I put down?" To which the sergeant replied in the blink of an eye and without even raising his head from the task at hand: "C of E." And so it was. Had that poor fellow died for Queen and Country in some corner of a foreign field that is forever England, he would doubtless have been buried, not only with full military honors, but also in accordance with the rites of the church by law established.

The established status of that church was brought home to us even more forcefully after about five or six weeks when our training had progressed enough to convince our superiors that we would no longer disgrace the regiment if seen by the world at large outside the perimeter of the high barrack walls that both concealed and confined us. The time: a crisp and clear Sunday morning late in October of that year. The place: the barrack square. The occasion: a parade of the full complement of recruits, now about halfway through their basic training and standing stiffly at attention with battle dress neatly pressed, belts and gaiters carefully blancoed, boots well shone, and highly polished brass accoutrements glinting bravely under the pale English sun. The adjutant had completed his inspection to make sure that this new lot would not embarrass the regiment if allowed (for the first time) to appear in public. For what was at hand was a particularly formal occasion. It was a *church* parade, which involved the company's marching smartly down through the town in order to take part in an Anglican service at the fine old parish church, in the nave of which the regimental colors and storied battle honors were on proud and permanent display. Before the march off through the gate of the barracks, however, one last formality had to be attended to. Regulations required the extension to the smallish minority of soldiers classified neither as members of the Church of England nor as Protestant Nonconformists of an opportunity to exercise their religious freedom. (It seemed to have simply been assumed that Nonconformists would make no fuss about conforming on such ceremonial occasions.) With that in mind, the regimental sergeant major bellowed out across the parade ground an order rather brutal in its specificity: "Roman

Catholics and Jews," he shouted, *"Fall Out!"* Whereupon just four of us, three Catholics and one Jew, a mere corporal's guard, turned smartly to our right, fell out of the formation, and marched to the edge of the parade ground, where we were immediately intercepted by a sergeant who ordered us to change into "fatigues" (working gear) and report to the cookhouse where we were to spend the rest of the morning peeling potatoes. Humility being usually viewed in religious terms as something of a virtue, I assume that that assignment could possibly be construed as an alternative and safely nondenominational form of spiritual exercise. I have often since thought that I would probably have enjoyed marching proudly through the streets of Preston, soaking up the beauty and serenity of that old church, and absorbing the lovely sonorities of the Book of Common Prayer. But this was still for us Catholics the pre–Vatican II era, when we were still firmly in the grip of religious tribalism and all too sensitive to the periodic attempts to nudge us into the sort of complicity with the Anglican religious establishment that our proud recusant forebears had been willing for centuries to accept civil disabilities in order to avoid.

As I watched from the reluctant sidelines as my comrades marched crisply through the gate of the barracks and off into the outside world— a brave sight—I realized that the tedious training and relentless drilling of the weeks preceding had succeeded, at least in making us *look* as if we were soldiers. That training had been multidimensional. It stretched from regular PT (physical training) sessions to the rather more challenging routine of being put through assault courses. Or from bayonet practice (accompanied by appropriately macho yells and shrieks) to extensive weapon training in the safe handling and effective use of the standard light arms (the Lee-Enfield 303 rifle, the Bren light machine gun, and the Sten gun, a species of submachine gun that had to be handled with caution if one didn't want to lose a finger or two, as it ejected its spent cartridges at high velocity from a slot on one side). Or, again, from tedious hours spent scrubbing and blancoing webbing belts, gaiters, and rifle slings to attempting, by assiduous and literal application of spit and polish, to produce a high shine on our rough and heavy boots or evoke a high, Brasso induced, sheen on our (brass) cap badges, belt clasps, and gaiter buckles. All of this was monitored by officers and NCOs by minute and intrusive inspection of one's person, appearance, and gear, with unpleasant but routine penalties imposed in response to any hint of sloppiness or inadequacy. Or, further, and now off the parade ground, from lectures on regimental history, intended to promote unit pride and solidarity, to admonitory sessions on the danger of venereal or sexually transmitted diseases, these last accompanied by truly terrifying visual aids and oft-repeated comic warnings to the effect that "only bishops contract VD from lavatory seats."

Such had dictated the tenor of our day-to-day lives. But looming over everything, it seemed, had been the long hours of relentless drilling we were put through in the parade ground every day by a seemingly inexhaustible supply of red-sashed drill sergeants. We jumped to attention smashing our metal-clad boots onto the hard surface, causing for the unfortunate among us the onset of a short but painful bout of the condition known as "guardsman's heel." We sloped arms; we ordered arms; we presented arms; we fixed and unfixed bayonets; we learned to salute properly (there was an inordinate amount of saluting in the British Army). We stood at attention; we stood at ease; we "stood easy." We turned smartly to the left; we turned equally smartly to the right; we executed a crisp about-face. We marched, wheeled, and countermarched; we learned the impressive ceremonial slow march used at funerals which so impressed JFK when he saw it executed in Dublin by Irish soldiers. To the order "Number from the left!" we shuffled to arms-length distance from our immediate left-hand neighbor, at the same time shouting out our positions in the line—one, two, three, four, five, and so on. Around that time the comic potential of this last maneuver was milked by a comedian on the radio bellowing out: "*Roman* legionnaires, number from the left," followed by a series of voices shouting out: "i, ii, iii, iv, v . . . ." Though punctuated by periodic short breaks geared to the amount of time it took to smoke a small, cheap "Woodbine" cigarette, close order drilling involving the hefting of heavy Lee-Enfield rifles could be very tiring. It could also be made to feel quite painful if the particular drill sergeant so wished. One of our drill sergeants clearly did so wish. He was a foul-mouthed bully of a man who clearly took pleasure not only in inflicting pain on the whole squad by means of excessive repetition of certain drill movements but also in the public humiliation of any soldier who showed signs of clumsiness. And in any squad there were always one or two of those whose right arms seemed to move instinctively in sync with their *right* rather than their left leg, thereby producing a swaying waddle akin to the walk of a giraffe.

Beyond the obvious external goal of this training regimen lay, or so I concluded, something deeper. It also surely involved an attempt to re-socialize us, to reshape our identities in such a way as to make us think of ourselves less as the particular individuals we had been in our previous civilian lives than as constituent members of a close-knit unit, inter-changeable parts who had let go of their earlier identities and become something new and different. It was an attempt, I think, that was more effective with the more malleable eighteen-year-olds than with those of us who were heading into our mid-twenties. And I would guess that it had been totally ineffective with the forty-year-olds whom the army had tried to turn into soldiers during the war. As a medievalist by calling, I could not help noticing that some of the socializing techniques being used had a lot in common with those employed for centuries by religious orders in the "formation" of the novices who had sought to enter the "narrow way" of the monastic life. We recruits, too, were under the tute-lage of a species of novice master—in our case the impressive staff ser-geant in charge of the whole intake. We, too, were separated radically from our earlier lives, dressed in a uniform habit, our previous, more individualized mode of dress now denied us. While we were not exactly tonsured, our hair was still cropped close. We ate and slept communally, we were immured in an all-male enclave, embedded in an unchanging, almost liturgical routine, subject in almost everything we did to the un-challengeable will of superiors, and, though we hadn't taken those tradi-tional vows, committed, however unwillingly, to a life of poverty, chastity, and obedience. Poverty, because the pay scale of conscripts in the British Army was set much lower than that of regular (professional) soldiers. Serving as orderly officer on payday later on, I discovered that one of my corporals, a regular soldier, was being paid more than I was as a National Service second lieutenant. As recruits, we private soldiers were paid only twenty-eight shillings a week, four shillings of which were deducted for the National Health Service (which, as soldiers, we were not entitled to use). Out of the remaining twenty-four shillings we had to pay for the boot polish Blanco, Brasso, and other cleaning materials we needed to keep ourselves presentable. The rest tended to go on cigarettes, beer, and the extra meals at the NAAFI we needed to assuage our hunger. Army food, if plentiful enough, was less than appetizing and we all needed to top it up with the more tasty (usually fried) NAAFI fare. We also drew on the contents of the food parcels that the more knowledgeable among our parents would send to their offspring. Not all recruits were lucky enough to get such parcels, but it was a striking fact that at Preston great pains were taken by the men to divide what was received into equal shares for everyone in a given barrack room. The practice was similar with the evening meal when one was on guard duty. On such occasions we all had to take our turns to go out in pairs on patrol for two-hour shifts, which was called "being on stag." If the meal arrived while one was out on stag it would be divided up meticulously into even servings for everyone, and one's share would be kept hot on the stove until one got back. These Lancashire lads seemed to be an instinctively decent, fair-minded lot. Later on, when I was at officer cadet school, I had reason to regret the absence among many of my comrades of those admirable qualities. There, returning to the guardroom after having been on stag, I was to find that the evening meal, having arrived in our absence, had been devoured in its entirety by the other members of the detail (most of them public school products), leaving nothing at all for the two of us. Fair-mindedness didn't seem to enter the picture. On such matters, at least, it seemed to be every man for himself. A very different group ethic.

The effort at resocialization reached also, in some ways, into what little spare time we had. On Saturday evenings we were rounded up and taken to the camp cinema where we were fed an unremitting diet of World War II films, some of which were pretty good, others blatant propaganda. At one level simple entertainment, I suppose, at another, continued indoctrination by more beguiling means. Interestingly enough, not all the films that had clearly been produced by the wartime propaganda machine were paeans to glorious victory. They were somewhat more subtle than that. During the first three to four years of the war, the British had had, after all, few victories to celebrate. Though I can't recall its title, one such film I remember quite clearly if for no other reason than that it spoke directly to our own condition. It was the story of the difficult shaping of an unpromising bunch of wartime recruits, many of them in their late thirties and forties and nearly all of them unfit, into a cohesive platoon, their subsequent deployment in the North African desert where they were confronted by resurgent enemy forces which surrounded them, cutting them off from reinforcements so that, their ranks depleted, they were left to fight on nobly in the face of almost certain defeat and death. A story that was, of course, quite clichéd and also, beyond that, a quintessentially *English* one in which the stoic confrontation of disaster with a measure of understated decency, nobility, comradeship, and compassion was ranked almost as highly as glorious victory. But what I took away from that film in particular was something else: a sense of the misery experienced by men who, in midlife, had been peremptorily uprooted from wives, children, jobs, and careers. For some, doubtless, it represented an unexpected and welcome delivery from lives that had come to smack of suffocating entrapment. But for most, I suspect, it may have bordered on the traumatic. And for those officers and NCOs charged with the task of trying to turn them into soldiers it must have presented an altogether different and much more testing challenge than that of shaping up a bunch of eighteen-year-olds.

The small group of us in our intake who were university graduates and a bit older than the average recruit, while we missed quite acutely the sort of freedom and intellectual stimulation to which we had become accustomed as students, seemed to adjust surprisingly well. In our barrack room we were spared the supervisory chivvying of a lance corporal because, our sergeant told us in a confessional moment, experience had taught them that people in our age group tended to get on with things and needed less supervision. Oddly enough, it seemed that university graduates, when left to themselves, tended to be better than average at such nonintellectual activities as polishing boots and brass and blancoing webbing. I myself found all that cleaning and polishing of gear tedious but doable, and the endless drilling and the physical demands made on us was equally manageable. The weapons training, moreover, was not uninteresting and had some diverting aspects. In their efforts to drive the pertinent points home, our NCO instructors were prone to employing highly (sometimes grotesquely) sexualized terminology—in the military, it seemed that was an honored and tried and true pedagogic tactic. Thus the parts of the weapons we were handling were aligned, by analogy, with cognate parts of the male and female anatomy. I can't recall precisely, but I think that it was in connection with clicking the Bren gun from single-shot into automatic machine gun mode that an instructor, without the slightest trace of self-consciousness, issued the following command: "Take your Saturday night finger, stick it up under here, and you will find you can release the catch."

All of this was behind us when, with the passage of time, we went on to shoot these various weapons and to spend an increasing amount of time on the range. There we alternated between shooting and patching up the targets, the latter chore calling for us to hunker down in a trench below the targets while the shooting was going on, with the result that one got habituated to the sound of bullets whizzing by two to three feet above one's head. So far as marksmanship went, I was disappointed to discover that, try though I might, I was no more than an indifferent shot with the rifle, though, oddly, I did much better firing the Bren gun in single-shot mode.

As our period of basic training drew to a close, the future, which for long weeks had seemed no longer to exist, began once more to intrude on the consciousness. Once finished, and after a few days leave, the bulk of our intake would move on for further infantry training with the regiment's first battalion which, after a spell overseas, had been rotated home to Castle Barnard in County Durham. As for me, my own future had become more complicated. Had I done nothing, I assume that I would have been moved on to some sort of further training with the Royal Army Education Corps. But a Corpus friend, now teaching Russian at the Army Language School, tipped me off to the fact that they had some vacancies in the Russian course (I would not have known otherwise) and that, should I apply, he was pretty sure I would get in. That prospect had some appeal. The school had a reputation for effective teaching, and if one graduated successfully after the better part of a year of intensive saturation instruction, one could expect to be posted with NCO rank to BAOR (the British Army of the Rhine) in Germany, there to spend one's time on shifts round the clock monitoring Russian military radio transmissions. And that, I thought, would have the further advantage of affording me an opportunity to improve my German. The alternative was to apply for a National Service commission. For that, I would have to get through a War Office Selection Board (familiarly known as WOSBY) and survive a long process of training at an Officer Cadet Training Unit (OCTU). While the latter option was a bit risky (I wasn't sure I would survive the weeding-out process), I told myself bravely that if

I was going to be an academic for the rest of my life I should really have the gumption to try for something distinctly nonacademic now. So I chose to follow this latter route and, having got through the not-very-demanding screening stage at the regimental level, was posted to a holding company at Formby, where I was to pursue what was billed as further infantry training while awaiting my WOSBY and its outcome.

During the war, Formby had functioned as a large-scale transit camp and I have since met several Americans who, having disembarked from a troop ship at Liverpool, spent a few days there before being shipped down to the southern coast and eventually over to Normandy. When I was there, ten years after the war had ended, it was a semi-deserted, slightly eerie place, its huts beginning to fall apart and providing inadequate shelter against the cold, damp winds sweeping in constantly from the Irish Sea. So bleak, indeed, that it was hard at the end of a vigorous day to get a decent night's sleep. Coming in, we would get the hut's potbellied stove going, filling it up with coal and coke until it was actually glowing red. Then, as early as 9:00 p.m., we would get into our bunks under a pile of blankets and greatcoats and go to sleep—but not for long. By about 3:00 a.m. we would all be waking up, freezing, and able to do no more than doze off intermittently until dawn.

WOSBYs had been introduced in the middle of the Second World War to provide a more effective screening device after it had been found that altogether too many officer candidates, selected presumably on social or educational grounds, were failing at OCTU and thereby wasting overburdened training resources. This selection process had been kept in place after the war, though the practice of assigning a psychiatrist to each selection panel had been discontinued. In my day, they had a reputation for effecting a pretty thorough shakedown of would-be candidates for officer training. Having gone through one, I would judge that that reputation was well deserved. The selection process, conducted down at Aldershot in Hampshire, was spread across two days and I can't remember everything we were called upon to do. But throughout those two days we were dressed in fatigues, wore no caps, and sported no names or identifying regimental or corps insignia. Assigned to groups of twelve, each supervised by a major, we were known and addressed only by the large number we wore on chest and back. Anonymity thus assured, the whole operation (presided over by a colonel) was cognate in a way to the kind of blind audition conducted by orchestras where the performer is concealed from his or her appraisers by a curtain.

The exercises we were put through were quite various, ranging from deskbound or indoor performances to the completion of an assault course involving the normal battery of obstacles to scramble over, ropes to be climbed or used to swing across a stream, and so on. We also had to complete closely observed and rather physically demanding leadership-oriented tasks, usually involving the manhandling with rope and tackle of some impossibly unwieldy object across a stream or across dead ground on which members of the team were not allowed to set foot. Intelligence tests of one sort or another were set; so, too, was a strategic problem for which we had to propose a solution in a fairly extended piece of writing which presumably served also as a test of writing ability. We were also called upon to participate both in group discussions on some set topic where no discussion leader was appointed and in others which one could be called upon to lead. Similarly, we were each called upon with little notice to make a short speech to the group on a topic not of one's own choosing. I myself got stuck with the topic "Hats." So far as the outdoor leadership tasks went, some were group tasks with no leader assigned. Others, each of us in turn had to lead. I had an idea that the former type of task was intended as much to reveal one's willingness to be a good team member as to test one's ability to seize control and I acted accordingly. But I was baffled by the task I was assigned to lead. I simply couldn't figure out how exactly to solve the problem set and I ended up with one member of my group swinging forlornly at the end of a rope above a stream.

We had begun all of this with fairly lengthy individual interviews conducted by the major in charge of our group; we ended with comparable interviews conducted by the colonel who was in overall command. In my own interview I acknowledged to him that I had messed up my assigned command task, but he didn't seem all that interested in the fact that I had failed to solve the problem. Instead, he wanted to talk about my background, what I had done at college and in Canada, and he ended up by asking me what sort of stuff I read for pleasure. Poetry and novels, I replied. That led him to probe a bit to find out what sort of novels, and when I mentioned, among others, those of Graham Greene, it turned out that he himself was a very well-read admirer of Greene's work. The interview was really quite pleasant and civilized but it left me with little sense of how good my prospects might be.

When the selection process had come to an end, those of us in our squad of twelve were lined up in numerical order and each presented with a small, folded piece of paper on which was indicated our fate. We had been told to expect one of three outcomes—"Pass," "Fail," or "Try Again"—and I was mightily relieved that, for good or ill, I was one of those who had passed. As we all, rather excitedly, exchanged notes and results, it turned out that one of those who had failed outright was a rather pushy, even bullying, sort of fellow who had missed no opportunity to try to seize control of the group. He was understandably furious about the outcome and unpleasant enough to express open incredulity about the fact that one fellow had not been failed outright but told to try again. The "Fails" and "Try Agains" were given the opportunity to seek an explanation (or a bit of advice) from the major. Having done so, this particular fellow proved to be so lacking in self-knowledge that he openly shared with the rest of us what he had been told. The major, it turned out, had bluntly informed him that the army would not dream of putting men under the command of somebody with his temperament and behavior patterns. Having heard that, and having passed myself, I quietly concluded (somewhat smugly, I am afraid) that the army's judgment could not, after all, be all that bad.

With this experience behind me, I returned to Formby for another two or three weeks of infantry stuff while awaiting my posting to Mons Officer Cadet School in Aldershot. At Mons, along with fellow cadets from the full range of army corps, including Tanks, I went through six weeks of infantry attack and defense up to the company level, with each of us being tested towards the end by being put in command of an attack or a defense. Mine involved the defense at nighttime of a long, sloping hill, punctuated by an impressive amount of whizz-bangs and periodically illuminated by the eerie white glow of parachute flares. It seemed to go well, though it wasn't clear to me how our superiors could arrive at an accurate judgment about the quality of one's effort.

It was standard practice for one to have to transfer upon commissioning from the regiment in which one had been a private soldier. My own hope (imagining myself seeing out my service in London in a capacity that did not call for the wearing of a uniform) was to get into the

Intelligence Corps and I submitted an application with that in mind. This led to a very strange interview somewhere near Watford in north London where I was quizzed at length by one captain in a tiny, cramped office, while another talked incessantly to someone else on the telephone. My interviewer seemed quite taken with the fact that I had studied Latin palaeography and dealt with old manuscripts, seeming to think that would equip me well for the business of deciphering aerial photographs. But in the middle of talking animatedly about that, he suddenly switched direction and interjected almost as an afterthought (but quite craftily, I sensed) the question: "I assume, Oakley, that you would have no objection to going through parachute training?" Though swallowing hard, I of course answered in the affirmative. But I need not have worried. In the end, it all turned out to be beside the point. The IRA was at that time very active in England attacking military camps, and as my parents were Irish born, I have the impression that I was denied the high level of security clearance required for work as an officer in the Intelligence Corps. As a result, I was to end up instead in the Royal Corps of Signals.

Apart from getting off some assignments by virtue of running regularly as a member of the Mons OCS cross-country team, the principal memory that stays with me from Mons concerns our regular, weekly passing-out parades. These occurred on Saturday mornings. They were spectacular affairs presided over by Sergeant-Major Brittain, one of the army's most senior warrant officers and a celebrated figure who, in his time at Mons, is said to have officiated at the passing-out ceremonies of as many as forty thousand cadets. These parades involved several hundred officer cadets and a full regimental band. Brittain was a very large man, possessed of a splendid voice, as mellifluous as it was powerful. His executive commands were as crisp and precise as the prelude was long. "Order-er-er (h) Arms!" he would bellow across the huge parade ground from the perch of the dais on which he stood, and one would hear the simultaneous slap of palms against the wood of the rifles, followed by the crunch of several hundred brass-bound rifle butts hitting the tarmac in well-drilled unison. The level of drill was really very high, our movements were well and finely coordinated, and our final march past the adjutant, who took the salute seated on a splendid white horse, was something to behold. That march past was usually executed to the tune of "The old, grey mare, she ain't what she used to be," and I must confess that it was a bit of a thrill to be part of it all.

The regimen at Catterick Camp up in the North Riding of Yorkshire, where the Royal Signals Officer Cadet School was located, was a good deal less romantic and more businesslike, demanding, and down-to-earth. We had all heard scare stories about the traditional miseries of the first fortnight there as well as the rotten nature of the assault course with which we would have to cope. And it is the memory of those first two weeks along with the last two that lingers clearly in my mind rather than that of what went on in between. The latter was certainly serious stuff, involving extended training in frontline telephonic and wireless communication, training in the erection of more permanent telephone lines (I still cast a nervous eye on the stresses and strains under which telephone poles manage somehow to remain standing in rural New England), and the conduct of ambitious wireless exercises culminating in one triangulated, long-distance effort that linked some of us, camping out uncomfortably in what little is left of Robin Hood's Sherwood Forest near Nottingham, with others operating up near Wallsend at the eastern terminus of Hadrian's Wall and with a third group situated near Bowness at its western terminus. Catterick Camp itself, in my day a huge complex which the Royal Signals shared with a Ghurka battalion, had its own historic connection with Hadrian's Wall. For it was situated on the site of a Roman legionary staging point (Cateractonium) on the military road that connected York (Eboracum), where at various times the VIth and IXth Roman Legions were stationed, with the crucial defensive line which the wall constituted. In winter, Catterick was a truly bleak place, with cold winds from the North Sea sweeping cruelly across the moors. Though I can remember, lying one day near sundown in a ditch during some maneuver when we were awaiting an attack by the "Blue Army," being moved by the sheer beauty of that moorland. Practically everyone suffered from chilblains, and it was common to joke mordantly that the place had almost certainly been better heated two millennia earlier under the Romans than it was in our time.

That may conceivably have been true, but signaling, at least, had improved a good deal since Roman times. The training in wireless and telephonic communication that we were put through was really quite sophisticated, and the fact that it is overshadowed in my memory by the physical demands placed on us in the first and last two weeks of our training is worthy of note. For those physical demands went beyond anything I had encountered either in the infantry as a private soldier or at Mons Officer Cadet School. Could it be that the Royal Corps of Signals, not being itself an infantry force, suffered from some sort of inferiority complex on the macho front and felt the need to compensate by cranking up the physical demands it made on its cadets? During the last couple of weeks prior to commissioning, we were all given some instruction in boxing technique, afforded the experience of some practice bouts in the gym, and then thrown compulsorily into a unit-wide boxing tournament staged (with no protective gear) in front of the entire cadet community as well as the assembled officers and NCOs. Each bout lasted for three rounds, beginning with randomly selected opponents and working up a ladder of competition designed to lead eventually to the identification of a unit champion. I don't know if this was really meant to be some final weed out exercise designed to make sure that we were all really possessed of the ineffable characteristic routinely referred to as "OQ" ("Officer Quality"), a very capacious and accommodating term. But the bouts could turn out to be quite rough. Split lips and facial bruising were common. Tony Hobbs, one of my comrades who was to become a good friend of mine over the course of the following year, had his nose broken within two minutes of stepping into the ring. And, in any case, even if one succeeded in sidestepping a fate that dire, three three-minute rounds could still be quite exhausting. I had found the instruction sessions very helpful and had discovered in the practice bouts that, even if my punches were not very powerful, my arms were long, my reflexes were quick, and my aggressive instincts strong enough at times to generate a flicker of fear in the eyes of opponents—this last was a somewhat corrupting capability. As a result, I had gained some confidence and, in the runoff bouts, did well enough to make it into the semifinals before meeting my comeuppance at the hands of an inelegant brawler. Having kept him at safe distance in the first round but having grown impatient in the second about my failure to land a really telling blow, I made the mistake of mixing it up and allowing him to get in a bit too close, only to be hit on the side of the head so hard as actually to see colored lights. I managed, fortunately, to stay on my feet and to recover enough to see the round out.

But the third round proved as inconclusive as the first, so I lost the bout on points and was out of the final phase of the competition.

If our pre-commissioning training was rounded out with this extended exercise in compulsory masculine bravado, the first fortnight of that training had also been one of marked physicality. Whatever else we had to do during those first two weeks, we had to end each day by making our way, equipped with rifle and backpack, over what was the most challenging assault course I was to encounter in the army. Our performance was timed, and we made our painful way over the series of obstacles dogged by the threat that if anyone in the unit came in over deadline we would all be required to do the whole course again. Enough to concentrate the mind. We had to begin by struggling, hip-deep, across a very cold stream and then continue by running for more than half a mile up a rough and rather steep hill before running on down to the area where the real obstacles began. Being a decent cross-country runner, used to making my way across rough terrain, and knowing that I was not all that well endowed with the upper body strength needed to surmount the obstacles quickly, I always went at the course quite hard at the beginning in order to get ahead of the pack and to leave myself with some extra time to deal with the obstacles. The latter began with an eight-foot wall, which called for us to collaborate in teams of three in order to surmount it, and went on to encompass all the usual miseries: diving headfirst through a window space (we had been taught how to do that safely in order to avoid presenting an inviting silhouette to a putative enemy shooter), crawling painfully through a long, eighteen-inch high, claustrophobia-inducing tunnel, climbing up rigging to cross a stream using a twenty-foot high three-rope bridge, and so on. One ended up breathless, with trembling legs, and with one's clothes and gear so covered with mud that the evenings had to be devoted to cleanup. As the clock ticked down towards the deadline, the same last man would always come in sight, tottering towards the finish, pursued by threats or urgent yells of encouragement from his comrades. It was almost as if he had planned it, for he always managed to finish with no more than a minute or so to spare, and did so with a broad grin and a cocky thumbs-up sign. He was an old Etonian, presumably German by descent, for his name was Fokke, a slim fellow with a milk and roses complexion who was possessed of a robust and mischievous sense of humor. With a name like Fokke, that sense of humor he must have needed at an English boarding school for boys as, indeed, he needed it in the army. One day, we were lined up and standing at attention while a new drill sergeant acquainted himself with us. As he looked down the list of names, nearly all of them standard English, Scots, Welsh, or Irish names, a look of incredulity crossed his face and he barked: "Which of you is Fock?" (his pronunciation). "Here, sarnt," said Fokke. Whereupon the sergeant strode over to him, invading his personal space, standing nose to nose with him in classic drill sergeant fashion and, taking his time, subjected him to a painstaking scrutiny. Finally came the judgment: "Fock," he said disgustedly, "You look like a fuckin' ruptured lettuce!" A not inapt appraisal, to which Fokke, not one to lose his cool, crisply responded: "Yes, sarnt!"

The passing-out parade at our commissioning in May 1956 was by no means as impressive as those grand Mons affairs. But it was preceded by a religious service (Anglican) at St. Martin's Garrison Church at Catterick, an event which, out of a sense of comradeship, I attended. It was a dignified affair at which the chaplain prayed (*inter alia*):

> May the strength of God uphold you, and
> > the power of God preserve you.
> May the wisdom of God instruct you, and
> > the way of God direct you.
> May the hand of God protect you, and
> > the shield of God defend you.
> We ask all this in the name of Him who
> > died in the service of man, our Lord and
> > Saviour, Jesus Christ. Amen.

We cadets then sang a couple of hymns concluding with:

> All praise and thanks to God
> > The Father now be given.
> The Son and Him who reigns,
> > With them in highest Heaven.
> The One Eternal God,
> > Whom earth and Heav'n adore,
> For thus it was, is now,
> > And shall be evermore.

After that, the chaplain sped us on our way, like consecrated medieval knights heading out to the Holy Land, with the exhortation:

> Go forth into the world in peace; be of good courage; hold fast that which is good; render to no men evil for evil; strengthen the fainthearted; support the weak; help the afflicted; honour all men; love and serve the Lord, rejoicing in the power of the Holy Spirit.

With a short leave behind us, we then returned to Catterick for several weeks of (more comfortable) post-commissioning training, and towards the end of that time we received our postings. As was customary at the time, half of our intake was to be posted abroad, the greater number to BAOR in Germany, the rest either to Malaya, where the counterinsurgency campaign was still grinding on though with lessening intensity, or to Cyprus. The latter was now altogether convulsed by the attempt of EOKA, the military wing of the enosis movement, to force union with Greece by a campaign of bombings, ambushes, and other attacks on British military installations and personnel. And before the conclusion of that campaign, more than 360 British personnel were in fact to lose their lives. My own fate, however, was to be given a home posting. This was to my great relief and delight for, by then, I knew that Claire-Ann was going to be able to come over to Europe under the auspices of the Experiment for International Living. Over the summer, she was to live with an Italian family at Cuneo in the Piemontese region of Italy and work on her Italian. But she had waited to apply for postgraduate status at a British university until she was sure that I would still be in the country. In the end, she was admitted by the English Department at the University of Bristol, only about an hour by train from Gloucester where I was to spend the rest of my army service. I was to be stationed, I discovered, at Robinswood Barracks, which one of the squadrons of the UK COMCAN Signal Regiment, along with the regimental headquarter's staff, shared with the Gloucester Regiment (infantry). Robinswood Barracks was simply our home base. Our principal duties lay elsewhere, some fifteen to twenty miles away up in the western Cotswolds where, at a classified site, the central signal center of COMCAN (Commonwealth Communications Army Network) was situated in the only truly modern facility I encountered in the British Army. Standing in about a couple of acres of land and cut off from the surrounding fields by a ten-foot-high chain-link fence, the facility consisted of a large, reinforced concrete monolith, sunk partly into the ground, accessible only through an entrance with heavy steel doors, and possessed of a flat, fifteen-foot thick roof that was allegedly proof against the conventional high-explosive bombs of the day. To the unconcealed delight of the men, who saw it as yet another proof of the incompetence and stupidity of the military, that roof somehow contrived to leak a bit in the aftermath of heavy rains. In addition to various offices, a locked and secured cypher room, and a large room containing the radios (fairly low-powered pieces of apparatus known, if I recall correctly, as E-4s), it housed a large traffic hall with rows of transmitting/receiving stations, each connected to its own large scrambling device capable of providing short-term (twenty-four-hour) security. Those devices were housed in large consoles containing, in one area, elements that heated up enough, as the men quickly discovered, to toast pieces of bread. It need hardly be said that the practice of using these sophisticated pieces of equipment as giant toasters was strongly (but ineffectively) discouraged. At one end of the traffic hall there was a raised walkway leading to a dais on which stood the desk of the duty signal officer (DSO) and which commanded a good view of the entire room. At the other end stood a desk occupied by the senior sergeant on duty.

This complex signal facility, of which the War Office in London (the red and blue shoulder flash of which we wore) was the main substation, functioned as the beating heart of a vast web of radio relay links that spanned much of the globe from Hong Kong to Ottawa and Scotland to Australia. That Commonwealth network was itself integrated, in turn, with the NATO radio network, using the same sophisticated but comparatively straightforward system of station prefixes to direct traffic to its destination. This system made it comparatively easy to originate a signal from an ordinary teleprinter at a small, remote army base and send it via Fontainebleau (still, in those pre–de Gaulle days, NATO headquarters) and a few other relay points to (say) the NATO commander in chief, Allied Forces South Europe, at Naples. Comparatively low-powered wireless transmission equipment was used, with the signal, in that pre-satellite era, being bounced off (reflected down by) the "F," or Appleton, layer of ionization in the earth's upper atmosphere. Under normal daytime conditions it was reliable enough. But with nightfall the Appleton layer shifts somewhat in its height above the earth and, although the (physical) angle of transmitters and receivers would accordingly be adjusted, transmissions sent around that time could often come through in garbled form, with the static causing the printer to stutter, producing a sometimes-unintelligible sequence of letters. Another signaling problem we confronted at that time stemmed from the fact that sunspot activity, following its normal eleven-year cycle, happened to peak around 1955–56, heightening the incidence of garbled transmissions.

We had been taught about none of this at officer cadet school, presumably because the number of National Service officers likely to be assigned to duty with the Commonwealth Communications Army Network was really miniscule. Those of us from my intake at Catterrick who were so assigned were all university graduates, a bit older, therefore, than the majority of the cadets, and were expected, simply, to learn on the job. Some, who had degrees in scientific fields, were assigned to supervise, on rotating shifts, the small group of technical specialists whose job it was to look after the wireless equipment and ensure its smooth operation. When on duty, they themselves were under the operational command of their fellow subalterns serving as duty signal officers (DSOs). It was to the latter role that my friend Tony Hobbs and I were assigned. We, along with two other DSOs, working in rotating shifts around the clock, were charged when on duty with command responsibilities for the actual running of the center's entire signaling operations. Those responsibilities were interesting and sometimes even quite stimulating, especially if one was called upon to figure out the best routing alternatives when poor transmission conditions were making it difficult to get signals through. Interesting and stimulating maybe, but also comparatively weighty. It is, perhaps, testimony to the latter fact that when it came time for us (all second lieutenants) to step down and hand over the responsibilities to our successors, those successors, now that the British Army was embarking on its long transition to a fully professional force, all turned out to hold the rank of major. Whatever else we and our predecessors had done during our period of service, we had saved the British taxpayer from the additional salary expenses that were now to ensue.

The lineage of the Royal Corps of Signals stretched back via the Royal Engineers to the cavalry. As a result, the smaller units that made up regiments were designated as squadrons and troops rather than companies and platoons. The duty signal officers, there were four of us, each commanded what was in effect an expanded or reinforced troop, including a sergeant-major or (more usually) a staff sergeant (equivalent to a master sergeant in the US Army), two other sergeants, five corporals, and about nine lance corporals, with the remainder of the troop being signalmen (private soldiers). In my own troop, all the senior NCOs and a couple of the corporals were regular soldiers, as were about twenty of the total complement of signalmen, and several of them were Irish enlistees from the Republic who, though we didn't think of them as such, were, in fact, foreign mercenaries.

In terms of command structure, we subalterns were subject to a slightly awkward form of dyarchy. While operating the signal center as DSOs, we fell under the authority of the chief duty signals officer (CDSO), a major who was, in effect, our commanding officer while we were on shift. But back at barracks, as troop commanders discharging the normal administrative duties attached to that role in any unit, we were subject to the authority of the officer commanding the squadron, another major, as well as, more immediately, that of his adjutant, a captain. In that role, we had to see to the welfare of our men and the condition of their housing (which we had to inspect regularly to see that it was shipshape); report any complaints about the quality of the food they were getting; make sure that they got enough drilling on the barrack square and were physically fit enough to manage assault courses and ten-mile marches; take them periodically for rifle practice at the shooting range; serve on rotation as camp payroll officer, as orderly officer, mounting and inspecting the guard, or as athletics officer, a job which I got stuck with since I was a runner; and so on. The chain of command did not run from the CDSO to the squadron OC but directly to the colonel commanding the regiment, to whom the OC also reported, but separately. And there was an unfortunate tendency on the part of the OC and adjutant to forget that it was our real purpose to manage efficiently the operation of an important signal center, not to spend all our time on make-work around the barracks. Thus it would happen that men who had been on shift all night, and who needed to get to bed, might be required to stay up to attend a chaplain's hour (where the main topic for discussion seemed to be football results) or that an officer similarly situated would be required to trail down to the South-Western District Headquarters at Taunton in Devon in order to help provide an audience for a lecture given by some itinerant staff officer. Some of those lectures, I should concede, were really pretty good. Senior officers who had made it through Staff College were clearly, intellectually speaking, a cut above our not-very-impressive superior officers in Gloucester. One such turned out to be none other than Glubb Pasha, Lieutenant-General Sir John Bagot Glubb, who, as its commanding officer from 1939 onwards, had led and trained Transjordan's Arab Legion until, in the context of the growing discord in 1956 concerning the status of the Suez Canal and of the serious riots that Nasser had succeeded in fomenting in Amman, King Hussein fired him as a sop to the Arab street. Something of a Lawrence of Arabia figure, he gave a very interesting lecture on the state of Near Eastern politics in the wake of the Suez debacle.

That was the state of affairs that those of us posted to the UK COMCAN Signals Regiment at Gloucester encountered when, after spending a bit of time at the remote transmitter and receiver sites (with huge batteries of aerials situated on high ground in different directions about thirty miles away from the signal center), we arrived at Robinswood Barracks late in the summer of 1956 and settled into the business of taking up our responsibilities and learning our jobs. Thus, rotating week by week through the four different shifts (which tended to wreak havoc at first with sleeping patterns), we gradually learned the routines and challenges of global signaling. We quickly grasped the significance of the various priority designations, from FLASH down through EMERGENCY, OPERATION IMMEDIATE, and so on, as well as the importance attached to the security coding of the various messages. The "language" of transmission was Murray Code, which sounded like prolonged gargling if one listened to it on the radio, but the messages printed out at reception on punched ticker tape. If the message had been transmitted via a twenty-four-hour scrambling device, it had to be channeled on receipt via an identical device or it would print out as a wholly unintelligible garble. "Secret" or "Top Secret" messages had to be formally encrypted and decrypted in secure cypher offices; these printed out in neat columns of five-letter groups (the men always referred to them as "groupers"). Our own cypher office, which none of us subalterns had the requisite level of security clearance even to enter, was presided over by a captain who reported directly to the CDSO. When, because of bad transmission conditions, we were having difficulty in getting a message through, the DSO had to work out the best alternative route, usually via the RAF or Royal Navy Networks, with the latter being more effective because the Navy used high-speed Morse code. If those alternative routings did not work and the message had a high priority but was UNCLASSIFIED, we would finally ship it over for delivery to Imperial Cable and Wireless. But if it was classified, our only remaining recourse was to ask Oakley Farm (sic!) at Cheltenham to deliver it, which, mysteriously, they always seemed able to do. We all assumed that Oakley Farm was the headquarters of the Foreign Office's radio network. Only later on, in the 1970s when, as a result of some serious breach of security, Oakley Farm put in an appearance on American TV, did I discover that it was in fact GCHQ (Government Communications Headquarters), the British intelligence agency that, among other things, serves the needs of MI5, the security/counterespionage service, and MI6, the Secret Intelligence Service that deals with clandestine operations overseas—none other than James Bond's fictional territory. Because of the time of day when they were characteristically sent (around nightfall when the Appleton layer was shifting), we frequently had difficulty with messages transmitted to us OPERATION IMMEDIATE from Ottawa. They usually listed the Ontario football results and were something of a nuisance because they were nearly always punctuated by garbles in the names of the various teams. They were being sent, I assume, as a morale booster for the Canadian soldiers serving at that time, along with their Indian and Polish equivalents, as monitors for the Indochina Truce Commission along the line dividing North Vietnam from South Vietnam that ran through the Demilitarized Zone. We routed them for onward dispatch to the Indian Army via the COMCAN station in New Delhi. Having lived in Ontario, I could often recognize through the garbles (and reconstitute) names like Guelph, Kitchener, Hamilton, Sudbury, Oshawa, Timmins, and so on, thereby saving my men the trouble of having repeatedly to request retransmission from Ottawa of partly unintelligible messages. I gained in their eyes, accordingly, the wholly unwarranted reputation of being a clever sort of a chap.

Throughout that late summer and early autumn period when I was working hard to get on top of my new responsibilities, I also had other (and happier) things on my mind. In early September, Claire-Ann had finally made it to England and stayed, on a temporary basis, in a professional women's residence on Cheyne Walk in Chelsea. It was on the site, I believe, of Sir Thomas More's house four centuries earlier, and round the corner, of all things, from Oakley Street. When I was able, by virtue of doing double shifts, to get a weekend off and make my way to London, I met her, and against all odds, more than a year after we had parted so emotionally on the St. Lawrence off Québec. The moment was a truly wonderful one, marked, despite the passage of time, by no awkwardness or reserve. We reconnected as if we had never been separated and, before I had reluctantly to report back at Gloucester, spent a blissful weekend staying with Lol and Suzanne O'Keeffe in Blackheath. We met thereafter, and right through the following academic year, occasionally in Gloucester or London, but more often in Bristol. There, she was comfortably ensconced, along with two English students, as a "paying guest" in digs just across Brunel's elegant Clifton Suspension Bridge spanning the Avon Gorge, close to Clifton College, and within easy walking distance across the bridge from Bristol University. She settled in quickly and happily, not only to life in England, but also to a course of postgraduate study in Italian and English literature, with a focus especially on Anglo-Saxon literature and Shakespeare. By dint of an arrangement with my friend, comrade, and fellow DSO, Tony Hobbs, I was able to get to Bristol almost every other weekend and spend most of Saturday and Sunday with her. He and I filled in for each other by doing double shifts on alternate weekends, which enabled him to get to London to see his fiancée, Truda, a lovely girl from a Dutch family settled in England. The only real drawback to this arrangement was the fact that I would often arrive in Bristol having been up all night. More than once, when we were sitting in the warmth and comfort of the evening, taking in a play at the Bristol Old Vic, a first-rate repertory theatre, Claire-Ann would have to nudge me repeatedly to keep me awake. And sometimes to no avail. One evening her nudgings were not enough to keep me waiting during what I understand was a fine production of Becket's comparatively new play, *Waiting for Godot*.

Though neither of us had much disposable income, we had a wonderfully enjoyable year. Bristol itself is an interesting and attractive city, not far from Bath, and the South West corner of England is replete with beautiful medieval churches, old stately homes, and other tourist attractions (like the Cheddar Gorge), less heavily frequented then than they came to be later on. We usually used our time to travel cheaply by bus to visit one or another of those attractions—it didn't really matter what it was. Whatever it was, it was mainly an occasion to be together and endlessly to talk. One such trip stands out in my memory, though for an odd reason. We had gone up to see Tewkesbury Abbey and the "bloody field of Tewkesbury" where, during the Wars of the Roses, Edward IV, with the support of the future Richard III, had inflicted a decisive defeat on Lancastrian forces. The "bloody field" itself—or what had been spared of it by modern housing sprawl—did not prove to be particularly memorable. It was not much bigger, in fact, than the meadow in Williamstown, Massachusetts, in which we were later to build the house in which we still live. It was hard to envisage an alleged nine thousand men being locked in mortal combat in so confined an area. But if the battle site itself didn't prove memorable, Claire-Ann's unabashed and commonsensical approach to eating what you paid for did. We had had a very nice afternoon tea in a neighboring hostelry when, noting that we hadn't demolished all the cakes and pastries served, she calmly wrapped in a napkin those that were left and put them in her tote for later consumption. Perfectly acceptable behavior in North America but my instant reaction was one of embarrassment. And that brought home to me the fact that, my time across the Atlantic notwithstanding, I had already slipped back into the embrace of more genteel and inhibited English norms of public behavior.

For me, then, that 1956–57 academic year involved an alternation between the steady and sometimes quite demanding grind of work as a DSO at the signal center and a troop commander at Robinswood Barracks and the happy and blissfully civilized time I was able to spend with Claire-Ann at Bristol or elsewhere. To the latter I will return later. So far as the military side of the equation went, three decidedly non-routine episodes may serve to convey some of its flavor. The first was really international, indeed, in its political ramifications, although for a couple of days it threatened to derail my personal life. The second was more purely personal. The third fell somewhere between the other two.

From the time of my arrival at the UK COMCAN signal center, we had found ourselves handling, with enough frequency to attract attention, signal traffic that referred to "Operation Musketeer" and often involved the transfer of various military specialists. While we, in our innocence, had assumed that it referred to some aspect of the annual NATO maneuvers in Germany, Operation Musketeer was eventually revealed to be the code word for the planned attack on Egypt by British and French forces in a vain attempt to put an end to the crisis precipitated by Gamal Abdel Nasser's nationalization/seizure of the Suez Canal in the wake of the American withdrawal of financing for his cherished Aswan High Dam project. On that front, we should have been quicker off the mark. For a good two months before the attack was launched (on October 29, 1956), convoys of desert-camouflaged military vehicles had been stopping at Robinswood Barracks for refueling as they made their way down to ports along the south coast. It was clear that something big was afoot. And yet I myself found it hard to believe that the prime minister, Anthony Eden, would commit the nation to so unwarranted and foolhardy a venture. In that, however, I was of course wrong. In the 1930s, Eden had needed to deal with the volatility of a Mussolini who failed to abide by his international agreements, and it was with Mussolini that he was tempted to align a similarly unreliable Nasser. At the time, the bulk of Europe's oil supply was still shipped through the canal and he saw Nasser as posing a potential threat to that supply line. For him, then, the canal simply had to be returned to Anglo-French management, and, beyond that, historians now tell us he was determined that Nasser had to go. There was a sense, then, as the huge banner headline carried by the *Daily Mirror* trumpeted, that this was, indeed, EDEN'S WAR. But Eden deluded himself about the willingness of the Americans to take a hands-off attitude while the British and French launched a military strike against Egypt. Whether or not any credence should be given to those revisionist historians who have since argued that there were sound geopolitical grounds for Eden's decision remains unclear. What is clear is that his decision brought to an end, not only Eden's own political career, but also Britain's position as the dominant power in the Middle East, as well as the ability of Britain and France, as fast-fading imperial powers, to throw their independent military weight around in the global arena.

For Britain there was a sense that, after 1945, the "big" war had never quite come to a definitive end but had dribbled off, instead, into a succession of smaller wars, conflicts, or skirmishes—Greece, Korea, Kenya, Malaya, Cyprus, Aden, and later on, of course, the Falklands and the grinding and prolonged struggle in Northern Ireland. If the big war had ended, peacetime never quite became what it was supposed to be. Certainly, throughout my time at COMCAN we were handling a steady trickle of casualty reports coming in from one miserable colonial conflict or another and such reports were so common as not to be seen as exceptional or as cause for comment. The only special attention given to them was that of ensuring they were cleared with minimum delay in order to avoid having the next of kin hear the sad news for the first time via the newspapers. But the Suez War, short though it was, was a good deal more than a skirmish. Even apart from the 175,000 troops the Israelis threw into action in the Sinai, the British and French assault on Port Said and the Canal Zone, which was preceded by a devastating period of Anglo-French bombing, involved the deployment of some 80,000 ground troops. And even if one brackets the civilian casualties for which there are no good estimates, the casualties sustained by the combatant forces (Egyptian, British, French) in the course of what was no more than a ten-day war (October 29–November 7) exceeded five thousand, with fatalities coming to at least two thousand. For those of us ensconced in our bomb-proof signal center up in the Cotswolds and beyond the reach of any conceivable enemy action, it was still a time of considerable pressure. The amount of signal traffic to be handled more than doubled, with messages bearing the arresting FLASH (top priority) designation coming through at the rate of about one an hour, whereas under more normal circumstances we could expect no more than one or two a month. Ours being a radio-relay system, standing orders required the DSO on duty to handle all such messages personally, recording and initialing in the log the times of receipt and retransmission. And, on top of that, we had to cope with nervous, deskbound staff officers at the War Office badgering us with telephone calls to assure themselves that the flood of signals they were sending for transmission to the Royal Navy Communications vessel anchored off Port Said had indeed been cleared with minimum delay.

Apart from the high incidence of sunspot activity in that period, other complications ensued. The NATO radio transmission system had been designed on the assumption that the Allies would be acting in unison against some common threat. It had not been envisaged that one or two might go it alone as the British and French had now done. The American military, therefore, cut off all communications with us, while the French used (or abused) our direct telegraphic link to send their signal traffic via NATO headquarters in Fontainebleau for transmission onward to Port Said. My men were interested in the unusual business of handling signals that printed out in French, and when we received a long, windy, and badly processed signal containing a speech by the then French prime minister, Guy Mollet, exhorting his paratroops to battle, they were curious enough about what it said to ask me to translate it. When I did, they reacted of course (it was of the "Courage mes enfants!" genre) with the same requisite measure of soldierly cynicism and disdain as, I suspect, his paratroopers did. Even for one who viewed the whole adventure as fundamentally wrong and misguided, which I did, the effect of all this high-pressured activity was, I am afraid to admit, quite invigorating. We were privy to the unfolding of events a good two days before the news became public, and as we followed the slow-moving progress of the merchant ships transporting the heavy equipment to the newly opened front, we got a vivid sense of the logistical challenges with which the British armed forces of the day were confronted. Sixty years later, I am not sure I can trust my memory on so specific a point, but I retain the distinct impression that those ships were still steaming along slowly somewhere *west* of Malta when hostilities were terminated. And in those frantically busy ten days I did get a sort of shamefaced appreciation for just how exciting involvement in a war can be—always provided, of course, that one's role keeps one at safe distance from the front lines.

Given the fact that most of the men and junior officers were comparatively inexperienced conscripts as well as the fact that the regular senior NCOs, a critical group in any military operation, were themselves of uneven quality, having the signaling side of this particular operation go off as efficiently as it did, with no notable mistakes made, was, after the event, cause as much for surprise as pride. There were, I think, only two untoward moments. The first was one that had some of our senior colleagues trembling for their careers. The British forces operating now in Egypt and its environs had come close to running out of functioning signal scrambling equipment of the type we used, so half a dozen of those large, rather cumbersome devices had been sent under heavy guard for shipment onwards by the RAF. But, instead of arriving, they simply vanished. Within days, investigators from MI5, the British counterespionage wing, had arrived in Gloucester to find out what had happened. This was a most unusual intrusion into Royal Signals affairs, and certainly one that no CDSO would want to see happening on his watch. Fortunately, in what was, it seems, a classic instance of interservice bungling, the RAF proved to be at fault. The devices were tracked down in Cyprus, found stacked at the edge of the RAF base in Nicosia, and, despite the day-to-day threat posed by EOKA, left unguarded. "Some sort of army junk," I can imagine a superior RAF type saying dismissively. "Just leave it there for the time being!" The second untoward incident was of a different type and came much closer to home. During the course of the Suez conflict I was due to spend a weekend in Bristol with Claire-Ann but had to call her at the last minute with the sad message that we had all, because of the emergency and not surprisingly, been confined to camp. I had also to tell her, more alarmingly, that some of us had been put on standby for shipping to Egypt, where some of our senior colleagues were already in place. In the event, the rapid, UN-brokered ceasefire precluded any need for that. But I have often since wondered what would have happened to the two of us if, after such a struggle to get together, we had been separated once more and I had been stuck, possibly for months, in the eastern Mediterranean.

The second episode I wish to mention is very different in nature and is of interest in that it affords something of a window into the operation of the army's system of justice, at least the system I encountered in the mid-1950s. Early in May 1957, just after I had begun a week of duty as DSO on the night shift, I was informed by the OC at Robinswood Barracks that I was to serve as defending officer at a forthcoming district court martial on camp. It had been convened to try a signalman in my troop. In a barrack-room altercation, he had not only used insubordinate language when the corporal in charge of the hut had ordered him to help get it ready for an upcoming inspection but had also punched the said corporal, breaking his nose. The signalman, a surly and resentful fellow, was a regular soldier; the corporal, a sober, serious, and reliable fellow— probably, in fact, my best corporal—was a National Serviceman. As was the normal procedure in such cases, a board or court of inquiry had been held on camp to try to ascertain the pertinent facts, and the summary of evidence taken by that board had been forwarded for appraisal by the legal branch at South-Western District Headquarters in Taunton. Had the lawyers there not found that the case warranted trial by court martial and that the evidence was likely to hold up in court, the accused would have been remanded to the OC for summary disciplinary action involving less severe penalties than those available to a court martial. In the event, the brigadier commanding the district had ordered the convening of a district court martial at which I was to be the defending officer and the adjutant, a captain, the prosecuting officer.

I still have a copy of the convening order and am puzzled by it on two grounds. First, because it lists as the president or presiding officer a major from an infantry regiment, with two other officers, a captain and a lieutenant, from neighboring units serving as the "Members of the Court." So far as legal expertise went, all were laymen. Some change must subsequently have been made, for the presiding officer turned out to be, in fact, a judge advocate (i.e., lawyer) with the rank of colonel. Second, the convening order is dated as having been issued only three days before the court martial was to take place, which would have given me minimal time to prepare a case. It is possible that I was tipped off earlier that a convening order was about to be issued. But, after almost sixty years, I simply can't remember if that was so. What I do remember is that the whole thing, given my other regular duties, involved something of a scramble.

Having, while on night duty, carefully perused the two pertinent law books, the *Army Act* and the *Queen's Regulations*, and gone over the summary of evidence in which, despite exculpatory protestations, the accused had succeeded in painting himself into something of a corner, I found myself with one important issue to check out as best I could. *Queen's Regulations* had, I discovered, a Miranda-like provision to protect those accused of an offense against witless self-incrimination. Before answering questions put to him at a court of inquiry, the accused had to be advised of his rights. But, when I interviewed this particular accused, he insisted that he had not been so advised. On the other hand, the officer who had presided over the court of inquiry (a captain on the staff at regimental headquarters) said that he had. But, when I put the question to him, he had responded in a somewhat hesitant and startled fashion. The regimental police who had been present when the accused was questioned could not remember his being advised of his rights, but they also couldn't swear to the fact that he hadn't. They seemed to have lapsed into some sort of coma during the whole proceeding. I was left, then, in doubt about the matter. The defendant had his rights and they should properly be vindicated. And the only way to make sure that they were was to have the matter adjudicated at the court martial itself. So, in order to ensure that that would happen, I indicated in advance that I would be pleading the defendant "not guilty" on the more serious charge against him, that of striking a superior officer.

I don't know how many district courts martial had been held at Robinswood Barracks within living memory, but it seemed that at none of them had a "not guilty" plea been turned in. That meant that all the prosecuting officer normally had to do was to lay out the evidence, with the sole duty of the defending officer being that of entering a plea in mitigation of sentence. My move, accordingly, which meant that the prosecuting officer would have to overcome a challenge to his case, stirred up a bit of a hornet's nest. The next day, when I had breakfasted after a night's duty as DSO and was about to go to bed, I received an order to report to the OC. It was a "boots and gaiters" order, which usually signaled that not only was one to dress in formal parade-ground style but also that one was in for some sort of dressing-down. When I turned up and saluted, the OC asked me to confirm that I was pleading the signalman not guilty. When I did so, he looked at me searchingly and said: "Oakley, I do hope you know what you are doing. Charles is very upset." "Charles" was the prosecuting officer and, being our adjutant, was in a good position to make my life utterly miserable during my remaining months of service. With that, I was dismissed. While the OC's admonitory remarks could be interpreted, I suppose, as an illicit intrusion into the course of justice, I was more concerned about the threat Charles could pose should he lose the case (with concomitant loss of face) and the defendant be acquitted. But there was nothing to be done about that now.

Fortunately for me, though not for the wretched accused, I was the one who lost the case and the adjutant, despite the trouble I had given him, proved, in the glow of victory, to be quite magnanimous in his attitude towards me. When the court convened, I was struck by how dauntingly formal and impressive an occasion it was. All of us, the president and members of the court, the adjutant and I, were in full-dress uniform, with those who had decorations wearing them. When he was marched in, however, the accused was in those surroundings a somewhat diminished figure. Deprived of his webbing belt and his beret, both of which had metal attachments which soldiers sometimes sharpened for use as weapons in brawls, he was not his normal cocky and truculent self. And I could see that he was taken aback by the solemnity and formality of the occasion. While I had decided that he would not make a good witness in his own defense on the substance of the charges, I had no choice about putting him on the stand on the procedural matter at stake. This was adjudicated in a sort of trial within a trial by the presiding officer alone and in the absence (if I remember correctly) of the other two members of the court. In response to my questioning, the accused swore that he had not, before testifying at the court of inquiry, been advised of his rights. Then the prosecuting officer cross-examined him and did so to devastating effect, tripping him up on factual matters, getting him to contradict himself, exposing his testimony as unreliable, and leading to the conclusion (probably correct) that he was simply lying. That, certainly, was the conclusion that the presiding officer drew, for he dismissed my procedural complaint and the trial on the substance of the charges then proceeded to its predictable conclusion. For the defense, it was downhill all the way. During cross-examination, I did my best to rattle the corporal who had had his nose broken, and to suggest that as senior rank present during the altercation he had permitted things to get out of hand, allowing the distinction between ranks to be obscured by argument rather than underlined by action. But to no avail. He proved to be a good, steady, believable witness, and it is not surprising that the court found the defendant guilty as charged. All that was left for me to do then was to submit the (rather strained) plea in mitigation of sentence that I had already drafted. I don't know if any such mitigation occurred, the less so in that the defendant by no means had a clean conduct record. All I know is that he was sentenced to 110 days in the military prison at Colchester, a place known to soldiers as "the Glass House" and possessed of the reputation of being a bit of a hellhole. Knowing the two parties involved and after what came out in the trial, I had little doubt that justice had been done. But I was left with the chastened and somewhat disillusioned realization that, at the district level at least, courts martial seemed to be basically liturgical affairs, proceeding to their preordained conclusion, with the defending officer's assigned role being simply that of pleading the defendant guilty and entering some sort of plea in mitigation of sentence. At that level, at least, there was something of a distressingly precooked feel to the whole process.

The third episode which is, I think, worth alluding to dates to the winter of 1956–57 and is different again. While it could have had a very serious outcome, it did not, and it lingers on in my memory under the rubric of the comic and bizarre. In Britain, the 1950s, in common with the late 1930s, were marked by a recrudescence of IRA activity. This time what was involved was not a bombing campaign against civilian targets but a series of surprise attacks on military installations, the objective being the seizure of weapons and ammunition for use in other attempts to weaken the British hold on Northern Ireland. With the exception of that latter province, the Britain of the time was an essentially peaceful country; the police, locally controlled, were not equipped with firearms, and the guards mounted at military installations, while parading around with rifles and bayonets, were not customarily issued with ammunition. The IRA was well aware of that practice and had more than once taken advantage of it. As a result, things were eventually to change. Flying into Manchester Airport in the early 1980s and at the peak of the renewed troubles in Northern Ireland, I was taken aback to see two uniformed policemen patrolling the concourse armed with submachine guns. It was not the England I remembered from the 1950s, though, even then, in the wake of the first IRA raids on military installations and under specifically threatening circumstances, guards were sometimes mounted with loaded weapons. Even on such occasions, however, the rules governing the actual use of those weapons were so restrictive in legal terms that, if a weapon were discharged, the threat of prosecution would loom large for the soldier concerned.

Such was the background to the episode in question. It occurred when I was on duty during a Friday-Saturday double shift. When I arrived, my friend and comrade in arms, Tony Hobbs, was wrapping up his shift and preparing to head off for the weekend to see Truda. As we went through the routine handover, I discovered that this time it was not altogether routine. With an "Oh, by the way," Tony pointed—rather gleefully, I thought—to a message lying on the desk. It was, of all things, from Scotland Yard, and it was alerting us to the fact that they had acquired intelligence, which they viewed as reliable, to the effect that our COM-CAN signal center might well be the target of an IRA attack that coming night. To me, that didn't seem too likely a possibility. While we might be a good target for purely propaganda purposes, we were not the repository of a large amount of weaponry. That was held, rather, in the armory at Robinswood Barracks. And, in any case, situated as we were at a remote, occluded rural site at the end of a tangle of minor roadways, we would be pretty hard to find. But, clearly, none of that could be taken for granted. We needed to take appropriate steps to beat off such an attack in the unlikely event of its taking place. So I unchained and unlocked our little emergency armory. It was just a trunk containing 12 Lee-Enfield rifles and 120 rounds of 303 ammunition, 10 for the magazine of each rifle. For the officer in command, there was a Webley service revolver along with 6 rounds but, inexplicably, no holster to carry it in. I had my staff sergeant work out a guard roster so that eight men would be standing guard outside at all times through the evening and night and on until dawn, with another four on standby in an improvised guardroom inside. The eight men outside were organized into two details of four, each led by a sergeant or corporal, and posted in the roof emplacements that existed at opposite corners of the building, thus affording a 360° view of the entire compound and of the illuminated perimeter fence. The men were all signalmen, not habituated like their infantry counterparts to the daily handling of weaponry. Mindful, then, of the potential for accidents, I had them, in accordance with a drill they had all learned in basic training, load the rifle magazines with 10 rounds each and then detach them and put them in their pockets. If events so dictated, those magazines could be slammed into place in an instant and, with a quick bolt action, the first round chambered. As for me, with no holster, I had to carry that heavy, loaded revolver somewhat apprehensively in my greatcoat pocket. The safety catch was on, of course, but had I been more accustomed to dealing with handguns, I would have taken the extra safety precaution of loading only five bullets, leaving empty the first chamber under the hammer. But at the time, that thought never occurred to me.

That done, we got on with our regular duties inside the signal center, handling the flow of traffic. Within, it was very much business as usual. Not so, outside. There, as the evening wore on, something of a fog developed and it became impossible to see the fields that lay beyond the floodlit perimeter fence, though one could hear, from beyond, the forlorn bleating of invisible sheep. Perhaps because of those changed conditions, I found, while making my periodic rounds outside, that the mood of the men on guard had undergone something of a shift. At the start, they had viewed the whole business as a bit of a lark, a welcome break from the dullness of routine. But as evening was overtaken by night and the compound was reduced in eerie fashion to an isolated, fogbound island, they began to betray occasional signs of nervousness. At one seemingly critical point, nervousness was indeed warranted. It was at the witching hour shortly after midnight. At that point, while at my desk inside and engaged in normal signal-related work, I received an urgent call from the regimental policeman at the gate, informing me that something was happening out of sight down the road. I went up, loaded revolver uneasily in pocket, to join him at the gate, noting that the guards on that side of the roof were covering the area in question with their weapons. And, sure enough, though we could still see nothing at all, we could hear, rising above the soft murmuring of sheep, the sound of a voice or voices. The words being spoken were at first undistinguishable. But as we strained our ears it eventually became clear that what we were hearing was a string of obscenities of the "Fuck!" "fuck!" "fucking hell!" variety. Then from the fog on the road leading up to the gate a wraithlike figure clad entirely in white slowly detached itself. Clearly confused and bewildered by what he was encountering and paying no attention to the rather frantic instructions given him (he, of course, knew nothing about our IRA-related state of high alert), the figure in question was in real danger of getting himself inadvertently shot. Having been yelled at by the guards to halt at once and identify himself, he was alarmingly slow to do so. Finally, having come to a grumbling stop, he responded, but not without asperity. What was all the bloody fuss about? he asked. Who the fuck did we think he was? He was the bloody cook, of course. It was not his choice to be there. He was just the poor bugger stuck with the job of bringing out the bloody night meal from the Robinswood Barracks cookhouse. Didn't we fuckers want it? And so on. The dialogue that ensued was less than immortal. As we eventually learned, he had been confused by the fog, missed a sharp bend in the nearby road, put two wheels of his light truck over the edge of a shallow ditch, and was now stuck in the mud, the truck canting over at an angle and the meal, contained in a large cauldron, beginning to slop over onto the floor. It was a real mess. Having first ascertained that he was indeed the person he claimed to be (in previous incidents that year and the year before, the IRA had resorted successfully to some tricky subterfuges, even placing one of their own as a recruit in one camp they eventually attacked), we accompanied him back to the truck and managed to manhandle it back onto the road and into the compound, and saved the bulk of the meal.

That, happily, was the most untoward occurrence that night. We kept up our guard until dawn but the IRA never put in an appearance. Either Scotland Yard's intelligence was faulty or the lads of the IRA had got lost as they tried to find their way through fogbound rural idiocy. I'd prefer to think that the latter was the case and to imagine a scenario in which they ended up drinking stout in the warm snug of a cozy Cotswolds pub, singing maudlin Irish nationalist songs and shedding the while a fugitive tear into their cups in memory of the heroic but doomed patriots of yesteryear:

> When all beside a vigil keep,
> The West's asleep, the West's asleep—
> Alas! and well may Erin weep,
> When Connaught lies in slumber deep.
> There lakes and plain smile fair and free,
> 'Mid rocks their guardian chivalry—
> Sing, oh! let man learn liberty
> From crashing wind and lashing sea.

> That chainless wave and lovely land,
> Freedom and nationhood demand—
> Be sure the great God never planned,
> For slumbering slaves, a home so grand.
> And, long a brave and haughty race
> Honoured and sentinelled the place—
> Sing oh! not e'en their sons' disgrace
> Can quite destroy their glory's trace.

> And if, when all a vigil keep,
> The West's asleep, the West's asleep—

Alas! and well may Erin weep,
That Connaught lies in slumber deep.
But, hark! some voice like thunder spake,
"The West's awake! the West's awake!"
Sing, oh, hurra! let England quake,
We'll watch till death for Erin's sake.

One last thing—knowing that I won't be believed, I've dithered to and fro about even mentioning it. The meal that the cook nearly got himself shot trying to deliver. What, after all, was it? Nothing other, in improbable fact, than IRISH STEW.

CHAPTER NINE

Lux et veritas

The conditions of life enjoyed by a junior officer at Robinswood Barracks, while not elegant—we lived in army-style huts—were not at all bad. I had a batman who made the bed, saw to it that my room was clean, and kept my uniform pressed, brasses polished, and boots well shone. The officer's mess itself was a reasonably comfortable place, our regular fare was quite decent, and on ceremonial occasions the fare was really pretty good. Two such occasions stick in my mind. The first was a New Year's dance. Claire-Ann, newly returned from spending Christmas with her Italian "family" in Cuneo and wearing a very fetching red dress was, I proudly thought, the belle of the ball and certainly boosted my reputation among my fellow officers. The second was a particularly elaborate regimental dinner, graced by a small military band which, among other things, played a few bars of the national anthem immediately after the proposing of each toast. The routine on such occasions was firmly fixed by tradition. Full-dress uniform was the order of the evening; the regimental silver was displayed on the table, though it was nothing in comparison with that of the Loyal Regiment in Preston (which I had glimpsed as a private soldier when I had to wash dishes on a similar occasion); and we were seated down the long dining table in order of rank, with the colonel of the regiment presiding at the head in his capacity as president of the dinner and the most junior subaltern (Mr. Vice) seated at the foot, serving by tradition as vice president. The rest of us subalterns were clustered around him along the lower reaches of the table. After the dishes were cleared, port glasses put out, and decanters placed before president and vice president and moved around in clockwise direction so that all could fill their glasses, the colonel rose to his feet and said "Mr. Vice, the Queen." Whereupon Mr. Vice in turn rose to his feet, raised his glass, and said "Gentlemen, the Queen." To which, having risen to their feet and raised their glasses, all said "The Queen" and drank. After a few (deafening) bars from the band, all sat down again, only to be raised to their feet by the second toast. "Mr. Vice," the president said, "our colonel in chief." Whereupon Mr. Vice, having risen to his feet, proposed the toast: "Gentlemen, the Princess Royal." To which, on our feet and before taking a sip, we would all respond by saying "The Princess Royal." After another few deafening bars, we were again reseated. But at the National Service subalterns' end of the table, and as at all such dinners, an informal ritual invariably unfolded. In accordance with a tradition handed down from time immemorial by our predecessors in rank and status, our glasses were raised no more than an inch from the table and we murmured *sotto voce* the National Serviceman's toast: "FTA" ("Fuck the Army!").

Such expressions of contempt for the military were, of course, *de rigueur* for those of us who were not professional soldiers and who were obsessively counting the days remaining before our demobilization, release from compulsory servitude, and recovery of the lost freedoms of civilian life. But if pressed later on, I suspect that we would all, though with differing degrees of reluctance, have been forced to confess that we had learned a great deal from our period of required service. And not just about the intricacies of global signaling and the like. The more important lessons lay elsewhere: in the responsibilities we had had to discharge; in what we had learned about our fellow countrymen in all their variety; about our own behavior and the behavior of men in general when thrown together with others under unpromising circumstances; about duty, the danger of irresponsibility, human decency and compassion, and the value of comradeship; and above all about ourselves, our good and bad qualities, our strengths and our weaknesses, our hopes and our fears. As a sixth-former at school, I had not been one of those whom the headmaster had chosen as a prefect and I had concluded, accordingly, that I must be altogether lacking in any sort of leadership potential. At officer cadet school, however, and later on when discharging my responsibilities at Gloucester, I learned that I was not quite as hopeless in those respects as I had gloomily concluded in the past. I was not deficient, I discovered, in powers of command. I was not uncomfortable with taking on responsibility. Taking charge carried with it no great terrors; it was clearly preferable to following somebody else's trumpet, especially so if that trumpet was an uncertain one. I was perfectly capable of being decisive, even crisply so, should the circumstances call for it. Perhaps more important, I had also learned that I took satisfaction in what, for better or worse, I would call the pastoral care and feeding of a group of men, some of them much older than I was. I tried to listen carefully and to think clearly in offering counsel when they brought to me their personal problems (a not-infrequent occurrence), often quite intricate in nature and calling really for the services of the solicitor whom they couldn't afford, and occasionally, given the chaos that seemed to have overtaken some of their personal lives, really quite poignant. It was all, for me, powerfully educative—about others, of course, but also about myself. Certainly, in the absence of that maturing experience, I very much doubt now that I would have been inclined later on to take on the sort of responsibilities involved in academic administration.

But such thoughts, of course, came along much later—the fruit, if you wish, of a species of emotion recollected in quasi-tranquility. At the time, as the winter of 1956–57 wore on, my thoughts and those of Claire-Ann were fixed on things more proximate, on our immediate futures, both individual and collective. For me, the default position was to follow the path I had mapped out before going to Canada: to return to Oxford and take up the Senior Scholarship that would see me through to the completion of a DPhil under the supervision of E. F. Jacob, something I thought I could do in two years. And that would have been fine by Claire-Ann, who had settled in to England and adjusted to English mores really quite happily. The problem, however, was "What then?" At the time, there seemed to be hardly any academic job openings in Britain and neither at Oxford nor later on at Yale did anyone seem conscious of the fact that the arrival of the baby boom generation at college age would almost certainly trigger a very significant expansion in the number of university places and, concomitantly, in the number of academic job openings. We wanted to get married and I was not enamored of the prospect of having to piece together a series of part-time tutorial jobs as I had seen others at Oxford having to do in order to make some sort of a hand-to-mouth living. Claire-Ann, moreover, had her own challenges. She wanted to teach school but, as she lacked British teaching certification, the public sector there would be closed to her and she would have to limit her job search to private schools. The latter might, conceivably, have worked out. Certainly, having submitted an application, she had initial success with a very good interview at Cheltenham Ladies College and was on the cusp of accepting a job there when we finally decided to pursue our futures in the United States.

That option we had been careful to keep open. Knowing that it was a long and convoluted process, I had begun, quite early, the application process for permanent resident status in the United States, which carried with it the "green card" that permitted one to work there. I had also done my best to investigate the current academic job status across the Atlantic. It wasn't particularly encouraging, but I concluded that I would probably be able to get a full-time job if I had a PhD, if only at some small and undistinguished college. I also concluded that, if I wished to pursue an academic career in the States, I would do well to finish my PhD work at an American graduate school and benefit from the job placement service it would provide. Being becalmed in an out-of-the-way military camp, it was difficult for me to find out much about a broad range of American graduate schools, so, wanting to graduate from a first-rate, high-profile institution, I had applied, with a singular lack of imagination, for graduate fellowships at Harvard and Yale. To my surprise and delight, both universities came through with decently funded fellowships. Meanwhile, Claire-Ann had learned that, because of the swelling of enrollments at American schools induced by the baby boom and the concomitant shortage of teachers, a fast-track certification route had been opened up for those who had graduated from a university or college with a degree in the liberal arts (that is, arts and sciences). All it involved was the completion of a summer certification program specifically tailored to their needs at a state university or state teacher's college. With that certification in hand, one could then apply for teaching jobs in the hard-pressed public sector.

Within the period of three weeks that we were given to respond to the Harvard and Yale offers, we had to make some fundamental and life-changing decisions. And that we did. The big one was for both of us to pursue our careers in America rather than England. The lesser one was for me to go to Yale rather than Harvard, even though I was familiar with the latter. I wish I could claim that I did so because the Yale motto (*Lux et veritas*) promised light as well as the truth signaled by its Harvard equivalent (*Veritas*). But the fact was that I could not afford to do otherwise. The Yale fellowship was worth $200 more than the Harvard one, at that time a not-inconsiderable sum of money. With our immediate futures now beginning to crystallize, the time seemed ripe for us to become formally engaged. Not that there was any need for earnest talk about "commitment" or formal proposals on either of our parts. We had long since slipped insensibly into the conclusion that we would be spending our lives together, as, indeed, we have for almost sixty years now. But because Claire-Ann's parents didn't know me, and because her mother had earlier needled her about "chasing off" to Europe after a boyfriend, we felt that I should write to her father asking formally, in good Victorian fashion, for the hand of his eldest daughter in marriage. And that I did. His (or, rather, their) response was warmly welcoming and reassuring. The reaction of my own parents, however, when I told them that I was getting engaged and going to Yale was less accommodating. The issue with them, I think, was less my choice of bride than the fact that I would be leaving again for the New World, this time for good. When I brought Claire-Ann up to Liverpool to meet them, it was not a happy occasion. While my father was fine and Noel was very welcoming, my mother and my sister Molly were, both of them, rather cool in the reception they gave her. Claire-Ann handled the situation with her characteristic aplomb, but I could not help feeling extremely upset and furious. My mother, after all, had left home at the tender age of fifteen, and she had married and moved away to England when she was just about my age. Why, I thought, and not without resentment, could she not accept the fact that her youngest son was about to do much the same thing? Why couldn't she let go gracefully? Why the need to indulge the temptation of unloading on him what in later parlance would be called a "guilt trip?"

Whatever the case, the last few months of my army service seemed to go by very quickly. I have a jumble of memories, some of them, doubtless, going back a bit earlier and most relating to duties on rotation as orderly officer. Thus I can remember having to go to the Gloucester Magistrate's Court on a Monday morning to testify to the conduct record and pay scale of soldiers who had been arrested for drunk and disorderly behavior in town on the previous Saturday night. Or going to the bank, accompanied by a guard armed only with a pickaxe handle, to sign for (rather nervously) and pick up the large amount of cash needed to pay the entire unit (the case containing it was handcuffed to one's wrist). Or going to check up on prisoners in the camp's cells to ensure they were not being mistreated or cheated out of their assigned cigarette ration, only to find our medical officer trying to look after one of them, a new eighteen-year-old recruit from some small Gloucestershire village who, my colleague told me, had been so shaken by his first encounter with military life that he lapsed into a (clinically defined) catatonic state. Or doing a routine check on the camp's rather disreputable cooks (a demeaning ritual that required them to line up and spread their fingers wide so that one could make sure that they were not handling food while suffering from scabies) only to find that they had casually left the door to the meat safe swinging open so that the sides of beef hanging there were covered by bluebottles. Or having to deal with a young mom, probably no more than eighteen years old, who had appeared at the camp gate having trudged right across Gloucester carrying her six-month-old baby. She and her husband, who was on duty overnight at the camp, had had some sort of domestic tiff and, frightened and consumed with anxiety, she needed to see him. We sat her down in the guardroom with a cup of tea (the universal English remedy for people in distress) until we found her (very embarrassed) husband and were able to give them some private time together to sort things out. But I still found my heart going out to her in the loneliness of her misery and thought that the least I could do was to pay for a taxi to get her and the baby safely home.

Finally, in June, Claire-Ann left for America to begin the accelerated teacher certification program at Central Connecticut State Teachers College, and within a month or so she had interviewed successfully for a teaching position in Vernon, Connecticut. In the meantime, looking ahead now to graduate school language requirements, I myself devoted much of the little spare time I had to trying to improve my German. The rest I devoted to combing over Gloucester Cathedral, a truly magnificent building that I got to know quite intimately. Despite the observable roughness of the juncture between the massive eleventh-twelfth century Romanesque Norman nave and the spectacular Perpendicular transepts and apse, what had been achieved, perhaps because the same Cotswold limestone had been employed to build both sections, was a splendidly harmonious whole. The Perpendicular section is of fourteenth-century provenance, a piece of bold remodeling undertaken after the tomb of Edward II was located in the building. While contemplating its glories I could not help thinking that had our modern type of historical preservation society existed at that time, the whole glorious enterprise would doubtless have been denounced as an intrusive example of outright philistinism. The only big event of note that summer was Tony Hobbs's wedding to Truda at a church in Wimbledon, a joyous occasion at which I had the privilege of serving as his best man. It was a military-style wedding which called for us both to appear in full-dress uniform equipped with (borrowed) swords, a touch that gave an agreeably Ruritanian feel to the whole affair. Not long after that, and as my term of service drew to a close, I handed over my troop to a rather grumpy major who seemed to find it hard to cope with night shifts without lapsing into crankiness at breakfast time. And my last official act was to turn up for a pre-demobilization interview with the colonel of the regiment who seemed stunned by the fact that a former subaltern of his might well envisage becoming a US citizen.

Demobilization formalities completed, I headed home to get my things together before embarking on the old *Queen Elizabeth* for the voyage from Southampton to New York. My few days at home, the last time I could use that designation for the house in which I had grown up, were not particularly happy ones. My mother was still finding it hard to come to terms with her youngest son's decision to relocate abroad and the atmosphere was gloomy and tense. My father accompanied me into town to see me off from Lime Street Station on the train for Southampton and I realized later, from something that he had said, that he had had some sort of a premonition that we would never see each other again. He was right. Two years later, just three months before Claire-Ann and I were due back for a visit to Liverpool, he died at the age of seventy-one of a massive stroke. My mother, ten years his junior, was destined to live on as a widow for another twenty-two years, living alone but surrounded by seven grandchildren and, Molly having become the busy headmistress of a secondary modern school, deeply involved in helping look after Molly's three young children.

Anxious as I was to get back to America, to reunite with Claire-Ann, and to pick up and mend the broken threads of my postgraduate education, I can recall only a couple of things about my return voyage on the *Queen Elizabeth*. The first is the fact that a fair number of French Fulbright students were among my fellow passengers, which made for lively conversation and much conviviality. The second is the fact that we encountered the tail end of a tropical storm or hurricane in the mid-Atlantic. It was the worst patch of weather I have ever encountered at sea, even though I was to crisscross the Atlantic a total of nine times by ship before capitulating to the convenience of flying. Stabilizers notwithstanding, that great vessel wallowed drunkenly as it made its painful way through the huge waves generated by the storm. Furniture had to be lashed down, crockery was smashed, and everyone, crew members no less than passengers, seemed to be in some measure seasick. Like all the older Cunard vessels, the *Queen Elizabeth* was a three-class ship with locked gates on deck dividing the separate areas and crew members policing the divisions. Under such stormy conditions, however, nobody was monitoring those symbols of English class structure and some of us, climbing over the barriers, were able to make our way forward until we were in an enclosed, windowed area right below the bridge. The sight that greeted our eyes as we peered forward towards the ship's prow was a stunning one. When viewed from pier-side in port, that huge ship loomed up above the quay almost like a high-rise building. But now, lurching, wallowing, and corkscrewing as it made its painful way ahead, it was actually burying its great prow beneath the oncoming waves and then, though not without a convulsive shuddering, raising that prow once more above the waves while shedding through the scuppers countless tons of water back into the ocean. It was a sight I shall never forget.

In that way, and at painfully reduced speed, we made our way through the tail of that storm until we broke free at last into the sunlit seas, fresh breezes, and calmer waters that lay on the other side to the west. As we did so, and succumbing without resistance to a sharp onset of the Pathetic Fallacy, I found myself imagining that Nature herself had chosen to echo the turbulence of my own emotions and to draw a firm line beneath the preoccupations of the Old World I was leaving—the nostalgic memories of a childhood long since gone, the loves, tensions, and resentments of the familial past, the poignant sense of place that had bound me to the insular landscape into which I had been born. From all of that I now felt sundered by the violent caesura of that storm and I began instead, future-oriented fellow that I was, to fix my eyes on the tests and challenges that lay ahead.

That, certainly, was the way I was thinking as the *Queen Elizabeth* felt its weary way into the shipping lanes that lay to the east and south of Long Island as they began to converge on the (still bridgeless) Verrazano Narrows, proceeding thence head-on to the towers and minarets of Manhattan Island which (in the absence of the Pan Am/MetLife building) presented at that time a sharper profile than it does today, then to be nudged by attendant tugs to its berth alongside its welcoming pier somewhere in the vicinity of West 40th Street, New York.

No sooner had we disembarked in New York than that city grasped us in its great maw and gave us a welcoming shake. Along with two of the French Fulbrights who, like me, had trains to catch, I took a taxi to Grand Central Station. We simply grabbed the cab that pulled up at the front of the line, but our choice proved not to be a felicitous one. The driver took off across town at a recklessly high speed, managing to sideswipe another cab on the way. We didn't stop, however, but simply slowed down for a while to see if the other driver wanted to make anything of it. He didn't seem to want to, so we rocketed on. That left my French companions a bit shaken, and they were even more shaken when, instead of pulling into the normal drop-off zone on Vanderbilt, our driver drove around to the side entrance of the station on Lexington and then, blandly ignoring the reading plainly visible on his meter, tried to double charge us. An immigrant himself (from eastern Europe, I would judge), and having heard French spoken among his newly disembarked passengers, he had clearly decided that we were a bunch of confused foreign innocents, ripe for the plucking. We were not, and the matter was quickly settled once we suggested getting hold of a cop. After fifty years and more in the United States and countless taxi rides in a host of other American cities as well as in New York, I have never had a similar experience. But it left my French companions clearly wondering if that particular taxi ride represented some sort of Wild West American norm. So I saw them to their respective platforms in Grand Central Station before going myself to pick up my own train on the old New York, New Haven, and Hartford railroad, which followed along the coastline of Long Island Sound up to New Haven before turning inland to make its way to Hartford.

There at the station I was met by Claire-Ann, who was looking wonderful and who drove me to her home in Manchester where, over a celebratory welcoming dinner, I was to meet for the first time her mother, father, and five curious siblings. Years later, when reminiscences were being exchanged at a meal after their mother's funeral, Claire-Ann's younger siblings shared with me the fact that they had been enthralled at the welcoming dinner to see me eating English-style, keeping my knife in my right hand and wielding the fork with my left. This was something that their mother, a stickler for good table manners, had taught them was poor form. One was permitted to cut one's meat using the knife in the right hand, but it had then to be put down on the plate and swapped for the fork with which one was properly to do one's eating. If that first dinner was perhaps a bit more formal than usual, the occasion was also a warmly welcoming one. The younger kids were unable quite to conceal their curiosity about their big sister's exotic fiancé, but in general I was not made to feel that I was being subjected to close scrutiny or critical assessment. Of course, with the experience under my belt of being a parent myself, I am pretty sure that that, however discreetly, was precisely what was happening. Fortunately, I seem to have passed muster. Tired clichés about mothers-in-law notwithstanding, Alice (my own future mother-in-law) and I were destined to get along very well, and she became in time almost as proud of me as my own mother (who could, I have reason to believe, be quite tiresome on that subject). And I certainly came to admire her very much. A strong, commanding figure with a firm will (I now see some of her more admirable traits in Claire-Ann), she for some years headed up the Nursery Teachers' Association in Connecticut and was active in Democratic Party politics in that state. She was possessed of a deep, though not ostentatious, Catholic piety that was grounded in (or had seen her through) a very tough time when she was a young mother with two small children. She had contracted tuberculosis and, in the absence of any other treatment, had to suffer the heartache of leaving her little tots behind in order to go into a sanatorium, there either to conquer the dread disease or to succumb to it. She conquered it and was to survive to the age of ninety, living alone in her last years as a confident and proudly independent person. One May when she was, I think, in her early eighties and when I, as president of Williams, had meetings to attend in Oxford, we brought her with us so that she could see the college gardens in their full seasonal glory. On that occasion, she proved to be an indefatigable tourist and a calmly poised guest of honor, seated at the right hand of the rector of Exeter at high table in that college's handsome Hall. She comported herself for all the world as if she had spent her life sipping wine and hobnobbing with Oxford dons. "What nice young men," she said afterwards, as we were making our way along the Broad heading back to the Randolph Hotel.

After a couple of wonderfully relaxing days in Manchester, I had to get down to New Haven to move into the room I had reserved in the Hall of Graduate Studies on York Street, to see the director of graduate studies in history in order to line up my course of studies for the year, and to take the required tests of reading ability in German and French. I hadn't quite finished my demobilization leave from the army when I found myself sitting down to take those tests, and it was something of a load off my mind later to find that I had passed both of them. One thing, at least, was out of the way. I quickly settled into my room, which turned out to be on the ground floor, its window separated by no more than three or four feet from the kitchen window of Mory's Temple Bar, the old club fronting onto York Street at which the Whiffenpoofs, the oldest college *a cappella* group in the United States, have been singing on Monday evenings for more than a century. So I associate that room, not only with the enticing aroma of food that was clearly of a quality beyond my means, but also with the celebrated Whiffenpoof song with which the group would always round out its evening performance. Its chorus is derived from a poem by Rudyard Kipling, "Gentlemen-rankers":

We're poor little lambs who've lost our way,
Baa! Baa! Baa!
We're little black sheep who've gone astray,
Baa-aa-aa!
Gentlemen [songsters] rankers out on a spree,
Damned from here to Eternity,
God ha' mercy on such as we,
Baa! Yah! Bah!

In my memory, the mournful sentimentality of those words is linked incongruously with the authors whose books I was sitting at my desk delving into on those Monday evenings—with Ernst Troeltsch, for example, the great historical sociologist of religion, or with Karl Popper and what he had to say about the logic of scientific discovery, or with Wilhelm Dilthey and R. G. Collingwood, with whose philosophies of history I was much concerned that year.

Shortly after arriving at Yale, I had a session with Franklin Le Van Baumer, the modern European intellectual historian who was at that time serving as director of graduate studies in the History Department. A grave, solemn, decent, and deeply conscientious man, he made it clear at the outset that only after the department had had the opportunity to arrive at their own judgment about my capabilities would it decide whether or not to take into account my previous graduate work and to permit me to proceed to take the comprehensive examinations after a single year of course work consisting of four graduate seminars. He also reacted with a twinge of impatience when I described my interests, which, while anchored in the Middle Ages, reached forward in some respects to straddle the traditional divide between medieval and what we now call early modern. Where did I see myself falling? he wanted to know. Into medieval or Renaissance-Reformation, two areas of scholarly specialization which, though chronologically cheek by jowl, were clearly deemed in accord with the academic norms then prevailing to inhabit two very distinct microworlds of intellectual endeavor. For the dominance of those norms, of course, something of an interpretative price was paid. Because of the nature of their training, medievalists tended to be ignorant about the early modern period, and "Ren-Ref" types reciprocated by being ignorant about the Middle Ages. Until the Dutch scholar Heiko Oberman began—

at the Harvard Divinity School in the 1960s—to train his Reformation-oriented students in late medieval theology, American specialists in Reformation history, while familiar with Renaissance history and the humanism of that era, characteristically knew very little about the late medieval scholasticism in terms of which Martin Luther himself had received his intellectual formation.

Confronted, however, with the necessity of making a stark choice between medieval and Renaissance-Reformation, I opted for the former only to discover that of the two medievalists in the department (the other, William Huse Dunham, specialized in English constitutional history), the one who dealt with continental Europe was on leave for the year. He was the Italian scholar, Robert Lopez, a distinguished and provocative specialist in medieval economic history, with some of whose work I was already familiar. For that absence I was later, or so I am now inclined to think, to pay a bit of a price. Although I got to know Bill Dunham quite well (he was very interested in the editing work I had done and was always very encouraging and supportive), I chose not to take his seminar because I judged that I was already pretty well prepared in English medieval history and needed now to focus on modern European intellectual history. For that was the required subfield outside my main area of specialization that I proposed to choose. So I signed up for Baumer's own (very well-constructed) seminar in modern European intellectual history, for the seminar in the philosophy of history offered by the German émigré historian, Hajo Holborn, and for a seminar in early modern English constitutional history and political thinking offered by Hartley Simpson, then dean of the graduate school and one of the several former students of Wallace Notestein who, ending up in the Yale department, left it with a marked oversupply of specialists in modern English history. For my fourth seminar, I opted for one taught at the Yale Divinity School by Roland Bainton, the prominent Reformation historian. It focused on the long history of Christian social teaching and would, I thought, help flesh out aspects of medieval religious history with which I was not well acquainted. And it did precisely that.

Later on, having for the first time read Perry Miller's *The New England Mind* and discovered the scholastic nature of Puritan theology and the degree to which (at least in natural theology) it was in direct continuity with late medieval scholastic modes of thought, I wished I had taken Edmund Morgan's seminar on colonial America. But, that not-withstanding, the choice of seminars I had made turned out to be more than satisfactory and, with the reading I had to undertake for them, helped make that year of graduate course work at Yale a very stimulating and valuable one. Indeed, in the work in the primary sources that I undertook for two of those seminars lay the seeds of lines of investigation that I was to pursue in my scholarly work for long years into the future, and two of the first scholarly articles I was to publish had their beginnings in research papers I wrote for those seminars. Baumer's seminar, which covered new territory for me, proved to be particularly helpful, bringing home to me just how important and fascinating the history of scientific thinking could be. During the course of the year we were all called upon to write two short papers for circulation to everyone else in the seminar. I chose to write mine on Thomas Henry Huxley and on Darwin, and I devoted my final research paper to the great Newton himself, whose understanding of the laws of nature I contrasted with that evident in the works of Hugo Grotius. It was not only, however, in my formal seminars that I found myself encountering new intellectual horizons. Living for a year in the Hall of Graduate Studies brought me into contact with a broad array of graduate students of varying intellectual backgrounds and who were pursuing PhD's in a wide range of disciplines. Talking and arguing with them on a day-to-day basis proved to be highly educative. One in particular, a rather eccentric English student, Benno Wasserman by name, a graduate of the London School of Economics and Political Science who was working on a topic in international relations, did me a great service by introducing me to the thinking of Karl Popper, who had been his teacher. I wasn't taken with Popper's treatment of the nature of historical understanding or with his popular *The Open Society and its Enemies* which, in its treatment of Plato, struck me as mired in anachronism. But I was impressed by his argument about the demarcation of scientific reasoning from other modes of thought, and I found his falsification theory far more compelling than the type of verificationism I had picked up at Oxford. It served to liberate me, I think, from thinking about the historical enterprise in terms of some sort of primitive, Baconian empiricism.

That year, then, was a good one. After the intellectual deprivation of army life I found the atmosphere at Yale enormously stimulating. And, in practical terms, the year came to a very satisfactory ending. One's grades in the graduate seminars were clearly very important. Only three positive possibilities were available—pass, honors, and highest honors—and it was clear that mere passes would not suffice if one wanted to proceed with graduate work. So I was enormously relieved to receive highest honors in all four seminars, to have my graduate fellowship renewed, to be excused from any further course work, to be cleared to take my comprehensive examinations in the fall, and to get on with my thesis. I cannot claim to have had anyone at Yale whom I could call my mentor. I already knew what I wanted to work on and the issue instead was to find someone willing to take me on as a thesis student writing on that topic. Fortunately, Roland Bainton was kind enough to assume the role of dissertation supervisor. I wasn't quite working in his field, but he knew enough about the later Middle Ages to save me from egregious error and proved to be prompt, efficient, and conscientious in his supervisory role, reading carefully my draft chapters as I submitted them to him and getting them back to me quickly. So far as my dealings with him went, things went very smoothly and I was able to complete my thesis in the course of the 1958–59 academic year. I was particularly touched, then, over forty years later, when the Sixteenth-Century Society and Conference awarded me its Roland Bainton Book Prize for my *The Conciliarist Tradition: Constitutionalism in the Catholic Church 1300–1870.*

I devoted the summer of 1958 to three things: picking up the threads of the work on Pierre d'Ailly I had needed to put to one side three years earlier, revising for the comprehensive examination which at Yale took the form of a two-hour oral, and cleaning up and painting the little third-floor apartment we had rented on Prospect Place, just off Prospect Street, opposite the old Berkeley (Episcopal) Divinity School, and close in to the central Yale campus. Claire-Ann had secured a good teaching position at a school in neighboring Hamden, we were planning to get married in August, and we needed to get the place shipshape before we moved in. So, while she made curtains, I spackled the damaged places in the walls and began the process of repainting almost the entire interior. It was the beginning of my house-decorating phase (which eventually extended to the more tricky and aggravating business of hanging wallpaper) as we moved from one residence to another over the course of five years—two in New Haven, then two in Williamstown, before we built our own house in 1965. The house decorating culminated in an orgy of painting at the house we built when the two of us, strapped for cash, took on the task of painting almost the entire interior wall space ourselves. We purchased a few pieces of furniture, were given a handsome settee that had belonged to Claire-Ann's deceased aunt, Loretta (it still graces our living room), along with an antiquated, heavy refrigerator of pre–World War II vintage that would start up with an enormous rattle and roar and dim the lights in the entire flat in the process. We needed to purchase a stove, and did so at a rather seedy New Haven establishment called Johnny's Swap Shop. It was a small, secondhand gas stove. When we first lit it, it proved to be home to a crowd of cockroaches. At that moment they were clearly as startled as we were, and we were able to dispose of them as they scurried around before they were able to set up home in our new abode. One of them, trapped in an unlit burner and unable to get out, waved its antennae through the small openings in a way that brought irresistibly to mind a striking scene from Carol Reed's film *The Third Man*, which I had just seen. There a wounded and exhausted Harry Lime (Orson Welles), trying to escape through the sewers of Vienna, was unable to budge a manhole cover in order to get out into the street. All that could be seen from the road were his wriggling fingers extending through the grating before slipping back down and out of sight. In my mind, then, Harry Lime and Johnny of Johnny's Swap Shop vie for possession of the memory of that first, prenuptial stove.

We were married on August 9, 1958, in Manchester, Connecticut, and after a brief honeymoon on Nantucket, off the coast of Cape Cod in Massachusetts (the first of many visits to that island), we settled in to happy married life on Prospect Place. Shortly thereafter, I took my comprehensive orals in the faculty lounge of the Hall of Graduate Studies, a room where, years later, I had to give a little speech of thanks on behalf of my fellow honorees at a lunch given for those of us who had just been awarded Wilbur Lucius Cross Medals by the Yale Graduate School Alumni Association. As graduate students we were required to stand for examination in one major and three minor fields. My major field was medieval religious and intellectual history. My minors were English history from the Anglo-Saxon invasion to 1215, English constitutional history and political thinking in the seventeenth century, and modern intellectual history. My examiners were Roland Bainton, Basil Duke

Henning (standing in for Bill Dunham, who was away), Hartley Simpson, and Frank Baumer. Though I thought I was a bit shaky in response to one of Baumer's questions, things in general went well and I even found myself involved in a stimulating disagreement with Bainton for a while on issues pertaining to Descartes' natural theology.

The gratifying upshot was that I passed with distinction, and not long thereafter I was told by George Pierson, chairman of the department, that if I were planning to go on the job market that year I should know that Yale itself would like to appoint me to a junior position in the department should they get clearance from the provost to make such an appointment. Whether or not that would be the case, they would not know until after the end of the calendar year, but he wanted me to be aware of that possibility, which he seemed to think was quite likely. This was, of course, wonderful news and, when it was finally confirmed, I found myself in line to become a full-time instructor in history at Yale College (the instructorship still being the starting rank) as of July 1, 1959.

What that meant was that by the spring of 1959 the only hurdle left to surmount, apart from the completion of my thesis, was the submission of a progress report to my PhD committee. That body consisted of Bainton himself, Robert Lopez, and, because I was writing on the history of political thought, Charles Blitzer of the Yale Department of Political Science. I was to encounter Blitzer again later on in life when he was serving as director of the Woodrow Wilson International Center for Scholars, Washington, DC, and I, having just stepped down in 1994 from the Williams presidency, was a fellow there and working hard to hit my scholarly stride again. By April 1959 when I submitted that progress report, I was well underway with the thesis and had encountered no criticism from Bainton about the several chapters I had already submitted to him. So I assumed that the submission of the report would be no more than a formality. For Bainton and Blitzer, indeed, it seemed to be precisely that. But not for Lopez. From him, instead, I received, not a piece of advice suggesting that I might do well to pay more attention to social and legal history (which could arguably have been a reasonable course correction) but, rather, a brief, formal note coldly informing me that the whole thesis appeared to be so involved with matters philosophical that he could not himself approve it for a doctoral degree in *history*.

Naturally, this left me quite shaken. Being literate enough, philosophically speaking, to be able to recognize the dividing line between philosophical and historical modes of reasoning, I was baffled by his stance. But if for me the philosophical as opposed to the historical denoted a different mode of reasoning, for him it seemed to refer, rather, to *subject matter* that was abstractly intellectual as opposed to the "factual" data of what he himself called "history proper"—presumably mainstream political, social, and economic history. And that was a position that struck me then, and now, as an unreflectively primitive one. But that notwithstanding, instead of seeing a green light opening up the way to a speedy conclusion to my student years, I was now confronted by something of an obstacle. Thinking (foolishly, it turned out) that a fuller explanation from me about the sort of work I was doing might remove the obstacle, I made an appointment with Lopez and went to see him in his office in Calhoun College. The session didn't go well or last long. I had hardly begun with my explanations when he interrupted me, reminding me that his judgment, not mine, was the important thing; he was the professor, I was just the graduate student. That was that! What had been a worrying amber light had now modulated, it seemed, into a more alarming red one prohibiting further progress towards the degree.

By this time, I was in a state of bewildered desperation. Everything seemed to be falling apart. The only way out, so far as I could see, was to avail myself of the avenue afforded by the rules and regulations for the resolution of such disagreements via the holding of a colloquium at which I could make my case to all of the professors on my dissertation committee. So I went to see Frank Baumer in his capacity as director of graduate studies to explain my dilemma and to request the convening of such a colloquium. His reaction was immediate. The last thing I needed, he told me, was to be involved in such a colloquium. I was to leave the matter in his hands and those of Bill Dunham; he would get back to me. Though he was both proper and discreet in what he said on that occasion, I learned much later that he must have known his man all too well. Lopez, a somewhat volatile fellow, possessed, it turned out, a somewhat unenviable reputation for giving graduate students (and especially so women students) a difficult time, and the department seemed to have learned the wisdom of dealing with the concomitant fallout via less formal means than the convening of potentially fractious colloquia. I don't know if the deliberations among my seniors were in any way contentious, but a sensible, face-saving solution was hit upon. I was to submit to Lopez three of the draft chapters I had already written so that he could make a more nuanced judgment about the nature of my scholarship. That I did and the approach worked. Having read the chapters and grumblingly conceded that they were scholarly, interesting, and even original, he gave me a bit of useful bibliographical advice about legal histories and permitted me to proceed on my chosen route towards the PhD. About all of this he wrote to Bainton who, with his permission, passed on the letter to me (I still have it). In that letter, and *inter alia*, he acknowledged that he might originally have come on a bit too strong. He was struggling at the time, he said, with a pileup of things calling for his attention after being in the hospital with a kidney stone attack (not, admittedly, the most propitious of moments to approach anyone)! But, while letting me proceed, he still insisted that my problematic was that of a philosopher rather than a historian and that my world was "a windowless thinker's world" to which "facts" beyond those dealt with by political philosophers were irrelevant. If I had "the ambition of becoming an historian," I would have "to open . . . [my] windows occasionally and look around." Noting that he had recommended me for an appointment in the department on the strength of what others had said about me and "of what I had heard him say at a lecture of Barraclough," he took pains to insist that he was "utterly unbiased" towards me. In fairness, that may well have been the case, though, in light of his deportment towards me over the next two years when I was a junior colleague of his, I began to have my doubts on that score. Though I was one of only two colleagues of his who were working on things medieval, he simply refused to acknowledge my presence or to speak to me or, even, to return my greetings when I spoke to him. For a young fellow just starting out, it wasn't much fun, and I began to wonder about what might lie behind the whole episode. Was there some previous history in the department about students of his whom he had tried to get appointed? That I didn't know. Or was he irritated by the fact that the department had opted to appoint a junior medievalist from Yale who had never been a student of his? That, too, I didn't know. It is true that he did write to me twice over the course of the next two years. First, to tell me he had nominated me for a position at Long Beach State College in California. If I recall correctly, history was not then (or not yet) a separate department at Long Beach; instead it was just a section within the humanities division. I wasn't interested in the job and let Lopez know that I wasn't going to pursue it. Whereupon I received another, oddly chatty and handwritten, letter from him in which he told me that I should bear in mind that I would still "have to find the permanent home that our department is not in a position to offer you." He was also already aware of the fact that, by that time (March 1961), George Pierson and Bill Dunham had recommended me for an opening at Williams, but he himself made a point of saying that "it does not look like a tailor-made opening for your measurements." I was left wondering what exactly he thought my measurements were. His attitude and the nature of his dealings with me have remained something of a singularly unpleasant mystery. Talk about the nasty micropolitics of academic life has long been fashionable. But it does not match my own experience which has been relatively benign. Across the course of a career that spanned over forty years, this was the only truly disturbing episode I was to encounter. Some years later when I was president of the New England Medieval Conference, at that time a very lively group, and when, accordingly, we hosted the annual meeting at Williams, my wife and I threw a dinner party at our place for the conference's steering committee. It was a very lively, convivial, and enjoyable occasion. And one of the most convivially engaged participants was none other than Robert Lopez himself. Though I caught him once or twice glancing speculatively at me, he appeared to have forgotten that we had ever encountered each other or had some previous history. After our guests had departed and we were embarking on the cleanup process, my wife, who had clearly enjoyed his company, asked who that "charming little Italian" was. I told her.

During those spring months of 1959 I also had another untoward, though less alarming, moment. This time it involved George Pierson, the chairman of the History Department. A distinguished Tocqueville scholar, he had moved on to immerse himself in the writing of a history of Yale College. He called me in to discuss my teaching responsibilities in the upcoming academic year and wanted to know to what subject I wanted to devote the senior honors seminar I had been fortunate enough to be invited to teach. History of medieval political thought, I hopefully suggested. No, he responded, because that pertained (though they didn't offer the subject) to the Political Science Department. Why not, then, the history of Anglo-Saxon England? Too specialized, he (probably correctly) responded. Medieval church and society, then? When I came up with that suggestion, he paused, looked at me searchingly, and then inquired if I thought I could be objective on such a topic. I was puzzled and taken aback by the question and didn't know quite how to respond. Then, as he himself began to betray signs of incipient embarrassment, it dawned on me what was going on. I had somehow been fingered as a Catholic who, as such, might not be possessed of the capacity for objectivity that clearly came naturally to people like him, members of a sort of WASP establishment who were, presumably, not caught up in the snares of any ideological entanglements. It was an awkward moment, for him, I suspect, almost as much as for me, and we had somehow to fumble our way through to an amicable resolution. At the time, I thought that his question was a spin-off from the sort of person he was and the class to which he clearly belonged. He was, after all, a rather patrician figure with deep ancestral roots at Yale College (he was a descendant of Yale's first rector and a relative of Yale's first student). I was not altogether surprised later on to read in Peter Novick's *That Noble Dream* (1988) of a report that Pierson had written in 1957 to Whitney Griswold, then president of Yale, complaining about the inadequate *social* backgrounds of the graduate students with which the History Department (unlike the English) was having to cope. Not, he fretted, "young men and women from the cultivated, professional and well-to-do classes," people, in effect, "*from able backgrounds*" (italics mine). Instead, the History Department was having to make do with the sons and daughters of janitors, mechanics, watchmen, pharmacists, railroad clerks, and the like. People, in effect, like me. But in time I came to realize that my embarrassing moment with him was not stimulated by considerations of class. Instead it was what it seemed on the face of it to be, one concerning religious commitments. It reflected, I believe, the profound doubts prevalent among the members of the American intellectual establishment at that time about the compatibility with American democratic individualism of the "authoritarian" Catholic mentality, as well as about the very commitment of the "Catholic mind" to critical rationality. Just as, a few years earlier, I had failed in my ignorance of things American to understand why my distant Irish American cousins might well be keen pro-McCarthyites, so too, now, my ignorance of the climate of opinion prevailing among American intellectuals (mainstream Protestants and Jews as well as unbelievers) was such that I failed to realize how deeply suspicious they were of Roman Catholicism. I had read Paul Blanshard's *American Freedom and Catholic Power* (1949, 1958) but had brushed it to one side as a piece of residual bigotry, a holdover from old-time Know-Nothingism. It hadn't quite sunk in that it was a national bestseller, a book of the month selection, lauded enthusiastically at the time by a stellar constellation of American academics and intellectuals from John Dewey to McGeorge Bundy, and generated sympathetic reverberations among such people as Albert Einstein and Lewis Mumford. I myself was instinctively interpreting the American academic and intellectual scene, I now realize, in terms of the British world where, established church notwithstanding, in the absence of any denominationally sponsored universities, members of the Catholic minority were more or less comfortably integrated into the student bodies and faculty ranks of places like Oxford and Cambridge and where public funds helped support denominationally sponsored school systems of Anglican, Roman Catholic, and Jewish provenance alike. And I had simply taken the apparent lack of a Catholic presence on the Yale faculty to reflect the fact that in the United States, unlike Britain, Catholics had chosen to segregate themselves in their own array of (at that time) not very intellectually impressive universities and colleges. In much of this, of course, as I was later to discover, I was wrong. It was none other than Perry Miller, whose work I so admired, who had written in the *New York Herald Tribune* just eight years earlier that Catholicism was antagonistic to both "the democratic way of life" and to "a free and critical education." As I was to discover in 1994 when reviewing George Marsden's *The Soul of the American University*, my own thesis supervisor, Roland Bainton of gentle Quaker disposition, had written in 1958 expressing his doubts about whether Catholics, Protestant fundamentalists, or Orthodox Jews could really "participate in the intellectual life of the university," and had wondered whether Catholicism could be "genuinely at home in any university other than a Catholic university."

Of all of this I was blissfully ignorant when I had my odd encounter with George Pierson, who was, in any case, basically kindly in his engagement with junior faculty. Nor was I really conscious in 1965 that

I might have been the first publicly observant, that is, "practicing" Catholic (an odd locution that—we are always "practicing" but don't seem to get very good at it) to be promoted to tenure at Williams. But, by that time, the old WASP ascendancy was disintegrating. In 1985, when I was elected president of Williams, while the local newspaper noted, somewhat awkwardly, that I was to be the first Catholic to hold that position, the student-run *Williams Record* showed no interest in the matter and, so far as I know, it wasn't a matter of comment on campus.

I missed the thesis submission deadline that would have enabled me to graduate at the Yale commencement of 1959 and had to wait until the next June formally to receive the degree. But all the work had been done and approved and, with my student years now over, I had been able to submit the bound copies of the thesis before sailing from Montreal for a stay of several weeks in England and France. My father having died suddenly in March, we wanted to spend a decent amount of time with my mother, the more so because Claire-Ann was now pregnant with our first child and we didn't know when we would be able to get back across the Atlantic again. And it was to be, in fact, our last holiday without children for almost a quarter of a century. We had a good time that summer, both in London visiting the O'Keeffe's and in Liverpool where we purchased a handsome Silver Cross perambulator, equipped with a nicely fringed surrey-type canopy for use during the summer months, and which later was recycled for inhabitation by our grandchildren. This we had shipped to Southampton, where it was picked up by the small Italian student ship on which we were sailing, and on which we would be embarking later on at Le Havre after our time in Paris and its environs. When we did so and enquired anxiously of a Genoese deckhand if the pram had indeed been picked up, his face broke out into a broad smile. "Carozella da bimba!" he exclaimed, and insisted on bringing us down a long ladder into the hold in order to show us that the pram, carefully stowed on its side and ensconced in protective wrapping, was indeed on board. By that time, Claire-Ann was clearly showing her condition and, on that return trip, entering into her Madonna phase, she was treated by the crew with marked solicitude and great kindness.

My two years as a member of the Yale History Department proved to be extremely busy and productive in more ways than one. Apart from getting my pedagogic feet on and my scholarly research off the ground, we were embarking on the great adventure of starting a family. Our daughter, Deirdre, was born at Grace New Haven Hospital in December 1959; our first son, Christopher, came along in April 1961. My teaching responsibilities involved, in addition to my honors seminar on "Church and Society in the Middle Ages," two discussion sections in the basic European history course which, over two semesters, covered the period from 800 to 1914. The latter was a carefully thought-out and well-framed course, combining a high-quality lecture series given by two of the more senior assistant professors in the department with a series of discussion sections taught by the rest of us (all full-time instructors, no graduate assistants). These sections were focused on sets of topically organized "problems" involving collections of primary historical documents—in some ways not altogether unlike the case studies favored by so many business schools. Though it was a leading research university, Yale was by no means prone to slighting its undergraduate teaching mission. Figured into our teaching load as instructors was a required weekly session led by the lecturer and devoted to the sharing of ideas about how to approach the teaching of the next week's topic. For one just starting out on his academic career, involvement in that course was highly educative and powerfully formative. So too was the seriousness of the teaching ethos that was conveyed. So much so, indeed, that even though I had been up all night with Claire-Ann in the hospital's labor room until, just before dawn, Deirdre finally consented to be born, it never occurred to me to think of cancelling that morning's weekly meeting of my seminar.

None of this left any time for research during that academic year, though, mindful of the publication expectations of places like Yale, I did manage to complete the translation of an exemplary conciliar tract by Pierre d'Ailly. In 1960, that appeared in print as my first article and was promptly anthologized. While I knew that my thesis on d'Ailly was fresh material and substantial enough to warrant turning into a book, I decided to put it to one side for a year in order to devote the summer of 1960 to the completion of two substantial articles. At the end of the day during that summer, Claire-Ann would often push Deirdre in her comfortable perambulator down to meet me outside Sterling Memorial Library when I emerged from my daylong labors in the stacks on those very articles. They were to be published over the course of the following year. So, too, was an article on William of Ockham's ethical thinking, begun originally at Toronto but read as a paper at a graduate seminar on natural law thinking that the distinguished Italian scholar Alessandro Passerin d'Entrèves (University of Turin) gave at Yale in the spring semester of 1960 in his capacity as Visiting Professor in Law, Philosophy, and Political Science. He had been Serena Professor of Italian Studies at Oxford when I was an undergraduate there, but I had not come into contact with him. Having since read and admired his books on medieval political thought and natural law theory, I decided to sit in on his seminar, and when at an organizing session he asked if somebody could get the proceedings started next time at the late medieval end of things, I volunteered to read the paper. Later on, he told me, rather disarmingly, that he was eternally grateful to me for doing so because he was always very nervous about getting his seminars off the ground. He really liked the paper and wrote me a lovely note telling me that it was "truly admirable" and represented the way in which "*Ideengeschichte* must be written" in order to be plausible. That was wonderful to hear, and he followed up his note by sending a cleaned up and annotated version of the piece to the journal *Natural Law Forum* (later *American Journal of Jurisprudence*), on whose editorial board he served, and they published it the following year.

Over the course of the next two years I got to know d'Entrèves quite well. Hailing from minor Italian aristocracy (he was the Count of Entrèves up in the Valle d'Aosta near Courmayeur), he had an English mother and was something of an anglophile. He had clearly loved his time at Oxford and he had happy memories of having been drawn into some of the meetings of the Inklings with C. S. Lewis, J. R. R. Tolkien, and others at Magdalen College. He was kind enough to give my thesis on d'Ailly a close reading and to pronounce it fit for publication. This was both helpful and reassuring, the more so in that, after it was accepted, I had not heard much by way of comment from either Bainton or Blitzer, and what I had heard from Lopez had obviously been a good deal less than encouraging. He also tried to interest me in taking on the editing of the *Consilia* of the fifteenth-century Italian canonist and conciliarist thinker, Francesco Zabarella, for a series of which he was the general editor. At that time, however, I already had too much on my plate with my line of research on Pierre d'Ailly, his great student Jean Gerson, and their early-sixteenth-century successors on the Parisian theology faculty, John Mair and Jacques Almain, to be able to take on that additional assignment even to please him. D'Entrèves was a warm, accessible, charming, and kindly man with whom I was to keep up a correspondence for a decade and more. On one occasion he came to tea at our little apartment (he missed the English ritual of afternoon tea) and made a characteristic and gratifying fuss over our little baby. From that occasion I carry in my mind a picture of him talking animatedly, teacup in hand, and sitting at one end of the couch while five-months-old Deirdre lay sleeping in a baby seat at the other.

D'Entrèves was not the only person at that time to invite me to commit to more editing work. I had got to know some of the people involved at that time on the big Yale project to edit the complete works of Sir Thomas More (among them Joe Trapp, the New Zealander who was later to become director of the Warburg Library in London) and had put together for them a little guide to the structure of the *Corpus Juris Canonici* and to the rather complex way in which texts from that great compilation were cited. It was that, I suspect, that led Dick Sylvester of the Yale English Department, then serving as the executive editor for the whole project, to ask me to take on the editing of More's *Confutation of Tyndale's Answer*. Though the text itself is not very ingratiating, the proposition itself was not unattractive as the project disposed of enough funding to "buy back" one's time—that is, to fund a leave of absence so that one could get on with the job. But again, rightly or wrongly, I decided that I would do well to forego that plum and to stick with the line of research to which I was already committed.

While such were the sorts of things that preoccupied me during my two years as a member of the Yale History Department, I also had my eye on the academic job market. Observation had taught me that those appointed to a junior position at a place like Yale should not succumb to the temptation of imagining that they might have a long-term future there. In the old days, as the makeup of the department itself suggested, that might well have been the case. But no more. Infrequent exceptions to the general rule of "out rather than up" there might well be. But with Lopez in the equation as one of the crucial senior people in my general field, the likelihood of my being such an exception hovered at or below the zero level. Not that my situation was an unenviable one. Yale was a good jumping-off ground for positions elsewhere. I could expect to be able to stay there for six or seven years and then, with my scholarly reputation firmly established, to move to a more senior position at another reputable institution. So I was not yet, at least in career terms, under any real pressure. In the end, however, I chose to move, and to do so earlier rather than later. In 1961, the medieval position at Williams College in Massachusetts opened up and George Pierson and Bill Dunham were kind enough to draw my name to the attention of Bob Scott, an American intellectual historian and himself a Yale product who was then chairman of the Williams History Department. I had met him two years earlier at a Yale "smoker" (reception) at the annual meeting of the American Historical Association and had found him to be a warm, approachable man. Bob contacted me to see if I might conceivably be interested. After driving up to Vermont the previous summer to attend the wedding of a graduate school friend, we had stopped over in Williamstown to visit with Bob and Diana Collins who had been our contemporaries as students at Yale. We were taken with the sheer beauty of the place and intrigued by what we picked up at a nice outdoor party about the atmosphere at the college. There was, we sensed, a real and appealing sense of collegial community there which seemed to be lacking in the Yale that we, at least, had encountered in our short time there. When Bob Scott contacted me, then, I told him that I might well be interested and I was invited up for an interview. Because Christopher was on the brink of being born (and, unlike Deirdre, he was to come very quickly), I could spend only a day in Williamstown. It was a day filled with meetings and interviews both at the college and departmental level. People were nice and it was all very pleasant. But I couldn't help being struck by the fact that nobody expressed much interest in what I was doing in my research. All the talk was about teaching and of that fact I took note.

After me, they had two other candidates to interview. Bob, I suspect, being himself a Yale product, didn't think I could be enticed to leave Yale. But he was not only a very bright, interesting, and engaging person, he was also a very good salesman for the college and it is ultimately to him that I attribute my decision to accept the Williams offer when finally it came. It did so during the spring break and, when I told him about it, George Pierson invited me over to his house to talk about it. He had, I think, my best interests at heart. He assured me, on the one hand, that I would be welcome to stay on at Yale and that, if I did so, I could expect other job offers to come my way. On the other hand, he spoke highly of

Williams. It was, he said, a fine old college which had always been home to some scholars of distinction. An offer from Williams was something to be taken seriously. It was, of course, he added, a "*Protestant* college," and he wondered, solicitously, if I would be comfortable in such a setting. That, in turn, led me to wonder where he thought I had been as an undergraduate, as also how well he actually knew Williams. Even I knew that it had been a very long time since the characterization of the place as "a Protestant college" had been accurately descriptive of the realities on the ground. But of that I said nothing, simply indicating instead that I anticipated no difficulty in settling in to pursue a career at such a place. And that, in the end, is what I chose to do.

I find it hard now to reconstruct the full range of reasons that led me to make that life-changing decision. Part of it was familial. We were not particularly enamored of New Haven. We already had two children and expected to have more. We realized that, though we lacked deep pockets, we would soon have to face up somehow to moving out from the center of campus to one or another of the outer suburbs. In comparison with the grubbiness of the city, the beauty and calm of the Berkshires had great appeal; so, too, did the fact that Williams maintained a considerable stock of its own rental housing, reserved for those in the junior ranks and situated more or less on campus. It was clearly a great place for young children and seemed, in fact, to be swarming with them. I also liked the idea of being the fellow who could shape the way in which medieval history was to be taught, and I found that there was something very appealing about the "feel" of the college in general, which somehow stirred up memories about my own student days at Corpus. The Yale History Department was a truly distinguished one to which I was proud to belong. But, at about sixty in size, it was also quite impersonal and it wasn't easy to get to know one's departmental colleagues, let alone colleagues in the university at large. In comparison, partly because of its size and intimacy of scale, Williams conveyed the sense of being a real intellectual community, and it was to prove to be precisely that. Finally, of course, and sadly, I had begun to find the experience at Yale of having a senior departmental colleague in my own field who wouldn't even speak to me to be, in the end, dispiriting, discouraging, and demoralizing. Whatever the case, and however the pros and cons lined up, our decision to leave Yale for Williams was not, in the end, a particularly fraught one. Nor have we ever regretted it.

During the summer of 1961 I had planned to embark upon the revision and rewriting of my thesis in order to turn it into a book. For that task I needed ready access to a research library and, that being so, we sweltered on into August amid the oppressive coastal humidity of New Haven. But then it was time to take our leave. Having shipped off our furniture and packed our belongings, we vacated the apartment into which we had put so much work, shook off from our feet the dust of New Haven, and set out for an overnight stay with Claire-Ann's family in Manchester. The next day we made our way via Springfield to the Massachusetts Turnpike which we followed westward to the higher ground and cooler reaches of the heavily forested Berkshires. Leaving the turnpike at Lee, we drove north on Route 7 through Pittsfield, then retracing in reverse the route I had traversed with the Breslin girls in 1954 when we drove down from Toronto for Christmas. We made our way through Lanesboro up to New Ashford, at the northern end of which the road begins to twist its way through a fairly narrow defile flanked on either side by steepish, heavily timbered slopes. Catching a momentary glimpse, at about eleven o'clock to the left and at about two hundred feet or so up the slopes, of a lovely upland meadow, a cleared island of light green grass floating in a dark green sea of trees, we entered upon a rather pronounced set of S-bends which, in turn, led us out into a straightish stretch bordered to the east by generously welcoming meadowland. That stretch was heralded by a prominent sign which said: ENTERING WILLIAMSTOWN, INC[ORPORATED] 1765. We entered, to be drawn for good into the embrace of its powerful magnetic field.

PART III

Williamstown

CHAPTER TEN

Williamstown and Its College

For those unacquainted with New England in general and the Commonwealth of Massachusetts in particular, let it be noted that Berkshire County is the latter's westernmost county. Its northern border abuts the state of Vermont and its southern border is shared with Connecticut, while across the length of its western border looms the immensity of New York state. In common with the other counties of Massachusetts, it is divided into townships which directly abut their neighbors, leaving no interstitial space to separate them one from another. The township of Williamstown occupies the northwest corner of both county and state, with the town center, the college to which it is home, and most of the township's population of around 7,500 clustered in close proximity to that northwestern corner. The point at which Vermont, Massachusetts, and New York state meet is located, in fact, on college property, falling within the 1600-acre confines of the Hopkins Memorial Forest, a protected area once managed by the US Forest Service but now, in more recent years, by the college's Center for Environmental Studies. Embracing in one section a precious stand of untouched primordial timber, it is punctuated by experimental stations generating longitudinal data about such things as water flows, changing climatic conditions, and the changing succession of second-growth timber that has come to engulf so much of the northern county.

In our geography classes at grammar school in England, we were taught to refer to the long eastern highland system that divides the North American coastal plain from the vast continental interior as "the old, folded Appalachian chain." The mountains of that chain constitute an eastern and much older counterpart to the younger and upstart Rocky Mountains of the West. They run for some 3,000 miles from Labrador and Newfoundland in the north all the way down to Alabama in the south. The township of Williamstown nestles within their more northerly reaches, and across it cuts the Appalachian hiking trail that runs for almost 2,800 miles from Mount Katahdin in Maine to Springer Mountain in Georgia. The town center is situated close to the confluence of three river valleys. One of these is formed by Hemlock Brook, and a second is formed by the Green River, which is fed by runoff from the Mount Greylock Massif that hems in the town to the southeast and which is clustered around Mount Greylock—at 3,491 feet, the highest mountain in Massachusetts. Both rivers run roughly northward, ending in the Hoosic (or "great") River which, emerging from the Hoosac Range looming to the northeast, and having scoured out a fairly broad valley, finds its way across a corner of Vermont into New York state, where it ends by pouring its waters into the Hudson River itself. Thus, bracketed by mountains to the north, northeast, and southeast, the township is also hemmed in on its westerly perimeter by the Taconic Range, along the 2,800-foot crest of which runs the border dividing Massachusetts from New York state. Within this formidably continuing circle of mountains, the valleys are watered by a series of small streams bearing such evocative names as Hopper Brook, Money Brook, and Roaring Brook, and punctuated by foothills such as Bee Hill, Northwest Hill, and Stone Hill. Looking to the northeast from the top of the meadow that marks the northerly end of Stone Hill and now overlooks the impressive campus of the Sterling and Francine Clark Art Institute, the town center and the buildings on the campus of Williams College can be seen, resting comfortably on the flatland abutting the Hoosic River, with the serene white steeple of the First Congregational Church and the grey neo-Gothic tower of Thompson Memorial Chapel (in configuration not altogether unlike Oxford's Merton tower) together marking the center of what seems (misleadingly) to be a secluded, tranquil, and self-contained village protected by its encompassing mountains from intrusion by the troubles of the larger world that lies beyond.

In the early eighteenth century, what is now Williamstown was basically a wilderness area, technically Mohican hunting territory but uninhabited on any permanent basis, lying athwart the principal north-south Indian trail which reached down from Canada via Lake Champlain, Lake George, and the Hoosic valley, and pointed like a dagger into the very heart of New England. Though situated some sixty to seventy miles southeast of Lake George, Williamstown still lies on the periphery of the contested area of "boundless woods," "interminable forest," and "bleak and savage wilderness" in which James Fenimore Cooper set his story of *The Last of the Mohicans* as it played out during the course of the Seven Years' War (also known as the French and Indian War) that ran from 1756 to 1763. A contemporary memoirist, indeed, spoke in 1753 of the whole area stretching northward from the Stockbridge settlement in the southern Berkshires as "that great and terrible wilderness of several hundred miles extent which reaches [up] to Canada." A century later, after the area had been settled and the great clearances somehow undertaken, it would have been eccentric to speak in such terms. But today, after the subsequent decline in farming and the forest's swift and greedy repossession of land once cleared with such pain and toil, it is not too hard to imagine oneself, having rounded a bend in one of the trails that cut across our mountainous and densely wooded terrain, coming face to face with Fenimore Cooper's noble Chingachgook, last of the Mohicans, or even, God forbid, with the fearsome Magua himself.

In the mid-eighteenth century, the northern Berkshires was still dangerous territory for Anglo-American settlers. At the beginning of the century it lay beyond the westerly line of settlement which then ran along the Connecticut River valley, with the town of Deerfield being the furthermost settlement in the northwest. As such, during the course of the Nine Years' War (also known as the War of the League of Augsburg, 1688–97) it had been exposed to repeated Indian attacks. Its great moment of trial, however, came later, after the outbreak of the War of Spanish Succession (1701–14), when, in 1704, a powerful French and Indian force, having taken the defenders by surprise and penetrated the town's protective stockade, destroyed half the dwellings and, having killed 21 of the inhabitants, departed for Canada along with some 112 captives. Among these, the best known was Deerfield's minister, John Williams, friend of Increase and Cotton Mather and member of a family prominent in the religious, political, and military affairs of western Massachusetts. Later ransomed along with most of his family, he went on to write a celebrated captivity narrative, *The Redeemed Captive Returning to Zion*. But his little daughter Eunice, only seven years old when taken into captivity, chose not to return and, having turned Catholic and later married a Mohawk, assimilated into native society. That society was a matrilineal one and I believe that descendants bearing the name "Williams" survive to this day in the small Mohawk territory of Kahnawake just south of Montreal.

I make a point of mentioning all of this because, fifty years later, it was a cousin of Eunice's (albeit more than once removed), Ephraim Williams, Jr., who was to bequeath the Williams name to West Hoosac, a new settlement further to the west. Lying athwart the main north-south Indian trail from Canada, West Hoosac replaced Deerfield as the northwesterly point of resistance to attempted French and Indian intrusions into New England. William Shirley, governor of the Bay State province, had ordered the building of a chain of forts along the northern border of the province, the westernmost of which, Fort Massachusetts, built in 1745, was situated along the Hoosic on what is now Route 2 in the town of North Adams. Remnants of its chimney (or a rebuilt version of that chimney) have survived into the present, jutting up incongruously from the parking lot of what was, until recently, the Pricechopper Supermarket. Captain (later Major) Ephraim Williams, Jr., had been placed in command of the whole line of forts, but he was not at Fort Massachusetts in 1746 when, after the War of Austrian Succession (1740–48) had spilled over into North America, its garrison of twenty-one was forced to capitulate to a French and Indian force over nine hundred strong and the fort itself was destroyed. In 1747 it was rebuilt and, with Williams now in direct command, succeeded in repulsing another French and Indian attack just before the end of the war in 1748.

In the short interval before Anglo-French hostilities along the frontier were resumed at the start of the Seven Years' War in May 1756, and partly as an additional defensive measure, the town of West Hoosac (the future Williamstown) was surveyed and laid out four miles further to the west of Fort Massachusetts, with members of that fort's garrison acquiring a goodly number of the available lots. For the protection of the settlers there, Fort West Hoosac (a blockhouse and stockade affair) was hastily built close to the center of the new town (located very close to the present-day Williams Inn and Field Park). While it succeeded in withstanding repeated Indian attacks, three of the local settlers were killed and scalped in the nearby Hemlock Brook valley when they made the mistake of venturing out to round up some stray cattle, and for the next two years life for the West Hoosac settlers remained fraught with danger. Then the tide of battle turned and Lord Jeffrey Amherst led the British and colonial forces to victory at Ticonderoga and Crown Point, thus relieving the pressure on the Massachusetts frontier. For Crown Point was the well-fortified French base on Lake Champlain from which devastating French and Indian raids had been launched against settlements in New York state and New England. In 1755 an earlier British and colonial attempt to seize it had failed, despite the defeat of French and Indian forces at the Battle of Lake George. And it was at the start of that battle on September 8, 1755, that Ephraim Williams, Jr., now a colonel and regimental commander, was killed.

During the previous July and before the expedition to seize Crown Point had left Albany, "not knowing how God in his Providence may dispose of my life," Williams had drawn up his last will and testament. The document is a quite lengthy and detailed one, but the only provision calling for our attention is one concerning matters educational. The Williams family, though they claimed Welsh descent, hailed from East Anglia. Robert Williams, Ephraim's ancestor, had settled in Roxbury, Massachusetts, in 1637, and he and his descendants had exhibited across time a strong commitment to the advancement of education in the colonies. They had participated in the founding of Roxbury Free Grammar School, Deerfield Academy, Mears Indian Charity School, and a school in Lakeman, Connecticut. In his will, Ephraim himself followed that family tradition by providing that the residual of his estate be used to support and maintain forever "a free school" in the township of West Hoosac. That provision, however, had two conditions attached to it. First, that "the Governour & General Court give the said township the name of Williamstown," a provision that was met in 1765 when the town was finally incorporated. Second, that "the said township fall within the jurisdiction of the Province of Massachusetts Bay," a matter that was not destined to be definitively settled until 1784 when the precise border between Massachusetts and New York state was finally determined.

In the meantime and while the educational provisions in Ephraim's will still languished in legal limbo, several members of the Williams family in the Connecticut valley had in 1762 attempted (in the teeth of opposition from Harvard College) to persuade the governor and legislature to charter a college in Hadley. But though (ironically) they had sought to enlist for that venture the backing of Lord Jeffrey Amherst, the attempt had failed, and it was to be in Williamstown that the second college in Massachusetts was to open its doors.

With the border issue finally settled, the executors of the will turned over in 1785 the pertinent assets to "the Trustees of the Donation of Ephraim Williams, Esq. for Maintaining a Free School in Williamstown." The latter then proceeded to construct a large and impressive brick building (the present-day West College) that was clearly grander and much more commodious than anything needed for the education of the town's children. When it opened in 1790–91, it accommodated not only the proposed, basically elementary, free school for the children of town residents but also a more advanced academy or grammar school for which tuition was charged. And in 1793 when the institution was incorporated as a degree-granting college for men, the trustees having successfully petitioned the legislature for a charter, the free school ceased to exist, though the academy lingered on for several years as a sort of preparatory school for those hoping to matriculate at the college.

As a college, Williams, though steeped in the Congregationalist tradition, was nonsectarian in the sense that it was not formally affiliated with any religious denomination and that its charter stipulated no religious test for its president, trustees, or faculty. It was also destined, in the words of the celebrated Supreme Court decision in the case of *Dartmouth College v. Woodward* (1819), to be classified as a private "eleemosynary institution" rather than a civil or public institution or, in any way, an "instrument of government." That, I assume, is clear enough. Less clear, however, may be the fact that the new institution was chartered as a college. For what, exactly, did that mean? The question is not as redundant as it might seem to be. In the twentieth century, the institutional status of colleges like Williams came to be dogged by uncertainty, in North America as well as Europe. In Europe, after all, "college" is a name frequently associated with institutions belonging to the secondary rather than the tertiary stage of education. My own grammar school in Liverpool was known as St. Francis Xavier's *College*. In the late nineteenth century, moreover, in the wake of the rise (under German influence) of the research university to a position of prominence on the North American higher educational scene, educational commentators were clearly tempted to assign the older colleges to the institutional stratum concerned with advanced *secondary* education. Thus David Starr Jordan, the distinguished founding president of Stanford University, confidently predicted that with time "the college will disappear, in fact if not in name. The best will *become* universities, the others will *return* to their place as academies"—return, that is, to being advanced-level secondary schools. With this interesting (if condescending) judgment, he betrayed his participation in the widespread confusion about the institutional origin and institutional status of the old American colleges which, starting with Harvard College itself in 1636, had constituted the norm in American higher education prior to the late nineteenth-century advent of the modern research university. Some of those old colleges, and Williams is a case in point, may well have started out as schools, but as *colleges* they did not trace their institutional lineage back to any sort of academy for secondary education. Their immediate forebears, instead, were the constituent colleges of Oxford and Cambridge. Thus the model for Harvard was Emmanuel College, Cambridge, and, for William and Mary, Queen's College, Oxford. But beyond that, and in a departure from the Oxford or Cambridge model, Harvard and the other old American colleges had been accorded a distinctive *university* prerogative—that of conferring (as the Williams charter puts it) "such Degrees as are usually conferred by Universities established for the education of Youth." By virtue of that fact, they were established ultimately on the model of the single-college universities that had appeared in the fifteenth and sixteenth centuries in Spain (Sigüenza), Scotland (Marischal College, Aberdeen), and, more famously, Ireland (Trinity College, Dublin). In this connection, it is worthy of note that Harvard College was sometimes referred to as "the University of Cambridge" just as Trinity was sometimes called Dublin University or, with greater legal and institutional precision, "the University of

Trinity College, Dublin." Similarly the argument for Yale in the 1899 case of *Yale University v. the Town of New Haven* spoke of "the University of Yale College" and stated that its founders, because of paucity of numbers, had chosen to adopt the Scottish and Irish model and to confer "upon the *same corporation* . . . the power of the university in granting degrees and of the college in government."

The sharp distinction, then, between college and university which people like President Jordan instinctively drew (and which people today all too often assume) is not one rooted in the earlier history of the American liberal arts college. It is, instead, something of a late nineteenth century American novelty. It is one spawned by the enormous contemporary admiration for the German research university and by the concomitant attempt, at places like Johns Hopkins, Clark, Cornell, Chicago, and Stanford, or, for that matter, at such older colleges as Harvard and Yale, to replicate its particular characteristics on American soil. That novel distinction has not proved to be a helpful one. It has tended to promote the idea that the freestanding, residential liberal arts college is something *less* than the modern American university rather than something *other* than that. It has even encouraged colleges to permit themselves to be defined by what they lack—great research libraries and laboratories, graduate and professional schools—rather than in terms of what they proudly possess, an undistracted and undiffused intensity of focus on a broadly based education in the arts and sciences which has long since become wholly extraordinary, not only abroad but increasingly so here in the United States, as well as the firm and unswerving commitment to bring to the education of *under*graduates the full resources pertaining to a small university. For that is what all the older colleges were and what those among them that, unlike Harvard and Yale, chose not to transform themselves into research universities still are—small college-universities devoted exclusively (or almost exclusively) to the education of undergraduates. And that is the type of institution whose faculty I joined in 1961 when I came to Williams.

Obviously, like Williamstown itself, it had undergone a great deal of change since it was chartered in 1793. At the heart of the campus, however, still stood its first building, West College (1790), situated on the east side of Main Street at the crest of what used to be called Consumption Hill. And right opposite it on the westerly side still stood the elegant house that General Sloane had built in 1801 and that has, for more than a century, served as the house of the college president. And such obvious symbols of continuity make it all too easy to forget just how different and, indeed, tiny the early college was. When Mark Hopkins, its fourth (and most celebrated) president, retired from that office in 1872, the student body numbered no more than 119 and the faculty amounted to no more than a handful of professors and tutors—these last playing much the same role as graduate assistants later on. To remind myself of that fact, I hung in my office as president a picture of Hopkins and his entire faculty, taken in 1866. They numbered only 10 and fitted easily, even posed in space-consuming Victorian casual style, on one half of the porch of the President's House. The administrative burdens shouldered by the president can hardly have been very pressing and, so far as I know, Hopkins didn't even have an office.

By 1961, with its decline as an agricultural community, Williamstown itself, with a population of around 7,500 (not very different from today) was well on the way to becoming a destination point for skiers and cultural tourists. The all-encompassing forest which, in the late-eighteenth and nineteenth centuries, had been pushed back and well up the slopes of the surrounding mountains, was now reclaiming with astonishingly rapid second growth the ground it had reluctantly yielded to the tenacity of the early settlers. And with that partial return of Fenimore Cooper's "boundless woods" was coming also, after a century of marginalization by agriculture, the return of an abundant wildlife: black bears, wild turkeys, coyotes, bobcats, possibly cougar (i.e., catamounts or mountain lions), the occasional lugubrious itinerant moose, and everywhere, it seems, white-tailed deer. It is interesting that the town history felt it noteworthy enough to record for posterity that in 1905 some "wild deer" had been sighted in the Hemlock Brook area. By 1961 that had come to be a phenomenon taken simply for granted.

If the town had changed, so, too, had the college, which now boasted a student body of some 1100. For its first seventy or eighty years, its main achievement was that of having survived to become a rather modest if reasonably stable institution whose mission it was to serve the needs of the region and locality, in the process sending a goodly proportion of its graduates into the ministry. That achievement was not something to be taken for granted. A great crisis had to be surmounted in 1821. In that year, the trustees having failed to persuade the legislature to move the college from its westerly rural backwater to the more civilized of environs of Northampton in the Connecticut valley, the then president, Zephaniah Swift Moore, took matters into his own hands and led some of its students over the mountains to establish a new college at Amherst. It was a secession reminiscent of the moves that had led, five centuries earlier, to the foundation of the University of Angers by secession from the University of Paris and to the foundation of Cambridge via a similar breakaway from Oxford. Williams somehow survived that moment of crisis, and by 1872 when Hopkins stepped down it had begun to attract students from the midwestern as well as the eastern states and, probably because of its missionary connections, from Hawaii and countries like China and Persia. It was also beginning to attract students from prosperous families with backgrounds in commerce, business, and finance. Its graduates were now beginning to pursue callings in those same realms, as well as in the professions at large, and the wealth controlled by its alumni was accordingly on the increase. While it had long been surpassed both in endowment and enrollment by Amherst and by Union College in Schenectady, New York, Williams began, in the late nineteenth and early twentieth centuries, to develop into a more prosperous institution, graced with an array of handsome collegiate buildings and possessed of the resources enabling it to mount a much richer array of curricular offerings, especially in the natural sciences. Its Latin requirement for admission tended to limit its applicant pool to students of privilege graduating from the old preparatory boarding schools. But when it dropped that requirement in the late 1930s, something of a quickening in intellectual tempo began to occur. Under two presidencies marked by a measure of activism, those of Tyler Dennet (1934–37) and James Phinney Baxter (1937–61), a good deal of accumulated deadwood was cleared from the ranks of the faculty and some stellar appointments made. At the same time, and especially in the wake of the influx of veterans on the GI Bill after the war, the nature of the student body had begun to change. It was becoming somewhat more diverse in religious and racial terms and an increasing number of gifted students from public schools nationwide matriculated.

Such developments, however, desirable though they might be, turned out to cause growing tension with the fraternity culture that had established itself so firmly at the college during the Gilded Age. That culture reached its apogee in the years leading up to the Second World War when fraternity membership climbed to as high as 80 percent of the student body and when it was no longer the college but the fraternities—independent, self-governing corporations—that had come to carry the primary responsibility for the feeding and housing of students. And it was the fraternities, with all their self-selecting exclusivisms, that had come to shape the social mores and dominate the social life of the campus. The bulk of their members periodically failed to meet even an average level of scholastic performance and they came increasingly to be seen as heading into collision with the college's academic mission and as constituting indeed, an impediment to its intellectual vibrancy.

The fraternities were closed during the war years and their functioning, once reopened and as the 1950s wore on, came to be dogged by controversy. They were shadowed by suspicion (sometimes well founded) that they were still following the racially and ethnically discriminatory practices encouraged by some of the national fraternal bodies with which they were affiliated. As a result, an enormous amount of institutional energy at the level both of the students themselves and of the president and trustees came to be devoted to the attempt to rectify any such wrongs and to align the functioning of fraternities more effectively with the college's institutional values and academic goals. Committee after committee was formed to address the intricate issues involved, but their recommendations (not always implemented) usually took the form of tinkering with the system rather than of calling it into question. Only one of them, the student Committee of 22, chose to bite the bullet, calling in 1957 for the outright abolition of fraternities at Williams and the substitution of a system of college-administered residential units to which students would be assigned via a system of random selection. But to no avail. If the drawbacks of the prevailing system were becoming daily more evident, the identification of generally acceptable solutions proved elusive.

Of all of this I was almost totally ignorant when I arrived at Williams in August 1961 as a new, wet-behind-the-ears member of the History Department. Never having been an undergraduate in the United States, I knew little or nothing about fraternities or about the degree of power they were capable of wielding over student life. I tended to view them, I think, as a species of self-selecting exclusive club that merely punctuated the general disposition of student living. Something akin, perhaps, to Yale's Skull and Bones, whose building I passed regularly on my way into campus and which, or so I assumed, was little more than a rather childish (if well-endowed) survival into the present of late-Victorian group sentimentalism. Nor did fraternity-related concerns come up as a topic of conversation when I first met Jack Sawyer (John E. Sawyer) in the spring of 1961 and not long after he had been elected to succeed Phinney Baxter as president of Williams. Robin Winks, a friend of his and a colleague of mine in the Yale History Department, had invited me along with Dan O'Connor (just appointed to the Williams Philosophy Department) to meet him over lunch at one of the Yale colleges. On that occasion, as I recall it, Jack talked mainly about the Williams faculty members he had known and admired, not least among them Richard Newhall, by then emeritus, a medieval historian of some distinction who, in his day, had been a student at Harvard of Charles Homer Haskins, the great pioneer of medieval historical studies in America. (The Newhalls were to extend a gracious welcome to us when we got to Williams and, by virtue of his kind gift, on my bookshelves proudly sit Mr. Newhall's six volumes of R. W. and A. J. Carlyle's *A History of Mediaeval Political Theory in the West*). At that time an associate professor of economics at Yale, Sawyer was a graduate of Williams, class of 1939, and as an insider to the fraternity scene and a long-standing trustee of Williams, had to have been acutely conscious of the mounting unease on campus about the way in which the fraternity system was now functioning. But he had not yet had to confront the urgencies of the situation created when, at the end of the 1960–61 academic year, a group of forty-five students, most of them campus leaders and fraternity men, submitted to President Baxter a petition requesting the formation of a committee charged with finding some alternative approach to the fraternity selection process that would involve collegiate decision rather than student election. That petition and Sawyer's ultimate reaction to it were to determine, not only the shape of his own presidency, but also much of the dynamics of institutional life at Williams as the transformative and eventually tumultuous 1960s unfolded.

My parents, Dublin 1922.

(right)
My kindergarten
picture, 1935–36.

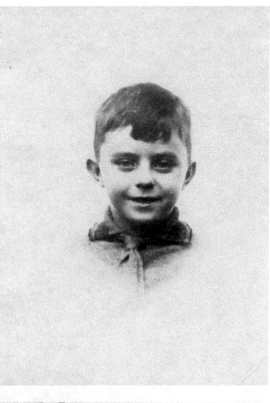

(below)
With my siblings,
Liverpool 1936.
Clockwise from me:
Noel, Vincent, Molly.

Corpus Christi College, Oxford, the main quad (1517).

Celebrating the end of Schools, the Corpus History crowd. I am at the right.

(right)
Second Lieutenant
F. C. Oakley,
Royal Signals,
Gloucester 1956.

(below)
At Noel and Monica's
wedding, Liverpool 1956.
Molly is next to me, my
parents are at the left.

With Tony Hobbs at his wedding, Wimbledon 1957.

Williamstown nestling in its valley.

Williams, West College (1790).

Williams, the President's House (1801).

A poke in the eye from Brian, our youngest, Williamstown 1965.

(right)
Book jacket photo
by my colleague
Charles Fuqua,
1969.

(below)
The next generation of
first cousins assembled,
Liverpool 1970. Deirdre
is second from the right;
Chris, Tim, and Brian are
the last three on the left.

(left)
Deirdre, Brian, Chris,
and Tim with Henry
Higgins, our first horse,
Williamstown 1971.

The two of us at home in 1984.

At my induction in 1985. Three Williams presidents: Jack Sawyer at the left, John Chandler at the right.

At my induction in 1985. Eldred Jones bringing greetings from Sierra Leone.

The honorees at our 1988 fall convocation, celebrating the 25th anniversary of the March on Washington. Counterclockwise from me: Charlayne Hunter-Gault, Congressman John Lewis, Rosa Parks, Ralph Abernathy, Ruth Batson, and Burke Marshall.

On the job: Arriving at Winfield House, Regent's Park, London, to address an alumni gathering hosted by Henry Catto, Williams class of 1952, then US ambassador to the UK.

Off the job around 1990: Skiing in Utah with Brian, Chris, Claire-Ann, and Deirdre.

At my retirement dinner, Mount Hope Farm, Williamstown, November 1993. Trying out the new saddle the trustees had just given me.

(right)
Farewell.
Christmas 1993.

(below)
The children and
grandchildren
assembled for our
50th wedding
anniversary,
Williamstown
2008.

CHAPTER ELEVEN

Encountering the Old Williams

That "old" Williams, it has to be confessed, did have its own charms. When we arrived in Williamstown in August 1961, like many others, of course, I was blissfully unprescient about the dimensions of the wave of institutional discontent and change that, by the end of the decade, was to break over the world of higher education. My own concerns, moreover, were parochially personal. They focused on matters familial, on the challenge of learning to teach effectively in a setting where good teaching was highly valued, and on the parallel challenge of keeping my research program going. This last was very important to me and certainly possible, though in my new liberal arts college setting it was clearly going to call for more stubbornly committed determination than it had at Yale. In the absence of the life-support systems provided by a great research library and the ready availability of the (non-travelling) rare books on which my own work was dependent, it was to call for more library-related travel and, in its more specialized and recondite aspects, could occasionally feel like a frustrating exercise in pushing water uphill. But it was doable and to me, even apart from considerations of career advancement, too important to let slip by the wayside. It was, after all, a compelling interest in matters intellectual in general, and historical in particular, that had led me to become an academic. And the business of teaching was for me so inexorably intertwined with that more general quest for understanding that I found altogether artificial any attempt to separate teaching and research. At that time, and indeed throughout my academic career until I embarked upon the open waters of retirement, the great challenge, instead, was always that of somehow protecting enough time to keep the project of the day moving ahead.

So far as family matters went, we had a lot on our plates. When we arrived at Williams we already had two small children; within the next three years we added two more, all four (no twins) born within a five-year period. We were happy to be able to settle in to the ground floor apartment we had been allotted in Williams Hall Annex, one of two old wooden-frame buildings situated on Lynde Lane within the future footprint of the Mission Park student residence that was to be built in 1971 to accommodate the influx of additional students when the college went coeducational and increased the size of its student body by a full third. In 1961, however, it was still a very quiet part of the campus. The apartment consisted of a largish kitchen, a bathroom, two bedrooms, no dining room, but a capacious bay-windowed living room that we really liked. That room looked out onto Mission Park and up its tree-clad slope to the monument memorializing the Haystack Prayer Meeting that took place on that spot during a thunderstorm in 1806 and to which the American foreign mission movement traces its origins. And, diagonally across to the left, one could catch a glimpse of some of the headstones in the college's cemetery, a place in which a goodly number of our faculty predecessors were resting from their earnest pedagogic labors, and to burial in which we and our spouses were entitled. It was a fringe benefit that we trusted would take even longer to kick in then the benefits of our TIAA-CREF pension scheme and was the source, accordingly, of many a mordant joke among the nontenured faculty who had more pressing insecurities to worry about.

Williams Hall Annex was a rather creaky, rambling structure that housed four faculty apartments in all. Laszlo and Dinny Versenyi and their two children, Adam and Andrea, occupied the other one on the ground floor. The two apartments upstairs belonged, respectively, to Warren and Alice Ilchmann (both of them future college presidents, he at the Pratt Institute, she at Sarah Lawrence) and to the Govans, whose son Michael was later to graduate from Williams and, in the fullness of time, to become director of the Los Angeles County Museum of Art and an esteemed fellow trustee on the board of the Sterling and Francine Clark Art Institute in Williamstown.

Laszlo Versenyi, a member of the Philosophy Department, turned out to be a fine colleague and a lively collaborator of mine in more than one curricular venture. An Hungarian émigré, like me he had come to Williams after teaching for a while at Yale. He was a truly interesting fellow, possessed of a formidable intelligence that was happily modulated by a characteristically droll sense of humor. After working on Heidegger, on whom he was later to publish a book, he had been drawn back in time by his love for the philosophy and literature of the ancient Greeks, and had switched to writing on the pre-Socratics and on Plato. Socrates (whom he portrayed, I think, in somewhat existentialist terms) was his hero; Aristotle, on the other hand, he viewed with a measure of distaste and tried, if possible, to avoid having to deal with him at all. He was a wonderfully challenging teacher in the Socratic, dialectical mode, and was capable of leaving an indelible imprint on the minds of those students who were fortunate enough to encounter him in the classroom. At his memorial service in 1988, Bill (William J.) Bennett, class of 1965, at that time secretary for education in the Reagan administration and a vigorously conservative combatant in the culture wars of the day, spoke with movingly affectionate wit about the startling and transformative impression Laszlo had made on him and his fellow football players when they encountered him in the introductory philosophy course. It had led them to become philosophy majors and it changed their lives. "He was a philosopher, a lover of wisdom," Bennett said. "He took us undergraduates as if we would be lovers of wisdom, too—and we were his."

Three memories of Laszlo are firmly fixed in my mind. The most recent, and saddest, is that of his walking into my office when he was chairman of the Philosophy Department and I president of the college. With characteristic directness he opened up the conversation by saying: "Frank, I am dying. What are we going to do about the department?" He was only in his late fifties at the time but he really was dying (of lung cancer). Within six months he was gone. The second memory stems from the years when we co-taught the required senior seminar for those majoring in our interdepartmental major in the history of ideas. It was focused on "The Idea of Law" and ranged broadly across the centuries from the classical Greeks to the celebrated Hart-Fuller debate in the twentieth century. Teaching with him proved to be a bracing experience. Until then, I hadn't realized that his characteristic mode of thinking was quite so exclusively philosophical and literary in nature. He didn't seem to have a single bone in his body that one could safely label as historical. The first time we taught the course we seemed (to the delight of the class) to disagree about practically everything. I can still see us, going at it into the twilight around the table in the old, handsomely paneled Preston Room, long after the seminar was supposed to have ended. Laszlo was a formidable dialectician and there were times, as he invoked Platonic dialogues with which I was not familiar, that I was led in my desperation to wonder if he was actually inventing them in order to make the clinching point. It was in many ways a marvelous and, certainly, an uncommonly stimulating experience. At least for us. Alumni who as students took that class have since assured me that they really enjoyed it. But I am inclined to suspect now, and certainly worried then, that the principal appeal it may have had for them was as an intrinsically interesting species of pedagogic spectator sport, deriving its charm from the fact that they were not accustomed to seeing two professors, both of whom (I have every reason to believe) they liked, respected, and certainly knew very well, disagreeing so tenaciously one with another without rancor but with great vigor.

The third, and happiest, memory goes back to the first summer after we arrived at Williams and when we and the Versenyis were still next-door neighbors in Williams Hall Annex. On nice evenings after dinner we used to sit outside on deck chairs drinking coffee and having a smoke, while the children milled around and Laszlo, who blossomed on such informal occasions, held forth wittily and irreverently about the philosophical world, the eccentricities of his colleagues, and the stupidity of all administrators. One such occasion is lodged firmly in my mind by the survival of a quick snapshot that Claire-Ann took. Our daughter Deirdre, not quite three and a busy little bee, deciding for some reason that she should give her daddy a pretend hair wash, had come up unnoticed behind my deck chair and had started scrubbing away at my scalp with her pretend soap. The "soap" was, in fact, a piece of hard wood and the procedure was obviously painful, for the snap shows my feet up in the air while I reached back to try to grab the "soap." It was a golden moment and remains a cherished memory.

Our entry into the life of the college was in general, then, a happy one. With an all-male student body of about 1100 (it's 2000 now, about half female) and a faculty and staff much smaller than today's, it had an intimacy of scale that doubtless had its drawbacks. It was the upside, however, that caught our attention. The college itself was less bureaucratized than it inevitably came to be and, for good or ill, concern with the purity of "process"—threatening sometimes to subvert a focus on matters substantive—was not yet as dominant as it was to become in the 1970s and subsequent decades. The place had a quite personal, face-to-face, feel about it and our senior colleagues put themselves out to make us feel welcome and to introduce us to colleagues in other disciplines. In the early to mid-1970s, the hallowed institution of the faculty dinner party was to fall victim, on ideological grounds, to derisive dismissal by the more recent additions to the faculty ranks and, on practical grounds, to the advent of demanding dual careers and the consequent shrinkage or marginalization of the cadre of faculty wives on whose generously extended efforts it had always depended. In the early 1960s, however, "faculty wife" was not yet a term of derogation or a focus of condescension, and the institution of the faculty dinner party was alive and well, still playing its traditionally important role in the stitching together of the collegiate community.

We were invited, then, to the homes of all our senior departmental colleagues in turn, and we, in response, as doubtless was expected, reciprocated. Not having a dining room in our place, we had to eat buffet style and, because the children's bedroom was right off the living room, we used to hang a blanket inside their door to muffle the sound of conversation and prevent their being woken up. Being of social disposition, we also involved ourselves in activities sponsored by the Faculty Club and, within a year or so, I was conned into taking on for a while the job of entertainments chairman. My main memory of that role is that of having cliff-hanger experiences when it looked as if our liquor supply might run out during the euphemistically entitled "tea dances" that took place after football home games. The veritable tsunami of cheap white wine that was eventually to engulf the academic profession had not yet begun to crest. Hard liquor was the order of the day, and, on those occasions, an enormous amount of it seemed customarily to be consumed. That being so, and because people insisted on having live music, I had to think creatively in order to stretch my rather meager budget to cover a series of these affairs without having to overprice them. To that end, I made the mistake on one occasion of hiring a comparatively inexpensive band from nearby Adams, which has a large population of Polish descent. It was called Andy Konopka's Trio and proved to be quite lively. Unfortunately, it turned out to play nothing but polkas all evening and while I myself enjoyed polkas, it became clear that not everyone shared my enthusiasm for them.

Whatever the case, by the fall of our second year at Williams, we had come to know enough people to think in terms of throwing a party of our own. To that end we teamed up with the Versenyis and invited forty or more people, most of whom accepted and showed up. As we didn't have enough space at home, we got the use of the old Alumni House on Spring Street, later to become a student pub and to be called "the Log." Having acquired a record player with the help of S & H Green Stamps accumulated via supermarket purchases, we were able to play records for dancing. I am amused in retrospect by the fact that we didn't hesitate to include the college president and his wife, Jack and Ann Sawyer, among our invitees and impressed by the fact that they actually showed up, mixing briefly with everybody and sipping tentatively a bit of the rather lethal "Artillery Punch" we were serving, the recipe for which I had borrowed from my father-in-law. Clearly, rather than taking the invitation as a piece of immature chutzpah, they had welcomed it as a nice collegial gesture.

Meanwhile, of course, there was work to be done. At Williams, student expectations of effective teaching were dauntingly high and the History Department itself certainly reinforced those expectations. At the time, I was called upon to put together a whole package of new courses and, in those early years, I spent an enormous amount of time on class preparation, sometimes having to get up at 5:00 a.m. to finish the task for an upcoming class. Classes being comparatively small, the preferred mode of instruction was not the formal lecture but a form of more or less directed discussion. To be effective, I quickly discovered, the type of discussion had to be tuned carefully to the particular subject and the type of material being taught, and, over the years, I experimented a lot with the degree to which I actually directed or controlled such discussions. Here, my previous classroom experience at Toronto and Yale proved to be helpful. Williams students, I soon realized, were of more or less the same quality as those at Yale, though, not feeling quite as consecrated as the latter by the mere fact of admission, they tended to put more energy into the task of being well prepared for class. Neither at that time nor later, and in this like most of my colleagues at Williams, was I able to relax into the comfortable assumption that the teaching I was doing was truly effective. Across time, student habits, attitudes, perspectives, and expectations change; a tried and true pedagogic tactic that once met with gratifying success could easily turn out, under changing conditions, to have lost its effectiveness, driving one accordingly back to the drawing board. In such a setting, the cliché of the lecturer droning on from yellowing lecture notes simply didn't hold. Across time, then, between the demands of teaching under such conditions and the increasing burden of committee responsibilities and the like, I was never able to get any research or writing done during the academic year. That was to remain a matter for the summer months and periodic sabbaticals, though there was something quite invigorating in the regular alternation between the intensity of the academic year and the contemplative space that the summer months afforded.

So far as the content of my teaching went, I responded to the growing interest in area studies which Jack Sawyer had encouraged at the college by reducing the amount of time devoted in the first semester to the early medieval centuries in Western Europe, at that time no more than a provincial backwater. Instead I gave equal time to Byzantium and Eastern Europe and also to the rise of the Arab Empire and the flowering of an Islamic civilization. Byzantium, after all, stood in direct continuity to the Roman Empire and the world of Islam also absorbed the Greek and Byzantine cultural legacy as well as that of Persia. That course I labeled, accordingly, the "Heirs of Rome." The second semester covered the Renaissance as well as the High and later Middle Ages and, being intrigued by the difficulties of periodizing history, I organized the latter part of it in such a way as to focus (with the help of colleagues in art, music, and literature) on "the problem of the Renaissance." I was also called upon unexpectedly (nobody had mentioned it when I interviewed for the job) to teach a course in Reformation history. Never having studied the subject either as an undergraduate or as a graduate student, I had to scramble hard to get on top of it, focusing the course fairly intently on the theologies of the various reformers, both magisterial and radical. It was eventually to mature into one of my favorite and most successful courses. And, among other courses in history and, later, history of ideas, I also developed an honors seminar on European political thinking from late antiquity to the early modern era. Over the years the regular teaching of this seminar gave me, among other things, the opportunity to come to terms with such demanding works as Augustine's *De civitate dei*, John of Paris's *Tractatus de regia potestate et papali*, and Marsiglio of Padua's *Defensor pacis*—this last perhaps the greatest of all medieval contributions to political philosophy. Teaching the successive groups of gifted students who gravitated to that seminar or to the tutorial I eventually developed out of it proved to be a very rewarding experience and proved also in the end to lay the indispensable groundwork for the attempt I was later to make in my retirement years to essay a broad-gauged reinterpretation of the development of Western political thinking from the Hellenistic era down to the mid-seventeenth century and to reshape the way in which we have been prone to conceptualizing the medieval phase.

In addition to courses in our own areas of specialization, all the Europeanists in the department, senior as well as junior, taught discussion sections in our yearlong, common syllabus, introductory course in European history. Covering the *longue durée* from 800 to 1914, it was the sort of survey course that seems since, for reasons both historiographic and practical, to have fallen out of fashion. On the historiographic side of the equation, the tightening grip of academic specialization, along with concomitant worries that the survey approach was likely to make for superficiality of understanding, have encouraged a privileging of the greater interpretative depth to be gained by narrowing the chronological reach of courses. It is true that since the 1980s world or global history has properly striven to find its place under the academic sun. But it has done so very much as yet another historiographic specialty and I don't sense that it has succeeded in making much of a dent on the historical imaginations of most Europeanists. As for things practical, over the past two or three decades, confronted by dauntingly restricted job prospects, nontenured faculty have become a bit paranoid about being called upon to teach anything lying clearly outside their areas of specialization over which they at least feel a measure of control. And the very prospect of having to co-teach in a course with a genuinely common syllabus seems now to have become totally unacceptable.

All of that said, History 101–102, the introductory history course in which we all taught, was on balance a good one, I think, though not quite as successful as the Yale equivalent on which it was modeled. Part of the reason for that shortfall was the fact that no one person was charged with giving the weekly lectures. Instead, we were all called upon to take our turn lecturing on appropriate topics chosen from those listed in the syllabus. The downside to this arrangement, apart from the fact that the lectures fluctuated in quality, was that the series as a whole was not as well integrated as its Yale equivalent. The correlative upside, however, for it was customary for all of us to attend the lectures, was the fact that it gave us the opportunity to observe and learn from the way in which our colleagues went about that task. The two senior members involved were highly experienced and capable hands, and one of them, Bob (R. G. L.) Waite, a specialist in the Weimar and Nazi periods in German history, was a truly gifted and compelling performer, with a sharp nose for the dramatic moment and a finely honed sense of rhetorical timing. We junior members did our best, and certainly took our lecturing assignments (four or five set pieces across the course of the academic year) with the utmost seriousness. We were conscious of the fact that our performances might constitute useful advertising among students for our own elective courses, and conscious, too, that those performances afforded our tenured colleagues the opportunity to observe directly and arrive at some sort of judgment about our capabilities in relation at least to that particular form of teaching. And we couldn't help being aware of the fact that the department chairman, who was an Americanist, was in the habit of sitting in discreetly when it was the turn of new members of the department to lecture.

Mildly intimidating, I suppose, especially given the importance of first impressions. But it was in some ways a plus. At the Williams of the day, there was still no formal method for garnering student judgments about the quality of faculty teaching. So far as I could tell, the chairman had to rely for that on generalized student scuttlebutt or what the senior history majors (whom he taught in the required senior course) had to say about it. Given the modern orientation of the history major (essentially nineteenth- and twentieth-century European and American

history), my elective courses lay outside its purview and many, sometimes most, of my students were majoring in such other disciplines as
classics, philosophy, and religion. So, Williams operating on a stringent
up or out tenure system, and teaching capability weighing heavily in
such decisions, I couldn't help worrying a bit about how he could learn
anything about the quality of my teaching in those electives. I was mildly
reassured, then, by the thought that the chairman and other senior colleagues would at least know that I could do a decent job in the formal
lecturing mode.

The other reason that our History 101–102 was not quite as successful as its Yale model was that the common syllabus had clearly been
subjected to a damaging amount of piecemeal tinkering, with various
members of the department replacing one or another of the Yale "Problems" with other materials they themselves thought worth reading. That
had served over time to threaten the course with a loss of depth and cohesion. And that bothered me. At one of our (infrequent) departmental
meetings when I was still quite new at the college and when the course
came up for discussion, I ventured (perhaps unwisely) to register my
dismay about the fact that the assignment for one recent discussion class
was no more than a mere fifteen pages in the Ferguson and Bruun textbook, a clear and not particularly demanding book that was in any case
required reading. It hardly called, I said, for extended discussion. To
which the chairman's acid and certainly crushing response was "Well,
Frank, nobody else seems to have found it difficult to teach." To which,
my hackles rising, I retorted, in turn, that it was the depth rather than
the teachability of the material that I was calling into question. After all,
I pointed out, we could teach the Manhattan telephone directory if we
had to. But why on earth would we want to? A bit cheeky for a new arrival, I suppose, and it wasn't to be the last time that I raised questions
about our customary modes of procedure. To his credit, Bob Scott never
seemed to hold it against me though I suspected, uneasily, that Fred Rudolph, a senior colleague in American studies and himself a graduate of
Williams, took a dim view of a new arrival's questioning the hallowed
norms of the department. But, then, after long observation of the behavior of colleagues, I have come to the firm conclusion that those who, as
nontenured faculty, fail to speak out on collegiate matters they deem important tend to be equally timid and passive after they have achieved the

security of tenure. Rather than job security, temperament seems to be what determines behavior on such matters. And the academic health and intellectual vibrancy of the institution eventually depend on the willingness of faculty members to speak out in dissent, even when it is likely to put them in an uncomfortable position.

In the early 1960s (though not always during the turbulent latter half of the decade), such moments of tension or dissension were infrequent. The department was mainly a congenial one, perhaps even a bit too congenial and teetering on the edge of being a bit boring. While many of its members would meet regularly for coffee in the Baxter Hall snack bar (which was eventually to become my spiritual home), the conversation rarely focused on matters intellectual. Instead, it tended somewhat obsessively to dwell on students from the past with whom the junior members were not acquainted. Although several of the senior members—Fred Rudolph, Bob Waite, and Dudley Bahlman—were themselves serious and active scholars, it was clearly not the done thing to talk on such occasions about one's research interests. Those tended to be referred to as "your own work" as if such work had nothing to do with the intellectual health of the college community as a whole. Rightly or wrongly (and it may well have been wrongly), one couldn't help getting the sense that talking too much about one's research interests might somehow give the damaging impression that one wasn't really serious about one's teaching responsibilities. So far as teaching and scholarship were concerned, the zero-sum appraisal seemed to dominate.

I am not sure what had happened to create this particular type of departmental culture, for, as I quickly discovered, it was rather at odds with that characteristic of several of the other large departments—not, it may be, with English, which at the time appeared torn with internal strife in a way that made the lot of the junior members an unenviable one, but certainly with economics. And I came much to admire the type of balance the latter had achieved between teaching and research, mounting what sounded like a very successful weekly seminar at which all members, senior as well as junior, were called upon in turn to share with their colleagues their own ongoing research efforts.

It turned out, then, during those early days at Williams, that for one reason or another much of the intellectual stimulus I received came from colleagues in other departments. One of the charms of the place, indeed, given its intimacy of scale, was the comparative ease with which one could get to know colleagues right across the college. In my case, that especially meant colleagues in classics, philosophy, religion, political science, and, once the subject was added to the curriculum, sociology. And I was led, accordingly, in the direction of exploring the possibility of pertinent interdepartmental studies. In the course of its curricular development, Williams had committed itself fully neither to the free elective system that Harvard had pioneered nor, by way of reaction, to the type of general education programs sponsored at places like Columbia and Chicago. Instead, it had chosen to combine distribution requirements in the three divisions—arts and humanities, social sciences, and natural sciences—with a regimen of tightly organized departmental majors. These last, framed on a model that made sense in clearly cumulative areas of study like the sciences and foreign languages, but much less so in subjects like literature and history, were organized fairly rigidly with a sequence of courses required of all majors. Though these courses were purported to build on one another and had to be taken sequentially across time, the realities of the matter stood at some distance from the curricular theory, and in the later sixties the whole system was to come under increasing pressure from student criticism and begin to crumble. Given the strength of the departmental ethos, interdisciplinary or interdepartmental studies were not as common as they would later come to be and were the target of a good deal of departmental skepticism. Of the two non-disciplinary majors then existing, political economy was managed via a reasonably stable collaboration between economics and political science. American history and literature (later to be named American studies), however, although rooted originally in a collaboration between the English and history departments, had by my time and for reasons that were easy enough to guess at fallen back into being a wholly owned subsidiary of the latter. The route to an expansion of interdepartmental programs was opened up in the mid-1960s by the establishment of coordinate programs (i.e., "minors," though that term was not used) in area studies, and when Laszlo Versenyi and I proposed the establishment in the freshman year of a program in ancient and medieval studies, we were able to secure faculty approval for it without any notable opposition. For the freshmen in the program, it involved the concentration of three of their five courses (in each of the two semesters) in Greek philosophy, literature, history, and their medieval equivalents. During the two years the program was offered, it was something of a success and attracted some very gifted and interesting students. Its defect was that it didn't lead anywhere in the subsequent sophomore, junior, and senior years. With that in mind, Dan O'Connor of the Philosophy Department and I collaborated in putting together, by way of a substitute, an interdepartmental major in the history of ideas, possessed of a firm foundation in things ancient and medieval but reaching forward into a choice of concentrations, modern as well as classical. We had already, in some ways, laid the grounds for that effort by collaborating for Scribner's Sons on a pedagogically oriented collection of readings which we entitled *Creation: The Impact of an Idea* (1969). Bringing that major into existence proved, however, to be something of a challenge. Some colleagues (including more than one in my own department) viewed it as a questionable novelty and an irritating motion to table carried the first time we brought it up for the requisite vote at a faculty meeting. After a modest (if reluctant) reduction in the requirements for the major, we were able to get it through late in the spring of 1969. We had built into the requirements a course in the history of science and, having persuaded the college-wide Committee on Appointments and Promotions that that subject really did belong in the college's curriculum, a successful search for an historian of science was pursued during the 1969–70 academic year and the program was launched in the fall of 1970. It succeeded from the start in attracting enough majors to make it viable and, during the (roughly) twenty years it stayed on the books, succeeded also in attracting to the college a remarkable series of gifted students, some of whom had studied Greek as well as Latin during their high school years. Teaching in that major came for me to be the source of an enormous amount of pleasure and intellectual stimulation, as did participation in the monthly cocurricular colloquia we mounted, using both local faculty talent and appropriate visiting speakers, which attracted a regular following of around forty. Running that program and teaching in it did impose on all of us some supererogatory labors. But whatever the additional burdens involved, they were undoubtedly worthwhile and I look back with pride on what we were able to accomplish.

Throughout those early years, and especially so in the mid- to late 1960s, I had other things, both personal and professional, on my mind. And, in retrospect, I can't help being struck by the degree to which the personal and professional intersected and intertwined. Though it was not to everyone's taste, that fact was one of the aspects of life at Williams that I found very attractive. Living, as we did, in the middle of the campus, we could take simply for granted the fact that the whole family could eat together every evening, something of a luxury, I was later to discover, for those pursuing other callings in less manageable settings. Until we moved to South Williamstown (no more than a ten-minute drive away), my office was within easy walking distance of our home. I don't think, as my children grew up, that there was anything mysterious for them about their daddy's work. They were surrounded, after all, by students, and the campus was in many ways their playground. With time they became accustomed to accompanying me to such things as the Saturday afternoon skating sessions at the college rink, at which I eventually tottered my way to a reasonable level of competence while they whizzed around with wild abandon. That would customarily be followed by hot chocolate and grilled honey buns (a *specialité de la maison*) at the college's crowded and convivial snack bar. In my own mind, indeed, some of my highly theoretical scholarly preoccupations ended up intertwined, in a manner too familiar to be altogether incongruous, with happy memories of familial distractions reaching back all the way to the days when the children were no more than toddlers.

On the professional side of things, my early years at Williams were punctuated, courtesy of a Social Science Research Council fellowship in political philosophy and legal theory, by a semester's leave of absence, during which we moved to London so that I could pursue research in the British Museum on late medieval natural law thinking. The move was not easy on Claire-Ann, and had she not been so competent a mom figure, well organized and infinitely patient (or so it seemed) with small, helpless creatures, we could not have done it. When, late in January 1963, we were due to embark in New York on the old Queen Mary for the voyage to Southampton, the dockworkers in New York chose to go on strike. As I would have to move our baggage across the picket lines myself, we scrambled to buy some footlockers that I could manage and to pack our belongings in them. As we had to drive down in what amounted to an ice storm, we covered them with a tarpaulin and tied them on the roof rack of our newly acquired Ford Falcon station wagon which we were taking with us on the ship for transport in England. Over there, though it was nothing more than a comparatively inexpensive compact vehicle, it turned out to attract much attention. This was the era when popular car mania was finally beginning to blossom in Britain and when the government had finally committed itself to building a series of closed-access motorways. At that time, a substantial section of the M1 (which paralleled the old Great North Road) had been completed, and while driving on that road, which in German autobahn fashion had then no speed limit, we were more than once overtaken by tiny Baby Austins and Morris Minors, shaking and steaming as their proud owners pushed them to speeds in excess of eighty miles an hour.

On that cold winter trip across the north Atlantic, poor Timothy, our third child and only four months old, contracted what we later learned to our horror was bronchitis. The ship's doctor misdiagnosed it and we arrived in London with a baby who was clearly seriously ill. Fortunately, we had a house in Blackheath already lined up and, after we got there, a neighboring GP, picked at random from the yellow pages, immediately recognized what was wrong (it was "the English disease" after all) and brought in a Harley Street specialist who also lived nearby and who proved to be very attentive, making several house visits until Timothy was safely on the mend. It was an enormous relief and we were left thinking very highly of the much-maligned National Health Service. The house we had rented in Blackheath was new, well appointed, and contemporary in style. It was the dream house of Lol and Suzanne O'Keeffe, but no sooner had they built it than he was posted for a few years to Greece, so it was available as a rental at just the right time for us. It did have some drawbacks, especially an overoptimistic electric heating system involving heating elements embedded in the quarry tile floor, with the pertinent electricity being supplied at night and at off-peak rates. Theoretically speaking, it sounded like a good scheme all round, but the way in which it actually functioned meant that one could almost fry an egg on the floor at 4:00 a.m., whereas by 4:00 p.m. the house was cold and uninviting and we were forced to build coal fires in the living room fireplace.

Apart from enabling me to keep my research program going, that spell of leave in London had two great side benefits: it enabled my mother to become acquainted with her new set of grandchildren and it introduced us to a whole new circle of friends in Blackheath. One of our neighbors there was the poet and novelist John Wain, whom I associated with Kingsley Amis, John Osborne, Alan Sillitoe, and other "Angry Young Men" on the English literary scene, though Wain himself struck me at the time as being neither convincingly angry nor particularly young. Strolling by, he would stop to chat and admire our modest Ford Falcon, which he always referred to, rather flatteringly, as a "shooting brake." The O'Keeffe's had been kind enough to line up their friends to welcome us, which they certainly did. They invited us to many a dinner party and helped us to find the necessary babysitters. From that time stemmed another wonderful and cherished lifelong friendship which was to involve many a happy encounter in London, Williamstown, and New York, and later on, as the McCalls entered upon their retirement years, at Guiting Power in the Cotswolds (a small village not too far from Stow-on-the-Wold). In the 1960s and 1970s, Ian and Creina McCall— close friends of the O'Keeffes—lived in an old Georgian house fronting directly onto the open space of Blackheath itself and they had three children of much the same age as ours. Ian owned a successful insurance business connected with Lloyds of London which he had begun to build up not long after coming down from Oxford (he was a loyal Oriel man). Prior to that, he had served as a midshipman on a Royal Indian Navy ship which had been in Bombay harbor in 1947 just prior to the British departure and the new dominion's declaration of independence. He had a vivid memory of the politically driven mutiny that broke out at that time among his Indian fellow officers. While it sounded like a rather genteel affair, the very idea of mutiny was more or less unthinkable for British Royal Navy types, and he recalled his captain, appalled that anything like that could happen on *his* ship, tossing into the harbor in sheer disgust a handsome presentation telescope he had in his hand.

Of Scottish descent, Ian was a big, outgoing fellow with a lively sense of humor and a gift for friendship. Though he died almost a decade or so ago now and though we had seen each other no more than once a year at most, I still miss him sorely. One thing especially sticks in the mind from that leave in 1963 when we first got to know him and Creina. Already fascinated by the micro society of which we had become part at Williams and in Williamstown, we had been trying over dinner to give them a sense of what it was like to live there and to serve on the faculty of an old New England college. At the time they had yet to visit North America, but Creina suddenly said "I've just read a novel that *has* to be about Williamstown." It was uncannily perceptive of her and she wasn't altogether off base. The novel she had in mind, which had just come out the previous year, was Alison Lurie's *Love and Friendship*, a story involving two faculty wives at an all-male college in New England. Lurie called it Convers College, but she was living at the time in Amherst, Massachusetts, where her husband was on the faculty of Amherst College, and it was clearly from Amherst, Williams's old offshoot, that she drew the inspiration for her collegiate picture. Around the same time, too, I must have regaled the McCalls with stories about the History Department's rather lively social life for, almost forty years later, Ian, while mixing drinks before lunch when we had driven over from Oxford to Guiting Power, observed: "I always had a fellow feeling for your old department chairman, what was his name?"—then finding it—"Bob Scott." Ian, who liked his whiskey, had never met Bob but was recalling my description of the latter's simply holding out his glass imperatively on social occasions when he was ready for another scotch.

While we were still in London, I was gratified to learn that Yale University Press had accepted my first book without calling for any extensive revisions. It was a monograph stemming from my dissertation on Pierre d'Ailly, the revision of which I had completed during the previous summer. Titled *The Political Thought of Pierre d'Ailly*, the book was published the following year and was well received by its scholarly reviewers. Around the same time, I was also invited to read a paper (my first) the following December at a joint session of the American Historical Association and the American Society for Reformation Research. I was thrilled to be asked. In those days there were far fewer occasions than there are today at which one might "strut one's stuff." And there were no general "calls for papers." Instead, one had to wait to be invited and given a chance. So, having been so invited, I worked hard to craft a strong and well-written paper, even trying it out on Claire-Ann over the dinner table while she struggled hard to keep a stiff upper lip and to avoid letting her eyes glaze over! When I came to read it at Philadelphia the following December, I could not help feeling a bit like a rustic backbencher from a small backwoods constituency. The session, attended by well over a hundred people, turned out to be an unexpectedly high-profile affair. Its organizer and chair was Bill (William J.) Bouwsma, the distinguished Renaissance historian from Berkeley. The other paper reader was Heiko Oberman, at that time established at the Harvard Divinity School and beginning to train a whole generation of pacesetting late medieval and Renaissance scholars. The leading Reformation scholar Jaroslav Pelikan, then at Yale I believe, commented on Oberman's paper while Brian Tierney of Cornell, already established as perhaps the leading scholar in my late medieval conciliar field, commented on mine. To my great relief, things went well and the paper was to be published a year later in the pages of the *American Historical Review*. The session itself, however, was punctuated by one unusual moment. During the discussion following the papers, Oberman said something that Tierney, rightly or wrongly, clearly took to be suggesting in condescending fashion that, as an historian, he was being over-responsive to the teaching authority claimed by the Roman Catholic Church. Somewhat quick of temper, Tierney leapt to his feet (so abruptly that his chair fell backward with a loud crash), strode over to the microphone, and snorted that he was not in the habit of clearing his historical judgments with the diocesan chancery. Undoubtedly true, as his later, demythologizing, and highly controversial *Origins of Papal Infallibility* (1972) made totally clear. But it was a highly unusual and dramatic moment of public misunderstanding at a characteristically staid scholarly event. Fortunately, over the years, it did not preclude the two men from becoming good friends. In 1995, at the 30th International Congress of Medieval Studies in Kalamazoo, Michigan, and at a session celebrating the fortieth anniversary of the publication of Tierney's classic and highly influential *Foundations of the Conciliar Theory*, Heiko and I read the two papers devoted to that fine book and Tierney's subsequent work. And one of the last scholarly papers I read (on scholastic reverberations in the natural philosophy of the great seventeenth-century chemist, Robert Boyle) was at an international symposium in Tucson celebrating Heiko's seventieth birthday and not long before his untimely death.

During the couple of years after we returned to Williamstown from London, it was other, more personal, concerns that were uppermost in my mind. Among them, housing my growing family loomed large. Much though we liked it, we had outgrown our original apartment and were delighted to have been allotted a small college house on Chapin Court, off South Street, close to the original center of town and, in fact, within about two hundred yards of the site once occupied by Fort West Hoosac. We loved that house. It had only one bathroom, but had a dining room (a big plus, given our social proclivities) and was possessed of a lovely, light-filled upper room that we turned into a playroom for our three (and soon to be four) children. Across the little street from us lived David and Clara (Claiborne) Park and their four children. David was a highly talented and literate theoretical physicist and Clara a gifted essayist and writer of nonfiction who was to receive great acclaim for her award-winning book, *The Siege.* It recounted their devoted struggle, at a time when the nature of autism had not been properly identified for what it was, to help their youngest and autistic daughter Jessie and to afford her the possibility of a stable and productive life. (Jessie was later to emerge as an artist of distinctive talent.) The Park household was a highly intellectual one and given the enormous amount of prose it was to produce across two generations (one of the children was to become a scholar, another a novelist), it can surely lay claim to a higher average word count than any other household in Williamstown. David had attached a swing to the bough of an old tree in the yard, and I can remember Katie, their eldest, who had long blonde hair cascading down to her waist, persistently swinging to and fro for hours, it seemed, and presumably deep in thought. She was to end up on the Harvard faculty as an early modern historian of distinction and, of more recent years, she and I had the pleasure of serving together as colleagues on the board of trustees of the National Humanities Center, Research Triangle, North Carolina.

Much as we liked that little house, however, with four children growing older we began to outgrow that, too, and began looking around for alternatives. As soon as I was promoted to the rank of associate professor with tenure and became, as a result, eligible for a college-funded, low-interest second mortgage (which would enable us to get an ordinary first mortgage from one or another of our local banks), we began to think about purchasing our own house. Not finding one that we really liked and could still afford, we began to think of building. The college had building lots available for purchase on a faculty housing development in town, but we had become enamored by then with the possibility of living further out in the country. Land available for purchase in Williamstown tended to come in forbiddingly large and expensive parcels. With a bit of luck, however, we were eventually able to purchase a smallish lot (with later additions it grew to about five acres) situated in a beautiful sloping meadow where Stone Hill begins to taper off into flatter land in South Williamstown. It was situated off Scott Hill Road, a dirt road linking Route 7 with Route 43 (Green River Road) that had been laid out in the 1760s in order to provide access for farmers to some of the eighty-acre lots of the township's fourth division. We fell in love with that meadow, which affords a stunning view of Mount Greylock and the valley head known as "the Hopper," framed to the north by Mount Williams and to the south by Deer Ridge. To maximize that view through the sliding glass doors that were to form the entire eastern side of the (upstairs) living room, we struggled mightily to angle the house properly. It is a split-level affair of barn style, post and beam construction, utilizing excellent materials (Douglas fir beams, mahogany window frames and doors, cedar siding and ceilings), and slotting neatly into the slope of the meadow rising behind it. It proved to be a wonderful place for children to grow up in and it has never lost its appeal for us, though given the number of steps involved—both exterior and interior—it is hardly the ideal house for old folk. For the children, its location proved to be an ideal setting. When we moved out there in 1966, there were more than a dozen other children of much the same age living within a half-mile radius at that southerly end of Stone Hill. Ensconced in an old farm house below us, and linked with us by a well-trodden path through the trees, were the two children of Jane and Lou Cuyler (Lou being a newspaperman by calling and at that time managing editor of the *North Adams Transcript*). Similarly, just above us were the children of Marilyn and Fran Coll—the latter a French teacher at Mount Greylock Regional High School. Delia, their third child, was to become a close friend of Deirdre's, singing with her in the school's madrigal group and, though they eventually went to different colleges (Delia to Wheaton in Massachusetts and Deirdre to Bowdoin in Maine), reconnecting and sharing an apartment later on in New York City. For a while they even worked together on the staff of *Vanity Fair* magazine during the editorship of

Tina Brown, a boss with *The Devil Wears Prada* proclivities of whom I suspect they were appropriately terrified. Further up the hill, there were other children—Hirsches, Goffs, and Scullins—and, over the years, the childhood friendships formed among the members of that "Stone Hill gang" have proved to be remarkably durable and have spawned some wonderfully spontaneous reunions when enough of them have been back in town. While as adolescents they were all understandably and restlessly anxious to experience the larger world that lay beyond our encircling mountains and nearly all of them now live and work in large cities, they have since been pleasantly haunted, or so I sense, by the unfadingly green memories of their Stone Hill childhood.

And why not? Our southerly end of Stone Hill was not then as impenetrably covered with brambles and second-growth timber as it has since become and it afforded them all a wonderfully welcoming natural playground. We were all of us, on weekends, able to ramble across it, remarking on the surviving cellars of long-gone farmhouses and marveling at the long stretches of loose stone walls dividing fields once cleared with so much labor but now well on the way to rejoining the "boundless woods" of which Fenimore Cooper wrote. I have two clearly etched memories of our first years out there. The first was of a familial nature when the kids were not yet in their teens, an incident precipitated by our gray thoroughbred, Lady. The second, a little earlier, concerns just the two of us. At night, Lady was accommodated in a large stall at the edge of her paddock and about halfway down the driveway. In the middle of one hot and humid night, we were all awakened by the sound of her (clearly terrified) shrieking and of her frantic thrashing around and kicking at the stall. The whole family piled out of bed and, still in pajamas, dashed down the driveway to find out what was amiss. When we got to the stall, we found that she was cast, lying on her side, drenched in sweat, and unable to get to her feet—a state of affairs very dangerous for a horse if allowed to persist. Because of the heat, we had left both the top and bottom half doors of the stall open and relied instead on a webbing stall guard to do the job of confining her. Unfortunately, rolling over in her sleep, she had somehow managed to put a hoof through one of the openings in the stall guard and get it caught there—hence her shrieking and frantic spasms of kicking in the futile attempt to free herself.

Because of her wild kicking, I could not get close for long enough to release the catches on the stall guard. Fortunately Chris had grabbed his
trusty scout's sheath knife when he jumped out of bed and brought it
with him. (I think as a weapon. Perhaps horse thieves were trying to
make off with Lady!) It was a blessedly sharp knife and I was able, between spasms of kicking, to lean in and quickly slash the webbing. When
the poor beast started kicking again, she found, accordingly, that her
hoof was now free and she was able to get very shakily to her feet. We
stayed with her long enough to calm and comfort her with a thorough
rubbing down. That done, we were able to get back and sleep the sleep
of the just. The other memory is of one freezing New Year's Eve in the
late 1960s when, along with our neighbors the Cuylers, we skied cross-
country across the southerly flank of Stone Hill to attend a party thrown
by colleagues at a house on Gale Road. Our way was illuminated by a
brilliant full moon and we pressed on, slipping and sliding as the tem-
perature dropped still further and snow conditions changed. But we still
stopped to light a fire, cook some small steaks, and drink a good deal of
wine before we finally arrived at the party, a little tipsy and glowing from
our exertions. It was all quite marvelous.

The only drawback to our decision to move to South Williamstown
and build a house there was that it left us for several years quite broke.
Both of us, therefore, were forced to scramble a bit to add modestly to
our income. Fortunately, the local public schools were more than adequate so that we were not forced to take on the added financial burden of
private schooling for the children. Even so, Claire-Ann began teaching
evening sections of the required world literature course at the newly
established Berkshire Community College, then still housed in the old
Pittsfield High School building. And she was later to teach part-time at
Pine Cobble School in Williamstown as well as teach English literature
full-time for a year to the seniors at Hoosac Valley High School in Adams.
Similarly, I myself taught some evening classes at North Adams State
College (later renamed Massachusetts College of Liberal Arts).

In both our cases, the remuneration for such evening classes was a
slender $500, which was paid only after one had submitted one's grades
for the term. Somewhat better remuneration (it was a bit of a lifesaver)
attached to the duties I undertook in 1966, 1967, and 1969 with summer

institutes in European cultural history held at Williams and funded under the provisions of the National Defense Education Act. I taught the medieval course and participated in the Great Books seminar at the 1966 and 1969 institutes (this last was great fun). And, in my first venture into academic administration, I organized and directed the 1967 institute. This summer teaching I found very stimulating. It was rewarding to have the opportunity to teach side by side with early modern specialists like Marvin Becker of Michigan and Orest Ranum of Johns Hopkins, and to get to know the talented and dedicated high school teachers who were our students. They were chosen via a competitive process, were awarded stipends to free them up from the necessity of finding summer jobs, and most of them proved to be serious, mature, and intellectually hungry people who were a pleasure to teach. That whole NDEA effort struck me as a very wise investment of taxpayers' dollars in the quality of American secondary education. And, during my year as director, I came also to be impressed by the crisp and careful way in which the budget officers in Washington monitored the expenditure of the comparatively modest funding allotted to us. Waste was clearly not to be tolerated.

As for us and our domestic economy, I'm not sure how we would have got by without that extra income. The only drawback to involvement in these eminently worthwhile endeavors was the threat it inevitably posed to my continuing commitment to scholarly research. For it took up much of the precious summertime on which one depended for that. And I could not help being aware of the concomitant price some of my senior colleagues had paid for permitting themselves to become locked, summer after summer, into directing or teaching in similar programs. So, for me, 1969 was the last year in which I was willing to forfeit those precious summer months.

That said, I cannot help being struck by how very busy I was in the late 1960s. To add to that busyness during those crowded years, another financially helpful and interesting opportunity came my way. Wally Scott, the dean of neighboring Bennington College, taught their course in medieval history and I was asked to come as a visitor to teach it while he went on sabbatical during the 1966–67 academic year. So, having secured permission from Williams to take on the assignment, I drove up to Bennington twice a week to teach the fifteen students who had signed up for the course. It was an instructive experience. While Bennington was another small, freestanding liberal arts college, it was very different in ethos and atmosphere from Williams. The fall that year was a particularly beautiful one and it was a great pleasure to drive up to the attractively planned and appealing campus situated on high ground in North Bennington. The college had been founded in 1932 as a nonsectarian, residential institution for women, one that prided itself on its experimental nature and that did in fact pioneer in integrating the visual and performing arts as central components of the liberal arts. In that, it was well ahead of most of its competition. In 1966 it was still a college for women (though within a few years it was to go coeducational), and it still retained some of its original experimental features: the long winter non-residential (or "field") term during which students took jobs or pursued internships elsewhere; the practice of individualized, self-constructed majors; descriptive (i.e., non-numerical) grading; formal student evaluation of the teaching performance of instructors; and so on. Poets like Howard Nemerov, Theodore Roethke, and (fleetingly) W. H. Auden had added luster to its faculty, as well as dancers like Martha Graham and novelists like Bernard Malamud and John Gardner. That being so, there was an artsy and intellectual feel to the place. And though there was some dating among students at the two colleges, there was a tendency among some, at least, of the Bennington women to look down on their male counterparts at Williams as no more than a bunch of jocks, crude in manner, simple of mind, and Philistine in proclivity.

Closer acquaintance with the college brought with it, however, some correctives to that picture. The artistic and literary luminaries at Bennington usually turned out to be part-timers commuting up from New York City to teach a course or two. And the regular faculty in residence were somewhat uneven in quality and not exactly luminaries. Some I got to know and admire, especially my colleagues in history who, poor salaries notwithstanding, were certainly capable academics and deeply conscientious in the discharge of their teaching responsibilities. But some others in the social science division struck me as rather dull dogs, surprisingly unimaginative and conservative in their educational thinking. And these last, it turned out, seemed to be the faculty members most deeply involved in the governance of the college. As for my students, while they, too, were uneven in quality, they were nonetheless an appealing lot who, when we got up to Gregory VII and the Investiture Contest, began one class by processing in, led by acolytes, clad in quasi-ecclesiastical garb, with one of them representing the person of the great pope himself—an amusing performance unthinkable in an all-male institution and unlikely in a coeducational setting. Whereas at Williams, where in my department the modernists ruled the roost, I had to work a bit to convince my students of the relevance of the medieval experience, my Bennington students took it altogether for granted. Indeed, too much for granted. The danger for them, in fact, was that of seeing things medieval through the appealing but distorting lens of terminal quaintness. One of those students, who had transferred in from a university and who planned to go on to medical school, was, I think, really quite brilliant and would have stood out anywhere. But, despite the seriousness of their interest, they were not as a group the intellectual equals of the students I was teaching at Williams. It was not the last time that I was to be reminded of the quality of the Williams student body.

From my brief time at Bennington I also took away some direct experience of two educational practices long since well established there but not, until some years later, to become a matter of interest for colleges closer to the mainstream of American higher education. The first concerned the use of descriptive, non-quantified grading. While at best it could be extraordinarily good, conveying important things both to and about the student concerned, it could also be vague and sloppy. Never having been called upon to grade in that way, I got permission to sample a cross section of such grades previously given at the college. The experience was for me something of a surprise. The grading done ranged from the totally irresponsible, via the unexceptionable, to extraordinarily detailed and subtle analyses of the strengths and weaknesses of a given student's performance, analyses that called for great insight, marked conscientiousness, and the willingness on the instructor's part to devote an enormous amount of time to the effort. The most irresponsible "grade" I came across emanated from an instructor in the dance program who had simply written diagonally across the evaluation sheet: "Lucy's [not her real name] a nice girl." And, so far as Bennington's own practice was concerned, this grading system as a whole was, I think, vitiated by the fact that, while the student herself was privy only to the descriptive grade, the instructor was also called upon to submit (for transcripts and external use) a parallel numerical equivalent. As I learned from the unhappy experience of a Bennington girlfriend of one of my students at Williams, descriptive grading might well convey to the student herself a more favorable estimate of her abilities than that conveyed by the numerical grades forwarded to a graduate school as part of an application process. Not a happy possibility.

The second piece of valuable experience picked up at Bennington was my first encounter with the (then highly unusual) practice of having students formally evaluate the teaching performance of their instructors. By long-established practice, it was routine at Bennington for one's students to do that twice in each semester—at the halfway point (with the goal of making possible needed midcourse corrections) and after the completion of the course. It was done in very direct fashion. The instructor would be asked to leave the room, and the members of the class would then elect from among their number a chair whose responsibility it then was to garner student opinion on how well the instructor was doing and how well the class was going, along with any pertinent suggestions for change or improvement. The elected chair would then meet with the instructor to convey her findings. In my case the experience was reassuring. I was pleased (relieved?) to hear that the class appeared to be going well and that no major course correction was called for, and I was happy to take on board a tentative suggestion or two for minor change. The whole process was handled with great maturity. It convinced me of the value to teachers of formal student feedback and encouraged me, a couple of years later, to collaborate with a student of mine at Williams who had devised an evaluative questionnaire and to administer it on an experimental basis in one of my classes there. In the early 1970s, a college-sponsored process of formal student evaluation of classroom performance was to be introduced at Williams. It involved both a quantitative instrument conducive to the cross-comparison of aggregated data that was designed and administered by the college and the collection of (unsigned) written student comments by the college that were then forwarded to the instructor concerned. While the majority of the faculty chose to involve themselves in this process, participation was not mandatory and its uneven nature tended to diminish the reliability and value of the comparative data conveyed back to instructors. It was, then, a significant improvement in 1988 during my presidency when we were able to secure a faculty vote making the use of such evaluative instruments mandatory for all courses taught at the college.

In the month immediately preceding our departure in 1963 on the old Queen Mary for that first leave in London, I had two pleasant surprises. First, I received a call from Kay O'Connell, secretary to the president, telling me that he wanted to see me. His purpose, as I discovered when I showed up in Hopkins Hall, was to launch a flattering species of pre-emptive strike. At the time, I didn't realize that was what it was, which made what he had to say all the more encouraging. At the time, Williams didn't have a dean of the faculty, but Jack, on that occasion, was in dean of the faculty mode. His purpose, it turned out, was to convey to me the reassuring conclusion that the department and the college-wide Committee on Appointments and Promotions had come to the conclusion that I was a likely lad. Or, to frame it more formally in the words in which he was later to put it in a letter to me, "having made our own basic judgment earlier this fall that you had demonstrated the qualities as teacher, scholar, and human being that we most want to encourage, we intend to have the arrangements here such that you find it rewarding to stay." My salary was, accordingly, to be adjusted upwards (if only slightly—Jack was a bit of a tightwad with the college's money), and I was to be accelerated through the assistant professor ranks so that I could look forward to a formal tenure decision no later than 1965. No more than a couple of days after that very encouraging meeting, I discovered what had precipitated it. I received a call from the chairman of the History Department at the University of California at Los Angeles about an opening for a medievalist in the department, and I was invited to go out there to lecture to their graduate students.

So I flew out (it was the first time I had ever flown) for what turned out to be a very exciting visit. My lecture went well, and I came to be very impressed with the quality of the department. (I learned that they believed themselves to be a stronger group than their Berkeley rivals). Lynn White, Jr., whose son, a future Chinese historian at Princeton, I had taught at Williams the previous year, was a provocatively original historian of medieval technology and a commanding presence in the department. Gerhart Ladner, a distinguished historian of medieval ideas, was due to join them in the following fall. And I was also warmly welcomed by two other medieval scholars with whose works I was familiar—Gustave von Grunebaum, the Islamicist, and Ernest Moody (Williams 1934), who specialized in late medieval philosophy and who had written the pioneering book on the logic of William of Ockham. As UCLA had been allotted (within the University of California system) the Center for Medieval and Renaissance Studies (Berkeley got the one in Asian Studies), these were scholars with whom I could expect to be in regular contact. Professionally speaking, it was all very appealing, and the prospect of being part of that constellation of medievalists (they were soon to launch their own journal *Viator*) was an exciting one. I was thrilled, then, to receive within a day or so of my return home an offer to join them. The decision to turn that offer down was not an easy one, and had I been a bachelor I might well have accepted it. But there were some downsides. Los Angeles didn't appeal to me and, unless they were people possessed of private means, the junior faculty members there lived, or so I thought, under very unattractive conditions. And the UCLA graduate students whom I met struck me as a less-gifted and less-interesting group of people than the undergraduates whom I had been privileged to teach at Yale and Williams. Williams and Williamstown, moreover, had already begun to weave those bonds of attachment which were to prove then, and over the years, too hard to break. So, without regrets or second thoughts, we turned the offer down and chose to stay.

If, at the time, this didn't seem to be any sort of determinative turning point, in retrospect I am inclined to think that it was precisely that. Having, thus far, done all my studying and much of my teaching at large research universities, that was the type of setting I had always assumed I would end up in. Over the next decade and more, and especially during the great expansion of American higher education when openings were plentiful (between 1965 and 1970 the number of new faculty positions added nationwide exceeded in size the entire American professoriate as it had stood in 1940), I was approached about job opportunities at a broad array of universities, some of which I chose to explore and from some of which offers eventuated. None of them, however, was as attractive professionally as the position at UCLA had been. I received "nibbles" from Columbia, Harvard, and Michigan, but they didn't mature into "bites." Most of those approaches came, rather, from research universities of what I would call the second or "aspiring" tier—places such as Notre Dame or the Stony Brook campus of the New York State University. Certainly interesting, perhaps tempting, and certainly worthy of consideration. Though it was clear, in the Williams setting, that one had to be careful about what one said on such matters. Some of our senior colleagues, or so one sensed, tended to take a dim view of any attempt on the part of their junior colleagues to cash in on favorable market conditions in order to enhance their position at Williams. In that connection, one sometimes heard amusingly evoked the dread specter of one's finding oneself on the receiving end of what was referred to as the "Phinney handshake." The reference was to a (probably apocryphal) episode involving James Phinney Baxter III, the long-serving tenth president of Williams (1937–61). Phinney, as everyone called him, had not only been a scholar of some distinction but also something of a character. He was possessed of a booming voice that easily carried across the campus, almost rendering redundant any wimpy recourse to telephonic means of communication. And the episode in question concerned an alleged encounter of his with a not, alas, particularly distinguished member of the faculty sometime in the 1950s, which were not good years for the academic profession—few jobs and miserable salaries. Somehow or other the fellow in question had managed to land a competitive job offer from the University of Saskatchewan in Canada. He had no wish to go to Canada but had foolishly thought that he could use the offer to extract from Williams some modest amelioration in his not so happy lot. So he went in to see the president and proudly shared his good news with him. Whereupon Phinney, who had, it seems, his own message to deliver, seized the occasion, leapt to his feet, leaned across his desk, warmly shook the poor fellow's hand, and boomed with unfeigned enthusiasm, "George, congratulations! Congratulations, my dear fellow!" and then slyly slipped in the words: "I do hope you and Myrtle will be happy in Saskatoon!"

"Happy in Saskatoon!" Words to reverberate across the campus, and in the mid-1960s, though Phinney was gone, our senior colleagues were not above evoking the dread specter of the "Phinney handshake" when the children showed any signs of getting out of line. Not that it really mattered very much to us by that time. We had both become increasingly attached to Williams itself and what it stood for as well as to the locality and the region. In effect, so far as Williams was concerned, though we didn't yet know it and though the term itself tends to be used in somewhat derogatory fashion, we were well on the way to becoming "lifers." And in that, taking the profession as a whole and widespread assumptions to the contrary, I am inclined to think that we were not truly exceptional.

In discussions of faculty attitudes, of course, it has long been customary to insist that the loyalties of faculty lie more to their particular disciplines or to the professorial guild at large than to the universities and colleges at which they serve. But, rightly or wrongly, I have come to take such sweeping claims with a pinch of salt. It is doubtless the case that the tiny minority of academic stars, hotly pursued by the topmost departments in their fields abroad as well as at home, can be tempted to flit from one prestigious and well-remunerated post to another without losing any sleep about the overall academic well-being of their current institutional perch. And something similar may be said today, though for much darker reasons, about the growing cadre of itinerant, part-time, adjunct faculty, many of them trying to piece together some sort of living in the academy by teaching a battery of poorly remunerated courses at more than one college or university. The institutions at which they teach can understandably not expect to command from them any significant degree of loyalty. But the story seems to be rather different when it comes to the central cadre of tenured or tenure-track faculty. From 1969 to 1994, at regular five-year intervals, the Carnegie Commission on Higher Education conducted valuable surveys of the expressed attitudes of American faculty on a broad array of issues. The standard clichés to the contrary, the survey data thus generated revealed that the vast majority of American faculty chose to affirm that their college or university was "very" or, at least, "fairly" important to them. Eighty percent of those teaching at research universities were willing to affirm that, while the percentage rose to ninety-one at the four-year liberal arts colleges and at the two-year colleges. Indeed, if one can believe the results of the 1984 and 1989 surveys, across those years institutional loyalty appears to have been intensifying.

While such global data run counter to the informally attested views that constitute the common coinage of sardonic faculty exchange, they may be more accurately revelatory of what people really believe. Certainly, they align with my own attitude as I settled in to work at Williams. They also align with the attitudes I sensed among my colleagues even during the transformative and increasingly turbulent conditions of campus life that set in as the late sixties and early seventies unfolded. Williamstown, unlike Berkeley and New Haven, may have afforded the benefits of rural seclusion, but Williams, in common with so many other leading colleges and universities, was not to be exempted from the malaise of the moment; nor was it to be spared the turmoil generated by the growing racial, political, and cultural tensions characteristic of that era.

CHAPTER TWELVE

The Transformative Sixties (i): The New Williams

Sexual intercourse began
In nineteen sixty-three
(Which was rather late for me)
Between the end of the Chatterley ban
And the Beatles' first LP.

Philip Larkin

That the 1960s at large did indeed prove to be transformative is not in question. That proved to be true of almost every dimension of social, intellectual, religious, and cultural life, not only in North America but also in Western Europe and beyond. Called peremptorily into question were the established modalities of political life and, with them, hallowed intellectual assumptions, long-prevailing attitudes towards race, class, ethnicity, and gender, as well as traditional marital and family roles and, as Larkin's poem amusingly signals, the deeply rooted sexual mores of yesteryear. Living through this great and multifaceted upheaval of the spirit, and especially so on a college campus, could be a destabilizing experience, as challenging as it was invigorating. Its reverberations proved to be long enduring. In some ways, we are still forced to maneuver uneasily today as we attempt to come finally to terms with the torrent of change that stemmed from that watershed era. And not least of all in the world of higher education at large, as well as in the small sector of free-standing liberal arts colleges to which Williams itself belongs.

By the end of the decade, the successful launching of *Change: The Magazine of Higher Learning* testified to the degree to which change had become the norm in institutions of higher education and stasis a thing of the past. And that shift had by then left a deep imprint on Williams. In 1961 when we arrived there, it was the "Old Williams" that we encountered—an all-male, fraternity-dominated institution, with the college still functioning firmly *in loco parentis* and its 1100 students (soon to be edged up in number to about 1250) subject to various parietal regulations and still required, some eighty years after Harvard had abandoned a similar rule, to attend Sunday chapel. Classes were still held on Saturday mornings and classroom attendance in general was both compulsory and carefully monitored, with only a stipulated number of cuts permitted. Students took five courses each semester, and opportunities for interdisciplinary studies were extremely limited; the available majors were nearly all departmentally based and tightly organized. They were built around a substantial core of required sequential courses and culminated in a reasonably muscular major or comprehensive examination. No more than a decade later, that firm institutional profile had been radically altered. Compulsory chapel was now a thing of the past; so, too, were Saturday classes and compulsory attendance at class. Fraternities had been dislodged from their long-standing pinnacle of prominence in student life, and membership in them had come in the end to be proscribed. Instead, students were now housed and fed in college-owned residential houses possessed of a measure of self-governance, and faculty associates were attached to each house. The semester course load had been reduced to four, and the academic calendar had been revamped to make room for a monthlong January (Winter Study) term in which students pursued—on a pass/fail basis—topics not usually taught during the two regular semesters, many of them experimental or experiential in nature. Interdisciplinary studies were beginning to proliferate and the various departmental majors were beginning to be reshaped in such a way as to respond more faithfully and flexibly to the specific characteristics of the various disciplines, while the culminating major examination was now on a species of life support and destined soon to be dropped. The size of the student body was in the process of being increased by a full third, with the additional 650 students being women and an increasing proportion of the overall student body being African American. The size of the faculty was also increasing, not proportionally but enough to permit the appointment of the first women faculty and the addition of such new subjects as anthropology, sociology, history of science, and environmental studies. Finally, having been declared by legislative fiat to be mature adults, students were no longer subject to the old parietal rules and had been given representation on some of the standing committees of the faculty. And while the notion of the college's standing *in loco parentis* had not altogether been abandoned, it had mutated uncomfortably into a more ambiguous form. As the chaplain of Harvard College was later dryly to observe, while students today are certainly intent upon preserving the autonomy conceded to them in the 1960s, they incline nevertheless to assume that colleges and universities are still burdened with the moral responsibility for shielding them from the consequences of the way in which they choose to exercise (or abuse) that autonomy.

In toto, this was an extraordinary amount of change to have been crammed within the narrow compass of a single decade. Nothing similar had happened before in the long course of the college's history; nothing of comparable dimensions has happened since. Coming to Williams in 1876, Bliss Perry had found that "his first Latin lesson, in the preface to Livy," was "exactly the same assignment" as his father had had in 1848 and, in 1916, his son was to confront that very same assignment. The 1960s were to make it clear that anything even approximating that type of curricular stability was altogether a thing of the past. Such being the case, one is led inexorably to ask what the factors were that made such sweeping changes possible.

The first factor, something not to be underestimated, was the mood, climate of opinion, and circumstances of the time. For higher education, the period stretching from the late 1950s to about 1970 stands out, in retrospect, as something of a golden age. The academic profession was enjoying an era of growing prosperity and high public esteem. While in

1983 a Harris poll was to reveal that no more than 36 percent of the populace reposed "a great deal of confidence" in those involved in the enterprise of higher education, in 1966 the comparable figure had stood at an impressive 61 percent. At the state as well as the federal level, government financial support was at an unprecedented high. On the West Coast, California's splendid state-sponsored university system was approaching its apogee. Back in the East, the State University of New York was making every effort to match its stature and achievement. Nationwide, as the 1960s wore on (and if one includes the burgeoning community college sector), new campuses were being opened up at the astonishing rate of one a week. "Bliss was it in that dawn to be alive, / But to be young was very heaven!" Not only was change in the very air that academics breathed, but for academic leaders the opportunity to effect change was wide open and to an unprecedented degree.

Those students of the phenomenon of leadership who resonate sympathetically to contingency theories of one sort or another (and are prone to locating its driving force, therefore, in external environmental factors) will be inclined to attribute to the circumstances of the time rather than to any individual agency the extraordinary wave of change that engulfed Williams over the course of the 1960s. And not altogether without reason. The abandonment of parietal hours and the like, the loosening up of the old curricular forms, the diversification of the student body in racial terms, the embrace of coeducation, and so on—it is hard to imagine such common institutional changes *not* having occurred, whoever was serving as president at the time. But they would doubtless have occurred in different and, I am inclined to think, less effective ways had they not taken place during Jack Sawyer's twelve-year presidency which stands out as an unquestionably transformative one. Hailing from Worcester, Massachusetts, Jack had attended Deerfield Academy prior to matriculating, like his father and older brother before him, at Williams. There, prior to going on to Harvard Graduate School, he had an exemplary undergraduate career and, again in the footsteps of father and brother, had served as president of the Zeta Psi fraternity. Thus, though he was later to prove that he could stand if necessary at a critical distance from it, he was certainly embedded in the deeply rooted culture of the Old Williams. His graduate studies were interrupted by four years of wartime service in the US Navy but upon his return to Harvard, he was elected to the

Society of Fellows there and served for a while on the Harvard faculty prior to joining the Yale Economics Department. As president of Williams, he proved to be a driving and very much a hands-on leader who involved himself not only in the framing of policy but also in its implementation, sometimes, indeed, irritatingly so, and down to the level of minute detail. And two major, transformative contributions were clearly his. The first is widely celebrated; the second, because of its nature, tends usually to be overlooked.

The first concerns, of course, the definitive removal of fraternities from the Williams scene, freeing up thereby for better purposes the wasteful amount of institutional time and energy previously devoted to the fraternity problem and eliminating a major obstacle to a tighter and undeflected focus on the college's primary academic mission. Confronted upon his arrival in office by an imperative student petition calling for a radical overhaul in the selection process for membership in fraternities, Sawyer's response had been quite traditional: he had appointed a committee to deliberate on the matter. It was a trustee, alumni, faculty, and student committee, chaired by Jay Angevine '11 (in his day a fraternity man) and carefully balanced between staunch fraternity supporters and others critical of the prevailing system. On that committee he imposed no precise mandate; nor did he himself attend its meetings. For many at the time it was simply yet another in a long series of similar committees, and from it nothing more was expected than another round of piecemeal tinkering. Things, however, were to turn out otherwise. The committee chose not to duck the central issue and in May 1962 it recommended that the college take over from the fraternities the responsibility of housing and feeding the student body. It stopped short of recommending the abolition of fraternities and, using diplomatically vague language, seemed to envisage some sort of continuing role for them. Or, at least, a continuing role for those among them financially able to maintain their existence under the changed campus circumstances of the future. That continuing role was not, however, to prove viable. As the complexities of the unfolding situation became increasingly clear to the Standing Committee (under the vigorous chairmanship of Talcott Banks '28) that succeeded the Angevine committee, and as the financial challenges involved in trying to maintain a continuing existence and paying for the fraternity house mortgages became increasingly apparent even to the staunchest of fraternity true believers, the tide of opinion began gradually to turn in the direction of outright abolition. And that was eventually to be decreed by trustee vote in November 1968.

Jack Sawyer himself, and perhaps also the board of trustees, seemed to be surprised by the comparatively sweeping nature of the Angevine committee's recommendations. Certainly, the initial public statement issued in June 1962 by way of response to those recommendations stopped short of indicating a willingness to accept and implement them. By October, however, president and trustees alike had rallied to the committee's position and now committed the college in unambiguous fashion to the major transformation in student residential life that the committee had envisaged and to effecting the necessary changes on an explicit and fairly tight timetable. Not surprisingly, given the traditional strength of the fraternity culture at Williams, the ensuing academic year was marked among alumni by widespread confusion deepening into dismay and, at worst, to splenetic outbursts of anger and resentment. For the president himself, an essentially cautious person averse to conflict (which sometimes even made him ill), it must have been a dreadful year. Indeed, at one particularly tense alumni meeting in Los Angeles he actually fainted.

In the early fall of 1985, during my own first semester as president, I had breakfast with Jack at the University Club in New York. We had met to discuss an idea I had for a potential seminar program focused on acculturating new faculty into the particular demands and opportunities that would confront them in a liberal arts college setting, a seminar program which he thought the Mellon Foundation might well be interested in funding. Business concluded, the conversation turned to other matters. Jack, it turned out, was concerned about the pressures I was coming under from the campus protest movement pushing relentlessly for total divestment by the college of stock held in multinational companies doing some of their business in South Africa. And, perhaps by way of reassurance, he confessed that there had been times during his presidency at Williams when he had not been sure he would get through the next two weeks, let alone the rest of the semester or the full academic year. Though he did not specify when exactly he had felt that way, I simply assumed that he was thinking back over that *annus horribilis* of 1962–63.

After that year, however, the tide rapidly began to turn and other important issues came gradually to the fore. Not least among them was the move that culminated in the decision to enlarge the college and to embrace coeducation. It now seems clear that Jack had been thinking about some version of this latter move from the very start of his presidency. A century earlier in 1868, John Bascom (one of those faculty members at Williams critical of Mark Hopkins and who was later to become president of the University of Wisconsin), while attacking the rising fraternity culture of the day as hostile to individualism and "independence of opinion," had also argued for the wisdom of admitting women students to the college. Now, as the 1960s wore on, the college was moving at last to follow in his footsteps, and the fact that the transition to coeducation at Williams went as smoothly as it did owes a great deal, I believe, to the prior exercise of firm presidential leadership culminating in the removal of fraternities and fraternity culture from the institutional equation.

About all of this, I should confess, I was not myself at the time all that clear. To reach that sort of clarity across time, I had to learn a good deal more about the college's specific history and to grasp more fully the nature of its distinctive collegiate culture. Nor, at the time, was I much clearer about the second major contribution I now believe Jack Sawyer to have made to the revitalization of Williams.

This was very different in nature from the first. It involved no single bold initiative or visibly decisive exercise of leadership. It was, instead, a consistent pattern of behavior embedded in his day by day work and deportment throughout the entirety of his presidency. Perhaps because of that it seems in marked degree to have flown under the radar. What I have in mind is a dimension of institutional leadership that I have come over the years to view as foundational. It involves the educational and instructional side of the leader's role and the building of a supportive followership. Theorists of leadership (who come in many shapes and sizes) usually classify it as cultural or symbolic in kind, and some describe it as involving an interpretative effort that pivots on what they call "the management of meaning." That term has something of an Orwellian ring to it, and it is not one that the sociologist Philip Selznick uses. But in an illuminating discussion, he does make the activity it denotes central to administrative leadership as he understands it. Bringing the perspective of humanistic sociology to his analysis of the phenomenon, he places his central emphasis firmly on the crucial role of the leader in defining and proclaiming on a day-in-day-out basis the institution's role and mission, in nurturing its "embodiment" of an enduring meaning and purpose, in himself (or herself) embodying that meaning, and in infusing it into the institution's very organizational structures and the routines of daily behavior within it. In its most fundamental reaches, the exercise of leadership as he understands it (and in this I believe him to be correct) pertains less to the exercise of power than to the vindication of the legitimacy of that power. Not merely a function of service in the cause of institutional maintenance, it extends beyond that, he says, "to the defense of institutional integrity," "the sustenance of the institutional core values, the framing, indeed, of the community's very identity."

It was only years later, after much brooding on the matter, that I came to grasp the central importance of this aspect of leadership on which I propose to dwell again later in this memoir. During the 1960s and early 1970s, however, as I became increasingly caught up as a faculty member in responsibilities pertaining to the governance of the college, I came to be better positioned to observe the way in which the president went about the discharge of his complex responsibilities. And, when that happened, I did begin to recognize and certainly to admire the way in which Jack went about things and I dimly began to perceive the degree to which his tenacious day-to-day commitment helped sustain and enhance the intellectual and academic vibrancy of the whole enterprise. Of course, being so positioned brought with it its own demands. As I settled into work at the college and began to get my head above water, I felt the need to become more faithful in my attendance at college-wide faculty meetings, where I was impressed by the vigor and seriousness with which my senior colleagues debated academic policy and with their willingness to engage college-wide curricular issues that extended well beyond their own particular departments. It brought home to me the fact that we constituted not a collection of departments merely gathered together for administrative convenience into a college, but a college divided for certain specified disciplinary functions into a group of departments. Though lacking in parties or even stable factions, I began to think of the faculty meeting as our own modest equivalent of the House of Commons, and, enjoying as I had always done the cut and thrust of debate, after a couple of years I summoned up my courage and began myself to intervene in its discussions. These meetings took place almost every month during the academic year. They were held in Griffin 3, a lovely room in the college's third-oldest building, an impressive, Georgian-style structure erected in 1828. That room, which has a fine elevation and handsome fenestration, had once been the college's chapel. It is a graceful and dignified space, an eminently appropriate setting for what, after all, is nothing less than the faculty's deliberative and legislative assembly over which, by immemorial tradition, the president himself presides. It is a room which echoes for me now with memories of crises past and battles long ago.

At about the same time as I fell under the thrall of Williams, I was being drawn into the beginnings of what was to turn out to be several decades of committee service. It is not uncommon for academics to dismiss the latter as a dreary waste of time. And I have to concede that that is sometimes the case. But by the mid-1960s I had garnered enough experience to realize that when that is indeed the case it usually reflects either the fact that the committee lacks a clearly identifiable mission or the fact that it is being badly led. Or sometimes, God forbid, a combination of both of those things. I served in those early days on two such committees. The first concerned student admissions and seemed to function as little more than the PR wing of the Office of Admission. Those of us on it who were faculty members simply didn't know enough about the intricacies of the admissions process either to participate in admission decisions themselves or to set sensible policy directions. The second was the Honors Degree Committee whose mission was, to say the least, opaque, and whose functions were destined soon to be absorbed by a reconstituted Committee on Educational Policy. On the other hand, I was also fortunate enough to serve on two other committees that were both possessed of clear and practical objectives and both ably led. From my service on them I learned a good deal about the college as a whole and about how a good chair should go about the task of leading a committee effectively. The first was the Pre-medical Committee, tasked in those days with doing the sort of hands-on work later assigned to an administrator. Its chair was Sam Matthews of the Biology Department, a courteous and kindly leader who was absolutely on top of his responsibilities. The Division I (arts and humanities) representative was Paul Hunter of the English Department, later on to become a scholar of note at the University of Chicago. And I was the (rather ignorant) representative of Division II (social sciences). The second such committee was the Committee of Three, charged, after the faculty had voted in the 4-1-4 calendar, with the task of getting the Winter Study Program off the ground. And that it did, under the steady leadership of Bill Oliver of the Mathematics Department, in quite an efficient manner. It was on that committee that I had the pleasure of getting to know Charles Samuels, then a junior member of the English Department. He had already acquired the reputation of being a very fine and challenging teacher and proved to be a highly intelligent and stimulating colleague. Bracingly dogmatic in the positions he took, he was also somewhat judgmental about his colleagues and prone to assuming that people were fools until they had proved to his satisfaction that they were not. But he was passionately committed to the life of the mind and determined to promote the overall intellectual well-being of the college. His tragic suicide in 1974 was an enormous loss not only to his family, to which he was devoted, but also to the college community at large, depriving us of a valued friend and colleague and a truly fine collegiate citizen.

For me personally the pace of involvement in the governance of the college had picked up fairly markedly in the fall of 1968. By the mid-1960s, talk either of linking our all-male college with a coordinate women's college or of making an outright commitment to coeducation was very much in the air. In 1967 the board of trustees had authorized the president to appoint a committee composed of trustees, faculty, and pertinent administrative officers "to explore the question of the desirability and feasibility of including women in the Williams College community and to recommend ways and means of accomplishing this if it appeared both desirable and feasible." In the fall of 1968 a further committee, known simply (if rather cutely) as Committee X and functioning basically as a curricular-oriented subcommittee of the principal body, was established under the chairmanship of Don Gifford of the English Department, with the provost serving as liaison with that main body and the other two members being our onetime neighbor David Park and myself. I was asked to serve, I assume, because I had just been appointed chairman of the Committee on Educational Policy. To this latter committee I had been elected the previous year as one of the Division II representatives, serving under the chairmanship of my colleague in history,

Dudley Bahlman, then dean of the faculty. And I had learned a good deal about the college at large from the annual round of assembling the package of courses, new and old, for the coming academic year and helping see it through to a vote of approval at the February faculty meeting. I am not sure why the decision was made to take the chairmanship out of administrative hands and to transfer it to a faculty member. I can only assume that, for purposes of perceived legitimacy, it may have been deemed prudent to take that step at what was proving to be a time of growing tensions within the college community on more than one front. Those were, of course, terrible times in the country at large, which had endured the assassinations of Martin Luther King and the Kennedy brothers, was bitterly divided over the escalation of the war in Vietnam, and was also being torn apart by mounting racial tensions. The years preceding 1968 had been punctuated by riots, usually racially triggered, in the nation's cities, from Rochester and Harlem, via Watts and Newark, to Chicago and Detroit. This last upheaval took place in 1967, was among the worst in US history, and ended only after the deployment in the city not only of the Michigan National Guard but also of elements of the 101st and 82nd Airborne Divisions. My brother-in-law, David, newly commissioned in the 101st and destined soon to be shipped off to Vietnam just in time for the Tet Offensive, was with one of the first federal units to arrive in Detroit and he has vivid memories of the chaos prevailing there and of the degree to which (at least in the eyes of the military) the Detroit police seemed to be out of control.

All of this, of course, generated destabilizing reverberations on the nation's campuses—perhaps especially so, ironically, on those where there had been a clear effort to diversify the student body racially and where a start had been made on integrating the African American experience into the curriculum. On such campuses the growing numbers of black students were becoming impatient with what they viewed as the glacial pace of change and were beginning to resort to peremptory forms of direct action, unmanageable protests, and the occupation of symbolic buildings. Berkeley, Columbia, Harvard, Yale, Cornell, and other large universities all went through their ordeal by fire. Cornell, where black students seized a building in protest against perceived racism in the university's judicial and disciplinary system, came to symbolize the campus upheavals of the era. It did so, especially, after Associated Press photographer Steve Starr's iconic, prizewinning picture of gun-wielding black students emerging from the building they had occupied was mainstreamed in the national press. And it did so still more in 1987 when Allan Bloom in his *Closing of the American Mind* highlighted the upheaval at Cornell in 1969 as having exemplified what he characterized as the shameful "dismantling of the structure of rational inquiry" which he portrayed as having taken place in the American universities of that era.

Such anomic upheavals of the spirit were not, moreover, limited to large urban campuses. Small colleges in settings like Amherst, Oberlin, and Swarthmore did not prove to be exempt. Nor did Williams. The occupation of Willard Straight Hall at Cornell took place on April 18, 1969. Less than two weeks earlier, members of the Afro-American Society at Williams, ventilating cognate grievances, had taken over and occupied Hopkins Hall, the building in which, along with some classrooms, the central administrative offices (including the president's) were housed. That explosive moment of truth had been some time in the making. Martin Luther King had preached in Thompson Memorial Chapel during the spring semester of 1961 and, at a time when there were no more than a handful of black students at the college, a lively enough interest in the civil rights movement had emerged on campus for some forty-eight students to participate in 1963 in the March on Washington and for others to participate in the Freedom Summer of 1964, joining other out-of-state students in the Mississippi campaign to register hitherto disenfranchised black voters.

At much the same time, back at Williams itself, the Office of Admission had launched a vigorous push to recruit academically qualified black students. Ever since Gaius Charles Bolin, proud son of a New York state freedman, had matriculated in 1885 as the first African American student at the college, there had (except during the brief and troubled presidency of Tyler Dennet, 1936–39) been a steady trickle of black students coming to Williams. Some had been students of marked talent, prominent among them Rayford Logan '17, pioneering historian of Haiti, and Alison and John Davis, classes of 1923 and 1933 respectively, both of them the valedictorians of their respective classes and both destined to become sociologists of distinction. But, as late as 1966, the numbers involved were still miniscule. In the years following, however, the Office of Admission (in this, I think, well ahead of the faculty) had moved vigorously to increase each year the percentage of black students admitted. By the 1967–68 academic year, the overall number had reached thirty-two, scaling up from four seniors to ten freshmen. And in the following year that overall number exceeded forty. A significant percentage of those students hailed from inner-city high schools and, as a small and self-conscious minority, their sense of isolation in—indeed, alienation from—the culture prevailing at a rural, privileged, all-male, and overwhelmingly white New England college campus is readily comprehensible. Given the racial turmoil in the nation at large, and as the black contingent at Williams itself came close to reaching critical mass, some sort of upheaval was well-nigh inevitable.

It was the assassination of Martin Luther King on April 4, 1968, with the inevitable outpouring of anguish, disillusionment, and rage that followed in its aftermath, that was to set things in motion. Immediately after that tragic event, the Williams Afro-American Society held a campus-wide meeting focused on the problem of racism in American society at large and on the inadequacy of the response of the Williams community to such matters. In the wake of that meeting, the society made a series of proposals for on-campus change, including "the start of a Black Area program which will seek to emphasize the role the Afro-American has played in American life," the establishment of a number of "Martin Luther King Scholarships" designed to help increase the number of black and other minority students at Williams, and the "start of an Afro-American fellowship room to increase the dialogue between white and black students." With a sense, I think, of time running out, the administration tried to respond in good faith and without delay to these and several other proposals. In the process, some of them found their way to me, for they were added to what was already a pretty full year's agenda for the Committee on Educational Policy (CEP).

Oddly enough, the administrator with whom I was to deal on such issues was neither the dean of the college nor the dean of the faculty, under the jurisdiction of whose offices one would have thought they would properly have fallen. My dealings instead were with the provost whose responsibilities under the Williams administrative configuration extended largely to budget formation and oversight, long-range financial planning, and the like. At that time the office was in the hands of a thirty- or thirty-one-year-old acting provost, Steve (Stephen R.) Lewis (Williams, class of 1960), a very bright young development economist whom we had somehow lured back to Williams from the Harvard Economics Department. He brought a wonderfully clearheaded intelligence and remarkably high energy to whatever he put his hand to. Later on in his career he was to serve for fifteen years and with great distinction as president of Carleton College in Minnesota. He was already a good friend and it was for me a great pleasure to see him in action that year and to work closely with him.

Apart from the annual round of assembling, vetting, and seeing the package of course changes, new courses, and so on through to a vote, the CEP had, at the start of the 1968–69 academic year, several other major items on its agenda: the question of whether or not to institute a system of student evaluation of faculty teaching and the choice of the form such a system might properly take; the need to come to some sort of conclusion about the continuing viability of the major (comprehensive) examination or the culminating moment in the college's major courses of study; an intriguing and creative proposal framed by Bob (Robert) Gaudino of the Political Science Department for a yearlong junior study-abroad program, experiential in nature, which he proposed to call "Williams in India"; and, already emerging on the horizon, a proposal for the institution of a new interdepartmental major in the history of ideas that Dan O'Connor and I were shaping. To these items, at Steve Lewis's fairly urgent prompting, we added the shaping of an interdepartmental coordinate (i.e., non-major) program in Afro-American studies. To deal with this last item, I appointed a subcommittee whose job it was, having liaised with the officers of the Afro-American Society and with the chairs of the departments most likely to be able to contribute courses, to draft a proposal to bring back to the full CEP. This it did in timely fashion, though the Afro-American Society was later to claim, rightly or wrongly, that it had not been adequately consulted. Whatever the case, and having consulted by phone with the man who was presumably going to be chairing the new program, we brought the proposal up for a vote at the February 8, 1969, faculty meeting where it was approved with little comment and with no dissent. The man in question, Joe (Joseph R.) Harris, a noted African historian who also taught Afro-American history, had been appointed professor earlier that year and was to begin his teaching at Williams in the fall of 1969. He proved to be a fine, thoughtful colleague and he and his wife, Rose, were to become good personal friends of ours. Williams was fortunate enough to be able to hold onto him until 1975, at which point he left to take up the chairmanship of the History Department at Howard University in Washington, DC, the country's premier predominantly black institution, and later to become a dean there.

The other related item of a pressing nature had been bequeathed to the CEP by the Admissions Committee at the end of the previous academic year. That committee being at the time little more than a wing of the Admissions Office, it had obviously been felt that the item in question should be handled by one of the faculty's standing committees. This indicated its belief that, on the matter of the college's admission policy towards "disadvantaged" students,

> the waters have gotten deep enough . . . to warrant the immediate attention of the CEP so that we can continue, effectively and honestly, to translate the educational objectives of Williams as we look to the future. The problem is really to try to define what should be the nature and extent of our institutional commitment to the disadvantaged students of this country. One writer on this general subject perhaps states the question best when he says that the heart of the problem is not what institutions of higher education are to *do*, but what they are to *be*.

It was the success of the Admissions Office in recruiting an increasing number of black students that had precipitated this move, and the rather vague and general way in which the issue was framed reflects, I believe, the delicacy or discomfort that still inhibited white academics at that time from speaking more forthrightly about the explicit targeting of admissions efforts on the recruitment of members of a particular racial minority. But the indirect or opaque way in which the issue was framed served also to introduce an unhelpful lack of clarity into the early phase, at least, of our deliberations. As a result, we were drawn into discussions that reached well beyond matters pertaining directly to admissions at Williams—discussions concerning the desirability of making Williams faculty available for temporary service at historically black colleges or of mounting summer remedial programs to help disadvantaged students about to enter other colleges, and the like.

We had made the issue the priority item in our fall committee meetings, and by the November 6 faculty meeting we were ready to report on our findings to date. The matter was such as to evoke from the faculty a sharply focused degree of attention. At the meeting, two members of the committee, Bill Moomaw of the Chemistry Department and Larry Graver of English, both of them very gifted colleagues, undertook to sharpen the focus of discussion by role-playing as firm advocates of competing positions. A very lively and helpful debate ensued and it was followed by a stream of suggestions submitted to the committee by individual members of the faculty.

All of these discussions and exchanges brought clearly home to those of us on the committee the need, if we hoped to bring the matter to any proximate conclusion, to insert into the debate a battery of distinctions capable of turning even a medieval scholastic pale with envy! With that in mind, I tried my hand at an appropriate memorandum and shared it with the committee, which approved it after a few pertinent revisions. That done, and in preparation for the December 18 faculty meeting, we shared the memorandum with the entire faculty. In that brief document we distinguished among the categories of students we had in mind and also among the various educational goals we might wish to pursue.

In relation to the former, we distinguished between black students in particular and disadvantaged students in general, as well as between *economically* and *educationally* disadvantaged students, with this last category being defined for our purposes to include all those "high risk" students whose educational background was such that they were not even marginally equipped to meet the academic standards currently prevailing at Williams. Such categories could obviously overlap but they were not identical. While increasing the number of black students admitted to the college would almost certainly mean an increase also in the number of economically disadvantaged students admitted, it would not *necessarily* also involve a commitment to admit students who were educationally disadvantaged.

In relation to the educational goals we had in mind, we suggested that we had been guilty of running unhelpfully together (and treating more or less as one) three basically different questions. First, how was the college to integrate its student body effectively? That is, the question of black admissions. Second, what should the college be doing to help the nation's economically disadvantaged? Third, should the college be seeking a radical social pluralization of its student body such that it would include a much larger number of students drawn from the ranks of the educationally disadvantaged?

While we acknowledged that these three questions were not mutually exclusive and were all of them deserving of close attention, we urged the need to set our priorities and to decide which of the three was the most central and pressing question—the question that we needed to confront immediately. The second and third questions, after all, reached in some ways beyond the matter of admissions policy and raised some far-reaching issues concerning the very nature of the college. Our immediate focus, we argued, should properly be the first question. There, all we would have to agree upon would be the proposition that a racially integrated student body was a worthwhile goal and should be given top priority in our admissions policies. If we thought we could achieve that goal without going further than we had into the business of admitting "high-risk" students, well and good. The Admissions Office had concluded that we could do this, and there were independent indicators that that appraisal was a correct one.

Having thus moved to clear the argumentative ground clutter, and having secured the reconstitution of the Committee on Admissions as a fully independent standing faculty committee, we brought to a vote at the faculty meeting on December 18, 1968, the following resolution:

That this Faculty:
1. Wishes to endorse the efforts which the Admissions Office has been making and is continuing to make to increase the number of academically qualified black students or other racial minorities at Williams College.
2. Urges upon the Admissions Office as aggressive a recruiting policy as feasible in order to achieve this goal.
3. Charges the newly reconstituted Faculty Committee on Admissions with the particular tasks of drawing up a coherent recruiting policy in the minority group area, of evaluating the results of

that policy, of responding to faculty and student initiatives relating to that policy and to its results, and of recommending to the Faculty and Admissions Office any changes in the policy which it deems appropriate.

Looking back on all of this from a vantage point of almost half a century later, I am tempted to view our earnest and protracted efforts as an instance of the mountain having been in labor and brought forth a mouse. And I have reason to believe that is precisely the (rather condescending) view that the Admissions Office took of the matter at the time. But it would be a mistake, I think, to do so. And I feel encouraged in that conclusion by the disagreements which the Supreme Court's recent deliberations in the case of *Fisher v. The University of Texas* have contrived to surface. Some, evoking the experience of Israeli universities, have argued that class-based admissions policies giving "socioeconomically disadvantaged applicants an edge" in university admissions would, in fact, "work to *diminish* racial and ethnic diversity." So that, in effect, "far from being complementary, broad diversity and race-neutrality are conflicting goals." Others, denying the pertinence of the Israeli experience, have argued for the compatibility of the two goals. But whatever the outcome of this more recent debate, it seems clear that our committee was correct, almost fifty years ago now, in its decision at least to engage the issue and forthrightly to acknowledge the fact that the policy we were recommending was racially oriented. We were acutely conscious of the fact that it was the faculty, after all, who would have to shoulder the responsibility of teaching the students admitted, and their heartfelt concurrence in the policy of vigorously recruiting academically qualified black students was vital to its successful implementation. The confusion involved in the overlapping questions noted above was present in the CEP's own early discussions of the matter and a glance at the (rather sparse) minutes of the November faculty meeting reveals it to have been evident in faculty debate then. Abetting such confusion, or so I would now judge, was the prevalence at that time of a nagging discomfort with framing an admissions policy on explicitly racial grounds. On balance, then, our careful teasing apart of the overlapping questions in play, however labored it may well seem in retrospect, was probably called for at the time. And the outcome, for the resolution carried without difficulty, was a clear and explicit endorsement by the faculty of the recruitment policy that the Admissions Office had pioneered. That commitment, fully shared by administration and board of trustees alike, has never since wavered, though it later became clear to me as I began to take on the task of addressing alumni chapters across the country that not all Williams alumni in the 1970s and 1980s necessarily embraced that commitment with any degree of enthusiasm.

It is possibly the case that comparable reservations were not altogether lacking among the faculty in the late 1960s. If so, those who shared them must have felt inhibited about giving them open expression. Certainly, I knew there to be misgivings about the establishment of an academic novelty like a program in Afro-American studies and when I brought that proposal up for a vote at the February 1969 faculty meeting, I was fully expecting to encounter opposition. And when it carried with a minimum of discussion, I could not help suspecting that an unhealthy measure of self-censorship was at work. I was also struck by the extent of the opposition that immediately surfaced in connection with the next item on the agenda—namely, our proposal for the establishment of an interdepartmental major in the history of ideas—and which culminated in its peremptory tabling, thus precluding any action on the proposal at that meeting. I could not help suspecting that that opposition reflected, at least in part, an element of displaced resentment over the need felt, in the climate of opinion then prevailing, for such self-censorship.

In the event, none of the steps the college had been taking to respond to the passionate dismay expressed by the Afro-American Society the previous spring succeeded in convincing the growing cohort of black students at Williams of the firmness or sincerity of the institution's commitment to respond to their expressed needs. In various written communications to the society, the dean of the college, provost, and president all pointed out, *inter alia*, that African history had been taught at the college since the beginning of the decade and Afro-American history since 1964 (when Fred Rudolph had launched an elective course entitled "The Negro in American History") and that the library had moved energetically to expand its holdings in both fields. Similarly, in 1966 Williams had established a summer ABC program aimed at promoting the college preparation of underprivileged students; during the 1968–69 academic year, the faculty had voted to establish an interdepartmental program in

Afro-American studies; space had been made available in Mears House for an Afro-American fellowship room; and two key appointments had been made to respond to the needs of black students—a senior black historian (Joe Harris) and a black assistant dean whose responsibilities would include helping with academic counseling and admissions. All of those things were worth pointing out then. And, with the object of keeping the historical record straight, they remain worth pointing out today. For, to judge by statements in *The Williams Record* (the student newspaper), already in the early 1970s campus mythology had it that all of these things had come about only as a result of the building occupation that had taken place in April 1969. The momentum leading up to that sort of direct student action had been quickened by the Afro-American Society's presentation to the college on March 12 of a set of demands. These were formulated in what was rapidly becoming the fashion of the day—not as proposals or requests but as a unified package of "non-negotiable demands," not one of which was to be "rejected, revised, redefined, or altered." Jack Sawyer's response, written April 3, the very eve of the student-stipulated deadline, was somewhat indirect in its wording and even, at some points, rather opaque. While courteous and diplomatic in tone, it indicated that it would be impossible to make "any complete response [to the demands] by April 4" and, quite understandably, insisted that the establishment of a "racially segregated residence" would run counter to "fundamental principles of educational philosophy to which the College and most educators are deeply committed."

In the wake of this communication, and of some rather frantic, last-minute discussions in which I participated, the members of the Afro-American Society sadly concluded that their set of demands had in fact been rejected. "Williams," they said, "has failed us." In the early morning hours of April 4, accordingly, the first anniversary of Martin Luther King's assassination, they took over Hopkins Hall, the college's central administrative building, and barricaded its entrances. While events of this sort have since become something of a tired cliché on the nation's campuses, at the time (at least so far as the twentieth century was concerned) they were something of a startling novelty, capable of shocking dignified administrators as well as faculty of traditionalist sympathies, causing outrage among the more conservative of alumni, and setting an entire campus on its ear.

About this particular moment of crisis, certain things stand out: first, the nature of the demands being made; second, the way in which the administration handled them; third, the deportment and behavior of the protesting students.

So far as the demands themselves went, they focused on Afro-American studies, admissions, and what was referred to as "administration" but which focused on housing issues in particular and the life of black students at Williams in general. In relation to the first two, while impatience was expressed with the dimensions and reach of the newly founded program in Afro-American studies and with the allegedly sluggish pace at which the number of black students at Williams was being increased, what was being demanded pertained to degree, not kind, and was readily open to negotiation once the society proved willing to involve itself in the (implicit) negotiation of demands it had previously stipulated as being in nature "non-negotiable." Similarly, the administrative issues which fell under the third heading, with one crucial exception. This last was the demand that the proposed Afro-American cultural center serve also as a residence for black students. The board of trustees had only just (November 1968) put the final nail in the coffin of the fraternity era at Williams and the very idea of the sort of segregated residence being demanded was, for the college, totally unacceptable. This particular demand was to be the great sticking point when the process of negotiation finally began. It was eventually to be resolved only when, in order to promote "the feeling of solidarity," the college eventually agreed to permit black upperclassmen to choose, if they so wished (not all did), to live in somewhat "larger concentration [than heretofore] . . . within the existing residential house system."

As for the way in which the administration chose to handle the demands, what struck me most forcefully at the time was the apparent absence of the president himself from the gritty process of arriving at the final accommodation. Or, perhaps more accurately, his comparative invisibility on campus during those critical days. He was, I know, prone to ear infections and attacks of shingles and, though he did preside over special meetings of the faculty on April 2 and (Sunday!) April 6, I got the impression, rightly or wrongly, that he may have been ill throughout this whole unhappy episode. Certainly when, after the occupation had been ended, he summoned a small group of us to meet with him to plan for the upcoming faculty meeting (that would be called in order to approve the settlement arrived at with the protestors), the meeting was held not in his office but at the President's House and on that occasion Jack himself appeared clad in a bathrobe. Instead of the president, the college's point person throughout had been our young acting provost, Steve Lewis. He it was who was called upon to shoulder the heavy burden of resolving the whole crisis and, so far as the administrative side of things went, he was in my view the hero of the whole episode.

So far as the dissident students themselves were concerned, I think it should be said that they were an impressively disciplined group that benefitted greatly from the charismatic leadership exerted by their chairman, Preston Washington '70, a person who combined admirably strong character traits with an essentially gentle temperament. After he graduated from Williams he returned to Harlem and spent the rest of his life ministering to a congregation in that community. Like many other students who had been involved in campus activism directed at putting pressure on the college, he was to become over the years a very loyal alumnus and to serve for several years as a trustee of the college. Under his leadership, the occupation of Hopkins Hall, which lasted until April 8, was a peaceful and orderly affair. Office papers were left untouched, files were not ransacked, and the occupying students made a point of tidying up behind them before vacating the premises. Nothing happened at Williams even remotely akin to the miseries that unfolded at Cornell just two weeks later, when white members of one of the fraternities went on the attack and tried (forcibly but unsuccessfully) to eject the black students who had occupied Willard Straight Hall. That was the episode that was to lead to the flourishing of firearms there. In contrast, and in contrast also with some of the later outbursts of student activism at Williams that were to have a rather jaded and manipulative feel to them, there was, I think, something comparatively pure about this particular episode in 1969. The occupiers clearly did not know what to expect as a result of the novel and risky action they had taken. In a moving statement issued after the Rubicon had been crossed and the occupation begun, they confessed that they knew their action would hardly be a popular one, that it might even have been "a grievous tactical error" on their part, and that they had much personally at stake. If "we have put our futures and our status as students at Williams on the line," it was because they sincerely believed that "the entire community" would "benefit from any change" that might "evolve from that incident."

In the event, and (it seems) in some measure to the surprise of the occupiers, the college's white students responded with broadly shared and publicly expressed sympathy with their plight and even with their goals. The college's administration also reacted with a measure of sympathetic understanding, indicating a readiness to proceed to further discussion of the demands even while the building was still occupied and making sure, in the meantime, that food was delivered to the occupiers.

At the time, no faculty steering committee existed. So the provost, feeling the need for an appropriate faculty body with which he could consult, requested the establishment of an ad hoc faculty advisory committee with a membership appropriately representative of the faculty's various ranks and of the most pertinent faculty committees (Admissions, Appointments and Promotions, Educational Policy, and Undergraduate Life). It was composed of two members drawn from the most senior ranks (Bill Gates of economics and Sam Matthews of biology), two from the middle ranks (Gordon Winston from economics and myself from history), and one from the nontenured ranks (Bill Bevis from English). We set up headquarters in Jesup Hall and met frequently throughout the occupation to discuss with Steve the progress of negotiations, to respond to his requests for advice, and, as the ice began to melt, to help draft putative public statements conveying the outcome. When a settlement seemed finally within reach, the Afro-American Society interposed a final hurdle by insisting that the provost's signature on the final agreement was not enough and that the concurrence of the faculty was called for. The president had declined our urgent request (conveyed via Sam Matthews) that he call a special faculty meeting to secure that concurrence, so it was left for us (if the occupation was to be ended without further, damaging delay) to provide a surrogate for that concurrence by cosigning with Steve a letter indicating our "unanimous agreement with the written understanding" he had reached with Preston Washington concerning the society's demands. Accepting that assurance, the students ended the occupation and the matter of formal faculty approval was left (somewhat uneasily) to a faculty meeting scheduled for later in that week.

At that meeting, Steve Lewis described in detail the course of events during the occupation and the nature of the agreement arrived at with the Afro-American Society. It then fell to me, representing the ad hoc faculty advisory committee, to introduce a motion to endorse that agreement and to speak briefly in support of that move. The motion carried by a simple voice vote and without protracted discussion.

With that dramatic and cathartic episode behind us, one had a strong sense that so far as the spring semester was concerned it was to be downhill all the way. All of us had to settle back into the mundane tasks of catching up on things that had been placed on hold during the crisis, wrapping up our courses, and setting and grading final examinations. So far as the work of the Committee on Educational Policy was concerned, our main tasks were seeing through the proposal to establish an interdepartmental major in the history of ideas to an affirmative vote and tying up any remaining loose ends pertaining to other curricular matters. As for Committee X, which across the course of the academic year had had some enormously stimulating curricular discussions, it had already reported back to its parent committee. When it did so, it had envisaged the possibility that a coordinate women's college might be established and, with that in mind, had proposed a pluralization of patterns of study, moving out from the existing core of strictly departmental majors to embrace a broad array of interdepartmental concentrations and even the notion of individually constructed major patterns of study. And, somewhat prophetically, it had even ventilated the idea (though somewhat vaguely and without explicit references to the Oxbridge model) of creating what it labeled as "tutorials" or "tutorial seminars."

In the event, however, having at the May faculty meeting secured the enthusiastic endorsement of the faculty for its recommendations, the Committee on Coordinate Education and Related Questions set to one side the idea for the creation of a coordinate women's college and opted wisely for outright coeducation at Williams itself. At the June 1969 meeting of the board, the trustees gave their approval to that approach. Williams, without reducing the number of male students from its current 1250 or so, was to begin to enroll significant numbers (650 was the stated target) of women students as regular members of the student body by 1971.

With that, the curtain was lowered on what had been a dramatic and truly hectic academic year—tension-filled, but also creative, exhilarating, and in many ways determinative of the future shape of the college. The next year was not to be a quiet one either; it was to end, after all, amid the upheavals of Cambodian Spring. But on campus, at least, it was to be a less divisive year and, in any case, not one in which I was destined to be involved. Knowing that I was due in 1969–70 for my first full year's sabbatical leave, I had applied to the American Council of Learned Societies for a (portable) senior research fellowship and had been lucky enough to be awarded one. We had been able, accordingly, to plan on spending that academic year as a family in London where I could pursue my research in the British Museum. We were due, accordingly, to depart from New York for Southampton (it was only the OPEC oil crisis in 1973 that was to sound the death knell for regular transatlantic passenger shipping) on the *France*, a splendid ship. In the interim, however, things were to be hectic for both of us. In the absence of women students at the college, it was customary for faculty wives to play the female roles in college theatrical productions. Claire-Ann, who had appeared as a dancer in the 1966 production of *Brigadoon* (not all that long after Brian, our fourth child, had been born!) and as one of the Bacchantes in a production of Euripides' *Bacchae*, had now been prevailed upon to dance in a 1969 production of *Guys and Dolls*. So, apart from making arrangements for the rental of our house to a nice couple working for Sprague Electric in North Adams, for the placement of our Irish setter Siobhan with another kindly couple who owned a farm nearby in Vermont, and for the discharge of her duties teaching in the evening division at Berkshire Community College, she was also caught up in rehearsals at the Adams Memorial Theatre. And I myself, apart from wrapping up my courses and committee responsibilities, was busy preparing to teach again during July in our NDEA Summer Institute in European Cultural History. But, one way or another, everything got done and the day after the Summer Institute ended and around the time of our eleventh wedding anniversary—jobs completed, dog comfortably accommodated, house let to plausible tenants, and everything packed for the year abroad—we made our way to

New York. After having ensconced the children in their own cabin next to ours (it proved to be high jinks all the way!), we collapsed with a welcome drink into deck chairs on the promenade deck as that wonderfully elegant ship slipped its moorings, hooted farewell to its attendant tugs, and, as a golden day drew to a close, made its majestic way through the Verrazano Narrows and out into the great and familiar waters that beckoned beyond.

CHAPTER THIRTEEN

The Transformative Sixties (ii): The Second Vatican Council

During this uniquely turbulent decade, not all of my personal and professional preoccupations linked up in any direct fashion with matters collegiate. Two, in particular, stood to one side of such matters. One involved the micropolitics surrounding public infrastructure projects in the United States; the other concerned the international macropolitics unleashed by Pope John XXIII's unexpected convocation of the Second Vatican Council.

So far as the first of these went, I became deeply involved towards the end of the decade with a local oppositional group whose goal it was to derail a putative and quite ham-fisted effort by the Massachusetts Department of Public Works (DPW) to construct (largely with federal funding) a monstrous four-lane bypass road designed to reroute long-distance traffic around Williamstown. Taking its departure from Five Corners in South Williamstown, it was designed to cut its way destructively across Stone Hill and to cross under Route 2 east of the town center before making its way north to rejoin Route 7 in Pownal, Vermont. As the only planned exit or crossing point was at the intersection with Route 2 (near the old Howard Johnson restaurant), Stone Hill (in particular) and the town (in general) would in effect have been cut into two parts. It was a case of gross overkill to remedy a not very clearly established traffic problem, and, in retrospect, it is hard to take the plan at all seriously. At the time, however, it all looked very threatening, and one didn't have to be a property owner affected by the necessary land-taking to come out in vigorous opposition to the whole scheme. In the end, in part because the DPW had simply ignored recent changes in federal regulations governing the use of federal funds (on a 90–10 percent basis) for such highway projects, the plan fell by the wayside and it has never been revived. If, at the time, the battle was an interesting and hard-fought one, and one from which I learned a good deal about local and county politics, it was also one that was too intricate to dwell upon here.

Instead, I propose to focus upon the international upheaval caused by the convocation and proceedings of the Second Vatican Council (1962–65), not simply because of the transformative impact upon any serious Catholic reasonably well informed on matters religious (and I would count myself as such), but also because it nudged me into developing another (more personal and religious) strand in my scholarly endeavors and brought home to me in the end just how deeply historical was the nature of my intellectual temperament. Unfortunately, in the attempt to convey what it was, exactly, that was at stake for me personally, I will be called upon to delineate at some length a stretch of history where the devil, alas, dwells in the details.

As we make our way now through the fiftieth anniversary of the great transformative decade that did so much to shape the late twentieth century imaginary, we hear a good deal from the commentators about the seismic political, social, and cultural shifts that distinguished that era. But large though they loomed at the time, especially in the realms of mysticism and spirituality, about the religious upheavals of the day we hear a good deal less. And about the mainstream religiosity of the 1960s the commentators tend to be silent. Allusions to the works of such as Norman O. Brown, Theodore Roszak, Allen Ginsberg, and Herbert Marcuse are commonplace enough, but, revolutionary though it was, we hear nothing about *Dignitatis humanae*, the Second Vatican Council's declaration on religious liberty—or, for that matter, about the other fifteen constitutions, decrees, and declarations that together form the legislative legacy resulting from that great assembly's labors between 1962 and 1965. Most people, I suspect, would find it incongruous to find such documents shelved cheek by jowl with Roszak's *The Making of a Counter Culture* even though they are alike the products of the transformative sixties. But for Catholics of intellectual bent it would probably not seem all that odd. And for me, certainly, not odd at all. In my own life, the various transformative upheavals of the day seemed to intersect in so natural a fashion as to preclude the need to tease them apart.

As an historical event, the Second Vatican Council was an enormous and wholly extraordinary affair. It is credibly claimed to have been the most significant religious event of the twentieth century. Indeed, with the number of its voting participants peaking in the neighborhood of 2,600, it can arguably lay claim also to having been the largest formally constituted meeting in the history of humankind. As such, it understandably attracted at the time a great deal of attention. While it is difficult to gauge the seriousness of the interest in its doings evinced by the European and North American intelligentsia at large, the depths of its impact on the lives of the billion-plus Catholics worldwide is not to be gainsaid. And not least of all on those living in non-Western societies, where the changes and reforms embedded in *Sacrosanctum concilium*, its Constitution on the Sacred Liturgy, opened the way once more, and this time irreversibly, for the type of acculturation and de-Europeanization of Catholic worship earlier attempted in the seventeenth century by Jesuit missionaries in China. For there the Jesuits (if not their Dominican counterparts) had boldly substituted Chinese for Latin in the liturgy and had embraced the traditional Chinese rites for the veneration of ancestors as compatible with the Christian faith. That earlier attempt at religious acculturation had proved to be evanescent; it had foundered in the eighteenth century on the rocks of inter-order missionary rivalry. But its twentieth-century successor was destined rapidly to become a worldwide phenomenon and Catholicism itself was freed likewise to take on the lineaments of a genuinely global religion with its center of gravity steadily shifting away from the West.

The council, then, and deservedly so, received a good deal of attention in the press, and not only in religiously oriented publications. Newspapers like *Le Monde* in Paris or the *Washington Post* and the *New York Times* in the United States covered its proceedings attentively. And the meaty and highly readable "Letters from Vatican City" published in *The*

New Yorker over the pseudonymous byline of "Xavier Rynne" (Fr. Francis Xavier Murphy) and republished during and after the council in four substantial volumes, were widely read. They did much, indeed, to shape the way in which its proceedings were understood by the wider literate public. It was easy enough, then, for interested Catholics to follow the exciting and turbulent unfolding of conciliar activity between 1962 and 1965, and it became all the easier after the *National Catholic Reporter*, an independent, lay-controlled weekly Catholic newspaper of unquestionably "progressive" bent was launched in Kansas City, Missouri, in 1964. Giving a blow-by-blow account of the conciliar debates and extra-conciliar maneuvering between the Majority (progressives) and Minority (conservative/traditionalist) factions that had emerged quite rapidly among the council fathers, and even publishing in English translation preliminary drafts of the documents still being debated and revised in council, it made for compelling reading. It is hard now, indeed, to convey the level of excitement and anticipation all of this generated among concerned Catholics of my generation. And especially so among those who, like me, were academics or people of intellectual bent, people committed to critical rationality who had long been restive with the attachment of the curial *immobilisti* at Rome to the maintenance of a narrow-minded, ghettoized form of Catholicism concerned above all to keep the modern world at bay even to the point of bracketing the familiar norms of rational judgment on which we ourselves relied in our chosen callings and daily living. We yearned to make our lives whole and, to that end, were keen to contribute whatever talents we possessed to the historic task of attaining the goal that John XXIII had labeled (somewhat loosely) as *aggiornamento* ("todaying").

It was as if a lid had been taken off the Catholic cauldron and, given the mounting ferment at Rome, we were beginning dimly to perceive that some of the most prominent features of the Catholicism in which as children we had been reared, far from being hallowed by age and anointed with timelessness were, in fact, of quite recent provenance. It was becoming increasingly clear that they were very much the product in general of the religious backlash against the destructiveness of the French Revolution and, in particular, of the papal reaction to the early twentieth-century Modernist crisis. The domination of the universal church by the Roman center and an imperial papacy, the latter's control over the appointment of bishops worldwide, its de facto (if not de jure) reduction of those bishops to the status of branch managers increasingly dependent upon the say-so of corporate headquarters at Rome, its monopolization of the church's doctrinal teaching authority, its constant effort to maintain within Catholic intellectual circles the hegemony to which the ultramontane Roman theological school had attained in the late nineteenth century—such things we had taken (however restively) to be some sort of age-old Catholic norm. But it was being revealed that that was not the case at all. That we had thought otherwise is powerfully reflective of the remarkably presentist orientation of modern Roman Catholicism. It may well be a religion that places great emphasis on Tradition, but it is also one that pays dangerously little attention to history. Certainly, in the mid-twentieth century, the dispositions of the present, however recent in provenance, tended to cast a long shadow back across the past and to take on an aura of timelessness. This was partly the result of habit. Less attractively, it also reflected an unfortunate degree of self-censorship on the part of those clerics who knew better. And, more alarmingly, it reflected a conscious politics of oblivion, evocative of the Party's motto in George Orwell's *1984*: "Who controls the present controls the past; who controls the past controls the future." Thus it was easy enough for most Catholics to assume that the popes had always appointed the bishops and had always been in the habit of issuing frequent encyclicals setting forth the acceptable doctrinal or moral stance on this or that issue, or even of defining doctrines like the Immaculate Conception (1854) or the Assumption of the Blessed Virgin into Heaven (1950) that had little or no scriptural grounding. Though such things were largely the offspring of nineteenth-century papalist innovation, that fact had become all the harder to discern in the wake of the condemnation in 1907, first by the Holy Office in the decree *Lamentabili sane* and then by Pius X himself in the encyclical *Pascendi dominici gregis*, of an amorphous collection of alleged heterodoxies to which the collective label of "Modernism" was attached. These condemnations had been followed by an anti-Modernist witch hunt of McCarthyesque proportions which had a devastating effect upon the morale of the clergy and upon Catholic intellectual life. As late as the 1950s, there had been a quickening of anti-Modernist sentiment that had led to the peremptory silencing by Rome of such theological luminaries as Henri de Lubac, Marie-Dominique

Chenu, and Yves Congar, all of them representatives of the French *nou-
velle théologie* and all of them destined within a decade to rise, ironically,
to great and influential prominence at Vatican II itself.

Attesting to the continuing strength of the attack on Modernism is
the fact that a very explicit anti-Modernist oath was imposed on all clerics
for almost half a century (1920–67). Revelatory of what lay at the root of
Roman fears was the fact that the oath required, of all those on whom it
was imposed, that they affirm "the *absolute* and *unchangeable* truth presented by the apostles from the beginning," that they reject "the heretical
invention of the evolution of dogmas to the effect that these would
change their meaning from that previously held by the Church," and that
they deny that "it would be lawful for the historian to hold views which
are in contradiction with the faith of the believer." What was reflected
here is, in effect, what the Canadian philosopher Charles Taylor has referred to as "the blind historical panic of much of the hierarchy" in the
wake of the French Revolution. It was history, with its critical foreground-
ing of the reality of change, that had clearly come to be seen as the sub-
versive science. One should not be surprised, then, that Cardinal Alfredo
Ottaviani, one of the leaders of the traditionalist Minority at Vatican II,
head of the Holy Office during the conciliar years and, as such, the official guardian of Roman Catholic orthodoxy, should have chosen as the
motto for his coat of arms *Semper idem*—"always the same." A joke circulating at Rome during the conciliar era well captured the feel of his
well-attested doctrinal stance. It related the story of his emerging one
morning from his apartment and, getting into his official car, saying "To
the Council." Whereupon the driver set off promptly for Trent.

Recognizing, however, the centrality of change to the new, historically oriented theological currents that had begun to flow so powerfully
at the time, the American theologian John Courtney Murray was to conclude that "development of doctrine" was "the issue underlying all issues
at Vatican II." And the terminal gloom that that fact generated among the
stubborn leaders of the traditionalist Minority reflected at its extreme the
unyielding posture exemplified already in the late nineteenth century by
the American Catholic Orestes Brownson when, denouncing Cardinal
Newman's *Essay on the Development of Christian Doctrine* as revealing
him to be "no Catholic," dismissed the work as being "utterly repugnant
to her [the church's] claims to be the authoritative and infallible Church

of God." For it was the view of that church that "there has been no progress, no increase, no variation in faith, that what she believes and teaches now is precisely what she always and everywhere taught and believed from the first."

If the horror generated by the threat of change was perhaps the dominant strand in the thoughts and feelings of the Minority at Vatican II, the course of events at the council reveals it to have been most profoundly felt when the waves of change threatened to break over the ultramontane or high papalist understanding of the papal primacy. And it also found at such moments a powerful resonance in the thinking of Pope Paul VI himself. John XXIII had died in 1963 when the council was already in midstream, and Paul had succeeded him. Though he was often portrayed as indecisive (John XXIII had dubbed him amusingly as *amletico*, or "Hamlet-like"), he had chosen not to terminate the council but to see it through to its conclusion. At the same time, however, he seemed to have become increasingly worried about the potentially radical nature of the changes the council fathers were proving themselves willing to entertain and of the degree to which they might come to threaten the papal teaching authority and papal primacy of jurisdiction. During the summer prior to the council's fourth and final session in 1965, he had begun in various allocutions to fret that the church was being threatened by a "crisis of obedience" or "crisis of authority," in that "truths that stand outside time because they are divine are being subjected to a historicism that strips them of their content and unchangeable character." And that concern, which led him to intervene repeatedly in matters conciliar during the last session, seemed always to peak when he saw the high papalist understanding of the papal primacy coming under threat. Ironically enough, on such occasions and in such matters it seems that he was ultimately skeptical about the likelihood that the thinking of the council fathers could reliably be assumed to reflect the promptings of the Holy Spirit. Thus the four issues which, by an exercise of his own supreme authority, he continued to prevent from becoming agenda items at the council—birth control, clerical celibacy, reform of the Roman Curia (or central administrative cadre), and the mechanism that could make episcopal collegiality an institutional reality—all touched intimately upon the papal authority. The last issue is a particularly revealing one. It concerns the relationship of the bishops as a whole when acting as a "College" (that is, collectively to the papal primate) and pivots upon the nature of the authority they exercised over the universal church when acting as such a collectivity. That issue was one that was hard-fought both in the discussions of the preparatory commission and in the debates of the council itself. So far as episcopal collegiality was concerned, the intuition involved was an ancient one. It was far older, certainly, than the high papalist, monarchical understanding of the papal primacy, though one that had come in the modern era to be increasingly marginalized. But *Lumen gentium*, Vatican II's great Constitution on the Church, emphasized in its crucial third chapter the collective or "collegial responsibility" of bishops worldwide (by "divine institution" successors to the original "apostolic college") for the mission and well-being of the whole church. "United with its head, the Roman pontiff, and never without its head," the Constitution declared, "the order of bishops is the subject [i.e., the bearer] of supreme and full power" over that universal Church, and that "supreme power is . . . solemnly exercised in an ecumenical council." To the conservatives of the Minority, this was an alarming claim. They saw it as being at odds with the monarchical primacy of the pope. It was a dangerous novelty, one that smacked of "conciliarism"—the late medieval view, so often condemned by the papacy, to the effect that the general council, acting apart from the pope, possessed in certain critical cases an authority over the universal Church superior to his. Paul VI himself appears to have shared that fear. During the course of debate and during the difficult "black" week—it was dubbed at the time as "la settimana nera"—he sent to the council via the Doctrinal Commission, and as the authentic norm governing the interpretation of *Lumen gentium*'s third chapter, a startling "Preliminary Explanatory Note" (*Nota explicativa praevia*). Both there, and in the final text of *Lumen gentium* itself, it was now made clear that the "solicitude" that the bishops are called upon to exercise for the whole Church is merely a *pastoral* solicitude, not one "exercised by an act of jurisdiction." At every point, indeed, the jurisdictional or juridical power would appear to be assigned to the episcopal college's head alone. Only in "hierarchical communion" with that head of the college and its members "can bishops exercise their various offices, governance included." Only through papal convocation and confirmation can a council be ecumenical. Only with papal approbation can conciliar acts become valid. Further than that, as head of the college, the pope "alone can perform certain acts which are in no way within the competence" of the bishops, can proceed, "taking into consideration the good of the Church" and "according to his own discretion" in "setting up, encouraging and approving collegial activity," and, "as supreme pastor of the Church, can exercise his power at all times *as he thinks best*" (italics mine).

For the general reader, I suppose, and probably for most Catholics even, this necessary but unhappily extended prolegomenon to my own involvement in the religious issues of the day is likely to seem pretty recondite stuff. But given the sort of research I had been doing, though it pertained directly, not to ecclesiology but to the history of political thought, much of it rang a bell. And that bell began to ring all the more imperatively after I began, in the mid-1960s, to acquaint myself with the new literature on general councils stimulated by John XXIII's unexpected convocation in 1959 of a new council. At Étienne Gilson's suggestion, I had begun my research on late medieval political thinking by focusing on the French philosopher/theologian Pierre d'Ailly (1350–1420), a prominent churchman whose political thinking overlapped with ecclesiological themes. And the unfolding events at Vatican II led me now to focus, in a way that I had not done previously, on the more purely ecclesiological aspect of his thinking.

Like the English philosopher William of Ockham, whose work he much admired, d'Ailly spoke of the natural right "which belongs to all those over whom any authority, either secular or ecclesiastical is placed— that is, the right to elect their rulers." But it was in relation to the Church, which he referred to as the "ecclesiastical polity," that he developed the theory of consent that this implied. And he did so in an attempt to arrive at a solution to the great crisis that had overtaken the Church in his own lifetime. The crisis in question was the Great Schism of the West, which, after the confused and disputed election of 1378, had seen two lines of claimants, Roman and Avignonese, vying destructively for the papal office. And then, still worse, after the failed attempt of the Council of Pisa to end the schism in 1409 by deposing the rival claimants and electing Pope Alexander V, it had seen the addition of a third (Pisan) line of claimants of which (the first) John XXIII was the second. Although at the time the Pisan line was widely accepted as the legitimate one, it did not quite succeed in carrying the day. John XXIII, as a result, was nudged by the emperor Sigismund into convoking the Council of Constance (1414–18) with the goal of bringing the schism to a definitive end. In the attempt to achieve that happy outcome, the churchmen whom we are accustomed to labeling as "conciliarists" (d'Ailly prominently among them) were led to argue that the general council, because it represented the universal Church or "congregation of the faithful," was possessed of the requisite authority to restore unity, even if that were to entail the judgment and formal deposition of the several papal claimants on the grounds that their obdurate clinging to office meant that they were acting not to build up the Church but to destroy it.

In 1415, then, confronted by the obduracy of John XXIII (who had fled the council and left it effectually headless), the council fathers formally promulgated the celebrated superiority decree *Haec sancta synodus*, an historic expression of the moderate version of what has come to be called conciliarism or conciliar theory. The decree declared that the Council of Constance was a legitimate general council representing the Catholic church militant, that it derived its authority immediately from Christ, and that all Christians—the pope included—were bound on pain of punishment to obey it and all future general councils on certain matters pertaining to the faith, to the ending of schism, and to the reform of the Church in head and members. The following month, even though they viewed him as the true pope, the council fathers acted on the provisions of that decree by trying and deposing John XXIII, who had been taken prisoner and returned to Constance. Shortly thereafter, though he had been deposed by the Council of Pisa, they moved pragmatically to negotiate the resignation of the Roman claimant Gregory XII. And, after failing to secure a similarly negotiated settlement with the Avignonese claimant, Benedict XIII, they proceeded in 1417 to try him in absentia, find him guilty, and declare him deposed. That done, and having first in the decree *Frequens* attempted to give constitutional teeth to *Haec sancta* by mandating, for the future, the regular and automatic assembly of general councils, they proceeded in November 1417 to elect as pope Martin V. He was originally one of the cardinals of the Roman obedience but, like many another churchman, had switched his allegiance to the Pisan line and, therefore, to John XXIII. Surrounded still by a tiny coterie of adamant supporters, Benedict XIII persisted right down to his death in 1423 in his forlorn claim to be the true pope. But, that notwithstanding, it has been customary to regard the Great Schism as having come to an end with the election of Martin V.

This is clearly a tangled story susceptible of successive rewritings. Martin V himself and his successor Eugenius IV, both of them acutely conscious of the fact that the legitimacy of their own papal titles depended on the validity of *Haec sancta* and the legitimacy of the actions that Constance had grounded in its provisions, abided by the stipulations of *Frequens* and convoked in succession the general councils of Pavia-Siena (1423) and Basel (1431–49). But during the bitter and protracted strife that broke out at the latter assembly, Eugenius IV changed course and initiated the papal policy of challenging the validity of *Haec sancta* and, with it, the overriding authority claimed in the Church by the general council. Hence the papal commitment to rewriting the pertinent history and the gradual emergence of a high papalist constitutive narrative that rose to prominence at Rome during the sixteenth and seventeenth centuries. Eventually, in its fully elaborated form and in the aftermath of Vatican I, it carried the day, dispatching into the outer darkness of heterodoxy the rival conciliarist narrative that had been entrenched for centuries at the University of Paris and taken for granted across the greater part of northern Europe. According to the now-dominant high papalist narrative, the whole conciliar episode was portrayed as emerging, once the ideological dust was allowed to settle, as nothing more than a stutter, hiccup, or interruption in the long history of the Roman Catholic Church. That it was an unfortunate, dangerous, and revolutionary episode was not to be gainsaid. But if it was radical in its origins, it was also rapid in its demise. The victory of Eugenius IV over the Council of Basel in the late 1440s marked the demise of the conciliar movement. And if conciliar theory survived a little longer, it was destined to end up as no more than a minor perturbation on the outermost orbit of the ecclesiological consciousness.

Such was the accepted narrative that had become embedded in the standard historical accounts, non-Catholic as well as Catholic, by the time I first became interested in d'Ailly and the Council of Constance. And I myself had taken that narrative simply for granted, not realizing that it was a piece of ultramontane historiography. My own interests being focused on political thinking rather than ecclesiology, I simply assumed that, so far as the constitution of the Church was concerned, conciliarism was a dead issue, something of interest only to the archaeologist of defunct ideologies.

In that casual assumption I proved to be utterly mistaken. With the dramatic unfolding of the early sessions of Vatican II, I was led, somewhat to my surprise, to call it sharply into question. The second John XXIII's unexpected convocation in 1959 of Vatican II had the effect of stimulating an enormous outburst of writing on general councils and their history, and I was naturally drawn to focus on what all this new work had to say about the Council of Constance and the question of the status of the decree *Haec sancta*. Three authors in particular caught my attention. The first was Karl August Fink of the University of Vienna, who had long since established himself as the reigning expert on the lead-in to Constance as well as on the doings of the council itself, and who had come to challenge at multiple points the traditional constitutive narrative. The second was the Benedictine church historian Paul de Vooght, a Belgian scholar with whose work on Jan Hus (the Czech reformer and national hero) I was already acquainted. The third was the young Swiss theologian Hans Küng. Already by 1960, de Vooght had come to argue for the validity of *Haec sancta*. At the time he drew no inferences from that fact to the contemporary ecclesiological situation. But he did portray *Haec sancta* as not merely an emergency measure relevant only to the activity of the Council of Constance but as a doctrinal decision concerning the competence of all general councils in matters pertaining to the faith and the unity and reform of the Church. And it was his conclusion that "there is no longer today any motive for maintaining the [traditional] ostracism of a dogmatic decree which clarifies and confirms a point of doctrine always admitted in the Church and always taught in the schools."

De Vooght's argument, clearly and forcefully presented, evoked an immediate and equally forceful response, positive as well as negative. And the clearest and most vigorous of the positive reactions came from Hans Küng in 1962 in his *Structures of the Church*, the first of several important ecclesiological works of his. There he went beyond de Vooght, pointing out that "the (traditionally understood) legitimacy of Martin V and all subsequent popes up to the present day depends on the legitimacy of the Council of Constance and its procedure in the question of the popes." At the same time he noted that modern Catholic theologians, nevertheless, "have not shrunk from pointing out the non-binding character of the Constance decrees, often with quite extraordinary, ostensibly historical arguments." Küng then goes on to summarize the findings of the most recent historical research on the subject and insists that "the binding character of the decrees of Constance [*Haec sancta* and *Frequens*] is not to be evaded." What they stipulated was that "an ecumenical council has the function of a 'control authority,' not only in connection with the emergency situation at that time, but also for the future on the premise that a possible future pope might again lapse into heresy, schism or the like." The Church, indeed, he added, "might have been able to avoid many misfortunes after the Council of Constance had the fundamental position . . . [of that council] papal primacy *and* a definite 'conciliar control' been upheld."

While at the time I was certainly intrigued by these startling findings and was beginning to realize that the work that I had been doing on conciliar theory was of more than historical interest and had an immediate relevance to contemporary ecclesiological tensions within Catholicism, I was also caught up in other historical work. And, so far as contemporary religious matters were concerned, I was still filled with great (and, alas, unrealistic) optimism about what Vatican II seemed on the brink of achieving. In the three years after the end of that council, however, things took a turn that, in retrospect, can be seen to have been signaled by Paul VI's increasingly nervous intrusion into the concluding work of the council. And, so far as I was concerned, it was very much a turn for the worse. In many parts of the United States, it is true, as in many other parts of the world, local ecclesiastical life presented to the casual observer a quite placid surface. And that was certainly true of New England. In such areas, while ecclesiastical feathers may often have been ruffled while Vatican II was in session, the apocalyptic winds of change seemed, since then, to have dwindled to the gentlest of institutional breezes. The traditional patterns of thought and the old ways of doing things appeared to be remarkably resilient. But for anyone who, like me, was willing to make the effort to track the drift of public opinion in the Church at large or who had struggled to keep his footing amid the astonishing surge of theological speculation then flooding from the presses, and despite the disconcerting undertow of papal and episcopal alarm that it helped generate, it was becoming clear that beneath the placid surface something was radically wrong. The Church, it seemed, was slipping into a state of quasi-revolutionary turmoil. Former loyalties were being shaken, familiar memories dimmed, old friendships threatened, and we were beginning to witness the startling exodus from religious practice of once-stalwart Catholics that has continued down to the present, creating a cadre of former Catholics in the United States (one third of the original total) that dwarfs in size most of the established Protestant denominations. Around that time, Hans Küng remarked that, while for all Christians "the problem of God is more important than the problem of the Church," it remains true that for most Catholics "the latter often . . . [stood] in the way of the former." And the problem of the Church that was now emerging was, in its most obviously practical dimensions, the problem of the nature and locus of ecclesiastical authority—the traditional jurisdictional pretensions and the magisterial (that is, doctrinal teaching claims) of the clerical hierarchy. More precisely, it was becoming increasingly clear that at the heart of the growing crisis confronting the Church stood the papal primacy as officially conceived and currently exercised. It was that, more than any other single factor, that was serving for many a troubled Catholic to erode the very credibility of the Roman Catholic Church itself. And despite the strenuous efforts of Paul VI, John Paul II, and Benedict XVI to turn the clock back in one way or another to the comforting ultramontane certainties of the preconciliar era, that has remained the case for the better part of fifty years down to the present.

By 1967, all of this had begun to weigh heavily on my mind and, having protected the summer of 1968 for research and writing, I was so disturbed by the Thermidorian reaction that was setting in at Rome that I decided to put my other work to one side and to devote whatever time I had to attempting an historically conditioned approach to the growing ecclesiastical crisis. What eventuated was a little book entitled *Council over Pope? Towards a Provisional Ecclesiology* (1969). It was a highly personal religious work, written with passion and at white heat. And, though pivoting on an historical base about which I felt quite confident, it reached also across the line that separated theology from history and eventuated in a passionately felt exercise by a non-theologian in a species of do-it-yourself theology.

The book was written across summer months punctuated dramatically by disturbing events in Rome. First, Paul VI's highly traditionalist
"New Credo" (*Solemni hac liturgia* or Credo of the People of God) written,
it seems, in response to the "New Catechism," endorsed by the Dutch
bishops but characterized by an alarmed committee of cardinals as "substituting one orthodoxy for another in the Church, a modern orthodoxy
for the traditional orthodoxy." And then, no more than a month later, his
catastrophic encyclical *Humanae vitae* on birth control. Traumatized, it
seems, by the call to make a change in the Church's teaching on contra-
ception and family limitation and by the possibility that such a dramatic
change might undermine papal authority, and despite the majority recommendation of the commission he had appointed to review the issue,
Paul VI rejected the commission's recommendations and, in the encyclical *Humanae vitae*, affirmed the standard teaching that went back to
Pius XI's *Casti connubii* (1930). But it turned out to be *Humanae vitae*
itself, which the vast majority of Catholics have simply declined to "receive," that turned out to call that papal teaching authority harshly into
question and also helped to precipitate, it seems, the subsequent virtual
collapse among the laity of the practice of sacramental confession. A
stunning development. The encyclical, in effect, transformed the problem of papal authority from a dark cloud on the horizon of ecumenism
to a question of conscience for vast numbers of faithful Catholics and a
matter of immediate concern for those economists and politicians whose
task it is to juggle the bleak equations of rising populations and deepening poverty in the developing world.

In the first and more purely historical section of my book, I set forth,
in counterpoint to the traditionally dominant ultramontane narrative, a
revised narrative of the Great Schism, its outbreak and course, the doings of the Council of Constance, and its aftermath which reflected the
accumulated historical research findings of the previous half century
and more. In so doing, I aligned myself with de Vooght's and Küng's endorsement of the legitimacy of Constance as a general council from the
very time of its convocation and of the validity of its superiority decree
Haec sancta synodus. I arrived at this latter conclusion in the teeth of traditionalist counterclaims. And as I did so, I was taken very much aback
by the willingness of Catholic theologians and church historians—even
scholars of the caliber of Hubert Jedin, the great historian of the Council

of Trent—to introduce anachronistic theological and canonistic criteria into what was properly an historical issue. Most of them clerics, they were permitting themselves to indulge in exercises of hermeneutical gymnastics or maneuvers of exegetical desperation in a frantic attempt to avoid the damaging conclusion that a legitimate general council had solemnly promulgated a fundamental teaching clearly at odds with the First Vatican Council's definitions of the papal primacy of jurisdiction and magisterial infallibility. For that was the neuralgic point at issue, just as it had been for the traditionalist Minority at Vatican II itself. But my own historical sensibilities, it turned out, were altogether too astringent to be compromised by such ideological maneuvers. If I didn't resonate to Lord Acton's Romantic propensity for discerning the validating finger of God in the stupefying scramble of events that we call history, I was altogether at one with him in the rock-hard conviction that "no ecclesiastical exigency can alter a fact." The celebrated words put in the mouth of Martin Luther as he grasped his destiny at the Diet of Worms in 1521 may conceivably be apocryphal. But I sensed now that they well caught an important conviction. Declaring himself to be captive to the Word of God, he is said to have blurted out before the emperor *"Ich kann nicht anderes"*—"I can do no other." And, without wishing to overdramatize the moment, the latter words spoke loudly to me now, confronted as I was by my own moment of truth. I was captive to the historical evidence; I could do no other. I had to forge ahead, my traditional Catholic loyalties notwithstanding, to tease out and identify the conclusions that would follow for the present from the recognition of the fact that *Haec sancta synodus* embodied the valid teaching of a legitimate general council.

This proved to be an uneasy and troubling task. I couldn't help being struck by the extreme caution with which even a Hans Küng had sidled up to the issues involved. In his later masterly ecclesiological treatise, *The Church*, Küng was to lay out what amounted to an almost-agnostic appraisal of the whole matter of a scripturally validated papal primacy. But in his earlier *Structures of the Church* (1962), what one gets is no more than a delicately diplomatic insistence on the continuing validity of the Constance decrees. Across the line of his argument falls the long shadow cast by the definitions of Vatican I. As a result, he seemed in that book content to subordinate the ecclesiology of Constance to that of Vatican I, to understand *Haec sancta* anachronistically in terms of the teaching of that later council, or, more precisely, to understand it in terms of the room left by Vatican I's teaching and by the prescriptions of the 1917 *Code of Canon Law* for the existence of limitations upon the exercise of the papal authority. Those limitations were so minimal as to lead me to accuse Küng of succumbing to a species of "deductive timidity." A bit brash, I suppose, and, though he didn't respond to that charge, he did make a point later on—tongue possibly in cheek—of sending me a copy of his far more radical *Infallible?: An Inquiry.*

Meanwhile, I had proceeded to draw my own conclusions about the ecclesiological implications flowing from a recognition of the validity of *Haec sancta.* At one level, of course, they were encouraging and relatively benign and no doubt in harmony with what Cardinal Koenig of Vienna had had in mind when, in 1964 and while Vatican II was still in session, he advocated (rather vaguely) a synthetizing of the disparate ecclesiological traditions stemming from Constance and Vatican I. Clearly, if *Haec sancta* and its essentially constitutionalist provisions were accepted as valid, then some modification of the current, absolutist understanding of papal monarchical power would necessarily be called for. The limitations on papal authority would have to be recognized as being far more extensive than those conceded by the standard modern theological and canonistic manuals. And the Roman Catholic ecclesiological tradition at large would have to be acknowledged to be richer and more pluralistic than commonly assumed—more polyphonic, if you wish, than the insistently high papalist melodic line of the past couple of centuries.

This was far from being an unattractive line of march and the arguments in its favor were not lightly to be dismissed. Unfortunately, they rested on the assumption that it was both possible and legitimate to affirm the validity of *Haec sancta* while somehow sidestepping the provisions of Vatican I's *Pastor aeternus* with its twin solemn definitions of papal infallibility and papal primacy of jurisdiction. But on what conceivable grounds could that be done? After all, Vatican II's *Lumen gentium* had itself made an explicit point of reaffirming both of those definitions. Clearly, I had to address the difficult question of their seemingly obvious incompatibility with the teaching of Constance. So I set about studying both *Pastor aeternus* and *Haec sancta* in historical context and in the light of the conciliar debates that helped produce them, taking into account also the changes they underwent in their various drafts and the commentaries that followed in the wake of their promulgation. Having done that, while I could perceive a certain narrowing in the gap or radical discontinuity between the thinking of the two councils, I could still see no way to bridge it. I concluded, therefore, and not without considerable discomfort as a traditionally brought up Catholic, that Constance's *Haec sancta* and Vatican I's *Pastor aeternus* confronted us with an instance in which two legitimate councils of the Latin Church were genuinely in contradiction with one another and on a truly fundamental doctrinal issue concerning the very locus of ultimate authority in the Church. In terms of long-standing ecclesiastical tradition, that was, of course, to think the unthinkable. In the early seventeenth century, indeed, Cardinal Bellarmine, that great "administrator of doctrine," when crossing dialectical swords with the acerbic Venetian theologian, Paolo Sarpi, had bluntly insisted as a matter of principle that legitimate general councils simply *could not* contradict one another. To suggest otherwise, he trumpeted, smacked of "the reasoning of heretics." For "that [council] alone is legitimate which asserts the authority of the pope to be superior to all councils." Q. E. D.!

Though many of our Catholic theologians remained (and remain?) under the spell of that essentially circular mode of reasoning, it was simply unacceptable to me. Stepping across the line dividing the theological from the historical and embarking somewhat impetuously on an exercise in amateur theologizing, I was led, however uneasily, to grasp the nettle, to abandon the anxious preoccupation with certitude that is so deeply rooted in the Catholic temperament, and to argue in radical fashion for the historically conditioned, reformable, and essentially provisional nature of all doctrinal formulations, ecclesiologies, and church structures—*all* ecclesiologies, conciliarist no less than ultramontane.

That, of course, did not go down well with mainstream Catholic commentators. When Herder and Herder, the American wing of Herder (the German religious publisher), released my book in 1969, it was received, it is true, with some enthusiasm in the Netherlands, at that time a stronghold of a liberal form of Catholicism. It also elicited from Paul de Vooght in Belgium a warmly supportive letter. But things were otherwise in the Anglophone world. Where it was not simply ignored (the politics of oblivion tactic), the tendency was to praise its historical section but to condescend to the ecclesiological conclusions drawn from the historical realities. Clearly, the book was not destined to make much of an impact on the thinking of our Catholic theologians, though the most negative response, oddly enough, was of Protestant rather than Catholic provenance. It came in a review written by the distinguished Methodist church historian, Albert Outler, who had served as an observer at the Second Vatican Council and may perhaps have become a little too cozy with Romanità and the Vatican establishment. Whatever the case, his review was an oddly angry and disheveled one, at more than one point sloppily misrepresenting the book's central argument. Moreover, while calling me "a brilliant historian," he accused me, nonetheless, of writing "pre-ecumenical church history" (whatever that might mean), and (really a bit cheeky for a Methodist) dismissed me condescendingly as a "professedly loyal Catholic." For one who had had to struggle hard with his traditional loyalties, this last, I must confess, hurt a bit.

It was all quite odd and really quite discouraging, coming as it did in the wake of what had been for me an emotionally draining intellectual journey. That journey had left me as a Catholic in a somewhat isolated position inhabiting the gloomy hinterlands of heterodoxy, unable fully to affirm or freely to let go. And there I was to remain in the years that followed, cast now in the role of a mere observer of the tide of reaction now gathering force and cresting during the distinguished but in many ways destructive pontificate of John Paul II. So far as Catholicism goes, I was then and have since remained no more than one of the vast grey horde of spiritual walking wounded, shuffling forward, more in hope than expectation, in the presumed direction of the Heavenly Jerusalem. That said, however, throughout my life I have never ceased to be acutely (and gratefully) conscious of the deep impress, no less on my temperament than on the ways of thinking natural to me, made by the sheer richness of the Catholic tradition and by the type of Christian humanism that I was fortunate enough to have imbibed at school.

Meanwhile, so far as the Church's leadership and the theological establishment at large went, the politics of oblivion seemed destined to prevail. The head-on collision between the ecclesiologies of Constance and Vatican I was somehow bracketed. But it was to linger on as what amounted to an historico-theological time bomb embedded in the Catholic consciousness, its presence ignored but its lethal fuse still intact. And that, too, has remained the case down to the present. But, as it was clear that my point of view was unlikely to gain any traction in the Catholic world, I turned back, so far as writing was concerned, to my more purely historical interests. I was not to return to the religious wars until my retirement years, and then only after being invited to co-edit and contribute to two volumes concerned with what by then had become a deepening and acute crisis of authority in Catholic modernity. And, so far as institutional engagement went, it was henceforth to focus more exclusively on the college, where I felt that I had at least a reasonable chance of being able to contribute something positive to its development.

CHAPTER FOURTEEN

Vita contemplativa: Teaching and Research

After the intensity of engagement that had characterized the previous academic year, and despite the challenges posed by relocating the family, the first weeks of our sabbatical year in London (1969–70) felt comparatively relaxed. We settled into the house on Blackheath Park which, with Creina McCall's assistance, we had managed to rent. It was a slightly shabby but roomy Edwardian structure possessed of a very nice walled-in back garden. And we enrolled all four children in a pleasant, if over-crowded, council school within easy walking distance of the house. The children were to have quite decent memories of that school, though they recalled being nagged at by the lunch ladies to "eat your greens!" "Greens" referred, in fact, to unpleasantly overboiled cabbage, though the children were convinced that it had to be some unfamiliar but un-questionably noxious vegetable native only to the British Isles. They were quite quick to make friends both in the neighborhood and at school, and I can still hear, running through my mind, a memorable jingle that Deirdre and her friends used to chant while skipping rope outside the house:

> Not last night but the night before,
> A pickle and a lemon came knocking at my door,
> When I went to let them in
> They hit me on the head with a rolling pin . . . .

And that endlessly repeated jingle eventually induced me to confer on her the affectionate nickname of "Pickle."

During the course of the year, we drove north for two weeklong visits with my mother in Liverpool, heading out at about 4:30 a.m. in order to avoid traffic, with the children dozing off on pillows in the back of the car as we passed by Big Ben and the parliament buildings. And we prefaced the second of those visits with an exploratory trip through the Welsh mountain country. In-between those visits I took each of the children up to Liverpool by train for individual weekend visits with their granny so that they could get to know each other better. In Blackheath itself, the year proved to be a rather social one, punctuated by dinner parties with the McCalls and other people we had come to know. But the big adventure proved to be the three-week trip we undertook in January 1970 in order to go skiing in Austria at a small place called Stuben which a colleague at Williams had put us on to. Situated in the Vorarlberg not far from the more fashionable Lech and Zürs, it turned out to be favored largely by German tourists. Apart from an English couple, we were the only visitors there from the Anglophone world.

In preparation for that trip, I had decided that I would do well to try to polish up my active speaking capacity in German and had enrolled for a few weeks of conversational lessons at a Berlitz language school on Oxford Street. This turned out to be a wise decision as I had to hit the ground running in German as soon as we got to Stuben. The only things I can remember clearly from those lessons, however, are that they took place in a room whose window fronted gloomily onto the grey-painted brick wall of an adjoining building and that the tutor assigned to me was a fiftyish Austrian who sipped tea and ate rather crumbly biscuits while he talked, so that his waistcoat tended to be adorned always with a scattering of crumbs. And one sad little moment lingers in the mind. While we were talking about skiing, which he had done as a younger man, he said, staring fixedly out of the window and at the grey wall that hemmed us in, "Ach, Herr Oakley, wie sind die Jahre geflogen"—"how the years have flown!"

To get to Stuben we had purchased a German Railway package which happily included couchettes, so we were able to get some sleep during what seemed like an interminable journey from London to Dover by train, thence by ship to Calais across a very turbulent English Channel, and then by train due east across northern France to Strasbourg, followed by an even longer stretch south along the Rhine valley to Switzerland and then east to Austria. At Stuben we settled in at a comfortable ski lodge and, language barrier notwithstanding, Brian and Tim were soon playing cards with the innkeeper's little boy—"Fish/Fisch" if I recall correctly. And, though we were to have a very enjoyable time there, the snow was so heavy that winter that the local slopes came to be closed one by one because of the danger of avalanches—signaled in one instance (and to the excitement of the locals who watched it all through binoculars) by the movement of mountain goats across the face of one of the mountains and away from an area where a small avalanche did indeed ensue. Shortly thereafter a German couple whom we had befriended and who had a car invited Chris and me to join them on a trip over to Lech where the skiing was better and we gladly accepted. They were a nice jovial couple in their fifties (I would say) but I was taken aback by their antipathy to Willi Brandt who had recently become chancellor of the German Federal Republic. Weren't English people upset about that, they wanted to know, and they were surprised when I told them that his election was viewed very favorably in London. After all, although I didn't say it, so far as possible Nazi affiliations went, he was clean, having spent the war in exile in Sweden. To this nice couple, however, the choice of exile was precisely the problem. They pointed out, quite unselfconsciously, that he was clearly no German patriot and that it was disgraceful that he should now be leading the country. With that, rather than pursuing the topic, I retreated behind the inadequacy of my German, but I couldn't help wondering, a little guiltily, where they had been and what had been their attitude during the war.

When it was time for us to leave for home, it was snowing so heavily that the road to the railway station at Stuben was blocked, so we missed our train. Early the next morning, on the advice of the innkeeper, we drove into Stuben as soon as the road was open and spent the rest of the day in a hotel room we had secured, waiting for the evening train. Meanwhile, I had to go to the station to get new tickets. When I got there my heart sank a bit as there was a long queue at the ticket booth, composed mainly, so far as I could make out, of restless commuters to Innsbruck. When I got to the front of the line I had to conduct my somewhat complicated business in my nervously flawed German, explaining why we had missed the train the day before and requesting replacement tickets, uneasily conscious all the while of the impatient people behind me. In the end, however, all went well. Replacement tickets proved to be no problem and I was even able to get reservations for three couchettes at least. And, as I left, the clerk asked me if I were Swiss. That I took to be a linguistic compliment, and it was followed by another, rather more precious one, when I got back to the hotel room proudly brandishing the couchette reservations. "Yeah for Daddy!" the children yelled, jumping excitedly up and down on the beds.

The electricity at the station had failed by the time we boarded our train and the journey itself was not to be without incident. With Claire-Ann and the children safely ensconced in their couchettes, I roamed the train looking for an empty compartment where I could stretch out and sleep. I found one but it proved to be First Class and I was ignominiously ejected from it in the morning when we reached the French border and a rather surly French train crew took over. We had all agreed to meet in the morning in the dining coach, which was up near the front of the train, and we were able to have a nice, leisurely breakfast there. When going back to the compartment which Claire-Ann and the children had occupied along with another woman, we were aghast to discover that the rear portion of the train in which that compartment was situated had been decoupled and was nowhere to be seen. All their luggage was in that compartment and, more important, Claire-Ann's passport and Deirdre's well-worn but cherished floppy and soft comfort toy, this last leading her to burst into tears and wail "My doggy! My doggy!" At that moment I could get little more out of the chef du train than "Coupé! Monsieur, coupé!" but I eventually learned that extra carriages coming up from Italy had been added to the train during the night and it had proved necessary, though no announcement had been made, to divide it into two. So our journey up the Rhine and across the flatlands of northern France was dogged by worries about the whereabouts of the second train, which was still nowhere to be seen. We were destined for Calais Maritime (the second station at Calais), where we were to pick up the boat for Dover. But, on the advice of the chef, I got off at the first station, Calais Ville, to await the second half of the train and to secure the luggage. I waved goodbye to the children, who were crowded forlornly at a window and clearly wondering if they would ever see their Daddy again.

And then, not without mounting apprehension, I waited. Finally, after about a quarter of an hour, I heard the puffing of an old steam engine and the train appeared. I caught a glimpse, leaning out of the window, of the woman who had shared Claire-Ann's compartment and who was by now becoming very concerned about what to do with the belongings Claire-Ann and the children had left there. In the event, everything proved to be fine, and it was with great relief that I found Claire-Ann's passport which, because I had only recently become an American citizen, covered all the children too. The Channel crossing was an uncharacteristically smooth one, and when we arrived finally at Blackheath Park, we had the distinct feeling, after all our adventures, of coming back to something more than a temporary home.

Right from the start of that year of leave I had settled into a regular routine of research in the British Museum. There, I gradually got to know several other scholars similarly occupied, among them Jinty Nelson of King's College, London (now Dame Janet Nelson and one of the world's leading experts on late Carolingian history). I had a twice-daily commute of about an hour in the morning via Southern Railway to Charing Cross, followed by a decent walk up to Bloomsbury and the museum; in the evening the reverse. But while I settled into a reasonably steady routine, I did succeed in making room, at least during the first few months, for a couple of avocational activities. Claire-Ann and I both signed up for riding lessons at some very nice stables in Mottingham, south of London, an establishment which boasted of an interestingly laid out cross-country course which I very much enjoyed. And, having decided that I should revive the violin playing that had provided so much fun when I was a student, I also started weekly violin lessons again, this time with a young teacher at a music conservatory in South London. But while he soon had me working away on Handel violin sonatas, it gradually became clear to me that if I wanted to make the sort of progress I was intent upon I would have to put in on a daily basis more than the hour's practice time that was all I could work in (usually late in the evening) between family time with the children, two hours of commuting, and the day's research work at the museum. And when we got back to Williamstown after that leave it proved to be even more difficult, in the face of proliferating professional obligations, to protect enough time for the

amount of practice needed. As a result, my playing became more intermittent and I eventually gave it up—a cause of great regret to me and of
a certain amount of self-recrimination about my lack of discipline. Other
things, especially research and writing, always competed more successfully for whatever time was left over from my regular professional and
family responsibilities.

While my central scholarly interest has always focused on the history of
ideas, especially political ideas, my initial work on Pierre d'Ailly, who was
a philosopher-theologian of some note before he became a bishop, cardinal, and ecclesiastical statesman of great eminence, had, in my further
scholarly work, pointed me in two, very different, directions, leading me
to engage with quite different issues as well as with different groups of
scholarly experts in North America and Europe. But as I found of quite
compelling interest both of the disparate areas involved, I tended across
time and down to the present to alternate between them.

The first area, and the one with which I have spent more time, was
the history of the conciliarist ecclesiology—in effect, a form of ecclesiastical constitutionalism and the role it played in the ending at the Council
of Constance of the Great Schism of the West, the greatest crisis and
scandal ever to have overtaken the medieval church. To that line of investigation I was to return again and again in a series of specialized articles and chapters contributed to books before bringing it all together.
This last I did (at the genial prompting of Heiko Oberman) by making
it the subject of the Berlin Lectures that I delivered at Oxford during the
Michaelmas term of 1999–2000 when I held the Sir Isaiah Berlin Visiting Professorship in the History of Ideas there. And in 2003 I developed
those lectures into a book for Oxford University Press entitled *The Conciliarist Tradition: Constitutionalism in the Catholic Church 1300–1870.*

The second direction was somewhat less gritty in nature, more abstract and philosophical, focusing on what I would call the voluntarist
theme in natural theology along with its subsequent impact on the early
modern period. That impact made itself felt, on the one hand, in the
arena of natural philosophy and the eventual emergence of the Newtonian science of nature and, on the other, in political theology as it found
expression in tangled and continuing debates about the prerogatives of
popes, emperors, and kings that stubbornly persisted across the years

from the mid-twelfth century down to at least the late seventeenth. At the heart of my interest in this area was the struggle of the medieval scholastics to reconcile disparate Greek and biblical views of the world and of the natural order. For they sought to bind together the ancient Greek notion of an eternal world possessed of an immanent and necessary order—the very foundation of its intelligibility—with the biblical notion of an omnipotent God who had created the world out of nothing, who could, had he so chosen, have created a plurality of vastly different worlds, and who, having by his will imposed an order on the world he had actually chosen to create, retained the power to abrogate that order or to act (miraculously) in ways that contravened it. That struggle, or so I concluded, was, in the end, nothing other than an attempt to render compatible the incompatible and harmonious the dissonant. For that reason, if I may evoke a terrestrial image, I have come to think of the landscape of our Western intellectual tradition as a highly conflicted one, riven by a profound geologic fault that runs right across its length, reflecting a sometimes invisible and half-forgotten line of troubled intersection between separate tectonic plates of rival Greek and biblical provenance. In their effort to come to terms with such issues, the late twelfth- and early thirteenth-century scholastics, in this like architects designing buildings for earthquake-prone areas, had tried so to position themselves that they could cope with the outbursts of seismic activity prone to occurring along that great geologic fault. On the one hand, they had to "manage" the threat to intelligibility that the concept of divine omnipotence could so easily pose. On the other, they had to try to deflect the threat to the freedom of the biblical God posed by the notion of an immanent and necessary world order that was part and parcel of the Greek philosophical legacy. In the end those scholastics did so by deploying across a broad array of theological and philosophical subfields the distinction between God's capacity and his volition. That is to say, the distinction between what God of his omnipotence *can* do, speaking hypothetically and *in abstracto*, and what he can do but taking now into account the orders of nature, morality, and grace that he has actually willed or ordained to establish. The distinction, in effect, and using the terminology that came in the early thirteenth century to be standard, between God's power considered as absolute and that power considered as ordained (*potentia dei absoluta et ordinata*). In so doing, they substituted for the typically Greek idea of a natural order that was immanent, necessary, and eternal one that was radically contingent, dependent as it was upon God's will and sustained only by his promise and covenant. And those disparate notions of order came across time to be reflected, and influentially so, in disparate notions of natural law and (physical) laws of nature.

With that recondite but important distinction I have spent over the years, from 1960 onwards, a great deal of time. In connection with it, at least in my own estimation, I did some of my most original work and I am not altogether sure, even now, that I am quite finished with it. It came to play a significant and fascinating role in the emergence of the Newtonian science. It also came to play, by self-conscious and explicit analogy (as I discovered in the mid-1960s), an important role in discussions in the canon and civil laws, as well as in French, imperial, Spanish, and English prerogative law concerning the power of popes, emperors, and kings. For there a crucial and analogous distinction came to be drawn between the absolute and ordained (or ordinary) power of the ruler. I began to publish articles on these issues in the early 1960s and I examined them in more broadly sweeping ways in my *Omnipotence, Covenant, and Order* (1984), a book based on the Mead-Swing Lectures that I had been invited to deliver at Oberlin College in the fall of 1981 at the instance of Marcia Colish, a distinguished historian of medieval religious and intellectual life whom I had known as a graduate student at Yale and who was now well on the way to becoming president of the Medieval Academy of America. I did so again in my *Natural Law, Laws of Nature, Natural Rights* (2005), a book destined eventually to find its way into Chinese translation, but based, this time, on the Merle Curti Lectures in intellectual history delivered in 2001 at the University of Wisconsin–Madison.

In the former book, having indicated discontent with some of the postmodern modes of thinking fashionable at that time and while indicating my broad sympathy with the approach to the history of political thought being pursued by Quentin Skinner and others affiliated with what was coming to be known as "the Cambridge School," I took sharp exception nonetheless to Skinner's casual dismissal of the approach to the history of ideas earlier advocated by Arthur O. Lovejoy of *The Great Chain of Being* fame. Lovejoy was a scholar possessed of a precise and discriminating philosophical mind. He had written extensively on metahistorical questions, and his methodological prescriptions clearly overlapped, in fact, with those of Skinner himself. While I had not had the pleasure of meeting Skinner, we had exchanged letters over the years and, even when he disagreed with me on one thing or another, I had always found him to be courteous, encouraging, and supportive. His sweeping claim, however, that Lovejoy's approach was a misguided one, wrong in principle, resting on a fundamental philosophical mistake, one, indeed, that could "never go right," inspired in me the uncharitable thought that he (Skinner) could comfortably plead innocent to the charge of having read him (Lovejoy) or, at least, of having read him with any degree of attention. And I was led to wonder if he was not guilty of assimilating Lovejoy's approach to the cruder one evident in J. B. Bury's *Idea of Progress*, a book which he also excoriated.

That being so, though not myself happy with Lovejoy's theoretical talk (based on an analogy drawn from analytic chemistry) about "unit ideas" (unchanging atomic particles that across time entered into or broke away from various idea-complexes), I did find his general attempt to write the history of an idea complex and, in effect, a tradition of thinking both warranted and illuminating. In my *Omnipotence* book, then, I set out, using a modified version of Lovejoy's approach, to chart across several centuries and in more than one realm of thought the history of the distinction between the absolute and the ordained power of God, treating it as a tradition of thought, the pivot of a coherent scheme of things entire which, during those centuries, constituted the chief rival to the notion of the great chain of being itself.

Because there was a good deal of disagreement about the very meaning of the distinction in question, this line of work involved me in a prolonged (if reasonably civil and certainly fruitful) scholarly controversy involving German, Italian, English, and American scholars, notable among them the distinguished medievalist William J. Courtenay of the University of Wisconsin. But as it became clear across time that the distinction had possessed more than one form right from the start, controversy subsided and in 2002 I was able, with a goodly measure of confidence, to analyze the distinction's historical significance and to sum up the scholarly state of play as it stood at the time in an Étienne Gilson Lecture delivered in 2002 at the Pontifical Institute of Mediaeval Studies,

Toronto. While I thought then that I had no more to say on the matter, about that I am no longer quite so sure.

Scholarly obsessions of this sort being apt to puzzle those not caught up in them, I can't help worrying that the gentle reader may well find all of this distressingly abstruse. And in some ways I suppose it is— though not for me. I would hasten to add, then, that across the years I have also undertaken writing projects broader in their reach and more readily obvious in their import. When I went on leave in 1969 it was my plan to write such a general book on the history of medieval political thought. But having begun my work with a close reading of the first three volumes of Eric Voegelin's splendid *Order and History*, I was drawn thence to probe the work of Old Testament scholars (mainly those affiliated with the so-called "Myth and Ritual" and "Uppsala" schools of interpretation). Thence, and beyond them, I was also led to probe the writings of cultural anthropologists and of students of comparative religion on the worldwide phenomenon of sacral kingship which came eventually to loom large in my preoccupations. This work, undertaken originally as preparatory ground clearing for my main project, I found eye-opening, enormously stimulating, and hard to relinquish. Pondering such broader perspectives, which I had come to realize were directly pertinent to our understanding of the medieval political experience, I realized that I could easily in my comparative ignorance be betrayed through impatience into messing up the project as a whole. So I put that project temporarily on hold. But, through teaching topics pertaining to it in seminars and tutorials to a fine succession of students over the course of thirty years and more, I learned a great deal that was to prove pertinent and that encouraged me to reshape the project. It was only in 2005, now in my retirement years, that I finally sat down to begin the writing of the book envisaged long before as a single volume but now planned as a trilogy. And it was after completing a draft of the third volume of that trilogy late in 2014 when, without having earlier thought of doing anything of the sort, I backed into the writing of this memoir.

One of the subsidiary efforts that had emerged from my initial work on the project in 1969–70 was an attempt to come to terms with the powerful interpretation of medieval political thinking being put forward around that time, and with great insistence, by Walter Ullmann, an

Austrian émigré who had risen after the war to professorial eminence at Cambridge. From that pivotal and influential position, for he was clearly a very gifted and inspiring teacher, he had succeeded in peopling history faculties across the length and breadth of Britain with former PhD students of his. And I had come to know and admire a group of them, along with Brian Tierney of Cornell, who had chosen to pursue a career in the United States. Their work came to enrich the type of medieval history hitherto cultivated in Britain, extending it to embrace topics in intellectual history and in the comparatively new but very promising subfield devoted to the history of canon law. The earlier work that had propelled Ullmann to scholarly prominence, though it had not been without its critics in Germany, had focused largely on the medieval papacy. In the 1960s, however, he had begun to scratch a persistent scholarly itch of a different type and in a whole series of acclaimed interpretations of the course of medieval political thought. The latter pivoted upon a rather rigid distinction between what he labeled as the "ascending" and "descending" theses of government and law. While his whole approach involved what I came to view as highly idiosyncratic readings of pivotal texts, and while I found myself increasingly puzzled by it and could not help noting that I was by no means alone in being so puzzled, it remained the fact that in the reviews of his work the voices of acclaim were more than balancing those of troubled dissent. Again and again, the reviewers had been moved to laud Ullmann's "mastery of the sources," the "richness" of his ideas, the "profundity" and "range" of his learning, the "subtlety" and "penetration" of his analyses, the "force" of his argumentation. References to "the magisterial sweep of Professor Ullmann's scholarship" and even (this in the staid old *English Historical Review* no less) to "the preternatural brilliance of his vision" represented merely the less restrained modulations of a laudatory theme to which his ear must long since have been no stranger. And the cumulative effect of such compliments served to make it clear that, in this series of studies, Ullmann had achieved a novel and powerful synthesis, with the fearful symmetries of which anyone seriously interested in medieval political and constitutional thinking had now to come to terms. So, having returned from London at the end of my sabbatical and having put my own attempts at synthesis on hold, that is precisely what I set about doing. I carefully reread all the books and articles of Ullmann with which I was already familiar and undertook a similarly close reading of the more recent ones I had not yet absorbed. Then I set about the composition of a lengthy critique which I entitled "Celestial Hierarchies Revisited: Walter Ullmann's Vision of Medieval Politics." The whole exercise proved to be a highly labor-intensive and demanding one and it took me more than half a year to bring it to completion. But, having hammered out a clear, if highly critical, appraisal, I was left with no doubt that that investment of time and effort had been worthwhile. As the critique concerned the work of the scholar who, at that time, could lay reasonable claim to being the leading authority in the Anglophone world on medieval political thought, I judged that the obvious periodical in which to try to place it was *Speculum*, the leading medieval journal in North America. With that move, however, I encountered a strange and unexpected snag.

Over the course of the decade since 1960 when I had published my first article, I had encountered little difficulty in placing my articles, translations, and notes in the appropriate scholarly journals—several of them, indeed, in such leading journals as the *American Historical Review*, the *Journal of the History of Ideas*, and *Speculum* itself. The two that I had a bit of difficulty with, one on late medieval theology and the emergence of the Newtonian science of nature and the other on Jacobean political theology, I now view as being among the most original of my efforts, and the untraditional point of view they expressed may well have got in the way of their ready acceptance. The latter paper, indeed, was returned to me from one journal with an oddly angry negative appraisal and looking for all the world as if the reader had eaten a contemptuous breakfast on it (bacon and eggs, if I interpreted the stains correctly, and perhaps also some sort of sausage!). This time, however, an impediment of an unusual type was involved. From the editor of *Speculum* I received a letter saying that, while the article was "lively" and "very well written," they viewed it as "too much of an attack *ad hominem*" to publish in that journal. I was very taken aback by this and, given the feedback from other scholars that I received after the article was eventually published (and, at that time, I heard from a lot of people), I had good reason for puzzlement. While my critique was largely a negative one, it was seen then to be reasonably dispassionate. And for good reason. The fact of the matter was that I did not know Ullmann and had no grounds whatsoever for launching any sort of personal attack on him. Quite the contrary. A

few years earlier he had given my *Pierre d'Ailly* book a favorable review—
a great relief at the time because he had a well-established reputation for
being capable of quite scathing reviews. Later on I was to hear via back
channels that I had fallen victim to what one might call the micropolitics
of international scholarship and that *Speculum*, as the leading American
journal in the field, was simply reluctant to publish so sweeping a critique of the work of a medieval scholar of such prominence on the British scene. Of course I didn't approve of editorial decision-making of that
sort. My critique was by no means vituperative, nor was it driven by any
sort of personal animus. Nor did the editors of the British journal *Past
and Present* view it as such. Despite its length (forty-three printed pages),
they published it without revisions and did not comment negatively on
its tone. That tone, indeed, can be gauged from its concluding words.
There I evoked as pertinent a remark once made by John Stuart Mill,
"For our part," he said,

> we have a large tolerance for one-eyed men, provided their eye is a
> penetrating one; if they saw more, they would probably not see so
> keenly, nor so eagerly pursue one course of inquiry. Almost all rich
> veins of original and striking speculation have been opened up by
> systematic half thinkers.

To which I myself added:

> Taking this statement, then, and applying it to Ullmann's vision of
> medieval politics, my own verdict overall would run very much as
> follows: Rich? Undoubtedly. Striking? Without question. Original?
> In no small degree. Speculative? More, perhaps than he would care
> to admit. But fundamentally valid as a key to the understanding of
> medieval political thought? I would argue not.

Though the piece was to attract a lot of attention, often from grateful former pupils of Ullmann's or (more distressingly) from mortal enemies
whom he had at some time offended, he himself never deigned to reply
to it. But subsequent scholarly commentary suggests that it did succeed
in undercutting the appeal of Ullmann's rather coercive descending/
ascending typology and, forty years later, his whole interpretative ap-

proach, which for a while had risen so high, appears now to retain surprisingly little appeal.

So far as I myself was concerned, the whole effort had at least succeeded in clearing the interpretative decks for my plan to embark eventually upon an appraisal of my own concerning the trajectory of medieval political thinking. And while, with eighteen years of administrative work supervening, it was to be a full three decades before I was finally able to sit down and begin the attempt to realize that ambitious plan, I had in the meantime tried my hand at writing two other books that were quite broad in their reach. The first, a sort of interpretative essay on the Middle Ages in general, written largely from an intellectual historical perspective, I undertook as a result of an invitation to contribute such a volume to a series being published by the now late and lamented Charles Scribner's Sons of New York. Once in print (1974), it was picked up almost immediately by a small publisher in England and then by Alianza Editorial of Madrid, who brought it out in Spanish translation. And, later on, it was selected by the Medieval Academy of America for inclusion in its Reprints for Teachers series (now published by the University of Toronto Press), and after forty years it still remains in print. The book was a joy to write, and if it took me little more than six months to produce it, that was in no small part because, in teaching a couple of courses several times, I had already hashed out most of the particular issues on which it focused. The first was a sequence course required for the history major concerned with topics in medieval and early modern European history approached from a comparative historical perspective. The second was one of the two introductory sequence courses required for the history of ideas major and entitled "The Christian Vision." Over the years it has been wonderfully encouraging to hear from readers in both the Spanish-speaking and Anglophone worlds who found the book a source of intellectual stimulation and a pleasure to read.

I undertook to write the other quite general (if somewhat more specialized) book in the mid- to late 1970s after returning from the best and most productive academic conference I have ever been fortunate enough to attend. Organized by Heiko Oberman—by then, I think, back in Europe at Tübingen—and Charles Trinkaus, the leading Renaissance historian at the University of Michigan, it was an invitational affair involving about fifty-seven scholars, all working in the field of late medieval and early modern religious history. Oberman and Trinkaus later published its proceedings under the title: *The Pursuit of Holiness in Late Medieval and Renaissance Religion* (1974), and this was to prove to be an influential landmark publication in the field. I felt, and feel, lucky to have been included in the conference. It helped acquaint me with new and stimulating lines of scholarly investigation in a field I had previously tended to view as being a bit torpid. It also encouraged me, as I was teaching a course on the Protestant and Catholic Reformations in the sixteenth century, to embark upon the writing of a book investigating the late medieval background of those great, transformative upheavals. The broadgauged research I undertook for that book came to inform quite deeply the way I was to teach that course in the future. At the kind suggestion of Geoffrey Barraclough, with whom I had been intermittently in touch, I submitted the completed manuscript in 1976 to Blackwell's Press in Oxford, then still presided over by the scholar-editor with whom he had dealt in the late 1930s when publishing a couple of books with them. This proved, however, to be a mistake. Having heard nothing for the better part of a year, and having inquired of them about the fate of my submission, I received a truly embarrassed reply to the effect that the reader to whom they had sent it for evaluation had contrived, somehow, to lose the manuscript! Maybe he had, but as an excuse for incompetent handling of an author's submission it strained credulity almost as much as the delinquent schoolboy's pathetic excuse to his teacher that the dog had eaten his homework! As a result, I withdrew the project from what appeared to be faltering hands at Blackwell's. (I was, however, to have a very good experience with them later on with another book after they had reorganized and modernized their whole publishing operation.) I went on to submit the manuscript to Cornell University Press, which accepted it without delay, proved to be very good to work with, and kept the book in print, in both hardback and paperback versions, for about thirty years. As the language of hungering and thirsting for God is present everywhere in late medieval spiritual and mystical writings, I had originally entitled the book *Hunger for the Divine: The Western Church in the Later Middle Ages* and I now regret that I didn't stand firm against editorial insistence that I drop that title and substitute for it simply the subtitle. Having kicked the original title around the editorial office a bit, they confessed to me that it had evoked for them above all the unfortunate image of "a missionary feast on Cannibal Island!" Faced with that measure of gentle derision, I had caved in on the issue.

Some of my more specialized scholarly efforts—technical articles, for example, on the contested attribution of various late medieval texts—had little direct relation to my teaching. My students, after all, were all undergraduates and not graduate students. But in one way or another most of my scholarly work did relate to my teaching, either helping to inform it or, alternatively, being informed by it, or, for that matter, both of those things. There was an identifiable interaction between my scholarship and my teaching and, as often as not, it was reciprocal in nature rather than unidirectional. The sense that attention to scholarly research somehow diminished one's commitment to teaching, a view that I had detected among some of my senior colleagues when I first joined the Williams History Department—in effect, the zero-sum game approach to the two—simply did not accord with the realities of my own experience as I pursued my career as teacher-scholar at a small liberal arts college that placed a marked emphasis on effective teaching. Nor, I suspect, was my own experience all that different from the experience of my colleagues. When, in 1986, in preparation for our decennial reaccreditation round at the hands of the New England Association of Schools and Colleges, the small committee that I chaired and which was charged with the task of writing a statement of mission and objectives for the college was able, without a moment's hesitation, to sign on to the affirmation that "among us . . . the proposition that teaching to be truly effective must be nourished and sustained by scholarship is not in dispute."

That being so, I was later taken aback by the fact that one of the subthemes emerging in the course of the culture wars, or battle of the books, that rose to prominence in the 1980s and 1990s, and reflected the profound and embittered alienation of neoconservatives from the American academic culture, turned out to be a refurbishing of the zero-sum game approach to the relationship between teaching and research. Beyond that, indeed, it eventuated in a vituperative onslaught on the quality, value, and significance of academic research in America. The titles of some of the books that appeared at that time are revelatory: Page Smith, *Killing the Spirit: Higher Education in America* (1990); Charles Sykes, *Profscam: Professors and the Demise of Higher Education* (1990);

Martin Anderson, *Impostors in the Temple: American Intellectuals are Destroying Our Universities and Cheating our Students of their Future* (1992). And the message such books conveyed was a singularly depressing one. At their harshest, they insisted that despite (or because of) the great emphasis that they saw the university placing on research, and the mounting body of publications resulting therefrom, much of what was being produced was trivial, dull, pedestrian, esoteric, or—God forbid!—some mind-numbing combination of all four. Academic research and writing, according to Anderson, constituted "the greatest intellectual fraud of the twentieth century." Similarly, for Sykes, "Much of what passes for knowledge creation . . . is merely humbug." Moreover, he argued that teaching was being radically undervalued by the academy, that in the frantic attempt to mount their overpriced and oversold research effort, academics had come increasingly to discharge their teaching responsibilities less conscientiously and less effectively than they had in the more distant past; that the academic culture (thus Sykes) is not merely "indifferent to teaching [but] is actively hostile to it"; and that "in the modern university," indeed, "no act of good teaching goes unpunished." And so on.

Such attacks, launched from outside the academy or from its fringes, unfortunately drew some support from people within the ranks of the professoriate itself. Hyperbolic though they were, they drew a fleeting measure of credibility from that fact. Thus, in 1992, an op. ed. piece in the *Chronicle of Higher Education* trumpeted, quite dogmatically, that there was "an inescapable incompatibility [between] the demands of teaching and research." Hence the rise to damaging prominence for a few years of attacks upon the so-called "publish or perish" syndrome and upon the threat that the university's allegedly characteristic lack of commitment to teaching was seen to pose to the quality of undergraduate education. That issue had clearly "arrived" in 1995 when it was made the focus of a classic *60 Minutes* exposé on CBS TV. The episode in question was entitled "Get Real!," those words constituting Lesley Stahl's considered response to the parental dream of a college-bound child heading off into a "wonderful intellectual world . . . [in which] great professors . . . [share] their ideas with eager freshmen: that sort of thing. The great professors are there," Stahl declaimed, "no doubt about it, but your soon-to-be freshman is not going to find it easy finding one. We had difficulty finding one at the University of Arizona." And so on. The segment then proceeded, via some fleeting footage of instructors mumbling away unintelligibly in Tucson, to glancing exchanges with sundry (but oddly obliging) academic types willing to say the most extraordinary things about the lack of attention paid to teaching at that particular university. One of them, indeed, cheerfully confessed by way of an arresting wrap-up to the whole segment that, because of that lack of attention, he himself was "waiting for some powerful parent to sue the university for consumer fraud!"

On this very issue some of us doubtless do have horror stories to relate. And such horror stories certainly found an honored place in the potpourri of anecdotage that the critics of American higher education were at that time substituting (on this as on other related issues) for any real attempt, however critical, to come to terms with what was actually known about the matter in question. Certainly, what they were saying was very much at odds with my own experience as an academic. And so bothered was I by the misleading picture of the academy that they were propagating that in 1995, as chairman of the American Council of Learned Societies (ACLS), I decided to focus on the issue of scholarship and teaching in my annual address to the assembled delegates of the learned societies. That address was later to be published as an ACLS Occasional Paper and then reprinted elsewhere. I had earlier touched upon the topic in a book on American higher education that I had published in 1992 when I was still president of Williams and I had at that time rummaged around a bit to see what sort of statistical information existed that might help nudge the issue out of the anecdotal realm in which it had come to be mired and onto the more secure footing provided by uncontroverted factual data. There turned out to be enough such data to render particularly puzzling the current reliance of the critics on episodic comments and tiresomely recycled anecdotage. For the period stretching from the late 1960s to the mid-1990s, we have in fact at our disposal quite rich sets of data concerning the attitude of faculty nationwide towards teaching and research, concerning the time they devoted to these and related activities, concerning research productivity as measured by the publication of articles, monographs, and books, and, more recently, concerning the correlation at our leading liberal arts colleges between the successful pursuit of scholarship and the effectiveness of teaching performance. These data have been analyzed (and have been added to over the years) by such accomplished social scientists and commentators on higher education as Everett Carll Ladd, Seymour Martin Lipset, Ernest Boyer, Martin Trow, Oliver Fulton, Howard Bowen, Jack Schuster, and Robert McCaughey. But it has been their fate to have been ignored almost entirely by those critics alleging the occurrence in the academy of some sort of "flight from teaching" and proclaiming the relationship between research and teaching to be a zero-sum game. More surprisingly, they have also been ignored by most academics themselves whose understanding of their own profession has been accordingly impoverished. Rarely, so far as I could make out, had either the critics or their bruised mainstream academic respondents attempted to take into account the broad and exceedingly diverse range of higher educational institutions in America or the differences in the priorities and preoccupations of those who were teaching in them. Instead, they tended to focus obsessively on what was alleged to be going on at a mere handful of leading research universities. Not least among the differences that marked the various institutional sectors was the variation in the degree of scholarly engagement that distinguished them one from another. "Publish or perish" was no doubt a hallowed and beloved cliché among academics and their acerbic critics alike, but, having perused the pertinent statistical data, I couldn't help noticing that American academics were clearly contriving, without perishing, to do little or no publishing. The available data sets had (and have) a great deal to tell us about the relationship between teaching and scholarship in the American system of higher education as a whole, much of it tending to reshape the issue among more complex lines, rendering it less rewarding material for those characteristically energized by the joys of polemic. And the most helpful of those data were those stemming from the surveys, every five years, of faculty attitudes and behavior conducted by the Carnegie Commission on Higher Education between 1969 and 1994. I much regret the discontinuation of that survey program. It leaves us threatened with an unhelpful return to the world of misleading (if frequently diverting) anecdotage and the insistently autobiographical mode of witness to the academic scene that, in our discussions of the state of higher education, has served us so very poorly in the past.

The Carnegie-generated data had been subjected, I found, to careful expert scrutiny, most revealingly by Trow and Fulton, who had published in the mid-1970s an intriguing analysis of the 1969 data. And those data, on the matter of teaching and research, turned out to be broadly consistent with those generated twenty years later by the 1989 survey. In their painstaking analysis, Trow and Fulton had extracted from those data a set of conclusions that would not have startled earlier researchers on the subject (people like Talcott Parsons and Gerald Platt) but would probably surprise many an academic at large today. And those conclusions should certainly serve to reassure any observers outside the academy whose views about faculty attitudes towards teaching have been formed by the sensationalist charges advanced by commentators like Anderson, Sykes, and Smith.

Naturally, a great diversity of attitudes proved to be evident among those teaching in the various institutional sectors of the academy, from our research universities to our two-year community colleges. That notwithstanding, I suspect that the reader may be surprised to learn that 77 percent of faculty overall and 50 percent of those at the high quality universities had indicated in 1969 that their primary interest lay in teaching rather than research. And that was true even of the faculty teaching at our largest public research universities—places where, one assumed, the "publish or perish" syndrome was most deeply entrenched. The analysts concluded, accordingly, that, judged at least by the faculty's "self-conceptions," the American higher education enterprise as a whole had to be recognized as primarily a teaching system and that, on the basis at least of the data collected, the widespread suspicion that a commitment to teaching was generally trumped by a preoccupation with research was simply not grounded in fact. Moreover, if one took the further step of working into the equation actual research productivity as measured by publication activity, the picture that emerged was broadly consonant with what faculty members themselves had reported about the primary focus of their interests. Overall, more than 50 percent appeared to have been inactive in research, and even for our leading research universities the figure exceeded 20 percent. Less than a fourth, other studies conducted in the 1970s revealed, were publishing at all extensively, and a surprisingly large proportion of the books and articles produced turned out to be the work of a smallish group (say, 6–10 percent) composed, one has to assume, of compulsive recidivists. Taking higher education as a whole, Trow and Fulton concluded, there was indeed something of a division between the so-called research and teaching institutions. But the division they detected was not one between the universities with a substantial commitment to graduate and professional education and the four- or two-year undergraduate colleges. Rather, it lay between the universities and the top tier of four-year colleges, on the one hand, and the less highly selective undergraduate colleges, on the other. On this they noted that, as on other matters, a veritable "fault line" ran between what they called the "high-quality four-year colleges" and the rest, with those high-quality colleges showing levels of research and publication activity approximating those prevailing at some, at least, of the research universities. And that same fault line was to be evident again in the data generated by the later Carnegie surveys.

Trow and Fulton went on to address a final set of questions pertaining to the relationship between teaching and other professional commitments at those research universities where most of the work was being done. And they had found that the faculty who published most frequently paid more or less as much attention to undergraduates, whether informally or in the office, as did their less research-active colleagues. At the leading research universities, indeed, the level of teaching activity turned out to be much the same among the researchers as it was among the non-researchers. And, so far as governance and administration were concerned, the most active researchers were "much more likely [than their less research-active colleagues] to be involved in the administrative processes of their departments and their institutions." The data being mined, of course, spoke no more to the *quality* of that teaching and administrative service than they did to the quality of the research being produced. But they do suggest that one should not simply assume that some sort of zero-sum game is necessarily involved. The common view that commitment to research is necessarily bought at the price of reduced attention to teaching is clearly not warranted. In aggregate, at least, it does not appear to be true even of highly productive scholars at our leading research universities. Such people seem to do more of everything, and the crucial variable distinguishing them from their less-active colleagues may well be, not differing priorities or interests, but differing levels of energy.

Assertions, then, of the "inescapable incompatibility of the demands of teaching and research" should be met with a robust measure of skepticism. They are not borne out by what we know of the behavior (at least in aggregate) of faculty teaching at our leading research universities and they come into direct collision with the truly impressive scholarly track record long since achieved by faculty teaching at our leading liberal arts colleges. There, student expectations for effective teaching are enormously high. There, too, the institutional commitment to the central importance of good teaching has remained clear, consistent, unwavering, and proudly so. In 1994–95, Robert McCaughey, dean of the faculty at Barnard College in New York, published the results of a careful, detailed, probing, and very "hands-on" investigation he had carried out of the scholarly and teaching activities pursued in the humanities and social science faculties of some two dozen of those leading liberal arts colleges (Williams among them), those institutions seen as accurately representative of a larger group probably numbering around three dozen. While faculty of those institutions, he said, "differ from [research] university faculty in accepting that the primary mission of their employing institutions is [that] of teaching undergraduates," they are nonetheless committed to the view that published "evidence of scholarly activity" should be necessary for the award of tenure and claim, at least, to "see no contradiction between their personal identities as scholars and their institutional responsibilities to be effective undergraduate teachers." Nor, according to McCaughey, were they indulging in wishful thinking. Using a control group composed of over seven hundred full-time faculty in the same disciplines at three of our major research universities (Columbia, Princeton, and Yale) and taking the humanities and social science faculties of his two dozen colleges as a whole, he concluded that about a quarter of the latter "perform at levels of scholarly activity typical among their colleagues at Columbia, Princeton, and Yale." And, of those, about a half "perform above those levels." He also concluded, after an intricate comparison of "externally generated scholarly ratings" of the faculty included in his study with "usable local ratings of . . . [their] teaching effectiveness," that there was an overall correlation between scholarly engagement and teaching effectiveness that was clearly positive.

That there was nothing idiosyncratic about those findings was strongly suggested by another, more broad-ranging study undertaken around the same time by Alexander Astin and others at the UCLA Higher Education Research Institute. It concerned "institutional climates" at a carefully balanced sample of some two hundred universities and colleges, public as well as private, of all levels of selectivity. Among other things, the study revealed that of the eleven institutions in that sample ranking "high" on both "student orientation" and "research orientation," all were private, highly selective, residential liberal arts colleges, Williams proudly among them. Astin and his colleagues also found, it is true, that the ten institutions ranking at the top in research orientation but at the bottom in student orientation were nearly all large, public research universities. But their findings and those of others about the leading liberal arts colleges serve to demonstrate that there is nothing in principle *necessary* about the existence of a conflict between a given institution's commitment to research and its commitment to effective teaching. At such colleges the two commitments contrive somehow to go hand in hand. In the sort of collegiate setting they provide, Astin concluded, it does seem possible in this respect to "have one's cake and eat it." In that judgment, having completed at one such college a career that spanned more than forty years, I heartily concur.

CHAPTER FIFTEEN

Vita activa (i): Matters of Governance

The ultimate heart of the matter for a college (apart from possession of the financial resources needed to support its academic mission) resides in the quality of the students it admits, the quality of the faculty it is able to recruit and retain, and the quality of what happens when those two groups encounter in classroom, laboratory, seminar, tutorial, and co-curricular settings. Everything else, or so I firmly believe, is ultimately nothing more than ancillary. Alumni, especially those who have sons or daughters at college, tend to be acutely conscious of the magnitude and complexity of the annual admissions round that makes possible the assembly of a capable, diverse, and well-rounded body of undergraduates. But they can sometimes be sublimely unconscious of the very existence of the parallel, equally painstaking annual process involved in the recruitment and ongoing evaluation of faculty. That process goes forward at the college-wide as well as the individual departmental level, and colleges, finely attuned as they are to the pressing imperative of quality control, characteristically devote an enormous amount of time and attention to it, with that attention understandably reaching its peak of intensity in relation to two things. First, the business of making their initial appointments of assistant professors, drawn directly from graduate school or from postdoctoral positions at research universities or, somewhat less frequently, from junior faculty positions at other institutions.

Deeply committed as they are to high-quality teaching, and conscious of the difficulties involved in trying to assess the teaching (as opposed to scholarly) skills of senior candidates from outside for appointment to the tenured ranks, liberal arts colleges tend to make the vast majority of their appointments from among the group of promising junior candidates just starting out on their careers so that the colleges can closely monitor the development of the junior faculty members' pedagogic skills across several years of probationary appointments. In effect, they prefer to "grow their own." Second, the challenging business of making "up or out" tenure decisions on those they have brought up through the junior ranks to that crucial moment of truth.

The commitment of the academy to that sort of tenure process is often misunderstood by those outside the profession and sometimes criticized, accordingly, as unnecessary, as conferring an unwise degree of lifelong security on those who are actually admitted to the tenured ranks. Tenure was put in place a century ago in order to afford a measure of job security and concomitant academic freedom to academics at a time when they were not infrequently in peril of peremptory dismissal simply for publicly expressing views that university or college administrators, alumni, financial supporters of the institution, or even the general public at large found offensive or unacceptable. And, at some institutions from time to time, it still serves that original purpose today. But at our leading colleges and universities its normal function, rather, is to serve as an instrumentality for quality control. As such, it is far from being an unwise redundancy. It is often suggested that a system of rolling term appointments (for three or five years, say), involving the ongoing possibility after careful evaluation of non-reappointment in cases of inadequate performance, would serve the same purpose, perhaps even more effectively. A reasonable theoretical case can indeed be made for such a system, and, in the late 1960s, some of the newly established academic institutions adopted it. Among them was Evergreen State College, an experimental liberal arts college in Washington state. In practical and psychologically conditioned terms, however, the case to be made is a good deal weaker. The demands on institutional time and energy that such a system of sequential and effective reappointment decisions for an entire faculty would create would be necessarily (perhaps unrealistically) heavy. Even if they were not, and though it is procedurally possible, the decision not to reappoint a colleague who has survived several such reappointment rounds turns out, in human terms, to be an exceedingly difficult thing to bring oneself to do. Far easier, of course, to "kick the can down the road," to postpone the miserable moment of truth for another (and, perhaps, yet another) reappointment round in the hope that sage counsel will lead to some sort of improvement. I once asked the pertinent dean at Evergreen State how well their reappointment system worked. He laughed and conceded that term reappointment decisions tended to be automatically positive. Rather than affording the possibility of non-reappointment, what their system really did was facilitate a process of periodic counseling for faculty whose performance left something to be desired. In contrast, the admittedly bleak virtue of the up-or-out tenure system is that it forces the institution at a single, given moment in a faculty member's career to marshal all the pertinent resources and to focus its energies on the task of deciding whether it could do better by declining to promote and going back to the market to find a replacement. In effect, the choice (in practice) is apparently not one between a non-tenure or tenure system but one between *de facto* tenure by indecision or default and *de jure* tenure by conscious, if difficult, decision. That being so, the latter, in my view, is unquestionably to be preferred.

That duly acknowledged, it has to be conceded that the tenure system often presents to those involved in the pertinent decision-making some testing challenges. Small departments, at least in my experience, intimately collegial as they may well be, often find it excruciatingly difficult, even when it is clearly warranted, to recommend the denial of tenure to a junior colleague. Because of their size they are not with any frequency called upon to face the miseries of such tenure decisions and there may well be no more than one or two senior members to make them. In such cases, especially, the involvement of some sort of experienced college-wide personnel committee is called for and all colleges tend to be possessed of a committee of that sort.

At Williams, the pertinent body is the Committee on Appointments and Promotions (CAP). This, the college's most important and hardworked standing committee, consists of three administrators—president, provost, and dean of the faculty (the last serving as its chair)—and, elected directly by the entire faculty from among the full professors in their respective divisions, three full professors. And the faculty at large seem always to have taken the task of electing colleagues to that pivotal committee with the utmost seriousness. It was service on that committee, in one capacity or another, that was to loom large in my day-to-day working life for the better part of a quarter of a century.

By the time we went on leave to London in 1969, I was aware of the fact that I could expect to be promoted to the rank of full professor in July 1970. But, as the pertinent election to the CAP took place before that date, I did not realize that my impending promotion would make me immediately eligible for election to the committee for the academic year beginning in July 1970. I was surprised, then, in early spring to receive a letter from Dudley Bahlman, dean of the faculty, telling me that my name had been placed in nomination as a candidate for election to the committee and asking me if I would let it go forward. In my view, and in that of most of my colleagues, it was a bit of an honor to be nominated in that way, so I answered in the affirmative. A month or so later I received another letter, this time from Jack Sawyer, informing me that I had indeed been elected as the faculty representative on the committee from Division II (social sciences) and that J. Hodge Markgraf, a gifted organic chemist who was a contemporary of mine, had been elected as the representative of Division III (natural sciences). When, a year or two later, Larry (Lawrence) Graver, chair of the English Department, was elected to fill the Division I (arts and humanities) slot, the divisional representatives were all in their late thirties, thus considerably younger than their predecessors. That meant that a whole generation of older faculty who could traditionally have expected to be the more likely candidates for election to that particular committee had been passed over by their colleagues. Given the institutional turmoil of the two years preceding, that may have been understandable. But it was not, I am inclined to think, an altogether healthy development, and it may well have generated a measure of resentment among those more senior colleagues.

Whatever the case, it was for me the beginning of almost a quarter of a century's continuous service on the CAP and, therefore, of intensive involvement in the college's central governance and administration. After serving for two three-year terms as the Division II elected representative, I became dean of the faculty for the better part of eight years before going on to serve as president of the college until January 1994. My presidency concluded with the yearlong celebration of our bicentennial year in 1993 and the successful completion of our Third Century Campaign. While, in the upcoming chapters, I will obviously dwell on what I was doing during those years, I cannot help worrying a little that it may well strike my imagined reader as dull old stuff. Not that it was for me. Though it was often quite stressful, I found it all highly stimulating and deeply fulfilling.

In any case, while college governance and administration loomed large during those years, it was far from being the whole of my life. Throughout that whole period I was still teaching in the History Department and the History of Ideas Program, though eventually on reduced time (during my presidential years, no more than intermittently). At the request of the students at Bryant House, one of our self-governing residential units, I also served for a couple of years as their senior faculty associate, spending a lot of time, usually over lunch or dinner, at the House and getting a different (and more revealing) glimpse of the texture of student life from that seen from the perspective of a classroom instructor. And I remember, as the highlight of that assignment, the afternoon we organized (on a voluntary sign-up basis) an autumn trail ride through the woods of nearby Vermont. Between thirty and forty students signed up, most of them non-riders. Getting all the horses tacked up and the posse organized at a stables in Pownal, Vermont, where Claire-Ann and I had both ridden previously, proved to be a bit of a challenge and left me wondering how cavalry units in the old days ever got any actual fighting done. The ride, mainly at a walk with occasional walk-trot interludes, proved to be very enjoyable, with the owner of the stables in the lead and I looking out for stragglers in the rear. But I was startled and induced to worry (a little late in the day) about insurance and matters of liability when the owner, coming out from the trail at the bottom of a meadow with a nice, gentle upward slope that positively invited a canter, gave a yell and put her horse into precisely that. Most of the other animals, being school horses, followed suit, with their (often terrified) riders bouncing around like sacks of potatoes. Fortunately, nobody came off, and the general sense when we got back to Bryant House seemed to be that the whole thing had been a bit of an adventure.

During the 1970s and 1980s I was also doing my best to keep my research and writing commitment alive, though as president I was to have no time for basic research and had to content myself with writing about higher education and, in an attempt to keep in touch with my own medieval field, reviewing a lot of scholarly works. More important, these were the years during which, as conscientious and attentive (though by no means "helicopter") parents, we were engaged in seeing our growing children through the ups and downs of adolescence, the challenges of high school, and, eventually, the transition to college. They were years punctuated, of course, by characteristic episodes of adolescent "acting out" and reciprocal parental moments of impatient exasperation. But no disasters, thank God. Over the years at family reunions, the boys have enjoyed regaling us (and their own wide-eyed children) with well-embroidered stories of alleged youthful escapades about which we are glad not to have known anything at the time. And Deirdre has often reminded us of a somewhat-fraught episode when she was still in her freshman year at high school. Concerned about the apparent lack of adult supervision at the household in question, we had refused her permission to accept a friend's invitation to overnight there. She could spend the evening there but had to be home by 11:00 p.m. As I drove her over to that friend's house, she turned on me with righteous indignation and blurted out: "You don't trust me!" To which I apparently replied: "That's right." Now in her fifties, Deirdre is willing to concede that that was an appropriate answer—or, at least, that it reflected an accurate assessment of the pertinent facts on the ground.

In relation to those teenage years, I would be remiss if I didn't also pay a measure of homage to some of the fine, dedicated teachers whom it was our children's good fortune to encounter at Mt. Greylock Regional High School in Williamstown. It was there that Chris was to discover, via a very imaginatively taught art class, the talent for drawing and painting that was eventually to point him in the direction of a stimulating and successful architectural career in Chicago. And it was also at Mt. Greylock, I believe, that Brian, our youngest, first discovered the interest in combining economics with environmental concerns that eventually led him, via a combined MBA/Masters of Environmental Management degree at Duke, to become involved in very interesting work as a partner in an environmental consulting firm in Washington, DC.

Cocurricular activities having their own importance, I would also pay tribute to the sensitive and humane coaching that three of the children (all, like me, keen cross-country runners) received in high school and which played, I believe, a significant role in their maturation as young people. Chris and Brian both became proud team captains at school and, later on, at Trinity College, Hartford, from which they both graduated. And Deirdre had the privilege at Bowdoin of being captain of a women's cross-country team that included among its members none other than Joan Benoit, the future Olympian.

During those teenage years we took brief family holidays to Truro on outer Cape Cod and, later, family skiing excursions to Park City, Utah, where the wonderful powder in Deer Valley and other nearby resorts was to spoil us permanently for the challengingly icy slopes of our local ski areas in the Berkshires. And, of course, as teenagers and on into their college years, the children also got caught up in summer jobs, the impact on them of that experience (an exercise in further education) being itself a very interesting thing to observe. The boys all caddied for a while at the Taconic Golf Club, Chris as a college student worked as a laborer during the summer months for the college's Buildings and Grounds Department, and, at one time or another during the tourist season, all four either washed dishes, served as busboys, or waited on tables at one or another of our local restaurants. Le Jardin, then a popular establishment on Route 7 just outside the town center, played an important part in their lives. Deirdre and Timothy, especially, put in a lot of time there, Deirdre waitressing and Timothy, who didn't enjoy "front of the house" work, putting in his time as dishwasher and developing his kitchen skills in food prepping before moving on to cooking itself. This sort of summer work provided valuable "real-life" experience for all four but proved, I think, to be most important for Tim. Noting that he seemed to like the work and clearly had an aptitude for it, Walter Hayn, the chef-proprietor of Le Jardin, took him under his wing and taught him the rudiments of cooking so effectively that, by the time he graduated from high school, Tim often served more or less as a sort of sous-chef at Le Jardin and had become interested in making a career of it. Walter himself was a graduate of the Culinary Institute of America (CIA), which by then had come to enjoy an enviable reputation and had relocated from New Haven (where it had been founded by the wife of a Yale president) to what had been a

Jesuit seminary overlooking the Hudson close to Hyde Park and Pough-keepsie. In its capacious grounds, interestingly enough, the celebrated but controversial Jesuit paleontologist, evolutionary theorist, and phi-losopher, Teilhard de Chardin, is buried. Having decided to follow in Walter's footsteps, Tim himself went on to become a CIA graduate. After his graduation, at which the principal speaker was a celebrated French chef, we all tucked into a splendid banquet in the institute's main dining hall. It had once been the seminary's chapel and still retained its original stained glass windows. In an atmosphere redolent of the sentiment "you are what you eat," we indulged ourselves incongruously under the watch-ful (disapproving?) gaze of such Jesuit worthies as Ignatius of Loyola and Francis Xavier.

After he began working as a chef, Tim concluded that he had re-ceived a first-rate practical training at the CIA but not much further edu-cation. After a few years, then, spent largely as a sous-chef at restaurants in the Hamptons on Long Island during the summers and at reputable establishments in northern New Jersey year-round, he took time off to complete an undergraduate degree at the University of Massachusetts Amherst. When he did that I was very impressed by the fact that, though his focus was on management, he was obliged to meet some general education requirements, among them courses in art history and Afro-American history. He very much enjoyed the latter, partly because it was clearly very well taught, but partly, too, because he had the sense that he could bring some life experience to the topics they would be exploring. His first job after graduating from the CIA had been at Colonial Wil-liamsburg in Virginia. There, it turned out, he had been the only white person among an overwhelmingly black kitchen staff. He was known, accordingly, (and ordered around) simply as "White Boy": "White Boy, how's the soup coming along?" "White Boy, where are those sand-wiches?" And so on.

Large universities with multiple schools, if I may return now to the more cloistered world of higher education, have more complex arrangements concerning faculty appointments and promotions than do small, free-standing liberal arts colleges. The latter usually have a single, college-wide, faculty appointments and/or tenure committee of one sort or another. To a surprising degree, however, and given different, historically conditioned collegiate cultures, such committees can differ in nature from college to college. Thus limiting myself to the New England liberal arts colleges often referred to as "the Little Three"—Amherst, Wesleyan, Williams—the pertinent committees differed from one another both in composition and standard operating procedures. And they so differ in quite significant ways. Amherst, where the senior academic administrators were almost always appointed from the outside, and where the gap (or habit of mistrust) prevalent between faculty and administration always struck me as being quite wide, had in my day a Committee of Six, composed entirely of faculty and in the deliberations of which the president was not allowed to participate. Instead, he was permitted to sit in as a silent observer before himself making the final, and independent, decision in reappointment and promotion cases. At Wesleyan, where the final recommendations to the president in tenure cases were in my day made (quite bizarrely) by the entire assembled tenured faculty, there was a university-wide Faculty Advisory Committee on the deliberations of which the president might or might not choose to sit in. While in all three colleges it was, of course, the president's responsibility to make to the board of trustees the final recommendation for reappointment, non-reappointment, and promotion or non-promotion to tenure, the relation of the role of the pertinent committee to that of the president differed from institution to institution.

Compared with its equivalents at the other two colleges, the Williams Committee on Appointments and Promotions, composed of administrators as well as faculty representatives, operated in comparatively simpler fashion. In its deliberations, official status played little or no role. The members, the president included, all participated in the lengthy discussions surrounding reappointment and promotion cases, especially those involving the award or denial of tenure, and they did so with what amounted to an equal voice. The recommendations which the president formally presented to the Instruction Committee of the Board of Trustees had emerged in collegial fashion from the deliberations of the committee as a whole. And the committee had striven mightily, even at the price of prolonging those deliberations, to arrive at a species of Quaker consensus. To my knowledge, no Williams president has ever presumed to override the considered views of the committee as a whole. And on the few occasions during my quarter-century-long experience on the committee when consensus proved to be stubbornly elusive and the final decision had to be left to the president, the divisions involved never pitted the faculty membership against the administrators but cut across both groups.

When I first joined the CAP in 1970, this mode of procedure struck me as wise and impressive. It was very much in tune with the college's general ethos, which reflected the tradition of appointing faculty members to serve for terms in the college's senior academic administrative positions. That meant, at least during my presidential years, that at any time there would always be a small cadre of experienced former administrators embedded in the ranks of the senior faculty. As a result, the (often silly) divisions and hostilities between faculty and administration which can hamper the effective functioning even of small colleges, while not altogether absent, were of comparatively low salience. This was all the more true because it fell within the CAP's prerogatives to determine, on an annual and reasonably rational basis, what the overall size of the faculty was to be and how any available slots were to be apportioned among the various departments. That involved, of course, a sort of twilight struggle to determine what sort of growth (if any) could be permitted and that dreary struggle could extend down to the level of mere fractions of full-time equivalents (FTEs). But it was ultimately worth the effort in that it represented for the faculty at large and the department chairs in particular a measure of assurance that such decisions were not simply an exercise of administrative fiat. Instead they reflected, even when they were viewed as being mistaken, the considered judgment of their senior faculty representatives who had often themselves served as department chairs.

For most of my time, and until, with the growth in size of the faculty, the sheer flow of numbers made it an impossible task, the CAP itself also interviewed all of those finalists for openings on the faculty who were brought to campus and then conveyed its reactions to the departments concerned. For members of the committee, however labor intensive the effort, this afforded across time a wonderfully enlightening education in the fascinating interconnections and differences among the broad array of disciplines in the arts and sciences, and for the interviewees themselves it involved an often-vigorous workout that some of those appointed were to remember as the high point of their campus visit. I immediately noted on joining the CAP that Jack Sawyer, who I tried to learn from and, later, tried as best I could to emulate, was particularly effective in such a setting. He was effective both because of the intensity of his engagement in the intellectual matter at hand and because of the obviously genuine nature of his interest in the candidate's research. In cases where Williams was having to compete with other institutions in the attempt to appoint some particularly attractive candidate, the involvement and deportment of the president on such occasions and the intensity (and flattering!) nature of his own interest in the candidate's work were unquestionably great for "sales."

If I must plead guilty to the charge of singing the praises of this particular committee at Williams, it is because over the course of a quarter of a century and from differing perspectives (faculty member, dean of the faculty, and president) I came to view it as a source of great institutional strength. And, for the president, it had the added advantage of occasionally providing something of a sounding board, as it was composed of highly experienced senior faculty in whom their colleagues had reposed a great deal of confidence and trust. It was a body with which he was accustomed to work on at least a weekly basis and one with which he could share some of the complex issues confronting him, secure in the knowledge that he could rely on the discretion of its members and the fact that confidentiality would be respected.

During the latter part of the 1960s when academic openings were plentiful and when for many a small institution the elusive lure of "university status" loomed large, Williams, like many another liberal arts college, often had to struggle hard to make the high-quality appointments it desired and had, from time to time, to settle for its second and even third choices among the finalist candidates. In the early to mid-1970s, then, as assistant professors appointed in the late 1960s came up for tenure, the CAP had to make some very tough decisions. As always, the basic question it had to put to itself was "Can we do better if we decline to promote and go back instead to the academic market?" Under the conditions of the day, when growth in PhD production had not as yet slowed down while growth in the number of available openings had ground to a sudden halt so that the pool of available gifted candidates had grown appreciably, the obvious answer was, not infrequently, that indeed we could.

During those harsh years, accordingly, the proportion of those coming up for tenure decisions and receiving a positive response sometimes fell as low as one in three. And even though that figure was to edge up somewhat as the decade wore on, its negative impact in the 1970s on the morale of the non-tenured faculty was quite palpable.

That decade was one in which a preoccupation with transparency and accountability and with matters procedural in general was everywhere high. It is hardly surprising, then, that the procedures that were followed in relation to faculty reappointments and promotions came under intense scrutiny. As a result, an appeals procedure available in cases of non-reappointment or non-promotion came to be instituted, as well as more clearly stipulated terms of service affording a somewhat-greater measure of job security for non-tenure-track faculty (instructors and lecturers) teaching part-time. To further the process of drafting the pertinent regulations and procedures, I was appointed as CAP representative to work on the matter in collaboration with a representative of the Faculty Steering Committee. I suspect that my colleagues chose me for that task because I had already demonstrated a minor talent for the rapid drafting of documents and memoranda—something I had discovered about myself when I was serving with the Royal Signals in the Commonwealth Communications Army Network. Being very interested in the flourishing of interdisciplinary studies at the college and having been co-founder of two interdepartmental programs, I had been troubled by the lack of any stable, college-wide system of organizing and looking after such programs. Wholly dependent as they were upon the departments for their staffing, and the Williams academic culture being by tradition so highly departmental, the programs always seemed potentially imperiled. They clearly needed to be given a more prominent place under the collegiate sun and afforded a greater measure of protection against departmental encroachment or indifference. What was clearly needed was some "constitutional" arrangement that would serve to underpin, protect, and support a sector of the curriculum that was the locus at that time of a lot of creativity and seemed to carry in its bones much promise for the future. That being so, I proposed that the college should henceforth view itself as being organized, for instructional purposes, not simply into departments, but into departments, programs, and program-sponsoring centers, and that such programs should each be supervised by an appropriately interdisciplinary faculty committee acting as a sort of departmental surrogate and led by a chair possessed of some of the prerogatives pertaining to department chairs. He or she was to be entitled to attend the meetings each semester of that latter group with the president and was required each year to report his or her program's staffing needs directly to the dean of the faculty and the CAP so that they would be in a position, should the occasion arise, to afford to the program involved some measure of protection and support. That proposal was approved by the CAP, the CEP concurred in it, and then it was presented at the May 1971 faculty meeting and approved there by simple voice vote and without prolonged discussion. And it was to remain, during the decades succeeding, the organizational structure underpinning all interdepartmental programs and sustaining their functioning.

In the process that led to that happy outcome there had been just one oddity. While it had initially been agreed upon in committee that at the faculty meeting it would fall to the CAP to move the adoption of this organizational or "constitutional" arrangement, at the very last moment Jack Sawyer had insisted that it should be moved only by the elected faculty members on the committee which meant, oddly, that the dean of the faculty would not appear as one of its proponents. I don't know why he did that and thought it was an unfortunate and counterproductive decision, the more so in that it implied, quite misleadingly, that in the deliberations of the committee its administrative and faculty members did not act in unison. In the event, while at the faculty meeting itself nobody came out in opposition to the proposal, it may be that somebody who did not sympathize with it had managed to catch the president's ear. Alternatively, Jack himself may simply have thought that the issue might be a controversial one and wanted to distance the administration from its advocacy. Whatever the case, it was a clear instance of the extreme caution which, from time to time, could characterize his mode of operation.

No comparable hesitation was to be evident in the part that John Chandler took, as president in the institution in 1975, in an appeals process for the reconsideration by department and/or CAP of negative reappointment and promotion decisions. As it involved terms of employment, the final decision lay with the college's corporate body—that is, in legal terms, "the president and board of trustees." But faculty concurrence in the president's placing the proposed process before the board was obviously greatly to be desired, and John indicated his own personal approval of that appeals process by circulating the final draft over his own signature. Although that draft was closely scrutinized at two regular meetings of the faculty in May 1975, with many a probing question put to the drafters, the faculty did vote to refer it to the trustees. That the move was not a controversial one probably reflects the fact that the procedures stipulated, while adapted to the circumstances characteristic of a small college, were closely aligned with those long since recommended by the American Association of University Professors (AAUP) and were possessed within the profession of a certain authoritative force.

It is the great merit of these recommended procedures that, while providing a channel for appeals, they are predicated upon an unambiguous affirmation of two fundamental distinctions. Those distinctions are constantly under pressure in a collegiate setting and aggrieved faculty recipients of negative decisions are (no doubt understandably) perennially tempted to lose sight of them. The first of those distinctions is that between "termination for cause" (e.g., because of discontinuation of a department or program, or because of *bona fide* institutional financial exigency) and non-reappointment at the end of a specified term of probationary service. In the case of the former, the burden of proof lies, appropriately enough, on the institution itself, which can rightly be called upon formally to justify its decision to terminate a faculty member. In the case of the latter, however, the institution is not required to shoulder that burden of proof and, as our procedures were to indicate (using AAUP language), the college is to be "accorded the widest latitude consistent with academic freedom, equal opportunity, and the standards of fairness" in discharging its responsibility "to recruit and retain the best-qualified faculty within its goals and means." Reappointment, then, to a specified term of further service, or involving promotion to tenure, is not to be viewed as a species of entitlement.

The second fundamental distinction, which the aggrieved and his or her supporters sometimes lose sight of, is between reconsideration on procedural grounds after a successful appeal by a person denied tenure or reappointment for a further specified term, and reconsideration based on the substantive merits of the appellant's case. As the original decision hinged ultimately on the exercise of considered judgment by colleagues, to permit reconsideration on the merits of the case would be to permit a review committee to substitute its own judgment for that of the CAP, thereby potentially opening the way to a series of sequential judgments and to the subversion of the whole decision-making process. In accord with AAUP norms, then, reconsideration on appeal was limited to the ascertaining of whether there had been any flaws, either at the departmental or at the college-wide level, in the original process of arriving at the negative decision in question. Such flaws were identified as falling into two potential categories, each calling for its own type of rectification process, the intricacies of which, out of kindness of heart, I will refrain from burdening my imagined gentle (and long-suffering) reader. The first (and more serious type) was called, in AAUP fashion, "improper consideration"—that is, consideration, for example, that may have involved discrimination or violation of academic freedom. The second, and far more common defect, was called "inadequate consideration" or, as the AAUP put it, "failure to accord adequate consideration to the candidate's performance" (as, for example, when the department, before framing its negative recommendation to the CAP, failed to seek out and consider all the pertinent evidence bearing on the candidate's performance). Should the review committee, given, of course, total access to the record, find that department or CAP was at fault with respect to either improper or inadequate consideration, the pertinent improprieties or inadequacies in the process would have to be rectified and, that done, the department and CAP in turn would have to go through the whole decision-making process again.

Such appeals procedures have undoubtedly increased for the faculty at large and the CAP in particular the burden of work involved in the task of arriving at often-fraught tenure decisions, but they have proved themselves to have teeth and, as a result, to be worthwhile. Although often approached by the faculty via a typically academic "hermeneutic of suspicion" and subjected periodically to moments of intense and critical scrutiny, so far as I can make out they seem to enjoy a measure of credibility among those whose interests they are intended to serve. As time has gone on, the one truly troubling thing I have sensed, as no more now than a sporadically interested outside observer, is a degree of increased pressure on the crucial distinction between simple non-reappointment and dismissal for cause, and a tendency among non-tenured faculty (and, perhaps, some of their seniors) to distance themselves emotionally and intellectually from the absoluteness of that distinction. And, in terms of the overall health and intellectual vibrancy of the college, that strikes me as an unfortunate and worrying development.

This complex appeals process, apart from the annual round of staffing allocations, interviewing, and reappointment and promotion decisions, was the sort of thing that preoccupied the Committee on Appointments and Promotions across the first half of the 1970s. The work was extremely interesting but also demanding and heavy, and it was the heavier because it was not yet customary to give any released time from teaching to the faculty representatives serving on the committee. That was to change only after Jack Sawyer announced in late 1972 his intention, after twelve years in office, to step down from the presidency on June 30, 1973. When he did so, he announced the formation of Williams's first Presidential Search Committee (such committees were now becoming customary). It was composed of several trustees, as well as representatives of the alumni, faculty, and student body. In so doing, he adroitly sidestepped the need for the faculty to hold a special election to pick the pertinent representatives. Instead, he simply identified the faculty's elected representatives on the CAP as the obvious people to fill the role. By virtue of their election to that committee and of their experience with appointments, they possessed after all a helpful degree of legitimacy and credibility. And that was to set the pattern at Williams for subsequent presidential search committees. At other places, the commitment to the direct election of faculty members to such committees has sometimes served, unfortunately, to politicize what is inevitably a complex process and has led to the introduction of competing agendas and counterproductive divisions between the trustees and faculty involved. And that, I believe, we have managed to avoid at Williams.

In our own case, certainly, back in 1972–73, and it was very much in the Williams tradition, nothing like that happened. Trustee, alumni, student, and faculty members (the last being Hodge Markgraf, Larry Graver, and myself) managed, without any noticeable difficulty, to interact with each other in a mood of natural respect. We ended, in fact, by bonding in so amicable a fashion that Ferdie (Ferdinand K.) Thun (class of 1930), a former trustee and our chair, became so attached to the group that in subsequent years, when he was back on campus for one or another alumni event, he threw several reunion cocktail parties to get everyone back together again.

The actual selection of the next president fell, of course, to the board of trustees. It was the job of the search committee simply to forward the process by advertising the position, identifying and soliciting further appropriate candidates, winnowing down what turned out to be a very substantial list, doing checkups and due diligence on those surviving to become part of the semifinal dozen and more selected for intensive interviews in New York at places like the Century Association and the University Club, and, those interviews completed, narrowing down the list to three or four finalists to bring up to campus for final interviews and evaluations.

Though we lost one of those finalists at the last minute (he accepted the provostship at his home university of which he was soon to become the president), the committee and the process worked well. While, of course, we disagreed among ourselves on this or that, those disagreements were far from being rancorous and, happily, no marked tensions emerged among the several constituencies represented on the committee. Those of us who were faculty members grew to like and admire our trustee colleagues, some of whom became good friends, and we were impressed by their obvious dedication to the college, their willingness to devote so much time to the search process in the midst of demanding, high-profile careers, and also by the quality of their judgment, which was in most cases calm, considered, and well-informed. They, in turn, proved willing to rely heavily on the faculty contribution. That was a fortunate thing, especially in light of the fact that, unlike similar searches later on, no search firm had been retained to help forward the process. It fell to us faculty members, as a result, to help move things along, using our contacts in the profession to help discover candidates in order to extend the list beyond those generated by nomination, word of mouth, or the college's advertising. From a friend who had served two years earlier as secretary to a presidential search committee at a comparable college, I was able, for comparative purposes, to get hold of their final list of candidates (over two hundred in all) and was interested to see on it many of the names that had been thrown into the hopper in our own Williams search. It was as if there was, floating around in the higher educational ether, an ur-list of likely lads (unlike the present, of course, there were then very

few names of likely lasses in play). In passing the list on to me, the friend
in question had taken the opportunity to warn me that I would find that
"the word doesn't often become flesh." And in that he proved to be right.
In our initial round of interviews of highly recommended people, we
were more than once disappointed and, indeed, sometimes baffled by
the fact that the candidate up for scrutiny bore so little resemblance to
the paragon so warmly described in the letters of recommendation. In
more than one way the whole search experience proved to be highly educative and enlightening. Those of us who were faculty were accustomed,
in the appointments process, to being able to focus on the narrower and
more readily identifiable professional expertise of the multiple candidates we had met and grilled. But it speedily became clear to us that we
were now having to sail across different and much more challenging
waters on which our trustee and alumni colleagues on the committee, by
virtue of the nature of their own careers, could sometimes prove to be
more skillful and experienced navigators than were we. The responsibilities attaching to a college presidency were so multifarious, the
constituencies to be dealt with so numerous, the requisite personal characteristics, temperament, and strengths called for so important, that we
soon realized that we were confronting a task more complex than we
normally faced in making regular academic appointments. We soon realized, too, as we went through our initial round of interviews, that the
task of identifying the most credible and suitable candidates and of piqu-
ing their own firm interest was not going to be an easy one.

But we soldiered on, learning on the job as our efforts progressed,
until, having brought the candidates for discreet interviews on campus
and seen them getting a sense of the place, we were in a position to
present a panel of three candidates to the board of trustees for their
decision. By that time, we had become so caught up and emotionally
involved in the whole process and had spent so much time working together to bring it to a conclusion that we all, I think, found it a bit hard
to let go and to get on with our normal lives. But let go, of course, we
had to. Our final duty was discharged when we met with the full board
of trustees and, one by one, shared with them our individual apprais-
als of the finalists. One of those finalists was John Chandler, who had
served at Williams as chairman of the Religion Department, as a faculty
leader in matters educational, as acting provost, and, finally, as dean of

the faculty before going on to serve for five years as president of Hamilton College in New York state, during which time he had also become a trustee of Williams. He had the great advantage of knowing Williams and its culture well, of being, in turn, an admired and known quantity among trustee and faculty colleagues alike, and of being possessed of a fine record of success in a series of senior leadership and administrative positions. Although it had been somewhat awkward for him as a sitting president at Hamilton, he had recognized that the search committee would properly need to check up on his performance there and had placed at the disposal of the faculty members of the committee a quiet room on the Hamilton campus where we spent the better part of a day talking to more than half a dozen members of the Hamilton community. Three of these he had himself suggested as likely to be informative; the others we ourselves had identified as likely to be helpful. And we had reported our findings back faithfully to the full search committee. In the end, it was John whom the trustees selected to be the new (twelfth) president of Williams, and he was to put in twelve challenging and fruitful years in that position. I don't think that the decision came as any great surprise to those on the campus who had known him as a kindly and compassionate academic leader.

When somebody said approvingly to Winston Churchill that Clement Attlee, his deputy prime minister in the wartime coalition cabinet, was "a modest man," Churchill is reported to have responded, cruelly, condescendingly, and ungratefully, that "yes, he had a lot to be modest about." Nobody could say anything like that about John Chandler. Orphaned during the Depression years in rural North Carolina, he grew up in a Baptist orphanage to which he has remained deeply enough attached to go back for annual reunions with his contemporaries, and to the teachers and administrators there he feels deeply indebted. Only in recent years has he opened up much about that early life experience, but it certainly serves to dramatize the most impressive trajectory of his life and career. Like Attlee, he, too, is by temperament an attractively modest person who, when elected president at Williams, didn't make great claims about himself. Like Attlee, he also, of course, had and has little to be modest about. Upon grasping the reins of the presidency, he saw his role, I think, above all as that of bringing to completion some of the major changes initiated under his predecessor, notably the complex

transition to coeducation, and of helping the greater Williams community to come to terms with other transformations (notably the ending of
fraternities) after more than a decade of change. In this respect it is significant, I think, that he devoted great and energetic attention to the care
and feeding of the alumni body. It was his great concern to see the college continue the rise to national preeminence that it had begun across
the two previous decades. And that he was to succeed in doing, while
staunchly promoting the college's central academic mission. No more
than anyone else, however, could he have foreseen the stern financial
challenges he was to face or the pressures to be generated by the distracting recrudescence of bruising student activism, especially that focused on the relation of the college's investment politics to conditions in
South Africa.

So far as matters financial went, it was his fate to have to struggle
with the fallout from the creation and policies of OPEC, the depressed
securities markets of the late seventies and early eighties, and the high
levels of inflation that accompanied them. It was only with great difficulty that the major fund drive he launched in 1974 was able at the end
of 1980 to reach its $80,000,000 goal. Only in 1985 at the end of his
presidential years did the college's endowment, after a very significant
and prolonged dip, make its painful way back in constant dollars to the
peak level it had attained as long ago as 1967. And it was to be another
three years before our annual fundraising efforts once more exceeded
(again, in constant dollars) the amount raised in 1967. But in the latter
part of his presidency, as financial conditions began to improve, John did
find it possible to address some of the college's outstanding needs in the
area of physical plant. He launched and saw through almost to completion two successive and very attractive expansions of the Williams College Museum of Art. The latter, designed by the architect Charles Moore,
created some beautiful new exhibition spaces as well as offices for the art
faculty and new classroom space. He also initiated the building of a new
college infirmary as well as an ambitious project to bring our obsolescent
athletic buildings up to par. Lasell Gymnasium, handsome though it is—
and I have put in many a long hour on its indoor running track—had
been built almost a century earlier, five years before the invention of bas-
ketball, which it later had to accommodate, and the old swimming pool

was far inferior to its grand, Olympic-size successor. That project was to be competed in 1987, two years after John stepped down.

Through service on the CAP I had seen a good deal of John in the mid-1970s and was used to working with him on the more purely academic side of the college's operations. I was truly delighted, then, before going on sabbatical leave in January 1976 to pursue research in the Yale libraries as a visiting fellow in my old department there, to be asked by him to take on the role of dean of the faculty upon my return in January 1977. I signed on without a moment's hesitation, the first of two senior administrative positions at Williams that I accepted without thinking to ask anything at all about the pertinent salary arrangements until later. Though, of course, I didn't realize it at the time, that was for me the beginning of a full sixteen years of senior administrative responsibility at Williams, a period stretching from my midforties to my early sixties, and it was to pose something of a bracing, though not in the end overwhelming, challenge to my ongoing commitment to the pursuit of scholarly work in my chosen medieval field.

CHAPTER SIXTEEN

Vita activa (ii): The Administrative Turn

My first impression of administrative life, when I started putting in full days at my Hopkins Hall office in January 1977, was how surprisingly tiring a day of end-to-end meetings could be. But I quickly adjusted to that and was later to find in turn, having stepped down from the presidency, that a full day open for research and writing without any interruption could seem virtually endless. At Williams, as at similar freestanding liberal arts colleges, the role of dean of the faculty is a significant and demanding one. In virtue of the responsibilities attached to it which relate directly to the college's central academic mission, however, it is also a compellingly interesting assignment. While, through my years of work on the CAP, I had become familiar with the dean's normal array of responsibilities (which focused largely in the crucial area of faculty appointments and promotions), I had also come to conclude that the role had some still-untapped potential for furthering the college's intellectual well-being. And I must confess that, when appointed as dean, I was already champing at the bit to see some of that potential realized. I remain grateful to John Chandler for having reposed his confidence in me and appreciative, too, for the degree to which, without anxious intrusion, he let me get on with the job. Unlike Jack Sawyer who, I'm told, could be something of a micromanager, John delegated confidently to those whom he had appointed to senior administrative positions and, while the dean's role could be challenging, demanding, and stressful, under that regime of generous delegation it proved also to be very satisfying and fulfilling. I look back to my seven-and-a-half years of deanly service with no small measure of pride in what I was able to achieve. Though I do so also, of course, with a keen sense of the support I received from my colleagues in administration as well as from the truly fine series of senior faculty members who served during those years as members of the CAP, prominent among them John Reichert of the English Department, Bernie (J. Bernard) Bucky of theatre, and Gary Jacobsohn of political science.

The dean of the faculty serves as chair or, better, chair-cum-secretary of the CAP, organizing and scheduling the work of the committee, forwarding to it in a timely manner the documentary materials it needs to discharge its responsibilities, keeping the records, handling communications between it and the department chairs, and, not infrequently, conveying the news of negative decisions to disappointed and sometimes distraught aspirants to tenure—spending time listening to them, in effect grieving with them, and advising them about their options for the future. My years in office were punctuated by some difficult times, some of them precipitated by the recrudescence of student activism and protest at the college, but more often involving the fallout from negative tenure decisions and the subsequent tangled unfolding of bitter appeals which, with time and the worsening condition of the academic job market, became more frequent and exacted a heavier toll on everyone involved. In all of this I would like to think, however, that I proved to be an efficient, judicious, and (I sincerely hope) empathetic supervisor of that whole, crucially important, appointments process. Certainly, I very much enjoyed the annual winter round of interviewing candidates brought up to campus as finalists for the various openings on the faculty and remain especially impressed by the ability of some of the mathematicians to deploy clever analogies in the attempt to render their (very abstract) research topics at least quasi-accessible to uncomprehending layfolk.

In the middle of one such interview, however (the moment remains, understandably, etched indelibly in my mind), a campus security officer diffidently interrupted the proceedings in order to give me a message. My wife had had a horse-related accident and I was to get home as quickly as possible. That I did, and as I drove down Scott Hill Road I saw

her standing, waiting for me, at the end of our driveway. She was holding to her face a bloodstained towel that covered her left eye. It was an
awful sight, but when she moved the towel so that I could see the wound
(which had bled very profusely) I saw to my enormous relief that she had
in fact been lucky; it could easily have been much worse. The accident
had happened when she was turning out into pasture our then-current
horse, a handsome grey thoroughbred called Lady. Delighted at being out
of the stable, Lady, once released, had whirled around in high-spirited
fashion and flipped up her rear feet in a rather high buck. Unfortunately,
Claire-Ann had been taken by surprise and was still a bit too close. During the winter months when the slopes of our pasture could sometimes
be rather icy, we were in the habit of having the farrier put sharp Borium
tips on the horseshoes so that the animal could get a secure footing. And
one of those sharp tips had missed Claire-Ann's left eye by less than an
inch and had gouged out the flesh for about an inch and a half across
the upper bridge of her nose. On the one hand, despite all the blood, it
was a superficial wound; on the other, unless stitched up in expert fashion it could leave an ugly scar. When I got her to the emergency room at
our rural hospital in North Adams, the doctor on rotational duty was a
markedly noninterventionist pediatrician prone to agonizing even about
giving an aspirin to a sick infant. When I told him that she was not altogether lacking in vanity about her looks, he panicked a bit and insisted
that what she really needed was the attention of a skilled plastic surgeon.
Such was not readily available in our area and he took some time to face
up to the fact that he might have to deal with the task himself. Treatment as a result had not got much further than an exercise in advanced
hand-wringing when Providence itself finally intervened. It did so with
the arrival in the emergency room of a fellow horse-lover from South
Williamstown, Roger Gould by name, by profession an upper maxillary
surgeon whose skill the nurses on duty clearly admired. He had done his
residency in the "Apache" zone of the South Bronx in New York and had
dealt with many a jagged knife wound. When he walked in, one had the
sense that the lights had suddenly been turned up. Striding over to the
gurney on which Claire-Ann was lying, and with the astonishing confidence that some surgeons seem to possess, he peered down quickly at
the wound and promptly said: "I can do that." If for no other reason than
he was a fellow horse-lover, Claire-Ann reacted with a reciprocal degree

of confidence and let him get on with the job. Neither his confidence nor hers was misplaced. He repaired the wound very skillfully (good hands!) so that all that was left when it finally healed was a fine, white line across the bridge of her nose. If some interviews of candidates stand out in my mind because they involved stellar performances, the one that I had to interrupt that day lingers on for less happy reasons.

Throughout my term of office as dean, I continued to teach two courses each year and I did not want to give that up. Partly because my services were needed, especially in the History of Ideas Program, but partly, too, because I wanted to signal in concrete terms that I was not as an administrator permitting myself to drift out of direct, personal touch with the sort of responsibilities my faculty colleagues were called upon to discharge. It would have been easier, of course, had I had the sort of help afforded later on when an associate dean of the faculty was appointed. But given the continuing adverse financial pressures of the late seventies and early eighties, I didn't feel I could reasonably make a case for any additional help. The less so in that I was still finding it possible to embark on some, at least, of the initiatives I had in mind.

At that time at Williams, as at American institutions of higher education at large, faculty salaries had been steadily losing ground in absolute terms to high levels of inflation and also in comparison with salaries in other occupations. Also at that time, with an oversupply of people with PhDs pursuing an undersupply of available academic openings, conditions were such that the receipt of a negative tenure decision could well threaten the end of any realistic chance to continue pursuing an academic career. Faculty morale, then, was understandably not very high, especially (though not exclusively) among the non-tenured cohort. Those of us in administration, accordingly, were acutely conscious of the need to do whatever we could to boost our colleagues' spirits. I myself had also become conscious, somewhat to my surprise, that even in a comparatively intimate collegiate setting like ours, individual faculty members might well be unaware of the presence in other departments of colleagues whose intellectual interests overlapped with theirs. There was clearly a need to do whatever we could to stitch together more effectively our particular community of learning.

My own response was twofold. First, perhaps a bit old-fashioned, I redoubled and expanded the amount of entertaining traditionally done by the dean of the faculty. So, taking care to mix together on each occasion faculty drawn from a range of different departments, we launched at our house an ongoing succession of cocktail parties, buffet dinners, and even small dancing parties for those whom we knew liked that sort of thing. Had we relied on caterers, our rather modest entertainment allowance would speedily have been exhausted, but Claire-Ann cheerfully came to the rescue by doing the cooking for our buffet dinners herself, and the barkeeping was done (if not by me) by one or another of my sons, who seemed to be amused by the large quantities of cheap white wine my colleagues cheerfully consumed. Being by temperament and habit rather social creatures, we tended to enjoy all of this and were certainly not prone to dismissing it as some sort of tiresome duty.

My second, related, venture, while it also pertained to community building in general, represented more specifically an attempt to enrich the intellectual experience of the collegiate community. After a year or so on the job, and in collaboration with colleagues at Amherst and Wesleyan, I was able in 1978 to get going a Little Three Faculty Colloquium which was destined to run on every year into the mid-1990s when the presidents of the Little Three colleges, all of them new to their positions, decided in rather peremptory fashion to terminate it. Being by that time out of administration, I was not privy to the reason for their decision. It can hardly have been financial because the colloquium really didn't cost all that much. Maybe it had simply run its course or, perhaps more likely, maybe the current deans of the faculty at the three colleges, all of them unfamiliar with the original intent behind these annual gatherings, had come by then to bridle a bit about the not-inconsiderable amount of time and effort they themselves had to invest in order to keep the colloquium going. Whatever the reason, I could not help regretting the decision to terminate. It is all too easy to let such programs go down the drain and much harder to get them going.

The beginnings of that particular effort went back to a conference at Williams in 1977 at which I had met several faculty members from Wesleyan including Richard Stamelman, a scholar of some distinction in French literature then serving as director of the Wesleyan Center for the Humanities. I had been impressed with the intellectual liveliness of the

Wesleyan group and had sensed that their center was either itself a re-flection of that liveliness or a stimulant to it. It had already launched *History and Theory*, a journal focused on metahistorical issues which had swiftly risen to a position of international prominence. A little later on I had attended (at Wesleyan, I believe) my first meeting with the Little Three administrators' group which met at the end of each academic year at one or another of the three colleges in rotation. Punctuated by enjoy-able dinners, it afforded one the opportunity to get to know one's op-posite numbers and to learn how the other colleges went about their business and under what conditions. In the group sessions, we shared quite candidly the triumphs, challenges, and disasters experienced on our several campuses during the previous academic year and brooded about the lessons to be learned from them. We also tried to identify the general trends affecting all our institutions and to get a clear fix on the challenges lying ahead. Of all the meetings of various administrative groupings I have attended, the Little Three meetings were by far the most helpful and enjoyable.

That was partly the case because of the characteristics that the three colleges shared in common. And that gave me the idea, working in col-laboration with Richard (a fine, imaginative colleague), to approach Prosser Gifford (whom I had known, years earlier, at Yale), then dean of the faculty at Amherst, to see if we could add to the Little Three athletic competition and the Little Three administrators' meetings a Little Three Faculty Colloquium. Though his faculty colleagues proved to be a bit lukewarm about that idea, Prosser himself embraced it enthusiastically and proved to be a fount of creative ideas. The plan was to meet towards the end of January each year at one or another of the three campuses in rotation for a (reasonably convivial) weekend of paper reading on a cho-sen topic, broad and interdisciplinary in nature. That topic would be in-troduced in a keynote address by a luminary from outside—thus, for example, Edmund O. Wilson when the chosen theme was "Sociobiol-ogy," René Girard when the theme was "Culture and Violence," and so on. And, for some years, we at Williams published the papers in a little regional magazine called the *Berkshire Review*. None of our departments were all that large and those occasions, attended regularly by about sixty conferees, were intended to provide the members of the three collegiate faculties an opportunity to get to know their opposite numbers at the sister colleges, thus enlarging the circle of colleagues in related fields. The gatherings were also intended to acquaint the faculty members with colleagues on their own faculties whom they might not have met, to nudge all of them out of their departmental silos, and to encourage a more ecumenical approach to the larger intellectual issues with which all would eventually have to grapple. All such goals struck me as eminently worthwhile, and these colloquia proved to be very stimulating intellectual events.

In terms of the ongoing building up of a community and the facilitating of a healthy measure of communication, other, more administratively oriented, measures were also called for, especially in relation to the body of academic department chairs. On the college's official table of organization (as quasi-fictional as all such documents tend to be), those chairs were represented as reporting to the dean of the faculty in presumably the same way as subordinate administrative officers report to their seniors. At most, that represents an exercise in wishful thinking. Those chairs, sometimes quasi-baronial figures, possess in fact a considerable measure of independence, bolstered by the confidence the other senior members of their departments have chosen to repose in them. And any dean of the faculty foolish enough to think that they worked *for* him rather than *with* him wouldn't last very long in the job. With that in mind, then, during my first week in office I made appointments with all those chairs, the people with whom I would have to work most closely and whose confidence I needed to enjoy. Thinking, rightly or wrongly, that some helpful symbolism might attach to it, I made a point of going over to see them on their own home turf rather than asking them to come to see me in my office. After my first year as dean, I also began the practice of holding, during the spring semester after the annual reappointment and promotion round was over, several dinner meetings with small groups of them at the Faculty Club. On those occasions, at which the discussion agenda was open-ended, I would have with me David Booth (the college's vice provost), partly because he was responsible for designing, managing, and monitoring the process whereby students were involved in the evaluation of teaching effectiveness, but also, and more important, because he was such a good, careful listener who could often pick up on nuances in what was being said that I myself might have missed. After each session was over, he and I would sit down to go over the evening's discussion to see if we agreed on what was to be learned from it. The chairs were constantly changing and always something of a mixed group, including not only more experienced and less experienced people but also those who by talent and temperament were more suited to their roles than were others. Some were impressively effective—I think, for example, from the generation ahead of mine, of people like Charlie Compton of chemistry or Bill Gates of economics, the latter a superb mentor to his junior faculty. Or, from my generation, people like Hodge Markgraf of chemistry, Larry Graver of English, and John Hyde of history. Others, especially from the small departments where there were fewer senior members available to choose from, were not necessarily very good at the job and I thought they might learn something valuable listening to how others went about their chairmanly duties. At each such meeting, then, I mixed the experienced with the inexperienced and made a point also of including chairs of the interdepartmental programs so that they could share the challenges they faced and hear, in turn, of the burdens that some chairs felt those programs placed on their departments.

Such occasions were not only highly informative but also quite enjoyable and, occasionally, even convivial. So, having gone through the cadre of chairs, I went on to work my way, across time in similar dinner meetings, through the entire tenured faculty. I listened closely to what they had to say when we moved on from general conversation over food and drink to more formal discussion, and I learned a great deal about their characteristic concerns and from the ideas that surfaced. So much so, indeed, that I tried to extend the process to assistant professors in their second term of appointment, but without success. Any views they had about the college and its well-being at large were understandably dwarfed by their obsession with their own upcoming tenure decisions. So I returned to the established cycle and began again with the constantly changing group of department chairs.

All of this activity directed at the stitching together of the fabric of community was, of course, quite labor-intensive and from time to time, when I was tired or felt a bit down, I couldn't help wondering if it really made much of a difference. I usually decided that it did, if only in a subtle sort of way, and I stuck with it throughout my time as dean. If nothing else, it meant that by the time I was elected president it had helped me get to know the faculty as a whole very well and, for good or ill, they had got to know me too. And I had been encouraged to keep on with the practice by an approving comment embedded in the 1978 report of the visiting committee that had conducted our decennial reaccreditation round.

Another initiative, dating this time to my last year as dean, reflected, like the founding of the annual Little Three Faculty Colloquium, a continuing attempt to promote the intellectual vibrancy of the faculty and, over the years, it has borne considerable fruit. In the spring of 1982 I met with Jim (James MacGregor) Burns of the Political Science Department and Mark Taylor of the Religion Department (both of them highly productive scholars of distinction) to discuss the role of faculty research at the college and its intersection with the college's teaching mission. At that time, the putative value of having some sort of humanities center at the college, one similar to the one at Wesleyan, was one of the topics of discussion. But we put it to one side in favor of a small program of senior seminars focused on the research interests of the faculty members teaching them. In the fall of 1984, however, the beginning of my last year as dean of the faculty, while driving back from the Albany-Rensselaer train station where I had just deposited Deirdre (who had to pick up a train to New York City where she was then working), I began to think that there might be a way in which a center, not just for the humanities but for the humanities and interpretative or humanistic social sciences as well, could be fitted into the life of the college. So I drafted a position paper on the subject, the first, in fact, of three, one of which explored ways in which we might fund such a center. I tried it out first on Mark, who responded with great interest and encouraged me to go ahead with the idea of getting together a small group of appropriate faculty to help shape a formal proposal. And we submitted that proposal, having encouraged a further and larger group of colleagues to sign on in support, to the president. As we ourselves constituted no more than an advocacy group, he then appointed a formal faculty committee to address the issue. That committee reframed the proposal slightly, submitted it to the president the following spring (1985), and endorsed it with enthusiasm. John Chandler held an open meeting to discuss it at which I spoke, affirming my own continuing commitment to the project, and a few days later

John confirmed that the proposed center would, indeed, be established. When he did so, he knew something that I did not. The weekend before, the board of trustees had arrived at a decision concerning who the new president of the college should be, and they were to assemble again in a few days' time to take the formal vote. That weekend, then, Pete (Pete S.) Parish '41, chairman of the board's executive committee, informed me that I had been elected as John's successor. For the nascent center that was good news as it put me in an excellent position to situate it appropriately (in a handsome college house located in a quiet spot on the edge of campus). It also put me in the right position to ensure that the raising of restricted funds to endow it for the long haul would be made part of the bicentennial fund drive that we were to launch publicly in 1989.

Since then, and after thirty years in operation, the center has come to flourish as an integral part of our collegiate life, sponsoring a rich variety of conferences, seminars, study groups, panels, and visiting speakers, and holding a weekly seminar at which the fellows currently in residence present papers relating to their research. As I have an office in the building (which is now named after me) and am privileged to take part in those seminars, I can attest to their liveliness. One of the reasons for the establishment of the center had been the greater difficulty faculty were beginning to experience, because of the demands of dual careers, in getting away from Williams while on leave and avoiding continuing (and distracting) entanglement in the life of the campus. From that life, which can be quite devouring, we needed to help them find a way to distance themselves while still in residence in order to concentrate on their own scholarship. The center, then, is a partial response to that need, and most of the fellows are Williams faculty, chosen as equitably as possible via a competitive process. Every other year or so, however, we tend to have a visiting fellow from one of our neighboring colleges. And every year, in collaboration with the Clark Art Institute's fine program for research scholars in art history, we appoint as Clark-Oakley fellow a scholar from home or abroad whose interests combine art history with another contiguous discipline and who, participating in the seminars of both programs, can serve as a helpful bridge between our group of scholars at the center and those brought together in the Clark program, the latter group being characteristically quite international in composition. This arrangement has worked very well, and the ongoing sponsorship of scholarly activity in the humanities by both the center and by the Clark has added significantly to the intellectual liveliness of our small community.

Not all my initiatives, of course, worked that well. One, indeed, involving an attempt to make a change in the college's curriculum overall, simply failed, foundering ultimately, I think, on the long-established and deeply rooted tradition of stubborn departmentalism at Williams. It may have foundered also, as, indeed, did every other college-wide curricular initiative right through the 1970s and most of the 1980s, on the unforgiving rock of changed faculty attitudes at the college. This is suggested interestingly in the little curricular history of the Chandler era that I asked Jim (James B.) Wood of the History Department to put together in 1985 by way of preparation for the curricular review we launched in that year. There he remarks that "by 1973 much of the senior faculty was tired and increasingly irritated by attempts to push the curriculum further away from the pre-1967 model." And, having noted that, he goes on to speculate that

> at the heart of this opposition were departmental concerns, often educational but also worries about staffing and enrollment implications of further modification of the curriculum. A common theme underlying the withdrawal and defeat of many measures [in this era] was also antipathy to increased requirements. To these [factors] can be added the increasing conservatism and more narrow professionalism of many junior faculty who, in an increasingly depressing job climate, resented any attempt to compel them to experiment outside what they did well and comfortably. Although the influx of more widely recruited faculty in the late 1960s and early 1970s had at first been an impetus for change, the steady increase in the variety of educational backgrounds since the mid-1970s has probably further *decreased* the chance for faculty consensus in terms of major structural changes on educational issues.

In the latter half of the 1970s, though not a great deal had come from it, a lot of concern had surfaced in the world of higher education at large about the inadequacies of the provisions for "general education" on our American campuses—that term being used to denote what went on in the part of the curriculum that lay outside the orbit of the various departmental majors. At the Williams of that day, by tradition highly disciplinary and departmental in its focus, the only real requirement that students had to meet beyond their major course of instruction was the stipulation that a minimum of two courses had to be taken in each of the three divisions (arts and humanities, social sciences, natural sciences), a regulation that served in practice if not in name as, above all, a science requirement. The principal concern at Williams, flagged in the years immediately preceding by the Committee on Educational Policy (CEP) and, again, by one of its subcommittees, was the failure of all too many of our students to avail themselves of courses offered in the pre-modern period, of courses pertaining to non-Western societies or to the African American and other minority American traditions, or of courses in women's studies. In effect, there was a prevalence of an undesirable degree of historical and cultural provincialism. Another concern was the lack of commonality in the intellectual experience of students and the obstacle that constituted to the emergence of a vital community of intellectual discourse among them. In the fall of the 1978–79 academic year, the president asked me to put together and chair a small working group with the charge of looking into this issue and, if it was deemed appropriate, proposing a pertinent reshaping of the student's non-major curricular experience at the college. The group was a good one and a privilege to work with. It was composed of Jim Wood, an early modern Europeanist in my own department whom I knew to have a good, creative head on matters of curricular import, David Park from the Physics Department, my old neighbor from Chapin Court and fellow member on Committee X, Michael Bell, an Americanist in the English Department and a highly energetic man possessed of a cracklingly sharp intelligence, and two students. One of those students, Jay Wallace, '79 (at that time a thesis student of mine in the history of ideas major), was later to become an esteemed senior member in the Berkeley Philosophy Department and one of the leading moral philosophers in the Anglophone world.

Benefiting from a series of earlier (if inconclusive) reports emanating from the CEP and one of its subcommittees, we were determined to end several years of fruitless discussion on the matter and to bring the issue to a moment of decision by the end of the academic year. So we went to work with dispatch and in committee sessions distinguished by their openness and intellectual liveliness. Michael Bell had volunteered to serve as secretary and was to bounce back highly literate minutes of our sessions with such rapidity that I was sometimes tempted to surmise that he had written them in advance of the sessions themselves. By December, having discussed our own curricular situation and canvassed the general education provisions at cognate institutions, we were able to circulate an interim report to which we requested responses. By the following spring, then, having sought out the views of our own students and faculty via both open meetings and a demanding effort to touch base individually with practically every faculty member currently in residence, we were able to circulate our final report with a view to thorough discussion at the April and May faculty meetings. The idea was to get to a preliminary vote warranting, if positive, the considerable effort that would be involved in the detailed planning for the courses and the way in which they would be staffed. Once that was done, we planned to present the overall detailed proposal for a final, definitive vote early in the fall semester of the following academic year. By now, we had done everything we could to familiarize the faculty with the general line of march we were pursuing and to encourage them to give it their careful consideration.

Products of institutions like Columbia and Chicago, which are still possessed of a strong general education tradition of the "great books" type, will doubtless be tempted to dismiss what we were proposing as very small beer indeed, no more than a minor tilt in the orientation of our highly departmentalized curriculum. For, apart from some recommendations for testing the standard of "numeracy" and "literacy" among our freshmen (a matter in dispute among the faculty), our principal recommendation was the college-wide institution of two required "great works" semester courses in the freshman year. Modest as that might seem, such a move was also very much at odds with long-standing and hallowed curricular tradition at Williams. That being so, and though it was supported by votes of both the CEP and the student College Council, the proposal sailed into a veritable storm of opposition in the April and May faculty meetings. It even generated a flicker of pamphlet warfare which served to inform and enliven debate at the second of those meetings. The working group's blue-covered report, signed by twenty-four faculty members and running to more than twenty pages, was countered over the spring break by a pink-covered oppositional document of comparable length, signed by an oppositional group composed of some two dozen senior members of the faculty. From internal evidence, I would judge that it was drafted largely by Russ (Russell H.) Bostert, an Americanist colleague of mine in the History Department who was a very good teacher and, on his watch, a fine chairman of that department. A deeply conscientious and engaged citizen of both department and college, he was also, however, a well-entrenched and stubborn opponent of college-wide curricular change. Highly polemical in tone and deploying adjectives concerning the proposed "great works" courses like "arbitrary" and "dogmatic," that pamphlet spoke disparagingly of "herding" freshmen into "compulsory" courses and of encouraging a superficial "dilettantism" among the faculty who, in relation to the great works under discussion, would not be "professionals" who "knew their material." Attributing to the working group "a serious misunderstanding of what a liberal education is," and stipulating that the "primary goal" of such an education was the production of "an informed and critical intelligence," the author(s) of the pamphlet argued that the type of general education requirement that the working group proposed was "a liability to be avoided," that, indeed, it would have "profoundly negative effects that would harm the educational mission of Williams College." Beyond that, it went on, reaching now the heights of plangent negativity, to predict disastrous consequences stemming from the impact of the proposed requirement on the distribution of course enrollments and its supposedly negative impact on introductory courses right across the college, as well as its possibly negative impact on faculty recruitment and departmental staffing. After all, 475 freshmen registrations each term would be shifted from departmental introductory courses into the general education courses being proposed, and (consolidating teaching factions) no less than 4.2 full-time faculty equivalents would be needed to staff those courses.

Fair enough, but in its last sentence the "pink pamphlet" did succeed in going one bridge too far. "Under the circumstances," it said, "we did not believe it appropriate to involve non-tenured faculty in the signing of this statement." While it archly avoided identifying what exactly those "circumstances" were, the implication was that non-tenured faculty might have something to fear, or might think that they had something to fear, if they came out openly in opposition to a proposal backed by the dean of the faculty. Though I myself viewed this as a shabby and

insulting sentiment for a group of senior colleagues to sign on to, all I
could do was to swallow hard. But I was heartened somewhat when one
non-tenured colleague got to his feet to object to it.

In any case, it was no more than an irritating distraction from the
matter at hand. The practical concerns being expressed were themselves
not irrational nor lightly to be dismissed. The working group itself had
felt bound to acknowledge that it could not predict with any degree of
certainty what the impacts on enrollment and staffing would be, but it
had properly insisted that

> Even on the most gloomy of predictions the perturbation in course
> registrations that the imposition of the new requirement would
> create *could* not simultaneously result in *every* department's "worst
> case." And planning that envisages simultaneously every "worst
> case" is unlikely to be productive.

In the end, however, the working group did so in vain, and the optimism of those who by temperament were prone to seeing the glass half
full was trumped by the pessimism of those who were habitually prone
to seeing it half empty. Nonetheless, though occasionally punctuated by
sardonic one-liners injected from the sidelines by the curricular agnos-
tics among us, the debates at those two faculty meetings proved to be
very animated and, at times, quite passionate in nature. Reading now,
some thirty-five years later, the minutes of those meetings, I cannot help
being impressed by the seriousness with which the pertinent issues
were engaged. I cannot help being struck, too, by the degree to which
they ultimately reflected, not simply the clash of differing temperaments, but also the hostile encounter of irreconcilable educational orientations. At the second of those two protracted faculty meetings and as the
debate proceeded, one could feel the tide of opinion turning in favor of
those prone to dismissing the "great books" approach as fostering superficiality in the students' reading and amateurishness and dilettantism
in the faculty's teaching. For the approval of a college-wide curricular
change, it was customary to stipulate the need for a 60 percent majority
vote, but, in the event, the vote in favor of the working group's proposal
came nowhere near that mark, falling just short of a simple majority.

The faculty had spoken, and had done so decisively. After years of inconclusive discussion at the college concerning general education, the core course approach, which had no roots in the college's instructional history, was now definitively extruded into the outer curricular darkness where there is wailing and gnashing of teeth.

While this outcome understandably left proponents in general and the members of the working group in particular in a rather bruised state, the extended debate involved—intense, deeply serious, and focused directly on fundamental educational issues—was, I believe, a significant contribution to the ongoing health of the college. If a constantly changing faculty had proved unwilling to approve the moves being proposed, it had at least reappropriated and made its own the curricular arrangements it had inherited. And that was no unimportant matter. Or so I assured the members of the group, to whom I was very much attached, when I took them out after the meeting for a dinner that was very enjoyable even if it was of necessity consolatory rather than celebratory in nature. In subsequent years, though we have gone through more than one important review of the curriculum, we have never again had anything quite like that great 1979 upheaval of the curricular spirit. And that, I am inclined to think, is a great pity.

One other thing from those years in the late 1970s and early 1980s deserves mention. Though it exacted its heaviest toll on the president himself and undoubtedly caused him some lost sleep, the other senior administrators were of necessity drawn into it. It was the recrudescence, after a period of relative calm, of the sort of organized student activism and protest directed against the college that had earlier peaked in the waning years of the 1960s. And that sort of activism, punctuated by vivid moments of protest (rallies, sit-ins, building occupations, hunger strikes even), was to persist on into and throughout my own presidency right down into the mid-1990s. At that time the tide finally ebbed, not to rise again during the twenty years that have since ensued, until the very recent past when flickers of activism focused on such things as institutionally based historical names or representations have made their disturbing presence felt.

Two moments of outrage precipitated the re-emergence of that sort of activism in 1977, the first in itself evanescent though leaving a quasi-permanent residue of disenchantment among the college's women faculty, at that time over twenty in number and now beginning to reach critical mass. The second, the 1976 uprising in Soweto, South Africa, was more far-reaching in its implications, giving birth eventually to a tradition of protest over the college's investment policies that was destined to persist until the collapse of South African apartheid in the early 1990s and, much later, to generate some feebler harmonics on matters relating to investment in the tobacco and coal industries.

The first precipitating incident was entirely homegrown, rooted in the continuing presence, in what had been an all-male student body but was now one more or less evenly divided between men and women, of a measure of crude and distressingly puerile sexism. On November 7, 1977, a group of sophomore men, singing obscene rugger songs, had thrown an inflated female mannequin, clad in what appeared to be blood-stained panties, down the steps into the library's reserve book room. What to them had doubtless seemed to be a good "guys' joke" backfired immediately, igniting furious expressions of outrage among some of their male as well as female classmates and leading to a passionate rally against sexism on campus attended by several hundred students, the organizers of which bitterly proclaimed that, despite the advent of coeducation, "Williams today remains essentially a school for men." As the correspondence columns of *The Williams Record* (the student newspaper) reveal, and despite a written apology to the community by the crestfallen sophomores involved, reverberations from that incident continued to be felt for several months. And not only within the student body but also within the ranks of women faculty who now organized themselves into their own, rather civil, activist group (Committee W), placing pressure on the college in connection with some of the issues that the deplorable incident had surfaced: the need to expand the number of courses addressing topics pertaining to women's studies, the effectiveness (or ineffectiveness) of our affirmative action efforts to increase the percentage of women on the faculty, and the very receptivity of the Williams community to the presence of women faculty. All three issues touched on my responsibilities as dean and, in response to urgent request, I prepared two, fairly meaty, memoranda for the group. These we went over at three lengthy meetings to see if we could reach agreement on the facts of the matter and, beyond that, on steps to be taken to improve the situation in which women found themselves upon arrival at Williams. At the first two of those meetings (in December and January 1977–78), the fear was expressed by some that a pattern might even exist at the college whereby women were prone to being appointed in disciplinary subfields that were not central to our curricular concerns, with the result that they were being appointed to what were, in effect, cul-de-sac positions so far as the possibility of promotion to tenure was concerned. When I first heard that, I immediately viewed it as inherently improbable, but I did, in response, go over the appointments record very carefully and felt justified at our third meeting in dismissing it as groundless. But I think it was revelatory of the mood of passionate dismay prevalent at that moment among many women on campus that such a fear had any currency at all.

So far as faculty appointments in general were concerned, in my capacity as affirmative action officer for faculty (a responsibility that had, three or four years earlier, simply been tacked onto the dean of the faculty's job), I had been keeping track of appointments statistics not only at Williams but also at an institutional cohort composed of some twenty colleges and five universities. Though they were not necessarily comparable, with the group of nine institutions that had historically been all male but had begun the transition to coeducation between 1969 and 1975, I also included six of the historic women's colleges as well as four of the colleges that had long been coeducational. The comparisons proved to be mildly reassuring. A decade earlier when Williams was beginning to think of going coeducational, we had only two women on the faculty (both teaching foreign languages), a tiny percentage. With the transition to coeducation, our stated policy had become that of recruiting women at a rate in excess of their presence in the PhD pool for the subject areas we needed to cover. With that, it turned out, we had had some success. With women now constituting, after eight or nine years of effort, some 14.8 percent of the Williams faculty, we were doing somewhat better than many of the other small colleges. The exceptions were women's colleges like Smith and Vassar, where the comparable percentage oscillated around the forty percent level, and Oberlin and Swarthmore, which had been coeducational since their early years and where the pertinent percentage fluctuated around nineteen percent. That the percentages of women on the faculties of those two colleges (and, indeed, at the women's colleges) were not higher reflects, I think, the declining presence of women in the academic profession at large during the years between the onset of the Great Depression and the 1960s. Only in the midsixties did the number of women choosing to enroll in PhD programs finally get back once more to pre-Depression levels. And even then, it is easy to forget that, as late as 1977–78, women constituted little more than a fifth of the PhDs graduated in the liberal arts fields that we were teaching.

But even if we were meeting our stated affirmative action goals, I am not sure how reassuring the members of Committee W found that fact. Clearly we still had a long way to go and other related problems to face. Doing the bulk of our recruiting at the entry level (and for good reason), it would be years before we could expect to have a significant number of women in the tenured ranks, and we also had good reason to be concerned about the fact that our retention rate for women was significantly lower than it was for men. There was, of course, little we could do about the rural isolation of Williamstown or the fact that it was such a small town. And that was clearly part of the problem. Williamstown had never been as attractive a location for single faculty as it had been for those who were married, especially those with children. And young women, working hard to get their careers off the ground, sometimes found it to be a lonely and uninviting setting.

So there was plenty to worry about. And greater cohesion among the group of women faculty already at the college, even if stimulated by a grotesque incident, was a helpful development. It certainly effected some appropriate consciousness raising among those of us (all male) in senior administrative positions. And, in the near term, it led to some useful advances. John Chandler decided to add an Affirmative Action Office with college-wide responsibility in relation to staff as well as faculty appointments and underlined its importance by making the position, assistant to the president for affirmative action and government relations, report directly to him. And I was to find Judy Allen, whom he recruited for that position, to be a fine, thoughtful colleague with whom it was a pleasure to collaborate. And there was another interesting development stimulated by this unpleasant episode and its subsequent fallout. It related to the presence of women's studies on campus. Recognizing that most faculty at that time—women as well as men—had little or no acquaintance with the emerging field of women's studies (let alone with feminist perspectives at large), some of the members of Committee W organized what turned out to be a splendid weekend conference on the subject. It was intended to serve the needs of all faculty (men as well as women), and I was happy to be able to provide the necessary funds to support it and to attend myself as many of its sessions as I could. Two of those sessions linger in my mind as having brought home to me how very illuminating feminist perspectives on traditional subject areas could be: one, on anthropology, by Professor Deborah Gewertz of Amherst College; the other, closer to my own interests, on political philosophy by Nan (Nannerl O.) Keohane. Then professor in the Stanford Political Science Department, the latter was later to become president, first of Wellesley College and then of Duke University. I was to see quite a bit of her at that stage as an admired presidential colleague in Massachusetts and, later, as a fellow board member at the National Humanities Center in North Carolina.

Among students, the passionate outpouring of anger and dismay that followed upon the mannequin incident somehow established interconnections with three other student causes: a push by the Williams gay rights organization to have the then comparatively new term "sexual orientation" included in the college's general nondiscrimination statement; a growing movement to pressure the board of trustees on investment policies, with the ultimate goal of seeing the college divest itself of all shares in companies with some of their operations in South Africa; and a more amorphous, late-sixties style effort to demand more democratic and direct student involvement in the governance of the whole institution. While the coming together of these disparate causes didn't quite constitute a perfect storm, it did eventuate in the formation of what came to be called the Thursday Night Coalition, a group that sought to mount pressure on the president and the board of trustees in order to wrest concessions that would advance the whole series of causes involved. The several meetings that ensued varied in tone, but they could be strident, accusatory, and unpleasant, punctuated by moments of student "acting

out," with administrators clearly being viewed as recalcitrant and trustees sometimes dismissed as devious. That was certainly true of one such
meeting between the president and members of the coalition that he
asked me to attend with him. On that occasion, as at similar occasions
later on when, as president, it fell to my lot to put in long sessions with
alienated students, it was clear to me that the student participants were
unusual mainly in the blinkered absolutism and impatience of their idealism, in the intensely serious and dramatic nature of their commitment, and unusual also, something that should not be overlooked, in the
extent of their (albeit wounded) institutional loyalty and the intensity of
their desire to make the college (in their terms) a better place. That said,
one should not permit twinges of nostalgia for the golden years of youth
to lead one to romanticize student protest. Youthful idealism is rarely,
in my experience, the full story. Commitment to campus protests has
the potential for being mildly corrupting for some of those involved in
it, and the protests themselves can be damaging to the institution. Certainly one should acknowledge that, to the Thursday Night Coalition
group (as to similar groups later on), devious, disheveled, unstable, or
manipulative temperaments were not altogether foreign. At the meeting
in question, though I can't now recall the point at issue, one student was
clearly lying and some, at least, of his comrades in arms, while silent on
the matter, appeared to me to have been uneasily aware of that fact.

In the event, despite its proclivity for unpleasant confrontation, the
disparate nature of the goals the coalition was intent upon pursuing un-
dercut its effectiveness and, perhaps because its future members had
become restively aware of that fact, the subgroup with an intense focus
on the investment issue separated out. And, known as both the Williams Students for Divestment and the Williams Anti-Apartheid Coalition (WAAC), it was to enjoy a long and somewhat tumultuous history
during the full decade ensuing and was to place as much pressure on
me as it had on John Chandler before me. And that pressure extended
also to the board of trustees, especially to those serving on the Trustee
Finance Committee who, over the years, were to have a whole series
of edgy meetings with a constantly changing succession of passionate,
bright, and often quite well-informed representatives of WAAC. Though
the trustees welcomed and usually enjoyed meeting with members of
the student body, I can't think that they enjoyed those particular meet-

ings, where the atmosphere could be self-righteous, accusatory, and even hostile. The most troubling of such encounters and, indeed, the worst moment in the relationship between WAAC, trustees, and administration was to occur in the context of the trustee meeting in January 1983. By that time the college had long since got its act together on the issue of divestment from the portfolio of multinational companies with some part of their operations in South Africa (usually a very small part), for that was what was at stake. Williams had no holdings in any South African companies.

It is not always realized that the practice of paying attention (at least in any systematic fashion) to the ethical aspects of college and university investment policies is a comparatively recent development. It predated by no more than a decade the upwelling of anguish and outrage across the Western world in the wake of the uprising of black high school students in Soweto on June 16, 1976, later dubbed as "the Day Apartheid Died." The precipitating factor had been the government's attempt to impose instruction in Afrikaans ("the language of the oppressor") on the schools but, with at least 176 students killed in the riots and upwards of a thousand injured, the whole upheaval quickly eventuated in a full-scale mobilization of the black South African population, spearheaded by the African National Congress, against the very apartheid system itself. And that whole struggle was to be intensified the following year by the death in police custody of the Black Power advocate Steven Biko.

By that time, the reverberations of that mobilization were being felt on American campuses in the form of the push for total divestment of all companies with any of their operations in South Africa. By the fall of 1977 that movement had made its impact felt in the Northeast, where two institutions in the Connecticut valley, the University of Massachusetts Amherst and Hampshire College (the latter after a building occupation), acceded to that approach. The trustees at Amherst College, however, despite considerable pressure on campus, declined to go that route, though in subsequent years they were eventually to crumble on the issue, as were their counterparts at Mt. Holyoke and Smith Colleges. Despite the miseries of campus turmoil, protest, and pressure, Williams and Wesleyan chose not to go that same route, committing themselves instead to versions of the intermediate route carved out carefully by TIAA-CREF, the large not-for-profit enterprise that manages the pension funds of most academics, and by universities like Harvard and Princeton under the firm, clearheaded, and articulate leadership of Derek Bok and William G. Bowen.

By the beginning of the 1978–79 academic year, Williams had adopted the mediating course which, with periodic modifications (and periodic paroxysms of on-campus opposition), it was to follow right down to the collapse of apartheid in the early 1990s. Given the intricacies, complexities, and, indeed, ironies—moral no less than financial—involved in the business of socially responsible investment, as well as the added complexities and uncertainties about attitudes and outcomes connected with the particular South African case, one might have expected that this would be a matter on which all parties involved would concede that people of good will could understandably differ. That proved, however, not to be so. Such was the mounting sense of impotent dismay over the manifest injustices of the apartheid regime that the thwarted proponents of total divestment, including, it may be, some faculty members who should have known better, displayed a disagreeable proclivity for imputing bad intentions or unworthy motives to those who had the gall to disagree with them. And that at Williams meant especially the president and the members of the board of trustees. For in a statement issued in August 1978 (revised somewhat in 1980 and 1981), the board, having emphasized the sheer complexity of the factors involved, rejected the goal of total divestment and opted for a case-by-case approach to multinational companies whose stock the college held and which conducted some part of their operations in South Africa. The relations of those companies with the South African apartheid regime and the quality of the conditions of employment they afforded to their black or "colored" employees were to be closely monitored with the help of a new on-campus Advisory Committee on Shareholder Responsibilities (ACSR) composed of faculty, students, alumni, and administrators, itself reliant on the pertinent and high-quality information gathered by the Investor Responsibility Research Center (IRRC). Using as a guideline the recently promulgated Sullivan principles proposed for the appropriate deportment of multinational companies in their South Africa operations, the college would use its proxies in voting pertinent shareholder resolutions, letters would be sent to management to solicit pertinent information and/or to urge

appropriate course corrections, and, as a last resort in the case of managerial recalcitrance, individual stocks were to be divested—a course which
the board took on several occasions across those troubled years.

As conditions in South Africa continued to deteriorate, however,
none of this proved to be enough for the impassioned advocates of total
divestment. A species of twilight warfare set in, characterized usually,
and depending on the current leadership of WAAC, by alternating periods of quiescence and/or tactical skirmish but punctuated from time to
time by some passionate upheavals that set the whole campus on its ear.
The nadir—or peak—of all of this, depending on one's point of view, occurred in 1983, in the context of the regular January meeting of the board
of trustees. It already had been agreed that at that time the president and
some of the members of the Trustee Finance Committee would meet in
a smallish seminar room in Hopkins Hall with a delegation of ten from
WAAC. This turned out, however, to be an unfortunate setup. If one
can believe testimony reported in *The Williams Record*, and there seems
to be no reason not to do so, the leadership of WAAC, frustrated by the
trustees' "inaction" on the matter of divestment, had been "considering
extreme action for a while." What they did was to hold a rally outside
Hopkins Hall immediately prior to the meeting in question. It was attended by 150–200 supporters and they then proceeded to cram into that
small room as many of that large group as they could. The rest, unable
to get in, remained in the corridor outside and crowded around the door.
It was clearly not something conducive to the promotion of rational discourse or the respectful exchange of opinions, and the students involved
may not have intended to hear the trustees out in the first place. What
was involved, instead, was an attempt at intimidation. They wanted to
"put the vibes" on the unquestionably irritated trustees, handing down a
series of demands and insisting on an immediate response. When they
didn't get it (the trustees responded that they would need to study those
demands), the WAAC leaders immediately proclaimed the onset of a
hunger strike in which (first three, and eventually six) students participated. It dragged on for no less than six days, placing an enormous burden of worry (for the health and welfare of the strikers who could easily
have done themselves some harm) on the president and the dean of the
college. The latter was my old friend Dan O'Connor of the Philosophy

Department, a fundamentally decent, deeply conscientious, highly principled, and essentially gentle person. And the president and the dean were certainly not helped by the fact that a group of about fifty faculty members, moved, no doubt, by the stern resolve of their students, signed a petition "to express solidarity with the hunger strikers and full support for the demands presented by WAAC" to the trustees. That had the effect, alas, of muddying the waters. Some of the signatories seemed oddly relaxed about endorsing both goals and tactics as a package. But other signatories, it turned out, had intended to signal support for the substantive demands concerning divestment while still harboring anxious reservations about the hunger strikers' choice of tactic. That the latter group of faculty had such misgivings is hardly cause for surprise. The hunger strikers themselves may well have believed that Gandhi's ghost was beaming down benevolently on their actions but, then, Williams was hardly the moral or political equivalent of the British Raj in India. We were a voluntary, not a compulsory, society and, beyond that, a highly intellectual community committed, as a bedrock principle, to the resolution of problems via a process of reasoned deliberation and consensus, and that process was not to be subverted by the triumph of any coercive moralizing will, however noble its cause might seem. And, in the event, the legitimacy or illegitimacy of the chosen tactic, which was an unquestionably coercive one operating via the manipulation of compassion, inevitably found its way close to the heart of debate at the two-session faculty meeting that swiftly followed upon the heels of the ending of the hunger strike itself.

We gathered together for that meeting on a dark and dreary late afternoon early in February under weather conditions not untypical for our region. Low-hanging clouds clung tenaciously to the slopes of our encircling mountains and the unfolding of our debates in Griffin 3 afforded no kindly light to lead us through the encircling gloom. John Chandler initiated the proceedings by describing the unfortunate nature of the meeting in Hopkins Hall which had ended with the declaration of the hunger strike. Dan O'Connor then picked up the narrative, noting that the crowding at the meeting had produced "conditions of physical intimidation and discomfort" and that the hunger strike had been planned in advance of the meeting. He continued with a detailed account of the unfolding of the strike and the course of the "negotiations" with the disaffected students that culminated in its ending. And he concluded by commenting on the regrettable nature of the tactic chosen. Following upon that I myself spoke, and not without a measure of passion, about the illegitimacy of that tactic in an open, voluntary society and of the need for a principled commitment by the members of our community to "the preservation of the conditions necessary for rational discourse." As the debate unfolded, however, it became increasingly clear that the faculty was deeply divided, and multiply so, not only on the goal of total divestment but also on the question of the student's chosen tactic and, beyond that, on subsidiary issues relating to the latter. Words, it seemed, could hardly wait upon thoughts and tended, more than once, to precede them. Two interventions have lingered in my mind, and not for happy reasons, leading me to go over the minutes of the meeting in question which make for interesting if not encouraging reading.

The first is a combination of two brief comments made by a member of the Political Science Department. He himself perceived the hunger strike, he proclaimed, "as an act of communication, as an advancement of discourse," because it had brought the divestment issue back into the focus of the community's attention. But he was "distressed by the breakdown in trust which [had] occurred; the fact that the WAAC students had not felt they could speak to the trustees without mass support . . . was one indication of that breakdown." The "cause of the breakdown," he was magnanimous enough to concede, was not "the cast of characters" (i.e., the particular people currently filling the senior administrative positions) but, rather, "certain aspects of the structure of the institution" itself. As his listeners sought to grapple with the profundity of that insight, he stressed, and "in particular" (though its relevance was far from being obvious), the fact that the president, not a faculty member, presided over our faculty meetings. Nonsense, of course, and no less nonsensical for being quite so portentous. Having been nudged thus to the brink of terminal academic silliness, one would have thought that things could hardly get any worse. But they did. Right at the start of the second session into which this particular faculty meeting ran, a colleague of mine from the History Department who was a very powerful speaker rose to his feet and said that he had a prepared statement he wished to share with the rest of us. He himself did not appear at that time to be an advocate of total divestment. That, on this occasion, was not the central burden of his plaint. The focus of his statement was rather, or so it seemed (the skein of his argument was a tangled one), the attitude of the deans towards student protest. What he was presumably referring to, though it wasn't altogether clear, was the fact that the dean and I had expressed strong disapproval of the hunger strike tactic. Students, of course, had every right to protest if they so desired, and, should there be need, the college would put itself out to protect that right. For us, the neuralgic point was not the fact that the students had chosen to exercise that right; it was, rather, their particular choice of tactic on this particular occasion. That distinction got lost, however, in what followed. Reaching, as was his wont, for a putative analogy drawn from the dismal annals of Nazi Germany, he argued that "one reason for the success of Nazism had been the silence of German academics," who had felt that "their overriding obligation was to academic pursuits, the life of the mind. . . ." He then evoked the 1943 incident at the University of Munich in which the Gestapo had seized, tortured, and killed two students who had publicly protested "the moral enormities of the Nazi regime." I don't believe he intended to suggest any moral equivalence between the stance of the deans and that of the Gestapo, though a careless listener might easily have assumed that was where he was heading. The [im]moral equivalence he appeared to have in mind was, rather, that between the Williams administration and the University of Munich faculty. The latter "kept public silence [about the killings]," he noted. "Many said in private that they were sorry it happened but [that] such moral protests had absolutely no place in an academic community. It is a line of reasoning," he added, driving his point home, "familiar to the deans of this college." Punkt! Perhaps the head of moralizing steam he was caught up in discharging had the effect of concealing from some of his hearers the shoddiness of the argument he was unfolding and the deeply offensive nature of the analogy he was invoking. I really don't know. What I do remember, however, is that when he sat down he received a round of enthusiastic applause from one segment of the faculty, not all of them, I would judge, believers in total divestment. And I still recall how disappointed and appalled I was by that fact, my habitual pride in being part of the academic profession momentarily shaken.

The outcome of this whole upheaval of the collegiate spirit was that nothing was really settled. WAAC proclaimed that the ending of the hunger strike was "really the beginning of the next chapter of protest" and that chapter was to involve various symbolic actions as well as an unsuccessful attempt to persuade Williams alumni to withhold their annual giving until the college embraced total divestment. Later that spring, the trustees held an open meeting on the divestment issue in Chapin Hall. It was quite well attended and, though the trustees exhibited varying degrees of discomfort under a barrage of basically hostile questions, they kept their balance and explained and defended their stance with patience and occasional flickers of good humor. The college also used the vehicle of *Williams Reports*, an occasional publication, to put out a detailed description and defense of its position on the divestment issue, to which was appended a history of the actions taken to date by the ACSR, along with various pertinent essays, including a lengthy "Open Letter to the Harvard Community" written by Derek Bok in 1979 and a "Statement on Corporate Social Responsibility" issued not long before by TIAA-CREF (whose retirement plan, involving a huge multibillion dollar portfolio, was providing retirement income for university and college people throughout the country). Faculty and staff at Williams were part of that plan and enjoyed, accordingly, voting rights in the election of the fund's officers. But I can recall no faculty move to pressure TIAA-CREF on its South African stance. Williams itself was clearly a softer target. That issue of *Williams Reports* also estimated that less than $9,000 of the income that Williams was receiving in 1983 could be attributed to the operations in South Africa of the pertinent multinationals in which it held stock. I don't know if that *Report* had any impact on faculty opinion. But I suspect that TIAA-CREF's considered judgment that "in general we don't consider divestiture a desirable, or even permissible, means of social protest" may have given some of my colleagues pause. Whatever the case, when I in my turn, a little more than two years later, had to cope with the longueurs of campus protest on the divestment issue, fewer than a half dozen faculty members appeared to be at all actively engaged in it.

Having witnessed at close hand the burdens it could place on the president, campus protest was on my mind in the fall of 1984 when, after

John Chandler announced that he would be stepping down from his position in June 1985, the newly formed presidential search committee informed me that my name had been placed in nomination for the position and asked me if I would permit it to go forward. By that time I had more or less concluded that I was not really interested in presidencies *as such*. But the presidency of Williams, a college to which I had come to be so deeply attached, was a different matter. I still thought long and hard, however, before replying in the affirmative. I had by then a very good sense of the downside of the job and of what I would be in for if I became president at that difficult time. That notwithstanding, I had also had some beguiling glimpses of how invigorating and rewarding the presidential role could be. And not least from the experience of two months or so during which, in accordance with the college's bylaws, I had served as acting president while John Chandler was away in France on a well-earned mini-sabbatical. Having also been nominated as a candidate for the presidencies of five other liberal arts colleges, all upper tier but of varying stature, I had had ample reason to reflect on whether or not I was suited to that presidential role. Two of those nominations I had declined, and in two of the other three searches I got no further than the intermediate interview round. In the third case, however, I had gone much further and would, I think, have had a good shot at election had I not decided to withdraw my name from competition. The college in question was Trinity College in Hartford, Connecticut. It was very much on Claire-Ann's home turf and Chris, our eldest boy, having responded to the appeal of a liberal arts college in an urban rather than a rural setting, was currently a freshman there. When informed, then, early in the spring semester, that someone had placed my name in nomination for the job, I had let it go forward. As the months went by and I heard no further word, I simply assumed that I was out of the running. As the end of the semester came within sight, my thoughts were fixed, rather, on spending my upcoming 1981–82 sabbatical year at the Institute for Advanced Study, Princeton, where I had been appointed as a member of the School of Historical Studies. I was also anxious to get to work on the series of four Mead-Swing Lectures I had been invited to give at Oberlin College early in the autumn. The Trinity search process, however, had clearly taken a course different from the norm to which I was accustomed.

The spring semester was almost over when I got a telephone call from the chairman of the Trinity Board of Trustees informing me that I had emerged as one of three finalists for the presidency of the college and asking if Claire-Ann and I could come up to the campus to meet with the search committee, other members of the board, the senior administrators, and a couple of faculty or faculty-staff interest groups. Given how late in the academic year it already was, I assumed that they had to be reconciled to some delay in the timing of the successful candidate's arrival to take up the position, so I accepted the invitation.

Our visit to the Trinity campus proved to be an interesting, informative, and energizing one. While I didn't get a clear sense of the dynamics on the Trinity Board of Trustees and am pretty sure that not all were present at the meeting, I found the chairman himself to be an open, attentive, kindly, and judicious person, the administrators to be courteous and helpful, and the faculty, who revealed somewhat indiscreetly how anxious they (and some of the board) were to see an academic installed as president, quite welcoming. One of the groups it was arranged for me to meet was composed of about fifty women faculty and staff members who had concerns not unlike those I had encountered at Williams four years earlier. Claire-Ann, who was also invited to attend the meeting, thought that it went well. At least, she assured me that I had managed to navigate my way through some delicate issues without quite putting my foot in it. Our final meeting before leaving was with the outgoing president and his wife. When we arrived, and before they showed us around the president's house, he apologized profusely for the fact that somebody on the faculty who had been involved in the search had leaked the names of the three finalists to the *Hartford Courant* so that everything had become public. And that, I must confess, bothered me. I cannot remember who the third finalist was, but, apart from myself, the other finalist was the incumbent vice president for finance at Trinity, Jim English by name, an alumnus of Trinity and a former insurance executive in Hartford who was well connected to the business community there. He was possibly, or so I had somehow sensed from one or another of the faculty or trustees, viewed as something of a front-runner in the search and he was, indeed, the person eventually elected.

One of the things that had become increasingly clear to me as our visit unfolded was the fact that they really wanted to have a new president who was able to hit the ground running immediately—that is, in July 1981. So, when we got home, I had a decision to make. It didn't prove to be too difficult. My heart was really set on the plans already made for the 1981–82 academic year, both my stay at the Princeton Institute and the delivery of the Oberlin Lectures. Neither of these was I prepared to give up, so I called the Trinity board chairman and told him that was the case and that I was, accordingly, withdrawing from candidacy for the presidency. While clearly a bit disappointed, he was also politely understanding. But, oddly, a couple of days later, and before his board had proceeded to a vote, I received a call from another Trinity trustee urging me to reconsider and to leave my name in contention. It was nice, of course, to have some evidence of being wanted, but I didn't find it a reassuring testimony to the smooth operation of the Trinity board. So I was not at all tempted to change my mind.

The Trinity adventure, however, had proved to be an educative one and, along with my earlier experience as member of a Williams presidential search committee, prepared me quite well for what I would encounter in 1985 as a candidate for the Williams presidency. I was morally certain that my candidacy would be taken seriously and it was. In January 1985, then, I was summoned to New York to be interviewed across the course of two hours by the search committee, which had divided itself for that purpose into two sections. Nor was I altogether surprised late in February, after the committee had recommended its three or four chosen finalists to the board, to be invited back to New York as a finalist for interview by the full board. But the circumstances were really quite unusual in that two of those finalists were members of the Williams faculty who had both served for some years as senior administrators at the college, whom most of the trustees had seen in action, and whom they knew quite well. I was one of the two; the other was my good friend Steve Lewis, with whom I had worked on more than one collegiate venture. A first-rate development economist with a good deal of advisory governmental experience in Botswana, he was from the outstanding Williams class of 1960 (two of whose members sat on the board), had put in two distinguished terms of service as provost of the college, and was, by any standards, a powerful candidate for the presidential office itself. Though from experience I could not help being conscious of the unpredictability of the selection process, he was, I thought in my heart of hearts (and depending on the quality of the unknown third or fourth (?) finalist), likely to be the one whom the trustees would finally tap for the job. I was prepared, then, for disappointment. But I was also proud of my own track record as a faculty member and administrator and possessed of confidence in my capabilities. I was, moreover, by temperament a competitive sort of fellow and was determined to give the challenge my best shot. And that I did, coming away from the exercise recognizing that my best shot might conceivably not have been good enough but content in the knowledge that, for good or ill, I had turned in a decent performance.

One of the senior trustees was Fay (Francis T.) Vincent, Jr., who was later to be baseball commissioner but at the time was chairman of Columbia Pictures. He had arranged for the use of the Columbia Pictures board suite at 711 Fifth Avenue, New York, and that is where the interview took place. The boardroom itself, where the walls on each side of the long table were punctuated by niches (each containing an Oscar), had a bit of a sacral feel to it. And I couldn't help wondering if any enterprising art historian had ever had the wit to undertake a study of corporate boardroom iconography. That was the setting. As for the process itself, it was both careful and complex. Each candidate and his spouse were to breakfast, lunch, or dine with the full board, which would then split into two groups, each of which in turn would interview the candidate for an hour while the other group entertained, chatted with, or grilled his or her spouse. This latter effort was not billed as any sort of interview—the proceedings were more indirect and genteel than that. But when Claire-Ann later described to me what it had been like, it sounded to me very much like a not unpleasant, low-key interview. And, in that setting, by her very deportment no less than what she had to say, I have no doubt that she mightily advanced my cause.

The Williams board at that time (predominantly male) still seemed to harbor the "vicar's wife" conception of the presidential spouse. She (as yet, so far as I know, no "he") was to expect no title, hold no official position, receive no remuneration. But she was certainly expected (though not technically obliged) to support her husband as a volunteer and work on behalf of the college. In effect, a two for the price of one sort of deal. Claire-Ann, it would be fair to say, understood the rules of engagement. At the time, she was very much immersed in the production of quite beautiful pieces of fiber art and had to her credit two successful solo exhibitions of her work. In 1985, moreover, she became very caught up in the foundation and nurturing of the Williamstown Rural Lands Foundation, a badly needed land conservation organization for which she was later to serve as chair of the board. Nonetheless, and in the event, she also threw herself into the traditional role of president's spouse with great enthusiasm, style, and success. It all began with her devoted supervision of the redecoration of the President's House (1801), the college's second-oldest building and a beautiful and elegant structure which had not had a thorough going-over since the Sawyers moved into it nearly a quarter of a century earlier. She didn't need to retain an interior decorator; that skill she supplied herself with the support of our Buildings and Grounds Department and good, sensitive advice from Bob (Robert F.) Dalzell, a friend and colleague in the History Department and future college marshal. And though she was not herself a college employee, she went on to interview and choose people for the house staff, training them to her own high standards of discreet table service and writing for the Personnel Office their annual performance reviews. She also organized in detailed fashion (and picked the menus for) the continual stream of social events at the house for trustees, students, faculty, alumni, major donors, movers and shakers around Berkshire County, and visiting dignitaries of all sorts—artists, poets, playwrights, politicians, state governors, ambassadors, the Aga Khan, and so forth. It was a commanding performance (for which she received from visitors many a flattering comment or note), and it was to be an enormous help to me in the discharge of my official duties. Without the assurance of her help and support I doubt if I would have wanted the job. She brought to her role an instinctive sense of style, and the elegance and warmth of the events she managed echoed the elegance and warmth of the fine old house in which they took place. She bonded at once with that house, for which she cared deeply, and though, being on the road so much and so busy when I was back in town, I myself didn't have all that much time to enjoy it, I did enjoy the constant

stream of entertaining there. It was one of the more relaxing and rewarding parts of the job, though I am not sure that I myself contributed much
to its success. Hers was the real contribution. I could simply relax into it
and enjoy myself, secure in the knowledge that the place looked so good
and that everything was organized so well. I couldn't help recognizing
with admiration and pride the alchemy with which she somehow routinely succeeded in conjuring up an atmosphere that was invitingly personal rather than blandly institutional. It was fun, and I much enjoyed
the sense of being a team that went with it. Hers was quite a performance, though with time she was to become uneasily conscious of the
fact that some of the women faculty and administrative staff, their feminist consciousness long since raised, probably thought her a bit foolish
for being willing to work so hard in a purely voluntary capacity and without much in the way of recognition. But, then, anyone curious about
the demands involved and the ambiguities and ironies embedded in the
role played by the traditional presidential spouse need only turn to the
pages of Jean Alexander Kemeny's tell-it-all *It's Different at Dartmouth: A
Memoir* (1979). There, the irrepressible wife of John George Kemeny, esteemed thirteenth president of Dartmouth College (1974–81), portrays
those demands, amusingly evokes those ironies and ambiguities, and
bluntly insists that she herself viewed the role, however interesting it
might be, as a truly demanding one that trustees would do well to recognize warranted official, salaried status.

At the interview weekend in New York, we had been a bit disappointed
to be assigned the breakfast shift; dinner, we thought, would have been
better and more enjoyable. But the members of the board already knew
both of us quite well and I assume that they wanted to reserve the longer
dinner session for an outside candidate whom they needed to get to
know from scratch. And I can't help thinking that the sort of questions
put to me, and, doubtless, also to Steve, may well have had a degree of
informed specificity lacking in those put to outside candidates whom the
trustees did not know. But that could just as easily have hindered our
candidacies as helped them. Whatever the case, I had the impression
somehow that it would take a couple of weeks before the entire board
could reassemble for a final vote. A week later, then, as I was preparing

to go into campus to start interviewing the students who had applied to go to Oxford the following year, I was taken by surprise when Pete (Preston S.) Parish, chairman of the board's Executive Committee and our senior trustee, called to tell me that I had been elected president and that, within two hours, he would be announcing that fact at an all-campus meeting in Chapin Hall. And from that moment onwards, my life underwent a change more dramatic, I think, than anything I had anticipated.

CHAPTER SEVENTEEN

Presidential Years (i): The Job: Nature, Range, and Variety

The university, it has been said, may possibly be the most internally diverse institution there is. And if universities are indeed dauntingly complex institutional entities, colleges, though smaller and simpler, are not altogether different in kind. If it were not quite so familiar and so very much taken for granted, the sheer multiplicity of activities characteristically pursued under their aegis would probably strike the observer as really quite odd. Those activities range from classroom teaching to the mounting of (sometimes quasi-professional) musical, artistic, and athletic events; from the deployment of security forces (unlike English bobbies, sometimes armed) to the construction, cyclical renovation, and routine maintenance of the large-scale physical plant as well as grounds, roads, and drainage and heating systems; and from the housing and feeding of thousands of students—a task calling for the sort of staff expertise one associates more readily with the hotel and tourist industry— to the running of infirmaries, libraries, theaters, studios, laboratories, and museums, and, beyond that, to the collective pursuit of research endeavors (sometimes of great magnitude). This whole, multiple enterprise calls, of course, for a large and variegated employee base and for overall financial resources large enough to bear comparison, at least in the case of our great research universities, with those at the disposal of the smaller nation-states around the globe.

Compounding that complexity, moreover, is the potential for tension and confusion residing in the bureaucratically ordered presence under one (rather capacious) institutional roof of a myriad of different types of substantive expertise, sometimes extremely technical in nature and often quite opaque or even mysterious, not only to the outside world beyond the academy but also to others within the university or college itself. Upon the institutional leader or president, then, falls the administrative task of recruiting, coordinating, facilitating, and sustaining the activities of a very disparate range of experts and, beyond that, the role of interpreting to some within the institution what others (within the same institution) are doing. The leader also has the role of interpreting (and sometimes symbolizing) the significance of their activities to an often-curious, sometimes-hostile, but usually uninitiated and not infrequently uncomprehending larger public.

Among commentators on American higher education, however, there is not a great deal of agreement about how well or effectively positioned university and college presidents are to discharge such complex and important responsibilities. In recent years, talk about "the shrinking college presidency" has become quite fashionable and, with it, twinges of nostalgia for the halcyon conditions that once made possible the great, commanding presidencies of yesteryear, such as those of Charles Eliot at Harvard, David Starr Jordan at Stanford, William Rainey Harper or, later, Robert Maynard Hutchins at Chicago. Contemporary portrayals of the college presidency can, in fact, be quite dispiriting, depicting it as a modest and essentially limited office, one so narrowly hemmed in by institutional constraints of one sort or another as to be essentially incapable of having any profound or truly enduring impact on the quality and direction of academic life. Classic among such dispiriting portrayals is that painted by Cohen and March in their *Leadership and Ambiguity*, a book which appeared in 1974 at what was one of the lower points in postwar academic fortunes. In that book they mounted a sustained (if sometimes hyperbolic) argument which, its admitted liveliness notwithstanding, falls well short of carrying conviction. According to that argument, colleges and universities are quintessential exemplars of the class of organizations that can properly be labeled as "organized anarchies." Such organizations are characterized by problematic or ambiguous goals, unclear procedures, unmeasurable outcomes, and a varying, intermittent, and fluid involvement by participants in the life of the whole. An organization of this sort can hardly be viewed as a "vehicle for solving well-defined problems," as a structure "within which conflict is resolved through bargaining," or as one which encompasses sets of procedures by means of which "organizational participants arrive at an interpretation of what they are doing and what they have done while doing it." Instead, it is to be viewed as "a collection of choices looking for problems, issues and feelings looking for decision situations in which they might be aired, solutions looking for issues to which they might be the answer, and decision makers looking for work." In such an institutional setting, the presidency, they argue, is essentially "a reactive job," indeed, "an illusion." The degree of control which the president can exercise over the course of things is but a modest one, "more commonly sporadic and symbolic than significant," with his or her particular contributions liable to being "swamped by outside events or the diffuse qualities of university decision making." Institutional performance being largely "an act of God," Cohen and March conclude arrestingly (and in a much-quoted passage) that the unfortunate president is "a bit like the driver of a skidding automobile. The marginal judgments he makes, his skill and his hands may possibly make some difference to the survival prospects for his riders. As a result, his responsibilities are heavy. But whether he is convicted of manslaughter or receives a medal for heroism is largely out of his control."

This sort of analysis doubtless makes for pungent and amusing reading. And it does catch some of the oddities and idiosyncrasies (at once both diverting and deplorable) of the academic institutional experience. But it strikes me as a bit over the top and certainly too clever by half. I don't find it really responsive to the day-to-day realities of the presidential role or, for that matter, to the administrative role in general, at least as I experienced them at a small, high-quality, freestanding liberal arts college from the late 1970s to the mid-1990s. Such sweeping claims for the marginality of the presidential role run afoul, moreover, of a veritable shoal of well-attested accounts to the contrary. Nor, in this connection, should we permit ourselves to be misled by the persistent drumbeat of contemporary concern about the contrast between the heroic stature of the robust presidencies of yesteryear and that of their pallid successors today—unquestionably somewhat diminished figures condemned to threading their cautious way through a minefield of governmental regulation, collegial inhibition, and institutional constraint. The fact is that if and when one makes the effort to compare them with their counterparts abroad, and especially those in continental Europe, North American university and college presidents emerge, in general, as comparatively strong figures, real executives possessed of a substantial measure of power and influence over the immediate operation and ultimate destiny of their institutions.

Of course, given the sheer number of American institutions of higher education (in my day, well over 3,500, great and small), and given the marked differences among them, one has to be cautious about any sweeping generalization purporting to apply to all of them. With the range and variety of the institutions involved, their presidencies are understandably quite various in their nature, reach, and style. They differ from one another for a variety of reasons, ranging from the size, age, and public or private status of the institutions involved, to their particular histories, and to the nature of the role played in their management by the senior administrative officer usually carrying the title of provost. Though in this respect, and at the level of individual institutions, all sorts of differences exist. At our largest universities, the provost tends to be a very consequential and often quite dominant figure whose purview is institution-wide and who, in the discharge of his responsibilities (which are largely analogous to those of a chief operating officer in the corporate world), often possesses a considerable measure of independence from the president to whom he reports in the latter's capacity of chief executive officer. At our small colleges, however, that tends not to be the case. If at such institutions the office of provost actually exists, and that is frequently not the case, the responsibilities attaching to it tend to be much more confined in scope, with the chief operating officer role falling, in effect, to the president who serves also as chief executive officer.

That was certainly the case at the Williams of my day, the administrative organization of which, conditioned by its own particular history, was somewhat unusual. The responsibilities discharged at many another college by a chief academic officer were, in fact, split between the dean of the faculty and the provost, with the latter also discharging some of the duties that fall elsewhere to a chief financial officer. While the college's bylaws stipulated that it was the dean of the faculty who should, in the prolonged absence of the president, serve as acting president, in other respects dean and provost were of much the same order of seniority, with the provost also reporting directly to the president and being possessed of his own distinct area of responsibility. Though they have since changed, those responsibilities extended in my administrative days to the framing of the annual college budget, long-range financial planning, and overseeing the library, the Center for Computing, the Williams College Museum of Art, the Bronfman Science Center, audio-visual services, the Office of Admission, the Office of Financial Aid, and Athletics. Recognizing the fact that, among the college's senior administrative officers, it was the president alone whose purview extended to the full range of collegiate operations, nonacademic as well as academic, and noting that it was traditional at Williams (and one of the sources of its strength) for the deans and provost to be drawn temporarily from the ranks of the faculty to serve terms in administration, more than one of the decennial reaccreditation teams assessing the health of the college have been moved to comment on the president's involvement in every aspect of the college's operations and to acknowledge the "strong tradition of presidential leadership at Williams." Concurring in that judgment, a former trustee with long years of devoted service on the board once told me that, when asked about it, he was accustomed to describing the Williams presidency as a strong one in that the president served also as chairman of the board of trustees, as presiding officer at faculty meetings, and as a visible presence in the community, residing in the fine old President's House at the very heart of the campus, right opposite West College (1790), our first building and the navel, as it were, of our collegiate universe.

I have to confess, however, that such, rather abstract, considerations and theories of leadership in general were far from my mind when, at the beginning of July 1985, I walked into the president's dingy little office in Hopkins Hall and sat down at Phinney Baxter's huge and rather battered double desk that filled most of the room. At officer cadet school, years earlier, I had heard enough portentous mystification about leadership in general to last a lifetime. There, after all, we had been solemnly graded on the degree to which we possessed the ineffable quality known as OQ ("Officer Quality"). And, in 1985, all I knew about theories pertaining specifically to academic leadership stemmed from an encounter, in a quasi-popular educational journal, with the genre of "self-help" piece that was often the work of a past or present president. And I had not been very impressed by that genre. It was characterized usually by a species of dully obvious didacticism and punctuated altogether too often by irritating lapses into terminal cuteness. Thus, for example, one was apt to be solemnly assured that "the position [of president] is full of paradoxes. Those who enjoy it are not very successful. And those who are successful are not very happy." Or, again, that "leadership is knowing where to go; management is knowing how to get there." Or, yet again, that "managers do things right; leaders do the right thing." The genre was lacking only, it seemed, upbeat exhortations to the effect that when the going gets tough the tough ought really to get going.

If my mind, then, was largely innocent of any real leadership theory, I was also not that well informed about the range of practical differences across the full spectrum of higher educational institutions in the status and positioning of the president. Never having served before on any board of trustees or directors, I was simply unaware of the fact that at institutions of higher education the president did not always (or, indeed, usually) serve also as chairman of the board. And though I knew, having attended faculty meetings at Yale, that it was the dean of Yale College rather than the president of the university who presided at such meetings there, I simply took it for granted that at a freestanding liberal arts college like Williams it was the president who should appropriately play that role. Similarly, I also took it for granted that the president and his family should live in the fine old President's House and was not unmindful of the symbolic importance of his presence there or of how much that seemed to mean, in those days at least, to loyal alumni who walked into that house as guests. And as for the president's involvement, in one degree or another, in every aspect of the college's operations, it was that, I soon discovered, that made the job so very interesting and energizing and that more or less ensured that, for good or ill, there would never be a dull day in the office.

Being, by well-established habit, an inveterate note-taker at meetings, I quickly fell into the practice of keeping such notes in a ledger, organized simply by date and time, with any actions to be taken as an outcome of such meetings highlighted in the margins. Thus, by going over those entries at the end of each week I could easily make sure that such actions had in fact been taken and any promise made faithfully fulfilled. By contemporary standards this was doubtless a fairly primitive system. But it seemed to work quite well for me. I still have those ledgers and, having casually perused them for the first time in more than twenty years, I am struck by the range of things I was attending to on a day-to-day basis. I am struck, too, by the sudden alterations in nature between the focus of one meeting and that of the next, as well as the gradual shift across time in the issues I was characteristically spending a disproportionate amount of time attending to.

Setting to one side the senior administrators who reported directly to me and who were in and out of the office on a regular basis, the range of people coming in to see me was really quite wide and varied. Across time I might well see, and in no predictable sequence, the college marshal, concerned with the ceremonial planning of an upcoming commencement or convocation, followed, say, by a couple of students wanting me to give them a tutorial in medieval political philosophy (we settled upon the lunch hour as one of the few times open and I pledged to provide sandwiches). Or I might see Nikos Psacharopoulos, director of the Williamstown [summer] Theatre Festival (WTF), wanting to talk about the edgy relationship between WTF and the college's Theatre Department, followed, perhaps, by a senior member of the faculty anxious to share his worries about the deterioration of collegial relations in his particular department. I could also see a resident of the town complaining about the behavior of Williams students who, having secured permission to live off campus in their senior year, were causing trouble in the neighborhood (beer cans on the lawn, etc.), followed, perhaps by Tom (Thomas) Krens, then director of the Williams College Museum of Art, pursuing his dream of creating a vast museum of contemporary art in the abandoned and decaying factory buildings of what had been the Sprague Electric Company in neighboring North Adams. Alternately, I might see Bob (Robert R.) Peck, director of athletics, stopping by to give me an excellent briefing in preparation for the upcoming meeting of presidents of the colleges belonging to the New England Small Colleges Athletic Conference (NESCAC), followed by two women students who, having organized an (evanescent) Croquet Club, wanted to know if they could stage a contest on the invitingly smooth lawn of the President's House. (Answer: "Yes, of course.") Or I might see Win (Winthrop M.) Wassenar, director of buildings and grounds, reporting on worrying signs of slope failure above one of the new linking roads at the site of the much-needed faculty housing development that we were laying out (somewhat controversially) on the lower slopes of Pine Cobble Mountain. And so on. The topics up for discussion at the endless succession of meetings of this sort could alternate, somewhat abruptly, between things like the state of race relations on campus to management problems at our Computer Center, or from a final appeal to the president being made by a student whom the faculty-student Discipline Committee had sentenced to expulsion for beating up his girlfriend (sentence upheld) to questions concerning campus lighting and security. They could also alternate from the health of the Williams Mystic Program in Maritime Studies to problems with the irrigation system at the Taconic Golf Club (a college property), or from the Williams-Exeter junior year abroad program at Oxford (a venture very close to my heart) to the antitrust case that a politically motivated Justice Department was pursuing against the Ivy League universities and a group of leading liberal arts colleges, Williams included, or, indeed, from the financial problems of the Village (Williamstown) Ambulance Service to the imperative need to bring to completion the *catalogue raisonné* of the paintings of Maurice and Charles Prendergast for which the Williams College Museum of Art had become the principal repository. One never quite knew what to expect next.

Perusing those ledgers again, I have been struck by several things. First, by how much time I seem to have spent between 1986 and early 1989 in discussion with Tom Krens about the unfolding MASS MoCA project. It reminds me of the extent to which, along with Will Reed who was also very active in the cause, I came to be engaged in the attempt to get it off the ground. Second, this time throughout the full course of my presidency, how constant was the flow of meetings with Hodge Markgraf and Mike Oman about development matters in general and the Third Century Campaign in particular. Such campaigns are akin to icebergs in that two-thirds of the activity they involve goes on below the more visible surface flow of speechmaking, dinner events, and donor solicitations. And if discussions with Tom often took an intriguingly serpentine course, meetings with Hodge and Mike tended to be crisp, practical, well-prepared, and briefer. Third, the fact that so many of the institutional concerns leading people to set up meetings with me were overwhelmingly concrete rather than more abstractly academic in nature. Matters that were often concrete, indeed, in more than a figurative sense. Bricks and mortar, pipes and parking lots, roads, wires, heating tunnels and running tracks, classrooms, museums, auditoria, and laboratories—such were the fustian things, at once both frustrating and rewarding, of a fair amount of day-to-day presidential engagement.

When I became president, more than one friend and acquaintance in the business world expressed surprise that a quintessentially academic type like me would take on (perhaps they really meant *could* take on but were too polite to put it in that way!) the management of a complex enterprise with more than nine hundred employees, a large physical plant, an endowment that was to move up across my term of office from slightly less than $200 million to $450 million, and an annual operating budget that likewise moved up from around $60 million to close to a $100 million. I was surprised by their surprise. It is true that the day-to-day management of such an enterprise could confront one with intricate and taxing problems. But there was nothing ineffable or truly extraordinary about them. The purely managerial side of my responsibilities, indeed, served often to call to mind some of the tasks I had become accustomed to dealing with in my army days. Most of our administrative and support staff and our hourly employees were decent, conscientious people who were glad to be working for the college and who wanted to do a good job. Sitting at the apex of the managerial pyramid, one could be sure, if one issued the pertinent orders, that *something* would happen. Perhaps not always quite what one had in mind but *something*—and, occasionally, more rather than less than one had intended. Here, I found, one had to be careful with buildings and grounds personnel who were prone to taking a "nothing but the best" point of view even where second or even third best would have been more than adequate. During my presidential years, the president of one of the great midwestern publicly funded research universities got into serious trouble over the ridiculously expensive nature of a fence or wall he had had constructed around the (publicly owned) presidential manse. In cost it was, apparently, the moral equivalent of the renowned thousand-dollar toilet seats reputed periodically to be embedded in the more occluded reaches of military budgeting. All he had wanted was a bit of privacy. But his loyal buildings and grounds troops, moved by a commendable desire to please combined, alas, with a lack of peripheral institutional vision, had gone over the top and left him struggling, in the end, with angry taxpayers and a public relations nightmare spawned by a minor issue peripheral to the overall functioning of his university.

But if, even at a private college, one had to keep a weather eye cocked for such inadvertences, the normal routines of management were by no means the most challenging part of my responsibilities. University presidents these days (although usually presidents in the public sector) sometimes refer to themselves, rather grandly, as chief executive officers. I don't particularly like that nomenclature but it does, I suppose, catch part of the story reflected in the typical collegiate organizational chart. And while it is part of the institutional story that is more or less invisible to students and one that the faculty is but dimly aware of, it is not, of course, to be dismissed as unimportant. Certainly, this executive/managerial function does take up a good deal of the president's time, even at a small college like Williams. The administrative corps has to be so organized that it functions effectively, so informed about the operation of the college as a whole that in its parts it does not lose sight of the overall mission and objectives of the institution, and so motivated that it wants to discharge its various responsibilities in an efficient, timely, imaginative, humane, and compassionate manner. Good things won't happen in a collegiate community without a lot of good, dedicated people in those roles, and, at Williams, we were blessed with a lot of such people. But they had to be led, and it was, and is, part of the president's job so to lead them—setting clear priorities; discouraging bureaucratic end-running around immediate supervisors (very demoralizing for an institution); maintaining the right balance between insufficient delegation and inadequate supervision; keeping the mission of the college as clearly as possible before the eyes of all (without that some administrative functions tend to be seen as ends in themselves—the great bureaucratic sin that I saw a lot of as a young army officer); doing one's best to exemplify through one's own actions, commitments, and achievements the very ethos of the place; demanding at least as much of oneself as of others; and pushing things along and keeping things moving, even if (especially when) it feels like wading through molasses. In the absence of this sort of exercise of executive/managerial leadership, the whole is still likely to keep on moving. But, if it does so, it is by some sort of inertial force, sluggishly and not necessarily in one particular direction or determined by any identifiable overall goal. Many colleges (and most, I suspect, at one or another point in their histories) have survived for years in that mode. But it is one that is surely inimical to the quest for institutional greatness. And it was that quest that was my driving force.

Of course, the standard administrative chart by no means tells the whole story; in some ways, indeed, it can be quite misleading. At Williams, for example, as at many colleges, the president not only reports to the board of trustees but also serves as one of its members. Indeed, in my day at least, the president served also as chairman of the board. Again, the standard organizational chart draws no attention to the role and importance of the alumni body or to the roles played by students, parents, the local public, or the public at large as stakeholders in the institution and people who exert considerable influence over the shaping of its destiny. And to the degree to which any such organizational chart suggests that the chairs of academic departments come under the dean of the faculty in the same way as subordinate administrators come under the superiors to whom they report, it clearly smacks of outright fantasy.

That there is, in fact, something almost schizophrenic about the governance system of American colleges and universities has been brought home to me quite forcefully by my recent year of interim service as a museum director. While at a college it is only those in managerial and administrative positions who can really be said to "work for" their superiors (all of them exercising what is ultimately a measure of authority delegated to them by the president), at a museum all employees/staff members, not only those in traditionally "managerial" roles, do so. And that includes the highly (academically) educated people in the curatorial, educational outreach, and publications departments. If it would be easy enough simply to assume that such people must enjoy a status comparable to that enjoyed by faculty members at a college or university, to do so would be quite wrong. Such people are, in fact, no less directly dependent on the director's authority (or whim!) than are those other employees working, say, in facilities, public relations, or food services. All, indeed, are employed "at will." At a college, on the other hand, faculty members—and especially so at old first-rate places like Williams—enjoy at least a shadow of the proudly independent governing role that the fellows of Oxbridge colleges (combining responsibilities that at American institutions are divided between the faculty and the trustee governing board) still discharge as full members of the corporate body. In North America that legal, corporate status was appropriated in the eighteenth century by boards of overseers or trustees who succeeded to the role once played by the original founders. But in terms at least of their *moral authority* in relation to curriculum, faculty appointments, and the general academic mission of the institution, faculties still enjoy something more than the power delegated to them by the president and trustees. No president can afford for a minute to forget that fact. A vote of no confidence by the faculty—sometimes, even, the threat of such a vote—has often constituted the death knell for a president unfortunate enough to have come into direct collision with widespread faculty sentiment.

Even though it occupies a good deal of time, then, the more demanding part of the president's role is not the executive/managerial side of things but the less clearly defined one of playing a finely balanced mediating role among a whole series of constituencies, each possessing in one way or another a measure of power independent of his—trustees, faculty, students, alumni, parents, the local public, and even, beyond the particular locality, the broader American public. The fluctuating views of this last concerning the mission, role, and health of American higher education at large serve, after all, to help shape governmental attitudes and policies and can have a very concrete impact on the financial well-being of our universities and colleges and on the ability of students to attend them. Public opinion obviously has its most direct impact on our public institutions of higher education, partially state-funded universities and colleges. But in terms especially of federal support for financial aid and faculty scientific research, it can have a marked impact also on our private institutions, Williams itself not excluded. And any president had and has in some measure to be attuned to such public frequencies. And especially so, given the degree to which the academy at large was in my day coming under attack from the political right. In the mid-1960s our colleges and universities had ridden high in public esteem and enjoyed substantial governmental support at both the state and federal levels. By the mid-1970s, however, in the wake of eye-catching turbulence on our campuses nationwide, they had forfeited much of that esteem. And by my own watch, from the mid-1980s to the mid-1990s, they were under fairly constant attack from the right-wing end of the political spectrum and even from at least one of the governmentally sponsored institutions academics had worked hard to establish. For the National Endowment for the Humanities, now politicized under the leadership first of William J. Bennett (Williams, class of 1965) and then of Lynne Cheney, came to take a very dim and really quite hostile view of the direction they thought American academic culture had taken across the two decades preceding; the picture as they seem to have seen it was clearly a gloomy one of downhill all the way. This I myself saw as a wanton misrepresentation of the pertinent realities, and I was so bothered by that fact that I set out to protect enough time in the summers to write what amounted to a historically conditioned work of rebuttal which I was able somehow to complete and see published in time for our bicentennial under the title *Community of Learning: The American College and the Liberal Arts Tradition* (1992).

For the president of a college like Williams, however, while he certainly had to keep his eye on the attitudes prevalent among the public at large, it was the stance of other, more immediate, constituencies that had necessarily to weigh more heavily on his mind. The interests and aspirations of such individual constituencies tend rarely to be unified in themselves. Nor do those interests and aspirations come close to coinciding with one another. At the same time, hardly any of those groups can be totally alienated if the institution is not to drift into crisis and if the president is long to retain his or her job. And all of them have to be at least reasonably content if the college is to prosper. The president, accordingly, has to be capable in some measure of fighting on all fronts simultaneously and redeploying his or her forces rapidly from one front to another as occasion demands.

But, then, if I may be permitted a turn that will take me into the more abstract realms of leadership theory, the military metaphor is probably not the one most congruent with the type of leadership called for when what is involved is the care, feeding, and management of the pertinent array of constituencies. It is true that data collected in the 1980s in the context of the Institutional Leadership Project, reflecting the views that college and university presidents themselves at that time held about leadership, reveal them characteristically to have understood in a highly directive top-down fashion the leadership they themselves were exerting; to them it seems to have been "a one-way process whose function it was to get others to comply with or conform to the leader's direction." It is far from clear to me, however, how that understanding of institutional leadership would fully catch even what happens on the executive/managerial side of a college president's functioning. And it certainly has little bearing on what I have identified as the more challenging aspect of presidential leadership, which calls for the careful balancing and management of multiple (sometimes competing) constituencies. So far as theories of leadership go, over the years since I myself stepped down from my presidential duties, I have come to conclude that the theories that are most pertinent and revelatory are those (casually brushed aside by Cohen and March) that fall at the cultural/symbolic end of the spectrum.

Fair enough, but what exactly do I have in mind? Here my thoughts go back to Jack Sawyer and to the major (if comparatively uncelebrated) contribution I believe him to have made to the revitalization of Williams. I noted earlier that what was involved in that effort was not any single bold initiative or some arrestingly visible exercise of what would readily be recognized as presidential leadership but, rather, a consistent pattern of behavior embedded in his deportment and his day-to-day work throughout the entirety of his presidency. It reflected a dimension of leadership that involves the educational and instructional side of the leader's role in the building of a necessary, supportive followership. And it is that aspect of leadership that has been studied much in recent years under the rubric of cultural and symbolic leadership.

When, long after I had put administrative office behind me, I began to read the relevant leadership literature under the genial promptings of Al (George R.) Goethals, friend and colleague and a gifted social psychologist who had served on my presidential watch first as acting dean of the faculty and then as provost, I was struck by its pertinence to the constituency aspect of the president's responsibilities and by the degree to which it made sense of what I myself, comparatively innocent of theory, had felt more or less instinctively moved to do.

However "constructivist" the intellectual inclinations of more recent years, mid-twentieth-century American sociology was persistently inclined to an overeager and exclusive embrace of the characteristically Durkheimian understanding of the social and institutional world as an alien and objective facticity set over against the individual in much the same way as the external reality of the world of nature is set over against the individual. And that sort of understanding tended also to be promoted in the presidential mind by the overwhelmingly concrete nature of so many of the institutional concerns that set the day-to-day agenda for academic leaders. That being so, the counterintuitive Weberian assumption that institutional life is a fragile social construction, the product of human creativity and fraught, therefore, with human meaning, is apt to seem as much at odds with its sheer facticity, otherness, weight, and inertial force as once was the novel Copernican heliocentrism with the ordinary person's commonsense conviction that it was he who stood immobile at the still point of a ceaselessly turning world. But few, I suspect, who have paused to ponder the fact that even states can fail, or who have been involved in the creation of any sort of start-up enterprise, are likely to harbor doubt about the rectitude of that Weberian intuition. And no one, I also suspect, who has been charged with the stewardship of an existing academic institution, however old and well established, can totally have escaped those moments of crisis, heightened sensibilities, exhausted reflection, or, simply, unexpected epiphany when the sheer *fragility* of institutions becomes suddenly quite palpable. And such moments are apt to bring with them the startled realization that, their massive concreteness notwithstanding, institutions are in the end nothing other than a frail tissue of human purpose, intentionality, aspiration, and hope, thrust boldly forward in the very teeth of the hostility of time.

In the face of this compelling epiphany, the more instrumental approaches to institutional leadership have little or nothing to offer. On the other hand, it is precisely at such daunting moments of truth that the seemingly hyper-theoretical cultural, symbolic, and broadly interpretative approaches come very much into their own, and sometimes in quite practical ways. They do so, I believe, because they helpfully shift the focus of concern from issues pertaining to the simple exercise of power, with which the more instrumental approaches are primarily concerned, to those more testing challenges that leaders confront as they reach out for the enabling warrants that will justify the actions they are taking and legitimate the changes they may be trying to engineer. And so reach out they must if in the exercise of their powers they are to be effective. For college and university presidents go about their business, not in some sort of unresponsive void, but in a rich context involving multiple group-ings fraught with expectations concerning the use to which they should at any moment be putting the not inconsiderable powers at their dis-posal. Whatever their particular institutional setting, simple power has somehow to be transformed into authority, for the would-be exercise of leadership is shadowed always by the problem of legitimation.

Close attention, therefore, must be devoted to the process that pro-ponents of the cultural and symbolic approach to leadership have some-times called "the management of meaning." As we have seen, however, and speaking specifically about educational institutions, Philip Selznick has described that process less portentously as pertaining to the crucial role that the leader plays in defining and proclaiming on a day-in-day-out basis the institution's role and mission, in nurturing its "embodiment" of an enduring meaning and purpose, in himself (or herself) somehow also embodying that meaning and infusing it into the very organization, structure, and routines of behavior within it, defending the institu-tion's integrity, and sustaining its core values. Selznick's emphasis, then, is very much on the educational and instructional nature of the leader's role, on the way in which the leader (as my late, revered colleague James MacGregor Burns was to put it when discussing what he called "trans-formative leadership") "shapes, alters and elevates the motives and val-ues of followers through the vital *teaching* role of leadership."

Commentators who have subsequently developed cultural and sym-bolic approaches have not so much abandoned that instructional perspec-tive on the leadership role as extended it and specified it more precisely. Assuming the socially constructed nature of institutional reality, con-cerned with the nature of institutional culture, and moved by the insights of interpretative anthropology, they have extended the instructional role to embrace not simply the forthright articulation and defense of enduring institutional values but, beyond that, the exploitation by leaders of myth, ritual, language, legend, symbol, and (perhaps above all) story. All of this to be done in the ongoing attempt to interpret for their followers and to shape, nurture, and develop in them the complex tissue of commonly shared understandings, perceptions, meanings, values, and beliefs which define, in effect, the institutional reality.

The importance attached in this and other versions of the cultural/symbolic/interpretative approach to the role played by *stories* should not escape our attention. This specific emphasis has been helpfully intensified of more recent years by Howard Gardner in a stimulating book entitled *Leading Minds: An Anatomy of Leadership* (1995). Arguing that "the arena in which leadership necessarily occurs" is that of "human minds," he claims that leaders make their impact in that arena not so much by the straightforward or static message or themes they attempt to convey as by the stories or narratives of an institutional drama unfolding in dynamic fashion across time. Such narratives, he goes on to argue, constitute "a uniquely powerful currency in human relationships." That is especially true of the most deeply rooted of the stories that leaders tend to relate, those that "concern issues of personal and group identity," narratives that, by helping "individuals think about and feel who they are, where they come from, and where they are headed, . . . constitute the single most powerful weapon in the leader's literary arsenal."

I can't help fretting, of course, that all of this may well strike even a reader interested in the "nature, range, and variety" of the presidential role as unhelpfully abstract and altogether too "academic." But against any such conclusion I feel bound to lean. And not least of all because I find that it has helped me make sense, in retrospect, of my own actions and inclinations as president. Whatever their pertinence or lack of pertinence to the leadership issue at large, both the cultural/symbolic/interpretative approach in general and Gardner's take on it in particular speak powerfully (and, I think, profoundly) to the leadership challenge confronting those who are called upon to preside over such quintessential communities of the word as institutions of higher education. And for more than one reason. Colleges and universities, especially if they have had a long, continuous history and (like Williams) still enjoy a humane intimacy of scale, are not only communities of the word—though that they certainly are—but they are also fine exemplars of what Robert

Bellah and others have dubbed "communities of memory." Such communities are those which, in an attempt to prevent the erosion of tradition and the consignment of their past to oblivion, persist in telling and retelling their "constitutive narrative," recalling to mind "the men and women who have embodied and exemplified the community's very meaning and identity." "The stories that make up a tradition," Bellah and his colleagues maintain,

> contain conceptions of character, of what a good person is like, and of the virtues that define such character. But the stories are not all exemplary, not all about successes and achievements. A genuine community of memory will also tell stories of shared suffering that sometimes creates deeper identities than success. . . . And if the community is completely honest, it will remember not only suffering received but suffering inflicted—dangerous memories, for they call the community to alter ancient evils. The communities of memory that tie us to the past also turn us to the future as communities of hope. They carry a context of memory that can allow us to connect our aspirations for ourselves and those closest to us with the aspirations of a larger whole and see our own efforts as being, in part, contributions to a common good.

Such insights about "communities of memory" in general are surely pertinent to what can constitute some of the greatest challenges college and university presidents can be called upon to face—those generated by the pressures and complex interplay of multiple constituencies, each comprised not of organizational subordinates but of a congeries of independent (sometimes entrepreneurial) figures, well or poorly informed, loosely or tightly organized, and betraying a whole range of disparate understandings of the nature, purpose, and destiny of the institution in question. If the college is simply to maintain its health, all of those constituencies have to be at least reasonably satisfied. And if, somehow, it is truly to thrive, the energies, loyalties, and commitments of all of them have to be marshaled in such a way that the whole collegiate enterprise can move forward confidently and with broadly shared conviction and in an assured and (if at all possible) agreed upon direction. Marshaled also, and accordingly (here Bellah's intuition comes into play), in a manner congruent with the hallowed legacy from the past, the acknowledged strength of the present, and the celebratory hopes for the future. And central to a presidential response to that energizing challenge is the framing, relating, and, if at all possible, the unambiguous personal embodiment of an institutional story that builds upon (even while it alters or extends) the traditional institutional saga, that fits the circumstances of the given historical moment, and that makes sense to the majority of constituents, however disparate they may be. Hence the mantra which, I now note, put in an appearance in many of my statements or speeches directed towards one or another segment of the greater Williams community. It was inspired by Edmund Burke's grand vision of society as a partnership in matters of such complexity, nobility, and enduring import that its end "cannot be obtained in many generations." So that, of necessity, "it becomes a [quasi-mystical] partnership" not only "between those who are living," but "between those who are living, those who are dead, and those who are to be born." And what was that mantra? Nothing other than this: "Pride in the past, confidence in the present, faith in the future." For mine, to borrow Albert Hirschman's phrase, was an ineluctable "bias for hope." And it was my abiding conviction that if we were to have faith in the promise of the future we were called upon, not only to have confidence in the integrity of the present, but also some measure of pride in the nobilities and achievements of the past.

CHAPTER EIGHTEEN

Presidential Years (ii): Organization, Appointments, and Initiatives

Descending now from the empyrean of lofty theoretical rumination to the sublunary practicalities of day-to-day reality, let me begin by reporting that when I was elected to the presidency in mid-March 1985, the trustees made a point of conveying to me their expectation that I would lead Williams through the proud celebration, in seemly fashion, of its bicentennial in 1993 and see through to a successful completion by the end of that bicentennial year an appropriately major capital fund drive. Across the better part of the nine years that ensued I was to do my level best to meet both expectations in a satisfactory manner.

In the aftermath of my election, however, I had to focus first, and with some intensity, on more immediately pressing matters. And I look back with a certain amount of retrospective horror on the two months that ensued until spring semester classes came to a merciful end. For during those two months I had to struggle very hard simply to keep my head above water. At the time, while I was still working to get our nascent Oxford program properly organized, I was also teaching the normal course load and (in an unfortunate coincidence) was teaching for the first time a new, required senior seminar I had put together for our history of ideas majors. This last was focused on the multiple (and shifting) interpretations across time of a great seventeenth-century classic in political philosophy, the *Leviathan* of Thomas Hobbes. After embarking on its teaching I had swiftly realized that, even for a group of smart seniors in that demanding major, the course as I had optimistically framed it was a bit too ambitious. So I was already in the middle of an attempt to reshape it on the run in order to be able to bring it to a reasonably successful conclusion. No easy task in itself but made the more difficult because my upcoming presidential responsibilities were unfortunately refusing to wait until July 1 and were already beginning to encroach on life. I was called upon immediately to make myself available to reporters from the local press and radio stations (a new experience for me) and called upon to make pronouncements about my plans for the future of the college. I was also deluged by a flood of letters of kindly congratulations and advice. The vast majority of those missives were generously encouraging and I felt bad about being unable to respond to them all individually. But I did receive two that left me feeling a bit rueful. They were from Jack Sawyer and Joe (Joseph) Kershaw, the economist and administrative colleague whom Jack had recruited from the Rand Corporation to become the college's first provost. While congratulatory in nature, of course, both were at pains to make it explicit that I had not been their preferred candidate. In itself, this came to me as no great surprise. I had assumed that they would be strong supporters of Steve Lewis, with whom they had worked closely and whom they understandably admired. What did surprise me, however, was that they felt it necessary (and appropriate) to underline that fact. It was not, exactly, an encouraging message to be given as one was struggling to get one's feet on the ground. But I couldn't afford to brood about it as I was already confronted by several important decisions which brooked no delay.

That notwithstanding, it is a sign of my anticipation of troubles to come that in the midst of all of this, and while focusing on some crucial appointments decisions, I still made time to convene a small meeting to discuss campus crises. Having been more than a sideline spectator during upheavals on the Williams campus from 1969 onwards, I wanted, in relation to such anomic events, to do whatever I could to be proactive rather than simply reactive. So, having put together all the pertinent records and affiliated materials we could find, I assembled the group of people who had been directly involved in one or more of those crises and, together, we went about the business of trying to pinpoint what if any lessons could be learned for the future. The effort proved to be more dispiriting than helpful. Each of the upheavals in question had been embedded in—or had sprung from—very specific contextual situations, and it proved hard to elicit from them any putative lines of action that could confidently be viewed as generally applicable in the future. From our deliberations, then, I was able to draw only two conclusions.

The first was that we owed it to our trustees, who were taking time from busy career obligations to work pro bono for the college, to afford them a measure of protection from the sort of miserable situation some of their predecessors had found themselves in during the 1983 crisis precipitated by the Williams Anti-Apartheid Coalition. Or, indeed, from the miseries inflicted on their counterparts elsewhere, where some had pig's blood thrown at them by protestors, or where, as at our sister college Wesleyan, trustees, in order to get into their board meeting, had been forced to pick their way over the recumbent bodies of protesting students. This last was memorialized in a photograph on one of the front pages of the *New York Times*, hardly the sort of publicity that any educational institution would want. Fortunately, few people at Williams seemed to know where our (then) boardroom was located—in an occluded if handsome space behind the stage of Chapin Hall. I was happy to keep it that way. And if any meeting was to be set up between members of the board and representatives of a student protest group, I was also determined to make sure that it would be held, not in any small seminar room that could, as in 1983, be intimidatingly packed, but in a large, capacious classroom that would not lend itself to that sort of miserable trick.

My second conclusion concerned communications and the importance of doing whatever we could to stem the circulation of damaging rumors during any future campus crisis, and especially so among the faculty who were, after all, in day-to-day contact with students and were well positioned, if they were convinced that it was appropriate, to exert a calming influence. In the absence of email, that posed more of a challenge than it would today. But I adopted the practice, under crisis conditions, of briefing as quickly as possible the Faculty Steering Committee, the faculty members of the Committee on Appointments and Promotions, and as many of the department chairmen as I could assemble. It was far from being an ideal solution, but later observation was to suggest that it did do something, at least, to curtail the damaging proliferation of misleading rumors—at least on campus. Given the eagerness with which the press covered signs of student unrest, off campus was another story. That challenge had to be met by our news director, though I myself was to do my best to keep the board informed by telephone calls and by the prompt dispatch of descriptive newsletters, of which I was called upon to write many.

While I was drawing these conclusions, two other things were also becoming clear to me. The first was that, unlike a president appointed from the outside, I couldn't really expect from the faculty much of the normal honeymoon period while I got to know the place and its people. I already knew both and it seemed clear that I would have to hit the ground running and somehow convey to the community without delay a reassuring sense of momentum. The second, and not altogether anticipated realization, was that during my first year my top priority would have to be that of devoting a lot of attention to purely administrative matters. At the level of the middle managers, a very important group if the college was to run smoothly and effectively, there seemed to be some general morale problems; I thought I could detect a certain restlessness and a sense that their work was not being fully appreciated. Over the course of the coming year, moreover, because of transfers, departures, or retirement, a whole series of positions needed to be filled, from director of the Oxford program to director of alumni relations, and from dean of the college to director of development, comptroller, registrar, director of personnel, and director of annual giving. And along with at least some of those appointments would occur a wholesale reorganization of the offices involved. While I did not have to be directly involved in the filling of all of those jobs, the more senior positions among them called for my immediate attention. I was fortunate enough to inherit from my predecessor three senior administrative colleagues whom I was used to working with and whom I both liked and admired: Neil Grabois, provost (and later to become the president of Colgate University), John Reichert, a first-rate dean of the faculty, and Will (William S.) Reed, vice president of administration and treasurer. But I still had some important personnel decisions to make that simply could not wait until I actually started my presidential term of service.

The first decision concerned the crucial job of running the president's office. Dorothy Kirkpatrick, secretary to the president (that is, his senior executive assistant and the most senior administrative assistant at the college) had been very seriously ill a couple of years earlier and, while she had made a reasonable recovery, had decided to retire at the same time as John Chandler. This was a worrying development. It meant that while I was new to the presidency the person on whom I would have to depend for a myriad of things pertaining to the day-to-day functioning of the office of the president would also be new to her duties. The potential for understandable mistakes and confusion would, accordingly, be quite high. So I didn't devote any time to mounting an extended search and quickly picked Julie Peterson, who had been my administrative assistant when I was dean of the faculty, for the role of secretary to the president. She knew me, knew my work habits, was a hard and deeply conscientious worker, was highly intelligent, possessed good, sensitive judgment, and could actually read my handwriting. This last was no mean achievement and was less trivial than it might seem. Over the years I had tried to dictate letters and memoranda but had given up on it. My dictated letters had struck me as akin to the efforts of somebody writing in a language foreign to them, replete with chunky sentences composed of clumsy prepackaged phrases. Having always ended up rewriting them in an effort to turn them into real English, I had returned to the practice of handwriting everything directly, which was something I could do at comparatively high speed. Like so many of the administrative assistants at the Williams of the day, Julie had not had the opportunity to go on to college after graduating from high school. But it was one of her great achievements, while serving as my executive assistant, to pursue her studies for an undergraduate degree by taking night and summer courses at North Adams State College (NASC—now the Massachusetts College of Liberal Arts). Her graduation in 1993 coincided with our bicentennial year at Williams and I was invited to give the commencement address at NASC. As Julie walked across the stage to accept her diploma, Tom Aceto, president of NASC, was kind enough to hand it to me so that I could give it to her. It was a truly great honor for me to be able to bestow that diploma on a wonderful person who had served Williams so well and who had managed somehow, despite the challenges of her job, to finish the degree. And I know that it was a very proud moment also for her only daughter who, with her mother's unfailing support, had gone on to fulfill her own dream of becoming an engineer. I never regretted my decision to bring Julie with me to the president's office, and I was to be greatly indebted to her, not least of all for the fact that we together managed the transition to our new responsibilities without any of the embarrassing mistakes that might reasonably have been anticipated.

That pressing issue taken care of, I immediately had to turn to the question of who was to take over (from me) the direction of our nascent Oxford program. At about two-thirds of the way through getting it organized and with the first batch of students to go there already chosen, I clearly had to move quickly if the program was to be launched, as planned, at the beginning of the upcoming Michaelmas (or autumn) term. As this was a new venture, the new incumbent should preferably be someone who had had senior administrative experience at Williams and could deal comfortably and credibly with his opposite numbers at Oxford. Having talked over the matter, John Chandler and I decided to approach Dan O'Connor, still at that time dean of the college but approaching the end of his term of service. Happily, though he was not familiar with the Oxford scene, he accepted the challenge with alacrity and was to meet it with great finesse. In order to orient him to the task, I took a quick trip with him to Oxford, along with his wife, Mary, and Win Wassenar, director of buildings and grounds. While Win and Mary went to London to pick out furnishings for the building on Moreton Road that we were remodeling as the director's residence, I took Dan around Oxford to introduce him to the pertinent people at the university with whom he would be dealing and went over with him what I had already done to organize the program and to assemble a cadre of tutors for its first year of operation. Completing that effort by October and settling students into quarters that were barely ready was to pose some testing challenges for him. But he met those challenges admirably and, to the astonishment of our colleagues at Exeter, we were able to launch the program successfully at the beginning of Michaelmas term, less than eight months after taking over the buildings and making a start on the thoroughgoing renovations that were called for. It was very much a success story.

But with Dan's heading out to Oxford, we had then to find a replacement for him as dean of the college in time for the upcoming academic year—which meant, at Williams, dean of students. The growing complexity of student life had made it increasing difficult to recruit faculty members for that role. Fortunately, I knew the faculty as a whole very well, and I was personally acquainted with all of the more credible candidates for the position. In what I view as one of my two best senior personnel decisions (it wasn't hard to make), I settled upon Steve (Stephen F.) Fix, a twenty-nine-year-old associate professor of English who had graduated *summa cum laude* from Boston College, where he had been president of the College Council and a student member of the board of trustees. For six long and (I can only assume) exhausting years for him, he proved to be a firm, wonderfully judicious, creative, and much-admired dean, with whom I was privileged to work closely under truly challenging conditions marked by complex racial tensions and recurrent student unrest. And the transition in the dean's office was helped by the willingness of Bob (Robert D.) Kavanaugh, associate dean and dean of freshmen, to stay on for a couple of years and serve under a dean who was younger than he was and junior to him in professorial rank. They made an excellent team and Bob's willingness to stay in his role was, I think, a fine example of the type of college citizenship characteristic of the Williams faculty of that era.

With that issue taken care of, I had then to face up to what to do about the college's Development Office, which was something of a crucial issue in the light of the forthcoming capital campaign. But that was an issue I was unable to resolve until the end of June, just before I took up the reins of the presidency. And in resolving it I was to make the second of my two best senior administrative appointments. I had come to the conclusion that the Development Office was not in particularly good shape. It was not well organized and struck me as having too many competing colonels and not enough willing foot soldiers. That view, I sensed, had been shared by an alumni development council that the previous director had formed, and that committee had also recommended that the Alumni Relations and Development Offices be brought under a single administrative umbrella. That recommendation John Chandler had accepted and he had brought the two functions together under the interim leadership of Jim (James R.) Briggs, a prominent alumnus and our baseball coach. Jim had agreed, out of loyalty and the goodness of his heart, to take on the assignment for a year. Anticipating the likelihood of a capital campaign, he had done some yeoman work during that year, setting up, across the country, sessions to assess the giving capacity of fellow alumni judged likely to be significant donors. Jim carried the title of executive director of alumni relations and development, which he thought, from the development point of view, was unhelpfully ambiguous, and he strongly recommended that his successor should carry the title of vice president.

That piece of advice I took to heart, so it was for such a vice president that we launched a search. We did so with the help of a consultant from Heidrich and Struggles who, being himself an alumnus, was well acquainted with the college. After he had taken the institutional pulse and familiarized himself with the prevailing state of affairs in the Development Office, he conveyed to me his strong sense that, rather than pursuing an external search, we would do well to focus on possible internal candidates, though not necessarily those involving people already in the office who had thrown their hats into the ring. The spotlight came quickly to focus, perhaps counterintuitively, not on a development professional but on a faculty member, and I opted to go in that direction. So I was led to approach my old friend and colleague Hodge (J. Hodge) Markgraf (Williams class of 1952), a fine teacher and active research scholar in organic chemistry who had previously served the college admirably in multiple capacities, from chairman of his department to three years as provost. He proved willing to consider taking on the assignment though he recognized that it would involve a move away from teaching and a fairly dramatic career shift for him. He thought long and hard, then, before signing on, asking only if I could provide him with some modest funding so that he could maintain his research lab and continue to work with senior thesis students. I was happy to oblige and also to reassure him that we would be creating a director of development position that would report to him and that it would be his first task to launch a search in order to fill that position. While he was totally confident about the alumni relations aspect of his new responsibilities, he felt he had a great deal to learn about development. In the event, he proved to be a quick learner and worked in colleagueship with Mike (Michael) Oman, a development professional who had worked in the Stanford Development Office and whom we appointed early in the fall of 1985 to fill the director's position, an assignment which he was to take on with great skill. Mike's strengths as a development officer lay on the

organizational (rather than the relational) side of development work, and
those strengths, which we badly needed, turned out to be formidable. He
was a down-to-earth Kansan, possessed of a fund of commonsense hid-
den behind a great stone face that could be disconcertingly hard to read.
Because of that, I tried to avoid looking at him if he was in the audience
when I was giving a speech. Once, however, when at some development
occasion I had given what I thought of as a rousing address, he actually
came up to me and said: "Frank, that wasn't bad." Coming from him,
that was flattery indeed and I dined out on it for at least a week!

Hodge signed on to his new position by the end of June 1985 and, so
far as administrative officers were concerned, I was able to turn my attention to the task of making sure that appropriate efforts were underway to identify suitable candidates for the other positions that were
already open or would soon be opening. In those efforts I was less immediately and personally involved than I had been with filling the most
senior positions, though I did keep a particularly close eye on the recruitment of a new comptroller. The comptroller reported to the treasurer,
Will Reed, and Will had shared with me the fact that he had developed
serious concerns about the current quality of the office and that he was
anxious to see the whole operation reorganized and upgraded. With an
operating budget standing at about $60 million, we clearly needed an
experienced professional with more than the comparatively local experience possessed by those who had previously filled the position and we
also needed to retain the services of an auditing firm with more than regional standing. Will and I both felt a good deal more secure when, in
the course of the 1985–86 academic year, we were able to install Saeed
Mughal as comptroller, an experienced professional of Pakistani origin
who, having reorganized the office, proved adept at training his staff to
his own high standards and was quick to recommend that we replace our
local auditing firm with Coopers and Lybrand, which had a first-rate department dedicated especially to the auditing needs of institutions in the
world of higher education.

While it was well into the 1985–86 academic year before we had the
positions of director of development, comptroller, and registrar filled, as
well as the other positions in personnel (human resources) and alumni
relations, the small group of senior administrators was happily in place
by the time I took over the presidency on July 1, 1985. Including me, there

were just six of us, the others being the dean of the faculty, dean of the college, provost, vice president for administration and treasurer, and the new vice president for alumni relations and development. That was my team. Known as the President's Executive Group, it was composed of a first-rate group of colleagues to whom I was warmly attached and came to be deeply indebted. As dean of the faculty I had been a member of the previous senior staff group which, for complex historical reasons, had become too large and too varied in composition, as it had included, along with the senior administrators, such middle management figures as the directors of admissions, of alumni relations, and of buildings and grounds. My own take on that predecessor grouping had been a rather critical one. It had clearly become too large and too varied in composition to be able to function effectively as a policy-making group and had come to serve, in effect, as little more than a "show and tell" operation. So I had determined to get rid of it, substituting for it the smaller President's Executive Group, which met weekly every Monday morning, and a much larger President's Administrative Group, which met monthly with all the senior administrators in attendance, and over which I also presided. The President's Administrative Group included the full range of middle managers who had previously, so far as I could make out, never considered themselves as a distinct, coherent group. The group was too big to function effectively in general as a policy group, though it did prove to be a valuable sounding board for proposed new departures and it played a significant role, for example, in the framing of a policy on AIDS and of campus-wide regulations concerning smoking. But it proved most effective, I think, in its "show and tell" functioning. I wanted to break down the comparative isolation of the various functions these managers supervised. I wanted, for example, admissions and alumni relations to have a decent sense of the challenges that career counseling was confronting, and the Comptroller's Office to be aware of the needs of the Development Office or the Office of Financial Aid. So, across the years and in turn, I had each of the managers make a presentation to the group as a whole concerning the responsibilities of his or her office and the problems that that office characteristically faced. Those presentations sometimes (though by no means always) stimulated lively and occasionally edgy exchanges. They were helpful to me, too, and I took the opportunity from time to time to follow up with a particular manager on issues that had surfaced after his or her presentation. For a while, I tried out a similar tactic at our monthly faculty meetings during the fall semesters when the agenda tended to be light, having one or another of our middle managers make a brief presentation on his or her operation. But while the managers themselves took the assignment very seriously, the faculty by and large did not. Presentations made by the directors of admissions and financial aid seemed to be of general interest. The rest, however, or so I quickly sensed, tended to be dismissed as "more time devoted to administrative-speak," and I was (rather naively, I suppose) taken aback by the lack of interest evinced by my faculty colleagues in the operation and functioning of the college as a whole (outside of its academic dimension). Apart from reports on admissions and financial aid, then, I gradually backed away from the practice of having the managers report with any regularity at faculty meetings.

So far as I could make out, Jack Sawyer had interacted with his senior administrative colleagues very much on a one-to-one, bilateral basis, so that one senior administrator might not be privy to some important issue that another might have been drawn into. And John Chandler, though less consistently so and to a less marked degree, had tended to follow that same pattern. That I wanted to change. Tending, by administrative temperament, to favor the participatory-collegial rather than the top-down hierarchical mode, I was determined to share as many of the policy issues confronting me as possible with the top five senior administrators who reported directly to me. And I also wanted each of them to be well aware of the problems with which the other four were having to grapple. On the last couple of days, then, before I had to pick up the reins of the presidency, I initiated a practice that I was to maintain on an annual basis throughout my time in office. I took them all off campus to a quiet Vermont resort for a planning retreat involving a series of quite intense working sessions punctuated, on our two evenings away, by purely social and enjoyable downtime over drinks and dinner. To that central group I added David Booth, our vice provost, who was very experienced, deeply thoughtful, and unusually insightful on matters institutional. Somewhat later, I also added to the group Nancy McIntire, who had succeeded Judy Allen as assistant to the president for affirmative action and government relations. In preparation for the retreat, I had asked everyone to submit any issues they thought needed discussion and attention and then, having folded in the matters I myself thought were pressing, put together an agenda along with all the pertinent documentation we might need to consult during our deliberations.

That agenda, a dauntingly formidable one, was broken down into sections: Administrative (Internal), Administrative (External), Students, Faculty, Physical Plant, and Other, and it was to provide the template for the agendas of our retreats in subsequent years. At the end of the 1985–86 academic year, moreover, I went over the action items stemming from that first retreat and created what I called an *Administrative Scorecard*. This indicated the items that had been disposed of satisfactorily, those that were still in process, as well as the small, residual group of issues in relation to which we could really claim to have done no more than engage in a handwringing exercise. I updated that *Scorecard* each year during my term of service, circulating it to the group along with the agendas for our upcoming off-campus retreats and sending a copy also to the chairman of the board's Executive Committee so that he could see what we had been up to and how we ourselves judged the success or failure of our efforts.

That first round of deliberations in the summer of 1985 went well and proved to be enormously helpful to me both immediately and in the long haul. Out of it came two sets of practices that we instituted in the fall of 1985 and made routine throughout my presidency. The first, which I am pretty sure was Steve Fix's idea, was to hold separate meetings in the fall just before the beginning of classes, not just as heretofore for the freshman class but for all four classes, and to tailor the topics to be addressed and the people to do the talking to the specific needs of the class in question, though the dean of the college and I would address all four. It gave us the opportunity before the academic year got underway to share what was on our minds directly with the students. And while, after the initial novelty wore off, it did not work as well with the sophomore and junior classes (whose members were now somewhat blasé and less likely to be faithful in their attendance), with the seniors no less than the freshmen it was really quite successful. The second innovation was the practice whereby the dean of the college, the dean of the faculty, the provost, and I would go each month during the academic year to one or other of the various residential houses in turn, have dinner with the students, and then make ourselves available after dinner to the members of the house in question—in open forum and without fixed agenda. Those visits, which we kept up month after month for the better part of nine years, constituted a basically proactive effort to make ourselves available to the student body. Again, once the novelty had worn off, those sessions were to be uneven in quality. We sometimes seemed destined to spend our time fielding questions concerning campus parking, the room allocation system, the vomit level at the house in question after the last weekend party, and even (from one or another buttoned-down aspirant to future hedge fund management) the performance of the college's investment portfolio. But, as is the case with one's teenage children, "quality time" isn't something that can be planned or programmed. One simply has to make oneself routinely available and every so often it will happen, quite serendipitously and, sometimes, quite movingly. Across the years all sorts of issues came up at those monthly sessions, from the crassly mundane to the highly intellectual. But at the most probing and moving sessions, the most intense interest tended to circle around racial and gender issues, matters of sexual identity, and somewhat querulous ruminations about relations with adults in general.

With reference to that last issue, one such session towards the end of my presidency in the early 1990s left us as administrators sitting around wondering what on earth, if anything, we would be able to do to ameliorate the yearning that had been expressed so touchingly and at such length. For what had been reflected in the discussion was the growing fallout from what has been called "the culture of neglect," the comparative absence from the earlier lives of the more recent cohorts of students of "authentic connection with adults." Students of that generation (early 1990s) struck me as having had somewhat less of a shaping, adult presence in their pre-collegiate lives than any I could remember in my own thirty years and more of teaching and administration. After a quarter of a century's interval during which their persistent tendency had been to distance themselves from adult involvement in their cocurricular lives, students were now, as we had discovered that evening, beginning to signal, and in ways no less compelling for being quite so self-absorbed, an inchoate yearning for an enhanced measure of adult guidance or, at least, presence. And they were doing so, alas, at a time when faculty, struggling to cope with the countervailing demands imposed by dual careers and the need to juggle far more complicated personal and professional lives than had their predecessors, were understandably finding it harder to maintain as much of a presence in the cocurricular and residential life of the campus. At the end of that evening we were left, then, with a good deal of discouraging food for thought.

With the principal administrative appointments made and searches underway to deal with the next tier of openings, and with the various routines I have described now firmly in place, I was able to turn my attention fairly early in the 1985–86 academic year to initiatives of a different kind.

Though it didn't lend itself to a quick resolution, I was at least able to make a start with the business of trying to sort out what had emerged for one reason or another as a worrying pileup of pending departures from the board of trustees at about the same time, a wave of departures which, if not spread out, would result in an undesirable discontinuity and loss of institutional memory within that very important group. For help in sorting out this tangle I am much indebted to a small and informal advisory group of senior trustees who arranged for some of their colleagues to step down before the scheduled ending of their terms and for others to stay a little longer. It is testimony to his loyalty and civic spirit that Pete Parish set the example by himself leading the early departures. That meant, of course, that his successor as chairman of the Executive Committee (senior trustee) had to be chosen and that task fell to me. There had been a tendency to allow that important choice to be determined simply by seniority of service on the board. That was clearly not a desirable way of going about things and I was able to avoid prolonging it by virtue of the fact that previous tinkering with terms of service had made it impossible to determine with any degree of certainty who could credibly lay claim to being the trustee senior to the rest. My solution to the issue was shaped in part by my sense (right or wrong) that people from the world of finance can be a bit too theoretical and lawyers too like academics in their inclination to postpone decisions. What we needed, or so I thought, was a chief executive type who was comfortable with making decisions while knowing that he could be wrong but recognizing, too, that no decision was itself a form of decision. So I turned to Pete (Peter S.) Willmott (class of 1959), an experienced and accomplished executive from the business world. At that time he was CEO of Carson

Pirie Scott in Chicago. He had already acceded to my request that he take on the national chairmanship of our upcoming Third Century Campaign, but, being a very devoted college citizen, that did not prevent his cheerfully saying "yes" to this added burden. I was to work most amicably with him in both those capacities and over the years our colleagueship was to deepen into a warm friendship. I feel very lucky to have had the opportunity to work so closely with him and for so long, not only at Williams but also, after that, at the Sterling and Francine Clark Art Institute where he was to succeed me as president (i.e., chairman) of the board and, with great conscientiousness, to see the Institute through to the triumphant conclusion of a truly major expansion project for which planning had begun already in the late 1990s. Pete is not only a thoughtful, conscientious, and hardworking person, he is also a kindly fellow and one possessed of a good sense of humor. As a result, while together discharging our responsibilities with an appropriate measure of seriousness, we also managed in the process to enjoy ourselves. We made, I think, a pretty good team.

At the first faculty meeting over which I presided as president (in September 1985) I said to my colleagues that I thought I had about three years during which I could focus on matters internal to the college in fairly uninterrupted fashion before the demands of the upcoming capital campaign would begin to to take over my time in a marked degree. In the event, it turned out to be more like two-and-a-half years and even during those years I needed to attend to normal non-development-connected alumni relations, visiting some twenty-one alumni chapters across the country and in England during the course of my first year in office, and doing likewise during my second. But my central focus as I said then and later, perhaps with a degree of tiresome insistence, was to make sure, before we set out to seek the very large gifts we were likely to be asking for, that we could honestly represent ourselves as a vibrant, imaginative, energetic, efficient enterprise that knew what it was about, had some vision for the future, and was responsive in what it did to that vision. So we had a lot to do and, in that effort, had made by 1988, or so I believe, significant progress.

Presidents tend to be given the credit for anything good that happens on their watch, even, classically, for an increase in the size of their institution's endowment. During my term of office, the Williams endowment more than doubled (at least in nominal dollars), and it reached almost $450 million by the time I stepped down. But apart from prudent, endowment-preserving budgetary policies and any increases stemming from the payment of campaign pledges, I can claim little or no credit for that doubling. That credit, instead, lay with market conditions, the success of the portfolio managers in navigating market crosscurrents, and the care with which the Trustee Finance Committee (led very ably by Charlie (Charles H.) Mott, class of 1953) had succeeded in monitoring and managing those managers. Of course, on the other hand, presidents tend also to be blamed for whatever goes wrong on their watch, even if it reflects external social, political, or macroeconomic developments, or even, simply, the malign deliverances of fortune. So there may be some rough justice in the customary apportioning of praise and blame.

In general, however, it should properly be acknowledged, and especially so if the president's characteristic administrative style is participatory and collegial (as was mine), that most collegiate initiatives emerge from a richly consultative matrix and no one person can usually claim any sort of overriding authorial credit for them. That said, of course, there may be a few that are purely presidential in conception and implementation alike. Similarly, there may well be others that would never have got off the ground, let alone reached implementation, had not the president made the ideas involved his own and thrown his full weight behind them.

In my own case, an example of the former would be the establishment of the residential Gaius Charles Bolin Fellowships for minority graduate students at the dissertation phase of their training. As dean of the faculty, I had become acutely conscious of the difficulties we were confronting in our efforts to recruit minority and especially African American faculty. Blacks and Hispanics constituted less than 3 percent of the PhD candidate pool in the arts and sciences subjects taught at Williams. Minority recruitment, moreover, was in the process of becoming even tougher. Over the previous decade, the number of blacks graduating with PhDs had dropped by no less than 27 percent. In some of the subjects we offered, moreover, the numbers were miniscule. In one year during the 1980s, for example, only four African Americans nationwide graduated with PhDs in mathematics. My idea, then, and I note now that

I had cleared it with the trustees while I was still president-elect, was to underline the importance Williams attached to the recruitment of able minority students into the academic profession by establishing fellowships that would bring into residence each year at the college a couple of minority graduate students who, while teaching at least one course (and thereby adding a little to the minority faculty presence in our classrooms), would devote the bulk of their time during the year to the completion of their dissertation work. It had been exactly a hundred years since Gaius Charles Bolin, our first black student, had matriculated at Williams, and given the fact that his grandson, Lionel Bolin, had just been elected as an alumni trustee, I sought the permission from the Bolin family to name these new awards as the Gaius Charles Bolin Fellowships. At my induction in October, then, with Lionel Bolin present on the stage, I was able to announce their establishment. These fellowships, which carried comparatively generous stipends, turned out to be hotly competed for and to attract first-rate candidates, most of whom (though in the first half dozen years we were able to appoint two of them to our own faculty) went on to fine faculty positions at places like Harvard, Yale, Stanford, Brown, and the Universities of Chicago, Pennsylvania, and Michigan. And, as a further manifestation of our commitment to encouraging minority entry into the academic profession, we were soon able, with foundation support, to add summer research awards and special mentoring to some of undergraduates who aspired to academic careers.

The prime instance of the latter sort of initiative—the sort that would probably not have made it off the ground without vigorous presidential support—was the college's decision to build a Jewish Religious Center at the very center of campus and (ironically) cheek by jowl with the former fraternity houses situated on what had once been called Fraternity Row. By the time I became president in 1985, what we as a college were doing, or failing to do, to meet the changing needs of our Jewish students was beginning to come into focus. Three interrelated issues were calling for action. First, it was becoming clear that the level of religious observance among our Jewish student population was rising and that the old Kuskin Room which had been used for that purpose was becoming a good deal less than adequate. Second, the symbolism involved in locating Jewish worship space in what was, in effect, the basement of an admittedly nondenominational but still essentially Christian chapel was, to say the least, unfortunate. Third, the efforts of the Office of Admission notwithstanding, Williams was not succeeding in drawing its appropriate share of gifted Jewish students from the leading high schools of the greater New York area. We were not alone in that. So far as the percentages of Jewish students at the various colleges went, it was as if a dividing line ran between the more northerly and more southerly of the highly selective colleges in the Northeast. That the dividing line should run between Williams and Amherst, leaving us unhappily on the northerly side of the divide, strongly suggested the persistence in the greater New York area (perhaps also in other metropolitan areas) of the unfortunate perception that Williams was the sort of place at which Jewish students might well feel uncomfortable. That that had once been the case was not in doubt. My conversations with older Jewish alumni from the fraternity era made that quite clear. That it was still the case in 1985 was a good deal less clear to me. But off-campus perceptions appeared still to be trumping on-campus realities and it was clear to me that the college really needed to respond without delay or foot-dragging to the three interrelated issues that were already on the table.

Being too small a campus to attract the attention of Hillel, I concluded that we were called upon to make the appropriate response ourselves, and that meant building our own Jewish Religious Center. And, with warm support from students, faculty, trustees, and alumni, that is precisely what we did. We quickly made the funding of the project one of the goals for the upcoming capital drive; we also moved ahead with a minimum of delay so that we were able to dedicate the building at a wonderful service in October 1990. To get to that point, however, some misgivings had to be overcome among our Jewish alumni and trustees. Some of our oldest alumni fretted that such a building might draw unwelcome, negative attention to the Jewish presence at Williams—a sad reminder of the darker side of the Williams of yesteryear. Others, somewhat younger, had to be convinced that what we had in mind was not something akin to a Jewish fraternity. To the idea of establishing such a fraternity, which had surfaced during their own undergraduate years, they had been staunchly opposed. And that same concern was reflected in the misgivings initially expressed by more than one of the Jewish members of the board of trustees. Those misgivings had to be assuaged by the firm insistence that what was envisaged was, rather, a religious building. That done, the entire board rallied to the support of the project. As we moved ahead with it, I was to rely heavily on Alan Berg, our Jewish chaplain, Beth Raffeld, later to be director of major gifts in our Development Office, and Peter Berek, a former dean of the college who was at that point special assistant to the president and was later to become dean of the faculty at Mount Holyoke College. Off campus, we benefitted greatly from the strongly supportive leadership of Edgar Bronfman, class of 1950, and Norman Redlich, class of 1947, with the latter undertaking to chair the pertinent fundraising committee.

For me, personally, this whole project was a wonderfully fulfilling venture, and I am left with vivid memories of the warmly emotional gathering that was called late in 1988 at the Harmonie Club in New York in order to get the effort underway. Accompanied on that occasion by Claire-Ann and two of my four children (then working in New York), and having acknowledged the dark strand of anti-Semitism woven into the older history of the college, I was moved to say that as a child I had been taught in my own religious tradition that a sacrament was an outward sign of inward grace, and that I regarded the building of our Jewish Religious Center as a sacramental moment in the college's history. It was, I believed, an outward sign of the inward grace that should surely inform our community, the grace of reconciliation, mutual respect, and grateful appreciation of the richness that our mutually various heritages bring to all of us. I meant what I said then and, thirty years later, I still mean it.

During my term of presidential service there was only one other moment when I was conscious of having to cope with real misgivings on the part of some of the trustees concerning a course of action I was intent on pursuing. But in that case, the misgivings went somewhat deeper and were not, I think, unwarranted. They concerned the college's public leadership of the effort to create a huge museum of contemporary art in the sprawling complex of empty nineteenth-century factory buildings once occupied by the Sprague Electric Company and situated at the very heart of North Adams, the old mill town about five miles to the east of Williamstown. Rereading the minutes of trustee meetings from that time, I see that such misgivings, though not expressed in a hard-edged way, surfaced repeatedly during the years from 1986 to the fall of 1988, at which time the college's direct involvement in the project came to an end. At that point, the entire work product from the extensive planning done over the two years preceding by staff members of the Williams College Museum of Art (WCMA) was handed over to the MASS MoCA Cultural Development Commission, a newly created public arm of the City of North Adams which was to be the recipient of initial state funding, was to be charged with launching the feasibility study (the precondition for any further state funding) for the subsequent rehabilitation of the physical plant, and was to oversee the planning and development of the proposed museum itself. At that point, moreover, the connection with Williams, however close it was to remain, became basically a personal and informal one. I served on the commission (until 2007, in fact), but simply as a citizen, not as a college representative. In 1993 I also became a member of the newly established board of the MASS MoCA Foundation (a private rather than a public entity), which was to function as the board of the museum itself, and in that capacity I co-chaired the Founders' Fund Campaign to raise bridge funding to facilitate the actual opening of the museum in 1999 and to see it through its first couple of years in operation. All of this was to leave me with a somewhat rueful insight into the ups and downs, roller-coaster turbulence, and alternation between exhilaration and despair that tend to dog large-scale start-up ventures of this sort.

From the beginning, some members of the Williams board had shared my excitement about the new venture, about the promise it held for complementing the strengths of the Williams College Museum of Art and of the Sterling and Francine Clark Art Institute, as well as about the opportunities it would open up for our students in art and its potential for enhancing still further the traditional importance attached to the visual arts at Williams. The hope, too, was that the project would have a beneficial economic impact upon North Adams, at that time still reeling under the impact of Sprague Electric's departure from the area and the concomitant deindustrialization of the city. At its peak in the 1960s, Sprague Electric had employed more than four thousand workers in North Adams. By 1985 that number had dropped substantially, the city was losing population, and the unemployment rate there, and in the northern Berkshires at large, was running well ahead of the national average. In response, Governor Dukakis had formed a Governor's Task

Force on Economic Development in the region. That task force had already issued a report acknowledging that the area would now have to face up to negotiating the difficult transition from a local economy based on manufacturing to one based more on service and oriented to tourism. Both Will Reed, our treasurer, and Neil Grabois, our provost, had served on that task force, and we were all acutely conscious of the difficulties confronting the region. Seeing the MASS MoCA project, then, as a potential contributor not only to the cultural life of the area but also, via construction work and cultural tourism, to its economic well-being, I also saw the project as a natural extension of our involvement as a "good neighbor" in the governor's efforts at economic revitalization.

But while they were not prone to denying the propriety of that involvement, some other members of the Williams board couldn't help being worried about its potential downside and on more than one ground. First, they were concerned that involvement in the project "could drain the time and energy of the president and administration." Second, should it go sour, the project could harm the reputation of the college. Third, the project could conceivably put the college's own financial resources at risk. If state funding proved not to be forthcoming, would not people in the region, thinking that the college had deep pockets, turn to it in expectation of financial support? In retrospect, I would judge none of these concerns to be unreasonable ones. While, at the time, I brushed the first to one side, I did not dismiss the other two out of hand and, from time to time, lost a bit of sleep worrying about them. But I still thought that our involvement was appropriate and worthwhile and, on balance though in slightly uneasy fashion, the board concurred.

I believe that it was early in 1986 that Tom Krens first raised the MASS MoCA issue directly with me. We were driving on one of our bi-annual pilgrimages down to Westport, Connecticut, to see Eugénie Prendergast, who had emerged as something more than a potential donor of great significance to the college's museum. From her late husband, Charles, she had taken over the devoted stewardship of the extensive oeuvre of his older brother Maurice Prendergast, the Canadian/American Postimpressionist, and she had lost no opportunity to promote his artistic reputation. Warren Adelson, founder of the Adelson Gallery in New York, once described her, indeed, as Prendergast's "one-woman marketing machine." By 1986 she was in the process of donating so many Prendergasts to the Williams College Museum of Art (WCMA), of which Tom Krens was currently the director, that it was to end up as the largest repository in the country of works by the two brothers (over four hundred, in fact, along with archival objects numbering around fifteen hundred). She had also provided most of the funding for a Prendergast catalogue raisonné project and had supported the addition of a Prendergast wing to WCMA. Eventually, indeed, she was to leave much of her estate to support exhibitions and research grounded in the collection. She was a very demanding and interesting person, a generous donor who warranted careful attention—hence our regular visits.

After driving down, a trip of about three-and-a-half hours, we would usually assemble, along with Mrs. Prendergast's advisory group (who always seemed rather suspicious of Tom), around her kitchen table. Tom would deliver his progress report, replete with formidable sets of spreadsheets, and Eugénie, a very strong and direct (though not unkindly) person, would then give him a hard time on one point or another for about half an hour, leaving him in appropriately (but uncharacteristically) bruised condition. That mission satisfactorily accomplished, she would then click into party mood, producing a couple of bottles of champagne along with repulsively bloated orange crunchies picked up at some convenience store, and, sitting around that kitchen table for what seemed like hours, we would become part of her social life. She was, I think, a rather lonely person who clearly enjoyed regaling us with anecdotes about the art dealers, critics, art historians, and collectors she had encountered during long years of immersion in the New York art world. It was fascinating stuff, as she seemed to have become acquainted with everyone in that world. Tom and I rarely had enough time to get any lunch, had a long drive ahead of us, and really needed to be on our way. But that did not prove to be easy; she never wanted to let us go. During those visits, as well as during her visits to Williamstown, I got to know her quite well and to like her. She was delighted to see that we had a Prendergast hanging in the grand living room of the President's House. And, being herself in her day a very fine cook, she recognized in Claire-Ann a fellow "foodie" and insisted on presenting her with her own annotated copy of *Larousse gastronomique*.

On the occasion in question, as we were driving down to see the formidable Eugénie, the issue that Tom raised had no connection with

Prendergastiana. He mentioned that he had recently been in Schaffhausen in Switzerland. With that, my ears pricked up. For me, it was the
place where, in 1415, the Emperor Sigismund's soldiers had captured (the
first) Pope John XXIII, a questionable figure who, by fleeing it, had tried
to bring the historic Council of Constance to an end, fearing, not without
reason, that it was about to force him to relinquish his high office. But
such historical memories were far from what was on Tom's mind. What
he wanted to talk about was the old factory building he had seen in
Schaffhausen that had been cleverly converted into a museum for contemporary art, not unlike, or so I imagined, the Temporary Contemporary then functioning in Los Angeles prior to the opening of the new Los
Angeles Museum of Contemporary Art. It had suggested to him that it
might be possible to do something similar but grander with the abandoned Sprague Electric complex of old factory buildings in North Adams.
In those huge spaces, appropriately remodeled and refurbished, it would
be possible (he thought) to exhibit the sort of gargantuan works of contemporary art that tended to dwarf traditional museum galleries. Vast
sculptures, for example, like those of Joseph Beuys, that would have to
be permitted to rise up through two floors of a traditional gallery. About
that possibility he waxed eloquent. What he needed from me, and he was
very proper about it, was permission to spend time on the project and to
have his young assistants—prominent among them Joe (Joseph) Thompson, who was to become the first director of MASS MoCA, and Michael
Govan, now director of the Los Angeles County Museum of Art—devote
a good deal of their time to drawing up the conceptual plans for the sort
of museum he envisaged. He also needed permission, and it was the important point, to use the name of the college in promoting the venture.

The idea was an intriguing one, Tom was very persuasive, and,
having given him the permission he sought, I, along with Will Reed,
was to become very involved in the great effort to promote and facilitate
the project. My own role was basically twofold. On the public relations
level it was that of putting a credible institutional face on what might
easily have been dismissed as one man's far-fetched pipe dream. After
all, even in the wake of the state legislature's voting in favor of some $35
million for capital costs associated with the project, the *Berkshire Eagle*
was still labeling it as "a long shot" and "imaginative madness." On the
more practical level, I used my official position to gain access for Tom

to the pertinent legislative leaders and went down with him to the State House in Boston so that I could introduce him and his case to George Kevarian, Speaker of the Massachusetts House of Representatives, to William ("Billy") Bulger, Senate President, and, I believe, to the chair of the House Ways and Means Committee. Similarly, I went with him and Will Reed to meet with Edward Kosnik, president and CEO of Sprague Technologies (basically a holding company), which owned the derelict Sprague factory buildings. At that meeting we explored with him the possibility of the company's donating those buildings to the putative MASS MoCA. Not quite chutzpah on our part as they almost certainly could not sell them and were clearly disinclined to spend the rather large sums of money that demolition would call for. I also made myself available to introduce Tom at various press conferences and to the editorial group at the *Berkshire Eagle*, the members of which, viewing him, it seemed, as some sort of snake oil salesman, gave the case he made for the project a surprisingly hostile reception.

But, as subsequent events were to prove, he was right and they were wrong. As I drive through North Adams today and past what is now a thriving artistic enterprise and perhaps the largest museum of contemporary art in the country, I can't help imagining the dismal picture that that sprawling complex of derelict and decaying factory buildings would have presented today, after thirty years of progressive deterioration, had not the project been realized. It would, I think, have looked like a set of ugly, decaying teeth dominating the center of the town and signaling to all who passed by the sad story of its decline and fall. So I remain very proud of the role that Williams and its people played in dreaming what seemed like an impossible dream and transforming that dream into a vibrant reality. At the same time, I have to confess that, at least in retrospect, the whole great effort strikes me as a rather delicate and risky enterprise for a small college to be caught up in. And not only in retrospect. I know that I was mightily relieved when the legislature voted in the funding needed to get the project off the ground. And relieved still more when the responsibility for managing the whole project and seeing it through to completion was finally lifted from our collegiate shoulders and assigned to the sort of public entity to which it more properly belonged.

The final, cliff-hanging maneuvers leading up to that happy outcome were quite dramatic and are worthy of mention. As we headed into the Christmas of 1987, we were informed, to our dismay, that during the legislative session that was now drawing to a conclusion, the legislators had failed to pass the Convention Centers Bill in which the putative funding of the MASS MoCA project had been embedded. The general sense was that the project was now doomed and I issued a press release indicating that the college's role in the matter was now ended and that we would be turning our attention to other things. In a parallel press release, Kosnik said that the offer to donate the buildings was now off the table and that Sprague Technologies would put them up for sale on the market. Neither of those eventualities came to pass. Almost immediately thereafter, I received a telephone call at home from Governor Dukakis asking me to prolong the college's commitment for a short time to permit him to introduce special legislation providing for the $35 million to defray MASS MoCA's capital costs. Tom Krens was the recipient of a similar call and was given the impression that this new, precisely targeted bill almost certainly would pass. It did, and the subsequent establishment of the MASS MoCA Cultural Development Commission, which would receive and be responsible for managing that funding, made it possible for us to begin the process of bringing the college's institutional role in the project to an end. Our last contribution, a modest financial one, was that of keeping Joe Thompson and his small planning team on the college's payroll until the state funding actually began to flow later on in the year. For with the departure of Tom Krens in July 1988 to become director of the Guggenheim Museum in New York, his formal role in the project was henceforth limited to that of serving for a few years as chairman of the commission. It was Joe who, as executive and as an employee of the Cultural Development Commission, was to direct the effort and he was to emerge very much as the hero of the whole start-up story, pursuing the elusive goal with courage, tenacity, optimism, and great steadiness of purpose through all the disconcerting ups and downs experienced across the following decade until the museum triumphantly opened its doors in 1999.

While the whole MASS MoCA saga was unfolding between 1986 and 1988, a lot of other new departures, these more central to its mission, were occurring at Williams. And I am struck, as I go over the record some thirty years later, by how very busy and lively a phase in the history of the college it seems to have been. Thus the faculty voted in a program of freshman residential seminars and finally acceded (somewhat nervously) to legislation making the use of the student course evaluation survey mandatory for every course taught at the college. For the previous quarter of a century it had been used on a purely voluntary basis, which had made it difficult to come up with reliable comparative data. Around the same time, Darra Goldstein of the German and Russian Department somehow coaxed into existence an interesting student exchange program with the University of Tbilisi in Soviet Georgia, whereby groups of students from both institutions would undertake two-week visits to each other's campuses. It was, she proudly proclaimed, "the first known direct contact between a Soviet university and an American liberal arts college." When the first group of Tbilisi students visited Williams, they turned out to be a rather sophisticated and (judging by their stylish and mainly Italian clothing) a rather privileged lot. They were also a bit older than our students and we were able, accordingly, to serve them white wine at a rather jolly welcoming reception at the President's House. But their KGB "minder," an older, rather tired fellow whom they seemed to view with amused disdain and who was clearly counting the days to retirement, asked if he could have a glass of Scotch and then settled into what promised to be an evening of heavy-duty consumption. Later on in the comparatively short life of this program, and at a time of marked civil unrest in the (now independent) state of Georgia, I was to receive a surprisingly personal letter from Eduard Shevardnadze, once the powerful Soviet Minister of Foreign Affairs under Mikhail Gorbachev and, at the time I received his letter, president of his native Georgia, apologizing for having had to cancel the upcoming visit of a group of our students because of concern about their safety.

During those same years, I was able to initiate (in the fall of 1986), with help of a grant from the Mellon Foundation, the bringing together of all our second-year faculty in a seminar presided over by a senior faculty mentor and to give them released time from one course to encourage their active participation. The idea was to help them, after their years at graduate school in large research universities, to adjust to the demands of teaching at a small liberal arts college and to acquaint them with the real opportunities their new institutional setting could afford them. In 1987, a generous grant from the Pew Foundation, for which we had been invited to compete and for which Bruce Kieffer of the German and Russian Department had written a successful proposal, also enabled me to bring the foreign language and literature departments together in loose affiliation with a newly established Center for Foreign Languages, Literatures, and Cultures. This center was equipped with a new, state-of-the-art language laboratory, was allotted adequate funding to bring in distinguished visiting speakers, and was presided over by a director of scholarly stature recruited at the senior level from the outside. My hope was to break down the comparative isolation of a series of small departments and to encourage them to participate across departmental lines in a somewhat larger intellectual community. Though I gather that the center has enjoyed across the years a modest degree of success, I don't believe that my own initial hopes were ever fully realized. The differences of interest and concern among the various language groupings were to have a persistently centrifugal effect, and at Williams, as elsewhere, the Romance Language Department (or, more accurately, its French wing) proved to be the rock on which the efforts of successive directors to realize the original idea and foster closer collaboration among the various language groups tended to founder.

The Center for Languages, Literatures, and Cultures, however, had been preceded, years earlier, by the establishment of two previous centers, both of them very successful: the Center for Development Economics and the Center for Environmental Studies. So we didn't hesitate in 1989, after first establishing a campus Commission on Race Relations and later visiting and studying the role of comparable centers on other campuses, to establish a Multicultural Center to serve as a focus of activities among our growing and increasingly diverse population of minority and international students and to afford them an increased measure of social and academic support.

In those early years we were also able to launch on a rotational basis an ongoing program of review of our academic departments by outside visiting committees. An attempt ten years earlier to do this had been sidelined after meeting vigorous faculty opposition. Mounting this more successful effort called for some intricate diplomacy and a certain amount of discreet indirection, but it was worthwhile and long overdue.

No such micropolitical difficulties attended upon my decision to revive from 1987 onwards the publication of an annual *President's Report* which had lapsed some decades earlier. I would not have been able to do that without the splendid help of two successive special assistants to the president—Peter Berek of the English Department and Jim (James B.) Wood of the History Department. The position they held was a staff position and not a line one; their task was to help me extend my reach. And the goal of reviving the *President's Report* was not only that of keeping the larger Williams community more adequately informed about the academic life of the college but also to create a new vehicle of communication that could be of service in the upcoming fund drive for which we had already begun the planning. Unlike the older versions of the *President's Report* which had simply been used to describe what had gone on at the college over the course of the previous year, each issue of this new version was to contain two things. First, a reasonably substantial essay by the president on some important aspect of the college's life and work—science at Williams, for example, or international programs, or the nature of the Williams faculty, or tuition and financial aid policy. And so on. Second, a report by the treasurer and the provost concerning the state of the endowment and budgetary matters, especially the differing proportions of our revenues spent across time on various aspects of our operations—instructional, administrative, financial aid, libraries, buildings and grounds, and so on. So far as the endowment was concerned, I was particularly anxious to disabuse our alumni body of any complacent assumption about our financial well-being that might have been encouraged by the traditional practice of reporting endowment figures across years marked by unusually high levels of inflation in nominal dollars only. So we reported these figures also in constant 1967 dollars with the purpose of making clear that in real terms the endowment had fallen for the better part of two decades to a level below its 1967 peak and had only recently clawed its way back to that level. We also made clear that, given the one-third increase in the size of the student body, our endowment per student had fallen well below the 1967 level. If we were going to be asking our potential donors for large amounts of money to support and enhance the quality of our operations, and we certainly were, I wanted it to be clear that we would be doing so out of real, not imagined, need.

In retrospect again, and from the longer-term perspective, I would say that the other significant initiatives that were at least launched in those early years (1985–89) were fourfold. First, the outcome of the two-year review of the entire curriculum with which, right at the start in the fall of 1985, I had tasked an expanded Committee on Educational Policy under the chairmanship of Tom (Thomas C.) Jorling, the director of our Center for Environmental Studies who was later to serve as environmental commissioner for New York state. At first it had looked as if we might end up with the curricular sail flapping against the mast, becalmed still in the doldrums that had prevailed now for two decades when it came to any attempt to effect college-wide change in the course of instruction. Thus, when the committee had field-tested proposals to establish college-wide departmental minors or to recalibrate the divisional requirement more finely into five rather than three groupings of courses, those proposed changes aroused no enthusiasm and had, quietly, to be dropped. In the end, however, it did prove possible to effect significant college-wide curricular change. In addition to establishing two other interdepartmental programs (one in Asian studies, the other in comparative literary studies and sponsored by the new Center for Languages, Literatures, and Cultures), the faculty also endorsed the CEP's proposal for the creation of an interdepartmental program of a different sort. It was one in cross-disciplinary and experimental studies and was intended to facilitate experimentation by providing an established administrative umbrella or serving as a sort of holding company for temporary experimental courses or clusters of courses. Most important of all, the faculty approved, with votes well above the 60 percent majority requirement, proposals to strengthen the divisional requirement by expanding it from two to three courses in each of the three divisions and also to extend to the home campus the mode of tutorial instruction adopted two years earlier for our Oxford program. As I recall it, the idea for making that move was raised in the CEP by two people. One was Tom Perkins (class of 1987), a member of the first group of students we had sent to Oxford who had become an enthusiastic proponent of the tutorial approach. The other was Dick (Richard H.) Sabot of the Economics Department, who had taken a DPhil at Oxford and himself done some tutoring there. The idea was to create tutorial courses operating on the Oxbridge model. They were to be limited to a total of ten students, broken down into five tutorial pairs. The instructor/tutor would meet with each tutorial pair for an hour each week. Each student would be required on alternative weeks either to deliver a seven-page analytical essay or to mount a critique of his or her tutorial partner's essay. Each, therefore, would, across the course of a semester, write six essays and six critiques, while the tutor, in addition to course preparation, would put in a total of five hours each week meeting with the successive tutorial pairs. Labor-intensive and expensive though it was likely to be, I reacted with great enthusiasm to the idea and, in order to ease the way for its approval and implementation, pledged in the event of its passage to add three full-time equivalents to the faculty.

Although some members of the faculty were dubious about the wisdom and practicality of that tutorial proposal (one complained that tutorials would impose a further burden of work on the faculty and went so far as to dismiss the whole idea as "romantic and naïve in the extreme"), the proposal caught the imagination of more than enough of their colleagues to pass handily. After a year of planning, then, we were able to launch our new program in the fall of 1988 with some twenty-four tutorial courses. Over the decade or so ensuing, the program was reviewed more than once, its tires were thoroughly kicked, and it was found to be popular both with the students who had taken tutorials and with the faculty who had served as tutors. Later on, under the presidency of Morty (Morton O.) Schapiro and at a time when the college's financial resources had grown enough to make such a move feasible, the tutorial program underwent a considerable expansion—to such a degree, indeed, that it has become what amounts to a signature feature of the Williams overall academic offerings. With that happy outcome I could not be more pleased.

Two other initiatives, embarked upon in my first two years but brought to fruition only later, concerned the faculty and their needs. The first concerned the housing provisions traditionally made for them. While we had a large pool of college-owned rental housing for faculty in Williamstown, those who received tenure were required to vacate that housing within five years so that its availability for new or more junior faculty could be ensured. To ease the transition and to encourage faculty to live for the long haul in town and within easy reach of the campus, the college had made two benefits available. The first was a low-interest second mortgage which eased the way for people to get a first mortgage from one of the local banks. Without that benefit, we ourselves would never have been able to build a house in town. The second had been to make available for purchase small building lots on land developed for faculty housing. This was called for because acreage in Williamstown for the building of new houses tended to be marketed in prohibitively large parcels well beyond the means of the vast majority of academics and administrators. But when I became president in 1985 I was dismayed to discover that our entire supply of available building lots had now been exhausted and that many of the houses built earlier on such lots had, with their unrestricted sale over the course of time, been allowed to pass out of the hands of owners connected with Williams. This turned out to be one of the urgent issues discussed at our first administrative retreat, and to Will Reed was assigned the task of finding suitable land already zoned as residential that we could purchase and develop in order to make available an array of building lots large enough to meet our needs for the next quarter century or so. That land, with Will's help, we did succeed in acquiring. While it was a beautiful site situated on the lower slopes of Pine Cobble Mountain, its development was to prove to be an aggravating undertaking, both because of the particular contours of the land and because a small group of local environmentalists was adamantly opposed, residential zoning notwithstanding, to any building on that particular site. The whole project, indeed, was almost brought to a halt when one member of the oppositional group, a talented amateur botanist, succeeded against all odds in finding on one corner of the site some samples of the hairy honeysuckle. This unattractively named species, though not uncommon elsewhere, was rare in Massachusetts and was protected under state law as an endangered species. It was to take a personal meeting on my part in Boston with the Massachusetts commissioner for the environment and his staff before it became once more possible, after foregoing for several years the development of several lots in the area in which the species had been discovered, to proceed with the project. In the end, after various mini-crises and the loss of a certain amount of sleep on my part, we were able in the early 1990s to complete the effort. The first house on the site was built soon thereafter and others followed rapidly in its wake.

The other faculty-related issue that we began to address in those early years, but that was not finally resolved until 1990, was the matter of instructional load. At Williams that was significantly heavier than it was at Amherst, Wesleyan, or even Bowdoin. It seemed clear that it was imposing some strain on the faculty. The 1988 report issued by our decennial reaccreditation visiting team confirmed that fact and we had to worry that it might well begin to affect our ability to attract the top-level candidates for faculty openings that we wished to appoint. While the college's financial resources at that time did not permit us to reduce our instructional expectations to the same level as those sister colleges, we needed to do something to alleviate the situation, and we were eventually able, though not before the 1990 academic year, to effect what approximated to a 10 percent reduction in the teaching load. Getting to that point, however, was not easy. Given their fundamental fiduciary responsibility, the trustees had properly to be convinced that such a move, which would call for an increase in the size of the faculty, would be sustainable even if economic conditions in the nation at large significantly worsened. With that in mind, and in order to test the waters, David Booth, our vice provost, produced a variety of long-range financial forecasts using the college's multivariate financial model. By bizarre coincidence, the plenary session of the board at which David presented a batch of such projections, including, to keep us honest, a disaster scenario predicated on a dramatic market downturn, took place on October 16, 1987. As the session wore on, one of our trustees, Art (Arthur) Levitt Jr., at that time chairman of the American Stock Exchange in New York, kept on leaving the room to make (or receive) urgent telephone calls. It turned out, of course, that the financial markets were heading into a dramatic correction and were being overtaken by their own, real-life disaster scenario that was to reach its peak on Monday, October 19, 1987, with a loss in market value of more than 22 percent—still less, however, than the one-third downturn we had projected in our own fictional disaster scenario.

The final development, already underway in those early years but destined to continue throughout my presidency, was not so much any new initiative as an intensification and acceleration of an effort that our Office of Admission had begun, as we have seen, in the early to mid-1960s—namely, the vigorous attempt to attract to Williams able minority students. That office was a highly competent and well-led operation, but successive decennial US Census reports were making it clear that we were pursuing a moving demographic target. The minority percentage of the national population was growing by leaps and bounds; it was also itself becoming increasingly diverse, with the growth in its Latino component accelerating markedly between the census of 1980 and that of 1990. To that shift we sought to respond with vigor and determination. As I affirmed repeatedly, both on campus and off at a host of alumni events, it was my passionate conviction that places like Williams, which produced among their highly able graduates a disproportionate number of the nation's leaders in so many different walks of life, had a bounden duty to ensure that those graduates reflected in their numbers the nation's rich diversity. Thus I note that at the first faculty meeting of the 1988–89 academic year, and in the wake of the on-campus racial tensions of the previous year, I reminded those present that Williams had "a long-standing commitment to building a genuinely pluralistic community" and reiterated my own heartfelt endorsement of that commitment. If, as one demographer put it after the 1990 census figures were released, the United States was now in rapid transition towards becoming the world's "first universal nation," I was convinced that colleges like ours had an important role to play in easing the birth pangs of that new, transformed nation. If the challenge was great, it was also one that responded to the country's deepest ideals.

In 1985 the percentage of American minorities in our student body stood at 12.5 percent. By 1994, now aligned with national norms, that percentage had been doubled to 25 percent with the Latino component much increased. In 1991, in the course of its ongoing (and usually controversial) annual rankings of American colleges and universities, *U.S. News and World Report* ranked Williams as the nation's number one liberal arts college. It was not the first time it had done so, and it was certainly not to be the last. But what stood out on that occasion, and in gratifying recognition of the determined efforts we had been making, was the fact that it chose to focus its accompanying article about Williams on the strength of our ongoing institutional drive to "build a multicultural community."

CHAPTER NINETEEN

Presidential Years (iii): Principal Challenges Confronted

Punctuating all the endeavors in which we were engaged during the years from 1985 to 1994 were challenges of one sort or another. While some of them were not unduly stretching, others among them proved to be quite testing and stressful. It would be tedious to list them all, but some warrant memorialization if only as testimony to the difficult conditions under which college presidents during that era had, perforce, to discharge their regular responsibilities. The challenges in question fall into several categories: those that the trustees had already signaled at the outset as part of the job at that juncture in the college's history; those that were totally unexpected and called for a rapid (if somewhat scrambled) response; those embedded in the sociopolitical conditions and racial tensions prevalent on American campuses in the 1980s and early 1990s, conditions that contrived to make the presidential lot a good deal more taxing than it had been in the past or would again be in the future; and those, finally, of the ideological nature prevalent at that time in the larger American intellectual and political scene, these last constituting the sort of challenge I could conceivably have been able to sidestep but chose instead to engage.

The two challenges falling into the first category involved the celebration in appropriate fashion of the college's bicentennial in 1993 and the completion by the end of that celebratory year of the major fund drive that came to be known as the Third Century Campaign. So far as the former was concerned it was my hope, which I acknowledged in 1989 when I established a Bicentennial Commission, "to put on an observance that combines dignity, joy, and a certain amount of pizzazz." And that commission, ably led by Dusty (Dustin H.) Griffin, distinguished member of the class of 1965 and trustee of the college, succeeded admirably in doing precisely that. Its members went about its business in highly creative fashion, among other things recommending the establishment of a continuing program of annual awards known as Bicentennial Medals, to be bestowed upon alumni for exemplary achievement in all walks of life. They also sponsored, as the bicentennial year drew near, a Bicentennial Games event modeled on the Centennial Games of 1893, a nationwide alumni blood drive, an exhibition at the Williams College Museum of Art of works loaned by the many art collectors in the alumni body, a diversity weekend on campus as well as a reunion of our former Rhodes and Marshall scholars, and a celebratory weekend that brought together Williams women from the first coeducational class of 1975 down to the present. As its bicentennial gift to the Williamstown community, the college built and donated a new facility to house the Village (Williamstown) Ambulance Service, and as a "thank you" to all of those in the Oxford University community who had helped us to make our Williams at Oxford program the flourishing enterprise it had by now become, we put on in September 1993 a celebratory dinner in Exeter College's splendid Hall. The members of the board of trustees who had come over for a special meeting devoted to international studies were all present for what proved to be a festive and memorable occasion.

The round of celebratory events across the country and abroad culminated on campus in October with a ceremonial Bicentennial Convocation at which the college was the focus of laudatory speeches delivered by the governor of the Commonwealth of Massachusetts, Bill (William F.) Weld and by Edward H. Williams, class of 1938, a lineal descendant of our founder, Ephraim Williams Jr., as well as by representatives of Harvard, Amherst, and Wesleyan. The campus was punctuated by tents for dining and festooned with bunting (that on West College reproducing the bunting displayed at our centennial in 1893). And the evening was marked by an array of receptions and dinners for visitors and students alike. Though it undoubtedly put a lot of pressure on those most intimately involved in the organization of the weekend—not least among them Hodge Markgraf and Bob Dalzell (our imaginative and indefatigable college marshal)—it was all great fun and did, I think, reflect the amalgam of joy, dignity, and pizzazz I had hoped for.

The events of that weekend amounted to the biggest, most elaborate, and certainly most complex social event that my wife and I had been called upon to host. And it was also, with one exception, to be the last big one. The previous year I had announced my intention to step down from the presidency of the college at the end of the bicentennial year in order to return, after an eighteen-month leave, to my primary calling as teacher and scholar in my old department. A presidential search committee had been formed and had gone about its work with great dispatch. As a result, in the spring of 1993, Hank (Harry C.) Payne, then serving as president of Hamilton College in New York state, had been elected to the Williams presidency, effective January 1, 1994. And the last big social event we mounted at the President's House was in fact a grand reception early in December to introduce Hank and Deborah Payne to a broad array of civic movers and shakers from the length and breadth of Berkshire County.

When we did that, those of us caught up in the college's development efforts were still working hard to push the Third Century Campaign as far as possible over the $150,000,000 goal which had already been met in September. This last effort generated a rather exciting surge in giving, and when the counting was finally completed, it turned out that we had reached a total just a few dollars short of $175,000,000—enough, in fact, to insure that we would hold, if only for a while, the small college campaign record. The great collaborative effort that brought us to that happy outcome reflected planning and organization going back as far as 1985–86, long before the formal launching of the campaign at a dinner held in the fall of 1989 at the Morgan Library in New York. It had begun with the reorganization of our Development Office under the leadership of Hodge Markgraf and Mike Oman, the formation of a national Campaign Planning Committee presided over by Pete Willmott, our national campaign chairman, and my drafting of a lengthy planning document to focus committee discussion and to indicate what I myself thought should be the pertinent priorities. Out of those discussions came the eventual case statement and the shaping of the campaign as essentially a "people and programs" rather than a "bricks-and-mortar" effort. The central focus was on the students and faculty, with a strong emphasis on building up the endowment supporting financial aid, funding faculty research, and financing a series of special five-year Third Century Professorships. Generous research funds were attached to each of those professorships and they were to be awarded on a rotating basis to our most distinguished faculty. The only bricks-and-mortar target initially included was the Jewish Religious Center, though, because of the receipt of a fine, targeted gift from a single donor, we were able later to fold in the building of a badly needed studio arts facility, which got underway during my last year in office.

A campaign of this sort had necessarily to be a highly collaborative effort involving not only the professionals in our Development Office but also a host of volunteers who gave most generously of their time and financial resources. Those volunteers included members of the board of trustees who were expected to set the example of generosity in giving, as well as alumni leaders from all over the country and those permanently residing abroad. It was also one of my major preoccupations throughout my presidency, and my modes of engagement in it were multiple. They included the original and continued planning for the whole effort (for the original planning committee mutated into a National Campaign Committee which met on a quarterly basis in New York City); the delivery of motivational speeches at the formal launching of the campaign in 1989 and, subsequently, at the sequential launching of multiple regional campaigns; and, in the spring semester of 1988, the hosting around the country of some twenty-one "consultative dinners" at which we field-tested our tentative goals and to which were invited, partly by way of initial cultivation, crucial groups of alumni leaders and potential donors. For other potential donors less closely connected with the college we mounted in Williamstown a series of invitational presidential colloquia which were quite intimate in nature (I don't believe any of them, including spouses, included more than sixteen people.) At those colloquia, punctuated by a reasonably elaborate dinner at the President's House (a purely social occasion, no speeches), faculty and senior administrators spoke with the group, as did I in a concluding, private, one-and-a-half-hour question and answer session. Labor-intensive though they were, these colloquia succeeded in proving their worth as the campaign wore on by reconnecting people with the college and enlarging our donor base. Finally, at the end of the line, I was of course deployed to "make the ask" of those potential major donors whose careful preparatory cultivation had brought them to that point.

Somewhat to my surprise, I was to find this whole effort a stimulating one and certainly not uncongenial. The objectives were clear, the need was real, and the cause was good and was one I deeply believed in. The people it brought me into contact with were nearly all of them loyal and committed people, alumni and parents who believed in and felt grateful to the college, and who wanted to help it, usually without attaching restrictions to their gifts. Many were also very interesting people to spend time with, and it was easy to see why some of them had been so very successful in their chosen careers. Of course, we encountered obstacles in our quest for support, but those obstacles were rarely because of the lack of philanthropic spirit on the part of those we approached. More often the difficulty stemmed from the fact that the potential donors had other charitable commitments, often in their home cities, that loomed larger in their priorities than did Williams. So while we had our moments of disappointment, they were rarely such as to leave a bad taste in the mouth.

In this whole campaign-related effort, indeed, I encountered only one episode that was personally upsetting. It came from a very unexpected quarter early on in the game and appears to have been triggered by loose talk emerging from our initial campaign-planning sessions in New York. It took the form of a lengthy (six-page) letter—fretful, condescendingly admonitory in tone, obliquely suggesting a lack of prudent financial planning on our part, and really very intrusive. And its author was one of my predecessors, none other than Jack Sawyer himself. Written in October 1987, it reflected his dismayed reaction to what he had picked up about our campaign planning and went so far as to urge "an intensive rethinking" of its whole direction. While, among other things, attributing to his classmates criticisms concerning the "extravagance" of the new athletic facilities (especially the Olympic-size swimming pool) John Chandler had built, he expressed his own doubts about the scope and value of our new Oxford program (a "delightful anachronism," he suspected), about the financial viability of our proposed tutorial program, and about the wisdom of launching a campaign with a target in excess of $100,000,000. But what really appears to have ticked him off was our declared wish to expand the faculty somewhat. I don't think he was aware of the fact that during the financially hard-pressed decade preceding, the student-faculty ratio had been allowed to drift as high as 13:1. Nor did he appear to be conscious of the need, if we were to be successfully competitive in our efforts to appoint the most attractive candidates for faculty positions, to effect something of a reduction in the teaching load our faculty carried. To achieve that goal, we would have to increase the size of the faculty, which would have the concomitant effect of improving the student-faculty ratio. It seems that somebody on the National Campaign Committee had (unwisely) passed on to him a draft planning document put together by the Development Office and intended to promote further and more clearly targeted discussion on that committee. In an attempt to render attractive the goal of increasing the size of the faculty, the drafters of that document had evoked the possibility of improving the student-faculty ratio to 10:1. (For comparative purposes I should note that, as of 2015, it stands at 7:1.) But to Jack the mention of a 10:1 goal was akin to waiving a red flag in front of a bull. Having himself for financial reasons and in the context of the move to coeducation increased that ratio to 12:1 from somewhere in the neighborhood of 10:1, he clearly viewed any reversal of that move as financially dangerous, and perhaps also as an implicit criticism of the direction taken by his own administration two decades earlier.

I must confess to being very taken aback by both the content and tone of that letter, the more so in that it came from so distinguished a predecessor. Despite the depth of Jack's knowledge of American higher education (and his dozen and more years heading up the Mellon Foundation had given him a privileged perch from which to view it), so far as Williams was concerned he still seemed locked into positions he had adopted during his own presidency two decades earlier. But despite the passage of time, it would be a bit of a disaster for us if his misgivings were somehow to become public. And, in this connection, I was not reassured by his statement that "Anne and I have put too much of our lives into Williams and have too many multi-general ties there to want to be anything but constructive" and that, therefore, he did "not plan to make this letter a public document." His very mention of such a possibility, after all, itself suggested that the thought of going public might well have occurred to him. Not much fun. So I consulted John Chandler to see what he thought. While not surprised about the fact of such an intrusion by Jack, and I found that interesting, he still seemed a bit bemused by its far-ranging nature. I also shared Jack's letter with our senior trustee, Pete Parish. Though, as always, he was appropriately discreet in what he had to say, his reaction was highly supportive and one of irritation and impatience with Jack. And I got the distinct impression that the latter may also have tried to make himself an intrusive presence during the course of the presidential search that had culminated with my election.

All of this gave me a lot to think about and I concluded that I might be wise to wait a week or so before writing a considered response. In so doing, and swallowing hard, I adopted a more or less conciliatory tone in what I had to say. I thanked him for his letter, acknowledged that it had given me much food for thought, assured him that at this point our campaign plans were far from being set in concrete, suggested that his "forceful observations" clearly deserved "a more substantive engagement than it would be possible to attempt" in a written response, and expressed the hope that we might find a moment to meet and to discuss his observations. At the same time, I did note that those observations involved three different strands that would have to be disentangled if such a future discussion was to be fruitful. They combined, I wrote:

> First, and in some measure, a misreading of our intentions for the Campaign—useful, because it suggests that the development document in its current form does not convey those intensions with sufficient clarity. Second, some assumptions about the quality, carefulness and scope of our current financial planning which are, in all honesty, somewhat at odds with the sober realities. Third, an element of straightforward disagreement about the goals that the College should be pursuing.

What I refrained from saying, though it was something about which I had strong feelings, was that his letter was not the sort of missive that any "sitting president" should expect to receive from a predecessor, nor one that I could imagine myself ever writing to any successor of mine. And that, I think, was wise. Jack's next letter, written by way of reply, expressed appreciation for my "civil and thoughtful response," and in its tone reflected, I sensed, some second thoughts or misgivings on his part about having written the original letter at all. It was several months before we could meet but when we did our exchanges were open and straightforward and the atmosphere was uncharged, friendly, and basically supportive. With that, the elements of disagreement seemed to fade in the background, though I couldn't help noting that Jack declined our invitation to attend the grand dinner at the Morgan Library when the campaign was launched. And that was a decision that Hodge Markgraf, one of his staunch admirers, found hard to forgive.

The denouement of this strange and disturbing episode was not, however, to occur until about three years later when the campaign was well on its way to success. And, when it did, it was touching, reassuring, and revelatory of Jack's human stature. In response to his invitation, I had stopped by the Sawyers' apartment in Manhattan, where, while chatting over a cup of coffee, he forthrightly apologized to me about having written the original letter in 1987. He explained to me that at that time, in the wake of his retirement from the presidency of the Mellon Foundation and the discovery that he had prostate cancer, he had suffered a bout of what amounted to depression. If I had been upset by the receipt of the letter he had written at that time and under those conditions, I was now moved by the knowledge that he had later fretted about having written it and had felt the need, proud and private person though he was, to convey to me his regret in a face-to-face meeting. I was touched and deeply impressed by that fact and took it as testimony to his fundamental decency and to his stature as a man. If I had long admired the way in which he had conducted his own presidency at Williams and hoped that I had learned something from it, I now admired him all the more, simply as a human being.

Turning now from those officially stipulated challenges that I had expected to confront to those that seemed to come from nowhere, let me say that three such, each of them different in kind, deserve at least a mention. The first surfaced in 1986 when Michael Card, the Williamstown building inspector, started closing down the use of Hopkins Hall for classroom instruction. An unrenovated, nineteenth-century Roman-esque Richardsonian structure, it had a large, open stairwell and was far behind the current building code. He made it clear that within a year no classroom use at all would be permitted. Over the course of the past half-dozen years or so we had done a lot of new building at the college and the last thing I wanted to have to undertake was the total renovation of an administration building, surely not the sexiest of projects. But the challenge had to be met and, if possible, turned into an opportunity. By taking on debt under the favorable conditions afforded by the Higher Education Financing Authority (HEFA), we were able to undertake not only a total renovation of the original building but also an expansion in order to provide additional office and classroom space, including some new-style banked "Socratic" classrooms. The outcome, though not uni-versally praised (especially by our resident astringent critics in the Art Department), was basically successful and, in my view, effected some modest improvement in the appearance of what had been a rather lumpy and ugly building. The project began with the rerouting of the heating tunnel on which the heating of much of the northern side of the campus depended, and the completion of that sub-project involved something of an anxiety-provoking cliff-hanger before the colder weather of late fall finally moved in upon us. The effort as a whole was to take a full two years, with one price tag attached to it being an inconvenient species of administrative diaspora as our offices had to be scattered right across the campus.

The two other unexpected challenges, which proved to be unfortu-nately juxtaposed, again came, it seemed, from nowhere. The first in-volved the receipt on July 1, 1989, of a Civil Investigative Demand (CID) from the Antitrust Division of the US Department of Justice requiring batteries of information concerning the procedures whereby we set sala-ries and tuition and awarded financial aid to students. In this we were not alone. Similar demands were received by the Ivy League universities (the real target, I think) as well as by an array of other universities and colleges. Fifty-seven institutions in all were the recipients of such de-mands. In its scope, or so the lawyers told us, this investigative effort involved an extraordinarily extensive commitment of government time and taxpayers' dollars.

One can only speculate about the real reasons behind this odd inquiry. But one cannot help noting that it came at a time when it was becoming fashionable in conservative political circles to launch attacks on the "liberal," northeastern "elite" universities. Moreover, the launching of the antitrust investigation was announced by US Attorney General Richard Thornburgh in Philadelphia not long before he also announced that he intended to run for election to the office of US senator from Pennsylvania. Whatever the underlying reasons for the investigation (and it is tempting to be cynical about them), the whole effort came eventually to center on the way in which this group of universities and colleges went about the business of awarding financial aid to needy students. And the latter were portrayed, not as the fortunate recipients of freely extended charitable help, but as consumers, "higher education shoppers," entitled via free competition to maximize their awards. As a result, the collaborative mechanisms traditionally used by many institutions in the targeted group to make sure that financial aid was indeed being allocated to students entirely on the basis of their demonstrated need were now denounced as a collusive effort by a "collegiate cartel" in restraint of free market competition and as falling, therefore, under the provisions of the Sherman Antitrust Act.

For those of us at leading institutions firmly committed to the twin principles of need-blind admission and strictly need-based financial aid (precluding, that is, the offering of merit scholarships irrespective of the recipient's financial need), this seemed to be a very odd way of looking at things. And in that reaction we were not alone. At the very end of the line, when the Justice Department finally agreed to dismiss the financial aid antitrust case against MIT, it did so in the wake of an appellate court's unequivocal reversal of an earlier ruling handed down against that institution. That appellate court ruled that the Sherman Antitrust Act simply did not apply. And on that occasion one of the three judges who handed down the ruling commented that "it does seem ironic . . . that the Sherman Act, intended to prevent plundering by the 'robber barons,' is being advanced as a means to punish . . . philanthropy."

Ironic, no doubt, but the consequences for those caught up in the toils of the investigation were depressingly concrete. While MIT had the fortitude to contest the antitrust charge, the eight Ivy League universities, anxious to avoid a costly legal battle but admitting no wrongdoing, had signed a consent decree precluding for ten years into the future the sort of inter-institutional cooperation in relation to financial aid that the Antitrust Division had chosen to target. And for every institution involved, even those which, like Williams, were not subjected to any formal charge, the legal costs incurred in simply responding to the CIDs proved to be substantial. In our own case, the half a million in unbudgeted legal costs, combined with the downturn in the economy and financial markets of 1990–91 and the concomitant drop in earnings from the endowment, nudged us into deficit. The fact that it was modest in comparison with the comparable deficits being recorded at places like Harvard, Yale, and Columbia afforded small solace. Our financial projections were telling us that, should the markets not improve, we would be facing proliferating and compounding deficits off into the foreseeable future. Projections, fortunately, are not predictions. Two or three years earlier we had embarked on an effort at cost control and we were now able to move that effort rapidly into high gear, committing ourselves to meeting the challenge by focusing on the expenditure rather than the revenue side. The story of what ensued was a happy one that reflected a wonderfully collaborative effort on the part of all managers under the energetic leadership of Al (George R.) Goethals, our provost. All of which enabled us, unlike many institutions, to claw our way back to financial equilibrium within little more than a year. By the time I stepped down at the end of our bicentennial year of 1993, our ten-year financial projections were happily able to indicate fiscal balance and what turned out to be an accurate promise of a deficit-free decade to come.

I am, I suspect, inordinately proud of that outcome, and mainly because it reflected what I believe to have been the sincere alignment of the college community as a whole with three fundamental commitments. First, the decision not to privilege the present over the future by dipping more deeply into the seed corn upon which future initiatives and creative new departures would depend. That is to say, we all declined to solve the problem in temptingly simple fashion by drawing down the endowment more aggressively. Instead, the solution was found on the expenditure rather than the revenue side. Second, the decision to privilege over other dimensions of our complex enterprise our core educational activities and the policies that sustained them. Though the size of the faculty was held at steady state, salaries were not, academic programs were not cut,

and the whole system of need-blind admissions and need-based financial aid, which had done so much to enhance the intellectual quality as
well as the social and racial diversity of the student body, was kept firmly
in place. Third, while those two commitments necessitated our effecting
the necessary savings elsewhere in our operations, we committed ourselves also, even if the process might as a result take longer, to finding
those savings without resorting to layoffs of any of our staff or hourly
employees. Deindustrialization had long since overtaken the northern
Berkshire region with resultant (and endemic) rates of unemployment
running well ahead of the national average. By the early 1990s Williams
had been thrust willy-nilly into the position of being the largest employer
in the region. Practically everyone in the Williams community was, I
think, appropriately and acutely conscious of the degree to which, not
only our own people, but also the local economy at large, had come to
depend upon our long-standing record as a stable employer. That record
we were careful to maintain.

If such were the unforeseen challenges with which we had to grapple
and which surfaced when least expected, what I recognize now as the
most testing, persistent, wearying, and stressful of the challenges we had
to confront during my presidential years was, in some ways at least,
wholly to have been expected. It was the challenge posed by the wave of
student activism that swept across the country in the 1980s and early
1990s that threatened constantly to derail carefully planned institutional
commitments, inevitably distracted institutional attention from the normal press of work at hand, and served, inevitably, to grind down the administrative spirit. In retrospect it seems clear that it had the effect
nationally of rendering the role of university or college president a more
stressful business than it had been at any time since the late 1960s. In
the early 1990s, indeed, it was reported that many a college presidency
lasted for no more than five years and that the average incumbent's tenure had dropped to a little less than seven years. At Williams the challenge handed down by this surge of student activism was not altogether
unexpected. The student-faculty push for total divestment of college
holdings in multinationals with some of their operations in South Africa
had now been underway, after all, for the better part of a decade. What
was less predictable was its modulation into a set of pressures focused

on the matter of campus race relations and coming to be centered characteristically on issues pertaining to affirmative action, especially as it related to the recruitment of minority faculty. At Williams, the student push for total divestment had been largely a white affair, but the Black Student Union became involved around 1986–87 and the focus on campus race relations began to become dominant.

Given the speed with which, at the time, we were increasing the size and internal diversity of the minority component in the student body, I am inclined to think in retrospect that even if campuses nationwide had not become roiled as they were by racial tensions, we ourselves would have experienced some turbulence. But, given the national situation, turbulence became well-nigh inevitable. Of course, a real irony was attached to the intensity of the activist concern with affirmative action as it pertained to minority faculty appointments. It is understandable that as our efforts to increase and diversify the minority student cohort gained traction, minority students should become increasingly aware of (and vocal about) the comparative paucity on campus of minority faculty. But they were doing so at a time when efforts on that front were becoming more difficult. The numbers of African Americans entering PhD programs with the goal of pursuing academic careers were actually dropping. I can recall one year, I believe in the late 1980s, when Harvard, which recruited a disproportionate percentage of the nation's most talented African American high school graduates, shamefacedly confessed that in the year in question not a single one of that target group in the graduating class had chosen to go on to PhD work. And the situation at Williams and its highly selective fellow colleges was not much better. I recall, too, that during my years as dean of the faculty when the affirmative action officer and I would meet at the beginning of the academic year with representatives of our Black Student Union to go over with them the list of faculty openings we would be seeking to fill, they characteristically showed little interest in my report on the percentages of minorities in the pertinent PhD cohorts now entering the job market, some of those disciplinary cohorts being really quite miniscule.

That notwithstanding, I don't believe that there was a single year during my presidency when, because of incidents or upheavals at Williams, or on neighboring campuses, or, indeed, on the national scene, we were not maneuvering anxiously to stay ahead (or get ahead) of the wave

of racial tension that seemed at that time to be inundating the nation's campuses, fueling edgy protests, building occupations, and the
like. Reading copies of the *Williams Record* from the late eighties, I can't
help being struck by the frequent appearance of op-ed pieces on the topic
of campus racism, as well by the sheer number of reports on race-related
upheavals on neighboring campuses. During that period such upheavals
occurred on more than a hundred campuses at large. In the Northeast
they occurred at Dartmouth, Brandeis, Smith, Hampshire, Amherst,
Wesleyan, Williams, and at the universities of Vermont, Massachusetts,
and Pennsylvania, with what was unquestionably the worst incident occurring in the spring of 1990 when the office of the Wesleyan president
was firebombed. During that period I myself gained some perspective
on why it was that student service professionals whose expertise and
focus was on campus race relations tended so often to "burn out" and
seek to take on other areas of responsibility.

If in this most difficult area we did achieve some successes, it has to
be acknowledged that they were comparatively modest ones. During the
1986–87 academic year, I established a Commission on Campus Race
Relations, and its efforts, along with good work by the Dean's Office,
did succeed on several occasions in defusing what could otherwise have
eventuated in quite incendiary situations. Moreover, largely because of
fine student leadership, reaction at Williams to the controversial California verdict in the Rodney King case (April–May 1992) took a remarkably
positive, community-enhancing direction. Elsewhere in New England
things sometimes took a very different tack, with passionate anger at the
initial verdict boiling over into protest directed at the college itself and
coming to focus on what were depicted as failures in the institution's recruitment of minority faculty and other minority-related issues. This was
true at Wellesley and the University of Massachusetts, and at Amherst
and Hampshire Colleges unrest eventuated in the seizure of administrative office buildings. On that occasion, however, and mercifully so, nothing of the sort happened at Williams. There, the focus was kept firmly on
the Rodney King case itself and on the call for federal judicial interven-
tion. A broad coalition of students organized a march down to the federal
building in Pittsfield (a distance of twenty-two miles) and, astonishingly,
more than a third of the student body took part—655 in all, with the
college itself shipping down box lunches and providing buses for the re-

turn trip. The march culminated, in collaboration with local civil rights groups, in an effectively focused and dignified protest. And in this case I could not help feeling proud about the thoughtful and constructive direction student protest had taken. But that, of course, was not always or even usually the case, and three semesters stand out in my memory because of the potentially destabilizing nature of campus unrest at the time.

The first was the spring semester of 1986, during my first year in office, and the issue that year was the continuing push of the Williams Anti-Apartheid Coalition (WAAC) for total divestment from companies conducting any of their operations in South Africa. The momentum of dissent had been building up all year. My induction in October had been picketed by protestors. Rumor, indeed, had it that I could expect to be interrupted while delivering my induction address, which was to be delivered in Chapin Hall before an audience of around thirteen hundred. So I had to prepare myself to cope with any such eventuality. While, to my great relief, nothing of the sort happened, not long afterwards candlelight vigils came to be held outside the President's House (usually around dinnertime), and later in the fall semester members of WAAC conducted a sit-in at the Admissions Office. Though they did not attempt to interfere with the flow of business there, they did take the opportunity to convey their view that the college's investment policies were racist to startled visitors who were there to check out Williams. This pro-divestment push came to a head, in characteristic student protest fashion, in April 1986 just after the spring break when, even in our northerly clime, the sun had finally reappeared, the sap was beginning to rise, the outdoors beckoned, and the pressure of final papers and examinations still seemed no more than a distant cloud on the horizon. What happened on that occasion, timed carefully to coincide with Parents' Weekend, was the erection on Baxter lawn, just outside Chapin Hall where I was to address the visiting parents, of a symbolic "shantytown." Doubtless no more than an exercise in symbolic protest, but it was one that would wear out its welcome if the shanties were left up long enough to arouse the ire of other students who took exception either to WAAC's goals or to its tactics or, indeed, to both. No administrator, certainly, conscious of the unfortunate ways in which similar protests had played out at places like Yale and Dartmouth, could fail to worry about the potential

that sort of protest had for violent confrontation and bodily harm. At Dartmouth, after all, students opposing that sort of protest had attacked the shanties with sledgehammers and pickaxes. At Williams, fortunately, the shanties remained standing for no more than eight days before we were able to prevail upon the protestors to take them down, and the whole protest passed off peacefully enough.

When the parents, having walked by the "shantytown," assembled in Chapin, I abandoned the remarks I had originally intended to make and, seeking to rescue something teachable from the moment, spoke instead to the matter of student protest on a campus like ours. I alluded first to a brief statement which the dean of the college had circulated the previous day. In that statement he had noted *inter alia* that just as the members of the Williams community held conflicting views about the question of divestment, so were they likely to hold various views about the particular form of protest that WAAC had adopted. The college fully expected, he had said, that all such views would be expressed "with the mutual respect and careful argument we owed to each other as members of an academic community." I myself then went on to focus on that last, central point. When I had spoken to their sons and daughters the previous September, I noted, I had acknowledged that there would be something sadly lacking in us as a community of learning if we somehow managed to prevent from intruding upon our consciousness the terrible things going on in the world at large. I also noted, quoting now my September address, that I had continued my remarks as follows:

On many such issues I myself hold strong views, and I am by temperament rarely shy about expressing them. But in my present capacity I have the overriding duty to do whatever is in my power to create and preserve the sort of institutional climate that will enable Williams to fill what is the oldest, the finest, the noblest, the most enduring mission of service to the larger society that colleges and universities have been called upon to pursue.

And what is that? Nothing other (I believe) than this: the provision of a sort of dialectical space wherein complex and difficult and testing issues can be vigorously debated and tenaciously explored in an atmosphere distinguished above all by its openness, its ratio-

nality, its civility, its generosity of spirit. Hence this plea—and it comes, believe me, from the heart.

Do not imagine, when the word *civility* is used, that what is intended is some genteel disinclination to raise controversial issues because by so doing you might upset others. No, what I have in mind is quite different. It is, rather, a certain moral stance towards argument and disagreement. And I think it can be summed up in three rather simple propositions:

First, that to be listened to with patience and courtesy one must oneself be prepared to listen to others with a similar degree of patience and courtesy.

Second, that our world being as much threatened by ignorance and confusion as it is by malice, there is something *wrong morally* about any too ready a willingness to impute bad motive to somebody else just because she or he has had the temerity to disagree with you.

Third, that in this our confused world, the arena of debate—and especially that of moral debate—is an unhappily shadowed one, that there endure stubborn issues on which enlightened people of good will end up in blank disagreement, that under such circumstances, in a college community committed by its very ethos to rational discourse, the only appropriate option then remaining is that of keeping the channels of communication open and of continuing discussion, however unsatisfactory that option may seem at the time.

For our part, I want you to know that those of us in administration will do our level best to practice what we preach and to keep our doors open to you.

You see, we need to hear your concerns and discontents. We need to be nudged by your criticism. We need to be invigorated by your imagination and your ideas. We need, even, to sense your encouragement and support. For we are engaged, after all, in a common enterprise. And what we truly believe, as it edges towards its bicentennial, is that this fine old college is called upon not simply to get by, not simply to endure, but to excel.

"That is what," (speaking now to the parents), "I had to say to your daughters and sons in September. That is what has framed my response to student dissent throughout the year. And that is what stands behind the position we have adopted towards the current demonstration. Williams, I like to think, is a robust community. It has nothing to lose and everything to gain from open and vigorous debate on the great divisive issues of our day. So long, of course, as that debate is conducted with the thoughtfulness and mutual respect that befits a community of learning. For *that*, after all, is what we are."

As the following summer wore on, as conditions in South Africa appeared to be deteriorating, and after its government gave a curt backhand to the representations of the Commonwealth's "Eminent Persons" group, I came to the conclusion that, while refraining from embracing total divestment, we should further modulate our mediating position and embrace the commitment to "disinvestment advocacy" that had just been adopted by TIAA-CREF after its own mission to South Africa had reported back on its discouraging findings. That is to say, that we should vote our shares in companies in support of shareholder resolutions in favor of those companies ceasing their operations in South Africa. And it was to be a striking fact that some of those resolutions were to receive an unprecedented level of support—as much, in fact, as 20 percent.

I had drafted a position paper advocating this policy of "disinvestment advocacy" and, having run it by my executive group, submitted it to the Trustee Finance Committee, which accepted my recommendation. In retrospect, if not necessarily so at the time, I am inclined now to think that that slight shift in our stance reinforced the moderate center and attracted enough support and sympathy among students and faculty to take at least some of the wind out of WAAC's sails. But if the divestment movement on campus began to decline, race-related discontent began to rise, and it came to something of a peak in the spring semester of the 1987–88 academic year.

That spring semester was one in which I presided, up and down the country, over some twenty-one campaign-related consultative dinners. That off-campus job we succeeded in getting done and the outcome was encouraging and energizing. On campus, however, things took a troubling direction, and I remember that spring semester as an exceedingly difficult one, marked by an atmosphere of unremitting gloom.

It all began with two deaths: one of a student, Charlie Hufford (class of 1989), who was killed in a car crash, the other that of Michael Knight, a much beloved and very effective member of the Theatre Department who had been ill for some time and who was to be sorely missed especially by our African American students. Those losses were followed in March by the death of my old philosopher friend, Laszlo Versenyi. And the final blow fell during the spring vacation when I was in San Francisco, just finishing up a series of visits to our alumni chapters up and down the West Coast. There I received a call from Will Reed breaking the terribly sad news that Jim (James) Skinner, chair of the Chemistry Department, devoted father of two teenage children, and somebody suffering, it turned out, from severe clinical depression, had taken his own life.

All of this for a small, tightly knit college community would have been devastating enough. And the semester was punctuated by wrenching memorial services. But it was also, just after the spring break, to be marked by serious race-related tensions that culminated, despite all efforts to the contrary, in the occupation, by a multiracial group of dissident minority students, of the deans' offices situated at that time, while the Hopkins Hall renovation was being completed, in Jenness House. The storm clouds had been gathering since February, when a violent racial incident at the Amherst campus of the University of Massachusetts that had culminated in the seizure of a building had generated reverberations on other New England campuses, notably at Hampshire College where a similar building occupation took place. These upheavals had attracted understandable attention among our own black students at Williams. And interest deepened into anger and unrest with the appearance in the *Williams Record* of a rather provocative article exploring the possibility that affirmative action might conceivably mean "reverse discrimination." This led, in turn, to the circulation of an anonymous document alleging that "Williams College has reneged" on "its commitment to affirmative action in faculty and staff recruitment." Given the amount of misinformation being disseminated, Al Goethals, acting dean of the faculty, and Nancy McIntire, our affirmative action officer, sought in a detailed report to the whole community to set the record straight. But, or so it seemed, to no avail. Early in March, a group of twenty-four minority students (black, Latino, and South Asian) delivered to the dean and to me a list of fourteen "demands" focused largely, though not exclusively, to matters pertaining to affirmative action. And to those demands they requested "an official written response" prior to the start of spring vacation.

The list of items demanded was a rather puzzling one, including, for example, a certain amount of pushing at an open door. Thus the demand for "the formal establishment of two Bolin Fellowships per year," a program that I had in fact initiated three years earlier, and another that there be a memorial for Michael Knight in the Adams Memorial Theatre. Closer to the heart of the matter, however, was the demand that in any given year the racial makeup of the faculty should reflect the proportion of black and Hispanic students enrolled (for example, a 6 percent black student body should entail a 6 percent minority faculty contingent "at all times," with the further stipulation that a third of any new minority faculty appointed should be women. This was obviously something I could not accede to, and for more than one reason. But not least among them was the fact, given the discouraging statistical realities, that it was a goal impossible of achievement. Indeed, for one reason or another, and as diplomatically as possible, I had to reject eight of the fourteen demands. In my response, then, while reaffirming the college's demonstrated commitment to affirmative action, I had to distinguish between those things that we could do, those that, for one reason or another, were out of the question, and those of their demands that were simply unclear. And in so doing I indicated my readiness to pursue further discussions with the group, which was now calling itself (somewhat tendentiously) CARE— that is, Coalition Against Racist Education.

In the end, after long hours of tiresomely repetitive negotiations, our discussions came to focus on no more than two or three items with one, in particular, becoming the stumbling block impeding an ending to what had by then become an outright confrontation. The spring vacation was now behind us and we had entered what seemed always to be the favored drop zone for campus protest. In the two weeks preceding, race-related incidents, demonstrations, and building takeovers had occurred in several neighboring campuses in the Northeast—including Smith, Yale, the University of Vermont, and Wellesley—and, at Williams, on Friday, April 22, members of CARE had occupied Jenness House. Across the ensuing weekend, then, and on into Monday morning, the dean of the college, provost, dean of the faculty, and I pursued (though not all at the same time) the wearisome path of negotiation.

For me, that weekend had something of a surreal feel to it. George Steinbrenner and a group of alumni friends of his were on campus for the dedication, in memory of two beloved coaches (Tony Plansky and Bobby Coombs), of a new running track and baseball diamond made possible by their generous donations. On the Saturday, then, I had to alternate between absorbing in the course of negotiation the woes of a group of alienated students, adjudicating complex wrangles between the Williamstown Theatre Festival and our own Theatre Department concerning the use of office space in the summer months, making appropriate speeches at dedication ceremonies, and hosting a celebratory dinner for the members of that visiting alumni group. They were well aware of the racial tensions roiling the campus but were, most of them, too polite to mention them. But if George said nothing to me about the building occupation, seated next to my wife at dinner he did observe to her (as if the thought had not occurred to us) that "the alumni won't like this."

On Monday afternoon I was scheduled to head out of town to preside over another of our Campaign Consultative Dinners and I had hoped to bring the building occupation to an end by Sunday night. That proved, however, to be impossible. The sticking point was the demand for the appointment of a "minority special assistant" to the president responsible for "non-student affirmative action," and that position to be filled by "a Black or Hispanic candidate." This demand was, in effect, an attempt to do an end-run around our existing affirmative action officer and I could not countenance it. Its implied criticism of Nancy McIntire's record as affirmative action officer was wholly unwarranted and unfair, and its racial implications were, to say the least, unfortunate. That single (largely symbolic) sticking point, the focus of about ten hours of tense and bitterly repetitive wrangling, prolonged the occupation until about noon on Monday when a compromise (suggested, I believe, by Steve Fix) was found. We agreed to engage consultants in the fall of 1988 to review the college's affirmative action program and the functioning of the Affirmative Action Office and to recommend ways to enhance the college's efforts to appoint minority faculty—including "if deemed advisable by the consultants, the addition of a minority assistant in that office." In the event, those consultants proved to be judicious and helpful, especially in relation to matters that had not been at issue in the confrontation. And they were to affirm the affirmative action program at Williams to be superior to that on many campuses. Dismissed as unnecessary was the idea of appointing a minority assistant in the office.

That was, I suppose, something of a vindication after the bruising confrontation of the previous spring. And if, for those of us in administration, that spring semester had been a pulverizing one, it was in the end brightened somewhat by the receipt of the formal letter of reaccreditation of the college from the New England Association of Schools and Colleges, Inc., Commission on Institutions of Higher Education. For it included a very positive appraisal of the state of the college. The summary judgment reproduced in that letter went as follows:

> We commend the College for its manifest strengths. Included among them are the most able administration which directs the affairs of the College with competence, energy, and feeling. In this regard, we would also note the President's clear and impressive sense of vision for the institution. The faculty are of high quality and devoted to their students, teaching, and the College. The quality of the student body is impressive academically and otherwise. The striking commitment of the entire Williams community to the values and objectives of the institution is no less commendable than are its rich array of resources.

Perhaps I may be forgiven for drawing some solace from that judgment and for reading it more than once.

The third semester that stands out in my memory as being unusually challenging and even a bit debilitating arrived in the spring of my last year as president. At the outset, things seemed in general to be going smoothly and well. The Third Century Campaign had been meeting all of its sequential benchmarks and I was confident that, working steadily, we would meet and surpass our goal. Jack Sawyer and John Chandler had agreed to team up with me by writing segments of my final *President's Report*, which was just about to be published. Jack's task was to look forward to the future of American higher education in general and

John was to do likewise for the liberal arts college sector in particular. My contribution was to be that of bringing the message home to Williams itself. Our collaboration during the course of our bicentennial year would, I hoped, symbolize for the larger Williams community the fairly seamless continuity in direction of the college's presidential leadership over the previous thirty years and more which had laid, or so I am now inclined to believe, the firm academic foundation on which the college's fine reputation has been erected. And, a related matter, I myself was receiving gratifyingly positive feedback concerning the little book I had just published—*Community of Learning: The American College and the Liberal Arts Tradition*—which I had dedicated to the larger Williams community, 1793–1993. The prospects right at the start looked good for a reasonably tranquil and satisfyingly productive final year on the job. But then we hit several patches of unpredictably rough water.

In January, the campus had had once more to come to terms with the death of a very popular and much-beloved student. While she had had a wonderfully broad array of friendships among students of all races, she herself was black and her African American fellow students were particularly hard hit by her death. On the morning of January 27, while they were still struggling to come to terms with their sense of loss, three racist messages were found posted to the front door of Rice House, where the office of the Williams Black Student Union (WBSU) was housed. They said:

—GO HOME NIGGERS!
—NIGGERS ARE WORTH LESS THAN
  THE DIRT UNDER THIS HOUSE!
—DIE NIGGERS!

Joan Edwards of the Biology Department, who had succeeded Steve Fix as dean of the college, was prompt in issuing a statement of condemnation, and the student College Council was quick to add its own. The general on-campus reaction to this miserable event was measured and mature, as was that of the coordinators of the WBSU. While a bit shaken by the threat involved, the latter were conscious of the fact that the perpetrator could be anyone, either off-campus or on, and could be of any race. The off-campus reaction was, alas, a good deal less measured, with the *Berkshire Eagle* (whose staff at that time was, I believe, entirely white in composition) treating the matter as front-page news, adopting a somewhat portentous and judgmental tone. Headline: "Racism rears head at Williams."

During the short break between the end of our Winter Study Period on January 28 and the start of our spring semester on February 4, it emerged that a black student had been responsible for the messages. Upset about the reaction to them, he had turned himself in to the dean, offering a rather confused explanation to the effect that he had wanted, as part of his Winter Study project, to stimulate "intellectual discussion" of racism. Without revealing his name or racial identity, the dean reported to the community on February 1 simply that the perpetrator was now known and was being charged with a disciplinary infraction. As is always the case under such circumstances, we were unable for reasons of confidentiality to say much more than that. The perpetrator, however, had also chosen to make his identity known to the WBSU and had met with some fifty of its members who had responded with varying degrees of anger, incomprehension, and compassion. With students back on campus on February 4, it was possible to assemble the faculty-student Discipline Committee and, the following day, after a very difficult meeting, it suspended the student perpetrator for one semester. That same day I had had to head out for Florida and, that evening, the pace of events began suddenly to quicken. Five minutes after checking into my hotel I learned that another student (white) who had been suspended for a minimum of one year (he was already on disciplinary probation for a previous infraction and had been warned that any further behavior that violated of the code of conduct would result in his suspension) for making harassing and sexually explicit telephone calls while posing as a gay Williams student who was currently abroad, had filed a civil suit in the US District Court at Springfield seeking from the court an injunction reinstating him at the college. He turned out to be one of a group of conservative students and may, alas, have been encouraged and supported in his maneuver by one or more like-minded alumni living in town. The court hearing was set for February 8, by which time our troubles had begun to mount. On February 6 the *Berkshire Eagle* made public the fact that the student responsible for writing and posting the racist messages was himself black, and we learned the following day that the paper was about to break the story that, the student in question having been suspended, a group of ten to fifteen black students (all of them sophomores if I remember correctly) were threatening to leave the college if the administration did not step in and rescind the Discipline Committee's sentence. That threat, if it was real, was never communicated directly to anyone in administration and the coordinators of the WBSU quietly conveyed to us the fact that it did not reflect their views on the matter. Our own subsequent meeting with some of the students concerned and with the perpetrator himself was civil enough and non-confrontational. Concerns were expressed but no insistent demands were made. Attention was focused on the college's disciplinary proceedings and on the right of any student found guilty of a disciplinary infraction to request on specific grounds reconsideration by the Discipline Committee of its decision. But I had to make it totally clear to them that there would be no presidential or administrative subversion of our established disciplinary procedures, and no referral of the case to some new committee (which is what they had requested).

That same day, the judge at Springfield crisply rejected the request for an injunction against the college in connection with our other discipline case. But in the immediate aftermath of that ruling (though not in the long haul) the student's lawyer appeared still to be intent upon continuing to pursue a civil suit against the college. Meanwhile, reporters from the *Boston Globe*, *Berkshire Eagle*, and *North Adams Transcript* continued to prowl the campus in the quest for further news. And the *Williams Record*, chafing at the dean's unwillingness to say much by way of comment while disciplinary proceedings were still continuing, and mistakenly assuming that it was the Dean's Office that had revealed to the WBSU the identity of the student responsible for the racist messages, chose in a very heavy-handed editorial to berate us all, administration and WBSU alike, for lack of "honesty and openness."

The central issue in both cases having now become the integrity of the college's disciplinary procedures, and delicate though the situation undoubtedly was, it seemed now clearly time for me, subject to legal advice, to issue some sort of statement, and the upcoming faculty meeting afforded an appropriate venue and opportunity for so doing. That statement, made on February 10, was made public the following morning in an all-campus mailing. It went as follows:

In the past few weeks our institutional commitments and standards here at Williams have been tested by a series of events that have generated a fair amount of press coverage and stimulated, no doubt, a good deal of rumor. To those events the College has responded with firmness and clarity, but because of the rules of confidentiality governing our disciplinary procedures, we in administration have been able to report to the community on the whole matter in only a very limited way. The Faculty Steering Committee has, of course, been briefed on the unfolding of events and I have greatly benefited from the advice of its members and of other concerned members of the faculty. I should now like to make a statement on what has been happening.

What was put to the test first were the standards to which we as a community are committed and which preclude as unacceptable behavior on the part of any member of the community either harassment on the grounds of sexual identity or threats (or what anyone would reasonably assume to be threats) grounded in the racial identity of those targeted as recipients. Clearly, such forms of behavior have no place in this community. They are utterly unacceptable.

Put to the test in the second place, and even more fundamentally, were the instrumentalities and carefully constructed procedures whereby we as an academic community determine whether or not such unacceptable behavior has indeed occurred and, if so, what disciplinary penalties must attach to it.

The first of the challenges involved took the form of an attempt to end-run our constituted disciplinary procedures, and a penalty of suspension emerging from them, by seeking from the US District Court in Springfield an injunction reinstating the student who had been suspended. The College made its case in court and the judge ruled very clearly and very firmly in the College's favor. I read in the press that notwithstanding his initial setback, the student involved intends to pursue his civil suit against the College for alleged breach of contract. If that happens, we will, of course, fight it.

The second of the challenges was a more complex one and, as the disciplinary process may still be incomplete (that we don't know for certain yet), there is not a great deal I can say about it beyond describing the sequence of events.

On January 27, threatening racist messages were placed by an unknown person on the door of the Black Student Union offices in Rice House. As you know from the all-campus mailing Dean Edwards sent out on February 1, a student subsequently admitted writing and posting those messages, and disciplinary proceedings were begun. That student subsequently chose to reveal his identity to members of the Black Student Union. Those disciplinary proceedings eventuated last Friday in the suspension for one semester of the student involved. On Saturday (February 6), the *Berkshire Eagle*, without identifying its informant, reported that the student was black. On Monday (February 8), again without identifying its source, it reported that between 10 and 15 black students at Williams were prepared to leave the College if the penalty of suspension was not rescinded. On Sunday (February 7) the deans met with several concerned students. On Monday (February 8) the deans and I met with the same students along with the student who had been suspended. At those meetings concerns were expressed and explored in thoughtful and civil fashion; no demands were made. Attention focused on the College's Discipline and Disciplinary Proceedings' (*Student Handbook*, pp. 68–70) including the right of a student found guilty of a disciplinary offense to "request reconsideration [by the Discipline Committee] of the Committee's decision on the basis of substantial new evidence or improper procedures" (*Student Handbook*, p. 70).

Where do things stand now? First, and as of the moment, the student involved has not requested reconsideration of his case though he still has the right to do so. Second, the disciplinary committee system and disciplinary procedures long since provided for in our established governance structures cannot and will not be bypassed.

What, then, can we all do to ensure the continued well-being of our community? Our student leadership in the Black Student Union and the College Council, as also, indeed, the concerned students with whom we met, have all comported themselves in an extraordinarily complex, difficult, confusing, and testing situation with admirable firmness, dignity, thoughtfulness, and compassion. Let us on the faculty do everything we can to assist them in that stance, and to encourage all our students to do likewise. And let us also, and with our help the students committed to our care, extract from this moment of turbulence the lessons that will enable us to go forward as a more open, more tolerant, healthier and more vital educational community.

What we are witnessing here, in this, the most plural, diverse, and integrated community in Berkshire County, what we are witnessing here in microcosm and, admittedly, in travail and labor, are the birth pangs of a new and vastly different society—edgy and conflicted, it may be, but full of vibrancy and creative promise. If pain now attends—and probably not for the last time—the delivery of that future, let us be careful to populate it, not with our fears but with our hopes. For as a college committed by our very mission to the education of a fine group of young people drawn from all sorts of backgrounds and from all races and religions, we are called upon to be a community, not of divisiveness and fear, but of compassion and hope.

I would like, of course, to be able to claim that these words succeeded in bringing this whole tangled contretemps to a close, but of course, they didn't. They did help the faculty, I think, to draw a line under the sequence of disruptive events that had preceded them. And for some students, or so I was assured, they were of some help. But not, I think, for the student body at large. Supporters of the two disciplined students tried, in uneasy coalition, to organize a rather confused effort to revise our disciplinary procedures, but without effect. They were not helped by the fact that the coordinators of the WBSU issued on February 10 a very forthright statement affirming "the College's action to discipline the [black] student," and *mirabile dictu* supporting "the College administration's quick response." Dissent, however, rumbled on and it was only the College Council's organization on February 22 of a forum attended by about a third of the student body that, however confused in its focus, provided the cathartic moment. With that, this miserable sequence of events began to move to the margins of campus attention.

But if it did so, it was rapidly to be replaced by another and in some ways more intractable challenge. In 1991, and in response to the needs and aspirations of our rapidly growing Latino student population, the college had committed itself to trying to make a regular appointment in US Latino Studies. Although a handful of distinguished scholars were working in that comparatively new field of specialization, it was one in which only a tiny number of new PhDs were being produced. So, despite vigorous recruitment efforts, that 1991 commitment had proved extremely difficult to deliver on. We had made a visiting appointment in history for the 1991–92 academic year and had embarked upon a multi-departmental search. That had culminated in the offer of a regular appointment in psychology, but the candidate had decided that to do her work she needed to be in a research university setting and we had had to content ourselves with renewing for another year the visiting appointment in history and with launching another, more targeted, search for a regular appointment. If it was frustrating for the faculty and the departments involved, it was even more frustrating for our impatient Latino/a students. The reasons for that failure were multiple. Among other things, the three finalists brought to campus were not deemed suitable for appointment either by the departments concerned or by the Latino/a students involved in the search. But it has to be acknowledged that there had also been some marginal posturing and foot-dragging on the part of one or two of the departments involved. The passionately engaged Latino/a students who had helped with the search had been quick to detect that fact and had become very frustrated with faculty and administration alike. Unfortunately, that frustration came to be focused on the History Department once it decided (and it was very firm on the matter) that it could not in good conscience recommend its visiting professor in US Latino Studies for a regular appointment. The students, desperate after a series of sequential disappointments, simply could not understand that decision and, over the course of the month ensuing, mounted increasing pressure on the department in the hope of inducing its members to change their minds. That hope was in vain and, despite sterling efforts made by Suzanne Graver (who had succeeded John Reichert as dean of the faculty) and by Joan Edwards, dean of the college, as well as exhaustive (and exhausting) rounds of discussion with the concerned students on the part of faculty and administrators alike, the students committed themselves finally on the Saturday of Parents' Weekend to direct action in the form of a hunger strike in which some

seventeen students participated (or claimed to be participating). It was
to last for three days. In so acting, they unwisely made some truly unrealistic and intractable demands that left, in effect, no room for anything
that could accurately be called "negotiation." In that respect, the language they used was revelatory. They said that they would "accept" the
appointment of a US Latino visiting professor for the 1993–94 academic
year and would "allow" placement of such a visitor in one or another of
the following departments: History, Political Science, and Anthropology
& Sociology. They insisted that the tenure-track appointment to be made
for the 1994–95 academic year "must" be in the History Department.
They insisted, too, that students "will" constitute one-third of the total
membership of the search committee for the new position, must have
full voting powers on that committee, and, indeed, must constitute one-
third of the voting power in its decisions.

Such demands, of course, trenched upon one of the faculty's most
fundamental prerogatives and there was little to be done beyond visiting
the hunger strikers to see that they were all right (that the dean and I
did), having our medical director keep a close eye on them, and pursuing, via a faculty liaison committee chaired by Dan O'Connor (our former dean), talks geared to convincing them that while (as in the past) an
advisory role for students in the making of faculty appointments was
perfectly acceptable, the extension of voting rights to them was out of the
question—as also was their counterproductive insistence that such an
appointment be made in any one given department.

Outside observers of anomic events such as this one seem often
to miss the fact that on campuses like ours the student protestors are
comprised—depending on one's term of choice—of late adolescents or
young adults, people still in the process of defining who they are and at a
vulnerable point in their development as individuals. By boldly handing
down what in the late 1960s used to be called "nonnegotiable demands,"
by breaching hallowed procedural norms and long-established patterns
of collegial governance in an impetuous attempt to impose on the institution the absoluteness of their will, they have contrived in effect, and
especially so in the case of building occupations and hunger strikes, to
paint themselves into something of a corner. In proceeding to negotiate
with them (the occasion off campus of a lot of Monday morning quarter-
backing and periodic spasms of alumni apoplexy), administrators—and,

in this case, faculty too—are engaging in an effort as educators to help young, idealistic people, who are, after all, *their* students, to extricate themselves from that corner. For administrators such negotiations have to avoid compromising concessions and characteristically involve the weathering of distressing gusts of alienation and the patient absorption of tiresome and self-indulgent bouts of "acting out"—all in the hope that the college will be able to find its way at long last to the crucial common ground on which minds can meet and can do so in such a way as to enable the institution to move forward again in a positive and, if at all possible, enhanced fashion. Though it is something that outside observers and critics are prone to missing, such negotiations also bring with them a somewhat stoic acceptance on the part of administrators of the necessity (in the interest of defusing resentment and permitting a modicum of face-saving) of conceding to the protesting students the dominant role in the framing after the event of the "constitutive narrative" of what exactly has taken place. Anybody who aspires to write a history of protest on any given campus, at least a history that is not thoroughly misleading, would do well in general to focus less on the institutional concessions (or seeming concessions) triumphantly claimed by the retiring protestors than on what is usually passed over in discreet silence—namely, the "demands" that the institution in question has wisely and firmly rejected. Here, as at other moments in the lives of educational institutions, the history of what was prevented from happening may well be as illuminating and as important as the history of what actually did happen.

In the particular case of the 1993 Latino/a hunger strike at Williams, resolution, because of the unwise and intractable nature of the demands involved, proved to be unusually difficult to reach. Before the students had committed themselves to direct action, we had already pledged to bring in as consultants for a renewed search a trio of distinguished scholars in the field of US Latina Studies. So that move could not now be used as a species of bargaining chip. Although, when faced with a firm and united stand by faculty and administration alike, the concerned students abandoned their unwise demand for votes in the appointment process and the insistence that the pertinent appointment be made in a particular department—for them very painful concessions—but they could not bring themselves immediately to abandon the hunger strike, though its purpose was no longer at all clear. It was only with the help of a new idea proposed by some of our more concerned younger faculty for the creation from their ranks of an *ad hoc* committee to offer supportive advice to the Latino/a students that the latter were finally able to let go and end the strike. While I was very relieved that it was over, my heart went out to them in their bitterness and sense of defeat. Of all the episodes of student protest and direct action on my watch as president this was the one that left me most deeply saddened.

That was far from being the case with my response to the last of the challenges on which I wish to comment. It involved a set of issues of a general nature that I could probably have sidestepped had I not found them to be of such compelling interest and so central to our own mission and to that of American higher education at large. What it involved was the "battle of the books," the great debate concerning the nature and quality of American undergraduate education that broke out early in the 1980s, peaked at the end of the decade, and finally petered out sometime in the mid-1990s. At its narrowest, that debate concerned the nature, shape, and quality of the undergraduate course of study in America. In some ways it represented no more than the resurfacing of a fluctuating but ongoing, century-long argument that had last recurred in quite intense form towards the end of the Second World War as American colleges and universities sought to prepare themselves for the return of peace and the entry of the veterans into institutions of higher education. At its broadest, however, while still encompassing that particular debate, the more recent battle of the books reached far beyond it, eventually warranting the label of the "culture wars" which academics came eventually to attach to it.

In this particular round, the debate had been initiated by the critics of American higher education in general and of contemporary undergraduate education in particular. And I think it fair to say that the combatants arrayed in the center of the line in this onslaught on the academy hailed from neoconservative territory. Undergraduate education in general, they said, had slipped into disarray. We were beset, they argued, by nothing less than "a crisis of liberal education" itself—a crisis reflecting (variously) the distortion of our universities and colleges by the research ethos and a concomitant neglect of teaching (thus, as we have seen earlier, Charles Sykes, Page Smith, Martin Anderson), the fragmentation of knowledge and the growth of hyper-specialization in the academic disciplines (thus William Bennett), the corrosive inroads of cultural relativism (thus Allan Bloom, Roger Kimball, William Bennett), the intrusion into the curriculum of a marketplace philosophy, the politicization and subordination "of our studies according to contemporary prejudices" (thus Bennett). Coupled with "a collective loss of nerve and faith on the part of the faculty and administrators during the late 1960s and early 1970s, as well as the abandonment of the old commitment (via required core curricula of one sort or another) to mediate to successive generations of students the richnesses of the Western cultural tradition" (thus Bennett), these developments were seen to have eventuated in nothing less than "the decay of the humanities" and the disintegration of the curriculum (thus Bloom, Bennett).

William J. Bennett was a graduate of Williams and a loyal member of the class of 1965, so it is safe to say that none of these issues were alien to the ongoing concerns of the greater Williams community. From time to time, alumni who resonated instinctively to the force and clarity of Bennett's critique of the undergraduate course of studies typical at American colleges and universities, or who were moved by Bloom's passionately quirky dissent from much that is commonplace in our contemporary intellectual life, would take the time to write to me to convey their concerns, or would question me directly at one or another alumni gathering across the country or at the open presidential question and answer session that we instituted as part of the annual alumni reunions in Williamstown. Similarly, if less happily, the scattering of alumni who, for one reason or another, reacted with sympathy to Sykes's truly shoddy and slipshod take on the deportment of the academic profession, and who echoed the view (so totally at odds with the established ethos and demonstrated track record of Williams) that a commitment on the part of the faculty to scholarly research was likely to undermine rather than strengthen the quality of their teaching performance.

As was made clear, however, by a survey we commissioned during the run-in to the bicentennial in 1993, such quizzical or angular voices, however seriously they should be taken, represented no more than a small minority of our alumni. And if they had some purchase on the views of the more conservative among our students, they had little noticeable resonance among faculty, staff, and students at large. This was hardly surprising. To the college's curricular culture and long-standing curricular tradition the core general education approach involving college-wide required courses pivoting on the Western tradition and possessed of a "great books" component had remained foreign. Contrary to the impression so often given, there was nothing timeless about that latter approach. It had risen to prominence only during the interwar years, had flourished for a while after the Second World War, but had failed to establish a firm foothold in the bulk of American colleges and universities. It had made its strongest appeal, by way of pushback it may be, at places like Chicago and Stanford where the free elective system championed by President Eliot at Harvard had been most enthusiastically embraced. And it had made little or no impact at colleges of comparatively conservative curricular bent whose traditionalism had served as a bulwark in the late nineteenth century against the inroads of the free elective system.

At Williams, which was certainly one of those colleges, it had become something of a mantra, long repeated in the college's catalog copy, that "not having abandoned itself to the elective principle in the nineteenth century, Williams did not need to rescue itself with the general education principle in the twentieth." And, as we had found out during the fierce curricular debate of 1979, most faculty were still disinclined to make even marginal moves in the direction of a college-wide core curriculum. During my term of office as president, while the pace of curricular change was really quite lively, it was basically evolutionary in nature. That being so, while the national "battle of the books" more or less coincided with my presidential years, my own personal interest and involvement in it, which led me to publish articles, give lectures, and, finally, write my *Community of Learning* book, were stimulated less by anything happening at Williams itself than by my own growing dismay at the direction being taken by a debate that might otherwise have borne considerable fruit. There were three grounds for that dismay of mine: the tone of the debate, the absence from it of any real degree of historical consciousness and institutional perspective, and the inattention to (or ignorance of) the pertinent empirical data on the part of those shaping it.

First, the tone that the latter-day critics of American higher education set for the debate was sarcastic, contemptuous, vituperative, and hyperbolic. That tone, while in some ways reminiscent of that adopted by such predecessor critics at the start of the century as Thorstein Veblen and Abraham Flexner, was placed at the service of a far less well-informed version of what was actually going on at our universities and colleges than had been the case with those earlier critics. Something comparably unflattering has also to be said about the tone adopted by more than one of the wounded academic respondents to those critiques (usually written from the "cultural left"), and especially to those focused on the allegedly deplorable current state of the humanities and its impact on the quality of American undergraduate education. The charge levied by the neoconservative critic, Roger Kimball, to the effect that Bennett's 1984 report, *To Reclaim a Legacy*, "occasioned paroxysms of rage" within the academy, if characteristically overstated, still comes depressingly close to the mark.

What stimulated those paroxysms of rage was Bennett's tight focus on issues of core, canon, and content no less than the *nature* of his recommended content. "[M]erely being exposed to a variety of subjects and points of view," he said, "is not enough. Learning to think critically and skeptically is not enough." What is crucial is that students be called upon to "master an explicit body of knowledge" and to "confront a series of important original texts." The determination of that content and the choice of those texts he viewed as hardly something to be left to the vagaries of faculty selection or the demonstrably uncertain sense among academics of what it took to enable us to "become participants in a common culture, *stakeholders* in our civilization." That content, indeed, he and fellow spirits saw as being so obvious that it did not call for extended justification. At its heart lay the mediation of the Western cultural tradition, a task to be effected above all through the required exposure of all students to the great works of that Western tradition. Those works were not to be approached exclusively as documents of time and place, manifestations of a particular time-bound historical moment. Instead, they had to be recognized as classics of timeless import precisely because of the profundity with which they addressed "perennial matters of human experience" and the power with which they mediated the culture's "lasting vision, its highest shared ideals and aspirations, and its heritage."

If that approach was open to criticism on more than one ground (and it certainly was), the virtues attaching to it were nonetheless considerable, not only because of the stature of the works usually proposed for study or the degree to which they would indeed serve to acquaint students with a sense of shared heritage (and, therefore with the inherited furnishings of their own minds), but also because it might serve, perhaps more effectively than any other approach, to foster among all students on a campus a rudimentary foundation on which to build a community of shared discourse. This last, certainly, had been what had moved some of us at Williams in 1979 to propose the insertion of a modest, required great books component into the freshman year curriculum.

The enthusiastic advocacy of something approximating Bennett's position, then, is not to be dismissed as some sort of oddity. Over the years it has served on countless campuses (our own included) to sharpen the endless and, in my experience, deeply thoughtful and conscientious debates about the undergraduate course of study into which college faculties cyclically fling themselves with remarkably good cheer. What was odd, however, and what served to set my own intellectual teeth on edge, was the *nature* of the advocacy of that position current in the 1980s and early 1990s, and the degree of unruffled confidence with which a particular curricular agenda was being pushed. That confidence was such that it came close to suggesting a serene and unreflecting assumption of self-evidence and to implying an impatiently condescending dismissal of alternative approaches, however widely followed. It also exhibited an edge of passionate dismay that led the proponents into betraying a disagreeable tendency to explain its otherwise inexplicable failure to carry the day by invoking the specters of intellectual confusion, laziness, and self-interest on the part of the faculty, compounded by a contemptible spinelessness and (post-1960s) failure of nerve on the part of administrators. And fueling that singularly unattractive tendency, at least in such critics as Allan Bloom and Roger Kimball, was a sense of profound alienation from the academic culture of the day and a marked hostility to the direction in which some of the most powerful intellectual currents of the postmodern era seemed now to be sweeping our universities and colleges.

Fueling that tendency, too, and deepening my own discontent with the critics, was a surprising absence of historical self-consciousness, one extending both to the recent history of educational debate in North America and to the more distant European past. So far as the former was concerned, though decline and fall was usually dated back to the political and cultural upheavals of the late 1960s, the transformative impact of the great wave of demographic change that had broken over American higher education in the postwar years and swept forward on into the present, was almost entirely ignored or overlooked. Demography may not admittedly be destiny, but it is simply impossible to comprehend the hopes and fears, achievements and failures, triumphs and tribulations of American higher education across the past half century if, somehow, we fail to take into account the wholly extraordinary demographic upheavals and swings that have characterized those years, bringing truly enormous pressures to bear on the whole institutional and educational apparatus. Periodically over the years that apparatus had needed to expand with great rapidity to meet one or another demographic challenge. In 1860, on the eve of the Civil War, some 250 colleges were in existence. By 1960 that number had expanded eightfold to 2000. By the time the critics were launching their attacks in the 1980s, almost a further doubling had taken place. And institutional growth had been matched during those years by a truly staggering increase in student enrollments—from about three million in 1960 (up already by a million since the end of the Second World War) to a figure in 1990 in excess of twelve million and still climbing. This fourfold increase was the most dramatic and sizable one in the entire history of American higher education. It was accompanied also by a dramatic increase in the size of the academic profession and, beyond that, by a marked diversification by race, gender, and class in the makeup of the student population. Already by 1980, in its report *Three Thousand Futures*, the Carnegie Council on Policy Studies in Higher Education was predicting (accurately, it turned out) that "roughly one-half of the students in the classroom of 2000 would not have been there if the composition [of the student body] of 1960 had been continued."

That in the 1980s and early 1990s such revolutionary changes should largely have escaped the contemporary critics of the academy, however deplorable, is hardly surprising. So many of those critics, after all, were drawing their negative conclusions from what was purported to be going on at little more than a dozen or so of the nation's leading research universities and liberal arts colleges. Their tendency was to glorify the 1950s as some sort of golden age of educational and curricular rectitude, and the impression was given that the core curricular great books approach (very much in fact a product of the interwar years and the first seepage of cultural self-doubt in the West) was some sort of timeless deliverance from an age-old past. In the very process of emphasizing the importance of knowledge of the Western cultural tradition, moreover, there was an ironic failure on the part of the critics to recognize how very conflicted in its intellectual commitments and educational ideals that tradition had been. In that very conflictedness, or so I would argue, may be found the wellsprings of the cultural singularity that the proponents of the great books approach rightly thought students should be helped to discern and understand. But of that one heard nothing. Nor was there anything really to suggest that those critics recognized the persistently destabilizing impact across the centuries of the fundamental tension between some of the positions characteristic of the Greek philosophical tradition and those other commitments, both intellectual and moral, that were ultimately of biblical provenance. Nor did they appear to realize that by their own emphasis on the required study of "the great works of the Western tradition," on the duty of the college or university to convey to students "the accumulated wisdom of our civilization," and on the duty of the scholars to "preserve the record of human accomplishment and to make it accessible in many ways," they themselves had tilted towards the rhetorical version of liberal education which, since the time of Isocrates in the fifth century BCE had been very much at odds with the philosophical tradition championed in that same era by Plato. And to say that, their reverential invocations of Socrates and Plato notwithstanding, means that they had also inclined away from what was, in effect, the Socratic heritage, the philosophico-scientific vision which has always been less concerned with the preservation and mediation of the cultural heritage than with discovery, critical originality, and the advancement of knowledge via the overthrow of received assumptions.

Given the passionate commitment of these critics to humanistic studies, this lack of historical consciousness was surprising. Surprising, too, was their lack of institutional perspective. And that was exacerbated further by their willingness to ignore or brush aside, even when they were readily available, accumulated sets of empirical data capable of throwing a more nuanced light on the complexities of what was actually happening. Typically drawing their negative conclusions in anecdotal fashion from the deplorable things supposed to be going on at a mere handful of elite institutions, these commentators on the ills of American higher education showed a surprisingly limited degree of interest in what might or might not be happening elsewhere in the more than 3,500 institutions that made up the whole and at which the vast majority of American students were enrolled. Nor did they respond with any visible enthusiasm to the comparative success of the much-maligned American system in adjusting to the enormous growth in both numbers and diversity of the undergraduate population since the Second World War, and in doing so without the swamping of existing institutions by students of differing expectations and capacities so evident in parts of Europe. That success, after all, might be taken to suggest (and despite the unevenness in academic quality that is their inevitable concomitant) that there might be something healthy and praiseworthy about the characteristics of independence, autonomy, and sheer institutional variety that distinguish the American from other systems of higher education in the industrialized nations abroad.

Of this, however, one heard nothing from the critics. Nor, as we have seen, from people like Sykes and Anderson who dined out so gleefully on the allegedly destructive effects of the "publish or perish" syndrome did one hear anything of the rich array of survey data suggesting a high degree of commitment to teaching as a calling on the part of the American professoriate. But that lack of interest in statistical data, I should in fairness acknowledge, was no monopoly of the neoconservative participants in this most recent round of the battle of the books. It was, instead, a characteristic feature of the whole debate, serving, unfortunately, to diminish its value and rendering it in many ways a lost opportunity. It is not reassuring, even in retrospect, to learn from survey data that, apocalyptic warnings to the contrary, what was universally deplored in the 1980s (by acerbic critics and anguished respondents alike) as a catastrophic decline nationwide in the traditional level of student interest in the humanities was, in fact, something of a statistical artefact. That is to say, that once one recovered and tracked the statistics back beyond the commonly chosen point of analytic departure in the late 1960s—a quite exceptional moment—one found that the startling and much-deplored decline in liberal arts enrollments in the 1970s and early 1980s represented no unprecedented declension from any long-term higher norm. Instead, it reflected a simple falling back from the all-time peak in such enrollments which had been produced by an unprecedented (and in part gender-related) surge of interest among a new and growing student population lasting from the late 1950s to around 1970. By tracing this statistical drama back to the earlier part of the century, it has since been established, moreover, that the effect of that falling back was merely to return us to something approximating the long-term "trajectory [of gradual decline] established over the past century."

Nor, similarly, and whatever one's ideological proclivities, is there really much cause for celebration in discovering, after decades of passionate debate about what more or less everyone took to be an indisputable decline across the nation in the amount of attention being given to the Western civilization component in the general education curriculum, that between 1970 and 1985 the percentage of colleges and universities requiring a course not merely in Western civilization but even, specifically, in the *history* of Western civilization had actually increased, and had done so by a little over 5 percent to a total of almost 50 percent. Nor, yet again, was there much joy in the unveiling of a celebrated (if inherently improbable) claim, that was for some years, and with much shaking of journalist jowl, treated as a documented matter of fact to be solemnly footnoted and enthusiastically recycled, as a simple piece of mythology. Namely, that Alice Walker's prizewinning novel *The Color Purple* was being "taught in more English courses today than all of Shakespeare's plays combined." The Modern Language Association's 1995 report on its survey data concerning what was being taught nationwide in introductory courses in British and American literature indicated otherwise. It revealed that, in the former, Chaucer was the author most frequently assigned (89 percent) with Shakespeare not far behind. In the case of the latter, Hawthorne headed the list at 66 percent with the other most frequently assigned authors being Melville, Whitman, Dickinson, Twain, and Emerson. No great surprises there either. Alice Walker, however, came in at less than 1 percent, trailing even Cotton Mather (2 percent), the not very user-friendly seventeenth-century Puritan divine.

This sort of thing nudged me, as I closed in on the writing of my *Community of Learning* book and of subsequent articles on American higher education, to the sobering conclusion that the real lesson to be learned from this last round in the cyclical battle of the books might well have nothing at all to do with the shape the undergraduate course of study should properly take. It might, instead, be an eminently conservative piece of wisdom suggesting that we would do well—acerbic critics and wounded respondents alike—under similar circumstances in the future to be careful to begin our vituperative exchanges by attending first to the basic facts. Accurate description of what *is* should surely precede uninhibited prescription of what *should be*. During this last (and largely futile) round, exhortation and prescription had been allowed to preempt description and analysis. We had been subjected to a barrage of disheveled anecdotalism, and a free-fire zone had been cleared for eye-catching and sensationalist claims matched all too often by analytically flaccid, apoplectic, and sloppy responses. Next time around, perhaps, those of us in the humanities will be more careful, before flinging ourselves into combat, to keep our powder dry and to pause awhile for a moment of historical reflection as well as for a little therapeutic consultation with our more patient, data-gathering colleagues in the social sciences. And it was that hope for a better-grounded argumentative future that was to lead me in my post-presidential years to involve myself quite so deeply in the protracted but ultimately successful effort sponsored by the American Academy of Arts & Sciences to produce a set of *Humanities Indicators* analogous to the *Science and Engineering Indicators* that had long since provided our colleagues in the natural sciences with a continuing flow of reliable data revelatory of what was actually going on in their respective fields.

Apart from the continuing effort to push the campaign total as far beyond the original goal as possible, all these challenges were more or less behind me during my last three months in office. In addition to making sure that no administrative loose end was left untied, my main concern was that we should all do everything we could to ensure a smooth transition in the college's leadership. To that end I asked all the members of the President's Executive Group to put together in ring binder folders any ideas about their own responsibilities and the functioning of Williams in general that they thought might be useful to an incoming president who was not familiar with the inner workings of the college, along with any informative documents they felt could be particularly useful to him. And I myself put together a similar collection of materials pertinent to the way in which the president's office had been operating over the course of the previous decade. In general, these were all the sorts of materials that I myself would have liked to have had drawn to my attention when I was taking up the presidency but which had not been. That being so, I was a bit taken aback by the fact that Hank Payne, my successor, seemed to be more amused than anything else when, at the first of our transition sessions, I presented these briefing books to him. I was also surprised, during those transition sessions, by what came through as an apparent lack of curiosity about the place and also by the speed with which, during those sessions, he began to betray unmistakable signs of boredom. Surprised and, let it be confessed, a bit embarrassed. Could it be, I wondered uneasily, that I was being a bit of a fusspot, tiresomely belaboring things with which he was quite familiar? After all, he had served for five years as president of Hamilton, one of our sister liberal arts colleges, and was almost as experienced a college president as was I. I worried, then, that our transition sessions, somewhat awkward in feeling, had not been as successful as I had hoped. Certainly, I myself came away from them with an uneasy sense of embarrassed puzzlement.

CHAPTER TWENTY

Aftermath

My last day in the President's Office was Saturday, December 31, 1993. And my ledger tells me that my last appointment, appropriately enough, was one with Steve Fix, my good friend and former colleague in administration, who needed to nail down some details concerning the chairmanship of the English Department which he was about to assume. Later in the day, leaving on the desk a note for Hank Payne, I left the office for the last time. I did so not without emotion. In 1985 I had concluded my Induction Address by pledging to bring to the fulfillment of my mission as president "whatever measure of energy and talent" I possessed. As I left the office that day, I did so secure in the knowledge that I had striven to do precisely that. I had fought the good fight, and in the wake of all the sequential challenges we had faced, I felt confident also that I had at least earned my keep.

The following afternoon we left the fine old President's House at the heart of the campus to which both of us had become so deeply attached and moved back to South Williamstown to get things organized and to settle in, once more, at the house we had built there nearly thirty years earlier. January that year was extremely cold, but for the fortnight we spent settling in at our old place, prior to my departure for Washington, DC (where I would move into a flat off Wisconsin Avenue close to the new Russian Embassy and take up a fellowship at the Wilson International Center for Scholars), I still enjoyed the unaccustomed luxury of being able to ski along Stone Hill Road (the old, discontinued, north-south colonial road) up to the wide meadowland above the Clark Art Institute every day in the beautiful late-afternoon light, there to take in the splendidly panoramic view it affords of Williamstown, nestling in the valley carved out in the distant past by the Hoosic River. But not for long. It was usually so cold that a premonitory tingling or prickling on nose and cheeks would quickly suggest the wisdom of hightailing it back into the comparative warmth of the woods and setting out on the two-mile trek back home.

I experienced no second thoughts about having relinquished the presidency. For the better part of nine years I had set myself a truly blistering pace, and I am not sure that I could have kept it up all that much longer even had I wanted to do so. I was proud of what we had accomplished. It had been a wonderfully satisfying experience to open up the throttle of a first-class institution, to hear the engine roar, and to feel the surge of power it generated. Moreover, challenges and accompanying stress notwithstanding, it had also been deeply fulfilling to have been called upon to bring into play every last ounce of energy, talent, and capacity I could muster. But other imperatives were beginning now to supervene. When I had announced to the faculty that I planned to step down at the end of our bicentennial year, I had noted among other things that my plans for various unwritten books were beginning to drone through my dreams like planes in a holding pattern over Kennedy Airport, and I sensed it was now time to start bringing them in to land before they started running out of gas. And that, of course, I couldn't even think of attempting while I was still in office. It was clearly time, then, to begin planning my return to my primary calling as teacher and scholar.

Having taught, though on a reduced basis, throughout my years as dean of the faculty, and having managed to do enough teaching as president (mainly during the Winter Study Period), I had no qualms about returning to the classroom. And, when I did so, I managed to add to my regular repertoire of courses a new one tailored to the needs of our Environmental Studies Program. It was entitled "The Idea of Nature" and ranged from Genesis and the *Enuma elish* (the Babylonian creation myth), via Plato's *Timaeus* and the interest it elicited during the Middle

Ages, all the way down to James Lovelock's Gaia hypothesis (evoking harmonics of the *Timaeus*, though I have no reason to believe he had ever
read it), as well as to Peter Singer's advocacy of animals' rights and Arne
Næss's quasi-mystical ruminations about "deep ecology." And while for
me that course posed something of a pedagogical challenge (most of the
students who took it were either science majors or policy-oriented in
their interests), it proved for me (and I have reason to believe for at least
some of the students as well) to be very thought provoking.

About my proposed reentry into the world of medieval scholarship,
however, I must confess to having been, at least at the outset, somewhat
less sanguine. While I had been writing a good deal about higher education and steadily reviewing books in my medieval field for the learned
journals, I had had no time at all to get to rare book rooms and to pursue
original research. And I had begun to sense, uneasily, that a gap was now
beginning to open up between where I stood, intellectually speaking,
and the rapidly advancing frontiers in medieval studies. Not a good feeling. So I decided to start again with basic research and to write a series
of fairly fundamental articles that I could then submit for peer review
by the pertinent scholarly journals. It felt a bit like starting out all over
again in the profession. But I thought it would serve to give me a sense
of how firm the intellectual ground was on which I was inclined to take
my stand. I had not at first intended to return to work on matters pertaining to conciliarism, but I was to change my mind when I discovered
that the great, Europe-wide ideological battle precipitated in 1606 by the
pope's imposition of an interdict on the Serenissima Repubblica of Venice and, in England, by Parliament's post–Gunpowder Plot imposition
of an Oath of Allegiance on Catholic recusants had constituted a species
of ideological relay station, picking up and clarifying the conciliarist signal and transmitting it forward in amplified form to future generations.
And this led me to a focus on the early seventeenth century and the
treatises of Edmond Richer, Gallican Syndic of the Sorbonne, and Paolo
Sarpi, the acerbic Venetian theologian who was in the forefront of the defense of Venice against papal pressure. It was while reading in the Folger
Shakespeare Library a collection of Sarpi's tracts that I had my reassuring moment of scholarly reawakening. For there, one morning, I suddenly discovered that I had become so engrossed in what he had to say
that I had moved on from reading one treatise written in Latin to another

written in Italian without even having noticed the linguistic transition. With that, I sensed that, so far as scholarly engagement was concerned, all would be well. And it turned out to be so. I was able to place my articles in the appropriate journals without any difficulty and began soon to be invited, once more, to contribute chapters to collective volumes. Those articles and chapters were focused on both of my enduring areas of scholarly interest and it was my purpose eventually to gather them together, along with several of my more important earlier articles, in a substantial volume for which I already had the title—*Politics and Eternity: Studies in the History of Medieval and Early-Modern Political Thought*. That accomplished, I was then able to settle in for the long haul to the business of tackling the book-length projects that long years of administrative service had necessitated my postponing. Over the course of the more than a decade and a half ensuing, I was able to get that task done, a business almost completed when I backed, almost accidentally, into the writing of this memoir.

I had framed (or bookended) the articles gathered together in my *Politics and Eternity* book with a revisiting of some of the metahistorical and methodological questions bearing on the history of ideas in general and the history of political thought in particular with which I had been seeking to come to terms over the two decades preceding. And my preoccupation with those questions, along with my active reengagement in historical scholarship, and eventually with my two major book projects, led me to brood (perhaps a little anxiously) on the ways in which historical scholarship in general had changed across the forty and more years since I had first immersed myself in it. In so doing, I was also led to ponder the degree to which my own most compelling interests had come to run counter to—or, at least, stand apart from—the powerful intellectual currents which, flowing so strongly in the last quarter of the twentieth century, had helped reshape the dominant contours of historical scholarship only a little less dramatically than those of neighboring disciplines like literary studies and art history.

It was clear to me, for example, that, at a time when the history of ideas was currently so preoccupied as a discipline with linguistic and contextual issues of one sort or another, my own compelling concerns were, by contrast, robustly "internalist" in nature, pushing at times right up to the borders of the histories of philosophy and theology and focused especially on the subtle networks of intellectual affiliation linking together such seemingly disparate realms of endeavor as political philosophy, ethics, epistemology, natural philosophy, metaphysics, and natural theology. And while, like many another, I had done some highly specialized scholarly work focused on issues bound tightly to a specific time and place, it was also clear to me that my most compelling interests were drawing me increasingly into the pursuit of the *longue durée*. Despite the currently fashionable emphasis on historical discontinuity and rupture, I remained more concerned with the exploration of the historical continuities I could discern unfolding across long (sometimes millennial) stretches of time. In effect, my interests lay with the attempt to reconstruct the history of complex traditions of thought. In the early 1980s I had immersed myself in the omnipresent theoretical literature of a fashionably poststructuralist bent, as well as in the very different theoretical disquisitions of the leading figures in what was coming to be called "the Cambridge School" in the history of ideas in general and the history of political thought in particular. And I had arrived (not without a measure of nervousness) at some tentative conclusions about where I myself stood on the metahistorical issues at stake. In 1984, then, I was led in the first chapter of my *Omnipotence, Covenant, and Order* book (subtitled *An Excursion in the History of Ideas from Abelard to Leibniz*) to delineate my own, somewhat unfashionable, methodological stance. And I entitled that chapter "Against the Stream: In Praise of Lovejoy." While critical of Arthur O. Lovejoy's controversial notion of "unit ideas," I had argued nonetheless for the methodological viability of his attempt to write the history of an idea complex or tradition of thought that was millennial in its duration across time. That enterprise, or so I had argued, was both warranted and illuminating. And when, after my presidential years, I was once more able to devote a decent (and increasing) amount of time to historical research and writing, that was to be the sort of enterprise to the pursuit of which I committed myself in both of my major, book-length projects: *The Conciliarist Tradition: Constitutionalism in the Catholic Church 1300–1870* and *The Emergence of Western Political Thought in the Latin Middle Ages*. The latter work, indeed, after an introductory exploration probing into deep antiquity, spanned the better part of two millennia from the Hellenistic era down to the mid-seventeenth century.

All of this, of course, set me somewhat at odds with the essentially monographic and intensely specialized nature of so much of contemporary historical scholarship, tightly wedded, as it so often is, to a very specific time and place. And I had to struggle mightily to come to terms as best I could with what seemed to be a constantly accelerating and mind-numbing cascade of specialized studies. A century ago, and in what was to become celebrated as a classic essay, Max Weber had proclaimed that the human sciences had committed themselves for good to a degree of specialization foreign to the scholarship of the centuries preceding. And, a half century later, as he in turn set out to make the case for history of ideas as a discipline, Lovejoy had commented wryly and amusingly on the degree to which the (Lovejovian) historian of ideas, as he cuts a swath across a whole series of intensely cultivated scholarly specialties, is burdened with the responsibility for coming to terms with a dauntingly disparate array of texts and is peculiarly susceptible, accordingly, to misreading the intricate scholarly controversies that trouble practically every field. He is, in effect, an exposed (if moving) target, drawing the irritated fire of successive platoons of specialists jealously guarding against outside intrusion the perimeters of their own well-fortified professional enclaves.

If that was true of the mid-twentieth-century scholarly world, it is, of course, even truer today, and not simply because of the tightening degree of specialization everywhere apparent. One has also to take into account an important side effect attendant upon the vast postwar expansion in the size of the professoriate—namely, the concomitant increase in the number of specialists contributing assiduously to the body of scholarly literature. Between 1965 and 1970, after all, the number of *new* faculty positions being created and filled in the United States alone exceeded the *totality* of faculty positions existing nationwide in 1940. As the postwar baby boom made its impact felt elsewhere, comparably massive expansions in the number of academic professionals were to take place. And in the wake of that era of expansion came a pulverizing proliferation in the amount of scholarly writing being done, much of it, in my own medieval field at least, analytically sophisticated and of high overall quality.

In that field, the increase in scholarly volume can be illustrated in quite concrete fashion. On the shelves in my office I still have a full run of the leading North American (multidisciplinary) medieval journal

Speculum from the January 1959 issue (received just after I got my first full-time job and became a member of the Medieval Academy of America, its publisher) all the way down the issue for January 2016. While I can readily access online any of the articles contained in all those issues, sentimentality if nothing else has induced me to hold on to the printed volumes. *Speculum* has always attempted to review as many as possible of the scholarly books written on medieval topics in English and in all the other major European languages. And it is a striking fact that whereas the January 1959 issue printed some twenty-eight book reviews occupying sixty-four pages, the January 2016 issue reviewed some eighty books, an almost threefold increase across little more than half a century, and those reviews, courtesy of the smaller typeface to which recourse had necessarily had to be made, occupied some hundred and sixteen pages.

This startling increase in the amount of scholarship to be mastered presents something of a bracing challenge even to those laborers in the scholarly vineyard whose interests are comparatively tightly focused. But for any historian drawn to pursue the "big picture" by reconstructing the millennial course of this or that tradition of thought, the challenge is, accordingly, much more severe. And that very fact must surely go some way towards explaining why the pursuit of "big picture" historical writing by professional scholars has of recent years become somewhat unfashionable. Certainly, the ten long years it took me to write my three volumes on the development of Western political thinking were years punctuated by moments of real discouragement and even of doubt about the very viability of the project to which I had committed myself. In my more "down" moments, in effect, I was periodically daunted by the prospect of having to come to terms with yet another intimidatingly large body of scholarship concerned with this or that topic, itself often the product of a lifetime of dedicated labor on the part of scholars who had devoted themselves as specialists to the subject in question, and I couldn't help thinking that it was a bit like riding in a steeplechase. No sooner had one made it safely across, say, a challenging hedge and ditch than one might be confronted with the need to position oneself to surmount some forbidding stone wall constituted by yet another formidable body of specialized scholarship. In this respect, there looms especially in my memory the challenge posed by the need to feel my way into the complex, highly sophisticated, tightly knit, and somehow claustrophobic world of Florentine historiography. Not to mention the challenge entailed by the effort involved in tackling the vast body of Dante scholarship. In that latter case, across the centuries and beginning with his oldest son's composition of a gloss on the *Divina Commedia*, the layers of commentary have come to attain to almost geologic proportions. But in that connection I was cheered on somewhat by the fact that, when speaking about that almost limitless archive of scholarship, Étienne Gilson himself (whose knowledge of medieval thought was truly encyclopedic) was moved nonetheless and wryly to confess that he couldn't "think of it without experiencing a kind of dizziness."

Such moments of misgiving notwithstanding, and however challenging the task, I remained convinced of the need to attempt, in quite self-conscious fashion, the framing of a constitutive narrative that would help reshape the way in which the unfolding of Western political thought has traditionally been understood. Of that need I was convinced all the more by the fact that "big picture" assumptions of one sort or another are by no means foreign to the more specialized works on the subject. And while such interpretative schemata are rarely foregrounded or subjected to explicit examination, they still contrive, hovering teasingly on the margin of consciousness, implicitly to exert a shaping influence on the choice of subjects to be addressed and the framing of arguments about those subjects. Thus, for example, in Hans Baron's *Crisis of the Early Italian Renaissance* (a book recently described as "possibly the most important monograph in Renaissance history written since the Second World War") the sweeping central argument that is elaborated depends for its force and coherence upon a taken-for-granted and really quite crude understanding of the distinction between "medieval" and "modern." Again, the refusal of so many historians to recognize any sacral dimension in the pre-Christian Germanic kingship of western and southern Europe during the late imperial age and the subsequent era of barbarian invasion would seem to pivot on an unreflective rejection of the pertinence of cross-cultural analogies even when the most direct of those analogies involved the unambiguously sacral kingship prevalent a little later on in the Scandinavian north. Beyond that, there is an equally dogmatic unwillingness to take into account the overwhelming testimony of cultural anthropologists and students of comparative religion to the global omnipresence of forms of sacral kingship and their millennial persistence.

Instead, the tendency has been to take a stand on the paucity of unambiguous direct evidence available to sustain a confident affirmation on the presence of sacral kingship among those pre-Christian Germanic peoples. Here, one of the brisk methodological observations that the distinguished anthropologist A. M. Hocart was prone to making strikes me as particularly apposite. Commenting admiringly on the way in which the astronomer "coolly reconstructs the history of the solar system for millions of years from observations of the present day only," he slyly compared that celestial endeavor with the way in which the terrestrial historian insists, in distinctly sublunary fashion, on pinning "his faith to direct evidence, to the writings of eyewitnesses, to coins, to ruins." Distrusting other sorts of evidence, the historian, he complained, persists instead in clinging "to his direct evidence as a timid sailor to the coast." The point is well taken and it encouraged me to insist, given the ubiquity and longevity of the sacral monarchy, that the burden of proof should properly lie, not (as historians have tended simply to assume) on the shoulders of those who claim its presence among the Germanic peoples of the pre-Christian era south of the Baltic, but rather on those who stubbornly persist in denying it, by so doing (though without acknowledging the fact) insisting on what amounts to the historical "exceptionality" of the Germanic political experience.

Such claims, of course, however confidently made, can stimulate and provide fuel for prolonged scholarly controversy—often bitter, and sometimes really quite unpleasant. Being acutely conscious of that fact, it was for me then, and in the end, something of a relief and no little cause for satisfaction to discover that I seemed to have succeeded in piloting my three volumes into what turned out (comparatively speaking) to be a reasonably welcoming harbor. Over the years, I had served on more than one book prize selection committee, including the Haskins Medal Committee whose difficult task it is to select the winning entry in a given year for the Medieval Academy of America's senior book prize. And I had come away from the experience with a sharp sense of the vagaries involved in the business of selecting the happy recipients of such awards. The outcome depended so much on the nature and strength of the competition in any given year. And beyond that (especially when the choice lay between books written by people in more than one scholarly discipline), in the particular scholarly sympathies of those making up the

selection committee in any given year. Such reservations notwithstanding, and with an acute sense of the complexities involved, I must still
confess to being inordinately thrilled when I was informed that my trilogy had been awarded the Haskins Medal for 2016. So much so that,
somewhat nervously, I half expected to hear my late mother's voice whis-
pering dryly in my ear that "Yes. He *does* break eggs with a *big* stick,
doesn't he?" But, then, having just brought to completion a project that,
though much less stressful, had been in its own way every bit as challenging as my earlier presidential assignment, I still permitted myself,
however shamefacedly, simply to be thrilled.

Exultation is the going
Of an inland soul to sea,
Past the houses, past the headlands,
Into deep eternity.

Bred as we, among the mountains,
Can the sailor understand
The divine intoxication
Of the first league out from land?

Emily Dickinson

My twenty and more post-presidential years, marked as they have been by an eminently satisfying return to the *vita contemplativa* of teaching, research, and writing, have proved for me to be years of great intellectual stimulation and, in that respect, I believe I have been a very lucky fellow. They have also been punctuated interestingly in more than one way: by the joy of watching the maturation of our grandchildren and by stints of lecturing at Oxford, at the University of Wisconsin–Madison, and to Williams alumni on a whole series of trips abroad—to France, Italy, Sicily, Scotland, Ireland, India, Russia, and the Baltic States. But those years, however beguiling in personal terms, do not warrant extended commentary. Some moments, of course, do stand out (at least for me): taking our two successive sets of grandchildren to New York City to see *The Lion King*, the story of which they already knew, though they had never encountered it in its stunning theatrical form; speaking about the potato famine—the Great Hunger—in Connaught, just a few miles from the tiny village that had been my mother's birthplace a century earlier; seeing the Red Fort in New Delhi and thinking of Bahadur Shah Zafar, the last of the Mughal emperors, nodding off during the course of the preposterous court martial that sentenced him to exile in Burma, where he was to die and to be interred in an unmarked grave; setting foot in the Examination Schools at Oxford to begin delivering my Berlin Lectures almost half a century after my fateful viva in those hallowed precincts; speaking about the Scandinavian role in World War II to a group of Yale and Williams alumni on the wonderful tall ship *Sea Cloud II* as she made her silent way, heeling gently to starboard under a full head of sail, in transit from Gdańsk to Stockholm; catching sight of something out of the corner of my eye as I bush-hogged the steep slopes of our paddock with our sturdy Kubota tractor and discovering, when I stopped the machine and turned around, that I was being very closely followed by a splendid hawk (intent, I suppose, on the moles that the tractor was scattering in terror)— a magnificent animal, proud of head, fierce of eye, and possessed of beautiful white socks.

But those are moments of purely personal resonance. Those years were punctuated also by my work as trustee on an increasing number of boards of not-for-profit institutions in the museum world and the world of higher education. That work was almost invariably interesting, and I learned a great deal from it. Like many another at my stage of life, however, I said "yes" a bit too often to such assignments, and I ended by finding myself overcommitted to an extent that was beginning to interpose obstacles to my scholarly efforts. And even though, having taken stock of my board commitments and begun then to slim down their number and range, I am still startled to discover that, since 1985 when I first embarked on that sort of activity, I have participated as trustee or director in some five hundred board meetings, some corporate but mainly in the not-for-profit sector, and presided as chairman over approximately a hundred of those meetings. For, in the end, I was to have put in some twenty-two consecutive years as chairman, sequentially, of the Williams board and of the boards of the American Council of Learned Societies (ACLS) in New York, the Sterling and Francine Clark Art Institute in Williamstown, and the National Humanities Center in North Carolina—not to mention the better part of two years as interim president (the executive role) at ACLS and, more recently, a year as interim director of the Clark.

Amidst all of this I find, as I grow older, that, intellectual type though I am, I feel something akin to the "resurrection of the ordinary" that Marilynne Robinson evokes so tellingly in one of her novels. I also find that the simple business of living or householding seems to take up more time than it used to, especially as we have encumbered our lives with animals—at peak, two horses, three goats, and two dogs. Partially as a result, though I am in New York City with some regularity and have had, from time to time, to undertake research trips to Chicago (the Newberry Library), Yale, Oxford, and the British Library in London, I travel a good deal less than I used to. And the tug and pull of home has become stronger. My spirits invariably rise when, driving in the evening into Williamstown along Route 43 from Rensselaer Railway Station in New York state, I catch a glimpse of the lights of the Store at Five Corners and know that I am about to reenter the valley in which we live, the familiar contours of which have come, somehow, to be embedded in my very being. There, the woods continue their silent encroachment on land once cleared for farming and the wildlife continues its progressive infiltration back into ancestral domains. White-tailed deer are everywhere and black bears seem to be growing in number. Nor is it uncommon for us now to catch a glimpse at breakfast time of a coyote slinking across the field, presumably heading for home after a night of successful predation. And given the number of wild turkeys in the area, it is hard to believe that in the 1970s they were designated as an endangered species in Massachusetts.

As I edge now into my mideighties, I sense that the shadows are beginning ineluctably to lengthen for me. But having taken on the interim directorship of the Clark Art Institute while we mounted a search for a new director, I found it hard, as I groped for an ending to this set of reminiscences, to evoke the sort of elegiac mood that would doubtless have been appropriate to the moment. At the same time, my typically academic skepticism and contra-suggestibility notwithstanding, I am *au fond* a religious sort of fellow, preoccupied with questions of ultimate meaning and prone to scratching the metaphysical itch. One who finds the universe a profoundly mysterious place and the darkened inner reaches of the human heart scarcely less so. I am occasionally tempted to think that I see the clouds of the great mystery parting (or at least thinning out a bit) and am moved to call to mind Alfred North White-head's splendid intuition that "the ultimate natures of things [do indeed] lie together in a harmony which excludes mere arbitrariness" and that "our experience, dim and fragmentary as it is, yet sounds the utmost depths of reality." No more than a fleeting epiphany, it may be, and like most of those I have experienced, somewhat sublunary, alas, in nature. Though I do have my moments. For reasons doubtless lodged deep in the lower Carboniferous of the psychic geology, I am also by tempera-ment an autumn and winter rather than a spring or summer sort of fel-low. And I am invariably moved in the late fall when, while walking the dogs or helping Claire-Ann out with the horses, I hear the honking and gobbling of the Canada geese as they sweep across the sky in their great V-formations on their way south for the winter. For they lead me to hope, as I contemplate my own impending flight to the eternal South, that my own departure will be as hopeful and animated as is theirs. Here I reso-nate powerfully to a poem of Emily Dickinson's that I love and that is printed as an epigraph in this postlude.

With such thoughts, moreover, there comes vividly to mind the sharply defined memory of a Christmas Day long ago when the children were small. The day of festivities had gone well and Claire-Ann, ex-hausted by her labors, had now retreated to bed. I had read the children their bedtime story. And I had later checked in to make sure that none of them had slipped down under the covers, destined, perhaps, to awaken, startled, with heart-wrenching cries of terror. That done, I had settled down by the fireplace, glass of Scotch in hand, looking across the room at the myriad of tiny white lights twinkling on the Christmas tree and listening, contentedly, to the gentle crepitation of burnt-out and disinte-grating logs as they gave up the ghost and settled down into a comforting bed of glowing embers. At that moment, what came to me—suddenly, it seemed from nowhere, and bringing tears to my eyes—was what I can only describe as an overwhelming, all-encompassing sense of gratitude. Then as, surely, now.

ACKNOWLEDGMENTS

For their kindness in reading over one or another version of the manuscript of this memoir and giving me the benefit of their encouragement and advice, I am much indebted to my daughter, Deirdre Oakley, and to my friends and colleagues at Williams—John Chandler, Dusty Griffin, Kenda Mutongi, and Dan O'Connor. Similarly to the fellows of the Oakley Center for the Humanities and Social Sciences at Williams, with whose weekly seminar I ventured to share a couple of chapters, and to Krista Birch, administrative director of the Oakley Center, for her generosity in extending a helping hand to one who, like the butler in Downton Abbey, did not quite come to terms with the telephone until his adult years and who still finds it a bit of a challenge to navigate the highways and byways of Computerland. To all of them I am most grateful, as also for the encouragement extended to me by the readers for the University of Notre Dame Press. *Commonweal* magazine gave me permission to incorporate in the chapter "Trajectories of Fear" material that first appeared under the title "Luftwaffe over Liverpool" in *Commonweal* 143, no. 2 (January 29, 2016). For permission to reproduce photographs they had taken, I am also indebted to Patrick Meyer Higgins, Charles Fuqua, and Leslie Reed Evans. And here, of course, I would be remiss if I did not once more, as with so many of my previous books, pay tribute to Donna Chenail for her fine work in preparing the manuscript for press. It has been, over the years, a great pleasure to work with her.

Williamstown, Massachusetts, January 2017   F.C.O.

p. ix: Edward Gibbon, *Autobiography*, ed. William B. Howell (Boston: Houghton Mifflin, 1877), 43.

p. 3: Brendan Behan, *Borstal Boy* (New York: Knopf, 1959), 3.

p. 7: James Joyce, *A Portrait of the Artist as a Young Man* (Oxford: Oxford University Press, 2000), 24–33.

p. 13: William Wordsworth, "The Solitary Reaper."

pp. 13–14: John Keats, "On First Looking into Chapman's Homer," "Ode to a Nightingale."

p. 17: William Wordsworth, "Lines Composed a Few Miles above Tintern Abbey, On Revisiting the Banks of the Wye during a Tour. July 13, 1798."

pp. 25–26: Rohinton Mistry, *Family Matters* (New York: Knopf, 2002), 98.

pp. 41–42: William Wordsworth, "The Prelude, or Growth of a Poet's Mind: 1. Childhood."

p. 51: Joyce, *A Portrait of the Artist as a Young Man*, 37.

p. 54: John Milton, "Il Penseroso."

p. 69: Alan Bennett, *The History Boys* (New York: Faber and Faber, 2006), 42.

p. 91: William Shakespeare, *The Tempest*, 1.2.50.

p. 102: Kenneth J. Dover, *Marginal Comment: A Memoir* (London: Duckworth, 1994), 146–48.

p. 105: Arthur O. Lovejoy, *The Great Chain of Being: A Study of the History of an Idea* (Cambridge, MA: Harvard University Press, 1936), 11.

pp. 132–33: Dover, *Marginal Comment*, 247–48.

p. 150: Robert Burns, "To a Mouse."

p. 151: Geoffrey Chaucer, "The Book of the Duchess." This is the earliest of his major poems.

pp. 194–95: Thomas Osborne Davis, "The West's Asleep." Davis was one of the leaders of the mid-nineteenth century "Young Ireland Movement." The poem is available online.

pp. 206–7: Rudyard Kipling, "Gentlemen-rankers."

p. 216: Peter Novick, *That Noble Dream: The "Objectivity Question" and the American Historical Profession* (Cambridge: Cambridge University Press, 1988), 366.

p. 217: George Marsden, *The Soul of the American University: From Protestant Establishment to Established Nonbelief* (New York: Oxford University Press, 1994), 415.

p. 229: James Fenimore Cooper, *The Last of the Mohicans: A Narrative of 1757* (New York: Charles Scribner's Sons, 1949), passim.

p. 229: Samuel Hopkins, cited in Wyllis E. Wright, *Colonel Ephraim Williams: A Documentary Life* (Pittsfield, MA: Berkshire County Historical Society, 1970), 6.

pp. 231–32: The will is printed in Wyllis E. Wright, *Colonel Ephraim Williams: A Documentary Life* (Pittsfield, MA: Berkshire County Historical Society, 1970), 151–57.

p. 233: Francis Oakley, *Community of Learning: The American College and the Liberal Arts Tradition* (New York: Oxford University Press, 1992), 26.

p. 234: Connecticut Law Reports, *Yale University vs the Town of New Haven*, 71 Conn. (Jan., 1899), 316–39.

p. 265: Letter from J. E. Sawyer to F. C. Oakley, January 28, 1963. Williams College Archives.

p. 270: Philip Larkin, "Annus mirabilis."

p. 272: Cited from Oakley, *Community of Learning*, 68.

p. 273: William Wordsworth, "The French Revolution as It Appeared to Enthusiasts at Its Commencement."

pp. 276–77: Philip Selznick, *Leadership in Administration: A Sociological Interpretation* (Evanston, IL: Row, Peterson, 1957), 62–66, 138–39, 151.

p. 281: Allan Bloom, *The Closing of the American Mind* (New York: Simon and Schuster, 1987), 313–56.

pp. 284–87: Minutes of the November 6 and December 18, 1968, faculty meetings, plus affiliated materials, Williams College Archives.

p. 300: George Orwell, *1984* (New York: New American Library, 1961), 32.

p. 301: An English translation of the oath is printed in Fergus Kerr, *Twentieth-Century Catholic Theologians* (Oxford: Blackwell, 2007), 223–25.

pp. 301–2: Orestes Brownson cited from Owen Chadwick, *From Bossuet to Newman*, 2nd ed. (Cambridge: Cambridge University Press, 1987), 171.

p. 302: Paul VI's words cited from John O'Malley, *What Happened at Vatican II?* (Cambridge, MA: Belknap Press of Harvard University Press, 2008), 253.

pp. 303–4: For *Lumen gentium* and the "Preliminary Explanatory Note," see Norman P. Tanner S.J., ed., *Decrees of the Ecumenical Councils*, 2 vols. (London and Washington, DC: Sheed & Ward and Georgetown University Press, 1990), 2:265–67, 899–900.

p. 307: Paul de Vooght, *Les pouvoirs du concile et l'autorité du pape au concile de Constance* (Paris: Cerf, 1965), 198.

pp. 307–8: Hans Küng, *Structures of the Church*, trans. Salvator Attanasio (New York: T. Nelson, 1964), 284–85, 301–2.

p. 313: Robert Cardinal Bellarmine, *Risposta di Card. Bellarmino al Trattato dei sette Theologi di Venetia sopra l'interdetto dello Santità di Nostio Signore Papa Paolo Quintio* (Rome: Guglielmo Facciotto, 1606), 22–28.

p. 314: Review by Albert C. Outler in *Journal of Ecumenical Studies* 7 (1970): 804–6, and my (puzzled) response, "Papacy under Fire: A Rejoinder," *Journal of Ecumenical Studies* 8 (1971): 382–84.

p. 328: Francis Oakley, "Celestial Hierarchies Revisited: Walter Ullmann's Vision of Medieval Politics," *Past and Present* 60 (1973), 3–48.

p. 332: Martin Anderson, *Impostors in the Temple: American Intellectuals are Destroying Our Universities and Cheating Our Students of their Future* (New York: Simon & Schuster, 1992), 85.

p. 332: Charles Sykes, *Profscam: Professors and the Demise of Higher Education* (New York: St. Martin's Press, 1990), 54.

pp. 332–33: Lesley Stahl, segment of *60 Minutes*, aired on February 26, 1998, on CBS.

p. 337: Robert A. McCaughey, *Scholars and Teachers: The Faculties of Select Liberal Arts Colleges and their Place in American Higher Learning* (New

York: Barnard College and the Mellon Foundation, 1995), esp. ix, 41–46, 92–93, 103–5.

pp. 337–38: Alexander W. Astin and Mitchell J. Chang, "Colleges That Emphasize Research and Teaching: Can You Have Your Cake and Eat It Too?," *Change* 27 (1995), 45–48.

p. 370: James B. Wood, *The Williams Curriculum, 1973–85: Action during the Presidency of John W. Chandler* (Williamstown, MA: Dec. 1985), 96. In Williams College Archives.

pp. 372–75: The "blue pamphlet," entitled *The Curriculum at Williams: Report on the Non-Major Segment*, was submitted to the faculty in April 1979 by the Ad Hoc Working Group on the Curriculum. And the "pink pamphlet," circulated among the faculty in May 1979, was entitled *Some Observations and Reservations Concerning the Working Group's Curricular Proposition*. See also the minutes of the meetings of the faculty on April 25 and May 16, 1979. All of these documents are in the Williams College Archives.

pp. 384–86: See the minutes for the February 9, 1983, meeting of the faculty, reconvened on February 16, 1983. In Williams College Archives.

pp. 396–97: Michael D. Cohen and James G. March, *Leadership and Ambiguity: The American College President*, 2nd ed. (Boston: Harvard Business School Press, 1986), 1–3, 81, 149, 203.

p. 410: Selznick, *Leadership in Administration*, 62–64, 138–39, 151.

p. 410: James MacGregor Burns, *Leadership* (New York: Harper & Row, 1979), 425.

p. 411: Howard Gardner, *Leading Minds: An Anatomy of Leadership* (New York: Basic Books, 1995), 14–15, 37, 42–43, 63, 203.

p. 412: Robert N. Bellah, et al., *Habits of the Heart: Individualism and Commitment in American Life* (Berkeley: University of California Press, 1996), 153–54.

p. 413: Edmund Burke, *Reflections on the Revolution in France* (Garden City, NY: Doubleday, 1961), 65.

pp. 451–54: Letters: J. E. Sawyer to F. C. Oakley, October 5, 1987; Oakley to Sawyer, October 13, 1987; Sawyer to Oakley, January 4, 1988; and Sawyer to Oakley, March 17, 1988. In Williams Colleges Archives.

pp. 472–74: President's remarks at the February 10, 1993, meeting of the faculty. In Williams College Archives.

p. 478: The books cited here are all listed and discussed in Oakley, *Community of Learning*.

p. 493: *The Emergence* consists of three volumes, all published by Yale University Press: *Empty Bottles of Gentilism* (2010), *The Mortgage of the Past* (2012), and *The Watershed of Modern Politics* (2015).

p. 496: Étienne Gilson, *Dante and Philosophy*, trans. David Moore (Gloucester, MA: Peter Smith, 1968), vii–x.

p. 496: James Hankins, ed. *Renaissance Civic Humanism: Reappraisals and Reflections* (Cambridge: Cambridge University Press, 2000), 1.

p. 497: A. M. Hocart, *Kings and Councillors: An Essay in the Comparative Anatomy of Human Society*, edited and with an introduction by Rodney Needham (Chicago: University of Chicago Press, 1970), 12.

p. 499: *Selected Poems of Emily Dickinson*, ed. James Reeves (London: Heinemann, 1959), 16.

p. 502: Alfred North Whitehead, *Science and the Modern World* (New York: New American Library, 1948), 19–20.

Francis Oakley is the Edward Dorr Griffin Professor of the History of Ideas Emeritus, and president emeritus of Williams College and of the American Council of Learned Societies in New York. He has written extensively (fifteen books and three co-edited volumes) on medieval intellectual and religious life and on American higher education.

CPSIA information can be obtained
at www.ICGtesting.com
Printed in the USA
LVHW011706031118
595860LV00017B/357/P

9 780268 104023